E. Paul Torrance: "THE CREATIVITY MAN"

an authorized biography

Garnet W. Millar

ABLEX PUBLISHING CORPORATION
NORWOOD, NEW JERSEY

Printed in the Unites States of America.

Library of Congress Cataloging-in-Publication Data

Millar, Garnet W.
E. Paul Torrance, "the creativity man" : an authorized biography / Garnet W. Millar.
p. cm.
Includes bibliographical references (p.) and index.
ISBN 1-56750-165-6 (cloth). -- ISBN 1-56750-166-4 (paper : alk. paper)
1. Torrance, E. Paul (Ellis Paul), 1915- . 2. College teachers--Georgia--Biography. I. Title.
LA2315.G4M54 1995
378.1'2'092--dc20
[B] 95-31875
CIP

Ablex Publishing Corporation
355 Chestnut Street
Norwood, New Jersey 07648

DEDICATION

This book is dedicated to my dear sister, Vivian (Millar) Krocker, who passed away while I was doing research for this biography; she wanted me to complete it... to my wife, Shirley, and sons, Christopher and Adam, for their understanding and patience with me while writing this book... and finally, to E. Paul Torrance—my highly respected subject and model for his exemplary life as a scholar and human being.

Contents

Acknowledgments vii

Foreward xi

Introduction xiii

1 The Early Years (1915–1935): *Life in Rural Georgia* 1

2 Teaching and Training (1936–1950): *The Making of a Scholar* 19

3 U.S. Air Force Advanced Survival School (1951–1957): *The Emergence of Creativity* 29

4 The Minnesota Years (1958–1966): *The Development of Creativity* 41

5 The Georgia Years (1966–1984): *The Return of the Native* 107

6 The Retirement Years (1966–Present): *Productive and Challenging Times* 180

Conclusion: *E. Paul Torrance—An Exemplary Beyonder* 240

Photo Section

Appendix A: *List of Publications of E. Paul Torrance* 245

Appendix B: *Questionnaire* 351

Appendix C: *Description of Creative Factors and Creative Strengths* 353

Appendix D: *Significant Events, Honors, and Distinctions in the Life of E. Paul Torrance* 359

Name Index 375

Acknowledgments

Tom Camden and Mary Ellen Brooks, archivist and curator, respectively, in the Hargrett Rare Book and Manuscript Library/University of Georgia Libraries, provided access to the Torrance Collection. I appreciated the many courtesies their staff extended to me.

Vicki Connell, Acting Director of the Torrance Center for Creative Studies in the College of Education, University of Georgia, provided funding so that I could conduct my research. I wish to thank her staff—Pam La Salle and Anita York—for their secretarial assistance.

Two individuals in Minneapolis, Minnesota, were extremely helpful to me: Dr. Berenice Bleedorn provided her "Torrance files" for my research and spent a good deal of time discussing his work; also, Dr. Charles Glotzbach was most helpful in locating information and putting me in contact with key individuals.

Suzanne Schaller, Editor-in-Chief of Scholastic Testing Services in Bensenville, Illinois, verified the dates of the tests developed by Paul Torrance.

The John F. Kennedy Space Center in Florida, NASA, granted permission to use the illustration on page 192. Dr. Mohinder Gill, at the Department of Art at Lock Haven University in Pennsylvania, granted permission to use the photograph of his painting "Doves." Dr. Gail Lewis-Robinson, head of the middle school in Episcopal of Acadiana, Cade, Louisiana, granted permission to use "A Likely Story." E. Paul Torrance granted permission to use the "Manifesto for Children" and the photographs from the Torrance Collection in the Hargrett Rare Book and Manuscript Library at the University of Georgia.

The following individuals offered to talk with me and gave freely of their time:

- Mr. Paul Anderson, Director, Future Problem-Solving Program, State of Minnesota
- Dr. Claire Clements, Head, Developmental and Rehabilitation Studies, University of Georgia
- Dr. Robert Clements, Professor, Department of Art Education, University of Georgia
- Vicki Connell, Acting Director, Torrance Center for Creative Studies, College of Education, University of Georgia
- Dr. Brad Courtenay, Professor, Adult Education, University of Georgia
- Dr. Bonnie Cramond, Associate Professor, Department of Educational Psychology, University of Georgia
- Dr. Pat Dwinell, Associate Professor, Developmental Studies, University of Georgia
- Dr. Mary Frasier, Director, Torrance Centre for Creative Studies, College of Education, University of Georgia
- Dr. Charles Glotzbach, Professor Emeritus, University of Minnesota
- Dr. Ram Gupta, Retired Professor of Educational Psychology, University of Alberta

Dr. Scott Hunsaker, Associate Professor, Department of Educational Psychology, University of Georgia

Dr. Felice Kaufmann, Consultant for Gifted Education, Washington, D.C.

Dr. Don MacEachern, Professor, College of Education, University of Minnesota

Mr. Christopher Nelson, Consultant for Gifted Education, State Department of Education, Atlanta, Georgia

Dr. Maynard Reynolds, Professor Emeritus, College of Education, University of Minnesota

Dr. Bert Richmond, Professor Emeritus, College of Education, University of Georgia

Mr. Jerry Rogers, Generalist, Curriculum Instruction, Clarke County Schools, Athens, Georgia

Dr. Tammy Safter, Former Assistant Professor, University of Georgia, Consultant in Gifted Education and Creativity, Aiken, South Carolina

Dr. Irving Sato, Consultant in Gifted Education, Los Angeles, California

Dr. Owen Scott, Retired Professor, Department of Educational Psychology, University of Georgia

Dr. Calvin Taylor, Professor Emeritus, University of Utah

Dr. Pearline Yeatts-Thomas, Professor, Early Childhood Education, University of Georgia

In addition, I received written answers to my questions about the life and work of E. Paul Torrance from the following people:

A. National Educators

Dr. James Alvino, Executive Director, Future Problem Solving Program, Ann Arbor, Michigan

Dr. Berenice Bleedorn, Assistant Professor and Director, Institute for Creative Studies, University of St. Thomas, St. Paul, MN

Dr. Bruce Bracken, Professor of Psychology, Department of Psychology, Memphis State University

Dr. Gary A. Davis, Professor of Educational Psychology, University of Wisconsin-Madison

Dr. Carolyn Falk, Adjunct Professor, Mattatuck Community College, U.S. Figure Skating Judge, Private Practice, Writer, Middlebury, Connecticut

Dr. Jerry Flack, President's Teaching Scholar, University of Colorado

Dr. Charles Glotzbach, Professor Emeritus, Educational Psychology, University of Minnesota

Dr. Kathy Goff, Inventor, Gerontologist, Assistant Professor, Medical School, University of Oklahoma

Marvin Gold, Editor, *The Gifted Child Today*, Mobile, Alabama

Dr. Eleanor Hall, Consultant, Tecumseh, Missouri

Dr. Lyle Johnson, Program Advisor for Minnesota Department of Human Services, Minneapolis, Minnesota

Dr. John D. Kauffman, Vice-President, Marketing, Scholastic Testing Service, Inc., Bensenville, Illinois

Dr. Joe Khatena, Professor of Psychology and Head of Department of Educational Psychology, University of Mississippi

Dr. Gail Lewis, Head, Middle School, Episcopal School of Acadiana, Cade, Louisiana

Laura Littleford, Writer, St. Paul, Minnesota

Dr. June Maker, Associate Professor, Department of Special Education and Rehabilitation, University of Arizona

Dr. Sam Micklus, Founder and Director, Odyssey of the Mind, Glassboro, New Jersey

Dr. Bruce Mitchell, Professor of Education, Eastern Washington State

Dr. Gordon Mork, Professor Emeritus, University of Minnesota

Dr. Rod Myers, Retired State Consultant, Professor, Writer, Eugene, Oregon

Dr. Sidney Parnes, Professor Emeritus of Creative Studies, Buffalo State University College

Dr. Harry Passow, Jacob H. Schiff Professor Emeritus of Education, Teachers College, Columbia University

Dr. Jack Presbury, Professor of Psychology, Department of Psychology, James Madison University

Dr. Joe Renzulli, Professor of Educational Psychology, Director of the National Research Center, The University of Connecticut

Dr. Cecil Reynolds, Professor of Educational Psychology, Texas A & M

Dr. Edwin H. Richardson, Retired Professor, Washington, D.C.

Dr. Mark Runco, Editor, *Creativity Research Journal*, Fullerton, California

Dr. Carol Schlichter, Professor and Chairperson, Program for Gifted and Talented, The University of Alabama

Dr. Doris Shallcross, Professor, University of Massachusetts

Mrs. Robin Shy, Director of Challenge Programs, Torrance Center for Creative Studies, University of Georgia

Dr. Betty Sloop, Professor, Mercer University

Dr. Joan Franklin Smutny, Director of the Center for Gifted, National-Louis University

Dr. Julian Stanley, Director, Study of Mathematically Precocious Youth, Professor of Psychology, John Hopkins University

Dr. Morris Stein, Professor Emeritus, Department of Psychology, New York University

Dr. Emily Stewart, Director, Laureate Program for the Gifted and Talented, Dallas, Texas

Dr. Don Treffinger, President, Center for Creative Living, Sarasota, Florida, Professor, Center for Studies in Creativity, Buffalo State College

Dr. Wilbur Williams, Retired Professor, University of Michigan

B. International Educators

Dr. Terutsugu Ando, Professor, Faculty of Education, Fukui University, Fukui-Shi, Japan

Dr. Nava Butler-Por, Head, Center for Evaluation and Management in Education, School of Education, University of Haifa, Haifa, Israel

Dr. John Carroll, Clinical Psychologist, Private Practice, Floreat Park, Western Australia
Dr. Nahig Sanei Dehlavi, Former Professor, University of Isfahan, Iran
Dr. Hesseen A. El-dreny, Dean, College of Education, Al-Azhar University, Cairo, Egypt
Dr. Noel Howieson, Associate Professor, Wembley Downs, Western Australia
Dr. George Kalushev, Director, Management Department, University of National and World Economics, Sofia, Bulgaria
Dr. John Karoussos, General Inspector of Master of Education Students (Retired), Athens, Greece
Dr. Francisco Menchén Bellón, Inspector of Schools, Madrid, Spain
Dr. Kobus Neethling, President, South Africa Creativity Foundation, Creativity Advisor to the Government, Pretoria, South Africa
Dr. Yoshio Nozu, Emeritus Professor, Shimane University, Shimane ken, Japan
Dr. Haruo Okabayashi, Associate Professor, Yamanshi University, Kofu-city, Yamanshi, Japan
Dr. Akira Onda, Professor of Psychology, Toyo University, Tokyo, Japan
Dr. M. K. Raina, Professor, School of Social Sciences, Jawaharlal Nehru University New Delhi, India
Dr. Aurora Roldan, Founder-President, Talented and Gifted Philippines Foundation, Inc., Greenhills, Manila
Dr. Saburo Sato, Professor Emeritus, Osaka City University, Osaka City, Japan
Ellen Smith, Principal, Ellerton Primary School, Three Anchor Bay, South Africa
Dr. Nayana Tara, Assistant Professor, Indian Institute of Management, Bangalore, India
Dr. Margery M. Vaughan, Professor Emeritus, University of Victoria, Mill Bay, British Columbia, Canada
Dr. Solange Wechsler, Psychology Professor, Pontificial Catholic, University of Campinas, San Paulo, Brazil

I am deeply grateful to my subject, Dr. E. Paul Torrance, for serving as a mentor for the past decade and during the research and writing of this biography. Dr. Torrance responded with remarkable swiftness to my many questions. I am indebted to him in many ways, not the least for authorizing the writing of his biography and finally reading it for accuracy in June 1993.

Thanks to Sandra Mukai who typed the manuscript and remained flexible and patient throughout the many revisions. Vicki Connell, Ralph Himsl, Dr. Bert Richmond and Dr. Carolyn Yewchuk were my primary readers and provided critical and constructive comments. Anita Jenkins provided editorial services.

Garnet Millar
Edmonton, Alberta, Canada
July 1995

Foreword

Accurate visions of the future and the will to act upon those visions so that they can become a reality are the essence of making our tomorrows what we wish them to be. Dr. Ellis Paul Torrance is the epitome of such a visionary. He accurately envisioned that the recognition and development of creative potential was the ultimate way that humankind could be progressively and positively productive in the face of ever-occurring challenges. This biography stands as an unprecedented marker of Dr. Torrance's work in the area of creativity research and practice. Chronicled within these pages is the record of a scholar who, early on in his life, "fell in love with" the study of creativity and developed this love in countless ways that have benefitted us all.

I first became acquainted with Dr. Torrance, the man and the researcher, in 1973 when I was a graduate student at The University of Connecticut. I remember a man who used a bunch of yellow jonquils when he made simple but powerful pronouncements to our graduate seminar about the creative potential in each of us. I don't remember the examples he used. But I do remember the day and the tremendous feeling of empowerment he imbued in me that I, too, could dream dreams and act upon those dreams so that they would become real.

I did not know it clearly at that time, but one of my dreams, soon to become a reality, was that I would come to The University of Georgia as an Assistant Professor to work with Dr. Torrance as one of his colleagues in the Department of Educational Psychology. At the time he was head of the Department of Educational Psychology; later he was a faculty member in our gifted and creative education program area. I got to witness firsthand his modeling of excellence as a scholar, an instructor, a mentor, and a friend. I always had the feeling that any request made of him no matter how large or small, was handled as if it were the most important request in the world. He was patient and thorough in his listening and in his teaching, whether it was in the classroom, in a doctoral oral examination, in a faculty meeting, or in response to a telephone or letter query.

The opportunities that I have had to work with him and to learn from him have had a significant impact on my life. I was at The University of Georgia when he started the Future Problem Solving Program and now have the unique opportunity to further its development through the Torrance Center for Creative Studies. I was at The University of Georgia when he wrote and published *The Search for Satori,* a book that continues to reveal great wisdom to me as can be seen by the tattered edges and the tape holding my copy together. I was at The University of Georgia and coordinated the planning of the sojourn of his *Torrance Tests of Creative Thinking* into space aboard the Challenger. I was at The University of Georgia when he retired and when he, along with Mrs. Torrance, approved my idea to begin the Torrance Center for Creative Studies as a place where his pioneering ideas could be further developed and embellished. I am presently at The University of Georgia where Dr. Torrance continues to write and make contributions to the field of creativity as a Distinguished Alumni Foundation Professor Emeritus; instruct individuals from far and near who still come to learn from him; mentor students and faculty who still seek him out for advice; and contribute to the development of his fellow human beings through his research on creativity in the elderly.

It would appear to be not only unfair, but impossible to attempt to capture the ongoing, lifetime contributions of so eloquent and prolific a scholar as Dr. Ellis Paul Torrance. Yet Dr. Garnet Millar, the author of this authorized biography of *E. Paul Torrance "The Creativity Man"* has undauntedly managed to capture the essence of this creativity giant under one cover—no easy task! In a skillful and insightful manner, Dr. Millar has presented a comprehensive synthesis of significant periods in Dr. Torrance's life and his passion for the study of creativity—from his beginnings in rural Georgia to his emergence as an eminent scholar, respected and revered worldwide by researchers, teachers, and students.

Dr. Millar's countless hours of research in the torrance archives, his numerous telephone and letter conversations with people around the world who know Dr. Torrance, his personal visits with Torrance in his home as a guest, his tenure at The University of Georgia as a Visiting Scholar, and his selection as the sixth E. Paul Torrance lecturer have resulted in a biography that will be of use to present and future scholars.

Under one cover Dr. Millar has provided the reader with not only an extensive documentation of Dr. Torrance's growth and development as a researcher, a mentor, a teacher, and a friend but also an exhaustive list of his publications. More importantly, Dr. Millar has portrayed the living reality of Dr. Torrance's dream that through the discovery and nurturance of creativity in children and adults, "We [can] give them all a fair chance to grow." Not only must this book be ready by everyone who has a professed interest in creativity—what it is, how to measure it, and how to use it—but also by those who are still trying to discover their creative potential and the impetus within themselves to make their dreams a reality.

— Dr. Mary M. Frasier, Professor Educational Psychology
Developer and Director, The Torrance Center for Creative Studies
The University of Georgia
Athens, Georgia
October, 1994

Introduction

While gathering the research for this biography, I wrote to many people from different cultures around the world. They responded enthusiastically, as if in concert, in praise and genuine gratitude for Paul Torrance—the man and his works. These are just some of the comments I received in letters:

> *There are few names in education who have had as much influence nationally and internationally as my friend and colleague, E. Paul Torrance.*[1]
>
> — Harry Passow
> New York City
> March 23, 1985

> *The Paul Torrances are the candle in the dark of the night.*
>
> — Pearline Yeatts-Thomas
> Athens, Georgia
> June, 1983

> *He has always been ahead of his time in every topic he's explored on creativity in education.*
>
> — Don Treffinger
> Sarasota, Florida
> May 18, 1992

> *He has been called the father of creativity. Everything he has written and accomplished expresses that designation. Always, one feels he or she is in the presence of someone very large, very warm, and very humble.*
>
> — Joan Franklin Smutny
> Evanston, Illinois
> July 11, 1992

---

[1] Letter from Harry Passow to E. Paul Torrance on the occasion of his retirement. March 23, 1985 (in the possession of the author).

I believe that few people have given so much to education of the gifted as Paul Torrance, perhaps no one at all. He not only produced significant research in creativity but he mentored outstanding persons who themselves are making an impact on education.

— Eleanor Hall
Tecumseh, Missouri
June 3, 1992

The name E. Paul Torrance will forever be synonymous with creativity research. But for those of us who have been privileged to know him personally, his name is also synonymous with the concern, humility, and generosity which are the marks of a truly great man. It's no wonder that he is so well loved!

— Aurora Roldan
Manila, Philippines
October, 1992

He generated an incubation process in me which I believe will never end—inspiring me to write, to teach, to do business, etc., etc.

— Kobus Neethling
Pretoria, South Africa
May 22, 1992

His twinkling eyes say—"I care" and "You are important."
His thoughtful manner that says, "welcome."
His tilted head that says,
"All who think are valued
All who try are prized."

— Carolyn Falk
Middlebury, Connecticut
May 6, 1992

Our hearts go out to him, in gratitude, and in hope that he will long be able to continue providing significant insights and support to creativity researchers.

— M. K. Raina
New Delhi, India
May 25, 1992

His unique contribution to our understanding of the creative spirit and the processes by which they can be developed in children of all cultures is universal and has benefitted scientists, educators, children and parents all over the world.

— Nava Butler-Por
Haifa, Israel
May 24, 1992

Paul Torrance's greatest contribution to the world has been that of a scientific entrepreneur: he has made what was magical into something empirical while in he still stands in awe of the creative process, he has tamed it and convinced other scientists that it is worthy of study. [2]

— Jack Presbury
Harrisonburg, Virginia
March 23, 1985

As I near retirement, I have learned that there are precious few Paul Torrances in the world. Dedicated, brilliant pioneers.

— Gary A. Davis
Madison, Wisconsin
June 28, 1993

Beneath the pines of Georgia and amid the dogwoods and magnolias lives a gentle genius. He has a brilliant record of achievement and has had an impact internationally. He is E. Paul Torrance—the father of modern creativity research. Paul Torrance literally wrote the book on creativity; in fact, he has written almost 2,000 books and articles on the subject. He, more than anyone else, has broadened the concept of intelligence to include measures of fluency, flexibility, elaboration, and originality—the basic components of creativity. Paul Torrance identified the creative child, who may very well come up with correct answers not found in "the books." The creative child is gifted with spontaneity, flexibility, originality, and a capacity to be puzzled. He identified a type of giftedness other than the IQ brand.

Paul Torrance has dispelled the myth that creativity is a gift doled out only to a minority, showing us that creativity is learnable and teachable and that it may bring ingenious solutions to impelling problems facing the world. He has been a teacher, in and out of university, and he is a mentor to those who come to learn. I once asked him, "How have you been able to do so much?" His answer was characteristically matter of fact: "I've had lots of time." This is a typical response from a man who is known for his generosity, approachability,

---

[2] "Paul Torrance's Greatest Contribution" by Jack Presbury in *Book of Letters* presented to E. Paul Torrance on the occasion of his retirement. March 23, 1985 (in the possession of the author).

accessibility, selflessness, and great sensitivity.

Paul Torrance developed a set of tests that measure the creative potential of individuals. With his wife, Pansy, he co-founded the Future Problem Solving Program, an international program involving over 250,000 students annually in all 50 states and several foreign countries. In 1985, the Torrance Center for Creative Studies was established at the University of Georgia as a living memorial to his work. It serves as an information center and network for the study of creativity for people in all parts of the world.

"E. Paul Torrance at the University of Minnesota is presently conducting research in the area of creativity which offers real promise." Such were the prophetic words of Norman J. Kleven, my child psychology master at Lakehead Teachers' College in Port Arthur, Ontario, Canada. The year was 1962, and as a teacher in training, I did not realize the full significance of those words. The seminal work on the nature and nurture of creativity was to have profound effects on the direction of education in Ontario, where I taught during the 1960s and early 1970s. The Report of the Provincial Committee on Aims and Objectives of Education in the Schools of Ontario, *Living and Learning* (1968), stated clearly that Ontario schools as fundamental principles governing their operation, should mandate that every school authority provide a child-centered learning continuum that invites learning by individual discovery and inquiry. One recommendation of that report referred directly to the importance of using a creative approach to schooling. It stated that schools need to "emphasize the creative nature of the learning process through methods of discovery, exploration, and inquiry." The quiet revolution in the goals and methods of education in Ontario, Canada and the United States had begun.

Over the years, this revolution has gradually placed a greater emphasis on creative problem solving and creative expression—on thinking or metacognition as opposed to rote memorization of subject content. An authoritarian atmosphere in schools has gradually given way to one that capitalizes on the interests and strengths of students, who are viewed as learners and thinkers.

Later, as a teacher, counselor, and psychologist in the 1970s and 1980s, I realized that there was a gap in my training. I knew there were students in my classes whom I was unable to reach. These students were bright but were often labelled as misfits. Educating them was a puzzle. The opportunity to overcome this apparent gap presented itself to me by my involvement in a professional organization called the National Association of School Psychologists. I was the representative from Canada and Mexico and met on a regular basis with other psychologists from various regions of the United States. At an executive meeting in New York City, I met and talked with Dr. Bert Richmond, who represented the state of Georgia. I explained my concern about understanding and helping students who were creative. I still remember vividly what Dr. Bert Richmond said: "I can help you. Paul Torrance is my department chairman and I will put you in touch with him."

Bert Richmond became my sponsor. I was able to take a study leave from my position with Alberta Education and work with Paul Torrance to learn how to use his tests of creativity. I had some difficulty obtaining other study leaves, however. On one occasion, I was startled to run into an assistant deputy minister who exclaimed that a short study leave I had requested was not necessary. "You already have your doctorate!" he said. However, I persisted and was able to complete two projects at the Torrance Center for Creative Studies, University of Georgia, for Alberta Education. One project dealt with "Entrepreneurship in the Alberta Curriculum"; the second one involved a new method of assessing students, using questioning skills.

In 1989, I was named a Research Fellow to the Torrance Center at the University of Georgia. The opportunity to work with the Center staff and Paul Torrance has greatly enhanced my understanding of the remarkable work of this pioneer in creativity. In addition, in October of 1990, the Torrance Center for Creative Studies invited me to present the Sixth Annual E. Paul Torrance Lecture, which focuses on creativity research and related issues.

To gather and organize the information for this biography, I undertook a number of key activities. First, I spent several months reading the books and articles written by E. Paul Torrance. This was a huge task (see list of publications in Appendix A). I had also had experience using the Torrance Tests of Creative Thinking with classes I taught at the University of Lethbridge (Alberta, Canada), and to screen students for admission to gifted programs. Next, I interviewed several key individuals in Georgia, Minnesota, and Alberta who had been colleagues or students of Paul Torrance, and I sent a questionnaire to colleagues, friends, and former students who live in various countries outside North America. (A copy of the questionnaire is provided in Appendix B.) In addition, I interviewed Paul Torrance several times. On several occasions, I stayed in his home in Athens, Georgia, and got to know him as a person. He also responded to many of my questions in writing; we carried on an extensive correspondence throughout the writing of this book. Finally, I spent a good deal of time in the Torrance Collection in the Hargrett Rare Book and Manuscript Library at the University of Georgia.

This book takes the reader through the life and times of E. Paul Torrance and highlights his prodigious contributions. His life is a story of excellence in scholarship and a study in persistence and single-minded pursuit of the nature and nurture of creativity. He has had the courage to follow his intuition when scientific data were lacking and the road map to knowledge was not clearly marked. Paul Torrance is, however, more than a highly productive phenomenon: He is also a soft-spoken, hard-working man of commitment, ethics, and courage—the courage to be a minority of one. This book records his frustrations and failures along with his successes and triumphs.

The book is organized into six chapters. Chapter 1 traces Paul's early days growing up in rural Georgia and relates significant school experiences. The development of his skills as a teacher and competencies as a psychologist are described in Chapter 2. Chapter 3 explains Paul's experiences as a research psychologist with the USAF Advanced Survival School, where he came to learn the importance of using creative skills in emergency and extreme situations. Chapter 4, the "Minnesota Years," relates the development of his creativity tests and programs and outlines how he met his future wife, Pansy. Chapter 5 relates the culmination of Paul's work at the University of Georgia and the development of a program that would affect students in all parts of the world. His activities since retirement are detailed in Chapter 6. He is still active in research, writing, and encouraging others in his chosen field. Each chapter contains footnotes and ends with references. The appendices contain supplementary and complementary information, including a complete list of Torrance's publications and a summary of significant events, honors, and distinctions in his career.

This world-renowned "Creativity Man" is aptly described by a term he coined himself: a "beyonder," which comes out of Torrance's 30-year longitudinal study of creative persons and their achievements. The study showed that many of these individuals were highly productive and creative throughout the years, continuing to produce books, poems, songs, plays, television scripts and performances; they have also made scientific discoveries, received patents, and so on. His tests predicted this kind of achievement back in 1959. Although the word "beyonder" is still not found in any dictionary, it communicates to us intuitively, describing a high achiever who may write hundreds of books or thousands of articles, invent countless inventions, or produce hundreds of films. E. Paul Torrance is an exemplary beyonder!

REFERENCES

Living and Learning (1968). The Report of the Provincial Committee on Aims and Objectives of Education in the Schools of Ontario. Ontario Department of Education. Toronto, ON: The Publications Office.

Millar, G.W. (1986). *Entrepreneurship in the Alberta Curriculum: A Monograph.* Edmonton, AB: Planning Services Branch, Alberta Education.

Millar, G.W. (1989). *Assessing student questioning skills... Toward an enhanced Alberta Student Achievement Testing Program.* Edmonton, AB: Student Evaluation and Records Branch, Alberta Education.

Torrance, E.P. (1993). The beyonders in a thirty-year longitudinal study of creative achievement. *Roeper Review—Special Issue on Longitudinal Studies*, ***15*** *(3)*, 131-134.

Chapter 1

The Early Years (1915-1935):

Life in Rural Georgia

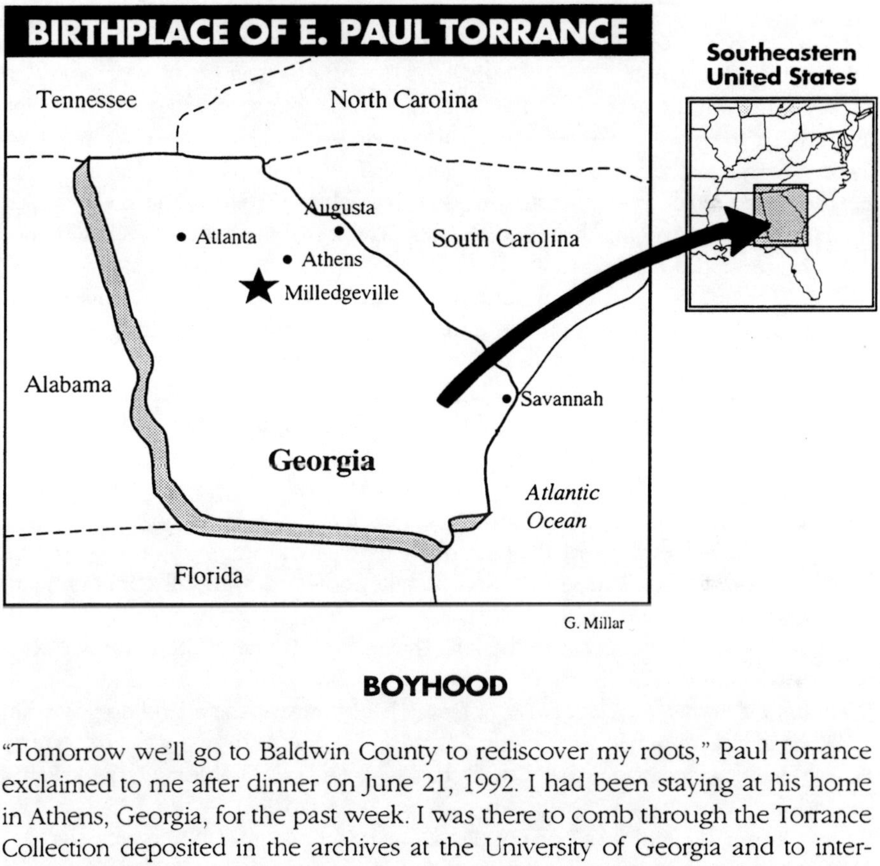

BOYHOOD

"Tomorrow we'll go to Baldwin County to rediscover my roots," Paul Torrance exclaimed to me after dinner on June 21, 1992. I had been staying at his home in Athens, Georgia, for the past week. I was there to comb through the Torrance Collection deposited in the archives at the University of Georgia and to interview individuals who had worked with or had been students of Dr. Torrance. I had been looking forward to this trip for some time; a previous attempt in March had been cancelled due to heavy rain and tornado warnings.

The drive by car from Athens to Milledgeville (the closest city to Paul Torrance's birthplace) was relatively short. We stopped at a roadside fruit stand by a peach grove to buy some famous Georgia peaches as well as pecans and peanuts. Following U.S. Highway 441 along the Antebellum Trail of the Old South, we also stopped at Eatonton in Putnam County to visit the Uncle Remus Museum, which depicts the antics of Brer Rabbit and other characters from the writings of Joel Chandler Harris.

Baldwin County is on the extreme southern border of the Piedmont Plateau area of the state. The majority of the soils are well adapted to production of cotton, grains, and peaches. Livestock, dairy, and poultry and their products make up about half the county's farm income.

Soon we were in Milledgeville, now a city with a population of 17,700. Hernando De Soto is said to have crossed the Oconee River just six miles from the city in 1540. Founded in 1803, Milledgeville was the state capital for 61 years, from 1807 to 1868. (Since 1868, the capital of Georgia has been Atlanta.) It was in Milledgeville, on January 19, 1861, that the Georgia Ordinance of Secession was passed. This was the agreement to collaborate with other southern states in pulling away from the northern states during the Civil War. In November 1864, on his famous March to the Sea, Federate General W. T. Sherman, the first practitioner of *blitzkrieg* and psychological tactics, passed through the city en route to Savannah on the coast. Sherman and his generals decided not to destroy the city's landmarks, although he had destroyed many cities in the northern part of the state.

Paul Torrance's great-great-grandfather fought with the Confederate Army. He was at Savannah, Georgia, at the time of the surrender to General Sherman, and he walked home from there to West Baldwin County, carrying a small magnolia tree that he planted near his home. The tree is still living today.

In Milledgeville, Dr. Torrance and I visited the Georgia Military College where he attended high school and junior college, and later served as a teacher and principal. We also visited the Museum and Archives of Georgia Education where some of Dr. Torrance's research on education in Georgia is deposited.

We left Milledgeville and headed 10 miles east on Stembridge Road to the Torrance homestead. The terrain here is hilly, covered with tall conifers, giant oaks, and groves of pecan trees.

"Slow the car down. Look to the left. There is the home of the country doctor who delivered me." Dr. Torrance explained that he was born in bed at home at 3:00 p.m. on Friday, October 8, 1915. Dr. O. F. Moran was the attending physician who made the two-mile trip to the Torrances' home with a horse and buggy. "There were no telephones so Daddy had to go to get Dr. Moran." Baby Paul's second and third toes were grown together on both feet—like his father, Ellis Watson Torrance. Paul was born under the astrological sign Libra, which signifies balance. Under Asian signs, his birth was in the Year of the Rabbit. Both signs predicted his future behavior fairly well. His father, Ellis, named his son after himself—Ellis Paul Torrance, but to avoid confusion, the son was always called Paul. When he started publishing it became E. Paul. The birth must have been a very happy occasion for Grandpa Torrance. He bought a Liberty Bond for Paul on his next trip into Milledgeville, something he never did for any of the other grandchildren.

As we drove down the road toward the homestead, Dr. Torrance noted, "At the time of my birth, my father and mother were in their mid-twenties. My father had only a seventh-grade education and my mother had eighth grade. Further education was unavailable. My mother always wished that she had kept up with me. She always wanted to be a teacher. Her maiden name was Jimmie Pearl Ennis. My father—Daddy—was a farmer, and my mother—Mamma—a farm wife." Both the Torrance and Ennis families settled in Baldwin County, Georgia, over 200 years ago. The Torrances came from Scotland by way of Virginia. There were a few stories about past generations in the Torrance family. "Torr" meant "hills," so the Torrances were hill people in Scotland. The story that has been passed down is that two Torrance brothers befriended Robert Bruce one time when he was out of favor. Robert Bruce was running from his enemies and needed to cross a lake to escape. He saw two Torrance brothers out on the lake in a boat. The Torrance brothers rowed him to safety, singing to distract the enemy. When Robert Bruce was back in power, the story goes that he gave his rescuers land around Stirling Castle and gave them a coat of arms. The coat of arms contained a farm animal, boat oars, and music symbols. Paul Torrance says that Robert Bruce and Robert have been popular names in the Torrance family for generations.

Dr. Torrance and I turned off the Stembridge Road just up from the country doctor's home. We were able to find the road that led to his original home, but it was overgrown and a fair distance to walk. I began to ask questions about his early childhood on the farm. Immediately, he held his head up, closed his eyes and said, "Ask one question at a time—let me rediscover my roots and reflect back."[1]

GM: Tell me about this farm where you grew up. Who lived next door?

PT: My grandfather, James Robert Torrance, owned the farm on which we lived—about 700 acres. We lived on the farthest western part of the farm. Daddy was a sharecropper, and he usually had one or two men who worked for him. Guy Stamp was one of these who lived in a house nearby with his wife Alma and son Johnny. I remember once that I was playing with Johnny and went to his house. When my father found me there, eating some of the cake batter which had been left in the mixing bowl, I was beaten [switched] and was informed that such behavior was not tolerated. I was given no reason. Johnny and I did not play with one another. We never discussed this in the family. It had been settled, but I remember it vividly.

My grandparents' home was about a quarter of a mile east of my home. We usually walked this distance and did so rather frequently. It was a large house and we enjoyed going there. The house was atop a hill which was part red clay and white clay [chalk]. This meant that it became very slippery

[1] All of Dr. Torrance's memories quoted here are taken from an interview with him at his home in Athens, Georgia in March of 1992.

when there were heavy rains. The farm was assayed two or three times for chalk deposits. About 15 miles away was a very large chalk mining industry. But the chalk on this hill was used for whitewashing houses, fences, flower boxes, and so on.

At the bottom of this hill were several houses used by the black families who worked on the farm.

One-half mile from my grandparents' big house lived Winnifred [Winnie] and Charlie Owen Ennis. Winnie was the oldest sister of my father and Charlie Owen [Chunk] was my mother's first cousin. He cut our hair, usually on Sunday or Saturday afternoon. The second grandchild was Owen, who was born six days before my sister Ellen.

GM: How many children were in your family?

PT: My only sibling, a sister, Martha Ellen Torrance was born at home January 15, 1919. It was all a big mystery. If I asked Mamma she would tell me to ask Daddy. If I asked Daddy he would tell me to ask Mamma. It was the same story all along. My parents never gave me any sex information. There was an air of excitement. My mother had a miscarriage and to this day it has never been mentioned to me. I saw the signs as a boy but I knew better than to mention it. It was never confirmed until Pansy discovered it several years after our marriage in giving my mother nursing care.

GM: What do you remember of your mother and father in these early years?

PT: My mother was very versatile. She was a better fisher and a better marksman than my father. She was also quite creative in house decoration, cooking, and sewing. We went through the Great Depression. Most of the time Daddy lost money on cotton, watermelons, and other crops. We raised our own vegetables and fruit. Most of our income came from eggs, chickens, beef, pork, butter, and cream. We were actually poor and always in debt, but we fared better than most of the people in the community. Most of our clothes were made of flour sacks. My parents were more creative and hardworking than others.

GM: At the time of your birth, what important events were taking place locally, nationally and internationally?

PT: Woodrow Wilson was President of the United States at the time of my birth and World War I was in progress. My father had been in the National Guard and had gone on maneuvers just before I was born. However, my family was pretty remote from all of this. The focus was on survival. What traveling was done was in a wagon or buggy. Daddy had had his buggy since he was 16 years old. The events of the time were quite distant from my family and there was not much communication—no radios and no newspapers. My grandfather obtained some news of local happenings from his associations as a member of the Baldwin County Board of Education, the Progressive Farmers' Club, Harmony Baptist Church, a member of the Black Springs Baptist Church, and Sons of the American Revolution. My father and grandfather heard some news when they went to town [Milledgeville]. Some news traveled by U.S. Mail. My Uncle Guy and his sister-in-law were the carriers. One of my first cousins is the carrier on this route now.

GM: What little stories have your parents told you about these early childhood years?

PT: This, again, is something my family never talked about. To my Torrance aunts I was a great nephew. I remember their delight when I walked at nine months. I also began talking at an early age, but I am not able to pinpoint this.

A visiting evangelist from Harmony Baptist Church said I had all the signs that would foretell a brilliant career. He used the head for his prediction—likely a practicing phrenologist!

I also have memories of a particular horse my father had. Once I was riding with him and we were thrown. We got a good scare but apparently received no physical injuries. Daddy never let me ride again with him on a horse.

My sister Ellen and I played with bottle dolls. We dressed them with scraps of cloth from Mamma's sewing. We would create a whole village and play school, play house, and so on. My aunts worried about this and thought I should have grown out of this because I was a boy. We persisted, and Mamma and Daddy did not interfere.

My sister and I each had a dog—terriers from the same litter—a girl dog for Ellen and a boy dog for me—Patsy and Pat. We played house, doctor, dentist with them. One day we were playing dentist. A log sawed up for firewood was the dentist's chair. Ellen took Patsy to me, the dentist, to pull her tooth. To our amazement, the tooth came out. I was afraid I had ruined the dog. We also dressed the dogs up, using scraps as we had done with the bottle dolls.

Pat was bigger than Patsy. Daddy gave Pat away to another boy who lived some distance from us. This broke my heart. I never knew why. Mamma and Ellen accepted it as a fact and I got no sympathy from either of them. Patsy lived to an old age, and killed many wharf rats—some almost as big as she was.

Ellen relates that she remembered all the family laughing about Paul and his Dad going in the buggy to Uncle Guy's store. Young Paul went to sleep and fell out of the buggy into a sand bed. He didn't wake up but scared his father. Another humorous incident she recalls was when Great Aunt Mamie Torrance tried to get Paul to eat something he didn't like. She told him to eat it so that he could grow up to farm like his Dad. Paul cried and said, "I don't want to farm."

GM: What were your greatest fears in those early years?

PT: I don't think I was fearful of anything during those years. I could climb the tallest tree. I could jump down from higher places than any of the other children. I could run faster than many of the older and taller boys.

I don't think I was afraid of people during these years. It was after I started to school that I became shy and timid. But I was aware that "children were to be seen and not heard" and that the "good child was the modest child," and I was not. I knew that I was different.

GM: What were your most vivid recollections of those early years?

PT: I suppose the most vivid recollection of my preschool years was walking at age nine months. The family thought this was so great and so unusual. On February 22, 1992, I visited my grandparents' old house and could point to the very spot where it occurred.

I also remember the feasts at my Torrance grandparents' house where all the family gathered. I remember my grandmother's pork and eggs pie. I have never seen it anywhere else.

I do not remember any rewards from my parents. I do remember the paddlings, switchings, and beatings I got when they thought I had done something bad. I tried not to do anything I thought they would consider bad.

There were some times when we got special treats like divinity candy, home-made chocolate bon bons, and Charlotte Russe. However, it was not for being especially good.

During this period, there were not many children to play with. Mother's oldest sister had many children and she would occasionally come and stay with us three or four days. We slept on pallets and this was fun. I remember once we were visiting them in Milledgeville. Mother's sister would give one of her children a nickel or dime and we would go to the bakery and get a loaf of bread. Then it would be broken up and all the children would have a hunk. This was the most wonderful bread I have ever had.

I never went to a summer camp until I finished the seventh grade. My parents never went on a vacation. At a later date my mother would go to Florida to see her sister, to a town nearby [Eatonton] to visit her other sisters, but Daddy never went. The train trip to Eatonton may have been while I was still a preschooler. At least I was very excited about it and remember it very vividly.

GM: Would you say your family was poor but didn't know it?

PT: Yes. We didn't have money to buy anything, and Daddy was in debt. We always had plenty of food—lots of fresh or canned vegetables and fruits, pork, beef, and chickens. We grew yams. When they were harvested, Daddy would dig a hole and would line it with pine straw, put the yams in the hole, and cover it with earth. Mamma would set traps for rabbits and possums.

Occasionally, Daddy would get a wild turkey or deer. We had fruit and nut trees. Eggs, butter, and milk were plentiful. Mamma was an expert seamstress, keeping us in clothes. We definitely fared better than most families.

I received a lot of love as a child from my parents and the rest of the family and felt loved. My Ennis relatives were somewhat more expressive than my Torrance relatives. In both families you were expected to kiss when you visited.

GM: What were your meals like, and what were your favorite foods?

PT: Our meals were usually happy affairs. I cannot recall having a meal to myself. Only occasionally there was some unpleasantness. My favorite food was dessert. My favorite desserts were home-made ice cream, peach cobbler, and Charlotte Russe. My least favorite food was collards. I ate everything but boiled okra. I was very fond of bananas, peaches, and apples. Coconut was a favorite, especially the juice or milk. Chicken liver was also a favorite, and Ellen and I were always claiming it.

GM: What were you interested in or curious about as a child?

PT: I was curious about almost everything and got into trouble handling things I was not supposed to. There are many very pleasant memories associated with my curiosities.

We visited the house that Dr. Torrance's paternal grandparents owned. The present owner invited us into the house for lemonade as it was 85°F outside. Mrs. Diane Pekar and her husband John bought the house in 1986 and are renovating it. She permitted us to explore around the house. As we were about to climb the stairs to the second story, Dr. Torrance declared, "I took my first step right here at age nine months!" He was able to remember back over 75 years. A swimming pool had been built at the back of the house—a good place to soak in the hot Georgia sun.

GM: When did you start school?

PT: My formal schooling did not begin until I was almost seven years of age. When I was six years old, my parents decided that I would not begin my schooling until the next year. I was told of this decision late in the summer before school opened. I had been counting on beginning in September. My parents thought that I was too frail to walk the three miles to the nearest school.

SCHOOL DAYS

We had left the Torrance homestead and had driven three miles down the road to an old, abandoned grocery store when I was instructed, "Stop here and pull over." We walked into a grassy field beside the dilapidated store.

"Here is where Union Point School stood. It was burned down several years ago," said Paul Torrance in his soft, Southern drawl. "I attended grades 1 through 9 here."

We walked through the now-grown-over playground and noticed an old building hidden in the brush. Sure enough, it was an old school building that may have been on the site when Paul attended first grade in September of 1922. We carefully entered the broken-down school. Alphabet cards were still on the walls, worn brown desks with inkwells were scattered about the room, and a cloak room was at the back.

> My first impression when I started to school was one of confusion. I can remember that first day quite vividly. The primary teacher had the first and second grades in one room. She called on one of the second graders to lead in prayer. Following the prayer, she began to call the roll without saying that that was what she was doing. My name was the first name on her list. I thought she wanted me to lead in prayer so I started repeating the Lord's Prayer. The correct response would have been, "Here." I was very embarrassed by this incident and do not remember very much after that. I just got the impression that there was confusion. All in all I enjoyed the day and felt that I had redeemed myself somewhat. I was not tearful or homesick. I was ready for the next day.
>
> I was very glad to start school. I knew a few of the children as I was related to many of them. My youngest uncle was in the ninth grade and some of my cousins were in the grades in between. As I remember, I had no trouble in getting along with the other kids. I did have trouble with one of my cousins that I had to walk home with. She had two or three older sisters, but she would beat up on me. I'm not sure why she did.
>
> There were no public high schools in the county at that time. The school, Union Point, was a small one enrolling nine grades—about 100 students. It was almost exactly three miles from my home. It was necessary to walk to school and walk home. My family lived in the same place that I was born until after I finished junior college and was working.
>
> Although I had to walk to school when I was in the first grade, I came in a covered wagon in the second grade, and in the third grade I came in a school bus, as consolidation in Baldwin County was underway. There were, of course, no wagons or buses for black children. Almost all of them went to one-room schools in bad repair. When my father was a member of the County Board of Education, he was assigned responsibility for looking after the condition of the rural black schools. Some improvement took place, but they were still in deplorable condition.
>
> I guess I liked the seventh grade better than any of the others. I also remember the third grade as being very exciting.
>
> I think the fourth grade was the worst experience I had in school. We had a sight singing teacher who came in extra. My singing was so bad that she ejected me from the class and made me go back to my regular seat and wait for the class to be over. My teacher in the third, fourth, and fifth grades recognized me for my

imaginative stories and other things that I wrote. There was plenty of time to write while the teacher was working with the other two classes. I think this teacher also liked English and writing and stories better than she liked mathematics. I think my experiences during this period were very influential in my later life. I had excellent mathematics teachers after I reached the sixth grade, and I continued to do well in mathematics throughout the rest of my school career.

I cannot remember when or how I learned to read. As long as I can remember I have been reading and enjoying it. I suppose my real addiction to reading and scholarship began when I was in the fourth grade and experienced an extended hospitalization and convalescence of six or seven months following a ruptured appendix. My father's three younger sisters kept me supplied with books to read, and I read everything in sight. I wrote books, edited them, and criticized them. I also began my letter writing at this time. I wrote the nurses, my teacher, my aunts, and my classmates, especially the girl I had a crush on at the time and the boy in my class who was my chum and best friend. I had little interference except from my sister who was four years younger than I but had started to school at age five.

In the years that followed, I was not to enjoy this pleasure again. There were always cows to round up and milk; cotton to plant, chop, weed, fertilize, dust, and pick; corn to plant, hoe, and harvest; firewood to chop or saw and haul; animals to slaughter, butcher, and prepare for marketing or home curing; or chickens, hogs, or cattle to feed. I disliked the haying and dusting the cotton with arsenic. I was somewhat inept at many of these tasks, at least in terms of the high standards of performance that my father set.

Thus, I was always relegated to work along with the lowest paid hired hands. One of these, Tom Swint, exerted considerable influence on my later life. He was perhaps the best teacher that I had during these early years. He was in the "low-pay ranks," not because of his lack of skills but because my father and neighboring farmers thought very poorly of him. He was regarded as a clever thief.

A more horrible crime, however, was that he had gone off to Detroit for a couple of years where whites and blacks mixed. Not only did this charming and unusually articulate black man teach me how to do the farm tasks at hand, but he taught me a great deal about another world—a black world, a world of big cities, a world of a black man's concern for his family that would not join him in Detroit. I suppose Tom was the only man I knew who had lived outside of Georgia. I expect knowing Tom helped give me the courage to go away to graduate school after I had finally finished college.

There were many superstitions flying about in those days. In the fifth grade we were given an assignment to collect superstitions. We had to recall all of the superstitions which we held and then ask other people to give their superstitions. The only ones that I can recall and still hang on with me are:

1. Never cut your fingernails on Sunday. The devil will be after you the whole week.
2. Friday the 13th is an unlucky day. Watch out!

I cannot remember having a crush on any of my teachers. I remember in the second and fourth grades that I did have a crush on some of the girls. The girls would tease the boys and then run to the outdoor toilet. We would chase them and have the privilege of kissing them if we caught them. I always tried to catch Catherine. In the fourth grade, while I was in the hospital, I started a correspondence with Frances. Daddy was the school bus driver and he would deliver my letter to her and her letter to me. She was the smartest girl in the class.

I never came home with a bad report card except in the second grade when I received a bad grade for penmanship. We did not have copybooks in the second grade so my mother made some copy for me on some ruled tablet. I practised using these whenever I had time on my hands, either at home or at school. At the blackboard my handwriting was very small and always slanted downward. On the copybook that my mother made me I was able to stay on a straight line.

I think my parents thought that I was being well taught and were pleased with my progress. I do not remember having received much punishment after I started to school.

There were many people who influenced me when I was a child. However, I think my mother exerted the most influence. She was very interested in what we were doing at school. She, herself, had wanted to be a teacher when she was in school. The last two years that she was in school I think she spent most of her time teaching the younger children. She loved it and probably would have made an excellent teacher. I could always learn those things that she taught me more easily than those that my father taught me. Several times, my father had tried unsuccessfully to teach me how to milk a cow. One time my father got on a hung jury and could not come home at night. When it came time to milk the cows, my mother said, "We will have to do it and you will have to help me, so come on and I will teach you how." And she did. After this, milking the cows was a daily chore throughout high school and junior college.

As a child, I think that I was fairly well coordinated because I could climb higher than any of the other children and jump farther. I could also shoot basketball goals pretty well. Other parts of the game were not so well liked. During elementary and high school I was very slim but not very strong. In fact, I never did develop good arm muscles in spite of the fact that I worked hard and exercised well. This has always been a mystery to me and something that I have been ashamed of.

During school days we played many games like Farmer's in the Dell, Marching Around the Level, Hopscotch, and Marbles. I did not learn to ride a bike or skate during this period. In our community, such things were almost unknown. We did, however, play softball, baseball, basketball, and once in a while we would play football. I was never much good as a tackler or blocker, but I could sure run if I got the ball. I could run the 100-yard dash faster than anyone else in the school.

Although I was inept at the higher-level farm tasks and could never plow a straight row, I succeeded in school and usually led my class. When I was in the sixth grade, I won a prize in a county-wide essay contest and repeated the feat in the seventh grade. Through some stroke of good fortune, I had excellent teachers and keen competition from my peers throughout the nine years that I attended the country school three miles from my home. When I was in the eighth grade, the third, fourth, and fifth grade teacher taught us Latin while our teacher taught her pupils arithmetic. She was an outstanding teacher and entered me in the state-wide

> Latin contest. I won first place in my district, placing above students in the large high schools in Macon, Milledgeville, and Augusta. This was the first objective indication that I had received that I might be learning as much as my peers in city schools. I was a first honor graduate of Union Point Elementary and Junior High School in 1929 and 1931 respectively.

As we left the old school building to go back to the car, Dr. Torrance bent over and picked a plant in the area of what had once been a playground. "Rabbit tobacco," he exclaimed. "The boys used to smoke it like tobacco behind the school house."

In the car Dr. Torrance described an important turning point in his life.

> We were eating supper—Daddy, Mamma, my sister Ellen, and I. I was 13 and shaving already. The mid-June day began before daylight with my helping to milk the cows and turn the separator. It ended after dark, the same way. I had spent the rest of the day chopping cotton.
>
> For supper, we had delicious fresh English peas from our own garden. The way Mamma cooked them, they had a delicious juice—or gravy. I was eating them with a spoon—a method that still seems sensible to me. Daddy stopped eating, looked at me, and said seriously and calmly, "It's plain now that you'll never be able to make a living on the farm. You'll have to go to town and you'll have to get an education. It's time you learned to eat peas with a fork!" [2]

There was no further discussion of the matter. From that point on, Paul Torrance was committed to "getting an education," even though a high school education seemed an impossible dream. It was all right with his family. That moment signified to Paul Torrance that his father accepted him as he was and that it was up to him to work out his own way of life. It put an end to years of desperate but unsuccessful attempts to master some of the more skilled farm tasks.

Paul obtained his first real sex education from an older student—Lewis—when he was in the seventh grade. Lewis was the oldest son in a large family and only came to school when he was not needed on the farm. He was about 15 and in the eighth or ninth grade. One day the seventh-grade boys were in the woods near the school. He enlightened Paul and the other boys and showed them some good places to copulate in the woods, including his favorite place. Lewis was a little rough but Paul liked him because he was so frank and outspoken. Later Lewis told Paul that he was smart but would never amount to much because he was not aggressive enough.

During Paul's junior high school years, an elderly man in the community, "Uncle Billy" Moran, recognized and encouraged him. Their association began when a railroad company and a civic club in Milledgeville decided to sponsor 10 boys from Baldwin County at Camp Wilkins, a Four-H camp in Athens,

---

[2] Torrance, E.P. (1969). It's time you learned to eat peas with a fork! *Theory Into Practice*, 8(5), 332–333.

Georgia. The participants were to be chosen by means of a test. Exactly 10 boys showed up to take the test, and the man in charge decided to give it anyway, although no one would be eliminated. The questions were about agriculture. Paul had just completed a required course in agriculture and knew all but one of the answers. The other boys would not speak up so he went ahead and answered all of them, although he knew it was not "good manners." The other boys didn't seem to mind and did not hold it against him.

Uncle Billy was the chaperon, and members of the civic club drove the boys to the camp at Athens. The camp was located on a spot just across the street from what is now Aderhold Hall (the building occupied by the College of Education). Uncle Billy was relaxed, played horseshoes with the boys, and talked with them as no relative had ever talked. Paul loved him, as did all of the boys. They talked about all sorts of things, went to a 10-cent movie every day together, and visited the YMCA, where there was a swimming pool for men only and where everybody swam nude. This was the first time Paul had been to Athens and the first time he had been away from home for this long.

A number of other individuals influenced Paul during this period. Among them were the substitute teacher who was afraid he would not get to go to high school, and the pastor who had studied phrenology and said that Paul Torrance would be a great man. Mr. and Mrs. Holland Strother and Mrs. Bessie Burton, teachers at Union Point School, were encouraging. Mr. Strother was the principal of the school and Paul's teacher in the eighth and ninth grades, as well as his coach in track and oratory. Later, Mr. Strother became principal of Midway Vocational School, where Paul was to teach in 1936–1937. Mrs. Strother, Paul's teacher in the seventh grade, gave him a book entitled *Success*. Mrs. Bessie Burton, Paul's teacher in the third, fourth and fifth grades, gave young Paul a love of literature and creative writing.

Paul Torrance describes his frustration about failing to learn to drive a car:

> I remember my attempts to learn to drive quite vividly. Usually, I attempted to drive on the way back from training union or some similar event. The car belonged to Aunt Mamie, who was wonderful to take us places, and she was very patient. I would become confused on sequencing and could not steer a straight course. I do not know whether this was from left hemisphere damage or what. I do remember I had an auto accident. I was sitting in the front seat and my sister was in the back seat. Daddy decided to cut through the woods and ran into a hole and it slammed me into the windshield. My head had a big knot on it for a long time afterwards. The knot on my skull and on my knee persisted for years. I received treatment on the knee for several years and there are slight traces even now. There were no tests, X-rays, or the like at that time. I was treated (with radium light) by an M.D. and by a chiropractor. Even now, I sometimes have pain in this knee.

We visited two churches that Paul Torrance and his family attended. Harmony Baptist Church is located very close to the Torrance homestead. Paul attended Sunday School and preaching service throughout his childhood. The Torrances later moved to another church, Black Springs Baptist Church, that had a young people's program. He was very active in it. Paul had an opportunity to teach Sunday School classes and be a leader in the Baptist Young People's Union. He knew then that he wanted to be a teacher or a writer.

We visited the cemetery adjoining the churchyard, where Dr. Torrance's paternal and maternal grandparents are buried, and also his wife Pansy, who died in November, 1988. After placing some flowers on his wife's grave and spending some moments in reflection, Dr. Torrance said, "This will be my final resting place."

Paul's family has always been religious. Paul attended Sunday School, training union, mid-week prayer service, and other church events. He started teaching Sunday School at an early age, held many offices in training union, including director in his local church and in the association, which included about three counties. He was elected deacon at a very early age. When he was in the twelfth grade, he wrote a Christmas dramatization and produced it.

Paul's parents were opposed to dancing and other teenage activities such as playing card games. This, coupled with the feeling that country kids were looked down upon as second-class citizens, made him somewhat of an isolate.

Paul Torrance has often said that the national climate for creative achievement is generally unfavorable. This was, and perhaps still is, further complicated in the United States and Canada by a climate that rather generally discouraged the full development of potentialities, except for certain types of athletics. The problem is especially severe in the Southern United States. Lillian Smith (1949), in *Killers of the Dream*, describes this problem eloquently. Creativity has been considered sinful. She describes the fact that society values beautiful things but imports them from other places, like Europe and Asia, and derogates our native sons and daughters who aspire to create art in various forms. Southerners, according to Smith, have generally feared hands that create but have accepted and honored hands that have destroyed. Paul Torrance recalls vividly that when he considered going to college, several of his friends and family members were afraid that he would be exposed to the sins of science. Curiosity was sinful. Imagination was sinful. Humor was sinful. Dancing was sinful. *Anything* creative was sinful.

It was mid-afternoon when we headed back to Milledgeville. Dr. Torrance explained that success in the Latin contest and in various county-wide essay contests probably did much to encourage him and some of his classmates to go beyond the ninth grade country school. Most of the students did continue in Milledgeville. The boys went to Georgia Military College, which was the county high school, and the girls went to Peabody High School, which was the laboratory school for the Education Department of Georgia State College for Women. None of the students from Union Point School had much difficulty in competing with their new classmates, and in algebra and Latin they were well ahead of them.

Middle Georgia Military and Agricultural College was established in 1879 by an act of the General Assembly of Georgia. It was renamed Georgia Military College (GMC) in 1900. The purpose of the school was to prepare young men for military service and to become productive members of society. The purpose of GMC was to develop character in each cadet by attention to the following goals:

- Intellectual curiosity quickened by proper study habits
- Attractive personality developed by social training and recreation
- A strong, healthy body built up by athletics and military exercises
- Higher spiritual values encouraged by religious training and service.

GMC began as a secondary school, and a junior college was added in 1930. In 1932, GMC was designated an Honor Military Institute by the U.S. Department of the Army. Today, in 1993, it is one of only six military junior colleges in the United States that offers its cadets the opportunity to obtain a commission after the first two years of college study.

At Georgia Military College, Paul Torrance was rejected for military training by the examining physician on account of his weak appendectomy incision and heart palpitations. This had two important results. First, it gave Paul at least one additional hour each day for study and reading while his classmates drilled and had classes in "Military Science and Tactics." For Paul, spending this time in the school library was sheer delight. The other result, which was not so delightful, was equally beneficial for Paul later throughout his life: He had to learn to live comfortably as a member of an "inferior minority." Not only was Paul unfit for military activity; he was also a country boy.

Again, it was Paul's ability to excel in school work that saved him. He had the support of his childhood chum, who was in most of his classes. He was able to make friends with some of the other country boys, most of whom happened to be outstanding students with high ambitions. Paul Torrance had many excellent teachers in his senior high school years at Georgia Military College, but two were particularly influential—Claude Ray, an English and physics teacher, and "Slap" Rentz, who taught history and political science. Claude Ray was exacting and held high standards. From him, Paul learned the importance of accuracy and precision. Slap Rentz had been a coach in his younger days. Some students still addressed him as "Coach" instead of "Major." He spoke out against the evils of the day: dishonesty and pretence, the deceit of people in high office, political corruption, and the grip of power and wealth. For example, he pointed out that people know how to make shoes that will last a lifetime, but power kept them off the market. "Boys, they have us by the balls on the downhill drag," he would exclaim. Paul remembers learning from him about courage and about "being in love with what you are doing." GMC President Colonel Joseph H. Jenkins has written in his memoirs that Paul Torrance was the most intelligent student he ever had.

Paul finished his high school career with the distinction of being first honor graduate and winning prizes in essay writing and oratory. He was voted by his classmates as the most intellectual. In May of 1984, Otis Dorough, one of Paul's teachers at GMC, wrote Paul a letter saying,

> At last I have caught up with you.... I, as one of your former humble teachers, am quite proud of you.... I was glad to be told by my daughter that teachers who are specializing in education at Georgia are required to take some of your courses.... Be assured that I am proud of you, one of the smartest young fellows I had in my classes at GMC.[3]

Paul Torrance's writing ability was developing at this time and was beginning to get some recognition. For example, the *Milledgeville Times* printed the notice reprinted here on April 1, 1936. In a carefully kept diary, Paul Torrance still has a copy of this notice along with a collection of the articles he wrote while at GMC.

> **Paul Torrance Times GMC Reporter**
>
> The Times takes pleasure in announcing that Paul Torrance, well-known GMC student and Baldwin county boy, has joined its staff for the covering of news about local cadets and others at the college.
>
> Mr. Torrance has had an outstanding record at the college and has also taken a prominent part in the work of the young people of the Baptist church. He is an accurate and prompt reporter, and his articles present the news just as it happens.
>
> He has been assistant to Miss Agnes Barnes, GMC librarian this year.

Following high school graduation, Paul Torrance was able to get a job during the summer measuring cotton acreages in his home county under the Agricultural Adjustment Administration. This provided him the necessary funds to attend the junior college department at Georgia Military College that fall. The job also gave him an opportunity to learn to work with an adult white man about the age of his father and to make contacts with almost every level of society in his home county. This gave him his first opportunity to visit

[3] Letter from Otis Dorough, May 23, 1984. E. Paul Torrance Collection Scrapbook MSS 2606 #031. Athens, GA: Hargrett Rare Book and Manuscript Library, University of Georgia

the famous Georgia congressman Carl Vinson. He was assigned to measure the cotton on his farm. His supervisors rated his work as superior. The following summer, he was given a job in the county office computing acreages from the measurements submitted by the field men. This netted the funds for his second year of college and the valuable experience of working "in town" and getting to know a few town people. The National Youth Administration helped Paul stay in college during this time. He worked as an assistant in the GMC library. He learned to classify books, which piqued his interest in research. During this time Paul continued to live at home, where he could ride the school bus to the College.

Paul Torrance's second year of college was, in his estimation, the highlight of his undergraduate years. He had excellent teachers who encouraged and facilitated his learning. His classes were small, and his classmates were able and serious students.

One of the highlights of this year was his French course. He was the only student; another student was to have taken the course with him but was killed in an automobile accident the week before classes began. The instructor, Dr. Ren Thorne, who hailed from Acadia University in Nova Scotia, Canada, was outstanding. Dr. Thorne foresaw Paul's future needs for this advanced work in French. He insisted that Paul continue in all three quarters. Paul read avidly in the whole field of French literature. Dr. Thorne left Paul on his own except for the times that he was reading old French and some of the more difficult dramas and poetry. Some weeks, Paul averaged reading one book per day. This skill in reading French was to help Paul many times in his career. When he needed an additional course to complete his A.B. degree, he was able to challenge successfully one of Mercer University's advanced French literature courses. Also, he was able to pass his doctoral examinations in French without additional preparation. Many times, both in his survival research and creativity research, he was able to get new insights from reading research reports and other documents in the French language.

At the age of 21, Paul again attained the distinction of first honor graduate on completing junior college at GMC. Paul's sister Ellen said that he would have won the West Point appointment, had he been a cadet. The night before graduation, Paul's mother was hospitalized for an appendectomy, but Ellen attended the ceremony.

This looked like the end of Paul's education. Personnel in the Agricultural Adjustment Administration office had changed and Paul was not re-employed for the summer. He had been promised a job with the *Milledgeville Times*, but that went to a graduate of the University of Georgia's School of Journalism. This was 1936—the middle of the Great Depression. No other jobs were to be had. Paul and his father decided that he might "make it" with watermelons, so they planted a large crop. The melon crop was great but the market hit "rock bottom." The freight charges on shipments to Chicago was greater than the sale price of the melons. The Torrances gave unlimited quantities of watermelons to their hungry neighbors and to their cattle and hogs.

On our return trip to Athens from Milledgeville, Dr. Torrance fell asleep, and I mulled over the day's events and activities. I concluded that Paul Torrance's early childhood days, at home and at school, had laid the foundation for his sensitivity to people and his scholarly pursuits. I attempted to make some links.

As a young person, Paul recognized the plight of poor people and the deplorable learning and living conditions of black children. Religion played an important role in his character development. He learned to respect and appreciate people, as well as nature and animals. Paul's many pleasant memories of childhood suggest he was allowed to play creatively and indulge his inquisitive nature. Yet, he had a strict upbringing, as he was young during the Great Depression and he was taught the orthodox Southern Baptist religion of his parents and relatives. His family provided psychological security and love but had to live frugally. As a physically inept country boy, Paul had to learn to live comfortably as a member of a minority. Significant individuals exerted a great influence on Paul's life. His mother was versatile and creative, whereas his father was strict and held high expectations for farm tasks. His father gave up on him as a farmer and encouraged him "to get an education." Young Paul encountered individuals in the community and at school who became role models and mentors to him. He learned the importance of friendliness to others, courage of convictions, and falling in love with something and pursuing it with intensity and persistence. Finally, in these formative years, Paul learned to love learning—reading, writing, and mathematics—and was rewarded for outstanding scholarship at all levels of schooling from elementary school to junior college.

Finally, we arrived home at 183 Cherokee Avenue in Athens June 22, 1992—what a significant day!

REFERENCES

Cook, A.N. (1978, revised edition). *History of Baldwin County Georgia*. Spartanburg, SC: The Reprint Company.

Smith, L. (1949). *Killers of the Dream*. New York: W.W. Norton.

Torrance, E. P. *Narrative Account of Career*. Unpublished manuscript, University of Georgia.

Chapter 2

Teaching and Training (1936–1950):

The Making of a Scholar

As a 13-year-old in June of 1928 (when his father ended a rare speech with, "It's time you learned to eat peas with a fork!"), Paul Torrance realized he had to accept himself as a student and that he had to excel as a student. He did well in high school and junior college, winning county-wide competitions in English and Latin and a scholarship to the state 4-H camp. He knew, however, that eventually he would have to compete with students from all over the United States and Central America. At the time, there were many Cubans and Central Americans at Georgia Military College. Most of them were from very wealthy families. Paul also saw that many were more intelligent than he was. To compensate for his deficiencies, he used greater imagination, creativity, and problem-solving skills. He achieved higher grades in mathematics and English because he could solve original problems and write original essays and compositions of high quality.

When it came time for Paul's university education, the financially troubling years of the Great Depression and the gloom of World War II became obstacles along his path. This section deals with Paul's single-minded dedication to developing his competencies as a psychologist and his skills as a teacher.

FIRST TEACHING EXPERIENCE

The year was 1936, and Paul Torrance was 21 years old. Further education did not seem to be an option, despite the efforts of Slap Rentz, Paul's former teacher and constant supporter. Major Rentz thought that Mercer University at Macon, Georgia, was the right school for Paul, and Paul had been offered a tuition scholarship there. Major Rentz took Paul to Macon, introducing him to friends who were in a position to provide part-time employment, including the publisher of the *Macon Telegraph*. When Paul flunked an interview with the newspaper (the publisher thought he was not aggressive enough), Slap told the publisher he would be hearing about Torrance—that Paul would make a name for himself.

As September approached, Paul applied in desperation to the Civilian Conservation Corps (C.C.C.), which President Roosevelt had created to employ young men in a kind of forestry camp to improve the environment. Just as he was about to be accepted into the C.C.C., Paul was offered a teaching position at Midway Vocational High School at Hardwick, Georgia, which is near Milledgeville. Although Paul had only a two-year provisional certificate from the State of Georgia Department of Education, he was allowed to teach.

The Midway Junior High School was being changed over to a senior high school. The principal had become ill, and Paul was to substitute for him. At this time Baldwin county had no senior high school. Midway had been a nine-grade junior high school. This year was the beginning of a transition and the tenth grade was being added. The next year the eleventh grade was to be added, and so on. In addition to trying to act as principal of this 10-grade school, Paul was to be responsible for all instruction in the eighth, ninth, and tenth grades. He managed fairly well for the first week, but the principal continued to be ill. It was an impossible and overwhelming task, and Paul knew he should not have taken it on. But he was desperate financially and he loved teaching.

Paul felt secure about his knowledge of the subject matter, but not about his pedagogical skills. By this time, the school's problem students had tested Paul sufficiently and had begun to harass him. When the principal returned, Torrance was asked to continue as a teacher of eighth grade English and algebra, and ninth grade history, Latin, and general science. He never studied so hard in his life. He was determined to be a good teacher, but he was being defeated by a few disruptive students. His worst discipline problems were two boys—one in grade eight and the other in grade nine. They were especially creative. The eighth grader later became Secretary of Labor in President Ford's Cabinet. The ninth grader became a very successful and innovative county school superintendent who established a county public high school that was separate from the Georgia Military College and the Georgia State College for Women.

Paul Torrance began to take education courses by correspondence during his first year of teaching. He enjoyed these and won approval from the professors. His monthly salary of $65 was not enough for him to save any money to attend Mercer University or the University of Georgia. However, that summer he was permitted to enroll in Georgia State College for Women as the only male student. Once again he was a social outcast, but he made the best of his two courses. He "discovered" psychology in a class given by an excellent teacher, Dr. Eurie Bell Bolton. She took a special interest in Paul and assured him that he could specialize in psychology. She sent him several encouraging letters after she retired, usually in response to articles Paul had published. Paul Torrance now had a sense of direction for the first time, and an interest that would continue to be exciting and all-consuming.

RETURN TO HIS ALMA MATER

In the fall of 1937, Paul Torrance was offered a teaching position at Georgia Military College—his alma mater. He taught Latin, French, algebra, and history, and gradually he became a more effective teacher. Paul lived in the barracks and received room and board for helping students during study hall, along with a salary of $75 per month. His family was also having a hard time; his sister had difficulty finding any kind of a job, but she finally got a position as a dietitian in a small hospital in Milledgeville. Paul was able to save almost enough to attend summer session at Mercer University. With a small bank loan—his first and only loan—he managed. He earned all As that first summer. He continued improving as a teacher at Georgia Military College and attended Mercer University during the summers until his graduation in August, 1940, summa cum laude. Mercer University provided a relaxing environment, and the quality of students and instruction were high. At Mercer University, Paul received support from several faculty members, including John Gregory, Dean John Clark, Major Ferguson, Dr. Otis Knight, and Dr. Smalley.

Paul is a highly respected alumnus of Mercer University. The *50-Year Reunion* booklet of the Class of 1940 describes Paul as follows:

> **TORRANCE, ELLIS PAUL**
> AB '40, MA '44 (University of Minnesota) Ph.D '51 (University of Michigan)
>
> Professor of educational psychology, Torrance Center for Creative Studies, College of Education, University of Georgia. Married Jessie Pansy Nigh. Member: American Psychological Association, American Creativity Association, American Educational Research Association, American Society of Group Psychotherapy and Psychodrama, Creative Education Foundation, Georgia Association of School Psychologists. Honorary life member and recipient of the Distinguished Scholars Award, National Association for Gifted Children; Fellow, Japanese Society for the Promotion of Science; Recipient of the Founders and Leadership Medal, Creative Education Foundation. Member, First Baptist Church of Athens. Present address: 183 Cherokee Avenue, Athens, GA, 30606-4350.[1]

While on the faculty at Georgia Military College, Torrance first faced a problem that was to come up on several occasions in his career—professional jealousy. His older colleagues held A.B. or M.A. degrees, while Paul had only two years of college. Paul worked very hard as a teacher and got excellent results from his students. He gave the boys at the college more help and was more available to them than the other faculty members. This increased his popularity with the students but at the same time produced some jealousy among his colleagues.

The situation became worse when the Dean started assigning boys who had

---

[1] Mercer University. (1990). *50-Year Reunion—Class of 1940.* Macon, GA: Office of the President.

failed during the fall quarter to Paul Torrance's algebra and plane geometry classes. Paul worked hard at teaching and motivating these students. He knew that many of them were highly intelligent and wanted to do well. He started all over and made up for their deficiencies. Paul knew that his colleagues would not believe how well his students performed, so he gave them national achievement tests at the end of the course. The boys scored well above national norms! Paul Torrance notes, "I do not think this dispelled their feelings of jealousy but it shut them up regarding my low standards. I offered to supply them with copies of the tests but none gave the tests to their classes."[2] Paul received his A.B. and M.A. degrees by taking summer courses, and he gained more teaching experience. The jealousy finally subsided.

There was little or no leisure time in those days for Paul. He attended an occasional movie and concert or play at Georgia State Women's College. His best friends were Colonel J.H. Jenkins (President of Georgia Military College), Colonel Ren Thorne (Dean), and Major Hilton Brown (his roommate). A few other individuals who supported and encouraged him in these years were Mrs. C. B. McCullar, Major Robert Christian, Major Herbert Walden, and Mr. P. N. Bivins, County School Superintendent (a childhood friend of Paul's father).

NORTH TO MINNESOTA

By now, Paul Torrance had decided that he wanted to do graduate work in counseling psychology, and that he wanted to pursue these studies at the University of Minnesota. He knew that professors such as E. G. Williamson, Donald Patterson, John Darley, and Gilbert Wrenn, all of the University of Minnesota, had done pioneering work in this area, had published most of the books in the field, and made up what was probably the most outstanding faculty in the counseling field at that time in the country. Paul applied for admission, was accepted, and Gilbert Wrenn was assigned to be his advisor. Paul's family objected to his going away so far from home during the summer, but they accepted his decision.

When Torrance registered in the summer of 1941, Wrenn was on leave, and Dr. Walter Cook became his advisor. Later Cook was to become his employer and friend. Minnesota was an exciting place for Paul. He loved his studies and succeeded in the courses in educational psychology. At Mercer University he had majored in English and had taken minors in history and education, so he lacked in-depth knowledge of psychology. After final examinations that first summer, he went home and enrolled through correspondence in more psychology courses. He majored in educational psychology with a minor in psychology. His thesis topic was "Predicting and Measuring Success in Plane Geometry."

[2] Interview with E. Paul Torrance. Athens, Georgia, March 1992.

By the time Paul completed his M.A. degree in August, 1944, he had been encouraged by Drs. Walter Cook, Gordon Anderson, and John Rufi to do a doctorate. Rufi, a visiting professor from the University of Missouri, had been very persuasive, and Cook had offered to appoint Torrance as his teaching assistant. But Paul had not managed to save any money beyond summer school expenses and could not make it, even with this financial assistance.

Back at the Georgia Military College, Paul had been promoted for his excellent teaching and his commitment to students. He was now principal of the high school department and registrar for the junior college department. Also, he had established an excellent guidance program that was recognized throughout the state. Paul served on a state-wide committee on high school guidance and made presentations at professional meetings.

On June 22, 1992, when Torrance and I took our day trip back to Milledgeville, we visited the Georgia Military College museum. The museum is located in what was once Paul Torrance's office, when he was principal of the high school program. The museum features a "wall of fame" containing photographs of selected graduates who have distinguished themselves by making significant contributions to society. Prominently displayed on this wall is a photograph of Dr. E. Paul Torrance.

COUNSELING VETERANS AT THE UNIVERSITY OF MINNESOTA

In December, 1944, Paul Torrance was offered a full-time counseling position in the Counseling Bureau at the University of Minnesota. Disabled veterans were returning to colleges and universities, and the Veterans Administration was establishing counseling centers to help them make decisions and adjust to college life. With this offer, Paul could still take one graduate course each quarter and work towards his doctorate. He gladly accepted and left Georgia Military College. Paul worked extremely hard, learned much, and was quite productive on the job. He had articles accepted for publication in the *Journal of Educational Psychology*, *Mathematics Teacher*, and *Occupations*.

Dean Williamson and Gordon Anderson worked hard to get permission from the draft board in Georgia for Paul to continue his work at the Veterans Counseling Center and to assume greater responsibility as its services expanded. In June, 1945, Paul was accepted for limited service.

CAUGHT IN THE DRAFT

Paul Torrance feels certain that if he had stayed on at Georgia Military College, he would never have been drafted. However, World War II was drawing to a close and they were admitting people at the height of their careers and even those with physical disabilities. Paul's examination showed that he was deficient in some of the physical requirements, so he was listed for limited service. He would not be sent into combat. Paul was glad to have this opportunity to work in a military setting. Although he was not a star student in basic training, he proved that he could stand up to the rigors of military training.

Paul's basic training began on June 19, 1945, at Camp Lee, Virginia. The weather was very hot. Paul's fellow trainees were younger and healthier. Since Paul could not keep step or hit a target, he was afraid he would be failed and would have to repeat the training, but he had good legs and could outwalk almost anyone. He also attended the adjutant general's course in Fort Ogelthorpe, Georgia, and made frequent trips into Chattanooga. He was next assigned to Fort Hancock, New Jersey—a quaint setting near New York City. He was able to get on the boat in the afternoon and get into New York City and return in the morning. On three-day passes he was able to go to New York City and explore the wealth of entertainment located there. At night he would attend the theater. During the daylight hours he would visit Coney Island, the Statue of Liberty, and similar sites. He was always able to get a bed at the Service Men's Club.

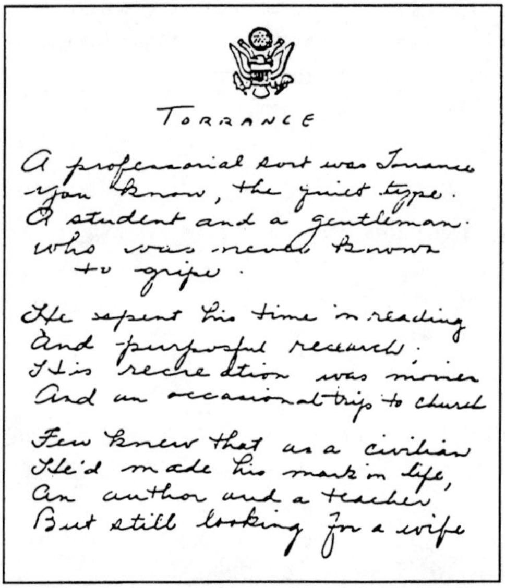
TORRANCE

A professorial sort was Torrance
you know, the quiet type.
A student and a gentleman
who was never known
to gripe.

He spent his time in reading
and purposeful research.
His recreation was movies
And an occasional trip to church

Few knew that as a civilian
He'd made his mark in life,
An author and a teacher
But still looking for a wife

The poem that is reprinted here was written by an army colleague named Joe. This gives us some insight into Paul Torrance's activities during this period.

Since Paul Torrance's unit was being activated, his first promotion was to sergeant, then to staff sergeant. He was recommended for another promotion to technical sergeant, but by this time, career soldiers were returning and being reassigned. This ended Paul Torrance's chances of promotion; a new first sergeant was reassigned to his unit.

AN ARMY PSYCHOLOGIST

Sergeant Paul Torrance was assigned to the Atlantic Coast Branch of the United States Disciplinary Barracks, as a psychiatric social worker and later a psychologist. Now able to use some of his professional skills, Paul could regain his identity and feelings of competence, both of which had been shattered by basic training. As a psychiatric social worker, Paul's job was to interview dishonorably discharged soldiers and prepare a classification report on them before discharge. Being experienced in dictating case histories at the Counseling Bureau in Minneapolis, he produced similar reports in his job as a psychiatric social worker. His typist, drawn from the prisoner pool, noticed that he stressed the strengths of each case as he had done with the disabled veterans in Minnesota. Through the grapevine in the prison, the typist told his buddies to try to get Sergeant Torrance as an interviewer, because he found something good about everybody.

Paul, as usual, was able to complete twice as many cases as anybody else, and again this caused difficulties between Paul and the other psychiatric social workers. However, Paul was soon promoted and able to avoid confrontation and conflict. He was reclassified as a psychologist and received training under Alexander Wolf, George Forlano, Garth Thomas, David Jenkins, Bernard Sless, and others. Dr. Wolf was famous for his analytic group psychotherapy theory and practice. Paul learned a great deal from him. In addition, Paul did a great deal of independent study while in the service. He became thoroughly familiar with the Rorschach Inkblot Test, the Bender Gestalt Test, and the Army Individual Intelligence Test. He conducted a program of group psychotherapy and group guidance for the men who were discharged from Fort Hancock, New Jersey. He would meet with them as a group in the morning and individually in the afternoon, administering vocational guidance and ability tests. Basically, the army was trying to prepare these men to re-enter civilian life, helping them to get out their hostilities over being dishonorably discharged and think positively about what they were going to do in the future.

In June of 1946, Dr. Maurice Woolf wrote to Paul and offered him a position in the Counseling Bureau for Veterans Administration, which Dr. Woolf was directing at Kansas State College. Paul accepted the position and left the Army on July 18, 1946, at Fort Bragg, North Carolina. Although he felt some sadness, he also felt good about the service he had been able to provide and the professional training he had gotten.

COUNSELING AT KANSAS STATE COLLEGE

Although Paul had worked with Dr. Woolf at the University of Minnesota Student Counseling Bureau, life in Manhattan, Kansas, was another world for him to conquer. In many ways, the young people there were different from those he had known in Georgia and Minnesota. They were preoccupied by another form of dust bowl. In career planning, they prepared for two occupations—one that they really wanted and one to fall back upon in case of "another dust bowl."

In 1947, Paul was appointed Dean of Men at Kansas State College, with additional counseling duties. According to his colleague and friend, Charles

Glotzbach, Paul set a splendid example as an instructor and counselor. He was very helpful to new graduate students. He was a good instructor in formal courses, and he often hosted groups of students at his apartment, where he provided food and stimulating discussions. He always had copies of new books available to attract the interest of students. It was partly because of Paul Torrance that Charles Glotzbach later went to the University of Minnesota to obtain his Ph.D. and work in the Student Counseling Department.

At Kansas State, Paul decided he wanted to improve his professional competencies but not pursue the doctorate. Therefore, in the summer of 1947 he arranged an exchange clinicianship at the University of Oklahoma under the direction of Dr. Bill Lemmon—a Rogerian. He also was given a further introduction to group psychotherapy that was different from the one he had received under Dr. Alexander Wolf. Next, Paul went for a month to study with Dr. Jacob L. Moreno at the Psychodramatic Institute in Beacon, New York. Paul was captivated by Beacon, by New York City, and by Moreno. In many ways, Moreno was the greatest teacher Paul Torrance ever had. At the time, Moreno had only five full-time students. Paul stated, "We worked on our own every morning, and during lunch Moreno debriefed us and taught us with his usual zest; each afternoon, he conducted psychodramatic and sociodramatic sessions, and these experiences became teaching materials during dinner with Moreno."[3] Twice each week, the students accompanied Moreno and his colleague and wife-to-be Zerka Toeman to New York City where they participated in Moreno's private and public sessions. Moreno was teaching every minute, from Beacon to New York City and then again at night from New York City to Beacon. This experience greatly influenced Torrance. He later used sociodrama as a technique to gain insights into human behavior with students in his classes at the University of Minnesota and at the University of Georgia.

During the 1948–49 academic year, Paul Torrance's teaching and counseling took on new dimensions. It was then that his skills in both these areas reached their greatest heights. His students were highly productive, and their achievements continue to amaze him today.

Professional jealousy showed up again in the Counseling Bureau at Kansas State. Paul failed to develop good relations with two members of the Department of Psychology. Most of the graduate students wanted Paul to be their advisor, and enrollments in his courses were higher than in other courses. While at Kansas State College, Paul received encouragement and support from Dr. Maurice Woolf, President Milton Eisenhower, Dr. Charles Glotzbach, Dr. Vera Gatch, Dr. Dorothy Mitchell-Lemmon, and Dr. Robert Wilson.

Moreno convinced Paul Torrance that he should complete a doctorate, and Dr. Maurice Woolf and his wife Jeanne at Kansas State College reinforced Paul's

---

[3] Torrance, E. P. (1972). *Narrative account of career.* Unpublished manuscript, University of Georgia.

decision to do so. In June, 1948, before leaving to do his doctoral studies, Paul conducted a workshop with Dr. Elwood Murray at the University of Denver. Each day, Dr. Murray would present some formulation in general semantics and Paul would then conduct a sociodrama to test and illustrate the concept. Apparently, every member of the class was an excellent actor or actress, so each sociodrama was a huge success and provided plenty of data for exciting insights into general semantics and human behavior.

FULL-TIME STUDIES

Paul Torrance chose the University of Michigan at Ann Arbor for his doctoral studies. His interests had shifted from counseling to classroom interaction. He chose the University of Michigan for three major reasons: First, the Research Center for Group Dynamics was moving there from M.I.T. (Massachusetts Institute of Technology), and he wanted to specialize in the sociopsychology of education; second, the psychology department at Michigan was outstanding; and third, Paul was awarded a Horace J. Rackham Special Fellowship and he had the advantages provided by the G.I. Bill of Rights.

This money—about $2,000—along with his savings enabled Paul to enjoy the year as a student. He was not disappointed. His one-year stay at the University of Michigan was the only time that Paul was a full-time student, completely dedicated to scholarship. There were approximately 25 graduate students at that time. They were all good students and very friendly people, and they were from different parts of the United States. Although he took a full doctoral program in one year, Paul found time to develop strong friendships with many of the students. For example, students and faculty from the sociopsychology program met every Sunday evening to discuss the most recent research in the field.

Paul considered that non-credit seminar the best course he ever took in his university career. In his words,

> I think I enjoyed this year, 1948 and 1949, more than any other time. It was a time that I devoted myself entirely to the program. Our time in the library and in study groups was a lot of fun. We developed many really strong relationships during our work together. There was a fair amount of interaction, and we enjoyed one another. Most of them were like me and had been officers in the armed forces in World War II, so there was a great deal of camaraderie.[4]

Paul's special friends during this year of doctoral study came largely from his study groups. They included Philip Mitchell, Evan Pattishall, Willard Bateson, Wilbur Williams, Roy Summerhill, and Julius Hill. While he was a student at the University of Michigan, Paul received support from a number of individuals: Dr.

[4] Interview with E. Paul Torrance. Athens, Georgia, March 1992.

Clark Trow, Dr. Claude Eggleston, Dr. Howard McCluskey, Dr. Angus Campbell, Dr. Arthur Moehlman, Dr. Harold Kelly, Dr. Albert Zander, Dr. Harold Guetzgow, and Dr. Theodore Newcom.

Paul left the University of Michigan in August, 1949, to return to Kansas State College as Director of the Counseling Bureau and professor of psychology. Maurice Woolf had become Dean of Students. The full-time counselors included Ira Gordon, Charles Glotzbach, and Dorothy Mitchell-Lemmon. This was a vigorous, dynamic, and hard-working group that pioneered many innovative programs under adverse conditions. During the 1949-50 term, Paul Torrance completed requirements in German and wrote his dissertation, *Self-Concepts and Their Significance in the Learning and Adjustment of College Freshmen*. His dissertation research and doctoral studies at Michigan, as well as some small experimental studies he had conducted at Kansas State College, had by now addicted Dr. Torrance to original research. At that time, there were almost no research jobs in educational psychology at universities. He had an opportunity for two jobs—a counseling job at Duke University and a research job with the Human Resources Research Laboratory with the U.S. Air Force. He decided to take the full-time research position and became director of a field unit in support of the United States Air Force's survival training program.

This period of Paul's young adulthood was marked by determination, dedication, and persistence to succeed academically despite the hardships of the Great Depression and the intrusion of World War II. Paul's teaching experiences, education at various universities, and army training helped prepare him for the original research that was to consume his interests, energies, and life. He was keenly aware of students who learned by unconventional means-creatively. Identifying and developing the creative process was to become his mission. In fact, he demonstrated the creative process in his teaching and learning. He earned high grades in his courses and graduated with distinction or summa cum laude. These achievements, the result of his hard work and great imagination, were harbingers of the prodigious contributions he would make to psychology and education in future years. A scholar was in the making.

Chapter Three

U.S. Air Force Advanced Survival School (1951-1957):

The Emergence of Creativity

> *"There is little question in my mind that you (Torrance) are the acknowledged authority in the U.S. on the psychological factors involved in small group and individual behavior under extreme conditions."* [1]
>
> — Capt. Keith Young (1957)

The U.S. Air Force Survival School was established in 1948, when General Curtis Le May expressed concern over the high percentage of bomber crews shot down in World War II who survived the bailout but didn't survive on the ground. Dr. Torrance's seven years with the school are best described as the "survival psychology" phase of his career. During this time, Dr. Torrance gained national and international recognition for his studies of the psychology of survival in emergencies and extreme conditions, the psychology of training men to cope more successfully with emergencies and extreme conditions, and the personalities of the American jet aces in the Korean War. At this time as well, Paul began developing his insights into giftedness and creativity.

In 1951, the Korean War had begun. Paul Torrance says:

> I should mention how I happened to get into the Korean War. At the University of Michigan doctoral program in educational psychology, I became acquainted with Colonel Philip Mitchell, who was on leave from the Pentagon to complete his doctorate. In 1951, back on duty after completing his doctorate, Luigi Petrullo was head of the Human Resources Research Laboratory (HRRL). Colonel Mitchell was assigned to work with HRRL to activate a research program at the USAF Advanced Survival School. Then there was the problem of staffing. It was a vast, unexplored field. Colonel Mitchell recommended me. I was enjoying life as Director of the

---

[1] Personal communication from Captain Keith Young to Dr. Torrance. March 9, 1957 (in possession of the author).

> Counseling Bureau at Kansas State, and I had also been offered a job in counseling at Duke University. There was something about the Survival School and developing a psychology of survival which attracted me and was very challenging. I accepted the job of heading the research field unit, got introduced to HRRL, located at Bolling Air Force Base in Washington, DC, and then headed for Colorado Springs to open up a Research Unit. Later the School moved to Stead Air Force Base at Reno, Nevada.[2]

In survival training, Paul witnessed and was part of a new kind of learning—experiential learning. To Paul, this was thrilling, exciting, real learning. Paul, as Director of the Research Unit, supervised a staff of eight people who were involved in three major areas of research: instructional methods and techniques for survival, personnel assessment (individual and group), and assessment and improvement of survival techniques.

PSYCHOLOGY OF SURVIVAL

Torrance and his staff developed materials to be used by combat aircrews. These materials dealt with teaching men global survival in all areas and under a variety of conditions. Survival schools were held in mountainous country (Plumas National Forest in northern California), jungle environs (Okeefenokee Swamp in southern Georgia), desert (Nevada), and cold conditions (Alaska). The psychology of survival was taught to groups of aircrew men, ranging from missile and scientific teams to DEW (Distant Early Warning) line teams. Every 17 days, new teams of aircrew personnel were trained at the survival school located at Stead Air Force Base in Reno, Nevada. This provided Torrance and his staff with ample opportunity to teach and conduct research on the psychology of survival. They doubled the amount of information available on survival psychology. Also, Torrance's Research Unit was able to read and summarize all the available relevant research that had been conducted prior to 1951–52.

One issue that Torrance and his Research Unit examined was leadership in the survival of small isolated groups. They identified five fundamental questions related to this issue:

- Is there a *need* for a leader in small isolated groups in emergency and extreme conditions?
- *Who* should be the *leader* under such conditions?
- What do people *expect* of a leader in emergencies and extreme conditions?
- How *do* leaders behave under such conditions?
- How *should* leaders behave under such conditions?

---

[2] Interview with E. Paul Torrance at his home in Athens, Georgia. June, 1992.

Their research related to these questions is important, as each affects the mental health of groups subjected to extreme stress. The answers to these questions are documented in a report written by Torrance (1957a). In the report, evidence is cited to support the conclusion that there is a definite need for a leader in small isolated groups under threat and that this concept needs to be taught widely to crews, teams, and other small groups exposed to danger. This information had particular relevance at the time of the Korean War and later the Vietnam War.

In his Psychology of Survival course taught to aircrew teams, Torrance lectured on a wide variety of topics, including brainwashing techniques employed by Communists and how they destroyed group dynamics. Basically, the Communists created dislike among group members, destroyed the power of the leader, broke down communications, and destroyed the group's goals. Torrance created posters and slides to illustrate the principles of survival that resulted from the research.[3]

As Director of the Survival Research Field Unit, Paul Torrance had to deliver a lecture on the psychology of survival, yet he felt so inadequate physically. Paul had never developed a strong physique. Somehow a legend in the USAF developed that Paul Torrance could endure all kinds of pain—that he was a kind of Superman. As a psychologist, Torrance helped prepare the aircrew teams before they went on survival training and then evaluated their success upon their return to base camp.

SURVIVING IN EXTREME CONDITIONS: EXPERIENTIAL LEARNING

Beginning on September 8, 1953, the Los Angeles *Daily News* carried a series of articles entitled "Survival! The Fantastic Story of a Lost B-36 Bomber Crew." The newspaper sent a reporter and photographer to document the seven-day, 50-mile survival trek through the rugged Plumas National Forest in the high Sierra Mountains of northern California.

[3] "Survival and Affect Linkages." E. Paul Torrance Collection Scrapbook MSS 2606 #053. Athens, GA: Hargrett Rare Book and Manuscript Library, University of Georgia.

Bomber crews were made up of men from the Bronx to Broadway, as well as country kids and lads from small towns. Many were products of an overly indulgent civilization. General Le May wanted to make his crews as capable and self-reliant on the ground as they were in the air. He felt that the air crews could be toughened up, taught to live off the land and survive anywhere, from the frigid arctic to the steaming jungles.

In May of 1951, Major Hans Marechal was given the job of commanding the 3904th Training Squadron, which ran the secret Survival School. He said, "I'll train these men to survive or else. I'll get them teed off at the world, to learn their reactions and behavior under stress" ("Survival!," 1953). That is what General Le May wanted—a rough-and-tumble outfit that could not only fly the atom bomb anywhere in the world, but could walk back if they got shot down a thousand miles from nowhere. The California newspaper detailed the "Survival Trek" of 22 men in the wilderness. Armed with an E-1 pack consisting of the barest essentials—a poncho, a vacuum-packed sleeping bag, two tins of SA-3 emergency rations, a knife, a compass, insect repellant, an axe, and three pounds of raw meat, the "walking air force" had to scrounge off the land for seven days. The grounded airmen had to learn to be resourceful. They were accompanied by a survival instructor who acted as a teacher–observer and decided which men would be sent back to their bases, either combat-ready or washed out. Each man lost many pounds, faced possible starvation, and reacted to various situations for which they had no previous learned response. The men learned to trap animals (porcupines and birds) and catch fish in order to survive. They learned what plants and mushrooms they could eat. A typical meal in the evening might be boiled sedge grass, squaw root, tree moss, wild onions, two frogs, and a trout.

The men learned to be self-reliant and to cooperate with others. They learned to tie knots and to fashion a rope from their nylon parachute risers that they could use to scale a mountain and rappel on a cliff. They had to stay clean to protect their personal .health, so they made a bathtub from a poncho laid in a shallow depression in the ground and filled with water from a stream. The men learned to slow their pace and conserve their strength.

Even though the training was rugged, none of the men died. However, all men had to draw on their personal resources and rely on each other. Some men became desperate and did foolish things. Once, two men slipped out of high camp in the mountains and walked 20 miles to a country store. They bought a big chunk of baloney. They got caught. At graduation, Major Hans Marechal said to them, "Everybody but you (two) men get diplomas showing they are real men. You guys get back the baloney!" ("Survival!," 1953).

Some 18,000 men graduated from the survival school during the 1951–57 period. These men learned an important lesson—to survive in extreme conditions and perhaps to stay alive behind enemy lines. There was no place in a bomber's crew for a mama's boy. If one was found, he was gotten rid of quickly.

When the men came out of the hills, half-starved, dog-tired, and footsore, they were assessed by the psychologist, Dr. E. Paul Torrance. He wrote a report on each man and determined with the survival instructors who was recommended for combat or who was dismissed.

The methods used by the survival school were criticized by some. The Torrance Archives at the University of Georgia contain a scrapbook on this period of research that deals specifically with controversy surrounding the training methods used by the United States Air Force Survival School. In 1955, a local "muck" magazine, aptly called *Cuckoo*, stated that part of the torture included orgies of brandy, champagne, and blondes through which the men had to wade. Further, this magazine stated, that the men were locked up in an upright coffin with a strip-teaser and not being able to move. No wonder many a man came out of this camp a gibbering idiot! If they had ever publicized this highly scandalous affair—why, every red-blooded young American under 70 wouldn't have joined.

Headlines in newspapers and magazines reflected this controversy:

"Brainwash—Courses in Cruelty by U.S. Services"
"Rigorous Training Practices at Stead (Reno, Nevada) Bring Repercussions (Trainees Are Given Taste of What Commies Do)"
"Training By Torture"
"Stead Officers Deny Tests Mistreat, Degrade Airmen"
"Education for Heroism?"
"Stead Air Force Base Under Investigation"

Newsweek magazine ran an article on the survival training methods at Stead, stating that the conditions and training paralleled those at Communist prisons in Korea—36-hour interrogation sessions, electric shocks, and standing in water for hours. Wing Commander Colonel McKenzie was called to Washington, DC, for a conference on the methods used at Stead.

The U.S. Air Force could not put up with this nonsense and decided to invite cameramen to observe things first-hand. About 100 accepted the invitation, which included a visit to the simulated prisoner-of-war camp on the base.

The consensus as a result of this open house was that the training taught men to evade the enemy or, if caught, to avoid brainwashing. "Tough but not inhuman" was the conclusion. It did not degrade men or goad them to the point of breaking.

This participatory learning was relatively new, and Torrance's research unit was giving it prominence. So little was known about how to train men to survive in extreme conditions, and every minute of training was precious. It had to make a difference. People's lives depended upon it.

Torrance and his research team identified these skills as being important to survival:

- inventiveness
- creativity
- imagination
- originality
- flexibility
- decision-making ability
- courage.

Much of the research on survival was reported in U.S. Air Force publications that were classified and not released to the public or to universities at the time. However, a summary of Torrance's (1957b) six years of survival research is now available. It deals with adapting to failure, pain, and torture; climatic extremes; food and water deprivation; and isolation and reduced stimulation. Paul Torrance's published articles on survival were widely quoted in group dynamics and sociology textbooks in the early 1960s.

THE STUDY OF THE JET ACE

In 1953, Paul Torrance headed up a research team that studied fighter interceptor combat effectiveness in Korea. This involved reviewing records, conducting interviews, and administering psychological tests to jet aces, near aces, and pilots who made no hits. The results of this study indicated that calculated risk taking was the factor that distinguished the jet aces from other pilots who were not as successful.

The basic question asked in this study was, "What makes a good jet-fighter pilot?" During the Korean War, U.S. Air Force officials kept wondering why some jet pilots with nearly the same educational backgrounds and physical skills as others were so outstandingly successful. These are the figures: A handful of jet pilots (38) bagged well over one third of the 823 MIG-15s shot down in the war. These jet aces represented only 5% of all of the Air Force fighter pilots at the time.

The research team closely matched the jet aces with other, less successful pilots, noting their ranks, ages, and World War II combat experience. The outstanding conclusion was that the ace is a man who has learned to get the best performance possible from himself. In this respect, he is similar to outstanding sports figures (for example, hockey's Wayne Gretzky or baseball's Nolan Ryan).

Through interviews and a biographical inventory (the Life Experience Inventory developed by Paul Torrance and Robert Ziller in 1957), the research team found that aces had a number of common characteristics that were different from those of their less successful aviation counterparts. The aces were aggressive, self-confident, and almost fanatically devoted to flying. They were unusually articulate, friendly, soft-spoken, enthusiastic, happy, colorful, and emotionally alive. The same emotional intensity was not found in less successful pilots. The jet ace's motivation was so strong that his fellow pilots had difficulty understanding his willingness to take calculated risks, his cool performance under stress, and his commitment to his job. Earl Nightingale, in a radio program called "Playing it Safe Can Be Risky" (1972), highlighted the essence of Torrance's study of the jet ace: "It is the wise person who learns the importance of risk-taking."

In "Portrait of an Ace" (1954) in *Time* magazine, Torrance's research was summed up: "I have nothing but great admiration for them... The jet ace is a man who goes out into life and meets it head on" (p. 38).

Torrance's later research on creativity revealed that the description of a jet ace—a courageous risk taker who is independent and committed—was also the description of a creative person.

After completing the study of the jet aces, Paul Torrance encountered a frustrating problem. He was invited to make a presentation at the annual meeting of the Western Psychological Association at Long Beach, California. He prepared his paper and a news release in advance and submitted it to Dr. Robert French, Director of the Crew Research Laboratory, under which the Survival Field Unit operated. Both the paper and the news release were approved. The Korean War was still on, but was grinding to a close at this time.

Newspaper reporters all jumped on the jet ace story and wanted to know more than the news release contained. *Time* magazine also latched onto the story. The Pentagon wanted a report. Paul Torrance prepared his own report and illustrated it with "Dennis the Menace" cartoons. Hank Ketchum, the cartoonist, was very interested, gave permission, and even designed a cover for the report. Dr. Robert French apparently liked the report and thought that the Pentagon officers would like it as well; Torrance was wary of this decision but went along with it. Pentagon personnel were not impressed with the "Dennis the Menace" version of the report, and it was never returned.

It appears that officials in the Pentagon were suspicious of Paul's research. His research uncovered the characteristics of an ace and theirs did not. The tests developed by the U.S. Air Force had been effective in pilot selection during World War II, but they did not differentiate between aces and the other types of flyers. Some were afraid that this finding posed a threat to the selection test battery, but the Director of the Personnel Research Laboratory did not feel threatened. The biographical inventory, if used, would differentiate aces from fighter pilots on personal factors. Several other agencies doing military research praised the report. It related significant early life experiences to later risk-taking tendencies, which were essential to be a jet ace. The research report on the use of a biographical inventory has been sought and used by scholars in many situations over the years.

RESEARCH CONTRIBUTIONS

Dr. Jacob L. Moreno (1957), editor of the *International Journal of Sociometry* commented on the research:

> It gives me great pleasure to assert that the researchers at Stead Field Unit No. 2, Survival Methods Branch, Office for Social Science Programs, Air Force Personnel & Training Center, have been a great stimulus to small group and group training research. The considerable number of papers which our Editorial Board has accepted previously in *Sociometry*, now in *Group Psychotherapy* and the *International Journal of Sociometry* is a token demonstration of our high regard of their scientific worth. Another objective demonstration of the high regard in which the Survival studies are held is that the papers of your group are widely referred to in bibliographies and footnotes throughout the literature, not only in American but also in foreign journals.[4]

Further evidence of the value of Paul Torrance's research was clearly articulated by Captain Keith Young:

> We may not always have agreed on minor points, Dr. Torrance, and at times I must admit that I have joined the crows on the fence derisively cawing, 'Head-shrinker!' and 'Bump-feeler!' but I can assure you, sir, that I have the utmost respect for the works you have produced. In general, I would describe them as unassailable and of particularly high value in the Evasion & Escape field.[5]

There were a number of influences on Paul Torrance's thinking during his "survival psychology" phase. In addition to the research team, the aircrew specialists, and the survival instructors and specialists, Dr. Torrance had two other major sources of influence: consultants and other survival researchers, and survivors themselves (past and present).

Perhaps the most influential consultant was Donald Super. He triggered many productive ideas and provided wise advice and support. The biographical inventory used in the Jet Ace study and later in the Risk Scale were inspired by Super's work. Albert Zander and Stan Schachter were also good mentors. They were very good at throwing group dynamics at Torrance and letting them

---

[4] Personal communication from Jacob L. Moreno to E. Paul Torrance. March 28, 1957 (in possession of the author).

[5] Personal communication from Captain Keith Young to Dr. Torrance. March 11, 1957 (in possession of the author).

trigger survival psychology ideas. Leon Festinger, a consultant in the social psychology field, was very good. He had a reputation for being hypercritical, but he was always supportive of Torrance and his associates in the survival research project. In addition, Thomas Harrell, Hans Strupp, Howard Houseman, Robert French, Raymond Bowers, and several other psychologists and sociologists were influential during this period.

Although critics have scoffed at Torrance's reliance upon the published and unpublished accounts by survivors of their emergency and extreme experiences, he found these data valid, and they triggered some of his best ideas. He interviewed a large number of survivors. One of Torrance's job-related hobbies at this time was collecting books on survival. He saw how emergency and extreme conditions require creative behavior, and he collected over 1,000 books on the subject, some of them autographed by the authors. Throughout his career, Paul Torrance always tried to read the most recent literature on a subject, issue, or problem he was interested in. He said it always paid off.

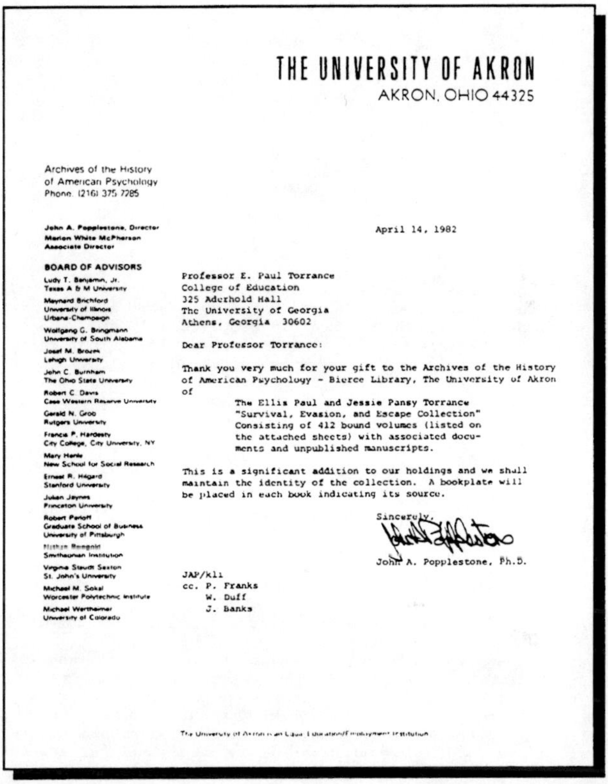

THE UNIVERSITY OF AKRON
AKRON, OHIO 44325

Archives of the History
of American Psychology
Phone (216) 375 7285

John A. Popplestone, Director
Marion White McPherson
Associate Director

BOARD OF ADVISORS
Ludy T. Benjamin, Jr.
Texas A & M University
Maynard Brichford
University of Illinois
Urbana-Champaign
Wolfgang G. Bringmann
University of South Alabama
Josef M. Brozek
Lehigh University
John C. Burnham
The Ohio State University
Robert C. Davis
Case Western Reserve University
Gerald N. Grob
Rutgers University
Francis P. Hardesty
City College, City University, NY
Mary Henle
New School for Social Research
Ernest R. Hilgard
Stanford University
Julian Jaynes
Princeton University
Robert Perloff
Graduate School of Business
University of Pittsburgh
Nathan Reingold
Smithsonian Institution
Virginia Staudt Sexton
St. John's University
Michael M. Sokal
Worcester Polytechnic Institute
Michael Wertheimer
University of Colorado

April 14, 1982

Professor E. Paul Torrance
College of Education
325 Aderhold Hall
The University of Georgia
Athens, Georgia 30602

Dear Professor Torrance:

Thank you very much for your gift to the Archives of the History of American Psychology - Bierce Library, The University of Akron of

The Ellis Paul and Jessie Pansy Torrance "Survival, Evasion, and Escape Collection" Consisting of 412 bound volumes (listed on the attached sheets) with associated documents and unpublished manuscripts.

This is a significant addition to our holdings and we shall maintain the identity of the collection. A bookplate will be placed in each book indicating its source.

Sincerely,

John A. Popplestone, Ph.D.

JAP/kli
cc. P. Franks
W. Duff
J. Banks

This collection of "survival" books has now been donated to the National Archives of the History of American Psychology at the University of Akron, to be used as a theme collection to show how psychologists get their information when they enter new fields. The University's letter acknowledging receipt of the collection is included above.[6]

As the war in Korea came to a close in the spring of 1957, Paul Torrance was

---

[6] Letter from John Poppleston, August 14, 1981. E. Paul Torrance Collection Scrapbook MSS 2606 #023. Athens, GA: Hargrett Rare Book and Manuscript Library, University of Georgia.

transferred to the Air Force Personnel and Training Research Center at Randolph Air Force Base in Texas. One of Torrance's staff, Dr. Edwin H. Richardson, wrote the unsolicited letter of introduction reproduced below.[7]

Of all the wars during Dr. Torrance's lifetime (World War I, World War II, Korea and Vietnam), the Korean Conflict was Paul Torrance's war. He was a civilian and was not officially in it, but the men who went through the sur-

Office for Social Science Programs
AIR FORCE PERSONNEL AND TRAINING RESEARCH CENTER
Air Research and Development Command
United States Air Force
Randolph Air Force Base, Texas

REFER REPLY TO:
Stead Field Unit Number 2 (Survival Methods Branch)
Office for Social Science Programs
Air Force Personnel and Training Research Center
Stead Air Force Base, Reno, Nevada — 15 February 1957

TO WHOM IT MAY CONCERN

It has indeed been a privilege to work under Dr. E. Paul Torrance. Dr. Paul Torrance has been the Director of our Survival Methods Branch Field Unit. It has been possible to know him both socially and vocationally. I would like to emphasize that Dr. Torrance has not asked for any letter of recommendation from me. This is totally spontaneous on my part, and it is in fact more a matter of appreciation. Paul Torrance is a proud man and not one to ask for favors, and consequently it gives me a real pleasure to be able to write such a letter.

Without any hesitation I can state that Dr. Torrance has been the finest man under whom I have had the privilege of working.

He has tireless energy. Despite the long hours of devotion to duty he is almost always in even temperament. In fact, he is so even tempered that he is prone to absorb discomforts and inconveniences without comment. Although most patient with personalities, his enthusiasm in his work obviously accounts for deep disappointment and frustration when his work is neither understood or appreciated. As a sensitive man he invests a tremendous amount of himself in his work and has a keen feeling for a job well done.

He is quiet, soft spoken, and a considerate man who will do anything for his staff. It is natural that he resents impositions made on his generosity. One of his outstanding characteristics is his organizational ability. His office, his home, his person, and his work shows the greatest utilization of adherence to facts and details. Despite any adherence for systems he has the flexibility and open mindedness so that he is neither dogmatic or opinionated. These facts along with his quiet but evident sense of good humor make him an easy man with whom to work.

His creativity is sparkled with a certain flair for the fancy that gives a variety and appeal to his work. He is straight forward, persistent, and goal-oriented. These factors and his natural ease in developing empathy with superiors, equals, and subordinates accounts for his indirect way of inspiring others. He is thorough but not excessively perfectionist. He is mild mannered, but definitely the boss. His desire for accomplishments makes him a thinker, a creator, and a doer - rather than a windy talker. In fact, I would say that his strength in leadership is through example rather than statement.

Edwin H. Richardson, Ph.D.

---

[7] Personal communication from Edwin H. Richardson to Dr. Torrance. Februaru 15, 1957 (in possession of the author).

vival training he was studying were in combat over Korea. His research unit studied their escape, evasion, and P.O.W. experiences. Paul Torrance lectured to these men on the psychological aspects of survival; he and his unit observed their performance in the field and in the P.O.W. compound. He felt split between two worlds—he was both in the midst of combat and in the civilian world, where few were interested in or cared about the Korean Conflict, and many would have preferred to deny that the U.S. was in a war at all. This split was even more severe after he had spent a month on Korean air bases during combat.

Torrance's research during this time laid the foundation for his lifelong pursuit: learning how to identify and develop creative potential. During the USAF survival research program, Torrance learned that the underlying element of survival is *creativity,* and that risk taking and other creative skills are essential for producing constructive behavior and unusual achievements. He learned about the important role of participatory learning and gained powerful new insights about group dynamics and interpersonal development. In a personal letter, Torrance reflects:

> Many of my ideas emerged from my survival research with the USAF. It was not until my retirement that I realized how much I have been influenced by this. ...In the survival schools, the goal was to train men to behave effectively in emergencies and extreme conditions. *I have held that whenever one is faced with a problem for which he has no practiced or learned solution, some degree of creativity is required.* [This came to be known as Paul's simple survival definition of creativity; emphasis added.] Of course, they were taught many solutions that others had used—from the American Indians to polar expeditions to survivors of World Wars I and II. I became a firm believer in experiential learning, cooperative learning in small groups, learning in all modalities, tolerance of disagreement in groups, the extreme importance of motivation and creative thinking.[8]

Paul Torrance's "survival definition," highlighted above, is the briefest and, in some ways, most satisfactory definition of creativity. The component parts of a creative solution can be taught, but the creative act itself must be self-discovered and self-disciplined. Therefore, it was important in survival training to involve men in practicing means of self-discovery, self-discipline, and the use of imagination.

Throughout this time (1951–1957), Paul kept up a regular correspondence with his mother, who was the letter writer of the family. He wrote at least one letter a week to her, and more often when he was on a trip. He tried to give his parents a feel for the wonders of the places he was visiting and what he was experiencing, because neither of them had traveled widely. He sent plenty of postcards and a few souvenirs. During this period, Paul went to busi-

---

[8] Personal communication from Dr. Torrance to the author. December 25, 1991 (in possession of the author).

ness/professional meetings in Japan, Korea, Hawaii, Guam, San Francisco, Los Angeles, New York City, Chicago, Paris, Brussels, Alaska, Las Vegas, Washington DC, and many air bases.

Finally, combat over Korea came to an end, and support for social science research by the United States Air Force was reduced. The survival research training program was phased out. It was time for Torrance to resume his career in higher education.

REFERENCES

Nightengale, E. (1972, December). Playing it safe can be risky (Broadcast #2352). In *Earl Nightengale: Our Changing World*. Chicago: WGN Radio.

Portrait of an ace. (1954, May 31). *Time,* p. 38.

Survival! The Fantastic Story of a Lost B-36 Bomber Crew. (1953, August 31). Los Angeles Daily News. pp. 10, 39.

Torrance, E.P. (1953). How groups behave when surviving. *Air Intelligence Training Bulletin, 5*, 360–370.

Torrance, E.P. (1954). The behavior of small groups under the stress conditions of survival. *American Sociology Review, 19*, 751–755.

Torrance, E.P. (1956). Will to survive: What combat aircrewmen believe about it. *Air Intelligence Training Bulletin, 8*, 11–22.

Torrance, E.P. (1957a). Leadership in the survival of small isolated groups. In *Symposium on Preventive and Social Psychiatry*. (pp. 309-327). Walter Reed Army Institute of Research. Washington, DC: U.S. Government Printing Office, April 15–17.

Torrance, E.P. (1957b). *Surviving emergencies and extreme conditions: A summary of six years of research*. Unpublished manuscript prepared at the Personnel Research Center at Lackland Air Force Base in Texas. [A copy is deposited in the Archives in the History of American Psychology at the University of Dayton.]

Torrance, E.P. (1957c). Group Decision-Making and Disagreement. *Social Forces, 35(4)*, 314–318.

Torrance, E.P., LaForge, G.R., & Mason, R. (1956). *Group adaptation in emergencies and extreme conditions*. Randolph Air Force Base, TX: Office for Social Science Programs, Air Force Personnel and Training Research Center. (Technical Memorandum OSSP-TM-56-4.)

Torrance, E.P., & Ziller, R.C. (1956, November). Crew decisions under conditions of uncertainty. Paper presented to National Research Council—Air Force Symposium on Personnel, Training, and Human Engineering Research, Washington, DC.

Torrance, E.P., & Ziller, R.C. (1957). *Risk and life experience: Development of a scale for measuring risk-taking tendencies*. Lackland Air Force Base, TX: Air Force Personnel and Training Research Center.

Chapter 4

The Minnesota Years (1958–1966):

The Development of Creativity

The Road Not Taken

Two roads diverged in a yellow wood,
And sorry I could not travel both
And be one traveler, long I stood
And looked down one as far as I could
To where it bent in the undergrowth;

Then took the other, as just as fair,
And having perhaps the better claim,
Because it was grassy and wanted wear;
Though as for that the passing there
Had worn them really about the same,

And both that morning equally lay
In leaves no step had trodden black.
Oh, I kept the first for another day!
Yet knowing how way leads on to way,
I doubted if I should ever come back.

I shall be telling this with a sigh
Somewhere ages and ages hence:
Two roads diverged in a wood, and I,
I took the one less traveled by,
And that has made all the difference.

— Robert Frost *

Paul Torrance had been involved in original research for several years, but the University of Minnesota provided an opportunity to do something quite different. Torrance struck out on the road "less traveled." And that "made all the difference." His choice set him apart from other contemporary psychologists and educators.

At the University of Minnesota in 1958, Torrance (following up on a recommendation of his advisory committee at the Bureau of Educational Research) initiated a program of research to understand the role of creativity in the education of gifted children. From the beginning, everyone, including the Dean of Education, was committed to a concept of a variety of kinds of giftedness. It was an easy decision for Torrance to begin work on the identification of the creatively gifted and the cultivation of creative thinking abilities.

---

* Reprinted with permission of the publisher, Henry Holt, & Co.

WORLD AND LOCAL EVENTS IN 1958: A FAVORABLE RESEARCH CLIMATE

The first two of eight highly productive years at the University of Minnesota, 1958 and 1959, were particularly eventful for Paul. He worked with stimulating, encouraging colleagues and hard-working, loyal students and research assistants. His research focused on the analysis of the definition and components of creativity, measuring creative potential, and developing creativity as a skill through various activities. As a professor, he made his course on Personality and Mental Health famous. It was also the venue through which he met his future wife.

There were a number of significant events in the world, the United States, and the Minneapolis area in 1958, and some of these events and issues had an indirect bearing on Torrance's research.

On January 27, 1958, the United States and the Soviet Union signed an agreement to expand cultural, educational, technical, and sports exchanges. The United States launched an artificial satellite—Explorer I—from Cape Canaveral, Florida. It weighed 31 pounds. The Russians simultaneously launched their first artificial satellite—Sputnik—on October 4, 1957. It weighed 3,000 pounds. The space race was on. The United States responded by announcing the establishment of the National Aeronautics and Space Administration (NASA) to administer the scientific exploration of space. During the latter part of 1958, the U.S. launched its first moon rocket; it failed to reach the moon but traveled 79,000 miles from Earth.

Education was given a boost in the United States on September 2, 1958, when President Eisenhower signed the National Defense Education Act (NDEA), which provided loans to college students, grants to schools for expanded facilities in the science and foreign languages, and fellowships for graduate students intending to teach. The NDEA was passed largely because Americans feared that Russia was outdistancing America in the space race.

Racial tensions heated up in the U.S. as desegregation of schools was attempted in the South. Governor Orval Faubus of Arkansas defied the Supreme Court by closing schools in Little Rock and reopening them as private segregated schools, thus frustrating the attempt by the U.S. Government to ensure equality of educational opportunity, especially for black Americans.

In 1958, the city of Minneapolis was finally surrounded by suburbs, and there was much talk about the deterioration of the inner city. Hard hit by the flight to the suburbs, the city started to plan redevelopment in several areas. Minneapolis and St. Paul had each developed in their own way, but they were finally forced to form organizations to foster common interests. Richfield's population had mushroomed to 37,350 by 1958, and, like other expanding suburbs, such as Edina, Bloomington, and St. Louis Park, it had to build new schools to keep pace with the growth and postwar baby boom.

Orville Freeman was the governor of Minnesota, but in the fall of 1958 he was elected to serve in the U.S. Senate with Hubert Humphrey. Freeman later became the Secretary of Agriculture under President John Kennedy.

In 1958, the state of Minnesota celebrated its 100th anniversary. The big celebration in May included royalty from Norway and Sweden. J. L. Morrill was president of the University of Minnesota, and the University was proceeding with plans to construct a new campus on the west bank of the Mississippi River. Murray Warmath, the football coach, was under fire for unproductive seasons; the regents finally decided he could stay. In 1958, a generation was growing accustomed to "drive-ins" for banking, movies, hamburgers, car washes, and dry cleaning.

The atmosphere was right for the emergence of creativity as a valid field of study, and it was particularly favorable at the University of Minnesota. Dean Walter Cook cultivated a research climate at the College of Education in which faculty members were free to move in the direction of their interests, with colleagues furnishing the stimulation and constructive criticism that is needed for such pursuits.

Albert Zander, a professor from the University of Michigan and a consultant to Paul during his survival research period, informed Dean Walter Cook and others at the University of Minnesota that Paul Torrance was leaving the Air Force job and would be available. The head of Student Counseling at the time, Charles Glotzbach (who was my host in July of 1992 while visiting Minneapolis and the University of Minnesota), told me that Dean Cook came to him before hiring Paul Torrance. He said, "I'm thinking of hiring Paul Torrance as a faculty member. He is still single. Do you think it'll cause any problems?" Glotzbach laughed and said he was sure it would not, assuring Dean Cook that "Paul was completely dedicated to his work." Glotzbach never told Paul Torrance about that conversation.

Paul Torrance chose to work at the University of Minnesota because he sensed an atmosphere in which people felt free to disagree with one another, yet respected one another greatly. From his survival research on groups under stress, he knew that this was a quality highly related to productive behavior.

Dean Cook provided a great deal of support to Paul and other faculty who did cutting-edge research in new fields. He felt it was his job to find financial support, space, equipment, research assistants, and clerks for investigators like Paul Torrance. Dean Cook's efforts to develop a research climate were reflected in his annual ringing challenge to faculty. Cook (1963) said, "At least fifty percent of what you are teaching your classes is untrue, and it is time you found out which half that is."

Paul Torrance understood and appreciated this challenge. He realized that we do have huge gaps in our knowledge about many areas, such as the human mind and personality and their workings, the learning process, instructional methods, curriculum development, and every other area of education. The recognition of these gaps in knowledge is the first step toward productive research; investigators can then search for clues from other bodies of knowledge, formulate guesses, test them, modify them, communicate the findings, and, lastly, apply them.

Dean Cook also encouraged a close liaison with schools in the state of Minnesota and was genuinely interested in their welfare. He maintained an open door to research in schools while he was dean. Walter Cook realized the need research workers have to maintain contacts with the scientific community, so he encouraged networking with researchers in other disciplines, as well as in other universities and countries. He also supported researchers' willingness to provide services on advisory boards at the local, national, and international levels. Finally, Dean Walter Cook encouraged faculty, including Paul Torrance, to publish the results of their research widely in journals, magazines, and newspapers, and also to make presentations to various audiences. Dean Cook was a powerful influence on the College of Education and on nationally and internationally known scholars, of which the University of Minnesota had its fair share.

Financial assistance was available from different sources for researchers in the College of Education. The Cooperative Research Program of the U.S. Office of Education had just been established and was offering grants for different kinds of research. The graduate school at the University of Minnesota also offered faculty members small grants from $3,000 to $25,000.

The University of Minnesota had established a tradition in educational research under the leadership of a number of well-known scholars; the Institute of Child and Family Development, which was part of the College of Education, had a similar tradition.

American education was making its first response to Sputnik III. In 1960, Paul Torrance predicted that:

> Tomorrow's schools will place an emphasis not only on learning but on thinking. More and more insistently, today's schools and colleges are being asked to produce men and women who can think, who can make new scientific discoveries, who can find more adequate solutions to impelling world problems.
>
> (Torrance, 1963, p. 4)

At the same time, scholars in many fields were beginning to observe that there appears to be a characteristic common to every person who makes a special contribution, whether it is technical, scientific, artistic, or social. That characteristic is creativity!

When Paul moved to Minneapolis in January of 1958, he lived in the home of Dr. Gilbert Wrenn, who was away on a sabbatical leave with his wife. Paul liked the neighborhood of Prospect Park and kept looking for a house to purchase there. When he saw the "For Sale" sign at 141 Warwick Street, he immediately made an offer, and it was accepted. The location of the house was important to Paul as it was only a few blocks from the university and the bus lines. Paul had no car and he was still unable to drive. By using the bus, Paul could go almost anywhere in Minneapolis, St. Paul, Bloomington, Richfield, St. Louis Park, Edina, and some of the other suburbs.

BURTON HALL: COLLEGE OF EDUCATION

Burton Hall, formerly the first library building at the University of Minnesota in Minneapolis, was erected in 1854 and became the College of Education in 1952. Above the entrance to the building is a 67-foot frieze of 56 figures divided into five groups. Each group represents an academic discipline: Science, Sculpture, Architecture, Painting, and Literature. Along the top of the building are etched the names of great scholars from the past: Montessori, Herbart, Descartes, Dewey, Dante, Plato, Copernicus, Goethe, and Darwin. The main entrance has eight huge Greek sandstone pillars of Doric architecture framing an entrance that leads to offices and classrooms on the ground floor and an atrium with a beautiful stained glass ceiling and offices on the second floor. A third floor houses additional offices for professors.

This is where Paul Torrance spent a great deal of time between 1958 and 1966, developing and implementing his tests of creativity and exploring studies with students on the nature and nurture of creativity.

The Faculty Advisory Committee to the Bureau of Educational Research in Burton Hall recommended that a 25-year pioneering research program on giftedness be initiated and developed. Dean Walter Cook was instrumental in this decision: He observed that in the laboratory school when students were tested for different abilities, their strengths lined up in different ways. As a result of Paul's work in the psychology of survival and interest in the written work of both Margaret Broadley and Johnson O'Connor, creativity became the focus of study of the Bureau of Educational Research.

FOCUS OF RESEARCH: CREATIVITY

Creativity has been thought of as a phenomenon or mysterious force that has forever kept humankind striving to improve their lot on earth. People have always been innovators, builders, composers, synthesizers, doers of things never done before, but very little was known about what makes them tick in this manner, or how they do it. Only in the last few decades has creativity been a subject for serious scientific investigation.

On the occasion of his election as president of the American Psychological Association in 1950, Dr. J. P. Guilford suggested that creativity be considered for serious study. Dr. Guilford said that at that time only about two-tenths of one percent of the literature in psychology was devoted to creativity. Obviously, it was a neglected area.

Guilford had been studying the mental operations of people and had developed a model called the Structure of the Intellect. One of the operations dealt with convergent/divergent thinking. In his book, *Way Beyond the IQ*, Guilford (1977) described divergent thinking as "a mental operation that involves production or generation of an answer; it is not given to you" (p. 92). He goes on to say that

> the greatest importance of divergent-production abilities is in connection with creative thinking, where many alternative ideas need to be brought to light with ease. Since creative thinking is an important aspect of problem-solving, these abilities are also important in that connection. (p. 108)

Torrance met J. P. Guilford several times at professional meetings, and he corresponded with him regularly. Calvin Taylor (in press), a professor of psychology at the University of Utah, has recently written an article called the "Three Giants of Creativity," in which he discusses Thurstone, Guilford, and Torrance. Taylor traces the genesis of the study of creativity to Thurstone, a mechanical engineer who worked for Thomas Edison. J. P. Guilford was a student at Northwestern University and knew the work of Thurstone well. Guilford "stood on the shoulders" of Thurstone and took creativity "way beyond the IQ." He developed a structure or model of the intellect composed of 120 abilities. Today's IQ tests measure only between seven and ten of those talents. In turn, Torrance "stood on the shoulders" of Guilford and developed ways to measure and teach creativity.

ORIGINS OF PAUL'S THINKING ABOUT CREATIVITY

The seeds of creativity—its measurement and development—had been sown in Paul Torrance as a teacher at Georgia Military College, as a part-time student at Mercer University, and at the University of Minnesota. He had read two significant books, *Ideaphoria* by Johnson O'Connor (1945) and *Square Pegs in Square Holes* by Margaret Broadley (1943). He also met many students and other people who according to Broadley were "too full of ideas" and were "like wild colts." His work as an Air Force research psychologist yielded more important insights about the creative person. The jet aces had once been "too full of ideas" and "like wild colts roaming the prairies." However, they had learned discipline and how to adapt successfully in the Air Force.

In January of 1958, Paul became Director of the Bureau of Educational Research (BER) at the University of Minnesota. According to Maynard Reynolds, the BER was a longstanding unit in the College of Education that provided services to faculty and students on research problems and statistical analysis.[1] It had operated since the late 1940s, had run down on the service side, and was in need of change. The Educational Psychology Department at Minnesota was a large department of 40 to 50 people. Paul Torrance also wanted to conduct his own research. The Faculty Advisory Board to the BER recommended the design and implementation of a pioneering research program on giftedness, to extend over the next 25 years. Dean Walter Cook had observed that children in the laboratory school varied greatly on different tests of ability, aptitude and intelligence. Basically, Cook was seeing the phenomenon developed by Calvin Taylor's (1968) Talent Totem Poles. Taylor demonstrated that a child may score high in one area (academic skills), average in another (decision-making skills), and low in yet another (forecasting ability). Needless to say, Paul Torrance chose creative abilities to be the special area for his study of giftedness.

Paul Torrance realized at the beginning of his research program that he would have to do a complete review of the literature on creativity to determine its current status. He needed to have measures of creative abilities, motivations, attitudes, and life experiences. He immediately assigned research assistants to do the necessary preliminary work. Victoria Punsulan was given the job of reviewing and summarizing articles and books on creativity. Paul Torrance still has those notes on 5" x 8" cards in the basement of his home in Athens, Georgia, and still occasionally refers to them.

Torrance wanted to develop a biographical inventory similar to the one developed in the jet ace study. Now he planned to use creative individuals—scientists, inventors, and explorers—as the basis of a new biographical inventory. Kenneth De Young was assigned the task of reading these accounts and designing statements that would link early life experiences to the development of creative characteristics. This research resulted in the *Life Experience Inventory* (Torrance & De Young, 1958). Dean Dauw (1965) used the biographical inventory with excellent results. It was not developed any further by Torrance, as Calvin Taylor at the University of Utah was developing this area and having good success with biographical inventories.

Torrance hypothesized that creative persons need to be motivated internally to make optimal use of their creative abilities. Torrance (1985) attempted to measure this kind of motivation by way of a *Creative Motivation Scale*—a kind of checklist of attitudes. Som Nath Ghei volunteered to do this task, and eight staff members judged the items. The scale has never been commercially published, although it has been used in some research studies.

---

[1] Interview with Dr. Maynard Reynolds at the College of Education, University of Minnesota, July 27, 1992.

DEFINING CREATIVITY

By February, 1958, Paul Torrance and two quarter-time research assistants had begun the search for a description or definition of creativity. Torrance spent several months early in 1958 reviewing over 50 existing definitions and examining his own observations of creative behavior from earlier studies and teaching. He categorized existing definitions in five areas: newness as a criterion; creativity vs. conformity; definitions that are true, generalizable, and surprising; definitions involving process; and a mental abilities approach. A good description of these categories of creative definitions is provided in Torrance (1988).

Torrance (1962) states his *research* definition of creativity as follows:

> Creativity is production of something new or unusual as a result of the processes of:
> - Sensing difficulties, problems, gaps in knowledge, missing elements, something askew,
> - Making guesses and formulating hypotheses about these deficiencies,
> - Evaluating and testing these guesses and hypotheses,
> - Possibly revising and retesting them, and
> - Finally, communicating the results. (p.16)

Embedded in this research definition are the major features of other definitions that have been previously proposed. Specifically, other definitions of creativity include such notions as "the production of something new" and "adventurous thinking"—permitting one thing to lead to another, and "truth"—shedding bias and being willing to discover the world as it actually is.

Paul Torrance chose a process definition of creativity for research purposes. It allowed him to determine what kind of person one must be to engage in the process successfully, what kinds of environments will facilitate it, and what products will result from successful operation of the process. Paul particularly liked this definition because it described creativity as a natural process arising from the need to satisfy tensions caused within individuals who sense something is incomplete. Creativity is therefore viewed as within the realm of all people, not just a few who accomplish a great deal. Creativity is possible at any age and, therefore, can be studied developmentally from preschool to graduate school and beyond.

"ARTISTIC" DEFINITION

Karl Anderson, a student in Paul Torrance's class while he was teaching at the University of California at Berkeley in the summer of 1964, created an "artistic" definition or description of creativity. Paul liked it immediately as it consisted of simple line drawings but communicated the essence of creativity meaningfully. Paul has lost the original Anderson drawings but Nancy Martin redrew the visu-

FIGURE 1
"Artistic" Definition of Creativity

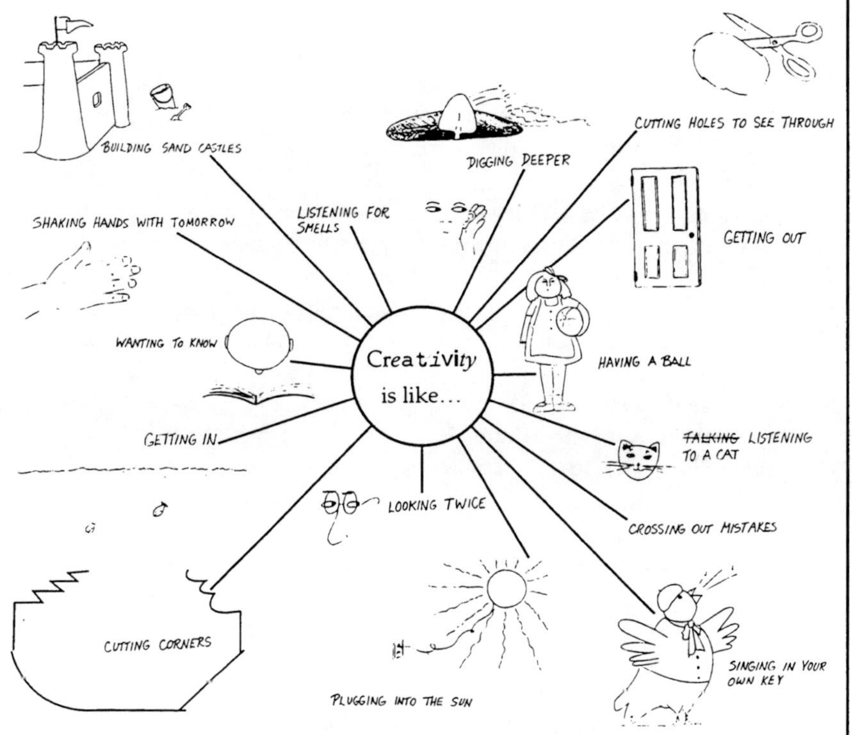

als in 1985, and they closely approximate the originals. To make the drawings meaningful, one has to look upon them as analogies. Figure 1 displays the drawings in an analogy which has inspired an infinity of meanings and ideas about creativity.

The elements of a creative art or solution can be taught; however, the creativity itself must be self-discovered and self-disciplined. A creative solution or art requires imaginatively gifted recombinations of old elements into new configurations. For example, Paul Torrance realized in his survival work that men needed to have information about how others survived (American Indians, early explorers, shipwreck survivors, airmen) in order to respond to unfamiliar situations in the Korean conflict. They then could draw upon that information and use it in the particular situations in which they found themselves. Creative thinking abilities have more recently been defined by Torrance and Ball (1984) as "that constellation of generalized mental abilities that is commonly presumed to be brought into play in creative achievement" (p. 1).

IDENTIFYING THE SKILLS OF CREATIVITY

Torrance undertook a closer analysis of Guilford's mental operations of convergent/divergent thinking in 1958, to better understand the nature of creative thinking and how it is different from abilities sampled by traditional measures of intelligence. He determined that convergent/divergent thinking consisted of a number of mental operations: namely, cognition (awareness), memory, two kinds of productive thinking (divergent thinking and convergent thinking), and evaluative abilities.

From his experiences as a psychologist, and from a study of Guilford's work and the work of other contemporary researchers such as Frank Barron and Calvin Taylor, Paul determined that there were a number of component skills involved in producing creative responses. The thinking abilities identified were sensitivity to problems, ideational fluency, flexibility, originality, penetration, analysis and synthesis, and redefinition. A description of these thinking abilities is important as they later determined the types of activities that Torrance and his associates designed for the Minnesota Tests of Creative Thinking.

Sensitivity to problems is the ability to see defects, needs, and deficiencies—what needs to be done. Questioning is the essence of this ability. Society in general and schools in particular are still quite intolerant of individuals who routinely practice this ability. The status of students in schools asking good questions is remedial at best. Ralph Himsl and the writer have developed a *Measure of Questioning Skills* (1993) and activities to enhance this important skill.

Ideational fluency is the ability to produce a variety of ideas or hypotheses concerning possible solutions to problems. During Paul's survival research, he demonstrated that groups find better solutions when there is a tolerance for divergence of ideas. To stimulate ideational fluency, one might ask individuals to think of all the possible uses of tin cans or bricks. In this era of conservation of our resources, we might think of other uses of newspapers, glass containers, and bags from the supermarket. Application of a research finding or well-established principle to an individual's professional career or personal life is another example of this type of thinking.

Flexibility is another important ability in creative thinking. It is the ability to adapt to changing conditions, to be free from inertia of thought, and to use a variety of approaches. This provides interest to our lives by viewing things from different approaches and considering alternative interpretations.

Originality is the ability to produce uncommon responses, unconventional associations, or cleverness. Originality is the most striking aspect of creative thinking and at the same time the most upsetting or disturbing. It invites the strongest sanctions from society. A creator of an original idea or product is either celebrated or derided. An original idea or product is either a fad or it makes a long-lasting contribution.

A newspaper article ran an example of a test of originality designed by Paul Torrance, something that is not assessed on IQ tests. The article, titled "Test Your

Originality" (1979) asked the reader to take 10 minutes and write down all the unusual uses he or she could imagine for junked autos. Instructions on how to score this test are in the box below.

Penetration is the ability to get underneath the problem and to view it in a different way.

Analysis and synthesis are the abilities necessary to puzzle out meanings more completely and more deeply, and then to organize these into some meaningful order.

Redefinition is the ability to reorganize what we see in new ways, to shift the function of an object and see it in a new context. This transformation makes thinking productive rather than reproductive. Classroom teaching often inhibits children's thinking by forcing them to do what they are told rather than what they think. Some children learn to work by textbook and by rule, reproductively rather than productively.

The above abilities and others that appeared to strengthen creative thinking were used by Paul Torrance in designing activities to obtain measures of creativity. These component skills of creativity can be scored and will predict future creative achievement. A description of the creative factors and creative strengths that are scored in the Minnesota Tests of Creative Thinking is found in Appendix C.

Following Sputnik and the beginning of the space race, the concern was the discovery and encouragement of creative scientific talent. At the 1960 Conference on The Space Age, held at the University of Minnesota, Paul Torrance and Margaret Mead were keynote speakers. Mead said to Torrance that creativity and education have come up for debate before. "Why do you think it'll amount to anything this time?" she said. She indicated that good reliable measures of creativity needed to be developed and used.

DEVELOPING THE *MINNESOTA TESTS OF CREATIVE THINKING*

Paul examined past efforts at measuring creativity. He chose some of the most

Check your answers against the following common replies. Give yourself a score of one for each answer that is *not* on this list:

- Make into an art object.
- Use as a pretend car on a kids' playground.
- Make it a safety warning for drivers.
- Plant flowers in it.
- Repair and sell it.
- Use the tires for a swing.
- Recap and sell tires.
- Make on good auto from several junked ones.
- Repair for demolition derby.
- Use as practice cars in teaching auto mechanics.
- Fix up for auto racing.
- Sell for scrap iron and spare parts.
- Smash with a hammer for tension reducer.

REMEMBER: The above answers score zero, all others score one each. If your score is five or below, it shows little originality; six to 14 is average; if your score is 15 and above, you're highly original.

promising activities and invented several of his own. In designing tasks or activities, his plan was to develop alternate forms of a battery of tests that could be used in kindergarten through graduate school. The activities had to be easy enough for the youngest and most disabled to make creative responses, and complex enough to challenge the most able.

By September of 1958, Paul and his research assistant, Som Nath Ghei, had developed a battery of tests of creativity for use with elementary and high school students. Paul also developed tests for use with graduate and senior students at the college level. Then Paul and another research assistant, Kaoru Yamamoto, administered a large number of them to a sample of individuals during the fall and winter of 1959–1960. They chose activities that were most different from one another yet had the greatest power to elicit creative responses. Thus, they chose and constructed activities that reflected what they knew about creative thinking processes, the qualities of creative products, and creative personalities. These batteries of activities came to be known as the Minnesota Tests of Creative Thinking. The activities had to be open-ended so that all individuals could respond based on their own experiences. Paul realized that this would be difficult, but he felt it was necessary in order to study stages of development and make group comparisons.

Paul administered the battery of activities and carefully screened out those that were unsuitable. The activities had to be an enjoyable experience for all. A number of test items or activities were devised and modified from existing tests. By November of 1958, Paul Torrance and Harold Michie, a research assistant, had developed a preliminary manual. It described the materials, instructions for administering and scoring, and interim norms for tests to appraise creative thinking in the early school years.

Since Paul's research definition of creativity was a process one, it was logical that the *Ask and Guess Activity* would be designed. It required the individual to examine a picture, then generate questions and guess both causes and consequences of what they saw. The "Ask" component revealed the individual's ability to sense and fill in gaps in information about the picture. The "Guess" component revealed the individual's ability to formulate hypotheses regarding cause and effect. The Ask and Guess Activity was scored for fluency and flexibility, that is, the number of relevant responses and the categories of responses. The statistical infrequency of the questions, causes, and consequences were scored as a measure of originality. The details incorporated in the questions and hypotheses yielded an elaboration score.

Much of our everyday creativity and invention requires that we improve something—a product, a process, or something in the environment. Paul and his associates were anxious to test this important creative skill. As a result, the *Product Improvement* and *Unusual Uses* activities were born. A stuffed baby animal was presented to the individual being tested in the Product Improvement Activity. The person was asked to think of the cleverest, most interesting, and most unusual ways to change the toy animal so that others would have fun playing with it. Individuals had eight minutes for this activity.

Adapted from a promotional brochure

In the Unusual Uses Activity, the person was asked to redefine the toy stuffed animal and think of the cleverest, most interesting, and most unusual uses for the toy. The uses could be for the toy as it was or as it could be changed. This is recognized as a test of improvisation with commonplace materials. For example, it could be used as a pin cushion or made larger and stronger and used to sit on. The time limit was originally set at eight minutes, and later changed to 10 minutes.

Both Product Improvement and Unusual Uses are popular with people of all ages and occupations. The activities make good sense to those taking the test.

The Consequences Activity in the Minnesota Tests of Creative Thinking was similar to Guilford's Consequences Test. Three improbable situations were devised for each form of the test, and five minutes were allocated for this task. An improbable situation might be, "What would happen if all pitchers in baseball had the same high skill level as Nolan Ryan of the Texas Rangers? However, Paul Torrance was not happy with the results, and test-takers did not seem to enjoy it. Paul had read a book by Alastair Reid called *Supposing* (1960) and found it exciting. He adapted the idea after trying it out on several elementary classes and research assistants. It was similar to the Consequences Test but had new twists, and individuals produced exciting responses. The *Just Suppose Activity* was an adaptation of the Consequences type of test. The test-taker was confronted with an improbable situation and then asked to list possible consequences. The verbal statement was accompanied by a black and white drawing of the situation. Paul Henrickson, an artist and a research assistant who worked for Paul Torrance, did several drawings to accompany the "just suppose" situations. One example was "Just suppose—a great fog were to fall all over the earth and all we could see would be feet." The drawing shown here was created by my son, Chris Millar.

To respond productively, individuals had to "play with the possibilities and imagine things that would happen as a consequence." Only one Just Suppose Activity was selected for each form on the verbal part of the Minnesota Tests of Creative Thinking.

The Figural Activities

Paul Torrance has said, "much of the world's creativity is expressed in a nonverbal, figural form.[2] The creativity expressed on the figural test is different from the verbal test; almost no correlation exists. Yet both types of creativity are important.

Torrance originally designed four different types of activities for the figural test. Each has a different creative tendency.

The *Picture Construction Activity* requires the test-taker to think of a picture in which the given shape is an integral part. It sets in motion the tendency to find a purpose for something that has no definite purpose by itself. Adding detail (elaboration) is required.

Adapted from a promotional brochure

The *Incomplete Figures* or *Picture Completion Activity* was an adaptation of a Drawing Completion Test used by Frank Barron and others. This task requires the individual to remain open and not close the figure prematurely. The instructions invite the test-taker to "make the drawing tell a story" and encourage elaboration.

Paul Torrance originally designed the *Circles and Squares Activity* to measure ideational fluency and flexibility, but later added the elements of originality and elaboration. It forced the test-taker to disrupt structure to create something new. It also required the ability to perceive the same stimulus in a different way.

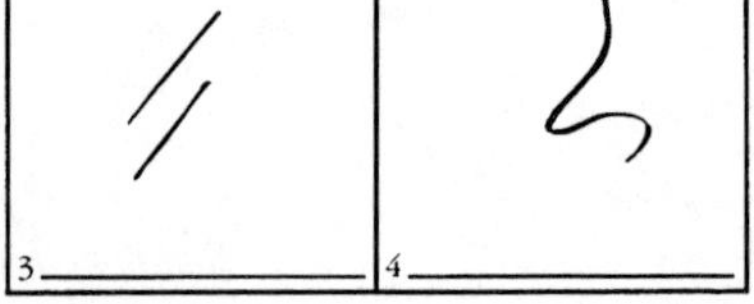

Adapted from a promotional brochure

A fourth activity that was part of the original test was called the *Creative Design Task*. It was developed by Paul Henrickson and involved creating designs or pictures from circles and strips of various sizes and colors. The shapes could be cut with scissors and glued into a four-page booklet. Scoring procedures were tested but were not perfected. This activity was dropped from the figural test.

Torrance found that the three activities discriminated between productive, original thinkers and good elaborators. Some produced a large number of very original ideas but failed to elaborate them well; some produced very few ideas but made them elaborate or "fancy"; and still others produced a large number

---

[2] Taken from *Research Newsletter*—College of Education, University of Minnesota, March 1961, p.1

of very commonplace ideas with little elaboration.

By 1961, the Minnesota Tests of Creative Thinking were ready to be used in exploratory studies on creativity. Researchers, students, and educators from many parts of the world were interested in using them.

Paul and his team of research assistants, notably Kaoru Yamamoto and Paul Henrickson, designed the original scoring manual that reflected the components of creativity and resulted in a total creativity score or index. In the early 1960s, when the Minnesota Tests of Creative Thinking were first used, people complained about the inordinate amount of time the test took to score and the energy it took to master. Others complained that the scoring placed too much emphasis on divergent thinking skills only and failed to capture other creative strengths or indicators elicited by the test activities.

The Minnesota Tests of Creative Thinking represented the first sustained and imaginative research to assess creativity. It consisted of a series of verbal and nonverbal or figural tasks. The verbal test included six activities that tap the mental factors or skills considered by Paul Torrance to be involved in creative thinking and achievement. The nonverbal or figural tasks consisted of three activities. Table 1 describes the tasks.

Table 1
Description of Activities/Tasks Involved in the Minnesota Tests of Creative Thinking (1958-59)

Verbal Tasks	Nonverbal (Figural) Tasks
• Ask and Guess Asking questions about a picture—questions that cannot be answered by looking	• Picture Construction Constructing new pictures from a given shape
• Guess Causes Listing causes of action in picture	• Figure Completion Completing open drawing
• Guess Consequences Listing things that resulted or might have happened in the future	• Circles, squares or parallel lines Elaborating common shapes to make unusual pictures
• Product Improvement Listing ideas for changing the toy (dog) to make it more fun to play with	
• Unusual Uses Listing cleverest, most interesting, and most unusual uses of the toy (dog)	
• Consequences Listing what would happen if… e.g., a hole were bored through the earth?	

Torrance and his associates experimented with the wording of instructions in the Minnesota Tests of Creative Thinking so they would provide the best creative responses from test-takers. For example, he found that the addition of the words, "Try to think of something no one else will think of" reduced the amount of copying from one another and increased originality of responses. Also, he observed that an overheated, stuffy classroom and time of year (May) decreased performance. Generally, experiments have shown that the administration instructions in the manual produced the most reliable and valid results.

ED PSYCH 159: THE COURSE MADE FAMOUS BY PAUL

In addition to his research activities, Paul taught a course. When Paul Torrance began as Director of the Bureau of Educational Research at the University of Minnesota, Dean Walter Cook wanted him to teach one course. It did not matter what the course was as long as Paul made it famous.

Paul chose to teach "Personality and Mental Health," which was already a fairly popular course. It had been taught previously by Drs. Gilbert Wrenn and Henry Borrow, who were both on sabbaticals at the time. There are several indicators that tell us Paul did indeed make it famous.

The first indicator is enrollments. The first time Paul taught the course, there was an enrollment of 35. His reputation as a teacher was already starting to spread on the University of Minnesota campus. Five of his graduate students from Kansas State University were top graduates at the University of Minnesota, and they had been bragging about his teaching. These students were Roger Wilk, Charles Glotzbach, Ted Volksy, Charles Halbauer, and Ruthetta Halbauer. Two men, Charles Hawkins and John Bowers, with whom Paul had worked on survival research in the Air Force, were also there.

The course attracted enrollments ranging from 50 to 150 thereafter, usually over 100 each time he offered it. Apparently, the advice given through the campus grapevine was, "Be sure to take it, but when you do, don't take anything else."

From the outset, Torrance required each student to prepare a paper proposing a new idea. Some middle-age or elderly person would come in saying, "I didn't think I could do it, but I did. This was the first paper that I have ever turned in, in which I used any of my own ideas." They would express a high degree of satisfaction about this.

Another indicator is the number of students who took the course and later became college teachers. One student told Paul Torrance that he wanted to teach this course but that he would never be satisfied unless he taught it like Paul did, and that would take too much work for him.

Paul also taught "Group Dynamics," but he decided to limit the enrollment to 55. He wanted to teach it as an experiential and theoretical course and to organize the students into ten groups of five each. He taught about five theories of group dynamics and used a group problem to test or challenge some aspect of the theory. With 55 students, usually 50 ended up staying. Some of the experiments were reported in *Climate for Creativity* by Calvin Taylor (1972). Some of these experiments have been published in French and Spanish journals.

Some departments at the University of Minnesota not previously requiring these courses started requiring them. Among the first departments to begin requiring them was the speech clinic, headed by the famous Dr. Bryng Bryngelson, as well as the art education department, the creative drama department, business education, industrial arts, and nursing school departments.

Remembering his positive and satisfying experience as a student at the University of Michigan, Paul was instrumental in establishing informal evening research seminars for educational psychology students. At the weekly seminars, set up in Burton Hall, students could discuss ongoing research projects. Paul Torrance was always at the center of those discussions. The first seminar dealt with research problems connected with the measurement of abilities and was led by Maynard Reynolds, Roger Wilk, and Robert Lathrop. Paul enjoyed working with students and was considered a creative teacher.

AN UNUSUAL STUDENT: PANSY NIGH

Paul's Ed Psych 159—Personality and Mental Health—continued to be very popular. It attracted students from many departments within the education faculty and from other faculties. One student—Pansy Nigh—was to have a real impact on Paul, not only as a student in class but as an individual out of class.

Jessie Pansy Nigh was born in Ralston, Oklahoma, on October 10, 1913. Her parents were poor and both died when Pansy was relatively young. Her father, a farmer, was often away from home looking for work, and her mother was housebound and ill most of the time. She had an older brother, William Clyde, and an older sister, Lelia, who were away from home, so Pansy had to be independent and take responsibility early in her life. As her mother was paralyzed from Parkinson's disease and suffered from pellagra—a vitamin deficiency—she had to look after her needs before and after school. The local doctor's wife befriended Pansy and lent all her books to her. Pansy learned about the larger world from those books, which included *The Reader's Digest*. An interesting account of her childhood is found in an article by Presbury and Henderson (1984).

In 1937, Pansy passed the Oklahoma State Board Nurses' Examination with the highest grade in the state. She worked as a public health nurse with the State Department and among various Indian tribes, especially the Creek and Seminole. After finishing her education in a Catholic nursing school in northern Oklahoma, she took a six-month training course in pediatrics in Chicago. She was a lobbyist for nursing standards and rights in Oklahoma and a member of the Oklahoma State Board of Nursing Registration and Nursing Education.

Before that, she had been a psychiatric nurse with the Oklahoma State Board of Mental Health, and she also had held a job in medical nursing at the University of Oklahoma. She obtained a bachelor's degree in nursing from the University of Minnesota after World War II. Jessie Pansy Nigh had returned to the University of Minnesota in 1959 to complete her Master of Education degree in psychiatric nursing and nursing education.

PANSY MEETS PAUL

Pansy Nigh was in Paul's "Personality and Mental Health" class during the Spring Quarter of 1959. Apparently, she did not want to take a course that she was supposed to take, so she asked her advisor if she could substitute. Her advisor told her of a new fellow in Educational Psychology who had a good reputation as a teacher and she might consider taking his course. She enrolled in this course "just for fun," with about 80 other graduate students who had varying backgrounds. The class met for two hours on Saturday morning, with an additional hour scheduled for laboratory work. Pansy signed up for the option that met early Saturday mornings to explore mental health problems through sociodrama. Since this group met for three hours, Pansy thought they should have coffee available to go with the cookies Paul furnished, which they had before the class began.

In many of the sociodramas, Paul selected Pansy for the rebellious teenager roles because of her liveliness and sensitivity. At 45 years of age, Pansy's outspoken nature must have been evident to Paul. Paul has indicated to me that it was not love at first sight—for either of them. However, he was attracted to her, on account of her warmth. He felt comfortable with her.

At the end of the course Pansy failed to turn in one of the required papers, so she received a grade of B rather than an A, which she had otherwise earned. She discovered the paper and came to the Bureau of Educational Research to give the paper to Paul. Needless to say, her grade was adjusted.

She and Paul began to see each other more regularly. In the summer quarter, Pansy would be sitting on the back steps of Burton Hall having her lunch. Since they both were Baptists and Paul could not drive a car, she began to give Paul a ride to the Baptist Church in Bloomington and they would often stop somewhere for lunch together. They were involved in beginning a new Baptist Church in St. Paul, which was nearer for both of them. In a strongly Lutheran and Catholic community, they were a member of a small minority group. This little group decided to have mid-week prayer service in a member's home. Pansy and Paul usually went to these meetings. On Sunday, they met in the St. Paul YMCA until a more permanent meeting place was obtained.

Pansy 'Pops the Question'

One night in October of 1959, when Paul was busy hosting the Second Minnesota Gifted Conference and his cat Hazel had just had six kittens, Pansy came over. Sitting on his lap, she said, "I want to marry you." Paul quickly said, "When?" Pansy hesitated some, and Paul suggested Thanksgiving Eve. Pansy agreed. The next morning, Pansy telephoned Paul to ask if he had changed his mind. He assured her that he had not and that he had been wondering if she would have him.

After this, Paul and Pansy began writing one another when they were traveling. They would not only write about their admiration for each other, but they would discuss their expectations about marriage. Paul has recently discovered that Pansy saved all of this correspondence. During the two months before their wedding, they ate out at nice restaurants more frequently, as well as at each other's places. When Paul's cat Hazel climbed up on the table, Paul said to Pansy, "Well, Hazel has accepted you now." About two Sundays before their wedding, Pansy was at Paul's house for lunch. While Paul was preparing lunch, Pansy went to the basement to see the kittens, then brought the kittens upstairs. Paul thought she looked lovely playing with them; however, he scolded her, as he wanted to delay their coming upstairs until he was sure they were housebroken. Their mutual love of cats began that day.

Before they were married, Paul and Pansy discussed the subject of having children. Pansy could not have children due to a medical condition. Paul had given the matter much thought even before he met Pansy; he had avoided marriage in the past because he was afraid to have children. He disclosed, "I don't think I could stand to see my child growing up with the physical characteristics that I had—muscles that would not develop, legs that looked like a girl's, and vision and a nervous system that would not let me drive. Paul had always felt so inferior physically that he never seriously considered marriage. However, with Pansy it was different. She knew most of his inadequacies and was willing to accept him as a husband.

Charles Glotzbach was surprised one day in the fall of 1959 when Paul Torrance came into his office and asked if he would be the best man at his wedding. Paul had known Charles as a student, colleague, and friend at Kansas State University, and Charles had come to the University of Minnesota partly because Paul had recommended it. Charles was in a department different from Paul's, and was terribly busy with being a graduate student and head of a young family of four children, so he did not get to see Paul much. From past experience at Kansas State, and knowing of his tremendous publications at the University of Minnesota, Charles was tempted to say, "I didn't know you were going with anyone." He was pleased to be Paul's best man.

Charles realized that Paul's work had been his "family" until that time and that Pansy Nigh would be an enthusiastic partner and supporter of Paul's work. Charles Glotzbach and his wife Helen were very pleased that Paul had found Pansy to share his life. They were struck by the great devotion between Paul and Pansy.

A 'Special' Thanksgiving in 1959

The day of the wedding arrived, Wednesday, November 25, 1959. Pansy Nigh had just turned 46 and Paul was 44. It was the day before Thanksgiving. It was business as usual for Paul: He arrived at his university office early—about 7:30 a.m.—and took care of some administrative details. He had a radio interview scheduled for 8:30 a.m. Pansy had told her friends and fellow students about it, so he knew they would be listening. The interview went smoothly. This was a good start to a memorable day.

Paul returned to his office to check a few matters—some business-related, others about the wedding. He checked with Herman Radig, a research assistant, to make sure that he was going to be present at the wedding to take photographs and Kaoru Yamamoto, a recent research fellow, to make sure that he would come to Paul's house in Prospect Park to care for Hazel and her two kittens.

Charles picked Paul up to go to the 8:00 p.m. wedding. It took place in the new Southtown Baptist Church in the Minneapolis suburb of Bloomington. It was near the airport and near the stadium where the Minnesota Twins played baseball and where the Vikings played football. It was also near the elementary school where Paul taught a class of gifted sixth graders as part of his educational research.

The guests at the wedding were members of the church that Paul and Pansy had helped found, University of Minnesota friends, and Pansy's nursing friends. Betty Thomley was the bridesmaid. The service was conducted by Reverend Warren Littleford, who was accompanied by his wife Anda.

The Littleford's daughter, Laura, nine years of age at the time, recalls one aspect of the wedding vividly. When her father pronounced Paul and Pansy husband and wife, she remembers that Paul passionately embraced Pansy. This "Hollywood movie-star kiss" was so spontaneous, Laura recounts, that Pansy was also surprised. Laura remembers women in the church looking at their husbands and saying through their gaze, "Why don't you kiss me like that?" For a middle-aged, Southern Baptist couple to publicly express their passion was revolutionary. It must have taken others by surprise as well, but Paul was different and used to being a minority of one.

Paul remembers being not exactly relaxed but not nervous either. None of their relatives were present, but they were surrounded by dear friends. Pansy's relatives were mostly in Oklahoma, and Paul's were in Georgia. All the arrangements went smoothly. Pansy had done most of the planning and coordinating, and the timing was perfect.

Paul and Pansy had decided to take a brief honeymoon of five days. They flew to Chicago, where it was snowing when they arrived. Paul recalls signing in at the Palmer House Hotel where he had made a reservation. "I signed in but did not enter Pansy's name. The desk clerk said I would have to add it. I explained that we had just married and this was the first time I had ever checked into a hotel with a wife. The desk clerk responded, 'Yes, I can see that.' Then I looked and saw that there was a lot of rice still clinging to my overcoat." They spent a good deal of their time in Chicago doing their Christmas shopping before returning to their little brown house at 141 S.E. Warwick Street in the Prospect Park Division of Minneapolis.

Paul's family did not meet Pansy until after the wedding, but Paul and Pansy had written them about their engagement and marriage. Paul's parents had waited a long time and had about given up hope. Mrs. Torrance was disappointed when she learned that Pansy was not able to have children; she dearly wanted a grandchild, and Paul's sister Ellen was also unable to bear children.

Paul and Pansy went to Georgia in April of 1960 during the Easter break following their wedding. Everything was beautiful, and all the flowers were in bloom. Paul recalls, "It was dark when we arrived, so the next morning when we awakened, Pansy saw the wisteria from our window and was thrilled over its great mass." While in Georgia, Paul was able to introduce Pansy to most of his close relatives. Paul's parents liked Pansy and came to love her.

Paul and Pansy shared similar backgrounds and interests. Both came from poor backgrounds and had had difficulty getting enough money together for school and college, working all the time. They both had high-achieving records throughout school and college.

Both Pansy and Paul always read a great deal. In the early years, Pansy had access to a doctor friend's library in Oklahoma and Paul had his aunt's library in Milledgeville. Both were brought up in Southern Baptist Churches, and Baptist Young People's Union had played important roles in their adolescence. Finally, both liked to write and had always written letters, stories, and articles.

Pansy and Paul were also different from each other, in a number of traits and activities: Pansy could express her emotions openly while Paul could not; Pansy could show affection openly and Paul could not; Pansy was liberal with money and Paul tried to be thrifty; Pansy did not hesitate to get a loan while Paul avoided getting one. Card or board games were commonplace in Pansy's home, whereas they were discouraged and disapproved of in Paul's home. Pansy would quickly see the humor in situations, where Paul brought insight to the partnership. Finally, Pansy was active in politics while Paul was not.

Their common backgrounds and traits, as well as their complementary roles, were to provide interesting dynamics in their life together. At middle-age, Paul had little trouble adjusting to Pansy after many years of bachelorhood. Pansy, too, appeared to have little difficulty in adjusting to Paul. Both were too absorbed in their own careers during the first few years of marriage to give enough support to one another. Paul kept trying to make changes so that he could give Pansy more of himself; he was painfully aware of a major conflict in his life, brought to consciousness by participation in Moreno's Psychodrama Institute a decade earlier—that of balancing his career with his home life. Pansy became the "flower" in Paul's life. Meanwhile, Paul was busy at Burton Hall conducting studies in creativity.

DEVELOPMENT OF CREATIVE THINKING: EXPLORATORY STUDIES

In October of 1959, the Cooperative Research Program of the United States Office of Education granted $25,175 to the Bureau of Educational Research. The grant was to be used to conduct a study on "Developing Children's Ability to Think Creatively." The focus of the study was to be on ways to provide a school environment that values creativity and on developing evaluative behaviors that lead children to think creatively.

Between 1960 and 1965, Paul Torrance and his students conducted a number of experimental studies in creativity to determine its nature, its limits, and the perceptions that others have about it. These studies, which arose out of Torrance's analyses of a variety of research studies into creativity and out of his own experience, are well documented in his book, *Education and the Creative Potential* (1963a) and in articles he wrote during this period. (See Appendix A.) The highlights of some of these studies are worth reporting here.

Paul explored the facets of creative thinking by engaging in six exploratory studies dealing with children in the early school years. Cooperating with Torrance in these studies were Dr. James Curtin, Principal of the University Elementary School; Dr. Orville Aftreth, Principal of Pratt Elementary School; and Dr. Arthur Jensen, Principal of Tuttle Elementary School. Paul asked these six key questions:

1. How do the genders respond to various test tasks that contain gender-specific materials on the Minnesota Tests of Creative Thinking?
2. What is the role of manipulation in generating inventive or original ideas?
3. How do groups affect their most creative member?
4. How can creativity be deliberately taught in primary classrooms?
5. What is the attitude of society toward boys and especially girls in learning science-related tasks?
6. What is the relationship of gender-role identification and creative thinking?

In the first experiment, the researchers found it desirable to provide stimuli appropriate to gender roles for children at the first-grade level. They also found that techniques needed to be developed to encourage girls at the second- and third-grade level to cultivate their inventiveness. Whatever the factors are that explain the scarcity of women among inventors and creative scientists, these factors seem to begin operating as early as the second or third grade. Efforts to cultivate the creative talents of women in science and technology cannot be delayed until the college/university years.

In the second experiment, the research team found a positive relationship between the degree of manipulation and the quantity and quality of responses. When children were able to manipulate objects, there was a significant increase in fluency and flexibility. Boys showed more increase in manipulation skills than girls and increased more from grade to grade. The importance of manipulativeness in creative and inventive activities was supported by the results of this experiment.

Creative persons have always met with opposition: Witness Copernicus, Columbus, and Edison. Therefore, children need to develop a feeling of confidence in their own original ideas and perceptions. The third experiment attempted to measure sanctions exercised by groups against their most creative members, and how children coped with or adapted to peer sanctions and organizational pressures. The groups were heterogeneously established by scores on the Bureau's creative tests. The study showed that creative children preferred to work alone, but this decreased in the higher grade levels. By grade six, creative children experienced a repertoire of controls imposed by other group members. The techniques of control included open aggression and hostility, criticism, rejection, indifference, and the imposing of power through the use of paperwork and administrative detail. The adaptive techniques used by the most creative members included compliance, counteraggressiveness, indomitable persistence, apparent unawareness of criticism, clowning, silence and apathy or preoccupation, filling in the gaps when others falter, and solitary activity.

The fourth study was conducted to debunk the myth that "you either have it (creativity) or you don't." The experiment, conducted in Tuttle Elementary School in Minneapolis, employed a variety of methods of encouraging creative thinking among children. The results indicate that, in a short period of time, children in the primary grades (with the possible exception of grade 1) can be taught a set of questions or principles that will stimulate new ideas and enable them to produce more and better ideas than they would have without training.

History reports few women who have achieved eminence as scientific discoverers or inventors. It may be that certain societal attitudes make it difficult for girls to develop competence in science fields. In the fifth experiment, groups composed of an equal number of boys and girls in grades 4, 5, and 6 were given a box of science toys and asked to discover what could be done with the toys. In 1959, boys demonstrated a significantly higher number of ideas and explained more scientific principles. However, when the experiment was replicated in 1960, girls equalled the boys in the number of ideas and scientific principles generated and they enjoyed it as much as the boys. However, the contribution of boys to the success of the group was rated more highly than the contribution of girls. (Several years later the experiment was repeated and no differences were found, reflecting social changes.)

Gender roles are a source of conflict for highly creative persons and are likely to interfere with a child's learning in school and with the igniting of a child's creative potential. In our society, the high degree of sensitivity that is part of creative thinking is considered distinctly feminine, while at the same time, the independence required in creative thinking is considered distinctly masculine. Therefore, the highly creative boy is likely to appear feminine and the highly creative girl may appear more masculine than others her age. Social sanctions against these children may cause them to sacrifice their creativity at an early age.

The sixth experiment was designed to compare highly creative individuals on feminine/masculine dimensions. It was hypothesized that highly creative persons would tend to rate higher on masculinity–femininity scales, in the direction of the opposite sex. The results indicate support for the hypothesis, but no statistical significance was achieved.

These early exploratory studies gave Paul Torrance and the Bureau of Educational Research at the University of Minnesota direction in focusing and clarifying their research program. More studies would be undertaken, some of which are documented in Torrance's book, *Rewarding Creative Behavior* (1965a).

LONGITUDINAL STUDIES OF CREATIVE TALENT LAUNCHED

Paul Torrance believed that the best way to learn about the nature of creativity was through testing and by deliberately teaching creative behavior. Also, he felt that the strongest evidence of a relationship between test behavior and later creative achievement would come from longitudinal studies. Torrance's longitudinal studies were designed to measure the predictive ability or validity of the Minnesota Tests of Creative Thinking (MTCT). He expected that individuals who scored high on the MTCT would be involved in creative achievements later in their lives. Beginning in 1958 and continuing for five years (until 1964), all pupils enrolled in two elementary schools in Minneapolis—the University of Minnesota Laboratory Elementary School and the Sidney Pratt Elementary School—were administered various batteries of the Minnesota Tests of Creative Thinking. Also, in September of 1959, all students (N=392) enrolled in grades 7 to 12 at the University of Minnesota High School took the tests.

In 1966, just before Torrance left the University of Minnesota, he collected data on the creative achievements of the high school seniors who had been tested in 1959. He felt it was his last chance to collect data before leaving Minnesota and was afraid he would not get good cooperation after his relocation to Georgia. The results of this follow-up and others will be discussed in Chapter 5 of this book.

Preliminary Longitudinal Studies of Creative Talent

Ted Clymer, Paul Torrance, and two of Torrance's graduate students—Tan and Allman—conducted a study on the predictive power of the Minnesota Tests of Creative Thinking, using college students as their subjects. The study began in 1958, when 328 students who were majoring in elementary education took the tests. The predictor instruments were the earliest developed batteries of the creativity tests. Six and a half years later, Torrance's team obtained follow-up data for 114 of the subjects, using a checklist that was developed to assess teachers' creative activity and achievement. Generally, the investigators found that the creativity test administered to teachers in training could predict classroom teaching behaviors eight years later. Those who scored high on the tests demonstrated creative achievement in the classroom, while those who scored low in creativity as a student teacher did not demonstrate creative behaviors as a practicing teacher. The results of this study were written up by Torrance, Tan, and Allman (1970). Paul was encouraged by this and other studies conducted with school students that showed an expected and significant relationship between creative test performance and later creative achievements. This indicated that the test had predictive validity; in other words, it measured accurately what it was intended to measure.

DEVELOPING INSTRUCTIONAL MATERIALS

In August of 1959, *Rewarding Creative Thinking*, an experimental manual prepared by four Twin City teachers, along with Paul Torrance, was distributed to eight elementary teachers who had expressed an interest in using it. The manual was also used in a controlled experiment in two elementary schools to improve the quantity and quality of creative thinking among students.

CROSS-CULTURAL STUDY OF CREATIVITY

In 1960–61, cross-cultural studies in creativity were conducted in various countries, using the Minnesota Tests of Creative Thinking. This research was supported by a 15-month grant of $30,000 from the United States Office of Education. Research on translating and developing normative data on the two types of creative thinking tests—verbal and figural—was conducted in the United States with white and black populations, as well as in Australia, Western Samoa, Norway, France, West Germany, India, Turkey, and Singapore. Torrance's purpose in doing this study was to find out what conditions in different societies permit persons to make creative discoveries. Arrangements were made to test children in grades 1 through 6. Several of Paul's graduate students and research fellows possessed various language skills and had received their early education outside of the United States. They included Kaoru Yamamoto (Japan), Balderjav Luther (India), Dietmar Schenitzki (Germany), Victoria Punsulan (the Philippines) and Dr. Kevsar Arsan (Turkey). Other former staff members who had returned to their native countries were also willing to assist with these cross-cultural studies. The tests of creative thinking were translated into German, Hindi, Chinese, Japanese, Malayan, Western Samoan, Tamil, Norwegian, and Italian.

Richard Johnson, a BER research assistant, tested children in Samoa (the South Pacific protectorate of New Zealand), and indicated that their imagination was extremely limited. Johnson, who had taught and counseled in the islands of Samoa before helping Paul Torrance administer the BER creativity battery to 1,100 children, stated that Samoan children have been pressured for centuries to obey instantly when told to do something. When faced with instructional tasks such as those on the Minnesota Tests of Creative Thinking, they were generally left very frustrated.

Johnson also discovered that originality or unusualness is culture-specific. For example, in the picture construction activity which requires the student to create a picture from a jelly-bean shape, one Samoan child drew a crab while another drew an apple.

CRAB

APPLE

An American would label the crab unusual (original) while an apple would be an expected or ordinary response. In Samoa, however, apples are expensive and difficult to obtain, while crabs are common.

The tests were translated into the Samoan language and normative data were developed. The same translation and norm preparation was compiled for children in grades 1 through 6 for Norway, France, and so on. A disturbing trend in the development of creativity was common across cultures.

THE "CREATIVITY CURVE": SLUMPS IN DEVELOPMENT

What do the numbers 5, 9, 13, and 17 have in common? These are the ages of lowest creativity development in children. Creativity dips were identified by analyzing the test results of children in the United States and other countries.

Figure 2 indicates that when a child enters school and adapts to it, there is a period of growth in the first through third grades. A rather sharp slump near the end of the third or beginning of the fourth grade is followed by another period of growth in the fifth and sixth grades. Entrance into junior high school is accompanied by another drop. Again, recovery and growth resumes until near the end of high school, at which time there is a slight slump or leveling off. Figure 2 depicts the shape of creative growth for children in the United States, but the graph is remarkably similar in other cultures.

Figure 2
Generalized Developmental Curve of the Creative Thinking Abilities

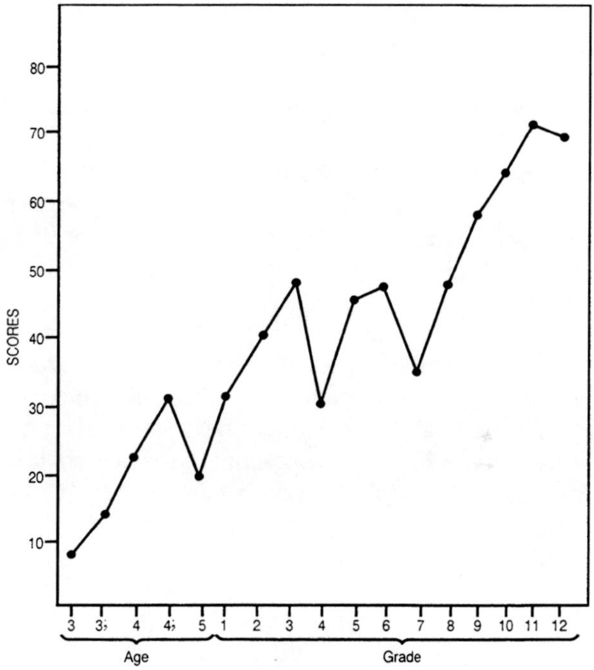

taken from Torrance, E.P. (1963). *Education and the Creative Potential.* p. 42.

Torrance identifies peer pressure as a possible explanation for the dips in creative development. Being creative requires independent thought, which often results in a minority-of-one status, with too few "anchors in reality." It may be that children surrender their creativity by conforming to peer and societal pressures.

An article appeared in the *Minneapolis Sunday Tribune* entitled "Does Creativity Dip at 9?" (1961). It described Paul Torrance's research on the fourth grade slump. Two days later, Paul received a letter from R. W. Lowry,[3] an ophthalmologist from Worthington, Minnesota. He expressed great interest in the finding and stated that the slump apparently occurs in other fields, too. Dr. Lowry has found that nine-year-olds have the worst possible visual organization, as compared to other ages, and they tend to be complacent, rarely reporting visual symptoms (blurring, doubling, eye watering). He said that it is not the best time for vision training or rehabilitation. Although the nine-year-old likes to practice endlessly, results are not readily forthcoming. Therefore, he found it best to delay therapy for six months to a year. He went on to say that in the

[3] Letter from R.W. Lowry to Paul Torrance, March 7, 1961 (in possession of the author).

landmark developmental work of Gesell and Ilg (1946), the nine-year-old was the "least understood" of any age they studied. However, Paul Torrance was optimistic that creativity could be revived at any age/stage with the proper atmosphere (school, home, community, state/province) and teaching methods.

UTAH CONFERENCE ON SCIENTIFIC CREATIVE TALENT

In June of 1959, Paul Torrance participated in the Third National Research Conference on the Identification of Creative Scientific Talent at Alta, Utah. At this conference, he made the first comprehensive report of the work on creativity. He also collaborated with Calvin Taylor on a new research project that would attempt to reduce the lag that occurs in applying scientific findings to classroom techniques. This was the beginning of a friendship between Calvin Taylor and Paul Torrance that has continued over their long careers, both of which have been devoted to "igniting" and pursuing creative potential.

Paul undertook the responsibility of preparing a report on the status of knowledge concerning education and creative talent. He had a project review team that included Calvin Taylor, John Holland, J. P. Guilford, and Frank Barron. A first draft of this report was ready in June of 1961. Paul's book, *Guiding Creative Talent* (1962a), included materials on approximately half of the studies conducted in the Bureau of Educational Research at the University of Minnesota. A summary report on the role of evaluation in creative thinking was also written for the United States Office of Education.

During the period between 1958 and 1963, a number of special grants and contracts supported the research program designed by Paul Torrance and his team at the Bureau of Educational Research in the College of Education. The Cooperative Research Program of the United States Office of Education had just been established, and it offered a variety of research grants. Also, the University of Minnesota offered faculty members small grants from a graduate school research fund.

Paul received grants for and was responsible for more projects than he could carry out. However, he had five or six outstanding doctoral students who worked as research assistants and enabled him to complete all of the studies. In 1963, in addition to Paul Torrance, who was the Director, the staff of the Bureau of Educational Research included the following individuals, all of whom devoted some of their time to research on creativity:

Mrs. Dorolese Wardwell, 50%-time, Office Supervisor and Assistant to the Director
Mrs. Darlene Ulrich, full-time, Secretary to the Director
Mrs. Gwendolyn Green, full-time, Secretary
Vincent Johnson, 50%-time, Supervisor of Statistical Work (Statistics)
Richard Dawson, 50%-time, Research Fellow (Group Dynamics)
Kaoru Yamamoto, 75%-time, Research Assistant (Educational and

Developmental Psychology)
Rod Myers, 50%-time, Research Assistant (Elementary Education)
Richard Johnson, 50%-time, Research Assistant (Counseling Psychology)
Gargi Luthra, 50%-time, Research Assistant (Curriculum and Instruction)
Noel Iverson, 50%-time, Research Assistant (Anthropology and Sociology)
Richard Peterson, 25%-time, Research Assistant (Exceptional Children)
Judson Harmon, 25%-time, Research Assistant (Counseling Psychology)
Bert Cunnington, full-time, Coordinator and Producer of Experimental Materials for Title VII Project (Speech and Journalism)

Paul was also busy supervising doctoral dissertations and master's theses concerning creative talent at the University of Minnesota. In addition, he was giving assistance to at least 100 research workers outside of the University who were using materials developed by the Bureau of Educational Research. The work completed by the Bureau was evaluated by many individuals and communicated to a host of groups and agencies.

About 60 draft reports of studies were disseminated to faculty of the College of Education, to participants in the research, and to other researchers in the field. Paul and his associates reported and discussed the results of their research program at national meetings of professional groups and held workshops for other universities, school faculties, groups of administrators and curriculum workers, and parent–teacher associations.

Discussion of the results and programming problems took place within the Bureau, with members of the Bureau's Advisory Committee and research participants, and in graduate and staff seminars from other departments at the University of Minnesota. Many of the reports were published in professional journals, and Paul gave progress reports on the research at the Utah Research Conferences on the Identification of Creative Scientific Talent and the Minnesota Conferences on Gifted Children.

It was difficult to provide a comprehensive review of the research program because of the urgency of daily demands of data collection, deadlines for reports, correspondence (400-500 letters per month), and the consequent lag in the completion of blocks of research that had to be evaluated and then reported.

Paul appealed to the Advisory Committee for more assistance to clear up the backlog of data that had to be analyzed, documented, and reported. He requested two full-time positions with some clerical support. He got his wish and work proceeded on unfinished studies.

SOUTHERN BAPTIST RELIGION AND PAUL TORRANCE

Religion had always played an important role in Paul's life, and the time had now come to apply some of his research findings to his religious beliefs and experiences.

Laura Littleford, in a personal letter[4] to me, answered some of my questions about the mission and passion of Southern Baptists, which I hoped to relate to the work of Paul Torrance. Laura, who has been writing on the subject, was brought up in the Southtown Baptist Church in Minneapolis, where her father was the minister. Paul and Pansy Torrance were members of this church, and they attended it regularly. They helped found churches at St. Paul, South St. Paul, and Roseville. Both taught Sunday School classes. Some of Paul Torrance's mission and passion in his research and teaching can be traced to his orthodox Southern Baptist upbringing.

Since their beginnings in England in the early 1600s, Baptists have been known as Separatists. In Colonial America, the Baptists formulated their strict position on absolute separation of church and state. At that time, of course, the Industrial Revolution was shaking up the previous church order—the rule of tradition—and in England, those economic changes were also reflected in the Separatist movement of churches—Presbyterians, Congregationalists, Quakers, Independents—as well as Baptists. This separation notion in the Baptist philosophy applies to Torrance's interest in creativity and to the nature of his research. The Baptist religion gave a kind of spiritual permission to go out and do something new and apart from the established order. It also gave that flavor to Torrance's research—separating out the creative gift from the intellectual gifts and talent, and making a distinction.

The concept of individual salvation is a part of the mission of the Southern Baptist. This gives a sense of urgency or passion to the mission. The mission of the Christian, once saved, is to witness to others, both by example and by word or teaching. One must bring this salvation and this teaching throughout the world. "Go ye into the world, and preach the gospel to every creature (Mark 16:15). I think that Torrance's work is weighted toward the verbal. Also, the Baptist's sense of mission is present in his written work/speaking engagements throughout the world and his interest in creative development in different cultures.

Paul Torrance is profoundly rooted in the culture of the South and the culture of Southern Baptists. He has taken the positive aspects of the Baptist mission and avoided the excesses or negativism. His work was pioneering. He had to break new ground to permit discussion and criticism. This is the burden of the pioneer. Unfortunately, the American South is so little understood and the stereotypes are so negative: redneck on one hand, and aristocratic on the other. Part of the Baptist history includes a trampling upon indigenous cultures and also a reputation for a frightful intolerance. Paul Torrance has broken away from this stereotype as he is exceptionally broad-minded and tolerant.

Passion is also a "Southern" thing—more emotional, very colorful, and yet very circumscribed. It is emotion within certain boundaries. A Southerner can feel passionate about many abstract things like patriotism, honor, and God, but

---

[4] Personal communication with Laura Littleford, September 6, 1992 (in possession of the author).

one does not express other things like family secrets and sins of the forefathers. Paul Torrance's passion is rooted in a sense of urgency, a sense of his passion about those who are misunderstood, the mislabeled "troublemaker" children whose gifts will be lost if a sympathetic mentor does not help them communicate or communicate for them.

Laura Littleford's mother, Anda, once stated that Paul Torrance was able to pour himself into his early work because he was single, which resulted in a single-minded focus, but after marrying Pansy, he learned another dimension to his work, the dimension of love. Paul Torrance's Baptist religion was extremely positive for him, and he decided to make a difference for people everywhere. Paul served as a deacon and as Sunday School Superintendent or Training Union Director in churches in Black Springs and Milledgeville, Georgia, and Bloomington, St. Paul (Minnesota), South St. Paul (Minnesota), and Roseville, Minnesota. Paul and Pansy were especially active in the church after their marriage. Paul studied the Bible more than he had at any other time. Paul and Pansy read the Scriptures aloud to each other. Paul also tried to study the lesson very thoroughly in preparing to teach Sunday School classes.

Creativity in Religion: Paul Lives by His Work

In 1960, at a conference on creativity in religious education, Paul Torrance cited several examples to show that God has commanded people to live creatively. He indicated that a human being's natural inclination is to learn creatively. Yet in education, we have traditionally insisted that people acquire knowledge by authority. In religious education, we have usually insisted that people acquire beliefs by authority. Learning by authority may be more efficient but is not long-lasting and meaningful.

At this conference, Paul gave examples of Jesus as a creative learner, thinker, and teacher. Jesus is often depicted asking questions—one of the basic techniques for learning creatively. This inquisitive tendency stayed with Jesus throughout his life, as it does with all really creative teachers. Price (1946) reported that the Scriptures record 154 questions asked by Jesus. Also as a teacher, Jesus aroused the curiosity of others. People asked him many questions, and he always treated their questions with respect and helped them to find answers.

Paul Torrance applied his research in creativity to the teaching of religion so that educators could leap the barriers from learning to thinking, and abandon teaching only by authority. Paul discussed the definition, value, and kinds of creative thinking. He proposed that the essence of creative teaching/learning is the relationship of teacher and student. Rather than being a reactive relationship (stimulus–response), it needed to be a co-experiencing one. It requires a willingness on the teacher's part to embark on a journey over untraveled pathways.

It means being open to experience and being willing to participate in the relationship, once it happens.

Paul's work as superintendent of Sunday School classes in the Baptist Church in Minneapolis revealed his love of teaching children creatively about God. He and Pansy worked together in the church. They wrote articles and a curriculum that had an impact upon the teaching of religion in the United States.

Ronald Goldman, a professor from Reading University near London, England, spent three months studying with Paul at the University of Minnesota. Paul co-authored a paper on "Meaning and Relevance of Learning Readiness for Curriculum Construction in Christian Education (1975), with Pansy and Ronald Goldman.

Paul and Pansy developed a curriculum for preschool children called "Ideas About God" which they published in "Creativity and Teaching Concepts of God" (1988) and taught. They chose three aspects of a mature definition of God on which to focus their program: love, infinity, and spirit. They designed a variety of experiences for preschoolers that helped move them along the path toward a mature concept of God. Paul and Pansy applied the findings from creativity research to teach the curriculum. The activities they designed incorporated the nature of the creative learning skills of preschoolers: interest span, ability to organize, looking at things differently, postponement of learning by authority, periods of silence and hesitation, taking a closer look, learning through fantasy, storytelling, and song-making. The curriculum provides ideas for teachers in teaching the key concepts of God—love, infinity, and spirit. For example, to teach the concept of *spirit*, Paul and Pansy dissolved a sugar cube in a glass of water. "Is the sugar still in the glass? they would ask. "Yes, but you can't see it, responded the children.

I quizzed Paul Torrance on some issues about religion and the church. Here are some of his thoughts:

> The debate about Creation and Evolution is like the one on Nature and Nurture in psychology. I am sure that both have taken place and are taking place. You will see the background for this statement illustrated in my article on "What Men May Become" (1989). I think and I hope that we are still evolving. I think there is modern-day evidence of this taking place in many areas of life mentioned in that article.
>
> Jesus was certainly a great teacher and accomplished miracles through his teaching and contacts. I use "miracle" here to refer to anything which involves going beyond the expected. You will find that I have spoken of teaching in public education about accomplishing these kinds of miracles when a child who is not learning and is predicted not to learn becomes a good learner. I have also written on this in several articles. I think the first is contained in my book *Education and the Creative Potential* (1963a). At the present time, I do not know whether the teachings of Christianity, Moslem, and other major religious groups are really different. Each reflects the moral culture of the people in which the religion evolves. It seems to me that God is the same in all of these major religions. The definition of God that we use in our material for four- and five-year-olds suits

me: God is love, God is spirit, and God is infinite. I think this definition would be acceptable in any religion. People seek God in different ways, knowing that there is some kind of higher intelligence that has created the Earth and the planets and that we must respect the authority of this intelligence or this creativity.

I think a similar relationship exists between reason and faith. I do not understand how some things happen, but I have never been able fully to understand the radio, the telephone, or many of the other marvels of the universe, yet I enjoy the benefits of all of these things. We should not think it strange when we see miracles taking place in our children and in our relationships with them.[5]

LOOK... NATIONAL RECOGNITION

"The tragedy of creative children is that they are often penalized—because they are 'different.'"

An event that occurred in late 1961 had a profound effect upon the work and life of Paul Torrance: The November 7, 1961 issue of *Look Magazine* published "The Creative Child" (Brossard, 1961), an article discussing Paul's research. The resulting avalanche of thousands of letters catapulted Paul Torrance into national prominence. It also upset the leaders of the day in gifted education and educational psychology and created a "paradigm shift."

Since joining the Bureau of Educational Research at the University of Minnesota, Paul Torrance had published several articles in professional journals in an attempt to communicate his findings to other educators. His efforts were largely futile as he was unable to reach a large number of influential people. He was hoping that a popular magazine like *Look* would speed up the process of gaining acceptance for a new educational concept among educators and the public. A popular estimate of the time was that it takes 75 years for a new idea to be put into practice in 50 percent of the schools.

The senior editor of *Look Magazine*, Chandler Brossard, was passionately interested in the study of children. He was an avid reader of the most recent books on child development and had written several articles on the education of children that demonstrated great sensitivity and understanding. He became interested in Paul Torrance's research at Minnesota and visited him in the spring of 1961. Chandler Brossard was fascinated with the subject of creativity and secured permission to do a story. He interviewed Paul Torrance and other members of the Bureau staff, and, with photographer John Vachon, visited a public school in Bloomington, Minnesota to take pictures and observe an 11-year-old named Jimmy De Schepper. Jimmy had scored extremely high in a series of creativity tests administered by Paul Torrance. The teachers regarded Jimmy as a

---

[5] Personal letter from E.P. Torrance to G.W. Millar, December 1, 1992 (in possession of the author).

problem student, while Brossard described him as a "self-possessed dreamer with great qualities of brilliance and originality."

The *Look* team translated the cold facts of research into the human dimension of a child's struggle to express himself *creatively*. The article answered a number of questions about the creative child. "What makes him different?" "How is he discriminated against?" "How is he overlooked?" "What often becomes of him?" "How can we utilize his mind?" (Brossard, p. 1).

The *Look* article criticized intelligence tests as measuring only a few abilities that favor only convergent thinking and memory-dependent individuals. Creativity tests like those developed by Torrance were an attempt to broaden the concept of intelligence.

Needless to say, prominent educators of the academically gifted and educational psychologists were disturbed. Torrance proposed a way to measure and teach another important human ability—creativity. The Bureau of Educational Research received over 2,000 letters in a period of 18 months. Paul Torrance analyzed 600 of the letters. The majority of readers of the article requested permission to use the creativity tests, asked for copies of the research reports, and expressed appreciation for and enthusiasm about the work of Paul Torrance and his associates. The article had aroused a great deal of interest among parents, counselors, curriculum coordinators, school psychologists, college/university faculty/students, educators of gifted students, elementary and secondary teachers, and creative individuals. These are samples of the comments in the correspondence that Paul received:

> The editorial concerning your work in the *Minneapolis Morning Tribune* sent me racing out to buy a copy of *Look* because it confirmed something I've been saying for years. I don't write fan letters as a rule; I have to in this case because your insight has given me new courage—and faith, that I'm not foolish to continue trying to do what I've been trying to accomplish for years.
>
> — Clare John Jansen, Minneapolis, MN. 11-16-61.

> A recent article in *Look Magazine* caught our attention and has resounded through the department here like an electric shock.
>
> — Patrick H. Poole, Kansas State College of Pittsburgh. 10-25-61.

> Please go on with your work, we are encouraged. Make a loud voice about it. If you reach the public directly as you did us in *Look*, school masters will be forced to take [the] lead.
>
> — Mrs. Reginald F. L. Moonan.

> It was with great interest that I read an account of your work "The Creative Child in a recent issue of *Look Magazine*. I certainly agree with the article in that new types of tests need to be developed to be used along with our conventional IQ tests.
>
> — Martin Garnick, Garden City Public Schools, Garden City, NY. 12-5-61.

> Please forgive the longhand. Thank God someone has finally realized there

is such a thing as a creative child.

— Mrs. Faith Broome, Washington, DC. 10-31-61.

I have just read the article in *Look Magazine* describing your intriguing work dealing with creativity in children. It seems to me that this is a significant piece of work, and that it points the way to much fruitful research in this area.

— Harold Miller, Westmont College, Santa Barbara, CA. 10-30-61.

Look's article on the creative child, based on your research, was one of the most hopeful, useful articles on education ever published in a popular magazine. Perhaps many more teachers than you realize are grateful for the balance your research provides.

— Dr. Marguerite Lienard, Bakersfield Center,
Fresno Street College, Bakersfield, CA. 2-5-62.

Over 300 teachers expressed an interest in using Torrance's new creativity tests. Immediately, 100,000 students were affected by taking the test. In the conclusion of his report (1963c), "The Torrance Report on the Response to *Look*," Paul Torrance wrote:

Most of the *Look* respondents set in motion some kind of action which has been reported through regular correspondence since the fall of 1961. Many others reported immediate actions of considerable consequence.

Principals and curriculum consultants re-evaluated their programs. Parents stimulated teachers and school psychologists to obtain information about testing for creative talent. And it is estimated that advice has been given to at least 300 graduate students concerning the conduct of doctoral and master's theses in this field. (p. 2).

Paul Torrance expressed one complaint about the *Look* article. He stated in his report (1963c):

An attempt to respond to over 2,000 letters and to meet a few of the demands for articles, speeches, and conferences all but halted our regular research program. The opportunities created by *Look*'s article far exceeded the resources of our organization. But it is to be hoped that the activity inspired by *Look* will more than compensate for this loss. (p. 3).

Paul Torrance, from this time forward, gained national acclaim for his work in the field of creative assessment and teaching.

COERCION TO CONFORM: SOCIETAL SANCTIONS AGAINST DIVERGENCY

"The ways in which a person is different from all others are his most priceless possessions and it is these differences which have made our country what it is and are essential to a democratic society." (Torrance, 1962a)

In a study that involved a creative writing task, Paul Torrance analyzed the written expression of 5,000 children from around the world to determine their perception of divergence and how society handles it. The overall purpose of the study was to determine the conditions in society that permit persons to make creative discoveries. Children in grades 3 through 9 wrote stories about animals or persons with some kind of divergent characteristic. Topics ranged from flying monkeys to lions that won't roar, girls who want to be engineers, and boys who want to be nurses. The stories revealed that the pressures of society against divergency are recognized by children as powerful forces. Divergence was even equated with mental illness. There was considerable variation among cultures.

Variations in perceptions were also evident in different American subcultures. School children from urban areas who attended classes made up of students of mixed ability showed the most severe pressures against creative kinds of achievement. The pressure came mainly from peers. Gifted children in special classes in urban areas were more optimistic about persisting in creative, divergent behavior. Stories written by children from small towns such as Hibbing, Minnesota, were more tolerant of divergence than their urban peers. The stories written by children in religious schools showed the most intolerance. Black children in a segregated school in Georgia reflected the greatest parental support of divergent talent.

Several cultures outside the United States were also studied. Stories written by French children showed the highest tolerance of divergence. Pressures to conform were viewed as relentless in almost every country—Turkey, India, Australia, and Canada. The pressure in these countries came from society in general rather than from the children's peers. Canada, in particular, has hung on to the British traditions of conforming to societal values.

My own doctoral dissertation (Millar, 1975) analyzed the psychological theory of security as proposed by William Blatz of the University of Toronto. One result of my longitudinal study was that a mentally healthy person was characterized by both independence, as demonstrated by competence in particular areas of life, and by cooperation with others. Those who were highly dependent upon others as children and tried to please excessively turned out to be highly dependent adults with few creative ideas. These findings are compatible with Torrance's finding that a high degree of tolerance for divergence is necessary for creative achievement and is a sign of a mentally healthy person.

This important cross-cultural study highlighted the pressures on children to conform and not display their differences or divergent tendencies. Paul Torrance believes that to be creative, one needs to have independence of mind and not be afraid to be a minority of one. He (Torrance, 1962b) offered this advice for parents:

> Stop equating divergency with mental illness or delinquency and help children recognize the values of their individual talents, for the ways in which a person is

different are his most priceless possessions and it is these differences which have made our country what it is.

WHO ARE THE HIGHLY CREATIVE?

Paul Torrance's research has helped us understand who the creatively gifted are and how to nurture that potential. He found that creative learners possess a different kind of giftedness than what is attributed primarily to academic ability or high intelligence.

Teachers indicated in the study of the Ideal Pupil (Torrance, 1963b) that they prefer highly intelligent children. They describe these children as more desirable, more hardworking, and more studious. On the other hand, highly creative children appear to learn as much as the highly intelligent child without appearing to work as hard. Paul Torrance believes that these highly creative children are learning and thinking when they appear to be "playing around." One five-year-old girl told Paul Torrance at a birthday party when she reached into a grab bag for favors, "That's how I get ideas—just reach in and scrunch around in my mind until I feel like pulling something out."

Paul Torrance quickly points out that regardless of the measure of IQ or scholastic aptitude used, about 70% of highly creative children are excluded from the gifted group. Children who demonstrate high levels of creativity are gifted children of a different sort. One study involved an experiment that distinguished highly creative children from those who were highly intelligent. Although there was an average of 25 IQ points between the two groups, both performed at the same level on achievement measures.

Creative children learn by questioning, inquiring, searching, manipulating, experimenting, and even playing around, but always trying to find the truth. Torrance (1977) has repeatedly said:

> Creative learning and thinking takes place in the process of sensing difficulties, problems, missing elements, gaps in knowledge, making guesses or formulating hypotheses about these deficiencies, testing these hypotheses and in communicating the results.

In 1961, Paul Torrance stated that gifted children may learn better, that is, more economically and effectively, by creative methods rather than by being told what and when to learn, that is, by traditional methods. Much of Torrance's research suggests that some children prefer to learn by authority and that others prefer to learn creatively. His five principles that encourage or reward creative thinking were reported in a Sacramento newspaper in 1961:

1. Be respectful of unusual questions, but tell children only what they cannot learn for themselves. Teach them the skills of inquiry and how to sustain a

question, to toss it back and forth, to refine it and to accept the questioning mood without the need for ready-made answers from parent or teacher.
2. Be respectful of unusual ideas and thinking.
3. Show children their ideas have value.
4. Provide opportunities for self-initiated learning and give credit for it. A mark of the highly creative individual is his self-starting ability.
5. Provide for a period of non-evaluated practice or learning. We do not have to evaluate everything. ("Gifted Children," 1961, p. A16)

Torrance declared, "external evaluation is always a threat and creates a need for defensiveness. There should be a time when a child can make a mistake without being criticized."

A creative person is never content to learn only by authority but persists in finding out for himself through constant questioning, probing, and experimenting. The work of Torrance and others in the area of creativity resulted in a revision of the definition or description of giftedness. In 1972, Sidney Marland, U.S. Commissioner of Education, stated:

> Gifted and talented pupils are those who by virtue of outstanding abilities are capable of exceptional performance. These are children who require differentiated provisions and/or programs beyond the regular school program to realize their contribution to self and society.
>
> Children capable of exceptional performance include those with demonstrated achievement and/or potential ability in one or several areas:
>
> a. general intellectual ability,
> b. specific academic aptitude,
> c. *creative and productive thinking* [emphasis added],
> d. visual and performing arts.

Personalities of Highly Creative Children

Paul Torrance analyzed personality data for highly creative children by way of sociometric position and drawings. The most creative boy and girl in each of 23 classrooms was studied. Three characteristics stood out: First, the highly creative child had a reputation for wild or silly ideas; second, their various productions tended to be off the beaten track; third, the work of the highly creative child was characterized by humor and playfulness.

When teachers were asked to describe highly creative children, their explanations illustrated an attitude of rejection. Teachers did not know them as well as other less creative children, regarded them as less desirable students, and rated them as less ambitious and hard-working. Simply put, teachers tended to reject many of the characteristics of highly creative individuals when describing the ideal pupil.

A result of studying creativity in young school children revealed that some phenomena inherent to the American/Canadian way of life inhibit creativity. These "stiflers" include:

- Success orientation or a preoccupation with prevention of failure.
- Contemporary pressure on the individual to conform.
- The "curiosity killed the cat" philosophy, which discourages questioning.
- Cultural tradition that has made sensitivity a feminine value and independence a masculine one.
- Belief that any divergence from behavioral norms is an indication of something abnormal or unhealthy.
- The culturally inspired tradition that one is supposed to hate work and love play.[6]

TEACHING RESEARCH SKILLS TO STUDENTS: IT'S ELEMENTARY

Paul's efforts with elementary students documented their ability to learn to conduct fairly complex research. In 1962, he developed a program with Rod Myers, a research assistant and former educator, to teach a group of students—the High Achievers of Riverside School in Bloomington, Minnesota—important research ideas and how to do their own probing into the unknown.

Objectives of the course included:

1. To familiarize the High Achievers with some of the most powerful concepts of research in the behavioral sciences, so that these concepts can become tools in their learning and thinking.
2. To communicate to them some of the excitement of doing research, exploring the unknown, and pushing forward our knowledge—and perhaps motivate some of them to choose and pursue careers in research.
3. To give them experience in participating in educational research and in conducting an experiment with real consequences.
4. To develop some skills in formulating hypotheses, testing hypotheses and reporting the results.

On the first day, December 11, 1962, the High Achievers learned that there are many things that teachers and other educators do not know about how to help boys and girls to learn most effectively. They were told that one of the ways of

[6] "Professional Studies 'Stiflers' of Children's Creativity." Newspaper clipping in Torrance Archives, University of Georgia (MSS 2606-1959-62, Volume I).

learning about these unknowns is through research—ways of digging into things, looking things up, and experimenting. They learned that research involves a more-or-less formal, systematic, intensive process of carrying on the scientific method. It is not mysterious, but systematic investigation. It is logical and objective. It involves applying every test for verification and organizing data in quantitative form. The students were involved in actual experiments to apply the principles of research. Finally, they learned about three major kinds of research—historical, descriptive, and experimental—and explored each first-hand during the week.

High Achievers could certainly learn to do research if given the skills and opportunity. Paul Torrance knew that students could also learn to become more creative by deliberately teaching those skills.

Laura Littleford, now a writer, actress, and former Montessori teacher in St. Paul, Minnesota, was in that grade 6 special class for bright children in the early 1960s. That was when she first encountered Paul Torrance as a teacher. Paul and Rod Myers taught research methods to her class. This was the post-Sputnik era when America was striving to be number one in the world. Her class adopted the "alter teacher" program, which involved a guest speaker program once a week. Laura remembers writing the Minnesota Tests of Creative Thinking. She, apparently, scored in the 90th percentile. In July of 1992, she indicated that on reflection of her special student status in the early 1960s, she felt it was "awful" and represented a "modified form of child abuse in the guise of gifted education."[7] She still corresponds with Paul Torrance when she needs affirmation about making a major change in her life.

Trust was the most important thing that Laura Littleford learned from Paul Torrance. Laura says, "to do something new is very scary, and I think a creative person has to have a trusted friend or mentor before he or she trusts their own gift, their own creativity."[8] Paul Torrance was one of the few adults she trusted as a child. Laura remembers that he had a sweet, genuine nature, and she felt completely at ease with him. She had no fear of his disapproval.

Minnesota Conferences on the Gifted and Creative

There were three Minnesota Conferences on the Gifted during this period (1958, 1959, 1960). Maynard Reynolds and Paul worked closely in organizing these pioneer conferences, which dealt with a variety of topics on giftedness and creativity. The conferences were a cooperative effort sponsored by the College of Education, the Bureau of Educational Research, the Division of Special Education, and the Institute of Child Development and Welfare at the University of Minnesota. Nationally known speakers, such as Calvin Taylor and J. W. Getzels, were invited

[7] Personal communication with Laura Littleford, September 6, 1992 (in possession of the author).
[8] Ibid.

to participate, along with local scholars. Three books resulted (Torrance 1960a, 1960b, 1961), detailing the proceedings of the conferences and providing reports on the progress of Paul and his students in various exploratory studies in creativity and on the status of the Minnesota Tests of Creative Thinking.

These conferences attracted leaders in the field of gifted and creativity education from all parts of the United States and Canada, and focused attention on the work of Paul Torrance and the Bureau of Educational Research at the University of Minnesota.

POPULARITY OF CREATIVITY RESEARCH

In February of 1959, Paul Torrance was invited by several groups to discuss the Bureau's studies of creative thinking in the early school years. On February 5, he met with the local Minneapolis Chapter of Psi Chi to discuss the work concerning peer pressure against the most creative members of groups. He addressed the elementary teachers of Northfield School on February 11, concerning some of the problems of identifying and developing creative talent in the early school years. On February 17, Paul was the guest of graduate students and staff members in the School of Home Economics at their regular seminar, where he talked about school experiences that foster and inhibit the development of creative activity. On February 24, he gave a lecture to Maynard Reynolds' class on the identification and development of creative talent.

This snapshot of his speaking engagements in February of 1959 indicates clearly that the work of Paul Torrance and the Bureau of Educational Research at the University of Minnesota was widespread, and it was capturing the interest of many groups and individuals in the Minneapolis region.

In the summer of 1959, Paul journeyed to Mount Mercy College in Cedar Rapids, Iowa, where he conducted a pre-college institute on "Improving College Teaching Through the Stimulation of Creative Thinking" and on "Problems of Counseling the Creative College Student."

His sphere of influence was evergrowing. In late 1960 and early 1961, Paul Torrance addressed many local, regional and national conferences and parent–teacher groups on the research generated by his Bureau of Educational Research. His calendar supports the nickname given to Torrance—"The Creativity Man." He summarized the research findings on creativity at meetings in several cities—Chicago, Ann Arbor, Detroit, Denver, and, needless to say, Minneapolis.

Newspapers and magazines often carried summaries of his speeches or talks. The archives revealed a sample of those talks:

- "Schools Cater to Retentive Memories"
- "Encouraging Children to Think"
- "Prof Goes to Bat for the Odd Ball"

- "'U' Educator Sees Creativity Stifled by Conformity"
- "Releasing Talent Through Teaching"
- "Keeping Creative Talent Alive—A Matter of Courage"
- "Developing Creative Readers"
- "Children's Creativity Gets Intensive Study"
- "Tests to Find the Creative Mind."

In the summer and fall of 1960, Paul Torrance carried the message of research on creativity to varied groups, which continued to create widespread comment. He lectured at the University of Illinois and Ohio State University; he conducted workshops for preschool and elementary teachers, as well as surgical technicians; and he talked to the Institute on Religious Education about "Making Religious Education More Effective by Stimulating Creative Thinking" (Torrance, 1960c).

Torrance strongly believed in accepting speaking invitations to promote an interest in his research on creative thinking. He was sought out by school authorities and universities to share his ideas about creativity with teachers, professors, and graduate students.

Emmet Williams, a superintendent of schools for independent School District No. 623 in Minnesota, wrote a newspaper article in support of the teaching of creativity. He indicated that every curricular field is fraught with possibilities for developing originality and insight on the part of boys and girls. He went on to say that creativity involves thinking and rationalizing about facts for life and not just memorizing them for tests.

In July of 1962, Paul Torrance was invited to present a "Great Ideas" seminar at Colorado State University at Greeley. He outlined three great ideas in the field of education. Paul called for expansion of the concept of the human mind, increased support for learning creatively rather than by authority, and development of creativity by a planned program rather than by chance.

Paul Torrance devised ingenious ways to communicate his research findings to others. He employed the usual methods of speeches and written pieces, but also a few that were more unconventional. A bulletin board display in Macalester College at the University of Minnesota in 1965 depicted the essence of creativity through a series of line drawings. Also, Torrance created several "info-posters" that communicated various findings about his creativity research, two of which are displayed in the photo section. Paul and Rod Myers developed activities and exercises to teach the skills of creativity.

EXERCISES TO TEACH CREATIVITY

"Give me a fish and I can eat for a day; teach me to fish and I'll eat for a lifetime."

Torrance and Rod Myers tested a series of idea books in 1963 with grade 4, 5, and 6 classes in Florida, North Carolina, Oregon, Hawaii, and Minnesota. Rod Myers had been an outstanding teacher in Oregon before returning to university to study creativity. He taught a grade 4 class at the University Elementary School in Minneapolis and, through his creative teaching, was able to avoid the fourth-grade slump.

Behind the paperbound workbooks (Myers & Torrance, 1963a, b, c) and accompanying teacher's manuals lie the authors' belief that children's capacity for original, creative thinking can be increased by exercises that "loosen up the imagination." The workbooks contain exercises that extend students' thinking. For example, Unit 4 in "Invitation to Thinking and Doing" is called "You, the Magician" and asks youngsters what they would change if they had magic powers. "What would you make sweeter so that it would taste better?" "What would you make go backwards in order to improve it?" Unit 6 contains "What if" exercises such as, "What would happen if lions were the size of cocker spaniels?"

Another aim of the authors was to get children to avoid "tired" words and ideas. Unit 8 offered the students a chance to make up their own comparisons, such as; "scary as __________," and "funny as __________."

Publishers of the early 1960s wanted Torrance and Myers to make the idea books subject-specific before they would publish them. However, the exercises were deliberately designed to range across all school subjects. To overcome this uncreative approach by publishers, they founded their own company—Perceptive Publishing. Torrance and Myers received letters from educators all over the United States volunteering their classes or schools for experiments in developing creativity. The books and teacher manuals were reprinted in 1986.

Torrance believed that by developing planned or programmed and guided experiences, teachers would develop boldness and courage to teach their students to be creative. Bert Cunnington initiated the idea of constructing tape-recorded materials that would bolster the teacher's spontaneity and ability to grip the imagination of students. The "Great Moments in Scientific Discovery" series was created for fourth-grade students (Torrance & Cunnington, 1965). The audiotapes focused on the role of creative problem solving, the importance of courage and other personality characteristics necessary for creative achievement, and planned, guided experiences in creative behavior. The experimental evidence indicated that planned, guided experiences in creative thinking can facilitate creative growth at grade four and tends not to interfere with the usual kinds of achievement. This is well documented by Paul Torrance and Ram Gupta (1964).

The success of this form of teaching for creative behavior will work if the teacher meets certain requirements. The teacher must be prepared to respond to the students' efforts to learn, think, and initiate further inquiries. Also, teachers need to relate the activities to regular curriculum content and develop the necessary skills. Paul Torrance demonstrated through deliberate teaching that creativity is not a gift doled out to only a minority. It is learnable and teachable, and it may bring ingenious solutions to problems facing the world.

THE CREATIVITY OF PRESCHOOLERS: UNUSUAL TESTS

Two of the tests of creativity that Paul Torrance developed came about serendipitously; however, these tests are not as well known as the Minnesota Tests of Creative Thinking.

Paul Torrance was not satisfied with the results of either the verbal or figural tests for preschool children. His tests required either verbal communication or drawing ability. Many creative young children would freeze up and not give any response to his tests, including his Mother Goose Problems Test. He was searching for a good way to assess their creative potential.

One day in the early 1960s, while Paul was working in a day-care center, he realized that these children had been walking and talking for only a short time, but had been moving all their lives. He observed their movement more carefully and noted that they solved most of their problems through action and movement. He went on to develop a test called *Thinking Creatively in Action and Movement* for preschool children (ages 3–6). Paul felt much better about the results. The test–retest reliability was good and had reasonably satisfactory validity. It was later refined at the University of Georgia.

Interpreting Sounds Creatively

Paul Torrance recalls the birth of the idea for another test of creative thinking. One Saturday morning, he met with Bert Cunnington to listen to his tape, *The Dog Named King*. Bert had been developing a number of audiotapes for use by classroom teachers to teach creativity. About halfway through the tape, there were some very unusual sound effects. Immediately, it suggested to Paul an idea for using a series of strange, ambiguous sounds and asking respondents to describe the images that the sound generated. Apparently, Cunnington immediately grasped the idea and produced a tape. It began with a simple, recognizable sound effect and progressed to stranger, more complex sounds. The fourth sound effect consisted of six rather strange sound elements. Cunnington and Torrance thought of ways that the tape could be used to stimulate creativity in visual art, dance, creative writing, and story telling.

The tape was used simultaneously as a test and as a teaching device. The manual and tape, *Sounds and Images*, was published by Ginn and Company in 1965. The results were most encouraging. Children produced very original artwork that was clearly more original and richer than usual. The same increase in originality and richness occurred in the children's creative writing and story telling. More work was needed in the months and years ahead to develop the test component of *Sounds and Images.*

At this time, Dr. John Gowan referred Joe Khatena to study with Paul Torrance. Dr. Gowan had engaged Joe Khatena as a young Singapore teacher while John Gowan was on a Fulbright Scholarship in Singapore in 1962 to collect responses to the Torrance Tests of Creative Thinking. Joe took his M.A. with John Gowan in Singapore. Joe also became a star pupil of Paul Torrance at the University of Georgia and established a brilliant scholastic record.

HEAVY DEMANDS TAKE TOLL...

The heavy load Paul was carrying at the University of Minnesota is noted in a letter written at Christmas, 1962. Pansy writes,

> About a year ago, Paul began to feel exhausted and for the first time in his life had to force himself to work. From teaching large classes, he had learned that the first 100 papers were fun to evaluate, but that the remainder were drudgery. Now, he began realizing that the first 100 speeches were fun, but that subsequent ones were exhausting. The first couple of thousand letters about his research were fun to answer, but the next five or six thousand have taken real effort.[9]

In July of 1962, Paul was exhausted and a break in his health occurred. The asthma season was upon him, and nights of sleeplessness made Paul an easy victim of the first virus of the season. This developed into a spastic cough and what appeared to be chronic bronchitis. He spent two weeks in bed and was hospitalized for a bronchioscopy and bronchiograph, which revealed an extremely spastic set of bronchi. In Pansy's words, "these findings will change our lives, but we are not yet sure what these will be."[10]

Maynard Reynolds indicated that while at the University of Minnesota, Paul would often fall asleep in faculty meetings while others were talking. To some people it appeared that he was uninterested in their work. However, it was the beginning of a medical problem that continued to affect Paul throughout his career. These untimely, irresistible attacks of sleep during normal waking hours were diagnosed as narcolepsy. This condition usually occurs after a heavy meal or a dull lecture, or when riding on a bus. This problem would continue to plague Paul and become more intense during his later years in Georgia.

By the end of 1962, there were many signs that the Minnesota Studies of Creative Thinking were having a definite impact on educational practices in many places. Most of the national educational organizations had extended invitations to Paul Torrance to speak at their annual meetings, and articles were

---

[9] Christmas letter from Pansy and Paul Torrance, 141 S.E. Warwick Street, Minneapolis, Minnesota, December 16, 1962.

[10] Ibid.

solicited from the *NEA Journal*, *Educational Leadership*, *Exceptional Children*, and the *Journal of Teacher Education*.

GUIDING CREATIVE TALENT (1962)

Paul's 1962 book, *Guiding Creative Talent* was selling well and reviews were extremely favorable. This book, which won the "Book of the Month" award for July, was dedicated to his third, fourth, and fifth grade teacher, Mrs. Bessie Burton, who taught him at Union Point School in Milledgeville. She instilled in Paul his love of literature and creative writing. In the dedication, he wrote:

> To—
> my parents
> my Aunts Clara, Mamie, and Lillian
> and "Miss Bessie," my teacher,
> who did most to keep alive
> a bit of my creativity
> through the "fourth grade slump."

The book won the annual American Personnel and Guidance Association award in 1963 for an outstanding contribution in original research. It contained a description of about half of the completed studies of the Bureau of Educational Research. It became very popular and has been reprinted 10 or 11 times. It was translated into three or four languages.

Saburo Sato translated it into Japanese in 1966. The book stimulated many Japanese educators to consider the importance of creative potential of children during a period when there was much discussion on how to reform Japanese education. His book is still a must-read for Japanese educators.

Mrs. Florence Foster of Westfield, New Jersey wrote Paul Torrance in 1962:

> Your new book, *Guiding Creative Talent*, which seemed to be so long in press, is at last in my hands and was well worth the waiting for. I have suggested that it be purchased for our school library (Newark State College) in hope that our teachers-to-be, as well as our graduate students, will read it and profit as I have. Of course, creativity is a subject near and dear to my heart, but your presentation should help to make it apparent that creativity should be the concern of all. Again, my congratulations. I believe your book is a real contribution to education.[11]

Ellen Smith, Principal of Ellerton Primary School in South Africa, wrote to me of Paul Torrance's impact on her school philosophy.

> It was through the pages of *Guiding Creative Talent* that I first encountered Paul

[11] Personal letter from Mrs. Florence Foster to Paul Torrance, July 25, 1962.

Torrance. The time was mid-seventies and I had been appointed principal of Ellerton Primary School in Three Anchor Bay.

I was searching for a better functioning education system—an improvement on the old left-hemispheric, linear-type learning currently practiced in all the schools.

It was through the writings of Paul Torrance that I found the key. Ideas such as this had fired my enthusiasm:

"There is little question but that the stifling of creativity cuts at the very roots of satisfaction in living and ultimately creates overwhelming tension and breakdown. There is also little doubt that one's creativity is the most valuable resource in coping with life's daily stresses."

It was an amalgam of Paul Torrance, Carl Rogers, Rollo May, and Maslow that finally provided me with the philosophy to form the foundation to the Ellerton Primary School model of learning.[12]

Overwhelmed by Interest

By 1963, Paul and his associates had become overwhelmed by public and professional interest in the creativity research being conducted by the Bureau of Educational Research. This interest seriously interfered with the Bureau's research, especially the contract research with the United States Office of Education. Hundreds of hours each month had to be devoted to answering correspondence and telephone calls, seeing visitors, reading manuscripts by other investigators, and conferring with students who were considering research projects involving creativity. From 1961 until the time Paul left the University in 1966, the number of inquiries concerning his research ranged from 3,000 to 5,000 per year.

By 1964, demands had become so overwhelming that Paul Torrance felt it necessary to resign as Director of the Bureau of Educational Research and accept a professorship in educational psychology. His major responsibility in this position was to develop the Department of Educational Psychology's program in the areas of personality development and social psychology. This was a very satisfying teaching experience for him. Many outstanding students enrolled in his courses and undertook exciting projects. The class sessions were a constant source of new ideas for Paul and his students. They accomplished a surprising amount of original research through class experiments in and out of the classroom.

John Karoussos, a retired chief inspector of schools in Greece and former student of Paul Torrance in Minneapolis, recalls that during a class Torrance had forgotten to zip his pants and his fly was open, and some students were whispering about it. John got up and told him in his ear what was happening. He, apparently, thanked John and continued teaching without any reaction, but

[12] Personal communication from Ellen Smith, Cape Town, South Africa, August 31, 1992.

after a few moments, he went to the overhead projector, wrote something, and deftly closed his zipper. John thought to himself, "That's what being a psychologist means!"

In Paul's words, "Perhaps the most disappointing aspect of my role that I assumed in 1964 was the lack of support for responding to national and international interest in my research" (Torrance, 1972c). Since he believed that his research was important in creating a better world, he could never ignore the requests that people made.

There were also individuals who questioned the validity of his work. Those who break new ground are often burdened by criticism.

DETRACTORS OF PAUL'S RESEARCH

The University of Minnesota had a history of strict quantitative methods and psychometrics, and some of Paul's colleagues and research assistants disagreed with some of his ideas. They questioned some of his research methods and the way he interpreted some of his findings, yet, no colleague ever attacked him or disparaged him while teaching a class. The limitations of accepted techniques should not limit the ideas of a thinker like Paul.

The detractors of Torrance's research interpretations were bound by historical psychometric procedures. Ram Gupta, a research assistant to Paul Torrance in 1962–63, says, "Dr. Paul was only concerned with the direction of the results of his research, not with the magnitude of statistical procedures used."[13] Ram Gupta, now a retired professor of educational psychology specializing in statistics from the University of Alberta in Canada, compared Torrance's statistical methods of the 1960s to the theory espoused by Nicolas Copernicus and later supported by Galileo. Just as the Polish astronomer was not believed by the scholars of the day, Torrance was surrounded by hard-headed statisticians who did not understand his research methods. Ram Gupta said in 1993 that Paul Torrance rejected the establishment regarding statistical procedures and followed his own hunches, which turned out to be true.

According to Maynard Reynolds, Paul's work was embraced by some individuals and criticized by others. His work produced ardent supporters and caustic sceptics. The criteria used to measure creativity were questioned. However, Paul dealt very well with this criticism, particularly with hard-nosed measurement types. He was viewed as an adventurer—ready to get out ahead and interpret his findings in a little more creative way.

Reynolds told me that E. G. Boring gave a speech at the University of Minnesota during the time of Paul's tenure. Boring was the chairman of the edu-

[13] Interview with Ram Gupta, Edmonton, Alberta, June 10, 1992.

cational psychology department at Harvard University and was the author of *History of Experimental Psychology*. In his speech he remarked that the "world's work is done by biased men." This remark reminded Reynolds of Paul's devotion and passion for his work.

Application of Creativity Research to Other Fields of Study

Torrance's research has been applied to many fields in education. For example, the *Journal of Health, Physical Education and Recreation* published an article on "Seven Guides to Creativity" (Torrance, 1965b). In a different vein, Dr. Susan Rose, a faculty member at Burton Hall, told me that she had used Torrance's tests of creativity while working with deaf children at Ohio State University.

WOES OF A RESEARCHER LIKE E. PAUL TORRANCE

Because researchers like Paul Torrance depend heavily on government funding, their fate is determined by whoever is in power and what is most valued at the time. In the post-Sputnik era of the late 1950s and early 1960s, creativity research was supported because America wanted to move forward scientifically and keep up with or go beyond Russia's impressive technological advances. The U.S. Office of Education provided many grants for educational research. However, the focus began to change as new personnel were hired and political mandates fluctuated.

For example, in 1965, Paul received a telephone call from the U.S. Office of Education. Officials there wanted him to write a mini-book for them on creativity. John Gardner, Secretary of Health, Education and Welfare at the time, had apparently told his subordinates to "get more creativity into their work." Paul was reluctant to take on this task because he was overwhelmed by important work he was trying to finish up before he left Minnesota to go to the University of Georgia. He finally gave in and wrote what his U.S. Office of Education monitor considered to be a masterpiece. However, by that time John Gardner had resigned and creativity was no longer in vogue. The U.S. Office of Education refused to publish the book, despite the protests and maneuvering of Paul's monitor, who also was on his way out.

At this point, the U.S. Office of Education began to favor the results of a few studies that had been designed to debunk the creativity research of the early and mid-1960s, even though the results of these studies were never made public. Paul Torrance had to find other sources of funding, and he did. He used his honoraria from speaking engagements and royalties to hire his own research assistants.

PANSY MAKES WAVES

Pansy and Paul had difficult times with critics over the years. Usually, one of them was able to see the humor in their attacks. Sometimes, though, the criticism hurt them both. Pansy tended to fire off scathing letters to critics to get it off her mind. In 1965, she felt that Vice President Hubert Humphrey was attacking university professors, which included her Paul, when he made a negative statement that was quoted in the July 22 edition of the *Minneapolis Morning Tribune.*

Pansy's letter to Humphrey (the reply is also included here) shows her staunch support for Paul and his work. This correspondence also illustrates clearly Paul's work ethic and Pansy's personality.

July 24, 1965

Dear Vice President Humphrey:

I am ANGRY, mad, FURIOUS, enraged, irritated, incensed, annoyed, infuriated, wrathful, indignant and IRATE with you, sir.

You are quoted in the July 22, 1965, Minneapolis Morning Tribune as saying:

> "The people who lead in educational research are at the universities. Let them quit playing games and go to battle."

You made such a sweeping incorrect statement which included my husband that I cannot be at peace with myself until I have told you a few facts about him.

He works about 16 hours a day. He was going all over the United States and Canada giving speeches to all kinds of groups, trying to get the whole population aroused as to needs in our schools. He also had had one book, Guiding Creative Talent, published, as well as having edited another, Talent and Education. I felt that his time was better spent in writing and getting the information he had learned disseminated more widely. He has concentrated on this aspect the past year, and will send you a list of his publications.

Now IN ADDITION, he teaches at the University of Minnesota, two classes first summer session, trying to teach teachers, counselors, nurses, and others to respect children and adults, to let them think, to teach them to really get at the essence of the problems which children have. He also is consultant to several groups, such as the workshop for judges and juvenile officers, speaking to them, and testing them to see how their ideas change in the treatment of delinquent children. Another workshop with which he helps is the one for principals of schools. He also teaches at least one class for teachers, and others, in another university or college each summer. Last summer he had about 175 enrolled at the University of California, Berkeley. He showed so much courage under direct attack from two or three members of the class, that the class gave him a "Notebook for a very broadminded person." The charge was that he was making the two or three think, something they had not attended the workshop for. They wanted to be bottle fed. He will teach next week at Wisconsin State College, Whitewater, Wis. He also speaks to PTA's, both in the Twin Cities areas, and in other states. Today we are trying to decide whether he should take a last minute offer from the University of Hawaii to conduct a one week workshop next month. The week is one which he had planned to spend in Oregon, working with another fellow who has also tried to fight the educational battle. He tested the 90 potential dropouts for Lincoln school area, Minneapolis, who were in a special program to prevent dropouts. Now let me tell you about the fellow he was going to see in Oregon.

Paul and Rod developed some materials which were not the usual sterile bland materials for teaching grade school children. No publisher would buy them. So they set up shop in our basement, with a Gestetner mimeograph machine and the two of them formed a publishing company to publish some materials, which after about 4 years, and after they had sold extremely well, Ginn and Company educational publishers, are now putting on the market. One of the publications was teaching research methods to sixth graders.

This is just what he does when he works. For recreation, we do church work. On Sunday mornings he is the Sunday School superintendent, and you know this extends into the week. Since 1958 he has been working in a mission in the Twin Cities area. We are now in the third mission. Sunday evenings he and I teach the 4 and 5 year olds for one hour. We try to apply the ideas he has found to be true from his extensive research and from his practical experience. We average about 5 children each Sunday evening. He also writes articles for many church publications. His classes at the University attract many ministers, and the nuns have decided one booklet, Struggle for Men's Minds, is the best preparation they have seen for their novitiates. This was prepared for the U.S. Air Force by him, and published for them. It is not being published at present.

He has not had a day off for over a year. We have been in other states, and in other places. His briefcase goes along and he continues to work. We had hoped to have a bit of time in January when we spent three days in Phoenix. He did go to dinner one evening with us, and took some pictures of the spectacular sunset. But unfortunately his asthma became worse, and with the work he did in the next two days he really was very exhausted when he went to northern California to give several speeches. Last summer we did go from Buffalo, N.Y. to Niagara, Canada, and spent the afternoon very leisurely, looking at the falls, going into shops and sightseeing. I cannot remember a day free from work since then.

I am not sure what you mean by "Let them quit playing games." He has been publicly attacked by the president of the American Psychological Association in the annual speech, because he continues to fight for better education teaching in our schools and more consideration of the children. This was printed in the American Psychologist. He has been attacked by many others. And people such as Benjamin Fine have used his ideas in a book, without crediting him for the ideas. If that isn't battle, I would hate to be in one. Perhaps you mean that he should start teaching in one school, to one class of maybe 30 or 40 students. I cannot agree with you. I know that you do need to do some horsetrading as a politician. (I was chairman of the Oklahoma State Nurses Association when we passed a bill for nursing in the state legislature.) But next time, please omit my husband when you say, "...go to battle."

Sincerely,

Mrs. E. Paul Torrance.

THE VICE PRESIDENT
WASHINGTON

August 4, 1965

Dear Mrs. Torrance:

I want to express my thanks for your irate letter and my tribute for your defense of your husband for his contributions toward improving the education of our children.

Actually, his contributions need no defense for his work is well known, even to people who are not involved closely with the new developments in education.

In my own defense I would like to say that my remark stating, "let them quit playing games and go to work" was quoted very much out of context. While not a part of my written text, it was delivered with reference to my remarks urging a closer liaison between educators at the University level and the slum schools often found in their proximity. Your husband, and a number of others, are outstanding examples of what is needed on a broader scale.

There was nothing in the deliberations of the White House Conference which could be considered as opposition to continued research and the early introduction of the findings into educational practice. Quite the contrary, there was a strong emphasis on the need for change at an accelerated rate and the need to establish a climate conducive to such a development. I am sorry if my remark has in any way diminished the opportunities for such action. The intent was quite the opposite.

I do want to compliment you for your obvious interest in this work and your sterling defense of your husband. Your unselfish devotion must be a great help.

Best wishes.

Sincerely,

Hubert H Humphrey

Hubert H. Humphrey

Mrs. E. Paul Torrance
141 Warwick Street, S.E.
Minneapolis, Minnesota

The Vice President also wrote to Paul Torrance at the same time, concluding his letter with, "I do want to take this opportunity to commend you for your work and to compliment you for that gallant woman who is your wife."

INFLUENTIAL COLLEAGUES

A number of well known professors and educators at the University of Minnesota gave Paul Torrance special encouragement and support during his years in Minneapolis, 1958 to 1966.

Dean Walter Cook had been Paul's advisor during his student days in summer courses (1941–1944). He was Dean of the College of Education when Paul Torrance returned in 1958. His untimely death in 1963 was a real loss to the University of Minnesota and to Paul personally.

Roger Wilk, head of the Department of Educational Psychology, had been a student of Paul's at Kansas State University. Roger was particularly encouraging, and he understood Paul's research.

Maynard Reynolds, head of Exceptional Children, played a key role in helping Paul plan the early conferences which eventually led to the University of Minnesota's annual conferences on gifted children.

Ned Flanders was in charge of all instruction on group dynamics, which was also a major emphasis in Educational Psychology. When he left the University of Minnesota, Paul began offering the two basic courses in group dynamics.

Guy Bond was one of the University of Minnesota faculty members who had a strong influence on Paul Torrance. Guy had had an outstanding academic record at Columbia University as a graduate student and research assistant with Dr. Arthur Gates, a national leader in the field of reading education. Bond went on to distinguish himself in the College of Education at Minneapolis, where for 29 years he was a prolific author in the field of reading instruction. Paul Torrance had read some of his books on reading before he went to Minnesota as a student. Paul took Guy's course on co-curricular activities while he was a student at the University of Minnesota. When Torrance went back to Minnesota as Director of the Bureau of Educational Research, Guy Bond encouraged his advisees to take Paul Torrance's courses. After Bond retired in 1980, he went to the University of Southern Illinois (USI) and tried (unsuccessfully) to recruit Paul Torrance.

Ted Clymer was a professor of elementary education who became editor of the Ginn reading programs.

Charles Glotzbach, best man at Paul's wedding, was a student colleague and a friend from Kansas State University. He was head of Student Counseling Bureau.

Marcia Edwards was associate dean. She was a charming woman who kept her finger on the pulse of the College of Education. She lived in Paul's neighborhood, Prospect Park, and he usually rode to the University with her and Theta Haganah.

Gilbert Wrenn was an extremely popular professor and one of Minnesota's great teachers. When Paul first came to the University he lived in Wrenn's house. (Wrenn was on sabbatical leave.)

E. G. Williamson, who was Dean of Students when Paul was in the Counseling Bureau in 1945, remained a long-time friend, and was always interested in Paul's teaching and his work as Director of the Bureau of Educational Research.

James Curtin, principal of the Laboratory Elementary School, was a good friend of Paul's. Curtin was interested in all of the research conducted in the elementary school and eagerly read the results. He provided a space in the school for creative art and inventions. He himself recorded an album of his own singing. He did many things to encourage the creativity of the children.

When Paul first went to the University of Minnesota, a rather famous internationally known personality was heading the English program. When she retired, she was gradually replaced by others. Paul Torrance asked Dean Cook why he didn't get another person of Dora Smith's stature. He replied that "he couldn't replace her. The best thing he could do was give someone else the opportunity to star in her role."[14] This person was Naomi Chase. She was a very good friend to Paul Torrance, who worked with several of her students. She also kept Paul current with what was happening in children's literature. She was an unusually good evaluator of children's books.

Dorolese Wardwell was the Executive Secretary of both the Bureau of Educational Research and the Bureau of Institutional Research—for 41 years. Everyone marveled at how she kept on top of these two agencies. Paul considers her a life-long friend. In a telephone interview with Dorolese Wardwell in 1992, she said she had worried about Paul Torrance because of the pace of his work. She stated, "Paul was a darling man, compassionate to others and passionate about his work. He was aware of every issue and problem before others."[15]

Willis Dugan was head of the counseling department while Paul was at the University of Minnesota. He always recognized Paul as a counselor, and Paul served on his counseling institutes. In 1963, when Paul won the annual research award from the American Personnel and Guidance Association, Dugan accepted it on behalf of Paul with great pride.

Reid Hastie was an inspiring professor of art education. Paul worked together with him and some of his advisees. Three of Hastie's doctoral students were Paul's research assistants at various times. Paul has several of Hastie's paintings.

Paul worked with Sam Popper and Clifford Hooker from the Faculty of School Administration. Clifford Hooker is now Head of Educational Administration at Ohio State University.

Robert Keller was principal of the Laboratory High School when Paul first went to the University of Minnesota. After Dean Cook's death, Keller became Dean of the College of Education.

---

[14] Personal communication from E. Paul Torrance to the author, November 30, 1992.

[15] Telephone interview with Dorolese Wardwell, Minneapolis, Minnesota, July 28, 1992.

Paul was pleased to have known John P. Anderson, who was Head of the Institute of Child Development. Anderson was a brilliant man who had read widely in the child development field. He took great pride in the Institute of Child Development, and tried to have a strong faculty. Every time Paul met him between Burton Hall and the Child Development Building, Anderson had read something quite recently about creativity research, and he always encouraged Paul. Dale Harris, also a very good friend, became Head of the Institute of Child Development after John P. Anderson, but soon left for Pennsylvania State University.

Probably the most illustrious woman in the College of Education was Ruth Eckert. She worked extremely hard and was interested in Paul Torrance's work. Another prominent woman at Minnesota was Mary Corcoran. She was on the staff of the Bureau of Institutional Research and was active in faculty governance. Today she remains active with the Minnesota Retired Teachers' Association.

Paul interacted with a number of different departments such as School Administration, Psychology, Vocational Education, Nursing, Creative Dramatics, Speech, and Sales and Merchandising. Paul was on dissertation committees in all of these fields.

As can be seen from this list, Paul Torrance was surrounded by competent, committed educators who were interested in his work and encouraged him to carry on during the Minnesota period. Paul also influenced many individuals—some of whom became avid followers.

Paul Influences Bee

Paul Torrance profoundly affected the professional career of Berenice "Bee" Bleedorn. Paul's research on creative potential and its development validated the perceptions and intuitions Bee had had in earlier teaching experiences. Although Bee did not have much interest in the counting and measuring processes of research, she was always intrigued and fortified by research conclusions in the field of creative studies. She has been able to collect a considerable amount of data for Paul Torrance's studies over the years—particularly since he left Minnesota. When he needed to follow up with students for his longitudinal study, she made contacts and found help in locating addresses of subjects. However, in Bee's words, "it has been his work and his constant pioneering efforts in issues related to creativity that have stimulated my own leadership in Thinking and Learning Styles, Creativity and Humor, Future Studies and Problem Solving Bowls, Mentorships, and Global Education."[16] Bee's success on many fronts is directly attributable to Paul Torrance's work

[16] Personal communication from Berenice "Bee" Bleedorn, November 22, 1992 (in possession of the author).

and his ongoing encouragement. (Bee has worked as the Minnesota State Consultant for the Gifted, developed the Master's Program in Gifted/Creative/Talented at the University of St. Thomas in St. Paul, and in teaching courses in Creative Problem Solving.) Bee says, "I am sure that I am passing on to students the support and encouragement that I had from Dr. Torrance. I am told so."[17]

SOME FORMER MINNESOTA STUDENTS AND COLLEAGUES REFLECT ON PAUL

Ram Gupta, a former student and research assistant of Paul Torrance in Minneapolis, stated in an interview that the most significant thing he learned from Paul was to be humble or ego-less and to live for your ideas and for your society, never for yourself. Ram said that Paul Torrance's research affected him in two ways: As a parent, he learned to be tolerant and to appreciate children's ideas and unusual behaviors; as a professional, he learned to encourage students' ideas. In summarizing Paul's persona, Ram said he displayed "a detachment from worldliness and attachment to ideas and people."[18]

I met Dr. Maynard Reynolds, now Professor Emeritus at Burton Hall (College of Education), to discuss Paul Torrance and the work he did at the University of Minnesota. Dr. Reynolds had worked closely with Paul Torrance during Paul's tenure as Director of the Bureau of Educational Research. Maynard Reynolds has had a distinguished career at Minnesota. He was the Director of the Psychoeducational Clinic, then Chairman of the Department of Special Education, and, more recently, a professor of educational psychology and special education. He has held executive positions with the Council of Exceptional Children and was involved in drafting PL 94-142—the Education for All Handicapped Children Act.

I asked Dr. Reynolds, "In all of Paul Torrance's work at the University of Minnesota, what has stood the test of time and remains as an important contribution?" After some thought, he responded, "Paul did follow through on Guilford's work and made it clear that we were operating on a limited concept of intelligence. Paul broadened the concept of intelligence to include divergent thinking, which caused a revision in the fundamental idea of mental ability. He detailed divergent thinking. Progress in society depends on creative thought, not just good memories. The whole world will change as a result of this broadened concept of intelligence."

Reynolds continued, "Paul also applied divergent or creative thinking in his

---

[17] Personal communication from Berenice "Bee" Bleedorn, November 22, 1992 (in possession of the author).

[18] Interview with Ram Gupta, Edmonton, Alberta, June 10, 1992.

classes. He would ask his students to read the works of authorities and not only understand the content of the reading, but to think of other ways of solving the same problem. He encouraged his students to go beyond memorizing content, to think of the problem and how to solve it. He made a difference in their habits of thinking."

Paul also influenced the schools in the state of Minnesota. He encouraged them to include activities for students that were characterized by production of new information, not merely reproduction of old information. He fostered individuals such as Berenice Bee Bleedorn, who have remained as leaders in creativity education.

Another significant result of his work at Minnesota was the development of the Minnesota Tests of Creative Thinking. Reynolds pointed out that Torrance had to work diligently to persuade hard-headed individuals about the criteria used to measure creativity. He sorted out the elements that make up creative products or achievements. Torrance was able to answer questions such as "How do you judge originality or flexibility?" These are reflected in his scoring scheme for the creativity tests.

Maynard Reynolds stated that much of Torrance's exploratory studies, such as the fourth-grade slump and developmental trends, yielded interesting results. His research raised important questions. "He was a pioneer in his day in pointing the way to creativity," concluded Reynolds.

Maynard Reynolds described Paul as single-minded about his work and the "hardest worker I have ever known." He said that Pansy dedicated her life to being a participant in Paul's work. She drove Paul to the University and to speaking engagements. Maynard noted that Paul never did much socializing, as his work filled his life.

Berenice "Bee" Bleedorn is a continuing influence in Minneapolis and other areas of the state. As an assistant professor at the University of St. Thomas in St. Paul and Director of the Institute for Creative Studies and Entrepreneurship, she actively promotes education for gifted and creative students. Bee recalls that her first encounter with Paul Torrance at the University of Minnesota was a turning point in her life. It was 1965. She had been married for many years to a suburban school administrator, and her two daughters had just graduated from high school. She had spent those years doing volunteer service in a suburban community. The time had come for her to break the routine, and she had decided to attend university classes in the fall quarter.

By chance, Paul Torrance conducted sessions on creativity for teachers in her husband's school, and Bee attended one such session. Bee knew instinctively that the ideas he represented had a future in her life, but she was hesitant to make the call that would connect her (housewife) with him (university professor). When she made herself dial his office number, she had a veritable anxiety attack. However, Paul answered the call and requested an interview in his special and encouraging style. She met with him, registered for the course in Group Dynamics that he was offering, and the rest is history. Bee was totally and irrevocably hooked.

Bee's second vivid memory is also a telephone conversation. Paul called her to offer her a special assistantship. The offer included a special privilege: She could arrange her work hours to allow her to take classes to finish the undergraduate degree she had begun earlier. Bee started the part-time assistantship immediately and finished her degree with honors.

Bee has many other vivid memories of times with Paul Torrance and Pansy, but none of those recollections are quite so special as the two telephone encounters that opened new doors. They represent the encouraging support of the master teacher, who quietly and consistently "gave her wings."

Don MacEachern, still a professor of statistics in the College of Education at the University of Minnesota, relates this anecdote about Paul in the early 1960s. Don's mother-in-law took a course from Paul. As usual, Paul spent an inordinate amount of time with his students. In fact, Paul had a ditto machine in the basement of his home so that he could reproduce materials for students. Paul told Don that "good ideas come at the last moment." Not too many other professors would have a duplicating machine in their home for the benefit of students.

Rod Myers, a teacher, professor, state consultant, and writer who is now retired, was a student, colleague, and friend of Paul Torrance at the University of Minnesota and later in Georgia. Rod recalls Paul's nearly boundless energy:

> On one occasion, I came to his home in Minneapolis to deliver a paper. As I approached the front door, I looked into the living room through the window. There was Paul, fast asleep, with a manuscript on his lap. I retreated quietly to my car, without ringing the bell. Undoubtedly he had come home from the University and was exhausted from his work there, and from the writing and reading he'd done in every spare moment. His efforts to write and to read were unrelenting, and his output has been prodigious. That is what has always impressed everyone—his enormous output. Paul has paid a price for his contributions to psychology and education, and it should be said clearly that his place was not obtained by trampling over others. He arrived there rather quickly through his own efforts, hampered by jealous colleagues and a fragile health, but powered by his tremendous store of energy.[19]

Lyle Johnson, now a program advisor for the Minnesota Department of Human Services, recalls Paul's thoughtfulness and consideration. Paul was Lyle's advisor for his doctoral work at the University of Minnesota. In 1965, Paul called Lyle into his office and discussed with him how he could complete his Ph.D., since Paul was leaving for Georgia. Paul returned to Minneapolis from Georgia for Lyle's oral defense.

---

[19] Personal communication with Rod Myers to the author, April 27, 1992.

MINNESOTA CORRESPONDENCE: REVELATIONS OF IMPACT

The letters that Torrance received between 1958 and 1966 reveal his broad influence during this stage of his career. A sample of quotations from this correspondence is provided here.

1959

Frank Barron returned from the Utah conference with a glowing report about your paper and the research which you are doing in the field of creativity. J. P. Guilford, on his way back from the conference, stopped in, and he, too, mentioned your work most enthusiastically.

Donald W. MacKinnon, University of California
Berkeley, California. 7-22-59.

1960

I wish to congratulate you on the article which you wrote for the current issue of the *Minnesota Education Association Journal*. I read it with a great deal of interest and pleasure and it helped me to see clearly some of the implications of your work to my field of interest, art education.

Dr. Reid Hastie, Art Education
11-7-60.

I want you to know that I am very interested in working with you in the future. I believe that the research in which you are engaged holds much promise for educational practices.

O. L. Davis, Junior Association for Supervision and Curriculum Development
Washington, DC. 4-7-60.

You certainly did a fine job at our PTA meeting last night—In addition to this let me also say that I thought I was familiar with all the work you have been doing in this work of creativity, but I must confess that I was astonished at the range of problems that you are investigating. It's all extremely fascinating, and I do hope that you can keep me in touch with these developments as they unfold.

James Curtin, University of Minnesota
11-3-60.

1961

I had the pleasure of hearing your presentation on *Flying Monkeys and Silent Lions* at the Council for Exceptional Children Convention last week. I was fascinated at your new research, as well as the unique presentation of the findings. Would that more educational research had the touch of humanity and humor, along with solid content, which was exemplified in yours!

Mrs. Barbara B. Iversen, Eastern Montana College of Education
Billings, Montana. 4-11-61.

I am not given to writing commentaries on articles that I have read; but the one on "The Creative Child," in the November 7th, 1961 issue of *Look Magazine* is one that I wish everyone connected with the education of our children, teenagers, and even adults; would not just read; but rather read, ponder, digest, meditate upon, consider, realize, perceive, comprehend and then act to do something about this situation.

Art Benson, Pacomia, California
10-20-61.

Congratulations on your fine work. Anything that you can do to modify the concept of intelligence in the United States will lend a significant contribution to school people, and teachers in particular.

Donald A. Davis, Western Michigan University
Kalamazoo, Michigan. 12-4-61.

1962

I had the opportunity to use your new book on *Guiding Creative Talent* in my short guidance seminar at Washington State University this summer and found that it contained a great deal of valuable information and many provocative ideas.

Calvin Taylor, University of Utah
8-15-62.

It was wonderful to have you at our 8th Annual Institute. The play-back so far received boils down to this: "By far the best yet."

Alex F. Osborn, Creative Education Foundation
Buffalo, New York. 7-6-62.

Actually, Paul, what irritates me is that too many psychologists use words to hide their vague notions, not clarify them. You don't. In simple, concise terms you explain what you see happen. For this reason alone I will always be grateful. For this reason alone, I am convinced you will have impact. I know you will.

Major Bert Decker, U.S. Air Force
Pease Air Force Base, New Hampshire. 6-5-62.

1963

I read with great interest the newspaper report on your study of currently popular IQ and aptitude tests. It comes like a breath of fresh air in an atmosphere of generally foggy thinking, polluted half-truths and stormy charges and countercharges on every side.

Arthur Henley Shelton, New York, New York
1-29-63.

Surely you are opening up a big field through your research on creativity—the most significant contribution I can think of. More power to you, Dr. Torrance.

Garry C. Myers, Highlights for Children
Honesdale, Pennsylvania. 4-8-63.

Congratulations on the selection of your book for the award! We rejoice in this achievement and it gives us another reason to be proud you are a Mercerian. We will run this note in *The Mercerian*.

Thomas J. Holmes, Mercer University
Macon, Georgia. 3-25-63.

1964

Your delightful article came today and it is with deep pleasure that we present it to the readers of *Living with Children*. To be more aware of how creativity can enrich the lives of children and ways it can be developed should help the Nursery parents to "let" their children create. To receive an article in such fine shape is one of the joys of an editor.

Mrs. Alma May, Scarborough Sunday School Board
7-30-64.

Accept my thanks... appreciation... and admiration for the very nice way in which you take care of requests for material on creativity... and for the tremendous catching up that you must do on what seems like a superhuman workload.

Peter Baycura, Commonwealth Bank
Butler, Pennsylvania. 5-22-64.

We want you to know that we appreciated greatly your coming to Baltimore to speak to the supervisors and principals of elementary schools. You gave an excellent presentation and contributed much to make the meeting a good one. There has been a great deal of comment and praise from members of the audience concerning your talk and the discussions. We plan to mimeograph your speech and send it to all of those who participated in the conference. We hope that it will be possible for you to return to Maryland at some future meeting and talk to us again. Thank you again and best wishes for a wonderful summer in California. I wish that it were possible for us to send a number of persons to your classes.

Grace Dorsey, Maryland State Department of Education
Baltimore, Maryland. 5-4-64.

1965

Having just finished your book *Rewarding Creative Behavior*, I must say thank you at once. It is going to make my task of teaching the development of creative potential much easier because it will convince the men in the classes that the research we have been stressing in Art Education is valid and valuable. All your books have been challenging, stimulating and filled with new things to think about.

Myrrl H. Krieger, Commonwealth of Pennsylvania
Department of Public Instruction, State Teachers College
Lock Haven, Pennsylvania. 7-7-65.

And was it not the apostle Paul himself who appeared in Athens? Now, what could be more appropriate than that young Paul from Milledgeville is now the famous Dr. Paul, the world renowned savant, returning to his native Georgia and its big and fine state university. Beyond the personality and physiological reasons, it would not at all be surprising that over the next couple of decades, Athens might even be a better fulcrum, as well as rostrum, for just exactly you and the creativity movement of which you are the apotheosis.

B. E. Bergesen, Personnel Press
Princeton, New Jersey. 7-9-65.

Your publication, *Constructive Behavior: Stress, Personality, and Mental Health*, by Torrance has been selected by the Book Review Committee of the Child Study Association to be included in our forthcoming listing, *Books of the Year, 1965*.

Liba Freccia, Child Study Association of America
New York, New York. 9-17-65.

LEAVING MINNEAPOLIS AND THE UNIVERSITY OF MINNESOTA

Torrance had been offered several distinguished professorships in 1965, but a visit to his parents in Milledgeville, Georgia, in April of that year changed his mind. At that time Paul also met with the faculty members at the University of Georgia in Athens, on the invitation of the Dean of Education, Joseph Williams.

On April 28, 1965, Dean Williams wrote to Paul and offered him the position of Head of the Department of Educational Psychology. Dr. Williams said the faculty members had expressed their hope that Paul would agree to join the faculty as chairperson. He added, "you are the person to furnish the leadership in our growing program of educational psychology."[20]

Paul sent his letter of acceptance in early May of 1965. He appreciated the fact that the job would not begin until September of 1966, as he wanted to complete reports for all his contract research projects and "finish up" or transfer his graduate student advisees. Ram Gupta told me that "Dr. Paul" spent so much time answering letters and giving talks that he had trouble submitting contract reports on time. This was a real frustration for him.

Associate Dean Marcia Edwards thought that Paul was making a mistake; she thought that he was changing from a first-rate university to a second-rate one. Associate Dean Edwards, Dean Keller, and Roger Wilk (his department head) were extremely generous in expediting his unfinished work. Paul had the

---

[20] Letter from Joseph Williams to E. Paul Torrance, April 28, 1965 (in possession of the author).

Winter Quarter free, but taught his regular load the other two quarters. Paul worked at home, but he would come to the university to work with advisees and committees. He was very productive at this time—publishing five books in 1965 and teaching successful classes at capacity enrollments.

Why did Paul Torrance decide to leave the University of Minnesota? There were a number of reasons. Paul had developed chronic bronchial asthma, and the climate of the Twin Cities was unfavorable to this condition. Paul's parents were aging and he wanted to be nearby to assist them. It may be that he felt he was no longer getting the support he needed to continue his research at the University of Minnesota. The University of Georgia was just entering a growth phase, and Paul likely sensed a greater opportunity to continue his work there. Also, he wanted the opportunity to work with the disadvantaged population in Georgia. Readjustment was taking place in Georgia as a result of racial integration in the schools. The position as Head of the Department of Educational Psychology would give Paul more responsibility for and influence over the direction of the expanding program in Georgia.

Robert Keller, Dean of the College of Education at Minneapolis, accepted Paul's resignation with deep regret. He said it was "indeed a shock" and stated, "I believe we have no graduate instruction which is better than yours; the level and extent of your research have been remarkable; and on advisory and service assignments, you have been unstinting of your time and energy."[21] Dean Keller concluded, "I want to tell you how grateful we are for all you have done as a member of the Minnesota family. Even though you will move from our area, we still shall regard you as one of us."

On reflecting on the College of Education at the University of Minnesota, Paul said it was freer of petty jealousies than any college he had known. There was freedom to speak out also. The only untoward incident Paul experienced was just as he was leaving. A newspaper reporter called and asked him if he was leaving because of interdepartmental disagreements. Paul stated that this rumor was untrue. He said he was leaving because of his worsening asthma condition, which was affected by the dust from the yeast factories and flour mills. He apparently also explained that his parents were growing old and he needed to be nearer to them. Nevertheless, the reporter's version of the story was on the 6:00 p.m. news, although the radio report did say that Paul had said that the rumor was untrue. It was embarrassing for Paul Torrance and he assured Dr. Roger Wilk, his department head, and Dean Robert Keller that he had not spread the rumor and that he had full confidence in them and appreciated their help.

One source of the rumor may have been the fact that in 1964 Paul had moved out of his job as Director of the Bureau of Educational Research to become a Professor of Educational Psychology. As mentioned earlier, this move was relat-

[21] Letter from Robert Keller to E. Paul Torrance, May 21, 1965 (in possession of the author).

ed to Paul's overwhelming work load and his desire to do more teaching.

One faculty member from the Department of School Administration later told Paul that he thought the Dean had eased Paul out of the Bureau of Educational Research. This faculty member reported that the Dean had made this remark at one of the Department of School Administration's meetings: "If we could get Paul Torrance to pack up his toys, we could get some things done." Going out of the meeting, the faculty member had said to a colleague, "I can see that we are to have a new Director of the Bureau of Educational Research soon." Shortly after this event, the change that Paul and others had been working on for some time was announced. When Paul left his position as Professor of Educational Psychology, two people were hired to take Paul's place, one to develop Group Dynamics and the other to develop the Personality area.

The week before they left, Pansy and Paul had supper with his department head and the Dean. On this occasion, the Dean told Paul that he had provided the College with something that had been lacking, something that the College needed, and something that could not be replaced. Paul brought world recognition to the University of Minnesota through his teaching and research. The Dean also said that many of the faculty had expressed to him their deep regrets that Paul was leaving.

When Paul left for Georgia, there was still a lot of unfinished University of Minnesota work to be completed: the cross-cultural study of the fourth-grade slump in creativity and several doctoral dissertations and final orals. A number of doctoral students followed him to Georgia.

At age 51, Paul Torrance looked forward to heading up the educational psychology program at the University of Georgia in Athens. He would be able to continue to develop the research he had started in his survival work with the U.S. Air Force and pioneered in Minnesota—the research that had captured the imagination of so many people in the educational and psychology communities. He was returning home, but could still count on support and friendship from his Minnesota family. His network and influence were ever-broadening. Minnesota suffered a double loss, but Georgia was to gain Paul and Pansy.

REFERENCES

Broadley, M. (1943). *Square pegs in square holes.* Garden City, NY: Doubleday.

Brossard, C. (1961, November). The creative child. *Look Magazine*, pp. 111, 112, 116.

Cook, W.W. (1963). Organization for Research of the college of Education at the University of Minnesota. *Scientia Paedogoica,* 9(1), 7-43

Dauw, D. C. (1965). *Life experiences, vocational needs and choices of original thinkers and good elaborators.* Unpublished doctoral dissertation, University of Minnesota, Minneapolis.

Does creativity dip at 9? (1961, March 5). *Minneapolis Sunday Tribune,* p.1 (feature section).

Gesell, A. & Ilg, F. (1946). *The child from five to ten*. New York: Harper & Row.

Gifted children may learn better by creative method. (1961, October 14). *The Sacramento Bee,* p. A16.

Guilford, J.P. (1977). *Way beyond the IQ: Guide to improving intelligence and creativity*. Buffalo, NY: Creative Education Foundation.

Himsl, R. & Millar, G.W. (1993). *Measure of questioning skills*. Bensenville, IL: Scholastic Testing Service.

Marland, S. (1972). *Education of the gifted and talented*. Report to Congress by the U.S. Commissioner of Education. Washington, DC: Government Printing Office.

Millar, G.W. (1975). *Blatz' security theory: An empirical study*. Unpublished dissertation. University of Alberta, Edmonton.

Myers, R.E. & Torrance, E.P. (1963a). *Can you imagine*. Albany, OR: Perceptive Publishing. [Reprinted in 1986]

Myers, R.E. & Torrance, E.P. (1963b). *For those who wonder*. Albany, OR: Perceptive Publishing. [Reprinted in 1986]

Myers, R.E. & Torrance, E.P. (1963c). *Invitations to thinking and doing*. Albany, OR: Perceptive Publishing. [Reprinted in 1986]

O'Connor, J. (1945). *Ideaphoria*. New York: Johnson O'Connor Research Foundation.

Presbury, J. & Henderson, M. (1984, March/April). Pansy Nigh Torrance. *G/C/T Magazine*, pp. 5-8.

Price, J.M. (1946). *Jesus the teacher*. Nashville, TN: Convention Press.

Reid, A. (1960). *Supposing*. Boston, MA: Little, Brown.

Taylor, C.W. (1968). Be talent developers as well as knowledge dispensers. *Today's Education, 57*, 67-68.

Taylor, C.W. (1972). *Climate for creativity*. New York: Pergamon.

Taylor, C.W. (in press). *Honoring three giants who pioneered creativity research: Thurstone, Guilford, and Torrance*.

Test your originality. (1979, June 15). *The Atlanta Constitution,* p. 11B.

Torrance, E.P. (1959). *Rewarding creative thinking*. Minneapolis, MN: Bureau of Educational Research, University of Minnesota.

Torrance, E.P. (1960a). *Talent and education*. Minneapolis: University of Minnesota Press.

Torrance, E.P. (Ed.). (1960b). *Creativity*. Minneapolis: Center for Continuing Study, General Extension Division, University of Minnesota.

Torrance, E.P. (1960c). *Creativity in Religious Education*. Minneapolis, MN: Center for Continuing Study, General Extension Division, University of Minnesota.

Torrance, E.P. (1960d, May 7). *The creative potential of school children in the space age*. Paper presented at the Education and Space Conference of the Minnesota Chapter of the Air Force Association, University of Minnesota, Minneapolis.

Torrance, E.P. (1961). *New educational ideas*. Minneapolis: Center for Continuing Study, General Extension Division, University of Minnesota.

Torrance, E.P. (1962a). *Guiding creative talent*. Englewood Cliffs, NJ: Prentice-Hall.

Torrance, E.P. (1962b). Curriculum frontiers for the elementary gifted pupil: Flying monkeys and silent lions. *Exceptional Children,* 28(3), 119-127.

Torrance, E.P. (1963a). *Education and the creative potential*. Minneapolis, MN: University of Minnesota Press.

Torrance, E.P. (1963b). The creative personality and the ideal pupil. *Teachers College Record*, 65, 220-226.

Torrance. E.P. (1965a). *Rewarding creative behavior*. Englewood Cliffs, NJ: Prentice-Hall.

Torrance, E.P. (1965b). Seven guides to creativity. *Journal of Health, Physical Education, and Recreation*, 36(4), 26-27, 68.

Torrance, E.P. (1972a). *Assessing creative potential: A description and sample of the Torrance Tests of Creative Thinking*. Princeton, NJ: Personnel Press.

Torrance, E.P. (1972b). Group dynamics and creative functioning. In C. W. Taylor (Ed.), *Climate for creativity*. (pp. 75-96). New York: Pergamon.

Torrance, E.P. (1972c). Narrative account of career. Unpublished manuscript, Department of Educational Psychology, University of Georgia, Athens.

Torrance, E.P. (1977). *What research says to the teacher: Creativity in the classroom*. Washington, DC: National Education Association.

Torrance, E.P. (1988). The nature of creativity as manifest in its testing. In R. Sternberg (Ed.), *The nature of creativity: Contemporary perspectives*. (pp. 43-75). New York: Cambridge University Press.

Torrance, E.P. (1989). On the shoulders of giants: What humans can become. *Educational Forum*, 53(2), 117-124.

Torrance, E.P. & Ball, O.E. (1984). *Torrance Tests of Creative Thinking: Streamlined (revised) manual—Figural A and B*. Bensenville, IL: Scholastic Testing Service.

Torrance, E.P. & Cunnington, B.F. (1965). *Sounds and images: Teachers' guide and recorded text (elementary version)*. Boston: Ginn and Company.

Torrance, E.P. & De Young, K. (1958). *Life experience inventory: Creativity form*. Minneapolis: Bureau of Educational Research, University of Minnesota.

Torrance, E.P., Goldman, R.J. & Torrance, J.P. (1975). The meaning and relevance of learning readiness for curriculum construction in Christian education: A study paper. *Character Potential: A Record of Research*, 7(3), pp. 118-141.

Torrance, E.P. & Gupta, R. (1964). *Development and evaluation of recorded programmed experiences in creative thinking in the fourth grade*. Minneapolis: Bureau of Educational Research, University of Minnesota.

Torrance, E.P. & *Look* Staff. (1963c). The Torrance report on the response to *Look*. *Look*.

Torrance, E.P., Tan, C.A. and Allman, T. (1970). Verbal originality and teacher behavior: A predictive validity study. *Journal of Teacher Education*, 21, pp. 335-341.

Torrance, E.P. and Torrance, J.P. (1988). Creativity and teaching concepts of god. In D. Ratcliffe (Ed.), *Handbook of preschool religious education*. Birmingham, AL: Religious Education Press.

Chapter 5

The Georgia Years (1966–1984):

Return of the Native

INTRODUCTION

Paul Torrance was returning home to Georgia after being away for 22 years. He was 21 years older and realized at age 51 that he would likely retire in his home state. Besides wanting to be closer to his parents and relatives, he knew that education in the state of Georgia was about to experience a growth spurt, and he wanted to contribute to it.

During his nearly 20 years at the University of Georgia, Paul Torrance shone as an administrator, teacher, and researcher. He had the support of Dean Joseph Williams to help reorganize and expand the University's Department of Educational Psychology, Measurement, and Research. He was determined to refine his tests of creative thinking and to develop new ways to teach the skills of creative thinking. He planned to develop new courses to make students aware of the significance of creativity in their personal and professional lives. In addition, this was the time when he would develop a school program that would affect the future thinking of thousands of children around the world. It is not surprising that the University of Georgia has established a center as a living memorial to the work of E. Paul Torrance. This part of Paul's life ended with his decision to retire due to Pansy's ill health.

THE SOCIAL/POLITICAL CONTEXT IN 1966

The World and Georgia in 1966

A number of significant changes occurred in the world, in the United States, and in Georgia during 1966, just as Paul Torrance was making his move.

The space race between the Russians and the Americans was heating up even more. The Soviet spacecraft, Luna 9, made a successful soft landing on the moon. Then the U.S. spacecraft, Surveyor I, made a soft landing on the moon and transmitted more than 11,000 T.V. images of the terrain. Edwin E. "Buzz" Aldrin stepped out of the Gemini 12 spacecraft in space for 129 minutes.

Charles De Gaulle was inaugurated for his second seven-year term as President of France. Mrs. Indira Gandhi, Nehru's daughter, became Prime Minister of India. United Sates President Lyndon Johnson went on a Far East Tour, and the Red Guard demonstrated in China against Western influences.

In the United States, 1966 was the year of an epidemic of racial unrest and riots. Chicago, Cleveland, Brooklyn, and San Francisco were ravaged by riots, burning, and looting. In Watts, a poor black section of Los Angeles, 28 blacks were dead after a riot. The Convention of Racial Equality held in Baltimore endorsed "black power," rejected the doctrine of nonviolence, demanded the withdrawal of U.S. forces in Vietnam, and supported resistance to the draft.

The Roman Catholic bishops ruled that U.S. Catholics were no longer required to abstain from eating meat on Fridays, except during Lent.

Alfred Hitchcock produced his 50th film, *Torn Curtain*. *Who's Afraid of Virginia Woolf?* starring Elizabeth Taylor and Richard Burton won the Academy Award as Best Picture. Walt Disney died at age 65. Two of the most popular songs in 1966 were "Born Free" and "Strangers in the Night."

Miniskirts came into fashion. Color television became popular. British yachtsman Francis Chichester arrived in Sydney, Australia, 107 days after sailing alone from London. And Jack Nicklaus won the Masters golf tournament for the second straight year in Augusta, Georgia—just 1½ hours down the road from Athens, where Paul and Pansy Torrance were settling into their new home on 185 Riverhill Drive on the Oconee River.

Education in Georgia

The year 1966 was an interesting one in the history of education in Georgia. Carl E. Sanders, Governor from 1963 to 1967, had held education as his number one priority. Sanders, who had played quarterback for the University of Georgia and received a law degree there, was a deacon in the Baptist Church in Augusta. During Sanders' tenure as Governor, there was tremendous growth in Georgia's schools: 6,000 classrooms and 10,000 teachers were added, teachers' salaries increased by an average of $1,500 per year, $176 million was allocated for building construction at the University of Georgia (more than had been received in the previous 30 years), and hundreds of university faculty members were added each year. Paul Torrance and Bert Richmond were among those hired during this time. Sanders ran for Governor again in 1970 but was defeated by Jimmy Carter from Plains, Georgia.

In 1966, the schools in Athens supported the Freedom of Choice plan. This meant that blacks and whites could go to any school they chose. However, few exercised that choice. There was one black high school, one black junior high, and three black elementary schools. By 1968, integration was mandated and students were transported by bus to get an appropriate mix.

The year 1966 was also the last full year of the tenure of Dr. O. C. Aderhold as president of the University of Georgia. He retired in June of 1967 and was replaced by Fred Davison. Aderhold had been a Professor in Education and had set in motion plans for a new building to house the Faculty of Education. When that new building was opened a few years later, it was named for him—Aderhold Hall.

The University of Georgia had been integrated in 1963 when two black students enrolled. One of them now occupies an administrative position at Grady Hospital in Atlanta and the other is an executive for CNN Television. There were a total of 19,923 students at the University of Georgia in 1966 as compared to 27,336 in the Winter Quarter of 1993.

In 1966, co-eds (female students) were not allowed to wear shorts except when participating in athletic events. They had to wear raincoats to hide their shorts. In early 1967, the rebellion began as co-eds started to wear see-through raincoats over their shorts. With the support of organized male students, sit-ins were staged in the Dean's offices all over campus, and the longstanding female dress code was broken in 1967. The shorts have been getting shorter ever since, but no complaints are heard from faculty or students.

Establishment of the University in Athens, Georgia: A Historical Perspective

In 1732, 21 Englishmen received a charter to found the colony of Georgia. They sought support to build a college before they settled there. In 1755, George Whitfield, an evangelical minister, sought permission to build the proposed college, but his efforts were thwarted because he was too fiery an evangelist.

In 1777, the Constitution of Georgia made no mention of a university. Abraham Baldwin, a Yale graduate, came to Georgia from Connecticut in 1783 and urged Governor Lyman Hall, another Yale graduate, to establish a university. Ezra Stiles, the President of Yale, worked with the two of them to draw up plans and get them approved by the legislature.

The legislature granted the charter in 1785. It was the first state charter for a university in the United States; all others were private. The charter forbade the exclusion of "any person of any religious denomination from free and equal liberty and advantage of education." However, another section of the charter required that all officers of the university should be of the Christian faith. Although chartered in 1785, there was no funding yet for buildings, teachers, or officers, nor had a site been selected.

The major center of population at this time was still around Savannah, where the colony had started. However, there was anti-urban sentiment against locating it in Savannah and political forces held sway, believing the remote frontier lands provided a more suitable environment for young people to learn. Land near the headwaters of the Oconee River was finally chosen for the university, and one of the committee members establishing the university—John Milledge—bought the land and gave it to the university in 1799.

Another Yale graduate, Josiah Meigs, was appointed Professor and was given the responsibility of formulating a curriculum. He was exiled to Georgia after he had been banished from his Professorship at Yale because of his liberal political views and had earlier been arrested for treason and imprisoned in Bermuda by the British. He was a scientist, not a minister. He traveled the State until 1803—two years after the formal opening of the University—and reported to the Board of Trustees that he had enrolled between 30 and 45 students. Classes began. His curriculum was extremely innovative and liberal for the time; his Code of Conduct for students and governance of them reflected the liberal ideas of Jefferson. The University conferred degrees upon its first graduates on May 31, 1804.

Religious forces soon began putting pressure on Meigs to make the University more puritanical and conservative. When Meigs was dismissed in 1810, he characterized the Board of Trustees as a "damned pack of... tories and speculators."

Athens was so named because early settlers wanted the place to be known as a classic city around a center of classic education. There had been no city there before the university opened in 1801.

In the early 1800s, there was a political campaign to move the University from Athens to a more populous center—to the capital in Milledgeville.

The University of Georgia celebrated its bicentennial in 1985. A special medal to mark the occasion was presented to distinguished Georgians, including Paul Torrance.

HEADING UP THE DEPARTMENT OF EDUCATIONAL PSYCHOLOGY—UNIVERSITY OF GEORGIA: GROWTH YEARS

When Paul's University of Minnesota friends told him he was leaving to go to a second-rate university, as it was viewed at the time, Paul knew it was probably true. He also knew, however, that the University of Georgia was ready to make some exciting changes. Paul took on the task of establishing the School Psychology Program and the Program in Gifted Education. The Department of Educational Psychology more than doubled in size in the first two years of Paul's chairmanship.

Table 1
Growth Statistics[a], 1960–1967
College of Education, University of Georgia

	1960–61	1966–67
Faculty	63	163
Outside Support (from government and non-government sources)	$188,156	$3,500,000
Enrollments (on Campus)		
• Undergraduate	900	2,242
• Graduate	101	430
• Ed.D. Doctoral	10	108
Graduate Student Support		
• Total Assisted	12	393
Degrees		
• Baccalaureate	346	573
• Masters	114	232
• Ed.D.	2	37

Until the 1967–68 school year, no courses on the psychology and education of the gifted had been ever been offered consistently at any college or university. Now, the Department of Educational Psychology at the University of Georgia was offering a master's and doctoral program in the area of giftedness, and legislation passed by the state of Georgia in March of 1968 specified that each school district would have a program for the gifted by 1976. A strong need was developing for trained teachers and consultants in this area, and the University of Georgia was responding to this need.

Table 1 presents some interesting statistics that illustrate the rapid growth of the College of Education at the University of Georgia between 1960 and 1967.

Paul's appointment as Professor and Head of the Department of Educational Psychology, Research, and Measurement marked the beginning of many changes at the University of Georgia. Under Paul's leadership, studies of the programs, courses, and curriculum were made. Changes were suggested, debated, and implemented. Since there was a shortage of school psychologists in the state, Paul initiated the "experienced teacher fellowship program in school psychology." The program trained 25 school psychologists, using a grant from the United States Office of Education. Research projects were undertaken to help culturally disadvantaged children and capitalize on their creative strengths.

Paul's great success combined with his modesty promoted confidence among even the most timid of graduate students or new faculty. Dr. Bert Richmond

[a] College of Education, University of Georgia, Growth Statistics, 1960–1967. Obtained from E. Paul Torrance, in possession of the author.

describes his first meeting with Paul Torrance. At the time, Richmond was a young counseling psychologist at the University of Georgia. He met Paul for lunch to discuss the possibility of his joining the Department of Educational Psychology. Although Paul already enjoyed a substantial international reputation, Bert Richmond was immediately aware of Paul's gentle, accepting, and positive attitude. Bert knew immediately that he could work well with Paul. Bert worked in the Counseling Department for 20 years before his retirement in 1986 as a professor emeritus.

In 1970, a Child Guidance Clinic was organized under Paul Torrance's leadership. Drs. Bert Richmond and Wayne Antenon were involved in establishing the clinic. Paul designed three new courses for the social psychology area. He felt they were necessary after reviewing and analyzing existing courses in his department. The courses were Group Dynamics and Mental Functioning, Interactional Analyses of Groups, and Complex Studies of Group Forces in Mental Functioning.

As a result of the rapid expansion in the department, the administrative requirements increased greatly. It was only with the full-time help from Pansy and the contributions from his royalties that Paul was able to keep his research going and find time to do his writing.

THE "AHA" HOUSE

The house at 185 Riverhill Drive was beautifully located on the Middle Oconee River, the river Paul had known and loved as a child at his parents' home in Milledgeville, Georgia. Paul and Pansy remodeled it, adding a "Pansy Room" with space for the freezer, sewing, ironing, laundry, Pansy's workshop materials, books, and clothes. The biggest addition was a library on top of the original house with 1½ miles of bookshelves, large closets, a bathroom, and a built-in space for filing cabinets. This would later make the house difficult to sell.

Students who often visited Paul and Pansy called it the "Aha" house. The interactions that took place there inevitably resulted in many "aha" experiences, or hatched ideas. I visited Paul and Pansy in this house in 1983. It was filled with memorabilia, like a museum. I remember looking through albums in Paul's upstairs library. Paul loved it all and took great pride in describing the flowers in the gardens that surrounded the house.

CONTINUATION OF RESEARCH IN CREATIVITY

Preventing "Slumps" in the Creative Development of Five-Year-Olds

In Minnesota, Paul Torrance had identified certain periods of discontinuity in the growth of creativity in children. The first "slump" or discontinuity appeared at age five—the time when most children enter school.

When Paul went to Georgia, he had an opportunity to discover whether growth in creativity can be continuous if a different approach is used for teaching kindergarten children. In 1966, Dr. Laura R. Fortson was promoting a creative–aesthetic approach to teaching five-year-olds, which involved carefully planned creative activities. The curriculum included activity centers, which fostered total involvement on the part of children and appealed to their natural curiosities. They engaged in activities such as role playing, painting, manipulating objects, interacting and cooperating with each other, constructing, relating and telling stories, and inquiring.

Paul designed an experiment to compare the effects of this creative–aesthetic approach with the traditional approach to teaching kindergarten children. (The traditional approach was more teacher-directed; the idea was to get children ready for reading and arithmetic.) The study was replicated over a three-year period. The children were given creativity tests at the beginning of the school year and again at the end. In each of the three years, the results indicated that the creative–aesthetic approach promoted continuous growth in creative development at a significant level. The creative–aesthetic approach was shown to enhance creative development and avoid the slump or discontinuity.

The author has been a consultant with the Department of Education in Alberta and is happy to report that twenty-seven years later, Alberta Education is still encouraging the use of a creative–aesthetic approach with five-year-old children in Early Childhood Services programs. Children are encouraged to learn at their own rate in a center-oriented classroom.

Ginn 360 Reading Program

An invitation to participate in the development of the Ginn Reading 360 Program allowed Paul Torrance to apply creativity to reading. He went to Boston in February of 1969 to meet with the authors and publishers. His former colleague from Minnesota, Ted Clymer, was editor and one of the principal authors. Paul devised the creativity strand for this popular reading program and in doing so influenced a whole generation of children in the 1970s. The Ginn 360 creativity strand included puzzles, mysteries, and questions that challenged all kids to think. This was the original impetus for the Incubation Model of Teaching.

PROFESSIONAL AFFILIATIONS

Paul was once again extremely busy during the late 1960s and early 1970s. Besides his teaching, writing, and administration duties as Head of the Department of Educational Psychology, he found time to serve several professional organizations. He was a member of the New York Academy of Science, a member of the editorial boards of the *Gifted Child Quarterly*, *Highlights for Children*, *Journal of Creative Behavior*, and *Personality: An International Journal;* he was also an editorial consultant of *Psychological Reports* and *Perceptual and Motor Skills*. He was a fellow in Division 15 (Educational Psychology), 10 (Psychology of the Arts), and 35 (State Associations) and a member of Division 16 (School Psychology) of the American Psychological Association. If these professional associations were not enough, he was also a member of the Georgia Psychological Association, Southeastern Psychological Association, American Educational Research Association, American Association for the Advancement of Science, National Association for the Gifted, the Association for the Gifted, Council on Exceptional Children, Association for Supervision and Curriculum Development, Association for Humanistic Psychology, American Association of Group Psychotherapy and Psychodrama, Creative Education Foundation, National Association for the Education of Young Children, National Society for the Study of Education, and Phi Delta Kappa. These affiliations demonstrate his wide interests and his commitment to keeping abreast of current activities in many fields of education and psychology.

SERVING DISADVANTAGED CHILDREN IN GEORGIA

In 1971, Paul's class on "Learning Problems of Disadvantaged Children" was involved in practicum experiences with children who lived in poverty. University students worked with disadvantaged children in Parkview Play School and a summer workshop at Dudley Park in Athens.

The university students became aware of the *real* problems encountered by poor children. For example, "older people fight and carry on" was one of the 70 problems expressed by underprivileged kids. Also, over 100 community problems facing disadvantaged children were revealed. For example, "There are too many bootleggers in the community. Police could find the bootleggers but do not."

University students were assigned areas to be responsible for in the Dudley Park "Creativity Workshop," including foods, photography, pantomime and creative dramatics, music and singing, science, puppets and creative dramatics, sculpture, storytelling, creative writing, and art. Pansy Torrance provided the general nursing services and acted as a health consultant. A daily news bulletin alerted the leaders of daily goals and important events.

These workshops, which were beneficial for university students as well as for the disadvantaged children, lasted for five consecutive summers. Many of these projects and workshops for disadvantaged children were financed by Paul's personal funds.

NATIONAL AND INTERNATIONAL PRESENTATIONS 1967–1977

Paul was invited to address delegates at many national and international conferences between 1967 and 1977. His honoraria for speaking at these presentations was used to pay for graduate assistants and researchers to continue his work in creativity. He saw these speaking engagements as a way to spread the word about his creativity research and instructional materials.

In 1967, Paul Torrance addressed the International Conference on New Methods of Testing in Berlin. He described the development of his tests of creativity. In 1969, Paul's book *Talent and Education: Present Status and Future Directions* was selected for display in the Education–U.S.A. exhibit that visited six cities in the Soviet Union. More than 1,200,000 Russians viewed this traveling book display.

Berlin, Germany (1967)
Paris, France (1971)
Liege, Belgium (1971)
Cincinnati, Ohio (1971)
Westbrook, Maine (1971)
Portland, Maine (1971)
Washington, DC (1971)
Ann Arbor, Michigan (1971)
Atlanta, Georgia (1971)
Athens, Georgia (1971)
Milledgeville, Georgia (1971)
Tampa, Florida (1973)
Atlanta, Georgia (1973)
Santa Rosa, California (1973)
New Orleans, Louisiana (1973)
Greensboro, North Carolina (1973)
Charlottesville, Virginia (1974)
Augusta, Georgia (1974)
Beacon, New York (1974)
Nashville, Tennessee (1974)
New Brighton, Minnesota (1974)
Birmingham, Alabama (1975)
Murfreesboro, Tennessee (1975)
Huntington, West Virginia (1975)
Ridgecrest, North Carolina (1975)
Los Angeles, California (1975)
Hartford, Connecticut (1975)
Florence, South Carolina (1975)
Macon, Georgia (1975)
London, England (1975)
Ellensburg, Washington (1976)
Houston, Texas (1976)
College Station, Texas (1976)
Valencia, Spain (1976)
New Orleans, Louisiana (1976)
Atlanta, Georgia (1976)
Winston-Salem, North Carolina (1976)
Philadelphia, Pennsylvania (1976)
Newnan, Georgia (1977)

MAJOR WORKSHOPS

Paul was involved in a number of national and international workshops on gifted and talented education over the years. In November of 1976, Paul was invited to participate in a two-week symposium on creativity in Valencia, Spain. Sponsored by UNESCO and the Creative Education Foundation in Buffalo, New York, the symposium brought together a team of five or six top-notch researchers in the field of creativity and a group of promising professors and graduate students.

In addition, he has worked with Joe Renzulli at the University of Connecticut and the Connecticut State Department of Education since the

Confratute Conference began in 1978. Also, Irving Sato has involved Paul in his Gifted Institutes in Hawaii.

CREATIVITY IN THE DEPARTMENT OF EDUCATION IN ALBERTA, CANADA

While researching the Torrance Collection in the archives at the University of Georgia, I came across an interesting article entitled "Clark Discloses Education Plan—More Emphasis on Creativity," which appeared in the *Calgary Herald* on December 14, 1965. Since I am an educator with the Department of Education in Alberta, I took special note of this clipping.

Across the top of the article, Paul Torrance had written "Looks interesting—doesn't it." The article was written only a few days after the Social Credit Party under Harry Strom had swept into power. The new Minister of Education and Youth, Bob Clark, was a 31-year-old former physical education teacher. The portfolio also included responsibility for universities and colleges. The article stated that "Alberta's new education minister today revealed fresh directions for the province's school system—an end to unbending authoritarian structures and a new focus on child creativity" ("Clark Discloses Education Plan," 1968).

I wanted to know more about how Mr. Clark went about "pushing hard to improve the quality and the nature of education offered in Alberta's classrooms."[1] I was filled with questions as I phoned Mr. Clark, now 55 years of age and recently appointed as Ethics Commissioner for the Alberta provincial government. He was very willing to talk with me and granted an interview.

Bob Clark recalls that a number of initiatives took place in the late 1960s and early 1970s to reform the Alberta education system and make it more child-centered. Clark created Athabasca University, which incorporates distance learning and serves the needs of people who cannot afford to be full-time students. Clark also wanted to make better use of the great amount of educational research being carried out in Alberta, particularly in the universities.

On the curriculum side, the Alberta Department of Education moved toward decentralization. Schools could develop their own courses and deliver them as options to students at the junior and senior high school levels. Work experience was added to give students an opportunity to know more about the world of work and the skills required. Social studies took on a values approach as opposed to the rigid acquiring of facts that had characterized the program previously. This approach forced students to think about issues. This period also saw the development of greater opportunities for the educationally handicapped. Dr. Jack Church headed up this area. At the time, creativity was viewed as responding to the needs of students and adults and

---

[1] Interview with Bob Clark by the author. Edmonton, Alberta, July 15, 1992.

providing meaningful experiences for them.

Paul Torrance would have agreed with the loosening of rigid course structures in Alberta, Canada but would also have recommended that students learn by creative means and creative teaching.

INFLUENCE ON PARENTING

Paul Torrance often spoke to parent groups in and around Athens, and he influenced their thinking through popular magazines and newspapers and through personal correspondence.

He liked to talk about how to develop the imagination of children. His advice to parents was the result of his research over the years. He would tell parents to provide materials (books), to permit time for thinking and daydreaming, to let children talk and tinker, and to love them and let them know they are loved.

Paul was a member of the "Giraffe Society," which believed in "sticking one's neck out" for the good of others.

[2]

The Giraffe Society

Charter Membership Expires Dec. 31, 1981

E. Paul Torrance
NAME

185 Riverhill Drive
ADDRESS

Athens, GA 30606
CITY STATE ZIP

The bearer of this card is a CHARTER MEMBER of THE GIRAFFE SOCIETY, fully empowered to assist the Society in its mission of finding and honoring all Americans who stick their necks out for the common good.

E. Paul Torrance
BEARER'S SIGNATURE

Editor
Quest/81 Magazine

"IDEAL CHILD" AS PERCEIVED BY TEACHERS

In a 1975 study designed to determine the characteristics of the ideal student, Paul Torrance found that most teachers felt it was far more important for students to be courteous than courageous. They also felt it was more important for pupils to do their work on time, and to be industrious, obedient, popular, and willing to accept the judgment of authorities.

These values, when combined, are more likely to produce students who are

---

[2] "The Giraffe Society" card in Torrance Collection MSS 2606 #021. Athens, GA: Hargrett Rare Book and Manuscript Library, University of Georgia.

ripe for brainwashing than students who are able to think creatively. The findings suggested that teachers were giving young children confusing signals about what behavior is most valued in society.

COMMUNITY INVOLVEMENT

Paul was active in his community as well as being committed to his research at the university. He was involved in a Summer Arts festival, which was sponsored by the Athens Recreational Department and open to talented young people. Paul was in charge of the creative component while other individuals looked after the art component. He also served as a judge in the tenth annual Design-An-Ad contest in November, 1978, sponsored by the local newspaper—the *Athens Banner-Herald*.

Peggy Hooper, a former student of Paul Torrance, administered the Torrance Tests of Creative Thinking to her class of gifted underachievers in Winston-Salem, North Carolina. This innovative teacher had her students individually write to Paul Torrance, and he took the time to reply to each one of them. Paul became a "pen pal" to each of the students over the course of the school year. As a culminating activity, Peggy Hooper organized a field trip to visit Paul Torrance in Athens. The 25 students made a three-day, 425-mile trip to Atlanta and then to Athens to visit sites and meet Paul Torrance at his office and have supper with him and Pansy at their home.

In 1977, Paul received a Distinguished Service Award from Georgia Military School in Milledgeville, Georgia. He was a library assistant when he was a student and has continued his interest in the GMC Library with gifts supporting a separate building for the library. He is now contributing to a fund for an addition to the library that will double its capacity. He has written the Governor of Georgia and others to raise funds for a new junior college building and for the restoration of the old capitol building. Paul has also contributed books and artifacts to the Museum of the History of Georgia Education located at Georgia College, which is also in Milledgeville.

Reverend Jon Appleton, pastor of the First Baptist Church of Athens, wrote to Paul: "You, along with Pansy, make a lasting contribution in the fellowship of the church, but especially in the experience of worship and training for our preschool children.... It is an honor for me to be your pastor." Paul has served as a deacon in the various churches he has attended over the years, but he has never been a deacon or other elected officer in his present church. He has quietly gone about involving himself in other ways—teaching a leadership course, writing material for the Southern Baptist Convention, consulting with them on their theological concepts project, and the like. Pansy has also conducted workshops in creative problem solving for editors and other headquarters personnel and at various Convention retreats. Paul is no longer able to attend Sunday school and worship services regularly or to engage in volunteer activities; however, he attends when he can. His Sunday School class helps with the food bank and serving meals for the local homeless shelter, and although he is unable to help with the work, he contributes food for these activities. He also offers special encouragement, books, and ideas to the Minister of Education and the Minister of Music.

Also not well known is Paul's involvement with the world community. Before his retirement he estimated that he devoted and average of four hours each day to correspondence, sending reprints and books and offering suggestions to people who write or call him. Now he estimates that he spends, on average, more than three hours a day in this kind activity. He now spends more time on foreign correspondence than on domestic correspondence.

ASSESSMENT OF CREATIVE THINKING: A BOLD VENTURE INTO ITS MYSTERIES

The Minnesota Tests of Creative Thinking were designed to be used for research and exploratory studies in the area of creativity. At about the time Paul arrived at the University of Georgia, research editions of the tests were published by Personnel Press, a division of Ginn and Company in Princeton, New Jersey. They were called the Torrance Tests of Creative Thinking (TTCT).

Assessing creativity has fascinated and frustrated educators and psychologists over the years. Like intelligence, creativity has many forms and it is expressed in many ways. As a result, many tests have been developed to assess creative abilities, and varied opinions have been expressed about this whole process. One cannot expect any single instrument to measure the whole field of "creativity." Paul Torrance did not claim that his tests measured every dimension of creativity, but that they measured the creative thinking abilities which he defined and that the overall result was an assessment of creative potential.

The 1966 version had two parts—a Verbal battery and a Figural battery. The Verbal battery contained seven subtests, namely, Asking Questions, Guessing Causes, Guessing Consequences, Product Improvement, Unusual Uses, Unusual Questions, and Just Suppose. The Figural battery consisted of three subtests, namely, Picture Construction, Picture Completion, and Parallel Lines. (These subtests are described in detail in Chapter 4 of this book, "The Minnesota Years.")

The subtests are scored on the basis of certain defined creative thinking abilities—fluency, flexibility, originality, and elaboration. The scores on the subtests result in a creative score or index that represents the creative *potential* of the individual.

Between 1966 and 1984, many refinements have been made to the TTCT. For example, Orlow Ball, a graduate student of Paul Torrance, streamlined the tedious scoring process. Paul added 13 creative strengths to the scoring system for the Figural tests. These relevant dimensions of creativity have added greatly to our understanding of the concept.

In 1984, Scholastic Testing Services in Bensenville, Illinois, published a new TTCT. According to Dr. John D. Kauffman, Vice-President and Director of Marketing, hundreds of thousands of the TTCT have been sold in the last several years. The TTCT continues to be the single most important creativity instrument. It is used for research, for evaluation, and for general instructional planning decisions. The TTCT is used in school systems to measure the growth of creativity as a result of a program that purportedly teaches creative skills. The TTCT is also used, mainly by school jurisdictions, as one of a battery of tests that identify gifted and talented students. It is usually used in conjunction with intelligence and achievement tests.

The TTCT has been published in 34 languages in 50 countries. Publication arrangements have been made with France, Italy, and, most recently, Hong Kong. The Department of Education in Bulgaria advocates its use in the schools of that country.

In a review of the TTCT in 1972, John Holland (1972) said, "whatever the eventual uses of the TTCT, Torrance has made a large, substantive contribution to our knowledge of creative imagination" (p.841). Don Treffinger concluded his review of the TTCT in 1985 with these words: "The TTCT offers useful insights into several relevant dimensions. The tests are complex tools which, like all psychological instruments, should be utilized with sensitivity and good judgement by qualified professionals" (p. 1634).

Paul Torrance has written and published three monographs that provide information about the uses of the TTCT in programs that develop creative skills. The Torrance Tests of Creative Thinking have been used throughout the world with the deaf, retarded, emotionally handicapped, and learning disabled, as well as with gifted children and adults.

Dr. Bob Clements, a Professor of Art Education at the University of Georgia and long-time colleague of Paul Torrance, believes that Paul's most significant contribution is the series of tests devised to measure creative potential. At last, he says, art educators have a means of measuring how art education makes a difference, and how art education enhances important creative skills. These skills can be applied in all areas of an individual's life. In the fifth edition of his textbook, *Emphasis Art: A Qualitative Art Program for Elementary and Middle Schools* (Clements & Wachowiak, 1993), a section is devoted to creativity and discusses the Torrance Tests of Creative Thinking. He describes the four aspects of creativity—fluency, flexibility, elaboration, and originality, and gives teachers ideas about how to develop these skills through art.

Dr. Bernie Schwartz and I have applied the ability to ask good questions—n important component of creativity—to art education. We have demonstrated how key questions can make students sensitive to good art pieces and aware of gaps in their own work.

Through correspondence and personal consultation, Paul has advised thousands of graduate students in other universities and experienced investigators in other research organizations regarding the research use of the tests of creative thinking. The TTCT is the most cited creativity instrument in the world today. As of 1990, the TTCT was reported to have been used in 1,779 studies. These publications cover the areas of validity, reliability, norms, administration and scoring use in evaluating programs, gender differences, race and socioeconomic class, and reviews.

Between 1960 and 1990 in the United States alone, over 160 universities produced 716 or more theses and dissertations that used the TTCT. The top 10 universities (those producing the largest number of such theses and dissertations) are:

Name of University and Location	**Number**
1. University of Georgia, Athens	92
2. University of Minnesota, Minneapolis	59
3. Indiana University, Bloomington	18
4. Fordham University, New York	15
5. Texas A and M University, College Station	15
6. Mississippi State University, Starkville	14
7. University of Michigan, Ann Arbor	13
8. University of Wisconsin, Madison	12
9. Ohio State University	12
10. Columbia University	11

In addition, 42 foreign universities have produced theses and dissertations using the TTCT. The foreign universities that have produced the most theses and dissertations using the TTCT are Panjabi University in India and the University of Toronto in Canada.

The topics of these theses and dissertations are wide-ranging; however, some of the most prominent topics over the years have been achievement, adjustment and mental health, attitude, black children, children, cognitive ability, college students, different cultures, disadvantaged students, elementary schools, environmental effects, gender issues, gifted/talented/creative students, imagery/imagination, intellectual ability, parental factors, personality traits, professional training, reading, retarded children, self-concept, socioeconomic status, special programs, teacher creativity, teaching methods, testing, thinking strategies, and training/fostering creativity.

To date, 191 professional journals from all over the world have published over 800 articles reporting studies using the TTCT. The top 10 journals (those publishing the largest number of such articles) are:

Name of Journal	Number
1. *Journal of Creative Behavior*	84
2. *Psychological Reports*	57
3. *Gifted Child Quarterly*	53
4. *Perceptual and Motor Skills*	47
5. *Journal of Educational Psychology*	24
6. *Creative Child and Adult Quarterly*	23
7. *Journal of Psychology*	20
8. *British Journal of Educational Psychology*	20
9. *Education and Training of the Mentally Retarded*	20
10. *Psychology in the Schools*	16

A cumulative bibliography (see Appendix A) on the TTCT lists all the university/college theses and dissertations and all published articles. Paul Torrance admits that some publications dealing with the applications of the TTCT may have been missed.

TTCT—Detractors

There are, and have been, individuals who do not believe that Paul Torrance's tests are sound. They ask, "How can you measure as complex a phenomenon as creativity with a paper-and-pencil test?" Some statisticians think that the tests are not reliable or valid. Psychologists know, for example, that intelligence tests tap only a few skills that contribute to intelligent behavior. So it is with creativity tests; only a potential to produce or be productive is measured. From the outset, Torrance maintained that there are many ways to use creativity—in asking questions, thinking of possible causes and consequences, thinking of possible changes for improving something, ideas for possible uses of commonplace materials, and thinking of possible consequences of future events. Paul's goal was to identify as many of these as possible and then devise tasks that would measure these abilities. Paul resisted pressures to combine these into one index of creativity that would give us a measure of general creativity. He finally had to give in to these pressures. Torrance now maintains the best of his tests to measure general creativity is the Sounds and Images test. This is true because all or almost all creativity involves imagery.

As James Delisle indicated in his recent book, *Guiding the Social and Emotional Development of Gifted Youth* (1992), the Torrance Tests of Creative Thinking have become the standard against which all other creativity tests are measured.

Dr. Joe Renzulli, Professor of Educational Psychology at the University of Connecticut and Director of the National Research Center on Giftedness, tells this story:

> When I was a beginning researcher I proposed a study entitled "Scoring Creativity Tests by Computer." A part of this research involved training human scorers with whom we could compare test scores that were analyzed by the computer. Since we were operating on a very limited budget the then publisher of the TTCT agreed to provide scorer training at no cost. I brought my group of student trainees to a meeting in New York City and to everyone's wonderment, Dr. Torrance "himself" arrived to work with us. He immediately made it clear that his name was "Paul," and that we were a group of peers attempting to solve a common problem. I, like the rest of my students, were literally shaking in our boots when Dr. Torrance entered the room; however, he reversed the atmosphere in literally seconds. This experience has remained in my mind for now more than a quarter of a decade. I learned something that day about greatness and kindness and humility that has provided me with a personal goal for my own work with others.[3]

Longitudinal Studies: Paper-and-Pencil Creativity Tests Predict Real-Life Creative Achievements

While he was in Minnesota, Torrance designed two major longitudinal studies to determine if his tests of creativity would predict creative achievements later in life. Longitudinal studies measure certain selected behaviors over a prolonged period of time to note stability or change. The real value of many tests is their ability to predict later performance. For example, students who score highly on an intelligence scale like the Wechsler Intelligence Scale for Children are likely to do well in school. Behavioral scientists refer to this quality as the predictive validity of a test.

In the first study, the 392 high school students who were administered the original version of the TTCT were followed up seven (1966) and twelve (1972) years later. Paul faced the usual problems inherent in longitudinal research—keeping contact with subjects, storing data, and financial support. The results generally showed that the Torrance Tests of Creative Thinking predicted later creative accomplishments on three dimensions, namely, creative quantity, creative quality, and creative motivation or aspiration.

The second study involved elementary school students who were followed up 22 years after being tested with the Torrance Tests of Creative Thinking in two Minneapolis elementary schools between 1958 and 1964. The subjects completed two questionnaires about their creative achievements. Five measures of creative achievement were derived from these questionnaires, namely, number of high school creative achievements, number of post-high school creative achievements, number of creative style-of-living achievements, quality of highest creative achievement (ratings), and quality of future career image. The

---

[3] Questionnaire completed by Joe Renzulli, May 14, 1992 (in possession of the author).

results indicated a significant relationship between the creativity test scores and creative accomplishments 22 years later.

Both longitudinal studies provide evidence of the power of the Torrance Tests of Creative Thinking to predict later creative achievements. Paul Torrance also found that it was important for the highly creative children to have mentors and to have a future career image or to have "fallen in love" with something that they pursued later in their lives.

From the 22-year longitudinal study, Paul Torrance wrote the "Manifesto for Children," which captures some of his important findings.

Reprinted with permission of E. Paul Torrance.

A 30-year follow-up of the 1958 group has been planned, and data have been collected. At the time of writing, Christopher Nelson, a consultant for gifted education with the Georgia State Department of Education in Atlanta, is completing the study as his doctoral dissertation. Paul Torrance and Kay Bruch are currently assisting him.

Torrance read a book by H. L. Ruben (1980) entitled *Competing: Understanding and Winning The Strategic Games We All Play*. In a personal letter to Joe Khatena, Paul said that Ruben agrees with him that "the only time to have a chance for success is when you play the game your way."[4] He agrees further that an unwillingness to change the rules, to walk away, to play our own games rather than those others present us with, create many personal tragedies. Paul found a great deal of support for this idea in the longitudinal study. The successful creative persons have for the most part created their own joys. Thus, the guidance of gifted students might involve helping them learn now to create their own jobs or careers rather than merely finding and keeping a job. There are of course many strategies for doing this. These could be brainstormed and tested through sociodrama.

Dr. James Alvino, former Director of the International Future Problem Solving Program, said that although it may sound silly, the "lesson" of lasting significance for him from Paul's work is the "Manifesto for Children." It is a courageous, even radical, statement to say "Don't worry about being well rounded; find something that you love and go for it!" James Alvino says, "Finding your *love* is the key."

Other Torrance Creativity Tests

Another of Paul Torrance's creativity tests, Thinking Creatively in Action and Movement (TCAM), is less well known. It was developed at the University of Georgia and was inspired by his observation of child behavior in a daycare center. Torrance had already tried to develop tests that required verbal and drawing responses, but was not satisified with them. He realized that 3 to 5-year-old children had been speaking and drawing only a short time, whereas they had been using movement and action all their lives.

The TCAM assesses the creativity of young children and is most effective from three years of age to age eight. The working time of the individually administered instrument is from 10 to 30 minutes.

TCAM does not require verbal responses, although they are accepted. Torrance believes that preschoolers best express their ideas in the kinaesthetic areas of actions and movement, not in words and drawings.

Fun activities and exercises are required of children, which sample their problem-solving capabilities. For example, the "How many ways?" activity samples the child's ability to produce alternative ways of moving.

---

[4] Personal communication by E.P. Torrance to Joe Khatena. Athens, Georgia, October 12, 1980.

TCAM can be used as part of a program to further develop promising creative talent among young children. Scores are available for fluency, originality, imagination, and total creativity.

A cumulative bibliography of Thinking Creatively in Action and Movement was compiled in 1992 by Paul Torrance and Laura Rose. It documented 115 studies that used this instrument. Two reviews of the TCAM were completed in 1985. A reviewer, Lynn Fox, concurs that the instrument should be used as a research tool and that its greatest value is its use for instructional purposes. The TCAM complements the TTCT and TCSW (the Thinking Creatively with Sounds and Words test).

The genesis of the TCSW occurred in Minnesota while Paul worked with a graduate student and a research assistant. This test assesses creativity by measuring the originality of ideas stimulated by abstract sounds and onomatopoeic words. The test consists of two batteries, Sounds and Images, and Onomatopoeia and Images. Both are presented on record albums or cassettes.

Sounds and Images was designed by Bert Cunnington and Paul Torrance. It is both a testing device to assess originality of thinking and a training method to motivate creative activities. It uses the free association process and the underlying principle that "creativity begets creativity." The test uses progressive warm-ups, makes divergent thinking legitimate, provides freedom from the threat of evaluation, and invites regression.

Onomatopoeia and Images was designed by Joe Khatena as a test of originality. He was a doctoral student of Paul Torrance, and he graduated from the University of Georgia in 1968. The test makes divergent thinking legitimate and allows the imagination freedom to create original images. It was published in 1973 by Personnel Press, and in 1980 Scholastic Testing Services took over publishing rights.

Style of Learning and Thinking: SOLAT

Paul Torrance, along with Bernice McCarthy, Mary Kolesinki, and Jamie Smith, developed an instrument that measures the different styles of thinking and learning that are apparent in students. The SOLAT indicates a student's learning strategy and brain-hemisphere preference in problem solving. It was Ted Riegel who got Paul Torrance interested in split-brain studies. Schools have been criticized for educating only "half of the mind"; that is, most activities performed in schools require logical, analytical thought as opposed to a creative, intuitive approaches. This instrument can help teachers discover which style of learning and thinking students prefer. The SOLAT was published in 1988 and is available in two forms—Elementary (K to Grade 3) and Youth (Grade 6 to Grade 12).

An upward extension and a different version of the SOLAT is the HIP Survey—Human Information Processing. It measures the processing preference of the brain—left, right, integrated, or mixed, at the college and adult level. Bill and Barbara Taggart of Florida International University in Miami were using the SOLAT in all kinds of workshops. They were anxious to have the SOLAT available commercially. Paul experienced a stroke in 1984 and has since that time had several mini-strokes, which have affected his left brain functioning. Some of the specialized functions of the left hemisphere have come back, while others have not. Whenever he has a mini-stroke, some of the functions that had recovered are again lost temporarily. This is especially true of speech, sequencing, and reasoning. When Paul had his stroke, he offered the Taggarts the opportunity to share authorship and royalties if they would get it ready for publication. They did so, and it became the HIP Survey.

J. P. Das of the University of Alberta, in reviewing the test, indicated that it is only of academic interest and that a theoretical rationale is missing. He states, "to put it simply, it is a myth to attribute separate and distinct styles of thinking to the left and right hemispheres of the brain" (Das, 1989, p. 363). More studies are necessary to validate this test. Torrance, however, has presented a rationale and considerable validity evidence in the manual.

An instrument called the Khatena–Torrance Creative Perception Inventory (KTCPI) was developed by Paul and his student and colleague of many years, Joe Khatena. The KTCPI consists of two separate paper-and-pencil instruments about creative self-perception—"Something About Myself" (SAM) and "What Kind of Person Are You?" (WKOPAY). It is described by the authors as a research edition to assist individuals in describing personal attributes that are considered creative. The SAM measures six creative attributes, namely, environmental sensitivity, initiative, self-strength, intellectuality, individuality, and artistry. The WKOPAY measures various creative attributes such as acceptance of authority, self-confidence, inquisitiveness, awareness of others, and disciplined imagination.

The KTCPI was first published by Stoelting Company in 1976, and Scholastic Testing Services is currently revising the test. A cumulative bibliography completed by Paul Torrance, Hsin-tai Lin, and Laura Rose showed that 135 studies have used the KTCPI.

Suzanne Schaller, Editor-in-Chief with Scholastic Testing Services in Bensenville, Illinois, tells me that the testing firm has a "pile" of never-published tests developed over the years by Paul Torrance. These tests, listed below, span a period of 21 years and illustrate his productivity and the result of incubated thought in the area of assessing creativity.

TORRANCE TESTS

Test of Creative Thinking (Counseling and Guidance Form)	1959
Non-Verbal Creative Thinking Tasks (Form NVA)	1960
Just Suppose	1960
Minnesota Tests of Creative Thinking (V & NV Form A)	1962
Minnesota Tests of Creative Thinking (Abbreviated Form VII)	1962

Scoring Guide for the Picture Construction Test (Triangle)	1963
Scoring Guide for Small Business Form Ask-and-Guess Test	1963
Administration and Scoring Guide for the Squares Test	1963
Problem Making Test	1965
Guide for Scoring Dot-Squares Test for Originality	1965
Guide for Scoring "Ding Dong Bell" Version of the Ask-and-Guess Test	1965
Minnesota Tests of Creative Thinking (Abbreviated Form 2)	1965
Thinking Creatively With Pictures	1966
Thinking Creatively With Words	1966
Pensando Creativamente Con Dibujos	1966
Scoring Guide for "How Good Is Your Imagination?" (Form B)	1966
Common Problems (Creative Children Form)	1966
Torrance Tests of Creative Thinking Norms-Technical Manual	1966
Administration and Scoring Guide for the Mother Goose Problems Test (Revised)	1969
Thinking Creatively About Teaching and Learning (Form B)	1974
Preliminary Norms-Technical Manual: Demonstrator Form A TTCT	1980

PROFESSOR AND MASTER TEACHER

"Paul Torrance is the template for the concept [of] teacher."[5]

During Paul's 18 years as a professor at the University of Georgia, he came to be known as an outstanding teacher. In 1973, the Board of Regents of the University of Georgia recognized this fact by awarding him the designation of "Alumni Foundation Distinguished Professor," an honor that is given for outstanding achievement in teaching, research, and community service.

He was well respected by students, especially for his concern about them and his attention to detail. He expected a lot from students and even more of himself. He marked student assignments and projects immediately—often handing them back the next day. He knew the importance of feedback and took his responsibility as a teacher seriously.

I had the privilege of attending his last class at the University of Georgia. It was a class on sociodrama and, as always, he had the students actively involved in various roles. He was the same as a teacher as he was in his personal, private life.

Paul always kept a heavy teaching load, as he was challenged by students and obtained a lot of his insights from interaction with them, as well as with other staff. Besides teaching EPY 822—Creative Thinking which he made famous, Paul taught a number of courses over his tenure at the University of

[5] Letter from Judith Preissle Goetz, Associate Professor, University of Georgia, to Paul Torrance on the occasion of his retirement. March 23, 1985.

Georgia: Research in Educational Psychology, Problems in Educational Psychology, Learning and Motivation, Seminar in Educational Research: Theories of Creativity, Learning Problems of Disadvantaged Children and Youth, Advanced Seminar on Creativity Research, Sociodrama, Seminar on Career Education, and Internship on Educational Psychology College Teaching, in addition to advising on independent studies, thesese, and dissertations.

In Paul's last year as a professor before retirement, he made a significant change in his Creative Thinking course: He changed one of the major requirements of the course, challenging his students to use the skills of creative problem solving to improve the quality of life somewhere in their environment, instead of just enhancing their own creative functioning. By all indications, students did enhance their personal creative functioning, *and* they also improved their larger environments.

In his annual report of 1983–84, Paul indicated that he intended to complete a textbook on the use of sociodrama in education and that his students would provide many insights for him. Paul was not able to locate a single text on the subject. He pretested the majority of the chapters of his book with students for about 10 years and incorporated their feedback and suggestions into the draft manuscript. Paul wrote this book with Mary Murdock and David Fletcher, and it is currently in press. It will be published in 1995 by Benedic Books of South Africa with the title "Creative Problem Solving Through Role Playing."

Paul always had more than his fair share of students who wanted him to advise them on their research papers, theses, or dissertations. For example, during the 1977–78 academic year, Paul was involved in 34 doctoral committees and he was the major professor in 14 of them. During that same year, he was an invited external examiner for doctoral dissertations in South Australia and India.

Testaments to Paul Torrance's Teaching Style

Paul's humanness "shone through" all his greatness, especially for students who took his classes. Julie Richards wrote this poem about her impressions of Paul:[6]

OUR TEACHER
by Julie Richards

He is quite a distinguished older man who gives a
first impression of being rather stern and hard-hearted.

He is not a very large man, but when he speaks to

[6] Poem, "Our Teacher," by Julie Richards, Spring 1969, in Torrance Collection MSS 2606 #006. Athens, GA: Hargrett Rare Book and Manuscript Library, University of Georgia.

you, you know that he commands the respect of a 6 foot 4 inch - 250 pounder.

The first day of class, he passes out an outline of your course and what is expected of you, explains it, and dismisses class. You leave the class bewildered. How on earth can he expect one to do reaction reports, teaching experiences, read the book, and stay in school? You are lost.

During the next few sessions of class you realize that you are being taught by the author of your textbook and the head of the Educational Psychology Department. You are petrified—how will you ever be able to understand a word that he says.

After a few lectures, you suddenly realize that he is not a battle-axe or a god, but rather, another human being. He is interesting because he talks to you on your own level, not as if he were talking to another doctor of psychology.

The first day that you walk into class and he hands you a test covering Chapter I, you automatically think—a pop test. But you find that he isn't interested in catching you off guard and checking up on whether you are keeping up. He is interested in providing for you a guided outline of study to let you see how well you are comprehending your textbook material.

He runs a very interesting classroom experience because he is so flexible. You never follow the same format in a class period if you have already followed that format in a previous period. This keeps things interesting. You never know exactly what to expect when you go to class, but you go to see what will be going on that day. If you don't like the way he teaches, he encourages any comments that you would like to make.

The day that he walks into class with hoola hoops and bean bags, you think that he has gone crazy.

> But then, he utilizes these toys to give you a better understanding of how to teach a skill. Rather than lecture, he involves the students in his teaching experiences.
>
> If you want to know anything about education or psychology, ask him. He sets aside a time period each day in which he answers any questions which you might have. If he can't answer your question, he will have an answer for it by the next class period.
>
> If you are still afraid of him toward the end of the quarter, look back at the times that he got tickled and laughed. He has one of the most jovial laughs you've ever heard. How can you be afraid of someone with a laugh like that, and most of all with someone who displays an understanding of and interest in you.

John Carroll had an embarrassing moment with Paul Torrance. He had just arrived from Western Australia for his first doctoral coursework at the University of Georgia. One was an independent study with just John and Paul Torrance in which readings were set and John would go to Paul's office to discuss them. John was very nervous in his first face-to-face meeting and started to tell Paul all about his readings. After a while he looked up and found Paul had gone to sleep. It was a bad moment. John thought, "Was I so boring? Should I go on and pretend I didn't notice, or cough or make a noise, or creep out, or what? Perhaps I should go back to Australia!" In a classic case of repression, John has no memory of what happened after that. He was told later that Paul was very embarrassed himself as he was taking medication and was prone to get sleepy if he stopped moving.

I posed one question to a number of individuals who have been influenced by Paul Torrance over the years: "What is your relationship to Paul Torrance—student, colleague, or friend?" Almost invariably, respondents said, "All of the above." This in itself is a compelling statement. Individuals have learned so much from Paul that they see themselves as *students*; they have worked with him over such an extended period of time that they are also *colleagues*; and they have developed a personal relationship with Paul and are therefore *friends* as well.

In 1980, Noel Howieson came to Georgia from Western Australia to study with Paul Torrance. She recalls a strange meeting with him in which they discussed her research topic. She had spent six months reading and preparing in a particular area, and intended to research that topic. Noel started to discuss her plans. Paul Torrance sat and nodded, looking interested but saying little. When she concluded, he sat thoughtfully for a while, offering no immediate response. Suddenly, with no forethought, she said, "Have you anything unfinished?" Paul's eyes twinkled and a smile swept his face. "Well, as a matter of fact, I do—I did a study several years ago across many cultures. I've followed up most but I never followed up in Western Australia." Noel Howieson was taken aback. How did she know to ask this question? Later, in 1983, she completed her study, "Long-Range Predictive Validity of the Torrance Tests of Creative Thinking Among Australian Children."

Diane Postniek recounts a vivid class period with Paul Torrance at the University of Georgia. Every class period with Paul Torrance was special, filled with unexpected delights and challenges, but this one particular class left quite an impression. In Diane's words:

> We arrived to find the room prepared for a celebration. The desk was arranged with a sheet cake and sweet punch—and a large bouquet of brightly colored crocheted flowers. After refreshments were served, Dr. Torrance invited each of us to select a flower to keep. He told us that his mother at age ninety-five had crocheted them in the nursing home. He asked us to keep the flower as a reminder that creativity could go on and on in our lives. It was then that he told us that his mother had died that morning.[7]

An Important Lesson

A student in Paul's Creative Thinking class, Lucy Guglielmino, recounts a particularly memorable experience in his class.

> Using a scrap of wood tumbled in a stone polisher, Dr. Torrance led me to an "aha!" (as he would describe it) that has had a major impact on my teaching and teacher-training. In a creative thinking class, he had each class member select one polished piece of wood from a box of thirty or more. He informed us that we would examine the piece we had selected, get to know it, and return it to the box. The pieces would then be shaken up and we would pick out "our" piece from the thirty others. We looked at the seemingly identical pieces of wood, and looked back at Dr. Torrance, unbelieving. He simply smiled and proceeded to offer the box to each of us in turn. As we struggled to find distinguishing features in these thirty similarly-shaped, similarly-colored pieces of wood, we were surprised. Small whorls and patterns in the grain began to make them unique. By the time we put them back into the box, most of us were confident that we could find them again—and all of us did. Pleased with the success of his experiment, Dr. Torrance then led us into a discussion of the value and uniqueness of the students we

[7] Letter from Diane Postniek to Paul Torrance on the occasion of his retirement. March 23, 1985.

> would encounter—their individual talents, skills and learning styles. I have that small piece of polished wood to this day.[8]

Another student, Mary Lee Platz, wrote to Paul in 1978 about her reaction to one of his lessons:

> I need to share with you how deeply moved I was in class yesterday by your presentation of the risks and dangers involved in deciding to be courageous and act creatively.... Many thanks! The misty eyes and lumped throats in our corner of the room yesterday were harbingers of applause—tribute to one man who exemplifies the challenge, cost and reward of trying, daring, and succeeding to influence the lives of others toward creative and constructive being and action.[9]

Bob Clements, a Professor of Art Education at the University of Georgia, spoke about Paul Torrance's willingness to meet students—in his home. Once a year, Dr. Clements would arrange with Paul to have his class visit him at home to discuss creativity and its role in art education. Other professors have also held discussion–socials with Paul Torrance in his home.

While I was visiting Paul in March of 1992, a conference call was set up and executed between Dr. Bill Nash's class in A & M University in College Station, Texas, and Paul in Athens. Each student was given an opportunity to ask Paul any question related to his research or some application of it. Paul always enjoyed these discussions and he considered them important in "spreading the word."

Morgan Henderson and Jack Presbury had been working on a cognitive model that they called "The Ways of Knowing," and Paul arranged for them to explain it to a group of his graduate students. Afterward, a group went to his house and were on his back patio. In typical Torrance style, he wished to give them critical feedback on their model without discouraging them. (No one does it better!) Paul plucked a flower from a large stalk growing in his garden (Night Blooming Ceres) and showed them the bloom. In his gentle guru manner, he said, "I find that all theories can be found in nature. Your model, for instance, might look like this flower." Morgan and Jack studied it, and subsequently made the revision in their theory that Jack was sure Paul had in mind, though he never criticized their ideas directly.

Throughout his career, Paul has displayed a pattern of paying unusual attention to foreign students. This is part of the reason why he has had such a worldwide influence. Paul has directed the most dissertations (110) in the history of the College of Education at the University of Georgia. Also, he has directed more dissertations on the disadvantaged than anyone else in the United States.

---

[8] Letter from Lucy Guglielmino to Paul Torrance on the occasion of his retirement. March 23, 1985.

[9] Personal letter from Mary Lee Platz to Paul Torrance. February 10, 1978.

Many of his doctoral students have taken key positions in colleges and universities, school jurisdictions, mental health facilities, and private practice.

Paul often presented guest lectures on his research and the theoretical foundations of creativity in the classes of other professors at the University of Georgia (those who were not threatened by his research and his prestige).

> Many would probably agree that the brilliant breakthrough work of Paul Torrance has encountered bureaucratic roadblocks along the way, and demanded the ultimate in patience and perseverance. There was never any doubt among his students that he was giving a lifetime of selfless leadership in the better understanding of the nature and nurture of creativity. His research, teaching, and his tireless mentoring, dedication, and support of students has created a network of devoted followers who continue to promote and further his work all over the world. I know so well. I am one of the network. There are thousands of others.[10]
>
> Bee Bleedorn
> University of St. Thomas
> St. Paul, Minnesota

THE FUTURE PROBLEM SOLVING PROGRAM

> *"The genius of the future will be the creative mind adapting itself to the shape of things to come. This will require Satori bursts of new insights. The skills of creative thinking must be recognized as mankind's most important adaptability skills. Such skills must become basic to the curriculum of schools, homes, business and other agencies."* [11]

In 1974, Paul and Pansy Torrance were invited to develop a month-long curriculum unit with 28 gifted students at Clarke Central High School in Athens, Georgia. Dr. Kay Bruch, a colleague of Paul Torrance, assisted Paul and Pansy in launching the program. This invitation provided Paul an excellent opportunity to address two of his foremost concerns—the decline of creativity among Americans and a lack of interest in the future. In September of 1975 at the World Conference on Gifted Children in London, England, Paul spoke to the delegates about his activities in what he called the Future Problem Solving Program. The response was enthusiastic, which made him more determined to make it a universal program.

Combining the six-step creative problem-solving process developed by Osborn and Parnes and some potential problems of the future, the Torrances launched what has grown to become one of the largest national and international programs for capable students—the Future Problem Solving (FPS)

---

[10] Questionnaire completed by Bee Bleedorn, November 22, 1992.

[11] Bleedorn, B. (1991). *Creativity*. An open letter to friends and colleagues of the Center for Creative Studies. St. Paul, MN: College of St. Thomas (summer).

Program. Each year an estimated 250,000 students in all 50 American states and several other countries, including Canada, are involved in the program. The program provides an opportunity for capable students to match wits using an interdisciplinary approach to studying and solving future problems.

The major educational objectives of the program include the development of creative problem solving skills, the improvement of teamwork and communication skills, the enlargement and enrichment of images of the future, the development and improvement of research techniques, responding to the challenges of difficult and unsolved problems, practice in evaluating alternatives, exercising control over issues that affect an individual's life, excellence in performance without threats of alienation from the peer group, and exposure to gaps in knowledge and new careers that may be pursued in the future.

The regular program is designed for students in grades 4 to 12, who work in teams of four. A primary division, which is available for pupils in the primary grades (K–3), is noncompetitive and instructional in nature. There are no Bowls or competitive aspects (as there are in the regular program), but it is an interesting way to prepare students for the regular program. Teachers or coaches assist the students in gathering information and refining their problem-solving and communication skills. The regular program involves three divisions based on grade level (grades 4–6, grades 7–9, grades 10–12). This arrangement allows teams to participate and compete against teams at their own level.

During the school year, teams work on three practice problems. When completed, the solutions are mailed to trained evaluators who critique the work and return it with suggestions for improvement. This feedback is considered one of the major strengths of the program.

The selection of scientific and social topics for each year is based on the results of a vote by the participating students, coaches, and state directors. A sampling of topics from the past includes robotics, UFOs, ocean communities, career alternatives, the Greenhouse Effect, nutrition, poverty, education, and acid rain.

Students who excel on the third practice problem receive invitations to participate in state/provincial Future Problem Solving Bowls held each spring. Winning teams in each of the three grade-level divisions at the state/provincial Bowls are automatically invited to participate in the International Future Problem Solving Bowl (which was held in the late spring of 1992 at the University of Michigan in Ann Arbor). Approximately 1,600 students representing grades 4 through 12, with their coaches and parents, convene from all over the United States and Canada for four days of competitive problem solving, cooperative educational seminars, and compatible social activities.

In addition to the problem-solving component, the Future Problem Solving Program offers a scenario-writing competition and a community problem solving division. Scenario writing involves youngsters submitting 1,200-word (or less) scenarios of the future. Forecasting the outcomes of possible decisions and solutions, the young people have a chance to demonstrate their creative writing skills. The writing should reflect the present situation and how the students feel about it. Students call on dreams they have for themselves, the way they see the world now, and the way they see the world is going to change. Many try to tackle problems that exist today as they project them into the future—for example, unemployment, or dehumanizing advances of technology in various professions such as education and medicine.

In the community problem solving division, students apply the problem-solving process to real-life situations in their communities. Reports of problem solving projects are evaluated, and winners at each grade-level division are invited to attend the FPS Conference.

To date, teams of students have implemented a wide range of community solutions, ranging from cleaning up hazardous waste in Utah to sending over 2,000 children's books from New York to a children's library in Fiji. The September, 1987 *Reader's Digest* published a story called "Kids Who Saved a Dying Town" (Henderson, 1987), based on the Georgia Community Future Problem Solving Program. Dr. Betty Sloop of Atlanta saw how involved students can become in the Future Problem Solving Program. Her sixth-grade students won first place for community involvement in the State Future Problem Solving Bowl. The students were involved with one problem—drunk driving—and became so excited that their enthusiasm led to a poster contest, a survey, a brochure, and letters to newspapers, legislators, school board members, County Commissioners, and radio and television stations. They were able to draw public attention to the problem through a special visit to the Capitol (in Atlanta) and a planned ceremony in which bumper stickers were put on county school buses. Paul Torrance's vision of students working to help solve problems facing society became a reality for Dr. Betty Sloop and her class.

In the first few years of the FPS Program, Pansy Torrance diligently wrote many of the problems the students were to solve. In addition, she developed the manual for evaluating the problems, scored the practice problems, provided helpful comments to the teachers or coaches, scored the Bowl problems, and trained thousands of teachers in the creative solving process. The Torrances were spending an excessive amount of their time on the program and a good deal of their personal resources. The program quickly grew beyond the borders of Georgia as other states wanted to run their own programs. Pansy wrote the handbooks on training coaches and evaluation of the solutions.[12] As early as

---

[12] Future Problem Solving Program Materials (available from the International Future Problem Solving Program, Suite 140-B, 315 W. Huron Street, Ann Arbor, MI 48198, 313-998-7876):

1. *Preparing for Tomorrow... Today: A Video Training Guide for the Future Problem Solving Program, 1992.*
2. *Coach's Guide to the Future Problem Solving Program.*
3. *For Coaches by Coaches.*
4. *The Evaluation Primer.*

1976, Paul realized the potential of the program. He wrote, "Gradually we are accumulating some experience with Future Problem Solving Bowls and I continue to be optimistic about their value in educating gifted and talented youngsters and in giving us alternative solutions for many of our puzzling problems of the future."[13]

In 1980, the Future Problem Solving Program received two donations for further development—from the National Association for Gifted Children and from the Lipper Foundation. Support of this national program was recognized by the state of Georgia with the proclamation of Georgia Future Problem Solving Week (April 8–14) by Governor Joe Frank Harris in 1984. In 1985, the Texas FPS Program made a donation to recognize Paul Torrance's retirement and to show appreciation for the wonderful difference Paul's "brainchild" has made in the lives of students and parents, and in the lives of teachers and coaches.

Between 1978 and 1981, the Nebraska Department of Education, Nebraska Association for the Gifted, and the University of Nebraska ran the national FPS program. Then, in 1981, the headquarters was transferred to Coe College in Cedar Rapids, Iowa, under the leadership of Dr. Anne Crabbe. In 1984, the program moved to St. Andrews College in Laurenberg, North Carolina, along with Dr. Crabbe. And in June of 1992, the International FPS Program was established in Ann Arbor, Michigan, under the leadership of Dr. James Alvino. A wide range of publications that support the program are available at the international headquarters, as well as information on implementing a program.

The benefits of the program to students have been well documented. The aim of the FPS Program is to help students enlarge, enrich, and make more accurate their images of the future. Some solutions resulting from the program have been sent to the Governor of Georgia and to the President of the United States for consideration. A complete issue of the *Gifted/Creative/Talented (G/C/T) Magazine* (1991) was devoted to an explanation of the program and its impact on participating coaches and students. Many students gave testimony that the program was the best thing that happened to them in their school experiences. One individual from Georgia wrote an appreciative note to the Torrance Center for Creative Studies and stated that he met a girl from West Virginia at the FPS Bowl at Coe College. The friendship made at the competition grew over the ensuing four years into a loving relationship that resulted in marriage. He ended his letter with appreciation for making it possible for him to find the woman of his dreams and for helping him to extract a very happy solution out of a difficult, "fuzzy" situation. Another student said that the FPS Program changed the course of his life. He attributes the motivation needed to complete his doctorate in gifted education directly to his experiences in the FPS Program. He is now taking on proactive advocacy roles in national associations like the Association for the Talented and Gifted (TAG) and the National Association for

---

[13] Letter from Dr. Torrance to Bee Bleedorn. February 14, 1976.

Gifted Children (NAGC). The FPS Program is equipping today's young people with the vision and skills needed to anticipate, understand, and solve the problems of tomorrow. Every year, Paul Torrance receives letters from children expressing their appreciation to him for conceptualizing and developing the program. Krystle Smith wrote Paul Torrance on June 22, 1993. She said:

> I am a FPSer from the East Orange, New Jersey junior team. I recently got the chance to compete in my first International Conference. It was a very enlightening experience. I wanted to thank you for developing the FPS program. It has done a lot for me including showing me that we need to be aware of the global problems we face. In using FPS it has made me begin to think about how we will be affected in the future by these problems. That's why I want to thank you.[14]

In 1984, Jerry Rogers, a teacher at Clarke Central High School in Athens, Georgia, wrote an unsolicited letter to Dr. Fred Davison, president of the University of Georgia, commenting on the success of the Future Problem Solving Program. He emphasized the inordinate amount of time that Paul Torrance gave the program in planning and in training coaches, judges, and coordinators, as well as the fact that he spent his own money for prizes and mementos. Rogers noted the most important thing Paul Torrance has given to the program is his devotion. His dedication to the program has resulted in an expansion of the program from one school in Athens, to the involvement of thousands of schools throughout the state, nation, and world. Rogers went on to say that Paul displayed a love for all involved—students, teachers, colleagues, all people. This type of behavior can perhaps be described as *agape*—a spontaneous self-giving love, expressed freely without calculation of cost or gain to the giver or merit on the part of the receiver.

The Future Problem Solving Program may be Paul Torrance's greatest legacy and the greatest tribute to his visionary power. He and his late wife Pansy were honored in 1989 at the 15th anniversary of the program. An award in Pansy's name, which recognizes her pioneering efforts with the program, is given annually to an exceptional coach.

Dr. James Alvino, former Director of the International Future Problem Solving Program, remembers meeting Paul for the first time. It was at an Olympics of the Mind Competition at Glassboro State College, and Paul was there to receive an award. Jim Alvino remembers thinking how low-key and pleasant this man was. (Alvino's biases at the time suggested to him that creative people would be flamboyant and flashy.) He also remembers thinking how graciously Paul Torrance accepted what was really a small award, given all his accomplishments and accolades, and how it was actually Paul who had honored the Odyssey of the Mind program by attending, since in some ways it was in competition with the FPS Program.

The FPS Program has created an intense admiration and loyalty for Paul

---

[14] Letter from Krystle Smith to E. Paul Torrance. June 22, 1993. (Obtained from E. Paul Torrance and in possession of the author.)

Torrance and his ideas among people in many countries of the world. He was one of the first to associate creativity with future studies. The widespread attention now being given to future studies is evident in a 1991 publication, *Future Research Directory*. It lists nearly 1,200 individuals who are professionally involved in studying the future, and 24 classified under "creativity and innovation."

A grade 12 student involved in the Future Problem Solving Program from Clark Central High School in Athens, Georgia, wrote Paul Torrance on the occasion of his retirement. The student said,

> Thank goodness Dr. Torrance was that someone who served as my impetus by giving me a reason and a chance to form and to give my own opinions on these matters in a society that often forgets or isn't able to give us "young kids" a say-so about the issues which will so drastically affect our future. He gave me, as well as high school students scattered throughout America, the opportunity to voice our opinions creatively and constructively. He provided a thoughtful, productive outlet for the frustrations I sometimes feel as a young person drowning in the policies of a distant government or out-of-reach adults.[15]

In 1986, Paul Torrance sent the FPS Program archives to Sidney Parnes for deposit in the library at the Creative Education Foundation at the State University in Buffalo, New York.

GOVERNOR'S HONOR PROGRAM

In 1971, Governor Jimmy Carter of Georgia asked Paul Torrance to evaluate the Governor's Honors Program. The program at the time involved 400 gifted and talented 11th-grade students in a 6-week summer activity. Governor Carter had hoped all along that the program would have a "spillover" effect on the public schools of Georgia. In 1977, when Jimmy Carter was president, an additional 200 students were appointed to an additional program that was targeted at the future and had a career education emphasis. This program was in existence for two years, and Paul Torrance and his graduate students did an evaluation that had a follow-up, which indicated that the program had excellent "spillover" effects in the schools from which they came.

Paul, along with Felice Kaufmann, Suzanne Gibbs, and Pansy, reviewed and evaluated the Career Development Program component of the Governor's Honors Program. It involved three clusters of study—current problems, future problems, and career education across regular curricular areas. Student ratings were high for "working with teachers who knew their business" and current information about college and other kinds of training.

---

[15] Letter by Lee anne Hutchinson to E. Paul Torrance on the occasion of his retirement. Book of Letters, March 23, 1985.

Executive Department
Atlanta 30334

Jimmy Carter
GOVERNOR

Hamilton Jordan
EXECUTIVE SECRETARY

October 4, 1971

Mr. E. Paul Torrance, Head
Department of Educational Psychology
The University of Georgia
325 Aderhold Hall
Athens, Georgia 30601

Dear Paul:

I have received and reviewed your excellent evaluation of the Governor's Honors Program.

This evaluation will be most helpful to me in implementing changes and improvements which are needed.

I hope that I will continue to have the benefit of your advice and support regarding the Governor's Honors Program and other issues and programs which vitally affect our state.

Sincerely,

Jimmy

Jimmy Carter

JC/jf

When Jimmy Carter received the evaluation results, he wrote a letter to Paul, which is shown above.

TROUBLING TIMES FOR CHAIRMAN PAUL TORRANCE

Paul spent 12 years as Head of the Department of Educational Psychology at the University of Georgia. Eventually, he felt the weight of his administrative responsibilities was detrimental to his teaching and professional commitments, and he decided to step down.

Probably the most difficult situation that occurred during those 12 years was related to one staff member. This individual's first assignment had been in the Research and Development Center. His work there was unsatisfactory, although Paul never learned why. However, one Sunday after a team from the U.S. Office of Education had visited the Center, Dean Williams called Paul and asked if he would accept the difficult staff member in the Department of Educational Psychology, Measurement, and Research. Paul agreed. At first the individual's work was satisfactory, both in teaching and research. When after the first year this person asked for a promotion, Paul was the only member of the Department to vote favorably. The following year, Paul's department approved the staff member's promotion without a dissenting vote, but the bid was rejected by the College of Education Committee on Promotions. This review brought up the individual's failures in the Research and Development Center. Paul appealed the decision, but it was refused. Paul went with him to appeal to the Dean, who called the Provost to see if his dossier could be sent to the All-University Committee on Promotions. Since it was contrary to university policies, the request was refused.

The individual started to make trouble for everyone, including Paul. He harassed faculty members, the Board of Regents, and even the president. He brought a lawsuit against Paul Torrance and three others, and a lawyer supplied by the Board of Regents defended them. The judge concluded that the professor had not presented any evidence that he should be promoted. This concluded a troubling chapter in Paul's career.

In a memorandum to staff in September of 1977, Paul outlined his goals and priorities for the upcoming academic year. He indicated his plans for a smooth transition to a new department head and his intention to conduct research in the Career Awareness Component of the 1977 Governor's Honors Program and to revise manuscripts and prepare reports that were crucial to his total career plan. He also stated that he planned to teach his course on Creative Thinking more effectively than ever before to make it an "unforgettable and valued experience for every student who enrolls."[16]

Pearline Yeatts-Thomas, a professor of early childhood education in Paul's department, expressed her sentiments to Paul, saying that she always thought of him as a scholar-researcher-writer rather than as a department head.

As a department head at the University of Georgia, Paul did exemplary work in initiating both the School Psychology and the Gifted Programs. His Gifted Program was considered the best in the United States during the 1970s. Paul's work has been recognized by appointment as a life member of the Georgia School Psychology Association and Georgia Supporters of the Gifted. He also has been given life memberships by the National Association of Gifted Children and the Creative Education Foundation.

---

[16] Memorandum from E. Paul Torrance to staff in Educational Psychology—*My Goals and Priorities for 1977–78*. September 4, 1977 (in possession of the author).

Faculty members strongly supported Paul in his position as Head of the Department. When Paul was bothered by one faculty member who was not teaching his classes and Paul had to confront him because of his irresponsible behavior, the faculty member tried to have Paul fired. However, 18 faculty members signed a letter of support to Dr. William Pelletier, Provost at the University of Georgia. They said, "Dr. Torrance is always willing to meet with faculty in an effort to help them in developing personal goals," and "we support the administration of Dr. Torrance and moreover we respect him highly as a scholar and as an individual sensitive to people."[17]

On June 21, 1978, Paul formally asked Dr. Joseph Williams, Dean of Education, to reassign him to full-time teaching and research. During Paul's time as head of the department, a doctoral program in the gifted and talented area had been established, the first for specialists in this area. During this period, Paul had also been criticized and regarded by some as not "mean enough" to discipline faculty who needed it. On the positive side, however, he was supportive of all faculty in his department—even those who viciously attacked him. He may not have been "mean enough" but certainly he was "good enough."

Paul plunged himself into his research and teaching as of July 1, 1978. In a letter to his colleagues (shown on page 143), he expressed his desires for the future.[18]

Administrative Skills Recognized

At this time, Dr. Joe Bledsoe, Professor of Educational Psychology at the University of Georgia, and Dr. Frederico Reissman, Head of Elementary Education at the University of Georgia, wrote letters nominating Paul Torrance for the American Psychological Foundation Distinguished Teaching Award. Drs. Bledsoe and Reissman extolled Paul's professional and personal virtues and stated that the expansion and reorganization of the Educational Psychology Department under Paul's leadership had made it the largest single graduate program in the College of Education and one that was recognized nationally and internationally for its excellence.

Paul's positive and firm leadership was apparent in a number of initiatives. Specifically, he reorganized the department into four areas, namely, Educational Psychology, School Psychology, Measurement and Research, and Specialists in Education for Gifted Children. Paul also established a Departmental Coordinating Committee to facilitate communication among staff members and

---

[17] Letter from 18 members of faculty to Dr. William Pelletier—October 22, 1973. E. Paul Torrance Collection MSS 2606 #18. Athens, GA: Hargrett Rare Book and Manuscript Library, University or Georgia.

[18] Letter to colleagues from E. Paul Torrance, July 1, 1978. E. Paul Torrance Collection MSS 2606 #18. Athens, GA: Hargrett Rare Book and Manuscript Library, University or Georgia.

provide a broader base for decisionmaking. He provided for a smooth transition of a department (Research and Development Center in Educational Stimulation) that was discontinued. In addition, Paul was instrumental in implementing a competency-based teacher education program.

Paul had won the professional admiration of his colleagues for his work in restructuring the department at the University of Georgia. His staff treated him with the highest respect, esteem, and affection.

THE UNIVERSITY OF GEORGIA
COLLEGE OF EDUCATION
DEPT. OF EDUCATIONAL PSYCHOLOGY
ATHENS, GEORGIA 30602

July 1, 1978

Dear Colleagues:

As I retire from my role as head of the Department of Educational Psychology and assume a different role, I would like to take this opportunity to express my appreciation for your support and cooperation during the past 12 years. Trying to respond to the needs of an ever-changing undergraduate program in teacher education, the needs for courses in the psychological foundations of education in a great variety of graduate programs, and similar needs in in-service prograsm; create excellent programs in school psychology and gifted/talented education and strengthen the programs in the preparation of college teachers of educational psychology and research design has been an exciting and frequently overwhelming experience. Your good will and support have been important in whatever success we have had and I am humbly grateful.

After 12 years as Department Head, I know it will be difficult to change your perception of me. Few people in similar circumstances even try. However, I want to try. I have managed to keep alive some of my earlier research and development work and even moved into some new areas. Now, I hope that I can make these efforts more generally useful to education and I shall be needing and seeking your help. In the past, I have participated with several of you in these joint explorations into new territory. I hope that these can be intensified and that new ventures with more of you will be developed.

My new office will be Room 577 of Aderhold Hall. I look forward to working with you during the next few years.

Gratefully,

E. Paul Torrance

E. Paul Torrance
Alumni Foundation
Distinguished Professor
of Educational Psychology

JAPAN: A SATORI EXPERIENCE

In late 1978, the Japanese Society for the Promotion of Science invited Paul Torrance to conduct research and present seminars and lectures to professional associations and university students in Japan.[19] The Society invites renowned academics from different disciplines including science, literature, history, law, and education to study in Japan for three months. Pansy accompanied Paul on this 73-day study trip to encourage international cooperation in scientific research.

Japanese Symbol for *Satori*

Paul and Pansy had a very full and busy itinerary. They were hosted by Dr. Sato, Professor of American Education and Dean of the Faculty of Letters, Osaka City University. Saburo Sato, a former Professor Emeritus of Osaka City, and now a Professor of Marketing and Distribution Sciences at the University in Kobe City, first studied in the United States in 1949–50. He was one of the first Japanese teachers to be in the U.S. while Japan was still occupied by Allied Powers. His research interests have been to follow the trends of American education in order to improve Japanese education (which has been greatly influenced by the American model).

Fundamentally, both the U.S. and Japan have adopted democratic systems of schooling, but educational practices in Japan have been characterized by conformity and standardization, thus suppressing the creative potential of students. Dr. Sato's research deals with how to make Japanese education more productive so that every child can benefit and develop according to his or her strengths. He attributes this concept of developing the strengths in *all* students to Paul Torrance. The Torrances were astounded by the high degree of creativity they observed in the preschool.

Saburo Sato had been awarded a Fulbright research scholarship in 1975 and had studied with Paul Torrance at the University of Georgia. Dr. Sato was very appreciative of the friendship and generosity of Paul and Pansy Torrance. In return for their kindness, he applied to the Japanese Society for the Promotion of Science on behalf of Paul. The government grant was normally awarded to natural scientists. Dr. Sato thinks that Paul's brilliant record of academic achievements made his application successful.

Paul had been in Japan briefly in May of 1953 during the Korean Conflict when he was Director of the Survival Research Field Unit of the U.S. Air Force, but on this trip, he encountered many changes and a different national attitude. Paul was well known in Japan; his research and writing were influential with many Japanese educators and psychologists. Several Japanese scholars, particularly Sato, had studied with Paul at the University of Georgia, and Sato had translated Paul's book, *Guiding Creative Talent,* into Japanese. Several other

[19] Torrance, E.P. (1979). Report to the Japan Society for the Promotion of Science, February 22 (in possession of the author).

Japanese scholars later translated books by Torrance.

This was a most interesting experience for Paul because the Japanese tend to value and honor intuition and creativity while the western world tends to respect and promote logic and intelligence. These age-old value differences between the East and West seem difficult to change.

Paul continued his research while in Japan and wrote the manuscript for his book *The Search for Satori and Creativity* (1979) which was later published by Bearly Limited. *Satori* (see the symbol or character for *satori* at the beginning of this section) is a Japanese word meaning the highest level of creative insight possible for man to obtain through enlightenment. The symbol represents a human mind totally open and receptive to new ideas and thought processes. This idea of illumination and perfection permeates Japanese culture.

During their stay in Japan, the Torrances visited 17 colleges and universities, 15 kindergartens, 7 professional associations, and 20 other educational, industrial, or government organizations. Paul lectured, led seminars, and talked with specialists. He was interviewed by a number of Japanese newspapers who were extremely interested in his tests of creativity, which have been translated and used with children in Japan, and in his Future Problem Solving Program. A copy of an interview with Mr. S. Inni, editor in chief of the *News for Private Education Institutions,* dated January 15, 1979, is reproduced below.[20]

-3- 昭和54年1月15日 私学ニュース

特集 "創造性"の教育

E・P・トーランス教授本誌に語る

対談
ジョージア州立大学教授 E・P・トーランス
聞き手 本誌主幹 乾 晴伍

—創造性の教育—それは、まさしく教育の柱であり、人類普遍のエネルギーの源泉である。来るべき二十一世紀を展望し「わが国の教育は如何にあるべきか」を問うことは、私学人共通の課題である。

—アメリカで学生に、将来最も早く廃れる職業は?というアンケートをしたところ、それは"先生"という職業だ との答がかえってきた。急激なテンポで進む技術革新で機械化がさらに進み、新たな教材が開発されるとやがて自主学習でまかなえる時代がやってくる。教師が惰眠を貪っているようでは、"教師"という職業はやがて廃れてしまう——。

このショッキングな話題を持って、「創造性の教育」の世界的な権威者であるアメリカ・ジョージア大学のE・ポール・トーランス教授が来日した。

我国の状況をみれば、過酷な受験競争の中で子供たちの創造性、自主性が損われており、創造的能力の開発、人間性の教育、教育の現代化が強く求められている。

そこで本誌は、トーランス教授に独占インタビューを試み同教授の「創造性の教育」の真髄に迫ってみた。なお、通訳と解説は、トーランス教授の学説を我国に翻訳・紹介した大阪市立大学の佐藤三郎教授にお願いした。

---

[20] Interview with Mr. S. Inni, Editor-in-Chief of the *News for Private Education Institutions,* January 15, 1979. In Torrance Collection MSS 2606 #80. Athens, GA: Hargrett Rare Book and Manuscript Library, University of Georgia.

Paul Honored by Japanese

The Japanese honored Paul Torrance with a *festschrift* called *Creative Ability—Its Development and Evaluation* (Onda & Sato 1978). This was a collection of writings by Japanese creativity researchers who have been influenced by his work. The volume contains one article by Paul.

The President of Hiroshima University presented Paul with the Phoenix Medal, which is given to highly respected individuals for their significant contributions to society. At Kurume, another of Japan's leading higher learning institutions, the head of the music department composed two songs in Paul's honor.

Besides writing the manuscript of *The Search for "Satori" and Creativity*, Paul collected data to do comparative studies of American and Japanese students. The studies dealt with styles of learning and thinking, self-directed learning readiness, and images of the future. The studies would be co-authored with Dr. Sato and two of his graduate students.

Informally, Paul devoted considerable time to reading and discussing books on Japanese culture, with special attention to the creative thinking and creative achievements of the Japanese. Also, he took great interest in the study of preschool education in Japan and took over 1,000 photographs of learning activities in preschool. The archives at the University of Georgia contain volumes of these interesting photographs.

Paul found that in Japan there was an excellent national climate for creativity. The Prime Minister has made it a national policy, stating that there is a need for valuing the creativity of each individual and that it is the responsibility of everyone to stimulate each person to develop his or her potential to the fullest. Paul was also impressed with creativity in the preschools (ages 3–5).

However, it was Paul's impression that there is very little research in Japan in education on creativity. He found a disappointing lack of interest in creativity research among graduate students, except for a few graduate students at Hiroshima University. In his discussions with university professors, Paul learned that there was little financial support to conduct research in creativity, although some encouraging research has been done by a few professors such as professor Sato of Osaka City University.

Paul identified a number of cultural differences that may contribute to what has been called "a nation of 115 million overachievers." The preschools in Japan are highly creative. Paul was totally unprepared for what he saw. The quality of creative expressiveness and problem solving seemed, to Paul, to be beyond their developmental age. This strong start in school may account for the fact that there are no reading problems in Japanese schools and an almost complete literacy.

Creativity is honored and is a common word in Japanese vocabulary, and creative accomplishments are recognized in Japanese culture. Annual awards are given for creative achievements in areas such as ballet, art exhibitions, musical performance, composition, creative writing, science, invention, and oratory.

Japanese students prefer to learn in creative, intuitive ways rather than through rational, logical thinking. The Japanese believe that excellence is achieved through persistence—hard work, self-discipline, diligence, energy, effort, competence, and expertness. There are no short cuts. To attain "satori" requires intense devotion, being "in love with" something, and constant practice. Also, the Japanese believe in a strong image of the future—a "long look." This provides the motivation for such persistence.

Many Japanese are involved in self-directed learning because university education is very expensive. They understand that information will be the source of power in this postindustrial society. Too much of our "education" in the West is teacher or professor-directed, rather than self-initiated.

One of the reasons for the high productivity of the Japanese is the emphasis on group learning and problem solving. Paul noted that much of a student's time is spent in group study. There is a fierce pride in accomplishments of the group or team. Individuals develop their identity in accordance with how well the group performs. It is all right for a group or team to "overachieve."

Finally, although the Japanese have rules for just about everything, they are free to diverge, invent, and innovate within those rules. Their ability to use freedom creatively makes the difference. Paul, although somewhat disappointed in the actual creativity research in Japan, observed and read about the many cultural differences that have made the Japanese "ichiban" (number one) in many areas.

Paul related an anecdote to me about a man named Masae Kitagawa who owns a preschool in Japan. His school was bombed by the Americans and completely destroyed during World War II. Masae was very angry and always hated Americans, but meeting with Paul and Pansy Torrance during their study tour in Japan helped him get over these feelings. At that time, Masae was preparing his son to take over and run the preschool. Masae later sent his son, Sadayuki, to the University of Georgia to study with Paul Torrance and others. During the course of his study period, Sadayuki traveled with Paul and Pansy to Savannah, Georgia, in December of 1980 to assist them in conducting a workshop on the Future Problem Solving Program. Pansy suffered her first severe stroke on the return trip. Sadayuki Kitagawa helped by driving the car back to Athens. Shortly after this event, Sadayuki received instructions from his father in Japan to stay in Georgia as long as Pansy and Paul needed him—a sure sign that their animosity for Americans had been replaced by gratitude, respect, and love.

Akira Onda, a Professor of Psychology at Toyo University in Japan, recalls having dinner with Paul and Pansy Torrance in a Japanese tempura restaurant. Paul was most impressed with the taste of the food. He believed that it was a masterpiece of fine cooking coming from the chef's experiences over many years and his knowledge of foods. Paul appreciated the creativity involved in cooking and presenting such a delightful meal.

Yoshio Nozu, a Professor at Shimane University in Matsue, Japan, translated Paul's book *Gifted Children in the Classroom* into the Japanese language. He vividly recalls taking Paul Torrance to an art museum after a lecture Paul had delivered to parents at the University High School. The art museum contains an important collection of paintings by Taikan—a distinguished Japanese painter. Most people go to the museum to see his artwork; however, Paul Torrance was most interested in the paintings for children's books. Yoshio was impressed with Paul's independent thinking.

While in Japan, Paul had time to keep up with his research back home. He wrote to his colleague, Bee Bleedorn, and asked her to obtain addresses of Minnesota students involved in the longitudinal study. He told Bee, "our visit here has been beyond description. At every hand we have been so loaded with gifts and tokens of appreciation and friendship that we constantly feel overwhelmed."[21]

During the Torrance's three-month stay, their host Saburo Sato never heard any complaints from either of them. Paul was writing his book on *satori* late at night after keeping a heavy schedule in the daytime. Paul and Pansy left Osaka City on February 23, 1979, filled with warm memories, and traveled from there to Taiwan to visit former students. Sato wrote in a letter in 1985 that Japan would like to have Paul and Pansy return again for a study and lecture tour.

SOCIODRAMA: A NEW FRONTIER

Paul Torrance taught a course at the University of Georgia on sociodrama as a technique for solving problems creatively. Sociodrama is a form of role-playing which results in heightened awareness of issues surrounding a conflict or problem and in a resolution of the conflict or problem that is acceptable to both sides. It involves use of various production techniques or tools such as role reversal and "the magic shop." Paul invented some of these techniques. In the past, creative problem solving as a discipline had not given much attention to sociodrama. Paul's book, *Creative Problem Solving Through Role Playing,* (Torrance, Murdock, & Fletcher, in press), will undoubtedly assist in the training of sociodramatic directors in the classroom or in the personal development or therapeutic setting.

Paul's interest in sociodrama began in 1945 while he was in the Army and working as a psychiatric social worker. There, he learned about psychodrama, sociodrama, and sociometry. He felt that the techniques had great potential and wanted to learn all about them. Jacob L. Moreno and his assistant (later his wife) Zerka were the most creative teachers he ever had. They sparked his interest at the Psychodramatic Institute in Beacon, New York. Paul went on to study with other great sociodramatists and had an opportunity to teach the skills of socio-

---

[21] Letter from E. Paul Torrance to Bee Bleedorn. Osaka, Japan, February 12, 1979 (in possession of the author).

drama in his classes and for community groups.

The main use of role playing is in the prevention of behavior problems among the disadvantaged and other high-risk populations. It has been used in specific treatment programs with adolescents who exhibit behavior problems and with young offenders. Role playing is useful to teach new social behaviors and to improve problem-solving behavior.

During role playing, a conflict situation is identified and then various members of a group are cast into roles which they act out. Paul has invented a number of techniques or strategies that are used to resolve the conflict situation. The sociodramatist's role is to keep the action moving toward resolution. Often multiple solutions are reached which offer individuals a choice in resolving issues.

PAUL TORRANCE: CREATIVELY GIFTED BUT LEARNING DISABLED

"Don't waste a lot of expensive, unproductive energy in trying to be well-rounded. Learn the skills of interdependence, giving freely from the infinity of your greatest strengths."[22]

— E. Paul Torrance

In a surprising presentation to the International Conference of the Association for Adults and Children with Learning Disabilities in Atlanta, Georgia, in 1982, Paul Torrance revealed that he has spent more than 65 years as a person with learning disabilities and challenged the audience to broaden their concept of learning disabilities. Paul described his experiences as a creatively gifted child and adult with learning disabilities.

Paul's learning disabilities were non-academic but nevertheless caused him a great deal of shame and frustration. By age six, Paul's parents were aware of his giftedness and his learning disabilities. He had learned to walk and talk at a precocious age and was a fast runner, but he was not very strong and there were many tasks for which he showed no aptitude at all. As a result, he was not sent to school until age seven, as his parents thought he was not capable of walking the six-mile round trip to school and defending himself from the attacks of older and stronger children. Paul felt the shame of his ineptitude in not being able to plow a straight line. In his agrarian setting, this inability was more shameful to him than not being able to read, write, or do arithmetic. When he was thirteen, his father freed him by recognizing his inabilities (and abilities) and permitting him to follow his interests and strengths—that is, to go into academic studies. Paul was permitted to get an education, and he never looked back. He was free to play his own game. This tacit approval to pursue his

---

[22] Torrance, 1982a, p. 35.

strengths alienated Paul from his family, but it salvaged his self-esteem.

In school, college, and university, Paul was a high achiever who found learning easy. However, his learning disability surfaced from time to time throughout his career. He could not learn to write on the blackboard in a straight line, or to drive an automobile and keep it straight on the road, or to sing in tune, play a harmonica, march or dance in step, or whistle. He could not learn to wink, shoot a target, swim, or type using the touch system.

His failures to learn these skills caused humiliation, shame, and disgrace. He tried "faking it." In singing classes, he tried to fake singing or playing the mouth organ. In the Army during World War II, the only way he could pass marksmanship was for the range sergeant to fudge his score a little. Paul got some good advice from a musically talented four-year-old when he tried to sing along with a group of four- and five-year-old children. He said to Paul, "If you can't sing in tune, why don't you stop?" Paul learned a lesson that day: One cannot be strong in all areas of ability but rather must learn to rely on other people and compensate where possible. He capitalized on his strengths to become highly successful and now gives advice to creatively gifted people with learning disabilities. These suggestions are some of the conclusions from his 22-year longitudinal study of creative behavior:

> 1. Know your strengths. Understand them deeply. Take pride in them. Practice, develop, use, and exploit them.
>
> 2. Learn to free yourself from the expectations of others and walk away from the games that others insist that you play, even though you have no interest or aptitude for such games. Free yourself to play your own games in your own way in such a manner as to make the best possible use of your strengths, your potentialities.
>
> 3. Do not waste a lot of expensive, unproductive energy in trying to be well-rounded. Master the skills of interdependence, giving freely of your strength. What you give in this way is far more valuable than all you could give with mediocre performances of achievements for which you have no aptitude or will. People are generally highest motivated for the things that they do best. (Torrance, 1982a, p. 35)

Professor Georgi Kalushev visited Paul Torrance on at least three different occasions and was a member of the Bulgarian delegation of educators who met Paul and Pansy Torrance in Athens in February of 1980. He recalls Pansy telling a story about Paul's poor orientation skills. Apparently, Paul got lost in his neighborhood and telephoned Pansy at home, describing what he saw across the street and asked to be picked up. Dr. Kalushev personally has poor orientation in space and it occurred to him that if Professor Torrance can be "lost in space" and still be what he is, then he need not worry, but just capitalize on his own strengths.

Chris Lee, a university student at the University of Georgia, describes his experiences of "faking it." He was able to hide his disability and still get through school. He was able to get assistance to compensate for his language deficits which affected his spelling and reading at university and wrote a book called *Faking It* (Lee & Jackson, 1992) with the Coordinator of the University's Learning Disabilities Adult Clinic. At the University of Georgia, he was captain of the swimming team in his senior year. The book describes Chris Lee as a creative learner as he, like Paul capitalized on his strengths.

Paul's job made use of his strengths and did not demand use of his weaknesses or disabilities. When he made his "Growing Up Creatively Gifted with Learning Disabilities" speech, he was asked by someone in the audience, "But weren't you handicapped in getting and holding a job by not being able to drive?" Someone in the audience answered for him, "He never wanted to be a truck driver." Paul likes to cite an apt example of an individual who capitalized on strengths. Quincy Jones has won 25 Grammy Awards and composed the scores for 38 films, including *The Color Purple* and *Roots*. He also gathered together 60 of America's top musical talents for an eight-hour recording session to produce "We Are The World" in 1985, which became the best-selling single of the decade. Creativity comes naturally to Jones. When composing, the ideas keep coming to him. He finds himself writing in taxis or in airplanes, using menus, gum wrappers, anything handy. Jones says, "It's no big deal because this is all I can do." He, too, couldn't learn to drive a car.

In February of 1992, Paul corresponded with a young person who was participating in the Creative Scholars Mentorship Program and was concerned with how to deal with her learning disability and her giftedness at the same time. Paul's response is enlightening:[23]

> Dear L.K.:
>
> I appreciated your excellent letter. I know Adrienne Kinkaid has been enjoying interaction with you. Your questions are very insightful and I shall try to respond to them as best I can.
>
> In my childhood and youth there was no such thing as an LD category. My own insights concerning my learning disabilities was a dawning over many years. I suppose the beginning of this dawning occurred when I was in the second grade. I received excellent grades in reading, arithmetic, and other subjects but I received a failing grade in writing. I wrote letters very small and not on a straight line. My mother, who was an excellent writer, made a copybook for me using lined paper. When I was not busy at school, she told me to practice writing using this home-made copybook. As a result of this experience I developed penmanship very close to the copy. When I began to learn farm tasks I became aware of other learning disabilities. This was also apparent to my mother and father. I was still doing good work at school, though they told me I would have to get an educa-

[23] Letter to L.K. from E. Paul Torrance. Athens, Georgia, February 26, 1992 (in possession of the author).

tion as I could never make a living on the farm. When it came time to learn how to drive an automobile my ineptitude was apparent. I could not steer an automobile just as I could not steer a mule and plow a straight row. Some of these, like handwriting, I was able to compensate for. For those tasks that I could not master, I stopped trying and devoted myself to things I could excel in.

Since we have become more knowledgeable about learning disabilities, I have met so many children who were gifted learners but whose educational progress was retarded by some kind of learning disability. I have seen many of them who developed wonderful compensation techniques. For example, one girl who was considered "dumb" throughout elementary school; however, she began learning some compensation techniques as she moved into high school. For example, in high school chemistry, the class she was in was required to learn the periodic table. She had always been very poor at memorization. To learn the periodic table she turned it into a song and dance, since she was very talented in music and movement. She earned an A on this assignment and remembers the periodic table in chemistry to this day. I am enclosing a paper that I wrote a few years ago in which I describe some other techniques. It is a matter of using your strength to overcome the disability.

You say that your strongest ability is in synthesis. This is a very important ability and will carry you far. The method that your boyfriend is using to teach you problem solving is very much like the problem solving method used by the Japanese. It requires synthesis and intuition. They put ideas on small cards or bits of paper and begin arranging them in clusters, much as your boyfriend does. I am also enclosing a reprint of an article that I co-authored on the Japanese method of problem solving. It relies very strongly on right-brain strategies. The method used by your boyfriend is apparently quite like this.

Your strengths are apparently specialized right-brain learning activities. You were taught Calculus apparently by a teacher who used left-brain strategies. You are apparently using right-brain strategies in your karate class. The other students and the teacher may be favoring left-brain strategies. Of the books that I have written, the *Search for Satori and Creativity* may be useful to you. It is out of print now but you may find it in your university library. I am in the middle of revising it and it will be published under a new title.

I believe you will also find useful some of the articles in *Education and the Creative Potential.* I am sending a copy of this book under separate cover. I am also sending you a copy of a poster which I believe you will find useful.

Yours cordially,

E. Paul Torrance

Paul Torrance is concerned about broadening the concept of learning disabilities to include non-academic disabilities. These individuals need support groups to help them invent creative ways of learning what their disabilities now prevent or make difficult.

MENTORING: WRITING ABOUT AND LIVING THE CONCEPT

Paul Torrance has researched and written a number of articles and books on mentorship, and he himself has been a personal mentor to many individuals around the world. A mentor is one who encourages, helps, prompts, teaches, supports, listens, and acts as a role model in the growth and development of the protege. Michael Shaughnessy (1991) has written an article about Paul Torrance and his contribution as a mentor.

Paul first discussed mentorship in his book *Guiding Creative Talent* in 1962. He said that, "Almost always, whenever creativity occurs and persists, there is some other individual or agent who plays the role of sponsor or mentor" (p. 8). Paul has demonstrated statistically that having a mentor aids creative achievement.

Besides writing about the importance of mentorship and creative achievement, Paul established, along with others at the Torrance Center for Creative Studies, a network of creative individuals who were willing to share their expertise with others. The Creative Scholars Mentor Program was initiated in 1985 by the Torrance Center and later was taken over by Scholastic Testing Services. However, it is no longer functioning due to the heavy administrative commitment required to keep it operating and limited funds. Paul got Harry Passow, president of the World Council on Gifted Children, interested in the program and the Council voted to take it over. A committee was appointed, but it was not able to attract the necessary funding.

Paul also implemented the International Network of Gifted Students and Their Teachers. The first year there were 6,000 members, and it ran for three years with good response. It put teachers and gifted students in touch with each other to share and encourage various interests.

Paul has made it a priority to continue his mentoring of people through letters, phone calls, and his care and concern for others. He is the consummate mentor.

Influence on Scholars

M. K. Raina, India's leading proponent of creativity, refers to Paul's interest in studying creativity in many cultures and countries as the "Torrance Phenomenon" (Raina, 1992). Dr. Raina quotes Gerald Middents, who recently expressed this "Torrance Phenomenom" in a different way:

> Throughout a wide range of countries and cultures, your hands have reached out. You have touched innumerable people directly or through your prolific writing and research. Inter-cultural understanding has widened horizons and countered

narrow ethnocentricism. Your fingers have pointed toward a better future in which people will creatively solve problems leading to global peace and justice."24

Unknown to most people, Paul Torrance has assisted scholars in many parts of the world, giving them advice on their research and their writing. M. K. Raina often sent Paul draft manuscripts of various papers and reports. They would come back meticulously edited and corrected, each line read carefully. His sense of perfection indeed brought fulfillment to others.

Dr. Berenice "Bee" Bleedorn is an excellent example of someone who has been mentored by Paul Torrance and who continues to spread the word about creativity to people everywhere she goes. In a letter to Paul, Bee recounts the impact she has had in Minnesota and beyond as a result of his research and good mentorship. As a Consultant for the Gifted and Talented with the Minnesota Department of Education in 1972–73, she brought the message of creative studies to countless teachers and administrators. She provided leadership by conducting workshops all over the state using a broadened concept of giftedness that included the creatively talented. In six months, over 1,000 teachers and administrators were trained and called "Contact Representatives." The Torrance-broadened concept of gifted and talented was well received.

Bee has since established her own consultantship called "Education for Creative Development." She took on a contract with Pike Lake School, north of St. Paul, to train the staff on the subject of creative teaching and learning. She promoted the concept of providing learning experiences in creative thinking for all kinds of students rather than just for those identified for special programs. As a result of her work at Pike Lake School, she and the principal, Harry Braunes, made a proposal for funding from the state. It was the beginning of Project Reach. Out-of-town authorities were brought in to help teach and stimulate interest in the creative process. Individuals such as Paul (and Pansy) Torrance, Frank Williams, Joe Khatena and Calvin Taylor helped make Project Reach prominent in Minnesota. It produced a line of teaching materials. Later, Joyce Juntune directed the program and brought it into national recognition. It may still be operating.

In 1973, Bee designed and introduced courses in Creative Problem Solving and Future Studies at Metropolitan State University in St. Paul, Minnesota. It was an alternative, degree-granting, community-based college. Classes were scheduled throughout the Twin Cities, as there was no campus. Since Bee left in 1980, Metropolitan State University has become more traditional.

Along the way, Bee and some of her students have made connections between the creative process and humor. She often presents workshops on "Humor and Creativity" and has published a book with the help of a student, Sara McKelvey, entitled *Humor: Lessons in Laughter for Learning and Living* (1984).

---

24 Letter from Gerald Middents to Paul Torrance on the occasion of his retirement. March 23, 1985 (in possession of the author).

Knowledge of Bee's work in creativity was spreading in the Minneapolis/St. Paul area, and in 1979, with the support of a faculty member and the Dean of Graduate Education at the College of St. Thomas, a program for teachers of the gifted and talented was started. Bee joined the faculty of the College of St. Thomas in 1980. Currently, a Master of Arts in gifted, creative, and talented education is offered at the College of St. Thomas in St. Paul. Two strands are available to students who wish either to study for a terminal Master's degree or who intend to seek degrees beyond the Master's level. Bee initiated the 11-course graduate program. As of 1993, Bee has a full-time split appointment in Entrepreneurship and Business Communication in the new St. Thomas campus building in downtown Minneapolis. She has presented at many conferences for educators and for the business community at the local, state, national and international levels. Berenice "Bee" Bleedorn continues to be a strong influence in Minnesota in promoting and teaching creative concepts espoused by her mentor, E. Paul Torrance.

Another individual who has been influenced by Paul Torrance's work is Dr. Julian Stanley, Director of the Study of Mathematically Precocious Youth and Professor of Psychology at John Hopkins University in Baltimore, Maryland. Paul and Dr. Stanley are contemporaries, they are fellow Georgians, and they have similar backgrounds. They are both vitally interested in talented youth. Julian was born in Macon, Georgia, and grew up in East Point—not far from the Torrance home near Milledgeville. Although Stanley is three years younger than Paul, he was so rapidly accelerated in high school and college that he graduated at about the same time as Paul. Both were teachers in Georgia—Paul at the Georgia Military College and Julian at Atlanta high schools (teaching science and mathematics from 1937 to 1942). Stanley then went to Harvard University to complete his graduate studies.

Julian Stanley has been at John Hopkins University since 1948. The professional careers of the two men have taken quite different paths. Julian Stanley has been interested in talented youth in the specific subject area of mathematics while Paul has explored the depths of creativity in all ages of people, but particularly children. The only interaction between the two men occurred in 1977 when Julian Stanley asked Paul to prepare a chapter for his edited book entitled *The Gifted and Creative: A Fifty-Year Perspective.*

Stanley said this to me about the different approach Paul Torrance took to study the creatively gifted: "I've had to ponder long and hard whether or not it is important to study what I sometimes harshly call 'creativity in a subject matter vacuum,' divorced from school subjects or disciplines such as mathematics. I've continued to prefer the subject-matter approach, but Dr. Torrance's work has certainly made me think."

Dr. Joe Khatena has been greatly influenced by the mentorship and friendship of Paul Torrance since 1964. Dr. Khatena has developed two creativity tests and has written several articles and books. In addition, Paul Torrance has helped further Joe's career. In 1975, Joe became a fellow of the American Psychological Association as a result of Paul's recommendation. Paul has been somewhere in the background as Joe has achieved many honors over the years, including a Headship of Educational Psychology at Mississippi State University, two Fulbright Professorships, and a recent appointment as Visiting Professor at the University of Malaya.

Dr. Khatena is only one example of the many scholars who have benefited from Paul's mentorship. Kobus Neethling of Capetown, South Africa, a leader in creativity studies in that country, is inspired by Paul Torrance. In the 1980s, he was the chief planner for the gifted. He trained people in gifted education, creative problem solving, and scoring and interpreting the Torrance Tests of Creative Thinking. He introduced the Future Problem Solving Program throughout the Cape province. When South Africa decided to establish a Bureau of Information, he was chosen to head the research division. Before he accepted the position, he was given permission to train all personnel in the Bureau of Information in creative problem solving. After his successes in this position, he was asked to train other departments in creative problem solving. Finally, he was asked to accept a position in the Ministry of Law and Order, where he set up a network of trainers. Having set this up, he currently serves only as a consultant to the Ministry to keep it going. He has now established a national foundation, which will permit him to work with the government as well as other groups.

There were significant changes in gifted education in South Africa during the 1980s, even though the planners in the Cape Education Department have been mostly ex-headmasters steeped in the traditions of Afrikaner's Christian National Education, formal learning, and a complete denial of the child's basic creative expression. Through awareness of the writings of American psychologists and educators, predominantly Paul Torrance, this vital aspect of a child's creative expression has been recognized and accepted.

A visiting scholar of Paul Torrance at the University of Georgia, Francisco Menchén Bellón, returned to his native Spain and wrote a book on creativity entitled *La Creatividad en la Educación* that has become very popular in that country. Torrance's work has widened the horizons in Spain, and his teachings are being used in many seats of learning including the universities in Madrid, Barcelona, Valencia, Sevilla, and Santiago de Compostela. Dr. Bell.n, as inspector of schools in Madrid, has introduced creativity—its development and evaluation—into the curricula and syllabi of the country's schools.

Dr. Bruce Mitchell, Professor of Education at Eastern Washington University, spent part of his sabbatical leave in 1979 with Paul at the University of Georgia. They worked on several projects together. Paul helped Dr. Mitchell realize that creative thinking is an integral part of intelligence. Moreover, he provided Dr. Mitchell with valuable ideas about the thinking potential of poor children and motivated Mitchell's interest in identifying poor children to participate in gifted and talented programs. In Bruce Mitchell's words, "More than any other educator, Paul's been my main source of inspiration. He has taught me to deal with adversity and maintain a professional bearing."

Paul has shared his materials with teachers who have expressed an interest in teaching for creativity. One such person was Doris Shallcross, who began the first high school class in creativity in 1965 at Cleveland Heights, Ohio. She used his work as the foundation for the program and still does today. Dr. Doris Shallcross now is a professor at the University of Massachusetts in Amherst and serves as president of the Board of Trustees with Paul Torrance at the Creative Education Foundation at Buffalo, New York.

June Maker, a contemporary advocate for the gifted and creative at the University of Arizona, credits Paul Torrance for her current research. She is developing a checklist of problem-solving behaviors for disadvantaged minority students. Torrance's research definition of creativity as problem solving has had a definite impact, as well as his checklist of creative positives.

Paul Torrance's ideas and work live in the hearts of his colleagues, friends, and students, and in the hearts of students of colleagues and friends of friends. His influence has been positive and far-reaching.

Dedications to E. Paul Torrance

> Personally, Professor Paul Torrance has been my guiding light and without him and his recognition of what we have achieved, I feel we would all have been professionally impoverished. His influence from even that great distance was fundamental.
>
> Ellen Smith, Principal
> Ellerton Primary School, Capetown, South Africa

Ellerton Primary School was the first desegregated school in South Africa. Under Ellen Smith, this school has been very successful with desegregation.

Several books written by colleagues, friends and/or students have been dedicated to Paul Torrance, such as the following from Maker and Schiever (1989):

TO

E. Paul Torrance

respected mentor and teacher
of many authors in this volume

who consistently, kindly, and tirelessly
has reminded all of us

"Differences are not deficits, but strengths."

The following note was handwritten on the inside cover of Mohamed Alieldin's dissertation, which was completely written in Egyptian.

> To my great professor
> Dr. E. Paul Torrance for the
> greatest guidance and support I
> have ever seen, and I have
> ever received.
>
> — Mohamed Alieldin, 1/30/78

Bruce Bracken (1993) a Professor at Memphis State University, recently developed a psychometric scale called the Assessment of Interpersonal Relations. As a former graduate student of Paul Torrance, he dedicated the scale to Paul and Pansy. He wrote:

> To Dr. E. Paul Torrance
> for stimulating my creative interests
> and in memory to Mrs. Pansy Torrance
> for her sincere interest in others.

Paul Torrance received a book from a woman who was among the students tested in Minneapolis in 1959. She fits Torrance's definition of a "beyonder." She has had a stunning array of creative accomplishments. The book is inscribed as follows:

> "To E. Paul Torrance, the mentor I've never met, with thanks!"

Visiting Scholars: Trek to Athens

During his later years at the University of Georgia, Paul's reputation as a leader in his field was recognized by professionals from all over the world. Many made trips to visit and study with him and sought his counsel on significant projects.

In the 1979–80 academic year, Paul met with visiting professors and post-doctoral scholars from several countries. Each of these visiting scholars was interested in Paul's research in creativity and was personally involved in work in this area. When these individuals visited Paul at the University of Georgia, he always entertained them at his home. Among those who visited for various lengths of time (one day to six months) were: Robert Livingston, M.D., Professor of Neurosciences, University of California at San Diego; Bruce Mitchell, Eastern Washington State University, Cheney, Washington; Professor Neil O'Conor and Dr. Hermelin, Medical Research Council, Developmental Psychology Unit, London, England; Jock L. Omond, Office for the Gifted and Talented, Port Elizabeth, South Africa; Abdalla Soliman, Professor of Psychology, University of

Kuwait; Nayana Tara, University of Bangalore, India; Professors Ronald and Juliette Goldman, School of Education, La Trobe University, Bundoora, Victoria, Australia; and Terutsugu Ando, Fukui University, Fukui-shi, Japan.

One of Paul's visiting scholars, Dr. Emily Stewart, Director of the Program for the Gifted and Talented in Dallas, Texas, was fascinated by his description of the research he had done as a young man serving in the military. This research, dealing with pilots who flew fighter planes in the Korean War (described in Chapter Three of this book), set Paul on his life-long quest to understand the risk taker. Dr. Stewart became acquainted with the traits of the ace fighter pilots and immediately saw the connection with and similarity to Paul's later work on characteristics of creative persons.

I too was fortunate to be one of the visiting scholars. In 1976, I was involved as the Director of the Canada/Mexico region of the National Association of School Psychologists. I had met the Georgia representative, Dr. Bert Richmond, in our executive meeting, and he became a professional colleague and friend. Bert worked with Paul Torrance in the Department of Educational Psychology and arranged for me to study with him. As a psychologist, I realized that my education was incomplete—I knew very little about the nature and nurture of creativity. In June of 1983, I spent two weeks in Athens, Georgia, learning from Paul Torrance how to score and interpret the Torrance Tests of Creative Thinking. Each day he gave me a test protocol to score, and we would meet the next morning to review my scoring and interpretation.

During my visit to the University of Georgia, a contingent of educators from Taiwan and two professors from James Madison University (Harrisburg, Virginia) and Temple University (Philadelphia, Pennsylvania) were visiting Paul as well. Later during the school year, scholars from Japan, England, Spain, Scotland, and India also made the trip to visit Paul and gain from his experience and creativity.

INCUBATION MODEL: TEACHING CREATIVE THINKING

Paul Torrance developed a method of teaching creative thinking that used a three-stage instructional model—the Incubation Model. The Incubation Model integrates creativity objectives with content or subject objectives. Paul first applied the model when he served as a consultant to Ginn and Company on their reading programs 360 and 720. For about ten years, the Ginn Reading Program was popular and successful, but the political situation was unfavorable and it was phased out.

The *Incubation Model of Teaching: Getting Beyond the Aha!* by Torrance and Safter was published in 1990 by Bearly Limited. It provides a model for teaching creatively that can be applied to all levels of schooling and post-school training. The book provides a model framework for lesson development and sample lessons that can be used by teachers. The lessons describe what happens not only during a lesson but before and after. The three stages of incubation are heightening anticipation, deepening expectations, and keeping it going. It makes explicit the methods that successful teachers use in helping their students become better thinkers.

While Paul has been criticized for using unorthodox research methods, as head of the Department of Educational Psychology, Research, and Measurement, he has been disappointed that the courses in research methods do not include historical methods, qualitative methods, the methods used by futurists, and special techniques such as Stephenson's Q-technique. Finally the Social Science Education Department has begun using qualitative methods and some of the Educational Psychology graduate students have taken some of these courses and found them valuable. Now, there is an annual meeting at the University of Georgia on qualitative research.

Dr. Tammy Safter, a consultant in gifted and creative education and a co-author with Paul Torrance, has become a spokesperson for creativity. Her modus operandi is to see creativity understood, fostered, and developed. In fact, her work in creativity is more important than anything else she does in the name of gifted education. She is trying to help teachers understand that teaching more creatively is good for everyone.

MANAGING CRITICISM

Joe Renzulli, professor of educational psychology at the University of Connecticut, learned something significant from Paul Torrance about dealing with critics. Renzulli and Torrance were visiting Don Treffinger in his home in Buffalo, New York, and they were discussing some criticism that had been leveled at creativity research and Paul's work in a recent article in a professional journal. Paul said that anyone and everyone had their right to comment and criticize, but that one must push ahead in a direction that one feels is important. What Paul did not say, but what the others in the room understood clearly, was that when one is on the cutting edge of knowledge and indeed in the forefront of major ideas about the study and understanding of human beings, one is always going to have people nipping at one's heels.

Paul's courage showed in the way he acknowledged people's right to criticize, and yet this did not deter him. This was a significant experience for Joe Renzulli as his theoretical work was just emerging and he had his fair share of critics. He learned that day that courage comes from accepting one's critics but not allowing them to discourage you from your quest. Indeed, Renzulli came to believe that the way one should approach the issue of criticism is to find out those aspects of your work that are being criticized the most, and then go out and do more work related to that criticism—because it is probably the only aspect of your work that is truly unique.

Harry Passow, professor emeritus at the Teachers' College at Columbia University in New York, said:

> There are few individuals who have had as great an impact on nurturing human potential as has Paul Torrance. He has been criticized and his work has been questioned, but Paul has responded with honesty and grace. I have always been sad that he has had to spend so much time defending his research and his work against critics who simply have not made a fraction of the contribution to the field that Paul has.[25]

PANSY AND PAUL: A LOVING RELATIONSHIP

While reviewing materials in the Torrance Collection at the University of Georgia, I came across countless valentines and other special day cards of endearment from Pansy to Paul or vice versa. Dr. Morris Stein told me that one cannot talk of Paul without mentioning Pansy. Whenever he attended meetings where the two of them were present, it was a pleasure to observe their loving relationship. In an age when so many of his colleagues were involved in multiple marriages and countless relationships with insignificant others, it was heartening and uplifting to watch Pansy and Paul working and being together. Mary Frasier, Director of the Torrance Center at the University of Georgia, considered Paul and Pansy's relationship to be "perfectly balanced."

Between 1967 and 1971, Paul and Pansy worked together on a series of articles for music teachers in grades 1, 2, and 3 in a quarterly journal called *Music for Primaries*. They applied their creative teaching approach to help music educators teach sounds—"Games with Sound." They also worked together in a variety of other ways, as described throughout this book.

Pansy felt a sincere concern for Paul's students. At one time, she became concerned that the marriages of many graduate assistants in the department of educational psychology were being broken by the stress of graduate school and inadequate finances. Pansy made it her mission to inquire and counsel students about the importance of their families. She apparently would stop the graduate students in the hall and ask them how their marriage was, explaining that she was distressed by all of the broken marriages. She even advised Paul to have the faculty stop working the doctoral-level graduate assistants so hard, and telephoned some of the wives and spoke with them about the difficulties of being married to a doctoral student.

Pansy was very much a free spirit. One amusing incident illustrates her idiosyncratic spirit and how Paul coped with that spirit. Paul was giving a guest lecture in a psychology class one day, when Pansy burst into the class and asked Paul what clothes he wanted to be packed for a trip he was about to take.

---

[25] Personal correspondence from Harry Passow. September, 1992.

Apparently, they chatted for a minute or two, and then Pansy turned to the class and asked, "Has Paul ever told you that he wears colored briefs?" The class laughed incessantly, while Paul blushed profusely. He merely shook his head in embarrassed disbelief and continued his lecture. This sort of outburst from Pansy became expected, and Paul almost seemed to enjoy being teased publicly by her.

The following incident, reported in *The Atlanta Constitution*, (Hudspeth, 1983), illustrates Pansy's strong resolve regarding inconsiderate and irresponsible behavior:

> This Pansy is no pansy: Athens' Pansy Torrance watched a man in a parked car set a paper cup outside his door on the parking lot. She walked over, picked up the cup and handed it to the man saying, "I believe this belongs to you." The man threw the cup out the window. Pansy picked it up and tossed it back in the car. The man angrily backed out, peeled off and as he did, tossed the cup out again. Pansy picked it up and put it in a waste can as a bystander noted, "Trash comes in many forms, doesn't it?"

The lighter side of Pansy Torrance was often evident in her verbal repartee. The following story appeared in *The Athens Banner-Herald* ("Dateline All Over Georgia," 1970):

> ATHENS, GA—Mrs. E. P. Torrance offers her sympathy because of the hubcap which keeps falling off of my pick-up camper. She also offers her own hubcap story:
>
> "One evening at the head of a long string of automobiles, I heard what sounded like a hubcap fall off. So I pulled over and the fellow behind me yelled, 'Hey, lady, you lost a hubcap.' So I thanked him, parked the car and started looking. While hunting along side the road, a highway patrolman came along, stopped and said, 'Are you in trouble?' I told him, 'No, I've just lost a hubcap.'
>
> "The patrolman walked around the car, then looked at me and said, 'Lady, you have four.'"
>
> Mrs. Torrance believes she is the only driver in Georgia who has "self-returning" hubcaps.

Pansy was often a special lecturer for Paul in his university classes on creative problem solving. One of Pansy's hobbies was using part of nature, such as a root, and transforming it into some whimsical creature or animal.

Pansy Joins Paul

In Georgia, Paul was still aware of the major conflict in his life—that of balancing the demands of the job with his home life. He tried to keep a reasonable balance, but the demands of his career were so great that he failed. There were times when Pansy wished that Paul could drive a car, and she could not understand that he could not learn. Pansy could not understand why he had not developed muscularly. Paul had always wondered, too, and he could not help her. The only real conflict was over Paul's having to work so hard, and such long hours. Ultimately, the conflict lessened at the University of Georgia when Paul's career became Pansy's career. She became a willing, supportive, and contributing partner in Paul's research and teaching activities.

Dr. Jack Presbury and Morgan Henderson wrote a song about Paul and Pansy entitled, "Nobody Said It Was Going To Be Easy."[26]

NOBODY SAID IT WAS GOING TO BE EASY

Written for Pansy and Paul Torrance
by Jack Presbury and Morgan Henderson

We've had our good times
We've had our bad times
But the hard times
Never seemed too hard to take.
And my love is as strong
As the day you came along
To teach me how to bend
And never break.

I see the others
Hurt by their lovers
Hoping just to live
To love again.
But I knew from the start
When I gave you my heart
That you would always be
My lover and my friend.

CHORUS: Nobody said it was going to be easy
Nobody said that our load would be light
Nobody said we could come this far together
And it was so easy
Nobody was right.

Those who have seen us
Think they know what's between us
And they wonder
How we found a love so true.
And how can we say
We just lived it each day
And hardly even noticed as it grew?

And if we should never
Make it through to forever
I still think
We made it all the way.
Give me sunshine or rain
Give me pleasure or pain
I wouldn't take forever
For today.

---

26 Unpublished poem written for Paul and Pansy Torrance (in possession of the author).

Pansy had a massive stroke in December 1980, when she and Paul were returning to Athens from Savannah, Georgia, after doing a workshop on the Future Problem Solving Program. At first they did not realize that it was a stroke. However, the partner of Pansy's heart doctor immediately suspected it and ordered a CAT scan. They found a blood clot about the size of a pancake on her brain. Surgery was performed.

Paul was forced to postpone a lot of his research and speaking engagements so that he could assist Pansy at home. At age 65, he began to contemplate retirement for the first time.

During this time, several people took advantage of Paul's trusting nature. Paul hired a person to do housework, but each time she came she borrowed more than she had earned. When she got $800 ahead of Paul, she didn't come back. A man cut the lawn once and promised to help in the future. Before he could come back to work, he stopped by five times to "borrow" money for prescriptions for his baby, a flat tire, and other "necessities," promising to do work in return for the loans. He also never returned. One of the nurses Paul employed for Pansy forged checks for a five-month period to the tune of $5,000. She removed the canceled checks from Paul's statements. Fortunately, the bank made photostatic copies of all checks cashed, and three people correctly identified the forgeries.

During the time of Pansy's illness, on March 17, 1982, a special event was organized in Minneapolis. At the instigation of Bee Bleedorn, Paul's friend and colleague, the College of St. Thomas, St. Paul Public Schools, and Honeywell Corporate Office honored Paul and Pansy for their work toward recognizing and fostering creativity.

Nava Butler-Por, a Professor from the University of Haifa in Israel who was on sabbatical leave in 1985, visited with Paul Torrance in Athens. She recalls arriving at his home, and there he was in the garden preparing a bouquet for Pansy. She says she was moved at the sight of Paul at the dining table holding Pansy's hand, who by this time was an invalid because of a series of severe strokes.

Dr. Tammy Safter, a consultant in gifted education and creativity in Aiken, South Carolina, says that her conversations with Paul during Pansy's illness stand out in her mind. Dr. Safter was vividly aware of their love, devotion, caring, and pain. Paul felt Pansy's pain at least as much as she did. Regardless of the situation, Paul put being with her and doing things for her first. His own health suffered as a result, but he would not have it any other way.

ESTABLISHMENT OF THE TORRANCE CENTER FOR CREATIVE STUDIES: A LIVING MEMORIAL

"His achievements have been recognized in many ways. Perhaps the most significant is the creation of the Torrance Center for Creative Studies at the University."

Opinions
Athens Banner-Herald, March 20, 1985

Dr. Mary Frasier provided the leadership for the establishment of the Torrance Center for Creative Studies. She is a personable South Carolinean who taught high school for 12 years before receiving her master's degree in guidance and counseling from South Carolina State College and a doctorate in gifted and talented education from the University of Connecticut under the supervision of Dr. Joe Renzulli. In anticipation of Paul Torrance's retirement, Dr. Frasier developed an ambitious proposal. She wanted to recognize his contributions to education and continue his research on the identification and development of creative potential. Mary Frasier developed a plan to create a center in Paul Torrance's name at the University of Georgia. The proposal was completed in August 1982.

The proposed plan was discussed and supported by several key individuals at the University of Georgia, including Dr. W. Louis Bashaw, Head of the Department of Educational Psychology, and Dr. Katherine Blake, acting Dean of the College of Education. The office of the Dean of Education, through Dr. Blake, indicated that they would support the concept of a Torrance Center as long as it did not require funding and if Mary Frasier could find available space. She did find the necessary space and ran the Center out of an office for a short time. It has since moved twice and now resides in a large office suite with adjacent space used as a reading room. Dr. Virginia Trotter, Vice President for Academic Affairs at that time, moved the proposal forward through the necessary university channels.

The Torrance Studies of Gifted, Creative, and Future Behaviors was established during the 1983–84 school year with Mary Frasier as director and Deborah Davis as administrative coordinator and secretary. Programs and services that were in existence before the establishment of the Center were continued and improved. These programs included the Future Problem Solving Program and the Challenge Program that reflected the philosophy and teaching of Paul Torrance. The establishment of the Torrance Studies of Gifted, Creative, and Future Behaviors at the University of Georgia was widely acclaimed by leaders of gifted/creative movements. Irving Sato, Director of the National/State Leadership Training Institute on the Gifted and Talented, represented that group when he wrote to Dr. Fred Davison, President of the University of Georgia: "Certainly he deserves recognition as a generous, intelligent, quietly enthusiastic, influential, and dedicated educator, and your university's action is such a fitting tribute and most appropriate climax to a career of distinction."[27] The Center was later renamed "Torrance Center for Creative Studies."

The general goals of the Torrance Center are to provide a research program, professional development opportunities, and publications. Specifically, the goals are:

---

[27] Letter from Irving Sato to Dr. F. Davidson, January 6, 1984. Torrance Collection MSS 2606 #30. Athens, GA: Hargrett Rare Book and Manuscript Library, University of Georgia.

Research Program
- To preserve, protect, and make available the papers of E. Paul Torrance for present and future researchers.
- To continue the seminal work of E. Paul Torrance in the identification of development of creative potential.
- To stimulate new research in creative, gifted, and future studies.

Professional Development
- To provide opportunities to educators, school children, as well as professionals in business and industry, for professional development and training in gifted, creative, and future behaviors.

Publications
- To provide learning resource materials for educators and the business community.

The research program has three components. The Visiting Scholars Program stimulates and supports research by national and international scholars on creative, gifted, and future studies. As of December of 1992, 25 visiting scholars had been invited to the Torrance Center to work on various projects. Many individuals from many countries of the world have come to study for brief periods of time, and the Center encourages them to do so. Many are interested in reading original manuscripts of E. Paul Torrance; others are engaged in original research in creativity and are seeking advice and further assistance; and still others wish to visit programs for the gifted and talented in and around Athens, Georgia. Table 2 lists visiting scholars and the purposes of their visit.

The Torrance Center for Creative Studies has established a program to provide recognition to scholars concerned with the identification and development of gifted and creative potential. Those recognized are named Torrance Research Fellows with initial appointments for a period of five years. Research Fellows collaborate with the Center on research projects and publications and promote the research and instructional goals of the Center. At the 1989 Annual E. Paul Torrance Lecture at the University of Georgia, five individuals were appointed as Torrance Research Fellows:

Dr. Kay Bruch, University of Georgia, Retired
Dr. Aileen Johnson, Lamar State University, Beaumont, Texas
Dr. Gail Lewis, Northwestern State University of Louisiana and the Louisiana School for Math, Science and the Arts
Dr. Garnet Millar, Coordinator, Special Educational Services, Education Response Centre, Edmonton, Alberta, Canada
Dr. Jeanette Parker, University of Southwestern Louisiana.

Kay Bruch is coordinating a model program for young creative scholars. The

Table 2
Selected Visiting Scholars—Torrance Center

Who	Where	Purpose
• Abdalla Soliman Professor of Psychology (1985–86)	Kuwait University	Techniques to Study and Develop Creativity in the Arab Countries
• Garnet Millar Consultant with Alberta Education (July, 1986)	Edmonton, Alberta, Canada	Entrepreneurship in the Alberta Curriculum
• M. K. Raina National Council of Educational Research and Training (September 1986–January 1987)	New Delhi, India	Creative Behavior: Perceptions of Parents and Teachers About the Ideal Child in India and the U.S.
• Kyoko Nakagawa Associate Professor	Nyogo, Japan	How Creativity is Fostered in Young Children
• Kari Tapid Uusikyla Associate Professor (July 1991–July 1992)	Helsinki, Finland	Theory of Giftedness/Creativity
• Mohamed Abdulla Al-Baili Assistant Professor	United Arab Emirates	Promoting Creativity in the Classroom
• B. K. Passi Professor and Head Department of Education D. A. University (June–September 1987)	Indore, India	Instructional Model for Enhancing Incubation for Teacher Educators in Georgia

program is being piloted in the State of Louisiana. Jeanette Parker and Gail Lewis are designing and conducting intensive services for creative children through day and residential summer programs. Aileen Johnson is providing a challenge program for young creative scholars at Lamar State University, using the Torrance Tests of Creative Thinking and instructional strategies derived from Torrance's research.

The **Reading Room**, which is adjacent to the Torrance Center in the College of Education, University of Georgia, is available to students, faculty, educators, and parents. It contains historical and current articles, books, and curriculum materials that pertain to the study and teaching of creative, gifted, and futures education.

The **E. Paul Torrance Archives** are located in the Hargrett Rare Book and Manuscript Library at the University of Georgia. The Torrance Archives contain the largest collection in the world of information on creative, gifted, and future studies. Among the Torrance Archives are a number of important collections:

- **Creativity Collection of Books, Monographs, and Other Printed Media.** Assembled over a period of 27 years, this is probably the largest collection of printed materials on creativity in existence.
- **Collection on Giftedness.** Not as large as the Creativity Collection, this collection contains printed material on giftedness. It is being constantly increased by gifts from leading authors in the field.
- **Collection of Future Studies.** A large portion of this collection has been donated to the National Headquarters of the Future Problem Solving Program. It is being increased, however, by gifts from leading authors in the field.
- **Collection of Creativity Tests.** This collection includes foreign language translations of the Torrance Tests of Creative Thinking and other instruments authored by Dr. Torrance, along with a growing collection of all present and past tests designed to study and/or assess creative thinking ability, creative functioning, and creative motivations.
- **Collection of Dissertations Directed by Dr. Torrance.** This collection contains dissertations directed by Paul Torrance at the University of Georgia and the University of Minnesota, as well as those in which he advised from other universities.
- **Scrapbook History of E. Paul Torrance's Work Beginning in 1958.** This collection consists of over 40 volumes of news clippings, photographs, letters, professional programs, certificate awards, and the like.
- **Collection of Torrance Writings.** This collection consists of over 1,600 books, papers, journal articles, monographs, test manuals, tests, and the like authored by Paul Torrance. It also includes over 500 additional unpublished papers, speeches, etc.
- **Collection of Medals, Plaques, Certificates and Other Public Recognitions of the Work of E. Paul and J. Pansy Torrance.** Items in this collection date from 1929 to the present.
- **Future Problem Solving (FPS) Collection.** This collection includes copies of the manuals for teaching participants about FPS, news clippings, notes about problems, and honors received.
- **Creativity Instructional Materials.** This collection includes instructional materials that Paul Torrance developed (e.g., the Imagi/Craft series), materials for which he served as creativity consultant (e.g., the Ginn Reading 360 and 720 Programs), materials developed by his former students (e.g., the *Blue Crystal Series* by Bert Cunnington, *Solving the Unknown* by Rod Myers, *Leader in a Box* by Marvin Johnson, etc.), and materials acquired by Paul Torrance for instructional purposes.
- **Japanese Creativity Collection.** This special theme collection was assembled by Paul Torrance during his visit to Japan and his ongoing study of

Japanese creativity. It includes Japanese language materials as well as English translations of Japanese writings on creativity.

- **Unpublished Test Collection.** This includes several tests as well as testing materials that Paul Torrance started to work on, but they were never fully developed and published.

The Center sponsors an annual **E. Paul Torrance Lecture**, which features a person of outstanding national or international reputation. The topic of the lectures is concerned with some area of research associated with gifted, creative, and/or future studies. There have been six Torrance Lectures presented at the University of Georgia. The presenters and topics are:

- 1985 Dr. E. Paul Torrance
  Alumni Foundation Distinguished Professor Emeritus
  University of Georgia
  "A Fair Chance to Grow"
- 1986 Dr. Sidney Parnes, Chairman
  Creative Education Foundation
  Buffalo, New York
  "The Magic of Your Mind"
- 1987 Dr. Don Treffinger, Director
  Center for Creative Learning
  Professor of Creative Studies
  State University of New York, Buffalo
  "Trends and Issues in Teaching Thinking Skills"
- 1988 Dr. Robert Strom, Professor
  Psychology in Education
  Arizona State University
  "Improving Our Expectations for Learning in the 1990s"
- 1989 Mr. Irving Sato, Director
  National/State Leadership Training Institute on the Gifted and Talented
  "Educating for Empowerment: Encouraging Innovative Behavior"
- 1990 Dr. Garnet W. Millar, Coordinator
  Special Educational Services
  Education Response Centre
  Alberta Education
  "The Power of Questioning: An Enabling Strategy to Enhance Learning"

Fittingly, Paul Torrance himself delivered the First Torrance Lecture at his retirement celebration on March 23, 1985. He chose not to discuss his achievements, but to celebrate those of his students, colleagues, and friends and describe what everyone *together* has achieved in giving children everywhere a fair chance to grow—creatively. He realized that others were involved in the dissertations he directed, as well as in the articles and books he wrote.

Many of Torrance's former students have gone on to establish networks of far-reaching significance. An international network for parent development, a network for family medicine, and a network of peace initiatives made up of ministers from the Soviet Union, Japan, and Europe are a few examples. Other former students have been enormously productive with innovative educational ideas, materials, books, programs, tests, and other creations. These are having a global effect, more than one man alone could create. A book (Torrance, 1985a) was collated from the responses that his former advisees provided when asked about their accomplishments and future aspirations. Paul Torrance (1985b) ended his lecture by making a plea: "Perhaps the most important thing that families, schools, churches, communities, cities, states—and our nation—can do today is to reorder priorities to provide every child a chance to learn, grow and live creatively."

I had the pleasure of delivering the Sixth Annual Torrance Lecture at the University of Georgia in October of 1990. I had been interested for some time in children's curiosity and how it manifests itself at school. A colleague, Mr. Ralph Himsl—Superintendent of Schools in Lethbridge, Alberta, Canada—and I had developed an assessment instrument called the Measure of Questioning Skills as part of a large project on teaching thinking skills to teachers and students. The ability to ask good questions proved to be one of the most important thinking skills. Students and teachers told us that questioning ability was critical to the management of information, in and out of school. Questioning is frequently used in the classroom, but rarely as a knowledge-seeking technique. Those who ask questions (teachers) are not seeking knowledge; those who should seek knowledge (students) do not ask questions. Little is known about student questions. I refined the Measure of Questioning Skills instrument and wrote a handbook for teachers on developing student questioning skills as a visiting scholar and research fellow at the Torrance Center for Creative Studies. I presented my research findings to a large audience made up of faculty, students, teachers, and the public.

I did question the success of my lecture when Paul Torrance fell asleep in the middle of my presentation. Although I realized that his medical condition of narcolepsy causes drowsiness, it was disconcerting. Albert Kingston, a professor of educational psychology (research and measurement) at the University of Georgia recounts a similar episode that "tickled" him. He wrote to Paul Torrance:

> One day the late Wendell W. Weaver emerged from a seminar shaking with laughter (and there was a lot of Wendell to shake). He told me that you had given him a laudatory introduction that pleased him greatly. As he started to speak, however, he glanced your way and observed that you were sound asleep. The contrast between your words and actions were the basis of his amusement. What Wendell didn't know was that many of us had been in oral examinations or committee meetings with you and had observed you in similar behavior. Although apparently

> sound asleep you would seemingly come to and make an urgent point or ask a candidate a pressing question. As a result no one was even certain whether or not you were asleep, bored or fully awake. Of all your many fine qualities this is indeed one I wish I also possessed.[28]

The Torrance Lectures will continue to focus attention annually on research and issues related to creativity and future studies.

Torrance Creative Scholars Program

In a keynote address to the National Association for Gifted Children in November of 1984, Paul Torrance spoke about "The Search for a Nation's Treasures." He called for a national effort to identify and serve the creatively gifted. Torrance stated that there was an increasing need for creative kinds of giftedness. He announced that Mary Frasier and the Torrance Center for Creative Studies were working to launch a national creative talent search and develop this talent once it has been identified. This innovative program is conducted in cooperation with Scholastic Testing Services. At present, approximately 400-500 creative individuals have been identified and will be provided with mentor services in the future. Currently, the program has a network of approximately 100 mentors located in the U.S. and 20 other countries around the world.

The Torrance Center for Creative Studies sponsors two direct services for students with high ability.

The Challenge Programs provide Saturday and summer laboratories for gifted and creative learners from preschool (four- and five-year-olds) to grade 8. Generally, the programs employ an interdisciplinary approach that includes math, science, language arts, geography, and art. The approach is simple—children learn by doing; all of the courses employ a hands-on approach to learning. The primary goal of the programs is to develop children's *creative* thinking skills. The Challenge Programs began in 1971 under the leadership of Dr. Kay Bruch and were continued by Dr. Mary Frasier and Dr. Gail Lewis.

During the first three years after the Torrance Center for Creative Studies assumed the leadership of the Challenge Programs, graduate students directed them. Mary Frasier was interested in getting a parent involved. In the fall of 1986, she found such a person in Robin Shy, who had a son in the program and was working in the Torrance Center library as a volunteer. She became a vital link between the community, schools, parents, and the University of Georgia.

---

[28] Letter from Albert Kingston quoted in Frasier & Weiner (1985).

The Challenge Programs have grown considerably in both number and size over the years. In 1985, most of the students were from Athens—about 60 per quarter (Fall, Winter, and Spring) and 125–150 during the summer. Today, in 1993, there are from 6 to 10 programs throughout the year and an average of 100–125 students per quarter. The summer program in 1992 provided experiences for 430 students. Students now come not only from Athens, but Atlanta and Columbus (Georgia), as well as from Tennessee, South Carolina, North Carolina, Alabama, Florida, and even Ohio and Michigan.

Teachers are from both public and private schools, as well as University of Georgia faculty and staff or people with a passion to share (horticulturists, artists, environmentalists, etc.). These people are treasured and utilize Paul Torrance's Incubation Model in all their lesson plans—with the hope that teachers will use it in their school classrooms.

The aim of the Challenge Programs is to stimulate students to develop interests in new areas and help them study an existing passion in depth. Speakers are brought in to show students that an interest can be developed into a career or hobby. The Center staff believe that all children are intrinsically motivated to learn. They are born natural scientists, constantly questioning the world around them. In an effort to keep their motivation alive, the programs are designed using Paul Torrance's Incubation Model of Teaching—helping both teachers and students view the world with a creative approach.

A description of one of the week-long programs—"The World of Science"—gives a glimpse of the program.

THE WORLD OF SCIENCE
July 20–24, 1992, 9 a.m.–12 noon

Discover the joy of science as we investigate the exciting and mysterious properties of chemistry, physics, and biology. Students will spend the week immersed in observing, questioning, analyzing, and predicting, as they are guided through scientific strategies. Join our search as we:

- see a liver enzyme at work
- find the holes in water
- determine the velocity of mechanical toys
- draw a map of your tongue
- measure your joules
- decode chemical formulas

Live the life of a scientist for a week as we discover what we do and don't know about the world around us. Learn how everyday events were explained in the past and how new explanations are created. Consider how our lives have been influenced by past scientific discoveries and how science may shape the future. Ask the questions scientists ask and use the creative process to find new answers.

Comments most often heard from the students in the Challenge Program include "Why isn't school like this?" and "Can I come to Challenge every day—not just Saturdays and in the summer?"

Robin Shy, who coordinates the Challenge Program, says, "The goal for Challenge would be to become obsolete... because schools need to adopt our methods and discover that children become most excited about learning when they are actually doing things (experiments, art, field trips, etc.)."[29]

The creativity research of Paul Torrance is being implemented in the Challenge Program and through the teachers into school programs.

The Georgia Future Problem Solving Program has been a direct service to educators and students in Georgia since 1978. Vicki Connell has been the director of the Georgia State program and currently is a member on the board of trustees that provides advice to the national and international program. The Future Problem Solving Program began as a pilot program involving 28 students from seven different high schools at Clarke Central High School in the 1974–75 school year. The program trains students to use creative problem-solving skills, teamwork, and constructive competition in solving future problems. The 1992–93 school year will see the involvement of several thousand students. Georgia has one of the highest rate of school, teacher, and student involvement in the U.S. and the world.

A number of programs and services are projected for future implementation. The Torrance Center recognizes the need to keep educators, parents, and business people current through a program of *continuing education* or *technical assistance*. Workshops, conferences and symposia will be held regularly for groups such as principals and superintendents, counselors and school psychologists, and personnel from business and industry.

Important publications on the teaching of creative, gifted and future behaviors will be produced and marketed through the Center. The intent is to contribute to the field materials that are practical as well as theoretical in the areas of creative, gifted, and future studies. Training in administering and interpreting the Torrance Tests of Creative Thinking will be coordinated through the Center. Activities and current announcements will be summarized in newsletters and bulletins regularly for university staff and patrons of the Center. A consultative team will provide advice on planning programs for and assessment of creatively gifted students. In addition, expertise will be offered, on a fee for service basis, for the evaluation of gifted programs at the school and/or jurisdiction levels.

The Torrance Center is providing mentorship. It acts to encourage, help, prompt, teach, support, listen to, provide a role model for, and support the growth and development of its proteges' behaviors. The Torrance Center is also a network. Some of its programs link scholars, students, and programs in the sharing and development of creative methods and materials. Both mentorship and networking imply creativity—that is, a situation in which one thing leads to another.

---

[29] Letter from Robin Shy to the author. Athens, Georgia, August 10, 1992.

The Torrance Center is operated through and is part of the Department of Educational Psychology, College of Education, University of Georgia. The activities of the Center are directed by a national and local advisory board through the head of the Center and her support staff. Paul Torrance still acts as a special advisor. The Center plans to expand its services, programs, and activities. Two funds were set up in 1985 to help ensure the continuity and expansion of the Center. The first fund is the Torrance Foundation Discretionary Fund, which was established to support the research, development, and instructional programs sponsored by the Center. The second fund is the E. Paul Torrance Endowment Fund, which was created to establish the E. Paul Torrance Chair at the University of Georgia for an outstanding professor in creative education to provide vital support for future educational quality.

For more information on the programs and services of the Torrance Center for Creative Studies or to make a tax deductible contribution, contact:

Dr. Mary M. Frasier, Director
Torrance Center for Creative Studies
Room 323, College of Education
Aderhold Hall, University of Georgia
Athens, Georgia 30602
(706) 542-5104

PREPARING FOR POSTERITY: THE ARCHIVES

In August of 1984, Paul and his research assistants, especially Nancy Martin, began preparing Paul's books, research papers, and other memorabilia for the archives. A big shipment of books and papers was made to the National Archives of the History of American Psychology in Akron, Ohio. Also, they prepared a shipment for the Museum and Archives of Georgia Education at Milledgeville and Joe Renzulli's historical collection at the University of Connecticut. In addition, they had already deposited many boxes of books, journals, and unpublished and published papers in the new quarters at the Torrance Studies of Creative Behavior in the College of Education, University of Georgia.

Paul continues today to prepare and contribute his professional work and documents and deposits them on a regular basis in the Torrance Collection at the Hargrett Rare Book and Manuscript Library, University of Georgia. Tom Camden, head of this library, told me that he had never seen a collection that was so well organized and documented. Paul presented two sets of materials to the archives of the Creative Education Foundation at State University of New York at Buffalo. One set consisted of manuals, reports, and memorabilia of the early days of the Future Problem Solving Program up until about 1986. The other consisted of materials related to creativity testing, including experimental tests and published tests that attempted to measure some aspect of creativity. The two sets of materials included about 250 items.

NASA INVITATION

Paul was invited to NASA to view the launch of the Space Shuttle (41-C) in April of 1984 at the John F. Kennedy Space Center in Florida. It was Dick Scobee's first flight. They had become friends through Dick's wife, June. The spaceplane's mission was to repair and restore a solar satellite stationed about 250 nautical miles above earth. Paul was unable to attend as Pansy was recovering at that time from a second stroke.

POPULARIZING CREATIVITY

Even *The National Enquirer* carried an article by Singer about creativity and Paul Torrance's ideas to develop these skills titled "How to Discover New $$—Making Ideas," in which Paul presented a number of ways to unleash great ideas:

- Read widely. Especially read books that illustrate creative people's imaginative development. If you read 40-50-year-old books you may find some good ideas that weren't recognized at the time.
- Build an idea file. Record your ideas as soon as they occur. From time to time, look them over and improve on them.
- Tap the minds of creative thinkers around you.
- Always ask questions.
- Develop your awareness of other uses for something that is already serving one need.
- When something irritates you, try to improve it with creative ideas instead of criticizing it.
- Talk with people in fields outside your usual circle. Read outside your main fields of interest.
- Keep an eye on new trends for the types of things people say they need.
- Remember that nothing is perfect—everything can be improved on.
- Avoid making premature judgments of your own ideas. Don't say right away, "That won't work." Talk and think about your ideas.
- Be true to yourself. Don't be afraid to follow your own ideas, impulses and imagination. Remember, any original idea usually singles you out from the crowd.

RETIREMENT

Paul and Pansy transposed their field into the spiritual realm. Paul's advocacy of creativity allowed him and Pansy to create an exciting curriculum for preschoolers in the Baptist Church, which is still used as a model. Paul's interest in and contribution to the church continued in the 1970s. In July of 1975, he presented a talk and dramatic presentation on "The Future of Religious Education" at the Eastern Baptist Religious Association in Ridgecrest, North Carolina.

In the fall of 1984, at the age of 69, Paul retired from the faculty at the University of Georgia so that he could care for Pansy. The separation notice from the University is dated October 11, 1984. He had given 18 years of service to the University of Georgia.

Paul had been planning for retirement for several years. He had planned to travel and use his time to complete many projects. However, Pansy's illness, along with the stroke he suffered a month after his retirement and subsequent mini-strokes, changed his life.

The 1984 March/April issue of *Gifted Child Today* was dedicated to Paul Torrance for his prolific work in the area and to thank him on the occasion of his formal retirement from the University of Georgia. He was the first person to whom an issue of *G/C/T* has been dedicated. Marvin Gold, editor and publisher of the popular magazine, praised Paul Torrance for his leadership in the area of creativity research. He indicated that Paul was involved with creativity while most other professionals were still thinking of ability in terms of IQ scores and that he pointed out the need for special help to disadvantaged groups while others were concerned only with the white middle class. The issue contained not only the dedication to Paul by editor Marvin Gold, but also lead stories about Paul and Pansy by Jack Presbury and Morgan Henderson. There were also articles written by Eleanor Hoomes on future problem solving and others by former students—Charlie Martin, Bonnie Cramond, Jeanette Parker, and Barbara Swicord.

This special issue on creativity of *G/C/T* was a complete surprise to Paul and Pansy. They found it on the kitchen table when they returned home from an appointment with Pansy's neurosurgeon. The doctor had given them bad news about Pansy's condition. They were both feeling low when they arrived home. The dedication and articles in *G/C/T* and "get well" wishes from friends combined at just the right moment to give them new energy, courage, and comfort to face the future with hope—and creativity.

REFERENCES

Bleedorn, B., & McKelvey, S. (1984). *Humor: lessons in laughter for learning and living.* Buffalo, NY: DOK Publishers.

Bracken, B.A. (1993). *Assessment of interpersonal relations.* Austin, TX: Pro-Ed, Inc.

Clark discloses education plan—More emphasis on creativity. (1968, December 14). *Calgary Herald*, p. 1.

Clements, R., & Wachowiak, F. (1993). *Emphasis art: A qualitative art program for elementary and middle schools* (5th Ed.). New York: Harper Collins.

Cramond, B. (in press). The Torrance Tests of Creative Thinking: From design through establishment of predictive validity. *Roeper Review.*

Das, J.P. (1989). Review of human information process survey. In J. Conoley & J. Kramer (Eds.), *The tenth mental measurements yearbook* (pp. 363-364). Lincoln: University of Nebraska Press.

Dateline all over Georgia. (1970, April 28). *Athens Benner-Herald.*

Delisle, J. (1992). *Guiding the social and emotional development of gifted youth: A practical guide for educators and counselors.* White Plains, NY: Longman.

Dyer, T. (1985). *The University of Georgia: A bicentennial history, 1785-1985.* Athens: The University of Georgia Press.

Fox, L. (1985). Review of Thinking Creatively with Sounds and Words. In J.V. Mitchell, Jr. (Ed.), *The ninth mental measurements yearbook* (Vol. 2, pp. 1621-1622). Lincoln: University of Nebraska Press.

Frasier, M.M., & Weiner, D. (1985). *E. Paul Torrance: His influence and his contributions.* Athens, GA: Torrance Center for Creative Studies, University of Georgia.

Glauser, V. (1980, July 21). Building a better brain: Could brain development boost productivity? *The Tulsa Tribune*, p. 10C.

Goff, K., & Torrance, E.P. (1991). *Mentor's guide and protege's handbook.* Bensenville, IL: Scholastic Testing Service.

Gold, M. (Ed.). (1991). Future Problem Solving Program [special issue]. *Gifted Child Today*, 14(2).

Henderson, B. (1987, September). Kids who saved a dying town. *Reader's Digest, 131*, 42-46.

Holland, J. (1972). Review of Torrance Tests of Creative Thinking. In O.K. Buros (Ed.), *The seventh mental measurements yearbook* (Vol. 1, pp. 840 841). Lincoln: University of Nebraska Press.

Hudspeth, R. (1983, November 7). This Pansy is no pansy. *The Atlanta Constitution*, p. 2B.

Lee, C., & Jackson, R. (1992). *Faking it: A look into the mind of a creative learner.* Portsmouth, NH: Heineman.

Maker, J., & Schiever, S. (1989). *Critical issues in gifted education: Defensible programs for cultural and ethnic minorities* (Vol. 2). Austin, TX: Pro-Ed, Inc.

McNeil, J. (1972). *Psychological education at the University of Georgia. Dissertation Abstracts* (University Microfilms No. 73-5741).

Myers, R.E., & Torrance, E.P. (1993). *Myers Torrance creative developments.* Bensenville, IL: Scholastic Testing Service.

Onda, A., & Sato, S. (1978). *Creative ability: Its development and evaluation.* Tokyo, Japan: Tokyo Shinri Publishers.

Raina, M.K. (1992). *The Torrance phenomenon: Extended creative research for Lord Vishvakarma.* Unpublished paper (in possession of the author).

Reilly, J.M. (1992). *Mentorship: The essential guide for schools and business.* Dayton: Ohio Psychology Press.

Renzulli, J.S. (1985). Review of Thinking Creatively in Action and Movement. In J.V. Mitchell, Jr. (Ed.), *The ninth mental measurements year book* (Vol. 2, pp. 1619-1621). Lincoln: University of Nebraska Press.

Ruben, H.L. (1980). *Competing: Understanding and winning the strategic games we all play*. New York: Lippincott & Crowell.

Rust, J.O. (1985). Review of Thinking Creatively in Action and Movement. in J.V. Mitchell, Jr. (Ed.), *The ninth mental measurements yearbook* (Vol. 2, p. 1621). Lincoln: University of Nebraska Press.

Schwartz, B., & Millar, G. (1992). The power of teaching questioning skill in art education: An enabling skill. *NAEA Advisory,* Spring.

Shaughnessy, M.F. (1991). Mentoring and E. Paul Torrance: His creative contributions. *The Creative Child and Adult Quarterly*, 16(2), 95-98.

Stanley, J.C., George, W.C., & Solano, C.H. (Eds.). (1977). The gifted and creative: A fifty-year perspective. *Revised and expanded proceedings of the seventh annual Hyman Blumberg Symposium on Research in Early Childhood Education*. Baltimore, MD: John Hopkins University Press.

Torrance, E.P. (1962). *Guiding creative talent*. Englewood Cliffs, NJ: Prentice Hall.

Torrance, E.P. (1969). *A three-year study of the influence of a creative-aesthetic approach to school readiness and beginning reading and arithmetic on creative development*. Athens, GA: Research and Development Center in Educational Stimulation, University of Georgia.

Torrance, E.P. (1975). Preliminary manual: Ideal Child Checklist. *The Gifted Child Quarterly,* 19(2), 130-139.

Torrance, E.P. (1979). *The Search for Satori and Creativity*. Buffalo, NY: Bearly Limited.

Torrance, E.P. (1980a). Lessons about giftedness and creativity from a nation of 115 million overachievers. *Gifted Child Quarterly*, *24(1)*, 10–14.

Torrance, E.P. (1980b). *Torrance Tests of Creative Thinking—Figural and Verbal Tests*. Bensenville, IL: Scholastic Testing Service, Inc.

Torrance, E.P. (1981a). Predicting the creativity of elementary school children (1959–1980) And the teacher who "made a difference." *Gifted Child Quarterly*, 25, 55–62.

Torrance, E.P. (1981b). *Thinking Creatively in Action and Movement*. Bensenville, IL: Scholastic Testing Service, Inc.

Torrance, E.P. (1982a). Growing up creatively gifted with learning disabilities. In W.M. Cruickshank & J.W. Lerner (Eds.), *Coming of age*. Syracuse, NY: Syracuse University Press.

Torrance, E.P. (1982b). Education for "quality circles" in Japanese schools. *Journal of Research and Development in Education*, 15*(2)*, 11–15.

Torrance, E.P. (1983). Role of mentors in creative achievement. *Creative Child and Adult Quarterly*, 8, 8–15, 18.

Torrance, E.P. (1984). *Mentor relationships: how they aid creative achievement, endure, change and die*. Buffalo, NY: Bearly Limited.

Torrance, E.P. (1985a). Letters to Dr. Torrance on the occasion of his retirement. Torrance Archives, University of Georgia.

Torrance, E.P. (1985b). Creative retirement provides a fair chance to grow. *The Creative Child and Adult Quarterly*, 10*(4)*, 214–222.

Torrance, E.P. (1987). *Torrance monograph series*. Bensenville, IL: Scholastic Testing Service, Inc.

Torrance, E.P. (1990). The Creative Scholars Mentors Program. In C. W. Taylor (Ed.), *Expanding awareness of creative potentials worldwide*. (pp. 56-58). Salt Lake City, UT: Brain Talent-Powers Press.

Torrance, E.P. (1991). Creatively gifted, disadvantaged children: Their desperate need for mentors. *Illinois Council for the Gifted*, 10, 4–6.

Torrance, E.P. (1992). Creatively gifted, learning disabled individuals. *The Educational Forum*, 56(4), 399–404.

Torrance, E.P. (1993). The beyonders in a thirty-year longitudinal study of creative achievement. *Roeper Review, 15(3)*, 131–134.

Torrance, E.P., & Goff, K. (1990). *Cumulative bibliography on the Torrance Tests of Creative Thinking*. Athens, GA: Georgia Studies of Creative Behavior.

Torrance, E.P., & Khatena, J. (1976). *Khatena–Torrance Creative Perception Inventory: KTCPI*. Bensenville, IL: Scholastic Testing Service, Inc.

Torrance, E.P., & Rose, L.H. (1992). *Cumulative bibliography of Thinking Creatively in Action and Movement (TCAM)*. Athens, GA: Georgia Studies of Creative Behavior.

Torrance, E.P., & Rose, L.H. (1992). *Cumulative bibliography: Thinking Creatively with Sounds and Words*. Athens, GA: Georgia Studies of Creative Behavior.

Torrance, E.P., & Safter, H.T. (1990). *The Incubation Model of Teaching—Getting Beyond the Aha!* Buffalo, NY: Bearly Limited.

Torrance, E.P., & Sato, S. (1979). Differences in Japanese and United States styles of thinking. *Creative Child and Adult Quarterly*, 4, 145–151.

Torrance, E.P., Cunnington, B., & Khatena, J. (1980). *Thinking Creatively with Sounds and Words*. Bensenville, IL: Scholastic Testing Service, Inc.

Torrance, E.P., Lin, Hsin-tai, & Rose, L.H. (1990). *Cumulative bibliography of Khatena–Torrance Creative Personality Inventory*. Athens, GA: Georgia Studies of Creative Behavior.

Torrance, E.P., Murdock, M.C., & Fletcher, D. (in press). *Creative problem solving through role-playing*. Pretoria, South Africa: Benedic Books.

Torrance, E.P., Sorkey, H., & Coone, J. (1968). *Evaluation of the University of Georgia 1967–68 Experienced Teacher Fellowship Program in School Psychology*. Athens: The University of Georgia.

Torrance, E.P., Taggart, W., & Taggart, B. (1984). *Human Information Processing Survey: HIP Survey*. Bensenville, IL: Scholastic Testing Service, Inc.

Torrance, E.P., McCarthy, B., Kolesinski, M., & Smith, J. (1988). *SOLAT—Your style of learning and thinking*. Bensenville, IL: Scholastic Testing Service, Inc.

Treffinger, D.J. (1985). Review of Torrance Tests of Creative Thinking. In J.V. Mitchell, Jr. (Ed.), *The ninth mental measurements yearbook* (Vol. II, pp. 1632–1634). Lincoln: The University of Nebraska Press.

World Future Society. (1991). *Addendum to the futures research directory of individuals*. Bethesda, MD: World Future Society.

Chapter 6

The Retirement Years (1966–Present):

Productive and Challenging Times

This chapter deals with the retirement years of Paul and Pansy Torrance, years that have been dominated by their courageous struggle to cope with health problems. Paul dedicated himself to helping Pansy, and in the process jeopardized his own health. At the same time, he continued to write and revise books. It was after his retirement that Paul's tests of creativity were recognized by the National Aeronautics and Space Agency (NASA) in Florida and carried aloft on a space mission. Pansy's death struck Paul hard, but he was able to focus again on his research. He became involved with the elderly, now his contemporaries, and was involved in a program to improve the quality of life of people with developmental disabilities.

In 1993, Paul spent a great deal of time corresponding with people from various countries of the world—scholars and others who were interested in creativity. This section ends with Paul's reflections on some of the important highlights of his life, a perspective of his many contributions, and a review of his life as a true "beyonder."

FORMAL RETIREMENT

"The light appears, flares, and fades like a brilliant flash struck on the matchbook sky. Paul and Pansy Torrance are passing. They are there somewhere between galaxies working together as they have always done. The mission is not new; only its time and place have changed."[1]

"The Comet's Tale" by
Mary Murdock
March 23, 1985

---

[1] Letter, "A Comet's Tale," from Mary Murdock to Paul and Pansy Torrance on the occasion of the retirement of Paul Torrance. March 23, 1985.

When Paul Torrance retired on October 1, 1984 to give Pansy full-time care, no celebration was held. On November 9, about a month after Paul's formal retirement, he had a stroke and spent about 10 days in Athens General Hospital. Meanwhile, Pansy was cared for by three health nurses. Now both Paul and Pansy required extensive care as they recuperated.

In the spring, Dr. Mary Frasier, Director of the Torrance Center at the University of Georgia, with the help of Center staff and students, planned a two-day retirement party for March 24–25, 1985. There was to be an Open House on Saturday and Sunday at the home of the Torrances and at the Torrance Center. The First Annual E. Paul Torrance Lecture was to be presented following the reception and banquet on Saturday night at the Georgia Center for Continuing Education on the University of Georgia's campus. Over 250 former students, friends, family members, and colleagues from all parts of the country returned to honor Paul. At the banquet, Dr. Pearline Yeatts-Thomas, an Early Childhood Professor at the University of Georgia, introduced Paul Torrance with an original poem:

Some of us see flowers
And think they are ours to keep
Others see beauty
And nurture them to bloom and grow

Some of us see rivers
And rush to build a dam
Others free the path
And let the waters flow

Some folks look at the mountains
And see but rock and stone
Others see a challenge
And reach to feel the snow

Some folks see the sun set
And thinks all is asleep
Others see the possibilities
And have promises to keep

Some folks see a child
And hear him wail and cry
Others see his smile
As he soars toward the sky

Some folks see a brother cry
They look and pass him by
Others feel the depths of hope
And reach to free his soul

Yes, some folks guide us to be our best
To never give up... never lose hope
But, to ever reach toward the sky
And in our reach to respect all men
That they too might fly

Those of us here tonight are honored to know such a man.
Friends, I am honored to present...

Dr. Paul Torrance.[2]

In preparing his speech, entitled "A Fair Chance To Grow," Paul had asked former students from around the world to comment on their creative impact and

[2] Letter from Pearline Yeatts-Thomas to the author. October 20, 1992.

future image. He used excerpts from these student letters, representing 32 countries and 26 states, as the basis for the first E. Paul Torrance Lecture. Although this was Paul's special day, he chose to highlight the careers and significant contributions of his students and to deflect the focus from himself. However, the fact that his students have developed a global network affecting millions of people clearly indicates the tremendous influence that Paul Torrance has had.

As a surprise, students, colleagues, and friends also contributed another set of letters describing their individual experiences and recalling anecdotes about their contact with Paul Torrance. The 87 letters revealed love, awe, respect, and inspiration, and showed that Paul is held in high esteem. The letter writers demonstrated their creative abilities—some sent poems, photographs, plays, drawings, and other creative expressions of their appreciation and love. Gail Lewis sent this piece of writing:

A LIKELY STORY
by Gail Lewis

One of a great many acts, the first scene

(As the lights come up, the halls are empty, the floor a highly polished, beige-ish tile. The building obviously belongs to the generic category, "college classroom buildings." The scene designer is welcome to take flights of fancy, but the set should never look like more than it is—there should be no warm colors, no atmosphere conducive to productive thinking. After all, the building has a utilitarian use as far as architects are concerned—the education of graduate students.

Lower stage left, a cut-away office reveals a standard secretary's desk, paper clips all neatly filed away, the day's work done. Only one person is visible on stage, a gray-haired man expertly typing on an IBM Selectric.

Gail Lewis walks in. She is tall and thin, with a decidedly dramatic personality.)

LEWIS: Excuse me, sir. (The man looks up, his concentration obviously broken.) I'm sorry to disturb you, but I'm looking for Dr. Torrance. I understood he could be found on this floor, but you're the only person here.

MAN: (A quietly impish grin breaks over his grandfatherly face. He maintains a balance between a busy interpersonal distance and a warm and encouraging manner—an ability given to few on God's earth.) Can I help you?

LEWIS: I'm afraid I really must see Dr. Torrance. Do you know him?

MAN: Quite well.

LEWIS: I must admit I'm rather anxious about meeting him. He's quite famous and I'm afraid I'll say something really stupid. Is he arrogant or friendly? I think of him as a hero. Does he look like a hero?

MAN: What does a hero look like?

LEWIS: Well, I have an image of a hero as someone who breathes confidence, commands audiences... someone who makes everyone stop and look when he enters the room. (She gestures dramatically.) Actors who are heroes usually look well-tanned and glisten as though they were expensively oiled.

MAN: How will you feel if Dr. Torrance doesn't look well-tanned and oiled? What if he's comfortable and grandfatherly and human, just like everyone else?

LEWIS: I'm not sure how I'd feel. I might have to change my image of hero to whatever he's like. You see, I don't know many heroes, but I'm sure he's one. He has had great ideas that can be measured in stacks upon stacks. I have heard that he never turns away a student, even when he's overloaded—that he gives of himself endlessly. Surely all of that makes him a great man.

MAN: (He turns to face her squarely.) Dr. Torrance is a human being—just like everyone else. He works hard and tries to inspire others to reach their full potential. He lives through daily routines of eating and sleeping and wishing, just as others do. He is sad sometimes and he makes mistakes sometimes. I've seen him frustrated and hurt, too.

LEWIS: Then what is that makes him different, able to produce so much and care so much?

MAN: He's disturbed by the gaps in what we know, by the inconsistencies. His efforts to fill those gaps explain his work—he has a creative spirit. But the same qualities that lead to new ideas also lead to new ways of relating to individuals. If one is disturbed by the gaps in what we know, he may also be puzzled by inconsistencies within the human personality, by questions about interpersonal relationships. Simply stated, he is aware of others as human beings and cares about them deeply.

LEWIS: I see. (She stands up.) I suppose I'd better resume my search for Dr. Torrance. It's getting rather late. He may go home before I find him. (She turns as she reaches the door.) What you said is rather important, you know. It's better if Dr. Torrance is a human being rather than a perfect, god-like being. If he's human, I have, as a human, a right to aspire to be like him. If he's perfect, or a god, I have no chance. That's a great relief, you know.

MAN: (Smiles warmly.) I hope you find him.

LEWIS: I think I will, now. I know what to look for. By the way, I don't mean to pry, but you look like a professor. May I ask why you're typing your own manuscript?

MAN: Well, you see, I don't have my own secretary. In order to meet that challenge, I asked myself, "In what ways might I get this manuscript done in time for the deadline?" One answer was to type it myself! (He laughs quietly.)

LEWIS: I see. Good luck. (She reaches the door and turns again.) You've been a big help. I hope we meet again.

(She exits. He types. The lights go out.)[3]

Besides the collection of students' letters, a *festschrift* was published to mark the occasion. It contains a chronology of events in Paul's career, research

---

[3] "A Likely Story," by Gail Lewis, sent to Mary Frasier for Paul Torrance on the occasion of his retirement. March 23, 1985.

insights, 25 provocative research results, and his last keynote address to the National Association for Gifted Children.

At the banquet, a number of presentations were made to Paul and Pansy Torrance. A proclamation from Georgia Governor Joe Frank Harris, issued in recognition of Paul Torrance's contributions, was presented by Dr. Virginia Trotter, Vice-President for Academic Affairs at the University of Georgia. The University honored Paul with a Bicentennial Medal, which was presented by Dr. Alphonse Buccino, Dean of the College of Education. University Archivist Tom Camden announced that the archives collection donated by Paul Torrance would soon be ready for public use. This collection of materials on gifted, creative, and future behaviors is the largest of its kind in the world. Also, it was formally announced that the Torrance Center for Studies in Gifted, Creative, and Future Behaviors would be established at the University of Georgia. This Center, initiated by Mary Frasier, an Associate Professor in the Department of Educational Psychology, would continue the tradition of scholarship and excellence exemplified in the work of E. Paul Torrance.

A number of firsts that Paul had achieved over his remarkable career were also announced:

- directed the most dissertations (110) in the history of the College of Education, the University of Georgia;
- directed the most dissertations on the disadvantaged in the United States;
- produced the most publications (more than 1,000) in the history of the College of Education, the University of Georgia;
- appeared in the top 100 citations in the Social Science Index (the only professor at the University of Georgia to do so);
- founded the Future Problem Solving Program;
- founded the International Network of Gifted Students;
- developed the Torrance Tests of Creative Thinking, the creativity tests that have been given to more children in the world than any other such test;
- had more books, tests, and articles published in Japanese than any other professor from the University of Georgia;
- had more books, tests, and articles translated into other foreign languages than any other professor from the University of Georgia.

In the conclusion of his speech "A Fair Chance To Grow," Paul challenged families, schools, communities, and the nation to reorder priorities to provide every child a chance to learn, grow, and live creatively. Ruth Noller, in a letter to Paul at his retirement celebration, aptly stated, "May your retirement years also be *refirement.*" Indeed they would be.

In April of 1985, shortly after the retirement banquet, Paul was awarded the Hall of Fame Plaque by the National Association for Creative Children and Adults (NACCA). It reads:

> **HALL OF FAME**
>
> AWARDED TO
>
> **E. PAUL TORRANCE**
>
> WHOSE SCHOLARLY RESEARCH
> AND ACTIVE INTEREST IN CREATIVITY
> HAS CHANGED THE FACE
> OF EDUCATION
>
> APRIL 14, 1985

Ann F. Isaacs, Executive Director of NACCA, composed a song for Paul in 1983 and presented it along with the award. Isaacs is a long-time supporter of Torrance.

In August of 1985, Paul Torrance was granted professor emeritus status by the University of Georgia. Paul's full academic title was now Alumni Foundation Distinguished Professor Emeritus of Education.

HEALTH DIFFICULTIES

Both Paul and Pansy suffered health-related problems in the 1980s. They dealt with these problems with courage and made creative adjustments. It was a difficult time for both of them as they had little privacy, and when they did have moments together it was not quality time.

Pansy suffered her first stroke in December of 1980 on her return to Athens from a Future Problem Solving Program workshop in Savannah, Georgia. She was 67 years old. Due to Pansy's poor health, Paul took over all the housekeeping duties. He cooked all the meals—including fruit pies, chocolate pecan pies, chocolate mousse pies, peach bread, casseroles, and quiches. Characteristically, he had planned to publish a cookbook entitled "Keep It Simple But Make It Exciting!" He also did the laundry and much of the outside work.

In January of 1984, a nurse came to care for Pansy's needs around the clock. On February 19, 1984, she had another stroke, after which she received assistance from a rehabilitation team at the St. Mary's Hospital in Athens—physical therapy, occupational therapy, speech therapy, and bladder therapy.

Also in January of 1984, Paul had a severe asthma attack in California. A young allergist was able to stabilize Paul to a near normal state. During that same time, his speech was affected; he had difficulty breathing, swallowing, and walking straight, and his feet became numb. His narcolepsy had gotten worse. Paul's health had broken as a result of sustained stress with helping Pansy. He had regular visits to the chiropractor. Paul's professional career had to be put on hold as he needed to care for Pansy. Consequently, he turned down an offer in July, 1984, to be a visiting professor at my alma mater, the University of Alberta in Edmonton, Alberta, Canada.

In October of the same year, Paul's number one priority was to make Pansy's days and nights as happy as possible. He decided to retire because he could not devote himself to both the University and to Pansy. Paul directed the activities of two shifts of health nurses, and he was frustrated with the medical system. He told me, "I could spend my whole time with medicare and Blue Cross, trying to collect claims for hospitalization, treatments, drugs, medical equipment and physicians."

At this time, Paul suffered a bad fall and had sore ribs and severe pain in his hips and left leg; one month after his official retirement, he suffered a stroke. The stroke affected Paul's left brain, and he had difficulty controlling his emotions. To compound matters, in November of 1986, Paul developed torticollis, a condition in which the muscles on one side of the neck are in a state of continual spasms, pulling the head into an unnatural position. It continued to bother him despite treatments of cervical traction and massages. He had trouble sleeping—about the only comfortable position was to sleep standing up. It has become chronic.

At times, his correspondence tended to accumulate as his own survival needs took over. To overcome his neck problem, he made adaptations to his chair so that he could resume some of his normal activities. He enlisted the assistance of a speech therapist and occupational therapist to help restore his functioning. All the while, he was trying to help Pansy.

Pansy had taken a bad fall and had broken her hip, which was replaced with a prosthesis. By July of 1985, she could not stand or walk alone but could move with the aid of a walker. She could talk and listen, and she was able to go in the car to church, to her doctors, and other places. Paul indicated in letters that Pansy was miraculously cheerful despite painful muscle spasms and little control of her right hand. In 1986, she had a fourth stroke—a hemorrhage the size of a lemon on the brain behind her right ear. This occurred on February 13, just before they moved from Riverhill Drive to Cherokee Avenue. She had surgery, which was successful, and she was hospitalized for two weeks. According to Paul, she insisted on eating everything with a fork.

In a letter eight days before Pansy's fatal stroke, Paul reported that she complained of pains in her chest; her incontinence increased, and there were times when she could not walk and had to use the wheelchair. Pansy died on November 13, 1988, and Paul wrote the letter shown on page 195 to friends one week later:

E. PAUL TORRANCE
Georgia Studies Of Creative Behavior
183 CHEROKEE AVENUE
ATHENS, GA 30606

November 20, 1988

Dear Friends:

I want to thank you for your support during Pansy's prolonged bout with strokes and during the past week when the final stroke came. It meant so much to both of us.

Her final day had been a very good one. She was preparing to go to church the next day. She had enjoyed her meals. She had had our Saturday night special – a good steak. She had watched the UGA football game and some other TV programs and had read. I put her to bed with the help of Princess, her kitten. She was very proud that she had remained continent all of the afternoon and evening and was more talkative than usual. Earlier in the evening the nurse had put the dress she had been wearing in the laundry and she had me to get it out to wear the next morning. I had not fallen asleep when I heard her gagging. Getting no response, I got her up with difficulty as the paralyzing effects of the stroke had already set in. Then I couldn't get her back to bed as the paralysis was pulling against me. I managed to prop her up so I could call an ambulance. Less than an hour had elapsed between her gagging and her arrival at St. Mary's Hospital. Dr. Novey thought that she would not last through the night. The stroke involved the brain stem but she held on until Sunday afternoon. She never spoke a word and I don't think she was ever conscious.

Had she been able to talk, I am sure she would have said, "I'm fine!" and smiled. She had said that she was ready to die. Throughout her eight years of strokes she had remained amazingly cheerful and smiling. I wondered how she did it. After her death I found this note on a card giving her philosophy of life written long ago:

> I'd rather say "fine" with a grin than let folks know the shape I'm in.

On this card was another bit of her wisdom – about priorities.

> When you're up to your neck in alligators, it's difficult to remember that your primary objective was to drain the swamp. In other words, first things first.

She enjoyed the colors of autumn, enjoyed the flowers and birds, and her drives with the nurses. Our own yard remained beautiful with hundreds of red roses, thousands of azuratum, mums, hydrangeas and red berries. Our big holly tree is loaded. She loved it.

I plan to be alone for Thanksgiving. Thanksgiving Eve and Thanksgiving Day were always a very special holiday for us. I need some time to be alone with my tears. We were married Thanksgiving Eve twenty-nine years ago in Bloomington, Minnesota (a suburb of Minneapolis).

I talked by long distance to my friend, Sid Parnes, about the challenges Pansy's death leaves me and he sent me an excellent paper on this topic and I will talk to him again tomorrow. Now, I must decide what the Lord wants me to do with the rest of my life, but I feel I must be very careful about establishing my priorities. I know one of my priorities must be "cheering others along." In 1986, when the spaceship Challenger went down, Jack Presbury wrote a poem dedicated to Christa McAuliffe and me, calling us great challenger-teachers. I liked it – especially the last four lines:

> The Challengers
> Are never dead and gone.
> They're always waiting somewhere
> To cheer the children on.

I put it on parchment paper, as an award to some of our great Challenger-Teachers and I also gave Pansy one. She had me to frame it and kept it in clear view in her bedroom. I must accept the challenge and continue "to cheer the children on." I know she will be cheering me and you on.

I think she knew that her time was getting short. She urged me on her last day, "Let's work on our Christmas letters and cards early." I promised her that we would. Last Saturday evening when we were alone, she asked me to talk to her about what I had been doing. I had been signing some papers to change the beneficiaries on one of my annuities. I explained that I was hoping I could leave enough to take care of her, that she might outlive me. She said, "I hope not."

Remember that both of us will be out there somewhere cheering you on. Keep up your good work.

Love,

Paul

E. Paul Torrance

When Pansy died, Paul wrote the following description of her to go under a photograph of her.

Pansy Nigh Torrance 1913–1988

Nurse, Nursing Educator and Crusader, Teacher Extraordinaire, Children's Rights Advocate, Mid-Wife to the Creative Process, Pioneer for Future Problem Solving

She was all of these and more to Paul.

Pansy's Funeral

At Pansy's funeral on November 16, 1988, Jon Appleton, her pastor at First Baptist Church in Athens, spoke these words:

Robert Frost wrote of "Devotion"—

The heart can think of no devotion

Greater than being shore to the ocean—
Holding the curve of one position,
Counting an endless repetition.

Pansy Torrance was a woman of deep devotion, who held the curve of *many* positions. She was a Christian, an active seeker of reconciliation and hope. She has been a giant of faith within our congregation and beyond. She served her church faithfully, faithfully holding the curve.

Pansy was a practical scholar, an advocate of overcoming problems in life. Where no hope was evident, she entered the room as an angel of hope. Where no care was evident, she arrived on the scene with sleeves rolled up, ready to move beyond despair toward building a block-house of possibility. She found great discomfort with closed doors. She spent her life opening those doors, because she believed that where there was life, there was hope. She faithfully held the curve.

Pansy was family. The names Paul and Pansy, devotedly linked for twenty-nine years, were, yes, a marriage in the true sense—but much, so very much, more. Together, they were devoted to Christ and to His church. Together, they found in their vocation, which was also their hobby, an interlinkage of research, study, practicum and experimentation. They were critics of one another, and their final papers, books, and theses had run the gamut of scientific and Christian interplay so that what they finally autographed was not only acceptable, but absolute. Faithfully, devotedly, they together held the curve.

A critic of Thomas Wolfe said of him—

"He had a song, his song lives
and that's the story of Thomas Wolfe."

Pansy had a song, her song lives.
Pansy had devotion, her devotion lives and that's the story of Pansy Torrance.[4]

In a letter written in December of 1989, Paul said he realized that he had grossly overestimated what he could do. He had struggled with his limitations and had had to reorient himself. He realized that his productivity would never be fully regained and had graciously accepted the role of encourager—"cheering the children on." He felt fortunate to have co-authors like Kathy Goff, Tammy Safter, Mary Murdock, Felice Kaufmann, and Zoa Rockenstein. He would give co-authors the data and tell them what he wanted to say. They would do the writing and see it through to publication. In 1990, Saburo Sato of Japan visited Paul in Athens, Georgia, to rekindle their friendship and to help console Paul after Pansy's death.

In December of 1990, Paul had attacks of tachycardia that reached a peak in both frequency and intensity. In September of 1992, Paul indicated that his narcolepsy had suddenly become worse and had him concerned. It prevented him from getting anything done.

---

[4] Personal correspondence from Pastor Jon Appleton to the author. December 29, 1992.

After prostate surgery in the fall of 1992, Paul had serious difficulties in regaining his productivity. It took him over six months to do this. As of March in 1993, Paul reported feeling much better. He has been more productive, is writing articles and chapters for books, and is answering correspondence.

After Pansy's death, Paul reflected on his status as widower and how he tried to carry on despite his terrible loss:

> I did not feel like a "fifth wheel." Of course, my life changed. For about eight years, there were nurses in and out all of the time except for the night shift. I got up about three or four times each night to help Pansy in some way. The nurses were a problem. I had to prepare meals with their requirements in mind. They all wanted to borrow money and made no effort to repay me. One forged about $5,000 in checks. One of them stole Pansy's wedding ring and her best pearl necklace. Many of the things I had stored in the basement disappeared. To be through with the nurses was a great relief, though I missed Pansy and this was sad.
>
> It left me with no one with whom I could talk intimately and with no threat, though she was not accessible to me for some time. Sometimes we would have a conversation before the nurse came in. If we continued the conversation, they were hurt and angry. Students and assistants provided a certain amount of frank conversation but it was limited. As time has gone along, I have developed a few friendships which provide this missing ingredient. Mohammed [Badaway] has provided most of it.
>
> I had already been retired for a little over four years, but I continued as much as I could. Since Pansy's death, I have continued this. I thought I would have more time for writing, research, and reading, but this has not happened. There are plenty of volunteer opportunities, but I have not been able to take advantage of them on account of my torticollis, incontinence, narcolepsy, and lack of transportation.[5]

FINANCING HIS OWN RESEARCH

While he was still at the University of Minnesota, Paul decided that he did not want to depend on grants to support his research. It was too difficult and frustrating to wait for grants and gifts from individuals and groups. He sought a creative solution. Paul decided to finance his own research by using 100% of his royalties from books and tests, as well as honoraria from speaking engagements. He would use this money to pay for his own research assistants. (Professors at universities normally pay for their research or graduate assistants through university or special grants and gifts.)

Shirley Anderson, Office Manager for the Department of Educational Psychology at the University of Georgia, says:

> In the case of Dr. E. Paul Torrance, Alumni Foundation Distinguished Professor Emeritus, for many years he has supplied funds from royalties of tests, books and

---

[5] Personal correspondence from E. Paul Torrance. February 26, 1993.

other writings for one or more research assistants each quarter. Account #GSCB—Georgia Studies of Creative Behavior was established for this purpose.[6]

This system of paying for his own research assistants and typists freed Paul to pursue studies in his areas of interest and removed the restrictions that are usually placed on what a researcher can study. It has also enabled Paul to continue producing despite a disabling stroke and other handicapping problems. However, Paul's creative solution did create a problem for him: He had to endure the jealousies of colleagues who would not believe that he had research assistants because he paid for them.

Financial Contributions

Paul Torrance has generously donated money to many U.S. national causes. A 1992 scrapbook in the Torrance Collection in the archives contains letters and certificates recognizing Paul's financial and personal support for several major issues and medical challenges facing modern society. The worthy causes include Alzheimer's Association, Mothers Against Drunk Driving, The Seniors Coalition, Arthritis Foundation, Blinded Veterans Association, National Foundation for Cancer Research, Citizens Against Government Waste, Special Olympics, National Federation of the Blind, Families USA, Cystic Fibrosis Foundation, and Americans Against Human Suffering (Freedom of Choice for Physician Aid in Dying).

TEACHER-IN-SPACE: "THE ULTIMATE FIELD TRIP"

"What are we doing here?
We're reaching for the stars...
I touch the Future.
I teach."

— Christa McAuliffe (1986)

The research of Paul Torrance and activities at the Torrance Center for Creative Studies at the University of Georgia had a special link with NASA's fatal "Teacher-in-Space" shuttle mission. On August 27, 1984, President Ronald Reagan announced plans to make a teacher the first private citizen to fly on the

[6] Letter from Shirley Anderson, office manager of the Department of Educational Psychology, College of Education, University of Georgia, to the IRS in Atlanta, Georgia. November 7, 1991.

space shuttle *Challenger* slated for January 1986. This was to be the flight for the common man, education, and human creativity. This flight was part of NASA's Space Flight Participant Program, which was designed to expand shuttle opportunities to a wider segment of private citizens. NASA coordinated the selection of the teacher with the Council of Chief State School Officers. Over 11,000 teachers applied for the opportunity to become the Teacher-in-Space.

Courtesy of NASA

On July 19, 1985, Vice President George Bush announced the selection of Christa McAuliffe with Barbara Morgan as back-up. Christa McAuliffe, a social studies teacher at Concord (New Hampshire) High School, began her training in September 1985 at Johnson Space Center in Houston, Texas. She became an instant celebrity but never lost sight of her purpose—to be an enthusiastic teacher who would bring the experience of space travel to students throughout the nation. She joined a highly competent shuttle crew—Commander Dick Scobee, Pilot Michael Smith, Mission Specialists Judy Resnick, Ellison Onizuka, Ron McNair and Payload Specialist Greg Jarvis. Their Shuttle Mission 51-L aboard the *Challenger* was to be a six-day mission leaving Kennedy Space Center in Florida on January 22 and returning January 28 to the same site. The mission was to carry and deploy two payloads—a pair of communication satellites to be stationed over the Atlantic and Pacific Oceans, and a device designed to make observations of the ultraviolet spectrum of Halley's Comet. In addition, a number of scientific experiments, including student-designed experiments, would be conducted. McAuliffe would describe these experiments plus other activities during her live lessons from space via satellite to the Public Broadcasting Service (PBS). This Teacher-in-Space mission would serve to emphasize the role of education in space research and exploration.

The research of Paul Torrance had influenced Dr. June Scobee, wife of Shuttle Commander Dick Scobee. June Scobee was professor at the University of Houston in Clear Lake, Texas and served as a member of the Advisory Board for the Torrance Studies for Gifted, Creative, and Future Behaviors at the University of Georgia. She had been a student of Dr. Bill Nash at Texas A & M University in College Station, Texas. Bill Nash had been a doctoral student of Dr. Torrance at the University of Georgia. The Scobees had met the Torrances, and the two couples had been attracted to each other through their mutual interest in creativity. Dick Scobee had been a fighter pilot in Vietnam and had studied the research conducted by Dr. Torrance on jet aces and fighter pilots of the Korean War. Dick and Dr. Torrance talked at considerable length about fighter pilots and the risks that they take. June Scobee especially liked the "Manifesto for Children" and suggested an alternative title, "How to Grow Up Creatively Gifted."

Astronaut Dick Scobee offered to take some product of Dr. Torrance's research in his preference kit on the *Challenger* flight. Dr. Torrance wanted it

In scientific advance and educational practice, progress has always been dependent to a large extent upon the development of instruments to make possible the kinds of research and practice not previously possible. In this respect, the Torrance Tests of Creative Thinking have been a breakthrough.

The Torrance Tests of Creative Thinking represent a step forward in the research and development of human intelligence. In search of an understanding of creative potential in all human beings, they have been administered to more children on Earth than any other such instruments. In keeping with the ideals and philosophy on which these tests were founded, they broke the metaphorical and physical boundaries of Earth's atmosphere with the launching of the *Teacher in Space* Space Shuttle.

PARTIAL LIST OF LANGUAGES INTO WHICH THE TORRANCE TESTS OF CREATIVE THINKING HAVE BEEN TRANSLATED

Arabic	Czechoslovakian	French	Hindi	Korean	Portuguese	Swedish	Urdu
Afrikaans	Farsee (Iran)	German	Hungarian	Malaysian	Punjabi	Tamil	Western Samoan
Bulgarian	Finnish	Greek	Italian	Norwegian	Romanian	Thai	Yugoslavian
Chinese	Flemish	Gujrati	Japanese	Oriya	Spanish	Turkish	Polish

E. Paul Torrance, Advisor
Torrance Studies

Mary M. Frasier, Director
Torrance Studies

Dick Scobee, Commander
1986 NASA 51-L Flight

Tests reprinted with permission from Scholastic Testing Service, Bensenville, Il

With special appreciation to Guest Printing Co., Inc., Athens, GA to be something of real significance, something symbolic to the world and the universe. After much debate and deliberation, it was decided to send a set of the Torrance Tests of Creative Thinking (TTCT). The TTCT represent a step forward in research on the measurement of human creativity. Translated into over 34 languages, the tests have been administered to more children worldwide than any other such instrument, and have been used to identify creative potential in children and adults, including special-needs populations such as the deaf, retarded, emotionally handicapped, learning disabled, and the gifted. The cover page of the package of creativity tests is displayed on page 201.

Prior to the launch of the *Challenger* mission, Paul Torrance received the following letter from the Scobees:

Dick Scobee
15026 Brookpoint Drive
Houston, Texas 77062

1-13-1986

Dear Dr Torrance & Pansy,

We want you to have this souvenir Shuttle Launch invitation for Flight 51-L.

Your Creativity tests will be aboard orbiting the Earth every 90 minutes. Someday they will be in the hands of people all over the world - not just over their heads.

This is <u>your</u> flight for creative people around the world.

Love, June & Dick

In addition, the College of Education at the University of Georgia, under the leadership of Dr. Mary Frasier, had a bronze medallion struck to commemorate the Teacher-in-Space flight. It also was to be carried aboard the Shuttle in Commander Scobee's preference kit.

A series of activities were planned to celebrate the Teacher-in-Space program at the College of Education in Athens, Georgia. The Scobees were to visit the University of Georgia campus in March to talk with students and the public. The College of Education had sponsored a future scenario writing competition for all Georgia schools called "Share Your Ideas with an Astronaut." Also at that time, Astronaut Scobee would officially present the medallion and the set of creativity tests taken on the shuttle flight to the University of Georgia.

Mary Frasier was invited to the NASA John F. Kennedy Space Center in Florida on January 28, 1986, to view the launch of the Space Shuttle Mission 51–L. This was to be the tenth flight of the Space Shuttle *Challenger* that would be propelled into a 153 nautical mile circular orbit. Many questions raced through Mary's mind as she awaited the launch: "How will this flight for education affect the thinking of millions of students who were watching the launch and would follow it over its seven-day duration? How will 'The Ultimate Field Trip' be received? and Can you imagine the sheer courage and commitment to exploration it would take to sit in a space plane atop enormous tubular bombs, some 36 stories high, gorged with several of the most explosive materials this side of nuclear fission, and let some NASA engineer light the fuse?"

Mary Frasier described her feelings of pride and joy *before* the actual launch:

> The opportunity to view the launch for the Teacher-in-Space expedition of the *Challenger* was an important event that only a few have the opportunity to experience. This was to be my second participation in a launch for, thanks to the Scobees, I had the opportunity earlier to witness a launch when the "seeds" project was the task at hand. But I did not personally know the astronauts involved. This time I did. So in this way it was more special. I knew the commander of this flight. That added to the excitement of being part of an event that also had a teacher, an educator like me, aboard. To be a part of this historical event was especially significant. In addition, I had the opportunity to help prepare the packet of Dr. Torrance's test that would be on the flight. Feeling fairly comfortable that this would be a successful mission, I was more disturbed by the weather conditions that were delaying the flight than anything else. I had the greatest confidence that this would be yet another triumph of mankind's exploration into a new frontier. The constant delays in the weather kept me from actually being there when the shuttle was launched for I had to return home. Responsibilities associated with my work and with arranging for the visit of the Scobees to the University of Georgia

campus precluded my staying longer. But I returned home with the idea that all would be well and had not the slightest feeling of the impending tragedy that would rock the world![7]

The rest is well documented history. The awful, unexpected event occurred at 11:59:13 a.m: The ship exploded in a fireball 73 seconds after launch, killing all seven "star sailors." The cheers in classrooms across America turned to tears as millions of students watched the explosion on television. According to the *U.S. News and World Report* by Huntley et al. (1986), despite the first-ever national trauma on television, NASA went ahead with its Space Ambassador project, using 104 teachers who were semifinalists in the Teacher-in-Space program to visit classrooms and discuss space careers with students. A day after the *Challenger* disaster, one of the ambassadors was in an elementary school in Maryland. He tried to keep a fine balance between being a parent and a counselor and still being enthusiastic about the program. When he finished his task, he asked students how many would like to go into space. Every hand went up.

Mary Frasier described her feelings of deep sadness *after* the launch:

> I was devastated when the news of the *Challenger* explosion was announced. Besides hurting over the tragedy in general, I was personally distraught because I knew the Scobees personally. I remembered my excitement over meeting Dick Scobee and visiting with him and June in their home. They both reminded me so much of Dr. Torrance in their humbleness in the face of their greatness. Piloting the *Challenger* was not just a job to Dick Scobee. It was a personal mission made more significant by his dedication to children and education. Both he and June always expressed the importance of education and the opportunities that their work afforded them both to contribute in so many ways. For example, I remember when Dick joined June at a summer workshop for children sponsored by Texas A & M to be a judge for a science experiment the children were doing. Not only was I excited to serve on the panel with him but I was impressed with the seriousness with which he carried out this task.
>
> I was somewhat disappointed with the turn of events because we had planned so carefully for the visit by Dick and June to the University of Georgia to personally present the Teacher-in-Space medallion and the packet of Torrance Tests that were on the space shuttle. Two things happened that affected very much my feelings after the *Challenger* explosion. The first was to find a way to let this be a valuable educational experience for the children in the state of Georgia who had invested some time and energy in preparing for the visit of the Scobees. Incidentally, the children were to be the main event. When the Scobees were contacted regarding the events that might be planned for their visit to our campus, they stressed the importance of meeting with children, not the obligatory dignitaries that normally mark such an event. The second thing that happened that has changed my feelings forever, was the courage and determination of June Scobee

[7] Personal letter from Mary Frasier to the author. October 11, 1992.

> that the program should take place as planned. She expressed the feelings about "risk taking," the essence of creativity so well when she explained how her husband and other astronauts understood that their pioneering efforts were always tempered by the risks they entailed. They knew, she noted, that the possibility of some mishap such as the explosion of the Challenger was always possible. But that was a risk they were willing to take. Explorations and experimentations must never be hampered by fears of failure for through failures as tragic as they may be we learn so much. Persons breaking new frontiers understand the dangers and prepare as well as they can to be as safe as is possible. But safety from all peril is never promised! [8]

America did go through a short period of self-analysis as to whether or not to continue the exploration of space that began in 1962. Some have asked, "Why bother with such a dangerous and costly space program?"

René Daumal, in his 1974 book *Mount Analogue: A Novel of Symbolically Authentic Non-Euclidean Adventures in Mountain Climbing,* gives a compelling reply:

> You cannot stay on the summit forever, you have to come down again. So why bother in the first place? Just this: What is above knows what is below, but what is below does not know what is above. One climbs. One sees. One descends. One sees no longer. But, one has seen. There's an art of conducting oneself in the lower regions by the memory of what one saw higher up. When one can no longer see, one can at least still know. (p. 115–116)

Walter Westrum, superintendent of Hall Township High School in Spring Valley, Illinois, said, "Isabella and Ferdinand (of Spain) didn't say, 'We'd better not send Christopher Columbus—somebody may get hurt'" ("Perspectives," 1986, p. 21). June Scobee responded to Vice President George Bush's talk to the astronauts' families, saying, "This incident must not slow up the exploration of space. We must go on (Torrance, 1986, p. 2). And finally, President Ronald Reagan expressed the courage and faith in dreams that have characterized Americans throughout the ages:

> Today, we promise that their dream lives on, that the future they worked so hard to build will become reality.... Man will continue his conquest of space. To reach out for new goals and ever greater achievements—that is the way we shall commemorate our seven *Challenger* heroes. (January 31, 1986) [9]

The University of Georgia's special link with the *Challenger* mission went ahead as planned despite the tragedy. Dr. June Scobee and astronaut Dr. Norm Thagard visited the university in May of 1986 to participate in the Georgia Space

---

[8] Ibid.

[9] *Challenger—We Remember.* Brochure distributed by the Challenger Center, Washington, DC.

Education Project. They spoke to students and faculty on the role of future leaders in supporting space research and exploration. Drs. Scobee and Thagard presented medallions to winners of the Georgia statewide scenario-writing competition. Students from elementary and secondary schools composed positive scenarios giving their ideas on how space travel and research will enhance the quality of life in the future. The medallions were replicas of the one Dick Scobee carried aboard the ill-fated *Challenger* space plane.

A memorial has been erected to the seven crew members killed in the *Challenger* at Arlington Memorial Cemetery in Washington, DC. Many Americans feel they would want us to carry on their mission—to explore space and to teach. In the fall of 1986, Dr. June Scobee, on behalf of the *Challenger* families, proposed Challenger Centers for Space Science Education. These centers would be the world's first interactive network of learning centers to bring the excitement of space to people everywhere. Through this initiative a major step will be taken toward reclaiming America's destiny to lead the way to the stars. The Challenger Centers will provide students and teachers with unique, hands-on learning experiences in science and mathematics skills. Since the first Challenger Center opened in Houston, Texas in 1988, more than 600,000 children have attended a center, and millions of others have benefited from resources developed by the program. The Challenger Centre in Edmonton, Alberta, Canada, where I live, has hosted more than 8,500 students since its opening in November 1991. Five "Mission Sites" have been planned—Space Life Station, Manned Base on Mars, a Lunar Mining Base, a Jupiter research outpost, and an Earth orbital science station. The living memorial to the *Challenger* crew is still developing. Twenty-five Challenger Learning Centers have been opened in 20 states and in Canada and have established a fine reputation.

In the recovery operation after the *Challenger* explosion, the set of creativity tests from Dick Scobee's preference kit was recovered completely intact. They are now a part of the Torrance Collection in the archives at the University of Georgia.

Dr. Jack Presbury, a student of Paul Torrance and Professor of Educational Psychology at James Madison University, wrote this poem after the *Challenger* tragedy and dedicated it to Paul, Christa McAuliffe, and other great teacher-challengers of the world:

ICARUS
by Jack Presbury
For E. Paul Torrance, Christa McAuliffe, and
the other great Teacher-Challengers of the world

Last night I dreamed of Icarus
And how he flew too high
With wax and feathers for his wings
He tried to touch the sky.
And some say
When we soar with pride

And lack humility
An angry God reminds us
Of the laws of gravity.

Last night I dreamed of Challenger
And seven souls who dared
How fire hurled them back to earth
And not one life was spared.
And some say
There's a secret vision
Only God should see
So we should stay here
Bound to earth
And let the heavens be.

But I say
When we try and fail
And dare to try once more
Something lives
Within our hearts
That wasn't there before.
And where our reach
Exceeds our grasp
Fantastic worlds begin
We touch the gates of heaven
And God invites us in.

Last night I dreamed of children
Who believe that they can fly
Who travel their imaginations
Far beyond the sky
Like Icarus,
The Challengers
Are never dead and gone
They're always waiting somewhere
To cheer the children on.

(Permission to use granted by Jack Presbury—October 8. 1992.)

TRAVELING DIFFICULTIES

In 1985–86, John Carroll, a clinical psychologist in private practice from Western Australia, spent a year at the University of Massachusetts on study leave and heard that Paul Torrance was coming to speak at a conference on creativity there. He was surprised to see the changes in Paul from 1979, mainly due to the stroke. Paul had some trouble with speech and movement, particularly of the neck, though there was nothing wrong with his memory as he recognized and recalled both John Carroll and his wife.

The address at the University of Massachusetts took place not long after the *Challenger* mishap, and a major theme of Paul's talk was on the quality of risk taking that is part of creativity. John had found Paul quite inspirational on occasion as a student, and he found himself incredibly moved by Paul's performance. Knowing that it would be difficult to pull this off, Paul had worked out a multimedia approach and had arranged for things like a special chair and audiovisual aids. However, the organizers did not provide the requested aids and Paul had immense difficulty in making his presentation.

John Carroll was tremendously proud of Paul and admired what he was doing. He was following his own advice and taking enormous personal risks to his self-esteem and reputation. John felt it was the most significant lesson Paul had ever taught him. The major speaker was a flamboyant personality whose material was glittery in presentation and trite in content. It occurred to John that the conference participants may have valued the other presentation more than the one given by Paul Torrance, and that saddened him.

Dr. Torrance also accepted a speaking engagement to address the Tenth Annual Conference on Creativity in Gifted Education at Houston, Texas, in March of 1989. He wanted to test himself to see if he was ready to resume this kind of activity. Although good friends assisted him in Texas, he had not traveled for five or six years and found that so many changes had taken place that he felt uncomfortable. For example, in his hotel room, he was not able to get either of the two TVs to work, even after hotel attendants told him how.

"MAKING THE CREATIVE LEAP BEYOND"

Paul and Tammy Safter revised and wrote new chapters for *The Search for Satori and Creativity.* Paul says that although the term *satori* is better known and understood in the Western world today than in 1979, it seemed desirable to change the title. The new title, *Making the Creative Leap Beyond,* has helped open up his own thinking about creativity and achievement.

In February of 1993, I received a package from Paul Torrance. It was a draft copy of his revised book, which has been submitted to the publisher, Bearly Limited. The foreword is by June Scobee Rodgers, and the book is dedicated "in loving memory of Jessie Pansy Nigh Torrance."

QUALITY OF LIFE PROJECT

The Quality of Life project is a program designed by Dr. Claire Clements and a group of assistants, including Paul Torrance, to use physical and creative activities to increase the self-sufficiency and independence of elderly people with developmental disabilities. The program is made up of 12 sessions that combine two or more elements of the arts, creativity, and physical fitness. Each session focuses on a theme descriptive of the current month or season.

Paul Torrance and Kathy Goff developed the creativity module, which provides information and sample lessons for instructors who will use the resource. Initial reports on the use of the materials are very positive. Elderly people enjoy the creativity lessons and use the skills to function more efficiently in their daily activities.

Kathy Goff and her colleague, Jamie McCracken, developed a game for older adults called "Senior Savvy—Brainstorming."[10] It was devised to foster communication with each other and to practice the valuable creative thinking skill of brainstorming. The game is an attempt to get the elderly to use their creative potential.

"BEYONDER" STUDY

Paul has demonstrated that a researcher can rely on intuition to go beyond the usual insights that can be gained from statistical analysis in a traditional research design. When Paul evaluated the information provided by subjects of his 30-year follow-up regarding their creative achievements during the past two decades, it became apparent to him that some individuals had achieved so much that they could not be placed on the same scale as their counterparts. He called them the "Beyonders." Paul Torrance determined that there are other strong forces that make a Beyonder, forces that are more dominant than creative ability, intelligence, and high academic achievement. These forces are love of one's work, persistence, purpose in life, love of challenge, diversity of experience, high energy level, and a sense of mission. These characteristics or strong forces seem most important in producing Beyonders. Paul found twelve who fit this label. The predictive factors that explained their unusual creative achievements were special abilities on the TTCT and other factors, such as a passionate love of what they were doing and a rich future image. Christopher Nelson, a consultant for gifted education with the Georgia State Department of Education, will detail these findings in his dissertation.

CORRESPONDENCE: "SPREADING THE WORD"

Letter Writing Began Early

Both Pansy and Paul were great letter writers. Both corresponded with friends in all parts of the world—particularly Paul. Paul still receives several hundred letters every month. Most are business-related: however, some are personal.

[10] Available from Elliot and Fitzpatrick, P.O. Box 1945, Athens, GA 30603.

Paul sent me a personal letter dated October 21, 1991, and enclosed the Japanese International Letter Writing Week commemorative stamps. The stamps were issued to promote world peace and cultural exchange through letter writing. Paul had received the stamps in appreciation from Sam Stern, who held the Japan Management Association Chair at the Tokyo Institute of Technology. Paul indicated that writing letters (and receiving them) sustained both him and Pansy, especially during difficult times and when they couldn't discuss their problems with the people around them.

Pansy began writing letters to a pen pal in Ohio when she was 10 years old. This friendship continued throughout the lifetime of her friend. After Pansy's friend was diagnosed with cancer, she created a painting for each of them. Paul's painting symbolized the predicament of gifted children; Pansy's symbolized her love of the State of Oklahoma, flowers, and education. Paul has given his painting to the Torrance Center for Creative Studies.

Pansy apparently saved every letter she received throughout her life. Paul and Pansy would write one another letters when they were away from each other. After Pansy's death, Paul discovered that she had kept all of these letters.

Paul also began his letter writing at age 10. He was hospitalized for a ruptured appendix and was out of school for six or seven months. He wrote everyone—the nurses, his teacher, his aunts, and his classmates, especially the girl he had a crush on at the time and the boy who was his best friend. Paul still enjoys writing letters, although he can't find the time to write letters that are as detailed and thoughtful as he would like.

Paul Torrance is deeply interested in nature. His letters are usually filled with reports of seasonal changes and the status of his own and local flowers: "The dogwood, hydrangeas, azaleas, redbud, pear, peach, and cherry had burst out in full bloom. Little violets are spread out all over our lawn. Kathy, my graduate assistant, has set out four tomato plants for me, and Mohammed's experimental plants had been growing."[11]

In most of Paul Torrance's correspondence, he manages to give the impression that the relationship has value for him, which is the essence of encouragement. For example, the few quotes below illustrate the personal quality of his letters to Bee Bleedorn in Minneapolis, Minnesota:

> Congratulations on the fine press you have been getting for the gifted program in Minnesota!
>
> Many, many thanks for your wonderful letter. It was at the same time cheering, supportive and inspirational.
>
> I appreciate you nominating me for the Temple Award for Creative Altruism and for all the nice things you said about me.[12]

---

[11] Personal correspondence from E. Paul Torrance to the author. April 10, 1992.

[12] Personal correspondence from E. Paul Torrance to Berenice Bleedorn.

Correspondence of E. Paul Torrance

As a graduate student, Don Treffinger wrote to Paul Torrance asking a question and wondered if he would ever get a response. Within a week, he had a personal letter back—in detail and full of support and encouragement. It gave him a tremendous boost. Today, Dr. Don Treffinger is President of the Center for Creative Learning in Sarasota, Florida, and presents workshops on creativity all over North America. Don Treffinger is, and has been, amazed at Paul's letter writing ability. He is extremely envious of how Paul can keep up to his correspondence and be so prompt.

International Correspondence: "Citizen of the World"

The work of Paul Torrance is well known throughout the world. Over the years, he has corresponded with many individuals—scholars, educators, and parents. He continues today to get requests from international persons for information about some aspect of his research and writings. An analysis of his international correspondence since his retirement reveals that his influence is universal and the scope of his work is wide-ranging.

From 1984 to 1992, his foreign correspondence com-

Argentina
Australia
Austria
Azerbaijan
Bahrain
Belgium
Bolivia
Brazil
Canada
Chile
China

Table 1
International Correspondence: Purpose*

1. Advice (examination, evaluation, review, help, cooperation on committees)	81
2. Reprints of Articles	69
3. Books and manuals	60
4. TTCT	52
5. SOLAT	38
6. Invitations (meetings, conferences, etc.)	31
7. Information	30
8. Other creativity tests	24
9. Visiting Scholar Program	16
10. Future Problem Solving Program	16
11. Translation of books, tests, and articles	15
12. Recommendation	14
13. HIPS	12
14. Torrance Creative Scholar/Mentor Network	11
15. Ideal Child and the Ideal Pupil Checklist	6
16. International Network of Gifted Children and Their Teachers	2

* Listed in order of frequency of requests

Costa Rica
Cuba
Czechoslovakia
Egypt
Estonia
Fiji
Finland
France
Germany
Great Britain
Greece
Guam
Hungary
India
Iran
Ireland
Israel
Italy
Japan
Jordan
Korea
Kuwait
Malaysia
Mexico
Netherlands
New Zealand
Nigeria
Philippines
Poland
Portugal
Qatar
Rumania
Saudi Arabia
South Africa
South America
Spain
Sweden
Switzerland
Taiwan
Thailand
Turkey
Ukraine
United Arab Emirates
Uruguay
U.S.S.R.
Venezuela
Yugoslavia
Zimbabwe

prised addresses in 59 countries and 341 different correspondents. One person from outside the country wrote extensively during this period, asking for assistance and advice. The top four countries involved in his foreign correspondence were India, Canada, South Africa and Japan.

The purposes of the correspondence have been wide-ranging, and the subjects can be classified in a number of categories. The topics of the letters are outlined in Table 1.

Requests from people in other countries fluctuate from time to time. Correspondence from India has been sustained over a long period of time, since well before Paul's retirement. There was interest shown in China for only a brief time, from about three years before the massacre at Tiananmen Square until immediately after that event. Now for the first time, there is interest in Paul's work in Russia and other eastern European countries.

The international interest in creativity demonstrates that the activities Paul recommends can be implemented in and across all cultures. Michael Jackson said at the 35th Annual Grammy Awards that "creativity is going to heal the wounds of the *world.*"

University Correspondence

I analyzed the sources and topics of correspondence that Paul received between 1978 and 1982, while he was a professor at the University of Georgia. The majority of the letters were from outside of the state. The major topic was requests for information or comments on a number of topics such as the Future Problem Solving Program, creativity, career education, and establishing gifted programs. Many individuals also asked Paul to write letters of reference for promotions. He was prompt and very complete in his response. His incredible work ethic and organizational ability shone through his correspondence.

PAUL TORRANCE REFLECTS ON...

This section discusses Paul Torrance's thinking on a number of important issues and situations related to his work and life.[13]

...Living on the "Edge" of His Competence

Paul Torrance feels that his career has served him well. It has not brought him from poverty to riches, but he has always lived on the "edge." It seemed that every ten years, Paul was pushed to develop a new expertise. His salary has been such that he could "get by." He has always lived on the "edge" in his career insofar as his ability and preparation are concerned.

Even during the latter part of his career, when he came to the University of Georgia, Paul had to had to learn new things: He had to become an expert on early childhood education. In Reno, Minneapolis, and even in Athens, he had had experience in working with preschool children in the churches to which he had belonged. However, he had no graduate school courses in preschool education. When the White House Conference on Children of 1970 came along, he was asked to chair the forum on children from birth to age two years on the emergence of identity. Paul demurred at first, saying that he was not an expert in the field. They quickly said, "Nobody is, but we have noticed that you have constantly gone into unknown areas and developed them." This itself was a challenge to Paul. The leaders of this forum were very helpful.

Since Paul and Pansy had not had any children, Paul had to get to know children and read lots of books that had previously been unknown to him. Paul made use of the members of his forum—a renowned child psychologist, a medical doctor, a cartoonist, a nurse, a folklorist, a kindergarten teacher, a poet, a psychologist, two educational media designers, a social worker, and others. Finally, they were ready. A number of resolutions were put forth and presented to the large White House Committee on Children. The forum participants in Paul's group wanted to protest President Nixon's lack of support for very young children, and they made a protest march around the White House. It became controversial. Paul was pleased with the resolutions of his committee, and several were used in the resolutions of the Conference as a whole. Delegates voted, and one of his group's resolutions received the most votes. It pertained to the rearrangement of U.S. national priorities to give all children a chance to grow creatively.

Another example of operating "on the edge" occurred just after Pansy's death in 1988. There was an editorial about her in the local newspaper, and next to it was a congratulatory note about a grant to Dr. Claire Clements on the Quality of

[13] Dr. Torrance's comments in this section are taken from a personal interview with him at his home in Athens, Georgia, June 1992.

Life program. This program was to be developed for caregivers of the elderly using drama, art, dance, and physical fitness. This inspired Paul to volunteer his services and those of his research assistant, Kathy Goff—a major in gerontology and adult education. They added Creativity as another discipline and the Incubation Model of Teaching as a method to organize and present various modules.

Before this, Paul had little expertise in gerontology. The field is a vast one, and Paul did manage to publish a few articles in the gerontology journals and in a gerontology encyclopedia. Paul, by now a septuagenarian, was using his research on creativity to assist his own generation. Yes, he was living on the edge, and still in front.

...25th Wedding Anniversary

Paul recalls his 25th wedding anniversary as his most memorable special day, although it was not all that good. He had planned for it; he had bought some bells and other things, and he had planned to invite some of their best friends. When the day came around, however, Pansy was in the hospital recuperating from a massive stroke. She was depressed and apparently had contemplated suicide. Paul went ahead and invited Craig and Doris Bryan, some of Pansy's closest friends, to the hospital. Paul had the cake but not the bells. Dr. David Butts, Head of Science Education, had his wife just across the hallway, so Paul invited them to have a piece of cake with them. It was not a jubilant occasion and not what Paul planned, but nevertheless it was memorable.

...A Fond Memory: 141 S.E. Warwick Street

In March of 1993, I asked Paul Torrance, "Of all the places you've lived, which holds the fondest memories for you?"

> This was difficult for me to decide. I have fond memories of every place I have ever lived. However, the house at 141 S.E. Warwick Street in Minneapolis, was the place where I "grew up." This was the first house I had ever owned and paid for. It was a very modest little house but I liked it. It only cost me $13,000 in 1958 and it sold for $13,500 in 1966, and I expected more than that because we had added many improvements—air conditioning, storm windows, painted the basement, put a ceiling in the basement, etc. However, this was 1966 and the price of housing had only begun to climb. It was near the University of Minnesota and I knew many of the people who lived there.
>
> It was in walking distance to a main busline which would take you to almost any address in Minneapolis or St. Paul. There was a small grocery store across the street from 141 Warwick S.E. As a matter of fact, this grocer was to be the central figure of one of my most pleasant memories. This grocer did many very

kind and thoughtful things for his customers, especially those who lived on Warwick (two blocks). One summer, Minneapolis Symphony offered itself to the group or individual who wrote the best letter describing how they would use the Symphony Orchestra. Pansy and the other women on Warwick got together proposing a street dance on Warwick Street to honor our grocer, Don Chergosky. They won and all of Don's customers were invited. This included the Mayor, our U.S. senator, a couple of congressmen, and many distinguished professors, lawyers, doctors, and businessmen. The street was roped off from traffic and card tables were placed in the street and Don's suppliers furnished the refreshments. Several of the houses had garages fronting on the street, and each of them had a deck. This was where the orchestra sat. After refreshments had been served and while the orchestra was playing, the people danced in the street, including the children. The headline in the newspaper read: "Posh it was not; fun it was."

Our neighborhood was beautifully cooperative, both in planning and cleaning up. Everything was cleaned up within an hour and we had expressed our appreciation to Don.

We entertained more while we lived here than at any other time—a great diversity of students, friends, visitors (publishers, *LOOK* writers and photographers, acquaintances from the past, past friends and professional colleagues, etc.) We had several large folding tables which we could set up in the basement. It was known as a small but warm and friendly place. I still receive letters from some of our neighbors who lived on Warwick Street and cherish those memories.

...Marriage

I think that empathy, love, caring, and mutual support are the major ingredients of a good marriage. If one or the other is having trouble, it's no time for the other to have trouble. The one above all needs emotional support—or whatever kind of support is needed. Above all else, keep communicating.

...Children

Paul Torrance spoke to me about the kind of children he and Pansy would like to have had, if they had been able:

> If I had had children, I would not have hesitated to love them and let them know I loved them. I think I would have encouraged such characteristics as curiosity, persistence, courage, honesty, integrity, independence and interdependence, a sense of humor, and a spirit of adventure. I think I would have encouraged them to see and experience the world and have an image of the future. I think I would have tried to help them feel comfortable as a minority of one and to choose something in life that they loved with a passion.

...Friendships

I asked Paul Torrance to discuss the friendships he has had over the years. He responded:

> I have always had lots of *good and loyal friends,* but only a few intimate friends. Now, most of my contemporaries have deceased. Most of the close friends have been classmates, Sunday school and church members, neighbors, and professional colleagues.
>
> The best and most intimate friend has been my late wife, Pansy. Now, I suppose my closet friends are my sister [Ellen] and Mohammed Badaway and Princess [his cat]. I tell most of my problems to them.
>
> I also feel rather close to Rod Myers (a former graduate student, co-author, and colleague), Kathy Goff (former graduate assistant and co-author), Tammy Safter (former student and co-author), Harrie Buswell (graduate student and creative person), Mary Murdock (student, co-author, etc.), Jack Presbury (colleague, co-author), Garnet Millar (visiting scholar and my biographer), Dorothy Funk-Werblo, Felice Kaufmann, Rose Arnold, Virginia Macagnoni, and Laura Rose.
>
> Then there is another group for whom I hold in equal affection and admiration, but my relation is less intimate and the contact is less frequent. One group is from the foreign students, visiting scholars, and visitors. Among them are: Conchita Tan-Willman (Philippines and Canada), M. K. Raina (India), Kobus Neethling (South Africa), Abdalla Soliman (student and visiting scholar, United Arab Emirates), Grigoire Nicola (visiting scholar, Romania), Saburo Sato (translator, visiting scholar, host), S. Nayana Tara (visiting scholar, India), and the Australian pair John Carroll and Noel Howieson.
>
> The other group is composed of my former students, advisees, and assistants. Among them are: Bill Nash, Jim Curry, Deborah Weiner, Orlow Ball, Jon Edwards, Alan Black, Ted Riegel, Bee Bleedorn, Bonnie Cramond, Bill Curry, Pat Dwinell, Jerry Flack, George Fujita, Paul Henrickson, Peggy Hooper, Marilyn Ivey, Lyle Johnson, Joe Khatena, Adrienne Kinkaid, Gail Lewis, Gerald Middents, Christopher Nelson, Larry and Lee Orcutt, Jeanette Parker, Mary Lee Platz, Jack Riley, Neil Satterfield, Howard and Norma Stevens, Barbara Swicord, David Templeton, Harry and Faith Turner, Anne Taylor, Mary Waterstreet and Kaoru Yamamoto.
>
> Then there are colleagues from Georgia Military College (GMC), University of Minnesota (UMn), Kansas State University (KSU), USAF Survival Research, University of Georgia (UGA), and other professional colleagues.[14] Among them are:

---

[14] Abbreviations mean:
FPSP—Future Problem Solving Program
CEF—Creative Education Foundation, Buffalo, NY;
NAGC—National Association for Gifted Children
UALA—University of Alabama
ACA—American Creativity Association
UAZ—University of Arizona.
NACCA—National Association for Creative Children and Adults
NS LTI GT—National/State Leadership Training Institute for the Gifted and Talented

Louis and Alice Andrews (GMC), Gladys Bellinger (KSU and UMn), Kay Bruch (UGA), Vicki Connell (UGA), Eleanor Conn (KSU), Lew and Lorena Cordell (GMC), Anne Crabbe (FPSP), Marie Friedel (Foundation for C/G Children), Mary Frasier (UGA), Ann F. Isaacs (NACCA), Joyce Juntune (NAGC and ACA), Ruth Noller (CEF), Sidney and Bea Parnes (CEF), Bert O. Richmond (UGA), Irving Sato (NS LTI GT), Carol Schlichter and Ross Palmer (UALA), Doris Shallcross (CEF), Dorothy Sisk (NAGC, CEF, ACA), Robert Strom (UAZ), Leatha Spratlin (UGA), Don Treffinger, and Robert Wilson (KSU).

There are many others whose friendship is valued but the contact is less frequent.

...Reading

Paul has always read a great deal. In college, he majored in English and American Literature. He usually read twice as many books as were required in literature, history, political science, educational psychology, and psychology. Paul managed to read a great deal of fiction until he had so much interesting professional reading to do. During the time he was Head of the Department of Educational Psychology, he felt that he should keep abreast of knowledge in all areas of educational psychology. He co-edited, with William White, a book of reading in general areas of educational psychology in 1970 and updated it in a second edition in 1975.

After Pansy and Paul founded the Future Problem Solving Program, there was another change in his reading. He then read the leading futurists, methods of futurists, and the frontiers that promised to bring about the most change and/or create the most problems.

Due to Paul's busy schedule, he bought thousands of books that remained unread. Pansy also read a great deal all her life, and she read books Paul had purchased but had no time to read. Pansy would read passages aloud to Paul, make notes, and mark the books with passages she thought Paul ought to read.

During Pansy's stroke illnesses, she liked to read the novels of Louis L'Amour, and before she died Bantam Books started to reprint all of his novels. Paul subscribed to it for her. Paul hopes that someday he will have time to read these books. Perhaps the collection will be donated to some library in honor of Pansy. Paul has already donated most of their religious books to the library of the First Baptist Church of Athens.

Throughout his career, Paul has always tried to read the old literature on the subject, issue, or problem that he is exploring. He says that it has always paid off.

Paul's greatest regret in moving from 185 Riverhill Drive in Athens was giving up his library and its 1½ miles of book shelves. He still finds it hard to part with his books or those belonging to Pansy.

...Music

All of Paul's attempts in the realm of music production have been utter failures. The only instrument he ever tried seriously was the harmonica. He made a little progress and participated in his group's concert, but he had to fake it. However, Paul likes to write and type to the accompaniment of classical music, and he enjoys country music and gospel music.

...Attempts at Vacations

Paul and Pansy took little time for recreation and holidays, as their work demanded so much of their time. They took many business trips together and this helped Paul, especially in giving more of himself to Pansy. They had some good trips associated with Paul's work, to Spain, Hawaii, and Japan. After an international conference of Applied Psychology in Liège, Belgium, they went on tour to England, France, Italy, Austria, Switzerland, and Holland.

In 1981, Paul bought Pansy and himself an Eastern Airlines Get Up and Go flight ticket with almost unlimited flights and stayovers on weekends. They went to Palm Springs, California, in January and stopped on the return trip at Pansy's niece's home in Huntington Beach for the weekend. A few days later, Pansy had a massive stroke and it put a stop to her traveling. As Pansy had one stroke after the other, and Paul suffered a stroke, they were together most of the time, but it was not quality time, and nurses were almost always around.

...Most Memorable Holiday

Paul and Pansy's most memorable holiday was spent in Lutzen, Minnesota. They sat on the shore of Lake Superior and watched the birds and waves. It was cool in August, and the food was wonderful. They walked the paths around the resort where there were wildflowers, berries, and small animals. Pansy played a little golf; they read some and rode around in the evening observing the bears in the garbage containers. On the final day, they stopped on the way back to Duluth. Paul took a beautiful picture of Pansy, the wildflowers, and the rocks on the bluff overlooking Lake Superior. He also took one of Pansy wearing a pink woolly-looking sweater and a blue dress with a cross and the mist in the background. Paul recalls that these were the best photographs he ever took of Pansy. In his words, "She looked quite beautiful!"

...His Parents

One of the main reasons Paul left Minneapolis was to be closer to his parents to assist them in any way possible. I asked him to reflect on his life with his parents. He used his last encounter with them to reveal his thinking and feelings about them.

The last time he saw his "Daddy" alive was the Sunday before Christmas in 1967. Paul and Pansy had gone down to the farm near Milledgeville to spend Christmas with his parents, his sister Ellen, and her husband Delmus.

Paul was under pressure to complete the report on the cross-cultural study of the fourth-grade slump on creativity. It had originally been scheduled for completion in 1964. The study was the most complex one he had ever attempted and also the biggest (with the largest number of subjects). He had been given an ultimatum that it must be completed by January 1, 1968. This was a monumental task, and he knew that if he took time out in the middle of this visit he could not finish it. Paul needed the grant money for the project, and he had already invested more than the amount of the grant from his own resources.

Just before they left, the weekend prior to Christman day, Paul sat by his father and explained his predicament to him. Daddy said, "If you can finish, I know it will be a great relief." During the ensuing week, some of the neighbors asked Mr. Torrance, "Where is that fat son of yours? Why isn't he here?" The reply was, "He is in Athens, working, but if I asked him to come down here, he would come."

Paul's father died of a heart attack that New Year's Eve in 1967. The autopsy confirmed a heart attack and showed some recurrence of prostate cancer.

Paul always thought that Daddy loved him and Ellen, but that he loved Ellen more. This did not bother Paul, however. Daddy never expressed his affection and neither did Mamma. Paul also thought of the many times his father had met his bus coming home. Paul recalled the time when he was discharged from the Army. He had not known when he would be discharged or when he would be able to catch a bus. Paul had thought that he would catch a cab or walk the ten miles from Milledgeville. It was about midnight when his bus arrived in Milledgeville, and there were no taxis, so he started walking, hoping that he could catch a ride, but there was not much traffic from Milledgeville to the place where his parents lived. As he neared his home, daybreak was on him. His parents were already up. They had been expecting him, but he has no recollection of embraces. They were glad that he was at home, but he would soon leave for his job at Kansas State.

Paul remembers his last visit to Mamma in the nursing home, before she became unable to recognize anyone. She had lost all of her sight, most of her hearing, and most of her speech. Paul just sat by her side with his arms around her and talked some. He does not know whether she understood anything he said, as she was so full of tranquilizers. She talked a little, but the thing that he remembers her saying was, "I always loved my children. I loved them too much." Paul knew that she did, but she never expressed it except in letters.

Paul's mother was very disappointed that she had never had any grandchildren. If it bothered Daddy, he never said anything about it. Mrs. Torrance also worried that Ellen and Paul had no children to take care of them in their later years.

When Paul's parents were younger, they were always busy. Mamma read a lot and crocheted a great deal. She could shoot a gun or rifle with greater accuracy than Daddy could. She would shoot hawks that bothered the chickens or snakes (rattlesnakes or moccasins). Daddy almost stopped farming in his last years, but he kept a rather large herd of beef cattle. Betty, a collie dog, was his constant companion until she died of old age. He also had cats—27 at one time. When Hazel died, Pansy went immediately to Milledgeville to get one of Daddy's cats for Paul. She selected a long-haired tabby for Paul, but it escaped. Daddy handed her one of the smaller ones, a brown tabby, and said, "This will make Paul a good pet."

Paul tells about a dream he had recently that sheds light on his relationship with his father:

> A few weeks ago, I had a very clear dream, without words. I had landed somewhere. There was something like an airport but no airplanes, but I was apparently moving in the direction of these buildings, but I did not know what it was all about.
>
> At first I did not recognize anyone. Finally as I approached the building, there was Daddy, wearing a gray top coat but it was not buttoned up. He was still slender, but was heavier than I had known him to be. He also looked younger than I had ever remembered him being, yet he was mature. I ran toward him and that was the end of the dream, but I have thought much about its meaning.

Valentine's Day must have always been Paul's favorite day. In assembling his archives, the oldest keepsake he could find was a valentine that he made for his mother when he was in second grade. His memories of this day are still very vivid. He recalls that one very beautiful little girl gave everyone in the class a store-bought valentine. He remembers the ambivalence of the other children in class about receiving it. Her mother was the community madam and apparently most of the parents of the children had told them to beware. Paul was naive; his parents had told him nothing. This girl's older sister was a friend of his first cousin. Paul remembers how scandalized everybody was when his cousin took this girl home with her.

...Some Significant Technological Changes

We have just progressed through what has been described as the most amazing 60 years in history with reference to science, medicine, education, entertainment, modern living, and the arts. Paul Torrance has experienced many technological changes in his lifetime that are too numerous to describe. However, the following pages highlight some of those changes and what they have meant to Paul, specifically the automobile and transportation in general, radio and television, and the typewriter.

The Automobile and Transportation in General

Paul's first memory of transportation is going to visit his maternal grandparents in a buggy. The night his father died, the undertaker told him a very interesting story about his father. When Paul's father was about 16 years old, he decided that he wanted a buggy. He went to the undertaker to make a deal on a buggy and gave his Uncle Charlie as a reference. The undertaker asked Uncle Charlie about it and was told that Paul's father would certainly pay him. So the first means of transportation that Paul encountered was the horse and buggy. He does not remember very clearly when his father bought his first Model T, but they did have it by the time Paul was in the third grade. His strongest memory of this car is the story recounted in Chapter 1 about his father driving where there was no road and running into a hole, which caused Paul's head to bump into the windshield.

The next transportation that he remembers was the school bus that his father drove. His father had sold the Model T by this time, and Paul does not think they had any other means of transportation other than the wagon; everywhere that they went, they went in the school bus. Paul was in the fourth grade, and he remembers driving over some steep red clay roads that were very slick when it rained. When Paul was hospitalized for three weeks with a burst appendix, his parents visited him almost every day after his father finished the bus route.

One humorous memory he has of the school bus is that their devoted dog Jack loved to ride in it. One Sunday, the Torrances had to shut Jack up in a chicken pen, but somehow he got out and followed the bus to church. The family was surprised to see Jack walking down the aisle of the church to join them.

The next automobile that the Torrances owned was a Whippet. The day his father bought the Whippet, he came by the school and got permission for Paul and his sister Ellen to go home and try out the new car. Paul remembers that they kept it for a long time and it gave them very good service. Some years later, his Aunt Mamie bought an automobile, and she drove them to many places throughout his later childhood and youth. Several times she attempted to teach him how to drive, but try as he might, he was unsuccessful. He could not steer the automobile in a straight line, so he finally gave up.

The next mode of transportation that Paul used was the Greyhound bus. He made his first long trip to Minneapolis in a bus; however, he rode the train the second time he went. Paul did not encounter air travel until after he received his Ph.D. degree, when he went to apply for a faculty position at Duke University. Paul decided to take another job offered by the Air Force as Director of the Survival Field Unit. From this time onward, he began to travel by air throughout the world.

Radio and Television

Other new technological developments were radio and television. Paul did not see a radio until he was about 12 years old. This radio was acquired by his Aunt Mamie and was at his grandparents' house. They enjoyed Amos and Andy, who were very popular at this time. They would walk the half mile to his grandfather's house several times a week to hear the "Amos and Andy" program. Paul did not own a radio or have one in his home until the second or third year that he was teaching. He bought a second-hand radio from one of the students at Georgia Military College while he was living in the barracks. After several years, he gave this radio to his parents. Paul did not have a television set until after he had married in 1958, and he did not get a color television until 1967. Paul did not have cable TV until 1986.

The Typewriter

Paul's first typewriter was acquired in the fall of 1936, in his third year of college. It cost $40 and was ordered from Sears, Roebuck, & Company. This was the first time that he had ever touched a typewriter, so he developed his own method of typing. The old Underwood served him through graduate school, the completion of his thesis in 1944 and through several years of teaching. He used this typewriter until he started to write a book in 1957 summarizing the seven years of survival research.

He bought an electric typewriter in about 1969, and this served him until 1980. It was not until later on that he acquired an electric typewriter that used a ball. Now he uses an IBM Wheelwriter given to him by Bill Nash, June Scobee, and Cecil Reynolds. He also has a word processor given to him by Jon Edwards, a former student.

Another technological advance of importance to Paul was the calculator. The statistics in his master's thesis were all done by hand. It was not until World War II that he learned about calculators and it was not until he had been at the University of Georgia that he had his statistics calculated by using the University of Georgia's Center for Statistics. In fact, it was not until about 1975 that Paul's department at the University of Georgia stopped using the hand calculator. When Paul thinks about computing, it seems to be a miracle that it is possible to run a program through the computer and do in a few minutes what a calculator could do in several months.

...Intergenerational Learning

Paul met Robert Strom in Minneapolis in the 1960s. Robert was teaching in St. Paul and took Paul's summer course. They collaborated on the book *Mental*

Health and Achievement, which was published in 1965. Paul has been good friends with Robert and his wife Shirley since those early Minnesota Years. Recently, Robert Strom published an inventory on the strengths and needs of grandparents. It emphasizes the significant role that grandparents have in teaching young people.

Paul Torrance, after his retirement, took up an interesting grandparent project. He collected a number of photographs illustrating grandparents in various learning situations with children in various cultures. Paul is a great believer in intergenerational learning; that is, he knows the time has come for the young to be teaching older individuals—computer skills was the example he always cited. Paul's research seemed to indicate that grandparents find it easier to enter "the world of the child" than parents do.

Paul is involved in an initiative called the "grandparent–grandchildren project." He is trying to capture the fun, learning, and growth of this relationship through natural photography (unrehearsed). He believes that these photographs can reveal many insights into this creative relationship. In addition, Paul Torrance feels that it will show parents, teachers, counselors, gerontologists, and others ways in which this resource may be used to benefit both grandparents and grandchildren.

...Challenging the "Golden Rule"

In a paper prepared for the American Creativity Association in April of 1991 in Houston, Texas, Paul discussed his many insights about creativity that have been questioned, rejected, ridiculed, and ignored. In Paul Torrance's 50 years of experience in creativity research, he has developed numerous insights about creative behavior that are counter to accepted and established ideas. This lack of acceptance is not surprising, as individuals like Paul Torrance, who have an original idea, are always in a minority of one, at least at first. Fortunately for Paul, he has had some support for his ideas, and this has encouraged him to continue.

Paul has noted that at times another person has come up with the same insight and it had been accepted. Paul cites the insight he had that being in love with something is important in creative achievement. He even reported research to support that insight, but it was not truly accepted until almost a decade later, when another individual came up with the same insight independently.

Paul has had the courage and vision to challenge ideas that are widely accepted and that no one dares to question. He questioned the Golden Rule, "Do unto others as you would have them do unto you," on the basis of his insight that we should "treat people like they want to be treated." He developed this idea through experience as a sociodramatist and from the great American Indian prayer, "Great Spirit, let me not judge a man (woman) until I have walked a mile in his (her) moccasins."

Paul cites the example of a high school boy who was "in love" with science. He had done well in elementary school and had done a lot of reading in science books prior to entering high school. The counselor told him that he could not take the General Science course as it would be too difficult for him. His family tried to intervene on his behalf but the counselor held firm, saying that he would fail, and lectured them on pushing him too hard.

The boy was able to find a science teacher in a nearby college to work with him. The teachere said the boy's understanding of chemistry was superior to that of college students. The boy was able to take high school science courses and he excelled in them. He won a scholarship for science talent in his senior year. The school principal could not believe his success and accused him of cheating. The boy was defended by one of his science teachers. It was discovered in his school record card that his home room number and IQ had been transposed. However, the science professor and teachers had treated him as he wanted to be treated.

A few other of Paul's insights are instructive and worth thinking about. Three are presented here to illustrate insights that are still not widely accepted.

1. *Insight:* Fourth graders are less creative than third graders.
   Accepted Belief and Practice: Creativity is developmental and consistently increases with age and education.
2. *Insight:* The willingness to disagree in a group facilitates creativity and making better decisions.
   Accepted Belief and Practice: Group cohesion and cooperation is the best facilitator of creativity and decision-making, and disagreement is disruptive to this process.
3. *Insight:* Young children can begin learning negotiation skills.
   Accepted Belief and Practice: Young children do not have the ability to learn negotiation skills, nor should they take time away from their basic skills instruction.

Many of these insights are supported by research, but none have been implemented in actual practice. Thank goodness for those who have the courage to question our beliefs and practices.

...His Health History and Secret of A Healthy Life

Throughout his life, Paul has been somewhat limited by health difficulties. When he was younger, he did not see how he could live a long or even average-length life, and he is amazed that he has lived as long as he has. However, he has always managed to keep going and has done an immense amount of work.

As a child and adolescent, Paul caught every communicable disease—

measles, mumps, whooping cough, and chicken pox. When he was examined at Georgia Military College, he was rejected for the officer training program and was made a non-cadet. He was never very strong and could not understand why he could not develop muscles, no matter how much he exercised. He often considered taking the Charles Atlas course in muscle-building.

It was the same story when Paul applied for life insurance. He was not accepted by some companies, although he was accepted grudgingly by others. When he was drafted during the Second World War, he was examined over and over and finally accepted for limited service.

As Paul entered the "old age" category, he has accumulated one diagnosis after another—stroke, anterocollis, arthritis (ankylosis spondylitis), fusing vertebrae, chronic bronchitis, asthma, many food and grass allergies, narcolepsy, prostatitis, tachycardia, and heart murmur. Some of these have continued; some of them have improved over the years; and others have gotten worse, as in the case of narcolepsy. Paul thinks that his narcolepsy is a serious handicap at the present time.

Narcolepsy is a neurological disorder characterized by serious symptoms such as excessive daytime sleepiness, sleep attacks, hallucinations, and loss of muscle tone. Paul reports that for him the symptoms of narcolepsy have intensified over the years. The milder symptoms of narcolepsy began appearing about 50 years ago in the form of falling asleep in church and at concerts. About 30 years ago, other symptoms began to appear: more frequent falling asleep in church, and while reading the newspaper, attending concerts, movies and plays, watching TV, and listening to lectures. Paul had observed these symptoms in his Grandfather Torrance, his uncles, and two of his first cousins. About 20 years ago, he began falling asleep while talking with students and others. If he recovered quickly, he apologized, saying he was fatigued. He usually continued the interview. If it was lengthy, Paul often found the student gone and a note on his desk.

In 1992, the above symptoms increased in frequency, and Paul also began falling asleep while standing and operating his photocopier, preparing a meal, drinking (letting his glass fall), typing, and writing. He has hallucinated several times (for example, thinking that he heard the doorbell when there was no one at the door). Worst of all, Paul has felt lazy or that he appears to be lazy. For one month he tried to make himself do two jobs. He would walk into his office intent on doing one of them but instead would decide to read something, pay some bills, watch TV for a while, pet his cat Princess... and the job did not get done that day.

Formula for Living a Health Life

Paul Torrance makes the following recommendations for living a healthy life:

I have never smoked and I would recommend this to anyone.
I have always eaten a lot of fruits and vegetables.

When I was in my mid-40s, I participated in a large-scale study of heart disease and cholesterol, and learned how to control my diet for cholesterol and I am thankful for this experience.

I have been a workaholic and I would not recommend this to anyone—put in time for exercise, relaxation, vacations, etc.

I did the best I knew about compensating for my disabilities. I have recommended that we not waste so much energy in being well-rounded or feel guilty about it. Accept interdependence as a way of life. Do your part but don't be afraid to accept help from others.

It is important to have a good family doctor who can be trusted, with whom you feel comfortable, who cares for you, and who is willing to refer when it is indicated. I have been very fortunate to have Dr. William O'Brian in Minneapolis and Dr. Jack Palmer in Athens.

As I have gotten older, I find that it is important to have good specialists, but usually your family physician can be depended upon because he knows you and what kind of a specialist can best meet your needs.

Be sure to have plenty of health insurance.

...His Purpose in Life and Regrets

Paul always felt that he had a purpose in life and still hopes that he has one. For over 50 years, he has felt that his main purpose was to love and encourage others "to be the most that they can be." Jack Presbury's poem, "Icarus," which was dedicated to Paul, Christa McAuliffe and other great teachers, echoed this purpose in the ending of the poem: "They're always waiting somewhere cheering the children on." Paul has been doing that all his professional life. For at least the last 30 years, he has been spending, on average, four hours a day on correspondence, encouraging and cheering his correspondents on. Paul says, "I can do this as long as I live."

Of course Paul has had regrets. "I shall always regret not giving more priority to my family—more love, more time. His greatest regret was his lack of courage in taking the initiative, and in not giving enough time and effort to Pansy, his sister, his mother, and his father. In the end, he did devote almost all of his time to Pansy and had planned to devote more time to her when she started having strokes.

Pick-A-Present Party—1986

Paul and Pansy realized that they had too many books and other personal belongings when they moved from the "Aha house" on 185 Riverhill Drive to 183 Cherokee Avenue in Athens, Georgia. They chose a unique solution to their problem: A "pick-a-present" party was held and many friends were invited. The friends chose books and other items collected over the years as keepsakes, and in turn helped the Torrances move more comfortably into a smaller house. (Paul is still having such parties, and he has given the Salvation Army three loads of material.)

TORRANCE CATS

Cherokee Chief, Cherokee Princess, Rascal, Little Brother, Amigo, Hazel, Ondine, Hilda, and Dickie were all Torrance cats. Anyone who knows Paul and Pansy personally is well aware of their love of cats. Paul understood cat behavior better than anyone I know. He would talk to them as if they were human. In a notation in April of 1968, Pansy wrote, "Paul said to Hilda, 'Sometimes you are a very sensitive cat—I was having so much trouble getting started on that speech (for the National Association for Gifted Children, Chicago, May 1) and you stayed here in the kitchen and didn't bother me on the desk'."[14] He got his love of cats naturally—his father had 27 at one time on the farm near Milledgeville.

Whenever I visited Paul Torrance in his home in Athens, I would begin my stay clear-headed and usually ended it red-eyed and stuffy due to my allergy to cats. Paul must have wondered why I wasn't affectionate to his cats and why I took a late night walk to clear my head. I did not want to tell Paul about my allergy as I knew how much Cherokee Princess meant to him. Medication did help me.

Yoshio Nozu and his wife, of Matsue, Japan, visited Paul and Pansy Torrance in Athens, Georgia, in 1984. They were impressed with Paul's warm and persistent affection toward animals, especially his cats. Adrienne Kinkaid, a student

[14] Handwritten notes of Pansy Torrance (in possession of the author).

of Paul in his Minnesota Years, recently wrote about the Torrance theory of house-breaking a reluctant cat. Put the litter pan where the cat wants to go, not where you think it should go. Paul used it as an example of problem-solving, but it is endlessly useful in dealing with young children.

"Amigo Torrance Cat" was killed by a pack of dogs that roamed in the ravine behind the Torrance home at 185 Riverhill Drive. The love and sensitivity Paul and Pansy felt toward their cat was reflected in this "obituary" written in May of 1986:

Amigo's Obituary

We mourn the passing of Amigo Torrance Cat on the night of May 26, 1986.

He was a faithful brother and pet.

He was a friendly companion.

Each day he patrolled our little acre several times.

He loved every inch of this acre that he had called home for 14 years.

Yet he was curious about every little thing and was always ready for an adventure.

He always had the loudest purr in catdom and shared his affection with all.

On his last day he had been in the house many times to check on us.

His communications were clear. When he jumped on this counter and sat, he was saying, "Give me a little milk, please."

He was murdered by a pack of vicious dogs in our back yard, just over the boundary.

Love, Paul Torrance, Pansy Torrance, Dickie and Little Brother Torrance Cat

Not long after Amigo's murder, two other Torrance cats, Dickie and Little Brother, were killed, presumably by the same pack of dogs. Paul put an article in the *Athens Banner-Herald*, warning residents of the pack of dogs that killed their cats.

The Arizona Future Problem Solving Program has founded an award in 1992 called "CAT" (Creativity Augments Thinking), which is given to teams for original ideas and for incorporating futuristic thinking and concepts into their solutions (Jackson, 1992). The award is designed for Paul Torrance, founder of the Future Problem Solving Program and in recognition of his love of cats. The winners receive the following let-

Dear Winners of the E. Paul Torrance Creative CAT Award,

Congratulations for your exceptional creative thinking!

Cats are exceptionally curious and creative. They are also exceptionally loving and loyal.

They are at the same time willing to take risks and cautious. They will consider many alternatives before risking. They see alternatives that others do not see. They are alert and use all their senses to find out the truth.

Even in old age they are playful and joyful. They enjoy watching nature and people. They communicate with they voice, eyes, ears, tail—their whole bodies.

Love,

E. Paul Torrance.

ter from Paul that reflects his fondness of cats:

Jennine Jackson of Tucson, Arizona,[15] developed the idea and designed the award.

The Torrance Collection in the archives at the University of Georgia contain a whole album entitled "Torrance Cats—We Are Family." It displays photographs of the cats with Paul and Pansy.

The E. Paul Torrance Creative CAT Certificate Awarded to Teams for Exceptional Creative Thinking

Date ____________________

A TYPICAL DAY IN THE LIFE OF E. PAUL TORRANCE

> *"Creative individuals are never content to work a forty-hour week. They cannot stop thinking and working."*
>
> Torrance (1962)

As a visiting scholar, I have had the opportunity on a number of occasions to stay in the home of E. Paul Torrance. On each occasion, I was struck with his caring, selfless demeanor, persistence, planning ability, and commitment to his work and research. I learned how a dedicated scholar lives on a daily basis.

His home is designed for productivity. For example, his study is lined on one side with a bank of five four-drawer file cabinets carefully organized with his articles and manuals. On the other side of the room are bookshelves from floor to ceiling. The books are ones he's authored along with others written on the subject of creativity and albums of recent photographs of friends and visiting scholars. His modest desk in front of two windows that look out on his veranda is usually piled with letters awaiting response. I can now understand why correspondents are amazed at his quick response to letters. He works diligently at it and often sends articles to accompany his personal remarks in each letter. To complete the working environment in his office, he has a photocopy machine that is used with regularity. A desk in his living room with a typewriter is the working environment for his secretary and/or graduate assistant. Most of his archival materials are prepared in this area.

The walls and shelves around his home are covered with paintings and adorned with sculptures. Usually they were given to Paul and Pansy by students

[15] Anyone interested in implementing the CAT Award in their program may contact Jennine Jackson, Amphitheatre Schools, 701 W. Wetmore, Tucson, AZ 85704.

My daily schedule usually runs something like the following:[16]

4:30 AM	Get up, let Princess out, let Princess in and feed her. Let Princess back out. Fix breakfast and eat. Clean up kitchen.
5:30	Get newspaper and read it.
6:30	Let Princess back in, shave, bathe, change clothes. Take pills and perform dental care.
7:30	Lay out work for the day, read correspondence to be answered.
8:30	Typist/assistant comes. Dictate correspondence and typist types it and does other jobs that are pressing four days a week, leaving one day a week to "catch up," go for medical and dental appointments, etc.
10:00	Write notes, collect material to fill requests of correspondents, etc.
11:15	Prepare lunch for me and Mohammed, answer telephone calls. (Calls always come when I am preparing or eating.)
12:00	Eat lunch and help Mohammed clean up, give typist/assistant further instructions, feed Princess. Take pills, perform dental care.
1:00 PM	Bed, rest, sleep.
2:00	Get up, drink water or fruit juice, exercise on stationary bicycle.
2:30	Read outgoing correspondence and prepare for mailing.
3:30	Get mail and process it. Drink water or fruit juice.
4:30	Get afternoon newspaper and read it and some of regular mail.
5:15	Prepare supper for me and Mohammed. Answer telephone calls. Eat and watch evening news. Take pills and perform dental care.
7:00	Read rest of mail, and do other unfinished tasks like preparing letters and packages for mailing. Write notes and plan work for next day.
9:00	Drink Metamucil and watch Larry King Live at least for 30 minutes.
9:30 or 10:00	Write of other demands do not intervene or I am not too tired.
11:00	Bring Princess in, if she's not already in. Pills, laxative, dental care.
11:15 PM	Retire and sleep (hopefully).

This is the usual except for visitors, students, classes, laundry days, special events, etc.

[16] As of February 26, 1993; personal communication to the author.

or as a special gift or honor. One of my favorite paintings depicts the great University of Georgia tailback Herschel Walker flying over the heads of Tennessee linesmen.

Paul Torrance always insisted on making well-balanced meals for me and for Mohammed Badaway. Mohammed is an Egyptian student who lives in the basement of Paul's home and assists him with daily chores such as getting groceries, cleaning the house, and general maintenance. Paul takes good care of Pansy's cat, Cherokee Princess. Princess is a great companion and comfort to him. Paul also insisted on doing my laundry. It would be done promptly on a selected day and would be neatly folded on my bed the next day. Before each evening meal, Paul would begin with this prayer:

> Thank you, Lord, for these and all
> your blessings.
> Please bless this food to our bodies
> and ourselves to your service.
> Amen.

I could always talk with Paul about the work in which I was involved. He would often present me with an article or book that was related to the topic of our discussions. I was constantly amazed at his meticulous response to my queries. I can well imagine how a student would feel with his attention, care, and respect for their questions.

One evening in March of 1993, while I was studying in my room, Paul took a conference call from Dr. Bill Nash and his graduate students from Texas A & M University in College Station. All the students had a chance to ask Paul questions about some aspect of his research that they had been studying. Paul would answer directly and often would elaborate with practical examples. He was delighted with their obvious interest in his work.

Paul's daily routine is the same except for when visitors come and on special occasions. Paul watches some television but only to keep current with national and international events. "Larry King Live" is his favorite program. He subscribes to many journals that relate to creativity and always has current books on topics such as health and photography.

Paul's house most often is filled with the fragrance of flowers from the gardens that surround his house. The scent from roses, gardenias, and hydrangeas permeates the air of the house—and the fruit bowl is filled with Georgia peaches when in season.

I felt fortunate to be able to stay with Paul Torrance and especially to have access to his advice in his own home while studying and doing the research for his biography. He demonstrated how his work is a labor of love. I understand that he has arranged to will his house to the University of Georgia for the use of visiting scholars who will undertake future research in the area of creativity at the University of Georgia.

A sampling of Torrance's best articles and unpublished papers over the years is being published by Ablex Publishing under the title *Why Fly? A Philosophy of Creativity*. A different sampling of articles and papers is being published by Benedic Books under the title *Just Wanting to Know*. In both books, Torrance prepared comments to show how each article or paper fits into the whole. He also tried to show how it reflects changes in perspective.

The letters I receive from Paul Torrance continue to reflect his high level of productivity. He complains when he is not able to continue at the pace he is normally accustomed to, but he still sets himself many goals and deadlines. He has tried unsuccessfully to slow down and take on some hobbies, but, I believe, his work ethic is such a part of his lifestyle that he is almost powerless to change.

PERSONA OF E. PAUL TORRANCE

"I will never forget his sweet eyes and smile whenever you presented him with a creative idea. He always smiled, like a child, facing a new thing."

Solange Wechsler
Professor
São Paulo, Brazil

In 1992, a questionnaire was completed by 76 students, colleagues, and friends who have known Paul Torrance through the years. The following is a summary of the responses given (in order of frequency) to the question, "What is it in

Paul Torrance's persona that has impressed you the most?" (A copy of the questionnaire is given in Appendix B.)

- Extremely kind, warm, caring, affirming and well-meaning towards people and students of all races and nationalities.
- Quiet, unassuming manner. Soft presence, unobtrusive.
- Extremely imaginative, creative and intelligent.
- Willingness to help and share with so many others (selflessness).
- Great desire to develop, support and respect the creative skills of people everywhere (worldwide).
- Remarkable, uncommon combination of childlike openness and scholarly thoroughness.
- Displays good nature and calm disposition.
- Unbelievably productive.
- An earnest Sadhak (a Hindi term referring to a person who is devoted to and in search of learning and knowledge), unswerving commitment to scholarship.
- A gentleman.
- Sincere (integrity).
- Takes pride in the achievements of others.
- The "Ttwinkle" in his eyes that appears with creative ideas.
- High regard for living things displays affection toward animals (cats) and appreciation for nature (flowers).
- Total congruence between the way he lives and what he teaches or public person is the same as the private person.
- Genuine love for Pansy.
- Punctual.
- Always accessible.
- Uncontrollable curiosity.
- Amazing organizational ability.
- Very generous.

On First Meeting Paul Torrance

Bruce Bracken was impressed with Paul's physical appearance. As an undergraduate student at the College of Charleston in South Carolina, Bruce had learned of Paul Torrance's work in creativity. He had imagined what Paul would look like, but learned that his idea was incorrect upon their first meeting. Bruce thought that Paul Torrance must be a dynamic, gregarious man with "sparks" flying from him as he spoke. He found that he was a quiet, unassuming man whose warmth was second to none. Though Bruce was initially disappointed in this man who looked more like Mr. Magoo than Mr. Creativity, he quickly realized that his expectations were naive and unfair.

Jack Presbury, Professor of Psychology at James Madison University in Virginia, described the first time he met Paul Torrance:

> In 1983, I wrote to Dr. T. and stated that if he would let me hang out with him for a month during the summer, that I would perform any work that he wished in return. He agreed and I met him face to face for the first time in his large office in Aderhold Hall at the University of Georgia. I was prepared to meet someone who was a "distinguished professor" and I expected that he was from Minnesota, and so would be formal and somewhat distant—sort of like Garrison Keillor's portrayal of the Norwegian Lutheran. Instead, there was this fellow who looked for all the world like the Happy Buddha speaking in this thick southern accent! He approached me, somewhat stooped-shouldered, and warmly grasped my hand, seemingly delighted to see me. This infectious delight, which he communicates to all, is the most memorable aspect of his personality for me.[17]

Aurora Roldan, Founder and President of the Talented and Gifted Philippines Foundation in Greenhills, wrote of her first meeting with Paul Torrance:

> But from that very first meeting in Manila (Fifth World Conference on Gifted and Talented Children), I sensed immediately that there was something different about this man. Since his reputation had definitely preceded him, I was not surprised by his expertise in his field—creativity. What did come as a wonderful surprise was his simplicity and gentleness of spirit. It was touching to see how devoted he was to his wife, Pansy, who was then an invalid but who had joined him on the long trip to Manila.[18]

Paul's unassuming manner revealed itself to June Maker, an Associate Professor at the University of Arizona. She recalls meeting Paul at a convention sponsored by the National Association for Gifted Children. At one of the luncheon sessions, June sat at a table with a group of people she did not know. She had no idea that the person sitting beside her was Paul Torrance. Everyone introduced themselves, and she was surprised when she heard his name. They had a wonderful conversation, and later Paul made a speech in which he took off his dress shirt to reveal a T-shirt with the words "I am a Creative Child" on it. June Maker was fascinated with his creativity, simplicity, and personal power.

Intelligence and Openness

Paul's intelligence is also legendary. He amazed students and faculty by his incredible ability to write and publish. He would sit at his desk and punch out manuscripts, one key at a time, with a literature review that came from memory. These

---

[17] Personal communication from Jack Presbury. October 8, 1992.

[18] Personal correspondence from Aurora Roldan, Greenhills, Manila, Philippines, October 1992.

first-draft manuscripts were submitted and accepted largely as they were.

Dr. Emily Stewart, Director of the Program for the Gifted and Talented in Dallas, Texas, has been most impressed by Paul Torrance's remarkable combination of childlike openness and scholarly thoroughness. The two qualities are seldom seen together, and so dramatically, in one person.

Dr. Morris Stein, Professor Emeritus in the Department of Psychology at New York University, indicated that Paul is a scholar and gentleman. He is one of the kindest, warmest and well meaning people that he knows. Paul himself is an extremely creative and intelligent individual. He is a quick and flexible thinker. Paul readily saw the significance of and implications of his own data and the work of others. He quickly took hold of any results which supported the notion that *all* persons had creative potential and the capacity to make creative contributions.

Dr. M. K. Raina, a Professor and a Senior Fellow to Jawaharlal Nehru University in New Delhi, India, has known Paul Torrance as a teacher, friend, and colleague for 25 years. He states, "Paul Torrance's gift to help and counsel, empathize and provide support are some of his remarkable peculiarities. The resilience to face life, take up challenges and a passionate devotion to inquiry, even in his late declining years, establish him as a real *Guru*."[19]

Dr. Hesseen Abedel-Azia El-Dreny, now Dean of the College of Education in Cairo, Egypt, expressed his deeply felt gratitude to Paul Torrance in his dissertation at the University of Georgia in 1976. It is instructive in understanding his persona:

> To the man who has dedicated his life to enhance the nation's creativity, to make everyone as happy as possible and who leads a highly creative life. To the man who works tirelessly as brilliant educator and psychologist, while at the same time receives me with his tender smile, encourages me to express myself, listens to me with incredible patience and never refuses my endless requests for his guidance, aid and support. To Dr. Paul Torrance, my deepest appreciation and sincerest gratitude. I hope I will be able to carry forth his teachings in my professional career and endeavor. Thanks my Lord for granting me this opportunity to be directed and cared of such a great and compassionate human being as Dr. Paul Torrance. (El-Dreny, 1976, p. iii)

Dr. Solange Wechsler, a former student of Paul Torrance and currently a Professor in Sao Paulo, Brazil, stated clearly that it was not only Paul's knowledge about creativity that affected her but his creative way of behaving. He lived what he taught.

Dr. Pat Dwinell, an Assistant Professor in Development Studies at the University of Georgia, indicated that, as a student of Paul Torrance, she saw a paradox in his persona. Although he was free in his thinking, he was very structured and had a definite plan in his classes. Being creative did not mean that

---

[19] Personal correspondence from M.K. Raina. New Delhi, India, May 25, 1992.

he was unorganized—without a plan. He attended to details and had a deep concern for his students. If Paul were asked for something (a tape, a book, or an article), he would have it the next day. He always had time for people. Pat Dwinell recalls an instant in a creativity workshop involving children when Paul became angry. This was the first time in 20 years that she remembered him getting frustrated. The children were fussing and not on task. He became frustrated, red in the face, and raised his voice. He was accustomed to using time well.

Kindness, Thoughtfulness, Compassion

During the many meals I have eaten in Paul Torrance's home, there was little general, idle conversation. Rather, talk revolved around my work or his work and events that would take place that day. One event that is still vivid in my mind occurred on June 23, 1992, the day my sister Vivian passed away in Calgary, Alberta. My wife had telephoned me at Paul Torrance's home to pass on the news. I was at the University in the Torrance Center at the time and was unavailable to take the call. Paul called me there and said, "Your wife called to say that your sister passed away last night. I'm sorry." When I arrived at Paul Torrance's home later that day, he had placed a sympathy card with a personal message on my desk. His thoughtfulness is uncommon.

Paul Torrance has demonstrated his empathy and compassion for students. For example, a Japanese student found himself in financial difficulty due to President Reagan's budget cut. Paul gave the student a job translating articles from Japanese to English.

Harry Passow, currently Jacob H. Schiff Professor Emeritus of Education at the Teachers College at Columbia University, has been influenced by Paul Torrance's work in the field of creativity since the 1950s. He had followed Paul's research and writings for many years before meeting him. Harry Passow considered Paul to be one of the seminal researchers who opened up new vistas for people in the field of gifted education. What struck Harry Passow about Paul when they met in London at the First World Conference on Gifted and Talented Children (1975) was his sincerity, his modesty, and his openness. Paul was anything but the "stuffed shirt" Harry Passow had come across in the field on too many occasions.

Leatha Spratlin, Paul's long-time secretary and office manager at the University of Georgia, revealed an aspect of Paul's character in the note reprinted on page 236.[20]

Dr. Jerry Flack, a President's Teaching Scholar at the University of Colorado in Colorado Springs, relates a personal anecdote that occurred between him and

---

[20] Note by Leatha Spratlin to Paul Torrance. June 7, 1972. Torrance Collection MSS 2606 #009 (1972). Athens, Georgia, Hargrett Rare Book and Manuscript Library, University of Georgia.

THE UNIVERSITY OF GEORGIA
COLLEGE OF EDUCATION
DEPT. OF EDUCATIONAL PSYCHOLOGY
ATHENS, GEORGIA 30601

Dr. Torrance:

Thank you very much for the dictionary for Clissa. I would probably never have remembered she would need one.

I just want to say you are the most thoughtful and considerate person and I think its too bad we don't have more people just like you in this world. I, personally, think our Department would be far better off if some of your qualities would rub off on many of the other members.

Thanks for being the kind of person you are.

Leatha
June 7, 1972

Paul Torrance. The first time Jerry Flack ever gave a presentation at a national conference (National Association for Gifted Children), he was very nervous. He became even more terrified when Paul Torrance showed up for his session—the session was on futures. However, Paul made him feel very confident and relaxed, and he stayed afterwards and talked to Jerry at some length as one colleague to another. Paul gave incredible support and encouragement to this young scholar.

Joe Khatena is a Professor Emeritus in the Psychology Department at Mississippi State University. He studied with Paul Torrance at the University of Georgia (1966–69) and was his research and teaching assistant. He describes Paul Torrance as a gentle, warm, and caring human being who continues to be loyal and supportive of his students long after they graduate and leave him. In addition, he has the greatness to stand aside when his students achieve prominence in their field and to let them grow. Paul's role then changes from mentor to colleague. He allows his students to self-actualize and takes great pride in them and their achievements.

Paul Torrance's humaneness is well known. He takes a deep interest in his students, friends, and colleagues. Francisco Menchén Bellón of Madrid, Spain, remembers with fondness the "Open House at the Torrances" at the end of the course on Gifted Children. The invitation cards stated plainly, among other usual details: "The wine from Dr. Francisco Menchén Bellón's native province of La Mancha (Don Quixote country) was bought as a gift for him."

Joan Franklin Smutny, Director of the Center for the Gifted at National-Louis University in Evanston, Illinois, writes succinctly about the element of Paul Torrance's persona that has impressed her: "Dr. Torrance expresses a compassion for mankind that is immensely endearing and appealing."[21] She indicated that she felt that Paul Torrance was as keenly interested in her and her work as he would have been in someone who had far greater leadership responsibilities. When she asked Paul Torrance to write a foreword to her book, *A Thoughtful Overview of Gifted Education* (Eby & Smutny, 1990), his affirmative responsiveness overwhelmed her.

Terutsugu Ando, a Professor in the College of Education at Fukui University in Japan, was a visiting scholar to the University of Georgia early in 1979. The thing that impressed him about Paul Torrance was that he never saw him get angry. Paul accepted everything.

Harry Passow, Professor Emeritus at Columbia University in New York, stated that he has "met very few people who combine Paul's humaneness, commitment and caring. Paul is a gentle soul, a gentleman, and a concerned human being, which is reflected in his work."[22]

Dr. Betty Sloop, now an Assistant Professor of Education at Mercer University in Atlanta, Georgia, wrote Paul Torrance three years after her graduation from the University of Georgia to express her appreciation of him. She chose three words to describe the qualities she experienced with him as a student and graduate assistant. She said that it is the combination of those qualities that have created a specialness about Paul Torrance: *caring*—about his students, his subject, the future, the students beyond his classroom, and the field of education; *creative*—making courses extremely adaptable and always useful; and *conscientious*—giving detailed feedback on assignments and being willing to let students redo them until they achieve the level of competence they desire.

Productivity and Work Ethic

Dr. Berenice Bee Bleedorn has been Paul Torrance's contact in Minnesota since he left in 1966. She has indicated that Paul's level of dedication to his work and to his students is unmatched. He has been the model mentor for her during some very traumatic professional experiences and has displayed empathetic

---

21 Personal communication from Joan Franklin Smutny. National-Louis University, Evanston, Illinois, July 1992.

22 Personal correspondence from Dr. Harry Passow. September 1992.

understanding not often found in persons of distinguished stature. Bee now recognizes the essence of his persona after reviewing a stack of letters from him between 1965 to 1993: selflessness and his capacity to support and applaud her efforts jump off the page. These characteristics are obvious in all his letters—he is and has been a great "letter listener."

A reception was held at the College of St. Thomas in St. Paul, Minnesota, in 1982 to honor Paul and Pansy Torrance. Bee Bleedorn wrote the following poem, which makes a strong statement about Paul's character:

> Torrance
> Mighty Man
> Mighty, modest man
> Mild and mellow
> Generous fellow.
> Networker
> Model extraordinary
> International champion
> Of Creativity.
> Intrepid. Authentic.
> Rare protector and defender
> Of Creative enterprises
> Of creative persons.
> Respected leader and friend
> Passing wisdom on and on.
> Minnesota has to salute you.
> We can't help it!

Sidney Parnes, Professor Emeritus of Creative Studies at Buffalo State University, has been impressed with Paul's productivity, his unassuming manner, his willingness to help so many people, and his organizational ability (photographs and other filed items). Paul's work ethic and productivity were evident in a workshop he conducted with Sidney Parnes. The participants produced significant products during the evening workshop. Paul took all the products (papers) with him and early the next morning he returned them all with an analysis. Sidney Parnes was amazed. Paul did not ask for any help and must have stayed up most of the night doing the work. Alex F. Osborn and Sidney Parnes wrote Paul in 1963, "We agree that you are as prolific as you are terrific."

Humility

Vicki Connell has been a student of Paul Torrance since 1978. Currently, she is the Director of the Georgia Future Problem Solving Program. When she first arrived in Georgia from Nebraska, she was struck with Paul's humility. Vicki was afraid to meet him at first. When she went to his office on the fifth floor of the College of Education, it was full of graduate students. Everyone was busy, including Paul Torrance, collating papers for the Future Problem Solving Program. He said, "Hey, Vicki, we need your help." Immediately, she felt that they were on the same level. Despite his international reputation, his humility is always present.

Cecil Reynolds, while a doctoral student at the University of Georgia, learned a lesson in humility from Paul Torrance, when they were co-authoring a paper. Cecil had written a first draft, and he asked Paul if he could give it to one of the department secretaries to type. Paul was Head of the Educational Psychology Department at the time. Paul remarked that they were overburdened with work, so he reached out, took the paper, and said, "I'll type it myself!" Cecil learned a tremendous lesson.

The thing about Paul Torrance that impresses most people is his kindness and humility. Joe Renzulli says he believes "it is because of these intensely favorable human characteristics that he has insights that lead to research on complex human behaviors that might often be overlooked by persons without an HQ (Humanity Quotient) that is as large as his intelligence and creativity quotients."[23]

Empathy

Laura Littleford, is the writer and former Montessori teacher in St. Paul, Minnesota who was a student of Torrance's in a gifted education/alter teacher program in Bloomington, Minnesota, in the early 1960s. She recalled what she learned from Paul Torrance.

> Trust is the most important thing I have learned from Dr. Torrance. Who and what to trust; and who and what not to trust. To do something new is very scary, and I think a creative person has to have a trusted friend or mentor before she or he trusts their own gift, their new creativity. I always "check in" with Dr. Torrance before I make major changes in my life; not for the actual career choice, but for that affirmation to change in my life, to go forward.[24]

Paul has always displayed a genuine interest in others. He and Pansy took a personal interest in students, faculty, and people in general. They both taught Sunday School classes, frequently spoke to elementary students, and often personally involved themselves in the lives of others in a quiet and sensitive fashion.

---

[23] Personal communication from Dr. Joe Renzulli. May 1992.

[24] Personal communication from Laura Littleford. St. Paul, Minnesota, September 6, 1992.

Qualities of a Great Teacher

Rod Myers, who was a student of Paul Torrance and co-authored two books with him, indicated to me that the essential ingredient in a good teacher's personality is *kindness*. When this ingredient is missing, it alters everything that happens between teacher and student. Paul Torrance had an abundance of kindness and patience. Sometimes it worked to his disadvantage. He would listen by the hour to students, who were grateful to have someone really listen to them. The price was often dear for Paul, since time was always precious to him—he had much to do.

This kindness was often coupled with thoughtfulness and insight. On one occasion at the University of Minnesota, he sent Rod Myers on a little photographic assignment with another graduate student. Rod later learned from the student that Paul put people in situations in which he thought they might grow and benefit. According to the student, he would pair people who might be mutually stimulating. It is an unusual person who would think of experiences like these to help his individual students.

Paul was terribly permissive, suggesting a course now and then, but leaving the direction and responsibility up to the student. For some, this nondirective approach was liberating, but others "swam in a sea" of indecision. He believed in students and trusted their creative potentials. He truly was a teacher who made a difference.

Paul Torrance modeled qualities that may be considered hallmarks of a great teacher. No one was too unimportant to receive Paul's time and energy. There was no hierarchy among the genuinely interested, nor was anyone too junior to help someone else in the learning process. He also modeled a lifetime commitment to a theory of creativity that he believed was important to pursue. He subjected the creativity theory to scientific examination, applied it in the community, and promoted its applications throughout the world—not with a commercial gain but rather to help all learners achieve their *creative* potential.

SIGNIFICANT LEARNINGS: PERCEPTIONS OF IMPORTANT OTHERS

"He has taken me to the edge of the cliff
and showed me the wonders of wings."

Kobus Neethling
Creativity Advisor to the Government
Pretoria, South Africa

Another question was posed in the 1992 questionnaire that was completed by students, colleagues, and friends who have known Paul Torrance through the years: "What is the most significant thing you have learned from Dr. Torrance?" The responses, in order of frequency, are listed here.

- Belief that *all* persons have creative potential and the capacity to make creative contributions. Respect for power and joy of a creative mind. "You don't have to stay between the lines."
- Tolerance and love of *all* people everywhere.
- Influence on so many persons from all parts of the world.
- Lives what he believes—life of integrity (remarkable commitment to his work, personal resources used to finance work, takes risks in topics explored and written about).
- Understanding of creativity in a psychological and psychometric sense. *Torrance Tests of Creative Thinking* can be used as a measure to predict future creative behaviors.
- Importance of keeping current in a field of study.
- Research and knowledge about children's creativity.
- Importance of childlike curiosity.
- Unbiased openness—acceptance of everyone's reality.
- Manifesto for Children—"Don't worry about being well-rounded, find something you love and go for it!"
- Future Problem Solving Program.
- To be supportive of the next generation of scholars.
- His research findings were practical—especially to education in general.
- His disciplined approach to producing.
- Sociodramatic approaches to creativity training.
- Scenario writing technique to help people clarify their image of the future.
- Suprarational factors of creativity—exploration of *satori* experiences.
- Differences are not deficits, but merely differences.
- Expect and accept criticism as the burden of the risk-taker and pioneer.
- *Development* of a strong network of people and his *interdependence* on them for ideas and stimulation.
- "Open style" of research.
- Being comfortable with ambiguity.

Significant Contributions

According to Harry Passow, Paul Torrance taught him the importance of "thinking creatively about creativity." He said that Paul broke the barriers and the boundaries and is recognized for having done so, and he went on to say that Paul taught him "belief in the potential of individuals—all kinds of individuals; belief in their potential for being productive; belief that they can extend their beliefs about their own capacity."

Passow also indicated that Paul's work and research affected his research and thinking by opening up the field of gifted education, both theoretically and practically. Guilford's Structure of the Intellect is often cited as having initiated teachers' efforts to nurture divergent thinking, productivity and creativity in the classroom—but anyone who was there at the time knows that it was Paul Torrance who was and is the most influential person in this regard. Harry Passow stated that "he certainly had a profound influence on my thinking."

Jack Presbury was a pretty hard-nosed, scientific type in the explanations he would accept for mental events. Paul Torrance opened him up to the "suprarational" aspects of thought as possessing their own wisdom.

The most significant thing that June Maker, an Associate Professor of Special Education and Rehabilitation at the University of Arizona, has learned from Paul Torrance is the concept that differences are not deficits, but merely differences. This idea can be applied to friends, family, types of giftedness, cultural groups, countries, social organizations, animals, plants, and the world we live in. June says that "Paul Torrance has lived this philosophy for many years, and it has permeated his writing, research and interactions with others." She has come a long way toward understanding and living this philosophy through his influence.

The most significant thing that Yoshio Nozu of Japan learned from Paul Torrance was his idea that "the most creative person has the ability to endure the most ambiguous situations." Dr. Nava Butler-Por, a Professor for Israel, learned from Paul Torrance the belief that *all* children can develop their creativity if they are provided with appropriate educational experiences in the care of knowledgeable mentors.

Dr. Kobus Neethling, President of the South Africa Creativity Foundation and creativity advisor to the Government in Pretoria, South Africa, has been a student of and a colleague with Paul Torrance for several years. The most significant thing he has learned from Paul is the power and joy of a creative mind—and the importance of having a vision of the future. He believes now that Paul Torrance becomes a permanent part of the people he sends out all over the world.

One of the most important things that Lyle Johnson, a former student in Minneapolis, learned from Paul Torrance was his open style of research. Paul used a research design that fit the nature of the data.

Love and Commitment

Dr. M. K. Raina, Professor in New Delhi, India, wrote to me about the most significant thing that he has learned from Paul Torrance. His response reflected two points—love and commitment. He said, "to answer your query, let me sing with the Baül (a group of people in Northern India who do not conform to established social convention) 'Love is my golden touch—it turns desire into service: Earth seeks to become Heaven, man to become God.'" As to commitment, he says that one should have "Total dedication to the field one is pursuing, even if it brings no rewards."[25]

Noel Howieson, a doctoral student at the University of Georgia from Western Australia, learned an important lesson from Paul Torrance one day. She had carried out research on creativity and hemispheric dominance and had written a paper integrating her readings. She was a beginning doctoral student and regarded her work on this topic as "probably wrong" or at best "poorly conceptualized" because she was a junior. Paul Torrance started to send her other students interested in the area who wished to talk things over. She protested, saying, "I'm no expert in this area." Paul looked at her for awhile and said, "Your major developmental task at this time is to redefine yourself." This statement registered as she saw her modesty as a lazy cop-out. It was easier to refer everyone to some other "expert" than think the issues through herself.

Jack Presbury has learned one significant thing from Paul Torrance—acceptance of everyone's reality. Jack has seen him remain open (resist premature closure or suspend disbelief) when someone is offering an idea which he had long since discarded as without merit, and he has seen this process result in sound and creative ideas, simply because Dr. Torrance was willing to stay with the idea until it bore fruit. Jack said, "I will never be able to do this in the way that he could, but I attempt to emulate it."

Morgan Henderson is a therapist and group psychologist who has read all of Paul's books and articles. She was always careful not to let her hobbies of writing poetry and creating rubberstamp art interfere with her serious work. To learn more from Paul Torrance she went to Georgia to spend a month with him in 1983. After the month, she wrote,

> Most of all, Dr. T. teaches me to push back my self-imposed fences. Fences that separate "serious work" from "play"; fences that separate "artistic creativity" from discipline and hard work. He helps me bring more flowers into my garden, and teaches me that everything—everything is seeds for new growth.[26]

Paul Torrance's contributions to the education of gifted children are inestimable. His life's work has been a celebration of children and their creativity. He has been remarkably productive during all of his professional career. His work has helped millions of youngsters.

Literature (Books and Journals)

Paul Torrance's research into the nature and nurture of creativity has endured

---

[25] Personal correspondence from M.K. Raina. New Delhi, India, May 25, 1992.

[26] "Paul Torrance as Gardener" by Morgan Henderson in book of letters on the occasion of the retirement of E. Paul Torrance. March 23, 1985.

through the years due to his single-minded focus or pursuit of this important topic. His work has been quoted widely in textbooks for students of psychology and education in the last 30 years.

Prior to 1960, no reference was made to creativity research and its relevance for educators and others in the human services. I did a sampling of textbooks in the area of educational psychology and testing, and the results support the fact that Paul Torrance's work has withstood the passage of time. For example, in 1959, a textbook entitled *Testing for Teachers* had no reference to creativity or to Paul Torrance. However, textbooks in the 1960s did make reference to his creativity tests and exploratory studies in problem solving and creative behavior. In the 1970s and 1980s, texts referred to Paul Torrance's work regarding ways to encourage creativity and specific skills of question-asking. His voluminous research is still being quoted in the 1990s by authors such as Eggen and Kauchak (1992) and Delisle (1992)—citing his definition of creativity and the significance of the Future Problem Solving Program.

Paul Torrance has been the main source of ideas about creativity and has clarified much of the mystery shrouding this important human ability. Dr. Mark Runco, editor of the *Creativity Research Journal*, wanted to comment on the lasting value of Paul Torrance's work. He stated that Paul is widely cited in the *Creativity Research Journal* and should be cited even more. Integration of creativity research is important to the field and Paul Torrance covered so many topics. He has uncovered issues that still require attention—opening the field and "finding gaps." Paul's research has stimulated a whole field of study.

Contribution to Other Gifted Movements in the United States

Carol Schlichter, Professor and Chairperson of the Program for Gifted and Talented at the University of Alabama, wrote me to indicate that Paul Torrance has been her professional "lode star" since her early graduate school days. He has made an important contribution to the development of Talents Unlimited, a current national model for teaching creative and critical thinking. Thirty years ago, when Carol was a student at George Peabody College, she learned of Paul's pioneering work in developing the creativity of children at the University of Minnesota. Through correspondence, Paul sent her a copy of *Invitations to Thinking and Doing* (1965), which encouraged her to explore children's problem solving.

Carol was impressed with Paul Torrance's discussion of three levels of student involvement that could be facilitated: (a) *initiating* activities, designed to puzzle and stimulate interest; (b) *exploring* activities, in which students are encouraged but not required to continue thinking about their first ideas; and (c) *follow-through* activities, an invitation to carry out ideas and projects in a hands-on fashion. This strategy, which was modeled in every activity, changed her way of thinking about instruction in every area of the curriculum and at every level she has taught—kindergarten to graduate school. In Carol Schlichter's words, "Paul Torrance's challenge to test the deep waters of learning and his practical strategies for helping students of all ages to stay afloat creatively have served well thousands of teachers committed to education for thinking."

Joe Renzulli, professor at the University of Connecticut, has stated that the Torrance Tests of Creative Thinking represent a contribution to the literature that ranks along with the work of Alfred Binet, Hermann Rorschach, David Wechsler, and a few other true pioneers in measurement of human behavior. Joe Renzulli's book, *New Directions in Creativity* (1973), was inspired by Paul Torrance's work as it relates to the development of creative thinking in young people. His ideas about more flexibility in the identification of students with high potential were a direct influence on some of Renzulli's major contributions to the field, the Three Ring Conception of Giftedness and the related Enrichment Triad Model. In addition to high intelligence, Renzulli describes gifted behavior as high levels of task commitment and *creativity*, which are brought to bear on general and specific performance areas.

CONTRIBUTIONS OF E. PAUL TORRANCE

It is difficult and even presumptuous for anyone to try to rank or prioritize the contributions of an individual like Paul Torrance. Who really is to say what is more valuable: the influence of a book like *Guiding Creative Talent,* or the creation of an instrument that permits a discipline to advance as a science such as the Torrance Tests of Creative Thinking? Or is the main contribution a program such as the Future Problem Solving Program, or an influence through individuals or networks such as that of Kobus Neethling in South Africa?

I believe that Paul Torrance will be remembered for two main contributions: The first deals with his "human network" or his teaching and work with and through people, and the second involves his achievements in research and program development. The correspondence I received from Paul Torrance's students, friends, and colleagues lends support to this statement.

Perhaps Paul Torrance's greatest achievements will be measured by the many disciples he has created through the years who are influencing millions of people all over the world. He has disseminated the germ of creativity through his work and through his person, and the effects have been felt far and wide and have been deep and lasting. Paul Torrance, with his quiet strength, sincere kindness, appreciation of beauty, and delightful sense of humor, radiates immense love. He lives what he teaches and inspires others to be the best that they can be. Paul engenders a feeling of power and worth in individuals, making them believe in their own creativity and capability to be productive persons. Paul and Pansy Torrance consistently worked with and through individuals to fulfil their priorities for:

- helping *children*, especially the disadvantaged, to develop unrecognized potential.
- helping *educational psychologists* to improve school conditions for learning and mental health.
- helping *parents* establish long-term respectful relationships with their children.

Paul Torrance forced us to re-examine the concept of intelligence. His significant seminal contributions to creativity have expanded our understanding of human abilities. He, along with others, developed ways to assess the creative potential of individuals. The Torrance Tests of Creative Thinking are widely used for research and practical purposes today.

Paul and his associates have developed ways or strategies to encourage creativity, and in the past decade they have designed the Future Problem Solving Program, which involves hundreds of thousands of students annually in many countries of the world. His participation in the Quality of Life Program will affect the lifestyles of countless elderly people and enrich their lives. Finally, the Torrance Center for Creative Studies at the University of Georgia will carry forward his excellent record of achievement in the area of creative development. It is comforting to know that Paul Torrance has been a teacher, a researcher, a writer, and an international scholar and still found time to be an engaging, endearing, warm, treasured, and winning human being.

REFERENCES

Buccino, A. (1986). *Next space shuttle to carry medallion and tests from U.G.A. College of Education*. Athens: The University of Georgia. News and Information Release (NIR 86–3), January 14.

Clements, C. et al. (1990). *The Arts/Fitness Quality of Life Program for Elderly Persons With and Without Developmental Disabilities*. Funded by Project of National Significance grant #90DD0148 from The Administration on Developmental Disabilities, The Administration of Children and Families, U.S. Department of Health and Human Services. Athens: The University of Georgia.

Daumal, R. (1974). *Mount Analogue: A novel of symbolically authentic non-Euclidean adventures in mountain climbing* (R. Shattuck, trans.). Baltimore: Penguin.

Delisle, J. (1992). *Guiding the social and emotional development of gifted youth: A practical guide for educators and counselors*. White Plains, NY: Longman.

Eby, J.W. & Smutny, J.F. (1990). *A thoughtful overview of gifted education*. White Plains, NY: Longman.

Eggen, P.D., & Kauchak, D. (1992). *Educational psychology: Classroom connections*. New York: MacMillan.

El-Dreny, H.A. (1976). *The effects of induced frustration on verbal dyadic creativity*. Unpublished dissertation, University of Georgia, Athens.

Garrett, H. (1959). *Testing for teachers*. New York: American Book.

Gray, P. (1986, February 10). Seven who flew for all of us. *Time*, pp. 32–35.

Huntley, S., Solorzano, L., Scherer, R., & Collins, D. (1986, February 10). A lesson in grief for the young. *U.S. News and World Report*. p. 24.

Frasier, M.M., et al. (Eds.). (1985). *Retirement celebration for Dr. E. Paul Torrance. March 23, 1985. Research insights over the years—A commemorative collection.* Athens: College of Education, University of Georgia.

Lindgren, H.C. (1968). *Readings in educational psychology*. New York: Wiley.

McDonald, F.J. (1965). *Educational psychology* (2nd Ed.). Belmont, CA: Wadsworth Publishing.

NASA. (1985) *Teacher in space project*. Washington, DC: Author.

Perspectives. (1986, February 10). *Newsweek*, p. 21.

Renzulli, J.S. (1973). *New directions in creativity*. New York: Harper & Row.

Rosser, R., & Nicholson, G. (1984). *Educational psychology: Principles in practice*. Boston: Little, Brown.

Ruben, H.L. (1980). *Competing: Understanding and winning the strategic games we all play*. New York: Lippincott & Crowell.

Smith, M.D. (1978). *Educational psychology and its classroom applications*. Boston: Allyn & Bacon.

Torrance, E.P. (1962, April 3). *Freeing creative intelligence through teaching*. Paper presented at the International Falls Citizen of the Year Award Dinner, International Falls, MN.

Torrance, E.P. (1986). Glimpses of the "promised land." *Roeper Review*, 8*(4)*, 243–245.

Torrance, E.P. (1986). *Reflections on the significance of the fatal flight into space of the TTCT and Christa McAuliffe*. Bensenville, IL: Scholastic Testing Service.

Torrance, E.P. (1991, April). *Insights about creativity: Questioned, rejected, ridiculed, ignored*. Paper prepared for the Second Annual Convention of the American Creativity Association, Houston, TX.

Torrance, E.P. (in press). *Why fly? A philosophy of creativity*. Norwood, NJ: Ablex.

Torrance, E.P. (in press). *Just wanting to know*. Pretoria, South Africa: Benedic Books.

Torrance, E.P., & Myers, R.E. (1965). *Invitations to thinking and doing*. Boston: Ginn and Co.

Conclusion

E. Paul Torrance: An Exemplary "Beyonder"

"He is number one in the world in his special field and research." [1]

Francisco Menchén Bellón
Inspector of Schools
Madrid, Spain

As a young teacher and psychologist, I came to know the name of E. Paul Torrance and I knew of some of his research. However, in the last decade, I have come to know him personally and professionally, and I have been truly amazed at his altruistic nature and remarkable achievements. Paul Torrance is an exemplary "beyonder."

"Beyonder" is a word that Paul uses to describe the high or ultra-achiever, the person who establishes a remarkable record and seems superhuman. Beyonders are individuals like Texas Ranger pitcher Nolan Ryan and Los Angeles Kings hockey player Wayne Gretzky, and those who write hundreds of books or thousands of articles, paint or sculpt hundreds of masterpieces, or produce hundreds of films or inventions.

Paul's concept of the beyonder came out of his longitudinal research on persons who had high creative potential, as measured by the Torrance Tests of Creative Thinking. The longitudinal research had indicated that a person's later achievements are significantly related to various measures of creativity and intelligence, and to achievement scores and sociometric data on creative factors. High creative potential generally predicts later creative achievements.

When Paul was doing a 30-year follow-up, analyzing the lives of certain individuals who had been included in this study, he found that there were other strong forces involved in creative achievement, forces that may be even more dominant than measured creative potential. Some subjects produced accomplishments far beyond what normally would have been expected of them, in terms of their test scores. The strong forces that Paul identified in the lives of these beyonders are love of one's work, having a clear and focused future self-image, never restricting one's field of exploration, love of challenge, diversity of

[1] Personal communication from Francisco Menchén Bellón to Garnet Millar. June 8, 1992.

experience, persistence, high energy level, feeling comfortable as a minority of one, and not being well rounded.

Paul Torrance certainly had the "stuff" to be successful in his life. He performed exceedingly well at school. He was an honor student in elementary school, high school, and junior college. He won several academic contests. He graduated with his bachelor's degree summa cum laude. He was voted the most intellectual cadet in high school at Georgia Military College. His IQ is estimated to be in excess of 120.

As Paul has said himself, there were other students in his early school years who were brighter than he was, but he was able to outperform them by using his creative ability. He wrote more original essays and was able to devise unique experiments and projects.

As well, there were other factors that shaped Paul Torrance's career and life. The "strong forces" that he attributes to beyonders are all present in large measure in his own history.

Clearly, Paul *loves what he is doing*. Complete devotion to his chosen field of study—creativity—permeates Paul's lifestyle. His daily schedule allows for little deviation from his central *purpose*—which is writing about creativity and encouraging others to pursue this important field of study. This characteristic created a major conflict in his life; he has always had great difficulty balancing work with time spent with loved ones. He always regretted not spending more time with Pansy and his relatives.

Paul has always had a clear, future-focused self-image. He knew, as a young boy, that his future career would be as an academic rather than as a farmer like his father. Despite financial difficulties, he was able to persist and find ways to achieve his future image. When Paul realized the importance of creativity in human behavior during his years of studying survival psychology, he continued to pursue creativity with intensity at the University of Minnesota and later at the University of Georgia.

Paul *never restricted his field of exploration*. He always read more than he needed to in his field. He realized the importance of reading about the past to understand present issues, the current situation, and future possibilities. He also read articles and books in other languages to obtain different cultural perspectives. Paul went well beyond the usual scope of a problem in trying to understand it.

Over and over, Paul has demonstrated that he *loves challenges*—mentally, psychologically, culturally, and creatively. He has always operated on the "edge" of his competence. He has constantly thrust himself into new fields because he was interested in creativity, and he knew creativity appears in many aspects of life. When he was asked to chair the White House Forum on Children, he had to do a lot of reading in the field of child development. When he applied creative problem solving to the study of the future, he was challenged to read widely again. His response to this challenge turned out to be one of his greatest legacies—the Future Problem Solving Program.

Diversity of experience is dominant in Paul's life. He has lived and experienced many places, cultures, kinds of work, and relationships. Paul traveled extensively to many countries in the course of his professional life, and he had a particularly fruitful relationship with Japan. His various roles in education have undoubtedly enriched his understanding of human behavior. He has been a teacher, counselor, principal, psychologist, researcher, professor, sociodramatist, administrator, and writer.

At every stage of his life, Paul has exhibited *persistence* and a *high energy level.* He has worked 18-hour days for the past three decades. His hundreds of books, articles, and presentations, in addition to his normal duties as a professor, reflect not only amazing organizational ability, but a high level of energy.

Paul has come to *feel comfortable as a minority of one.* He has displayed great courage in questioning the status quo in education and psychology. His foray into the field of creativity has been single-minded. Some of his findings have challenged the ideas of traditional scholars and educators. His original research has often made him a minority of one. Paul was raised in the deep South on a farm. The pressures to conform were strong in his society and no one expected him to become a world-renowned scholar. He had learned to be a minority of one by age 10.

Paul Torrance is *not a well-rounded person.* There are many ordinary things, such as driving a car, that he cannot do. His learning disabilities did not interfere with his academic pursuits, but they did prevent him from participating fully in society. They made Paul different.

E. Paul Torrance, a beyonder, has made many significant contributions to education, to psychology, to other areas of life, and especially to the people around him. The Gentle Genius of Georgia has truly made a difference.

My purpose in writing this book was not only to explore the life and career of E. Paul Torrance but also to let more people know about his greatness. There are a number of common themes that have permeated the various periods of Paul's life. Paul did not depend upon grants from universities, government, or other agencies to finance his research. He realized that relying upon such external assistance would not allow him to use his incubated thoughts on a topic or area of study. Paul was able to examine creativity in many of its manifestations over the years because he financed his own research.

Paul's research occurred during a time generally characterized by a progressive view of society. A climate conducive to developing the potential of individuals existed in the United States and in many other countries, especially after World War II and the post-Sputnik era. Paul conducted his research in and across many cultures to explore the meaning, trends, and developmental aspects of creativity. He attracted students from many cultures who have in turn applied the principles and skills of creativity in their various countries. As a result, his work is well known and used in many countries such as Brazil, Spain, Bulgaria, Greece, Japan, Canada, Malaysia, South Africa, Australia, Turkey,

India, Germany, and the Philippines.

Another common theme in Paul's work was his unorthodox research methodology. He was not limited to rigid, established statistical procedures but instead followed his hunches. Paul recognized certain gaps in knowledge, searched for clues from other bodies of knowledge, and then applied the research to solving problems in education and other facets of life. His longitudinal studies allowed him to determine the creative potential of people and isolate other factors that contributed to their creative achievements. Paul's notion of good leadership was also developed over the course of his career. During his survival psychology period, he learned that to facilitate creativity and make good decisions, a leader must allow for diversity of opinion and disagreement. A good leader will expect this and use the strengths of people for the benefit of all. Aircrews in the Korean War held together when the commander allowed for diversity of ideas and disagreement and used the information to help the crew. This notion of leadership is currently used in the Future Problem Solving Program by teams choosing solutions acceptable to all. A better solution results after much open discussion.

Finally, Paul has always been able to work with people and draw out their strengths. He is a leader who motivates individuals to apply their energy and creative abilities to make the world a better place in which to live.

REFERENCES

Briggs, J., et al. (1991). *Nolan Ryan: The authorized pictorial history*. Fort Worth, TX: The Summit Group.

Gretzky, W., & Reilly, R. (1990). *Gretzky: An autobiography*. Toronto, ON: Harper Collins.

Taylor, J. (1994). *Wayne Gretzky—The authorized pictorial biography*. Vancouver, British Columbia: Opus Productions.

Torrance, E.P. (1991). The Beyonders and their characteristics. *The Creative Child and Adult Quarterly, 16* (2), 69–79.

Torrance, E.P. (1993). The Beyonders in a thirty-year longitudinal study of creative achievement. [Special Issue on Longitudinal Studies in Gifted Education]. *Roeper Review, 15(3)*, 131–134.

The Early Years

Paul and his sister Ellen at the Torrance family farm near Milledgeville, GA. Paul was about 6 and Ellen about 2½ (circa 1921). (Courtesy of the Hargrett Rare Book and Manuscript Library/University of Georgia Libraries)

Ellen, Paul with his dog Jack, and first cousin Owen Ennis (circa 1922). (Courtesy of the Hargrett Rare Book and Manuscript Library/University of Georgia Libraries)

Paul and his dog Jack, a rat terrier (circa 1922). Jack was very good at catching wharf rats. (Courtesy of the Hargrett Rare Book and Manuscript Library/ University of Georgia Libraries)

Jessie Pansy Nigh on a special occasion at Ralston, OK (circa 1918). She would much later become Mrs. Paul Torrance. (Courtesy of the Hargrett Rare Book and Manuscript Library/University of Georgia Libraries)

Circa 1900

The "Big House" in Baldwin County near Milledgeville, GA, which was owned by Paul Torrance's paternal grandparents—James Robert Torrance and Mattie Hatfield Torrance. Paul lived with his parents on a farm only a short distance away. In 1986, Diane and John Pekar or Long Island, NY, purchased this house. (Courtesy of Garnet Millar)

1992

School Days

In 1992, Paul Torrance stands in his old school playground in Baldwin County near Milledgeville, GA. The building behind Paul in this photo is an old school, but not the one he attended. Paul went to Union Point School, which burned down in the early 1960s.
(Courtesy of Garnet Millar)

In 1941, Paul Torrance was principal of the high school department and registrar for the junior college department at Georgia Military College (GMC) in Milledgeville, GA. He had also been a student and teacher at GMC.
(Courtesy of E. Paul Torrance)

On June 22, 1992, Paul returned to visit his alma mater, Georgia Military College. (Courtesy of Garnet Millar)

Paul Torrance in his old office at Georgia Military College, which is now a museum. Over his right shoulder (lower right) are his two GMC mentors, Colonel J. H. Jenkins and Colonel Ren Thorne (1922). (Courtesy of Garnet Millar)

Wall of Distinguished Graduates in the Museum at Georgia Military College. To the left of Paul's photo is a shot of Wallace Butts, who coached football at GMC and later became famous as coach of the Bulldawgs at the University of Georgia (1922).
(Courtesy of Garnet Millar)

Paul stands on the "viewing block" overlooking the parade square at Georgia Military College and recalls his days as a student, teacher, and principal (1922).
(Courtesy of Garnet Millar)

The Making of a Scholar

Dr. Jacob L. Moreno, a Romanian-born psychiatrist who had been a student of Sigmund Freud, established the Psychodramatic Institute in Beacon, NY. Paul studied with Moreno in 1947, and called him his greatest teacher. (Courtesy of the Hargrett Rare Book and Manuscript Library/University of Georgia Libraries)

"The Emergence of Creativity"

Survival training at Big Delta, AK. Paul was Director of the Survival Field Unit of the USAF Advanced Survival School. His Unit helped prepare aircrew teams to survive and manage in extreme and emergent conditions. Creativity was the key to survival. (Courtesy of the Hargrett Rare Book and Manuscript Library/University of Georgia Libraries)

The Minnesota Years

Burton Hall, College of Education, University of Minnesota, Minneapolis, MN, erected in 1894. "Home" to the Bureau of Educational Research and to Paul Torrance, 1958–1966. (Courtesy of Garnet Millar)

E. Paul Torrance, the new Director of the Bureau of Educational Research, University of Minnesota, circa 1966. Research into creativity would later bring him national and international recognition. (Courtesy of the Hargrett Rare Book and Manuscript Library/University of Georgia Libraries)

Paul purchased the little brown house at 141 S.E. Warwick Street in Prospect Park, Minneapolis, so that he would be within walking distance of the University of Minnesota campus.
(Courtesy of the Hargrett Rare Book and Manuscript Library/University of Georgia Libraries)

Paul and "Hilda" in the cold Minneapolis winter (circa 1960).
(Courtesy of the Hargrett Rare Book and Manuscript Library/University of Georgia Libraries)

Paul Torrance and Pansy Nigh become engaged, October 1959. (Courtesy of the Hargrett Rare Book and Manuscript Library/University of Georgia Libraries)

Southtown Baptist Church in Bloomington, Minneapolis, where Paul and Pansy were married on November 25, 1959. (Courtesy of Garnet Millar)

The Torrance wedding party in Bloomington, MN: Betty Thomley, Pansy, Paul, Charles J. Glotzbach, Reverend Warren and Ms. Anda Littleford (November 25, 1959). (Courtesy of Bee Bleedorn)

Dean Walter Cook at the University of Minnesota, who supported Paul's creativity research (circa 1959). (Courtesy of the Torrance Center for Creative Studies/University of Georgia)

Paul in his office at the University of Minnesota (circa 1959).
(Courtesy of the Hargrett Rare Book and Manuscript Library/University of Georgia Libraries)

The University of Minnesota High School, where Paul's longitudinal study was launched. This school, which is on the edge of the campus, is now a University Technology Center.
(Courtesy of Garnet Millar)

Paul administers part of the creativity test to a youngster (circa 1966). The development of the Torrance Tests of Creative Thinking evolved over several years. (Courtesy of the Hargrett Rare Book and Manuscript Library/University of Georgia Libraries)

Kaoru Yamamoto was instrumental in developing the series of tests that came to be known as the Minnesota Tests of Creative Thinking and later the Torrance Tests of Creative Thinking (circa 1960).
(Courtesy of the Hargrett Rare Book and Manuscript Library/University of Georgia Libraries)

Paul understood the importance of communicating his research findings. These "info posters," designed to describe important aspects of his research, were displayed at conferences and universities, and even in shopping malls. (Courtesy of the Torrance Center for Creative Studies/University of Georgia)

T R A N S L A T I O N of R E S E A R C H
R E S U L T S I N T O M A T E R I A L S
I N S T R U C T I O N A L M E T H O D S . . .

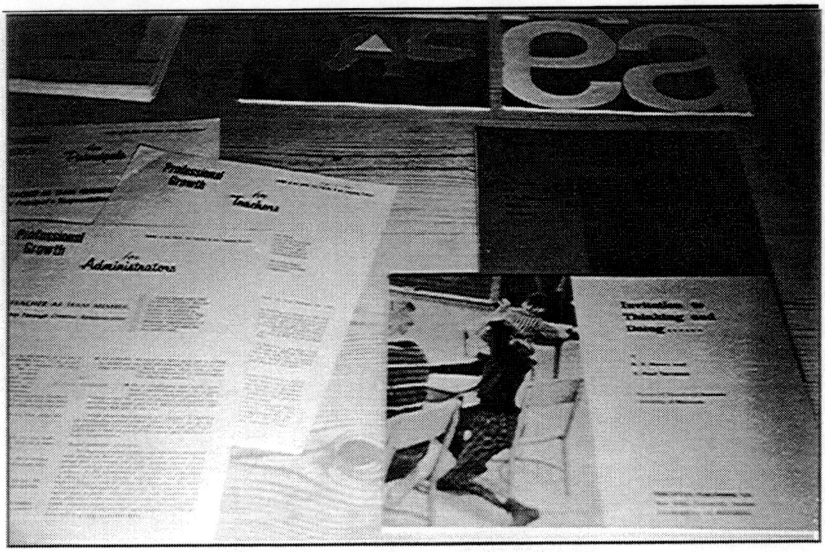

A deliberate attempt is being made by the staff of the Bureau of Educational Research at the University of Minnesota to translate research results related to creative growth into tested materials and instructional methods. Examples of early efforts are these PROFESSIONAL GROWTH LEAFLETS and the workbook entitled INVITATIONS TO THINKING AND DOING. A sample set of the workbook and manual is $2 and may be ordered from Perceptive Pub. Co.

Perceptive Publishing Co.
Box 4086, University Station
Minneapolis 14, Minnesota

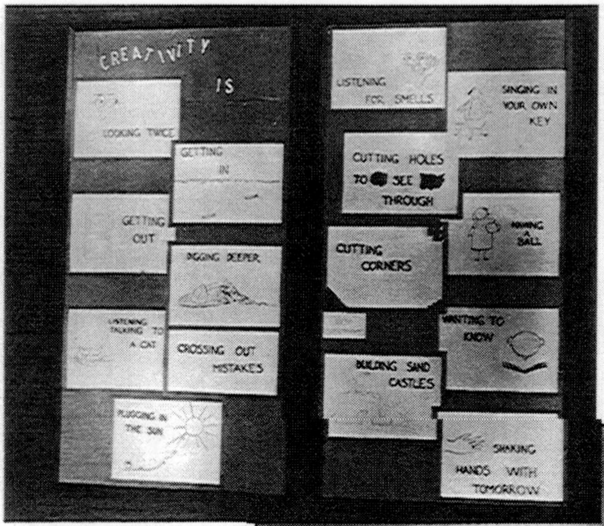

A display visually depicts creativity on a bulletin board at Macalester University in Minneapolis (circa 1965). (Courtesy of the Hargrett Rare Book and Manuscript Library/ University of Georgia Libraries)

Paul set up a publishing company in the basement of his home in Minneapolis (circa 1965). He was highly productive in 1965-1966. (Courtesy of the Hargrett Rare Book and Manuscript Library/ University of Georgia Libraries)

Mrs. Bert Cunnington teaching the skills of creativity to a demonstration class in a Minneapolis shopping mall—Richfield (circa 1964). (Courtesy of the Hargrett Rare Book and Manuscript Library/University of Georgia Libraries)

Bee Bleedorn became a student and research assistant during the latter part of Paul's tenure at the University of Minnesota. She later became Paul's Minnesota "contact" for the longitudinal study. (Courtesy of the Torrance Center for Creative Studies/University of Georgia)

Paul and Pansy receive an award from their "Minnesota Friends"—St. Thomas University, St. Paul, MN, March 17, 1982. (Courtesy of the Hargrett Rare Book and Manuscript Library/University of Georgia Libraries)

The Georgia Years

The University of Georgia Arch leads to the campus from the city of Athens. The city and university were designed and developed at the same time. (Courtesy of Garnet Millar)

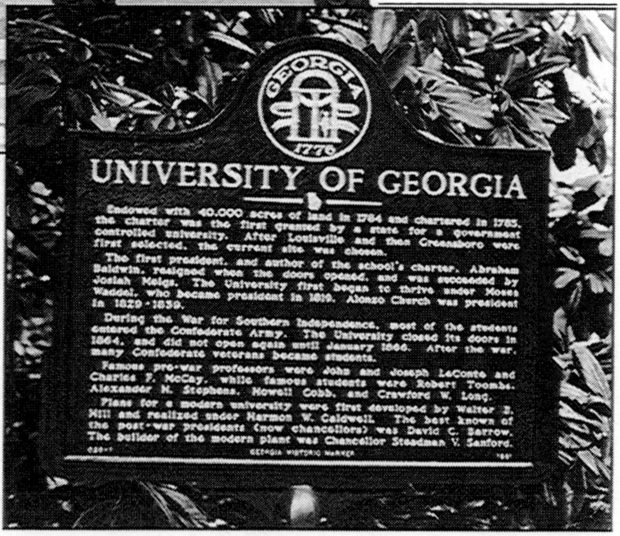

The University of Georgia celebrated its bicentennial in 1985—the year of Paul's retirement celebration. (Courtesy of Garnet Millar)

Aderhold Hall, College of Education at the University of Georgia. Paul spent 18 years working in this building. The Torrance Center for Creative Studies, established in 1984, is housed here. (Courtesy of Garnet Millar)

Paul with friend and colleague, Dr. John Gowan (circa 1974). (Courtesy of the Torrance Center for Creative Studies/University Georgia)

Paul with his mother and father at the homestead near Milledgeville, GA (circa 1966). (Courtesy of the Hargrett Rare Book and Manuscript Library/University of Georgia Libraries)

Dr. Rod Myers, student, colleague, and friend of Paul, at both the University of Minnesota and the University of Georgia. Paul and Rod collaborated on a number of books and intructional materials (circa 1970). (Courtesy of the Hargrett Rare Book and Manuscript Library/University of Georgia Libraries)

Paul during the shooting of a film on the "Magic Net Technique," a creative method used with children to resolve problems. (Courtesy of the Torrance Center for Creative Studies/University of Georgia)

Paul and his students conducted summer creativity workshops for disadvantaged children at Dudley Park in Athens, GA. Painting, poetry, and creative movement were some components of the program (circa 1973). (Courtesy of the Hargrett Rare Book and Manuscript Library/University of Georgia Libraries)

Paul with Prof. Saburo Sato in Osaka City, Japan (circa 1979). Paul was a visiting scholar in Japan in 1978–1979. (Courtesy of the Hargrett Rare Book and Manuscript Library/University of Georgia Libraries)

The Phoenix Medal, presented to Paul by Hiroshima University (Japan) in 1979, is an emblem of respect and admiration. Paul has donated it to the Museum and Archives of Georgia Education in Milledgeville, GA. (Courtesy of Garnet Millar)

Paul and Pansy enjoy time together in Hawaii during a conference on the gifted and talented (circa 1978). (Courtesy of the Hargrett Rare Book and Manuscript Library/University of Georgia Libraries)

Paul and "Amigo" behind the Torrances' 185 Riverhill Drive home on the banks of the Oconee River (circa 1984). (Courtesy of the Hargrett Rare Book and Manuscript Library/University of Georgia Libraries)

Dr. Nayana Tara from Bangalore, India, and Dr. Calvin Taylor participate in a Creativity Conference of the National State Training Institute for the Gifted and Talented at Dallas, TX (circa 1983). (Courtesy of the Hargrett Rare Book and Manuscript Library/University of Georgia Libraries)

Torrance Center staff (left to right). Vicki Connell, Assistant Director; Dr. Mary Frasier, Director; and Pam La Salle, Office Manager (1990). (Courtesy of Garnet Millar)

Paul in his office as Head, Department of Educational Psychology, University of Georgia. He held this position for 12 years (1966–1978). (Courtesy of the Hargrett Rare Book and Manuscript Library/University of Georgia Libraries)

What Paul teaches and how he behaves are congruent. (Courtesy of the Hargrett Rare Book and Manuscript Library/University of Georgia Libraries)

Paul receives the Arthur Lipper Award of the World Olympics of the Mind for outstanding original contributions to the development of human creativity. Arthur Lipper is making the presentation (1982). (Courtesy of the Hargrett Rare Book and Manuscript Library/University of Georgia Libraries)

Two Torrance advocates—Dr. Doris Shallcross from the University of Massachusetts and executive member of the Creative Education Foundation in Buffalo, NY and Dr. Nayana Tara from the Institute for Research on Social and Economic Change in Bangalore, India. (Courtesy of the Hargrett Rare Book and Manuscript Library/University of Georgia Libraries)

Paul and Pansy attend and participate in the World Gifted Conference in Manila, Philippines, 1983. (Courtesy of the Hargrett Rare Book and Manuscript Library/University of Georgia Libraries)

GOVERNOR HARRIS PROCLAIMS "GEORGIA FUTURE PROBLEM SOLVING WEEK"
On January 25, 1984, Governor Joe Frank Harris proclaimed Georgia Future Problem Solving Week to be observed throughout the State during the week of April 8–14, 1984. Governor Harris acted upon the recommendation of participants in the 1983 Georgia Future Problem Solving Bowl and the Advisory Board of the Georgia Future Problem Solving Program. Witnessing the signing of the proclamation in the Governor's Office are (left to right): Dr. Betty Sloop, Advisory Board Member; Dr. E. Paul Torrance, Co-Founder of the Program; Mr. Christopher Nelson (behind Dr. Torrance), Consultant, Georgia State Department of Education; Mrs. Pansy Torrance, Co-Founder; and Ms. Ruth Cowan, Georgia Society for the Gifted President. (Courtesy of the Hargrett Rare Book and Manuscript Library/University of Georgia Libraries)

Paul was a master teacher. He required his students to think for themselves and create new information (circa 1984). (Courtesy of the Hargrett Rare Book and Manuscript Library/University of Georgia Libraries)

On the occasion of his graduation from the University of Georgia, Mohinder Gill presented this painting to Paul. The painting, which depicts Paul and Pansy as two love doves, was given as a token of appreciation for Paul's unconditional kindness to Mohinder Gill while he was a student. (Courtesy of Mohinder Gill)

The Retirement Years

Pansy and Paul at retirement celebration held March 23, 1985. They were presented with a number of gifts and awards, including a book of letters from former students. (Courtesy of the Hargrett Rare Book and Manuscript Library/University of Georgia Libraries)

E. Paul Torrance—Alumni Foundation Distinguished Professor Emeritus—University of Georgia (UGA)—1985. Paul was presented with the University bicentennial medal for serving the University with high distinction. His achievements as a professor at UGA are unmatched. (Courtesy of David Dwinell)

Despite the NASA Challenger tragedy in January 1986, astronaut Dr. Norm Thagard and Dr. June Scobee, widow of Challenger Commander Dick Scobee, visited the University of Georgia in May 1986 to meet the finalists in the Georgia Space Education Project. The contest involved writing about the value of space travel and exploration. Among the 12 finalists were (left to right): Jeanna Gregory (Vienna, GA), Reggie Soloman (Americus, GA), and Matthew Holloway (Americus, GA). (Courtesy of the Hargrett Rare Book and Manuscript Library/University of Georgia Libraries)

The 1990 E. Paul Torrance Annual Lecture was presented by Dr. Garnet Millar. Paul presented Dr. Millar with a plaque commemorating the event. Also in the photo are (left to right): Vicki Connell, Assistant Director of the Torrance Center for Creative Studies, and Dr. Mary Frasier, Director of the Torrance Center. (Courtesy of the Torrance Center for Creative Studies/University of Georgia)

Ellen (Torrance) Steele (circa 1940), Paul's sister, currently lives with Paul in Athens, Georgia.
(Courtesy of Dr. Torrance)

Paul at the Museum and Archives of Georgia Education. Paul has donated several of his books and memorabilia to their collection (1992). (Courtesy of Garnet Millar)

Paul with his "girls"—students, colleagues, and now friends, Dr. Felice Kaufmann, Consultant for Gifted and Talented, and Vicki Connell, Acting Director of the Torrance Center for Creative Studies (1992). (Courtesy of Garnet Millar)

Paul in his office at home in Athens, GA (1992).
(Courtesy of Garnet Millar)

Appendix A

LIST OF PUBLICATIONS OF E. PAUL TORRANCE 1940–1995

This list represents a complete record of the publications of E. Paul Torrance over a 53-year period of his career. The list is organized by year, and by category within each year to illustrate the breadth of his writing and presentations, including keynote addresses. Key periods or eras in the career of Paul Torrance are also used as organizers and relate to the parts of the biography.

The seven categories of publications are as follows: Books and monographs (88); Parts of books, contributions to cooperative volumes (256); Articles in professional and research journals (408); Reports, manuals, handbooks, tests, instructional materials (538); Articles in popular or trade type journals and magazines—applications of research (162); Papers presented at seminars/conferences (355); and Foreword(s)/Preface(s) and book reviews (64). The total number of publications and presentations, to date, is 1,871.

Some of these publications are available at local public libraries, many at university libraries, and all in the Torrance Collection in the archives located in the Hargrett Rare Book and Manuscript Library at the University of Georgia, in Athens, Georgia, 30602. Paul Torrance continues to write and publish today at his home in Athens, Georgia.

In 1990, I asked Paul Torrance to provide me with a collection of the most influential articles written by him. At the time, Mary Frasier and I had planned to publish a commemorative book on the occasion of his 75th birthday, to be presented to individuals attending a Stewardship Dinner after the 1990 Torrance Lecture at the University of Georgia. Those articles are indicated with a double asterisk and in bold.

TEACHING AND TRAINING

1940

Articles in Popular or Trade Type Journals and Magazines—Applications of Research

1. Staff Budgets Time to Avoid Trouble. *The Scholastic Editor*, ***19****(9)*, 209.

1943

Articles in Professional and Research Journals

1. Victory Corps Series. *Guidance Manual*, 7. Athens, GA: State Department of Education.

1944

Reports, Manuals, Handbooks, Tests, and Instructional Materials

1. Predicting and Measuring Success in Plane Geometry. In partial fulfillment of the requirements for the Degree of Master of Arts. Submitted in Educational Psychology, University of Minnesota, Minneapolis, MN.

1945

Articles in Professional and Research Journals

1. The Influence ofthe Broken Home on Adolescent Adjustment. *Journal of Educational Sociology*, ***18***, 359-364.

1946

Articles in Professional and Research Journals

1. Mathematics Interest—Fundamental or Not? *Mathematics Teacher*, ***39***, 24-25.
2. More About Using Part IV, D.O.T. *Occupations (The Vocational Guidance Magazine)*, ***24***, 208-210.

1948

Articles in Professional and Research Journals

1. Getting More Than an I.Q. from Testing Elementary School Children. *The Elementary School Journal*, ***49****(10)*, 550-556.

Reports, Manuals, Handbooks, Tests, and Instructional Materials

1. The Role of Projective Methods in the Evaluation of Attitudes. Unpublished paper prepared for national project on evaluation of general education.
2. An Analysis of the Phenomenon of Resistance in a College Class Situation. Unpublished term report for Education C201: Advanced Educational Psychology: The Growth of the Self. Kansas State College, Manhattan, KS.

1949

Parts of Books, Contributions to Cooperative Volumes

1. "Psychodramatic Methods in the College Student Personnel Program." In R. Haas (Ed.), *Psychodrama and Sociodrama in Education*. Beacon, NY: Beacon House.

Articles in Professional and Research Journals

1. The Role Concept in a Vocational Guidance Program. *Childhood Education*, ***25****(9)*, 413-416.
2. Psychodramatic Methods in the College Student Personnel Program. *Sociometry*, ***2***, 368-375.

Reports, Manuals, Handbooks, Tests, Instructional Materials

1. *Faculty Advisers' Handbook for Kansas State College (Revision)*. Manhattan, KS: Counseling Bureau, Kansas State College.
2. *Faculty Advising at Kansas State College, Reports, Plans, Evaluation, Suggestions, New Tools, Resources* (a supplement to the *Faculty Advisers' Handbook*). Manhattan, KS: Counseling Bureau, Kansas State College.

1950

Parts of Books, Contributions to Cooperative Volumes

1. "Changing Attitudes Concerning 'Academic Discipline' in the College of Literature, Science and the Arts of the University of Michigan." In C. Eggertsen (Ed.), *Studies in the History of Higher Education in Michigan*. Ann Arbor, MI: University of Michigan School of Education.

Articles in Professional and Research Journals

1. The Phenomenon of Resistance in Learning. *The Journal of Abnormal and Social Psychology*, ***45****(4)*, 592-597.
2. The Principale of *Pragnänz* as a Frame of Reference for Psychotherapy. *Journal of Consulting Psychology*, ***14****(6)*, 452-457.

Papers Presented at Seminars/Conferences

1. "Perception of Self and Other's Roles Related to Sociometric Choice Patterns." Paper presented to Midwestern Psychological Association, Detroit, MI, April.

U.S. ADVANCED SURVIVAL SCHOOL

1951

Articles in Professional and Research Journals

1. Getting mental hygiene practices into action through a college class. *Mental Hygiene, 35(1),* 88–95.

Reports, Manuals, Handbooks, Tests, Instructional Materials

1. (With M. Taylor) *Incomplete Sentences Blank Designed to Assess Attitudes of Respect for the Worth and Dignity of Individuals.* Manhattan, KS: Counseling Bureau, Kansas State College.
2. *Summary of Counseling Bureau Studies Completed Between September, 1950 and June, 1951.* Manhattan, KS: Counseling Bureau, Kansas State College.
3. Self-Concepts and Their Significance in the Learning and Adjustment of College Freshmen. Doctoral Dissertation. Ann Arbor, MI: The University of Michigan.

Papers Presented at Seminars/Conferences

1. "Personality Development and Characteristics of Scholastic Over-, Under-, and Accurate Self-Evaluators." Paper presented to Midwestern Psychological Association, Chicago, IL, May.
2. "Some Uses of Stephenson's Q-Technique in the Quantification of the Individual." Paper presented to Kansas Academy of Sciences, Lawrence, KS, May. (Transaction of the Kansas Academy of Science, 55(1), 92–97.)
3. "Rationalizations About Test Performance and Self-Concepts." Paper presented to Kansas Academy of Sciences, Lawrence, KS.
4. (With M. Taylor) "Self-Concept as a Determinant of Socioeconomic Status." Paper presented at Midwestern Psychological Association meeting, Chicago, IL, April.

1952

Reports, Manuals, Handbooks, Tests, Instructional Materials

1. *Survival Research: A Report of the First Year of Development.* Washington, DC: Human Resources Research Laboratory, Air Research and Development Command.

Papers Presented at Seminars/Conferences

1. "The Relationship of Attitudes and Attitude Changes Toward Survival Adequacy to the Achievement of Survival Knowledge." Paper presented to Rocky Mountain Psychological Association, Boulder, CO, May 3.

1953

Parts of Books, Contributions to Cooperative Volumes

1. "Some Human Factors Operations Research Findings of Interest to Intelligence

Personnel." In R. Work (Ed.), *First World-Wide Evasion and Escape Conference.* Stead Air Force Base, NV: USAF Advanced Survival School.

Articles in Professional and Research Journals

1. Perception of Group Functioning as a Predictor of Group Performance. *Research Studies of the University of Washington,* ***21****(3)*, 262-265.
2. Methods of Conducting Critiques of Group Problem-Solving Performance. *Journal of Applied Psychology,* ***37****(5)*, 394-398.

Reports, Manuals, Handbooks, Tests, Instructional Materials

1. *Psychological Aspects of Survival: A Survey of the Literature.* Washington, DC: Human Factors Operations Research Laboratories.
2. *Crew Performance in a Test Situation as a Predictor of Field and Combat Performance.* Washington, DC: Human Factors Operations Research Laboratories.
3. *Problems Faced by Officers in Maintaining the Respect of the Airmen of Their Crews During Survival Training.* Reno, NV: Human Factors Operations Research Laboratories.
4. (With M. Levi and G. O. Pletts) *Sociometric Studies of Combat Aircrews in Survival Training.* Washington, DC: Human Factors Operations Research Laboratories.
5. *Survival Research Documentary Series—Psychological Aspects of Survival.* Washington, DC: Human Factors Operations Research Laboratories.
6. *Survival Psychology: Some Things the Combat Aircrewman Should Know About the Psychological Aspects of Survival (Memo 42).* Washington, DC: Human Factors Operations Research Laboratories.

Articles in Popular or Trade Type Journals and Magazines—Applications of Research

1. Fear in Survival. *Second Air Force Intelligence Digest*, July.
2. How Groups Behave When Surviving. *SAC Survival Trends*, February.
3. The Survivor-Evadee and People in Hostile Territory. *SAC Survival Trends*, March.
4. What Would You Do? How Groups Behave When Surviving. *Air Intelligence Training Bulletin,* ***5****(6)*, 360-371.
5. You, the Survivor-Evadee and Fear. *SAC Survival Trends*, May.

Papers Presented at Seminars/Conferences

1. "Research in Group Development in Survival Training." Paper presented to American Personnel and Guidance Association, Chicago, IL, March.
2. "Some Human Factors Operations Research Findings of Interest to Intelligence Personnel." Paper presented to First World-Wide Evasion and Escape Conference, Stead Air Force Base, NV, April.
3. "Some Current Contributions of Human Factors Operations Research Laboratory to the Psychology of Learning." Paper presented to American Psychological Association, September.

1954

Articles in Professional and Research Journals

1. Leadership Training to Improve Aircrew Group Performance. *Air Training Command Instructors Journal*, ***5***, 25-35.
2. Some Consequences of Power Differences in Decision Making in Permanent and Temporary Three-Man Groups. *Research Studies of the State College of Washington*, ***22****(2)*, 120-130.
3. The Behavior of Small Groups Under the Stress Conditions of "Survival." *American Sociological Review*, ***19****(6)*, 751-755.
4. Rationalizations about Test Performance as a Function of Self-Concepts. *The Journal of Social Psychology*, ***39***, 211-217.
5. Some Practical Uses of a Knowledge of Self-Concepts in Counseling and Guidance. *Educational and Psychological Measurement*, ***14****(1)*, 120-127.
6. (With M. Levi and G. O. Pletts) Sociometric Studies of Combat Aircrews in Survival Training. *Sociometry*, ***17***, 304-328.
7. The Relationship of Attitudes and Changes in Attitudes Toward Survival Adequacy to the Achievement of Survival Knowledge. *The Journal of Social Psychology*, ***40***, 259-265.
8. Leadership Training to Improve Group Performance. *Instructors Journal*, ***5****(1)*, 25-35.

Reports, Manuals, Handbooks, Tests, Instructional Materials

1. *Survival Psychology: What the Combat Aircrewman Should Know About the Psychological Aspects of Survival*. Washington, DC: Human Factors Operations Research Laboratories.
2. *Psychological Aspects of Survival: A Study of Survival Behavior*. Washington, DC: Human Factors Operations Research Laboratories.
3. *Psychological Aspects of Survival: Teaching the Psychological Aspects of Survival*. Washington, DC: Human Factors Operations Research Laboratories.
4. (With R. C. Ziller) *Teaching Men to Survive*. Reno, NV: USAF Advanced Survival School.
5. *The Development of a Preliminary Life Experience Inventory for the Study of Fighter Interceptor Combat Effectiveness*. San Antonio, TX: Air Force Personnel and Training Research Center.
6. *Some Consequences of Power Differences on Decisions in B-26 Crews. Research Bulletin*. San Antonio, TX: Air Force Personnel and Training Research Center.
7. *Leadership and Organizational Factors in Fighter Interceptor Combat Effectiveness*. Randolph Air Force Base, TX: Crew Research Laboratory, Air Force Personnel and Training Research Center.
8. *Exit the Tiger: Survival Psychology for the ADC Tiger*. Colorado Springs, CO: Air Force Air Defense Command.
9. (E.P. Torrance et al.) *Survival Research: A Report of the Second Year of Development*. Randolf, TX: Crew Research Laboratory, Air Force Personnel and Training Research Center.
10. *Survival Research: A Report of the Third Year of Development*. Randolf, TX: Crew Research Laboratory, Air Force Personnel and Training Research Center.
11. *Feedback and the Design of Experiments*. Reno, NV: Crew Research Laboratory, Air Force Personnel and Training Research Center.

12. *The "Can You Drink Sea Water?" Controversy: Its Psychological Aspects and A Proposal for Arbitration.* Reno, NV: Crew Research Laboratory, Air Force Personnel and Training Research Center.
13. *The Use of Evasion and Escape Reports in the Study of Personality Requirements for Survival.* Reno, NV: Crew Research Laboratory, Air Force Personnel and Training Research Center.
14. *Teaching the Psychological Aspects of Survival.* Washington, DC: Human Factors Operations Research Laboratories.
15. *Some Psychological Aspects of Survival Ration Acceptability.* Reno, NV: Crew Research Laboratory, Air Force Personnel and Training Research Center.

Articles in Popular or Trade Type Journals and Magazines—Applications of Research

1. Portrait of an Ace. *Time Magazine, 38.*
2. Traits of Jet Aces Traced. *Los Angeles Examiner, 1.*

Papers Presented at Seminars/Conferences

1. "Some Consequences of Power Differences in Decision Making in Permanent and Temporary Three-Man Groups." Paper presented to Western Sociological Association, Corvallis, OR, April.
2. "A Psychological Study of American Jet Aces." Paper presented to Western Psychological Association, Long Beach, CA, May 20.
3. "Additional Personnel and Training Research of Interest to Escape and Evasion Officers." Paper presented to Second World-Wide Evasion and Escape Conference, Stead Air Force Base, NV, November 30.
4. "The Making of Jet Aces." Paper presented at Western Psychological Association, Long Beach, CA, May.

1955

Parts of Books, Contributions to Cooperative Volumes

(* Indicates a previously published journal article.)

1. *"Methods of Conducting Critiques of Group Problem-Solving Performance." In P. Hare, E. F. Borgatta, and R. F. Bales (Eds.), *Small Groups.* New York, NY: Alfred Knopf, Pp. 560-567.
2. *"Some Consequences of Power Differences in Decision-Making in Permanent and Temporary Three-Man Groups." In P. Hare, E. F. Borgatta, and R. F. Bales (Eds.), *Small Groups.* New York, NY: Alfred Knopf, Pp. 482-491.
3. Techniques for Studying Individual and Group Adaptation in Emergencies and Extreme Conditions. In National Academy of Sciences, *Air Force Human Engineering Personnel and Training Research.* Washington, DC: National Academy of Sciences, National Research Council.

Articles in Professional and Research Journals

1. Perception of Group Functioning as a Predictor of Group Performance. *Journal of*

Social Psychology, ***42***, 271-282.
2. Survival Psychology. *Air Intelligence Training Bulletin, 7,* 2–19. (Also in *Air, 7*(11), 2–19.)

Reports, Manuals, Handbooks, Tests, Instructional Materials

1. (With R. Mason) *Problems of Recall of Personal Data*. Randolph Air Force Base, TX: Crew Research Laboratory, Air Force Personnel and Training Research Center.
2. *Personality Factors and Survival Ration Acceptability*. Randolph Air Force Base, TX: Crew Research Laboratory, Air Force Personnel and Training Research Center.
3. *Communist Techniques for Disrupting Groups*. Randolph Air Force Base, TX: Crew Research Laboratory, Air Force Personnel and Training Research Center.
4. *The Will-to-Resist: An Exploratory Study of the Combat Aircrewman*. Randolph Air Force Base, TX: Randolph Training Research Center.
5. *Attitude-Change Research and How to Resist the Enemy*. Randolph Air Force Base, TX: Crew Research Laboratory, Air Force Personnel and Training Research Center.
6. *The Will to Survive*. Reno, NV: Air Force Personnel and Training Research Center.
7. *Personnel and Training Problems in Survival Equipment*. Reno, NV: Stead Air Force Base.
8. *Laboratory Note—Personnel and Training Problems in Surviving Equipment*. Reno, NV: Air Force Personnel and Training Research Center.
9. *Adaptation to Living and Working in the Arctic*. Randolph, TX: Crew Research Laboratory, Air Force Personnel and Training Research Center.
10. *Laboratory Note—Adaptation to Living and Working in the Arctic*. Reno, NV: Crew Research Laboratory, Air Force Personnel and Training Research Center.
11. *How "Open" is the Open Mind?* Reno, NV: Crew Research Laboratory, Air Force Personnel and Training Research Center.
12. *Survival Research—A Report of the Fourth Year of Development*. Reno, NV: Air Force Personnel and Training Research Center.
13. *Sports and Stress Resistance*. Reno, NV: Crew Research Laboratory, Air Force Personnel and Training Research Center.
14. *Fifteen Days with a B-29 Crew*. Reno, NV: Crew Research Laboratory, Air Force Personnel and Training Research Center.
15. (With A. C. Higgins) *The Development and Preliminary Validation of a Method for Studying Frustration Behavior in Survival Situations*. Reno, NV: Survival Research Field Unit, Crew Research Laboratory, Air Force Personnel and Training Research Center, Stead Air Force Base.
16. *A Preliminary Life Experience Inventory for Studying Susceptibility to Stress*. Reno, NV: Air Force Personnel and Training Research Center.
17. *A Proposal for Assessing "Attitude" in Survival Training*. Reno, NV: Crew Research Laboratory, Air Force Personnel and Training Research Center.
18. *Some Issues Regarding Power Roles in Emergencies and Extreme Conditions*. Reno, NV: Air Force Personnel and Training Research Center.
19. *Frustration Behavior and Personality*. Randolph, TX: Air Force Personnel and Training Research Center.
20. *Food Prejudices and Survival*. Reno, NV: Survival Research Field Unit, Crew Research Laboratory, USAF Survival Training, Stead Air Force Base.

Papers Presented at Seminars/Conferences

1. "Function of Expressed Disagreement in Small Group Processes." Paper presented to Annual Meeting of The Institute of Management Sciences, New York, NY, October 21.
2. "Some Issues Regarding Power Roles in Emergencies and Extreme Conditions." Paper presented to Social Science Research Council—West Coast Society for the Study of Small Groups Conference, Monterey, CA, April 24-26.
3. "Psychological Adaptation to Living and Working in the Arctic." Paper presented at SAC Conference on Arctic Research and Indoctrination, Maxwell Air Force Base, AL, June.

1956

Parts of Books, Contributions to Cooperative Volumes

1. "Sociometric Techniques for Diagnosing Group Ills." In J. L. Moreno (Ed.), *Sociometry and the Science of Man*. New York, NY: Beacon House, Pp. 341-356.
2. "Techniques for Studying Individual and Group Adaption in Emergencies and Extreme Conditions." In G. Finch and F. Cameron (Eds.), *Symposium on Air Force Human Engineering, Personnel, and Training Research*. Washington, DC: National Academy of Sciences, Pp. 286-297.
3. "Conditions for Creative Growth." In L. D. Haskew and J. C. McClendon (Eds.), *This is Teaching*. Glenview, IL: Scott, Foresman and Company, Pp. 329-333.

Articles in Professional and Research Journals

1. (With R. Mason) The Indigenous Leader in Changing Attitudes and Behavior. *International Journal of Sociometry*, ***1***, 23-28.
2. Will to Survive: What Combat Aircrewmen Believe About It. *Air Intelligence Training Bulletin*, ***8****(2)*, 11-12.

Reports, Manuals, Handbooks, Tests, Instructional Materials

1. *How to Use the "POW Grapevine."* Randolph Air Force Base, TX: Crew Research Laboratory, Air Force Personnel and Training Research Center.
2. (With R. Mason) *Management of Stresses in Resistance Training*. Randolph Air Force Base, TX: Crew Research Laboratory, Air Force Personnel and Training Research Laboratory.
3. (With G. R. LaForge and R. Mason) *Group Adaptation in Emergencies and Extreme Conditions: The Blizzard Study*. Randolph Air Force Base, TX: Crew Research Laboratory, Air Force Personnel and Training Research Center.
4. *Concurrent Emphasis on "First and Second Lines of Defense" and Confidence in Ability to Adhere to the POW Code*. Stead Air Force Base, NV: Crew Research Field Unit, Air Force Personnel and Training Research Center.
5. *Confidential versus Anonymous Responses: Confidence in Ability to Live Up to the POW Code*. Stead Air Force Base, NV: Crew Research Field Unit, Air Force Personnel and Training Research Center.
6. *Personal Factors Related to Capture in a Simulated Escape and Evasion Exercise*. Stead Air Force Base, NV: Crew Research Field Unit, Air Force Personnel and Training Research Center.

7. *Personal Factors Related to Expressed Confidence in Ability to Adhere to the POW Code of Conduct.* Stead Air Force Base, NV: Crew Research Field Unit, Air Force Personnel and Training Research Center.
8. *Personality Adaptation in Survival: Case Studies of USAF Survivor-Evadees in Korea.* Stead Air Force Base, NV: Crew Research Field Unit, Air Force Personnel and Training Research Center.
9. *Possible Consequences of Training for a "Second Line of Defense."* Stead Air Force Base, NV: Crew Research Field Unit, Air Force Personnel and Training Research Center.
10. *The Use of Evasion and Escape Reports in the Study of Personality Requirements for Survival.* Stead Air Force Base, NV: Crew Research Field Unit, Air Force Personnel and Training Research Center.
11. *"Survivance de l'Avieteur Hostile Aspects Medicaux" translated by E. Evrard.* Stead Air Force Base, NV: Crew Research Field Unit, Air Force Personnel and Training Research Center.
12. *Volunteers for Experiments Involving Discomfort.* Stead Air Force Base, NV: Crew Research Field Unit, Air Force Personnel and Training Research Center.
13. (With P. W. Buck, R. Mason and E. H. Richardson) *The Psychology of Interrogation: A Syllabus for Training Interrogators for Air Force Code of Conduct Training.* Stead Air Force Base, NV: Crew Research Field Unit, Air Force Personnel and Training Research Center.
14. (With R. C. Ziller) *Experiments on Decision-Making in Small Groups.* Stead Air Force Base, NV: Crew Research Field Unit, Air Force Personnel and Training Research Center.
15. (With R. C. Ziller) *Negative Identification as a Function of Personality Differences.* Stead Air Force Base, NV: Crew Research Field Unit, Air Force Personnel and Training Research Center.
16. *Survival of the Aviator in a Hostile Environment: Medical Aspects.* Reno, NV: Air Force Personnel and Training Research Center.

Articles in Popular or Trade Type Journals and Magazines—Applications of Research

1. Adapting to the Arctic. *Survival Trends, February-March*, 3-27.
2. Group Factors in a Combat Team. *General Training, 2(13).* (Continental Air Command)
3. What Combat Aircrewmen Think About the Will-to-Survive. *Survival Trends, April-May*, 1-20.

Papers Presented at Seminars/Conferences

1. "How 'Open' Is the 'Open Mind'?" Prior Expectations and Acceptance of Survival Rations. Paper presented to Western Psychological Association, Berkeley, CA, March.
2. "Experiments on Decision-Making in Small Groups." Paper presented to West Coast Society for the Study of Small Groups, Berkeley, CA, March.
3. "A Study of Group Adaptation Under Blizzard Conditions." Paper presented to Aero Medical Association, Chicago, IL, April.
4. "Research Problems in Applying Research Findings: Examples from a Military Setting." Paper presented to American Sociological Association, Detroit, MI, September.

5. "Training Factors Affecting Survival Ration Acceptability." Paper presented to Department of Defense Coordination Conference on Research and Development in Foods, Wright-Patterson Air Force Base, OH, October.
6. "Fallacies About the Psychological Aspects of Survival." Lecture given to Survival School Trainees, 1952-1956.

1957

Books and Monographs

1. *Emergency and Extreme Conditions Part II*. Lackland Air Force Base, TX: Personnel and Training Research Center.

Parts of Books, Contributions to Cooperative Volumes

1. "Food Attitudes in Survival Situations." In *Stress and Food Problems*. Chicago, IL: Quartermaster Food and Container Institutes for the Armed Forces, Pp. 46-52.
2. (With R. Mason) "Psychologic and Sociologic Aspects of Survival Ration Acceptability." In J. Brozek (Ed.), *Symposium on Nutrition and Behavior*. New York, NY: National Vitamin Foundation, Inc. (Nutrition Symposium Series 14), Pp. 176-179. (Also in *American Journal of Clinical Nutrition, 5,* 176–179.)
3. What Happens to Sociometric Structure in Emergencies and Extreme Conditions. *Proceedings of the 15th International Congress of Psychology*. Amsterdam, Brussells, Belgium: North Holland Publishing Company.

Articles in Professional and Research Journals

1. Group Decision-Making and Disagreement. *Social Forces*, ***35****(4)*, 314-318.
2. What Happens to Sociometric Structure in Small Groups in Emergencies and Extreme Conditions. *Group Psychotherapy*, ***10***, 212-220.

Reports, Manuals, Handbooks, Tests, Instructional Materials

1. (With R. C. Ziller) *Risk and Life Experiences: Development of a Scale for Measuring Risk-Taking Tendencies*. San Antonio, TX: Air Force Personnel and Training Research Center.
2. *Frustration Behavior in Survival Training: Its Observation and Prediction*. Randolph Air Force Base, TX: Crew Research Laboratory, Air Force Personnel and Training Research Center.
3. (With C. E. Hawkins) *Structuredness of Commands and Compliance in Frustrating Situations*. Randolph Air Force Base, TX: Crew Research Laboratory, Air Force Personnel and Training Research Center.
4. (With C. E. Hawkins) *Humor, Profanity, Non-Responsiveness, and Carelessness in a Test Situation as a Predictor of Performance in a Simulated Survival Exercise*. Randolph Air Force Base, TX: Crew Research Laboratory, Air Force Personnel and Training Research Center.
5. *Effects of Non-Segregation of Officers and Airmen on Respect for Officers in a Simulated Survival Situation*. Randolph Air Force Base, TX: Crew Research Laboratory, Air Force Personnel and Training Research Center.

6. *Training Combat Aircrewmen for Confidence in Ability to Adhere to the Code of Conduct.* Lackland Air Force Base, TX: Air Force Personnel and Training Research Center. (*Development Report* AFPTRC-TN-57-00, ASTIA Document No. 134220.)
7. (With C. H. Rush, H. B. Kohn, and J. M. Doughty) *Factors in Fighter-Interceptor Pilot Combat Effectiveness: A Summary Report.* Lackland Air Force Base, TX: Air Force Personnel and Training Research Center. (*Technical Report* AFPTRC-TN-57-23, ASTIA Document 098926.)
8. *Reports of the Survival Methods Research Program.* Lackland Air Force Base, TX: Air Force Personnel and Training Research Center.
9. *Ideology of Combat Aircrewmen Concerning Leadership in Small Groups Under Stress.* Randolf, TX: Air Force Personnel and Training Research Center.
10. *Survival Research: Summary of Research from October 1955 to February 1957.* Randolf, TX: Air Force Personnel and Training Research Center.

Papers Presented at Seminars/Conferences

1. "Leadership in the Survival of Small Isolated Groups." Paper presented at Symposium on Preventive and Social Psychiatry, Walter Reed Army Institute of Research National Academy of Sciences, Washington, DC, April 15-17.
2. "Criterion Problems in Studies of Leadership and Group Effectiveness Under Stress." Paper presented to Western Psychological Association, Eugene, OR, May 9-11.
3. "Research on Interpersonal Perception Under Stress." Paper presented to Western Psychological Association, Eugene, OR, May 9-11.
4. "Group Factors in Survival Ration Acceptability." Paper presented to Department of Defense Coordination Conference on Research and Development in Foods, Boston, MA, May.
5. "Changes in Sociometric Structure Under Stress." International Congress of Psychology, Brussels, Belgium, July.

THE MINNESOTA YEARS

1958

Parts of Books, Contributions to Cooperative Volumes

1. (With R. Mason) "Instructor Effort to Influence: An Experimental Evaluation of Six Approaches." In *Symposium on Air Force Human Engineering, Personnel and Training Research.* Washington, DC: National Academy of Sciences—National Research Council, Pp. 1-9.
2. (With R. C. Ziller) "Crew Decisions Under Conditions of Uncertainty." In *Symposium on Air Force Human Engineering, Personnel and Training Research.* Washington, DC: National Academy of Sciences National Research Council, Pp. 20-26.

Articles in Professional and Research Journals

1. Sensitization Versus Adaptability in Preparing for Emergencies: Prior Experience with an Emergency Ration and Its Acceptability in a Simulated Survival

Situation. *Journal of Applied Psychology*, ***42(1)***, 63-67.

2. How Minnesota Science Teachers Are Meeting the Challenge. *The Minnesota Journal of Science*, ***2**(1)*, 22-25.
3. Interpersonal Aggression and Submission in Ability to Endure Pain and Discomfort. *Journal of Social Psychology*, ***48***, 205-210.
4. Visuals Used in Brainstorming Experiment in 1958. *Elementary School Journal*, ***62***, 34-41 (1961).

Reports, Manuals, Handbooks, Tests, Instructional Materials

1. *Minnesota Secondary School Administrators Look at Their Mathematics and Science Programs*. Minneapolis, MN: Bureau of Educational Research, University of Minnesota. (*Research Memorandum* BER-58-1.)
2. *Minnesota Secondary School Teachers Look at Their Mathematics and Science Programs*. Minneapolis, MN: Bureau of Educational Research, University of Minnesota. (*Research Memorandum* BER-58-2.)
3. (With S. N. Ghei) *Recent Research and Expert Opinion Concerning Secondary School Mathematics and Science*. Minneapolis, MN: Bureau of Educational Research, University of Minnesota. (*Research Memorandum* BER-58-3.)
4. *Mastery of Stress: School Counselor Notes on Space Age Critical Job Areas*. Wright-Patterson Air Force Base, OH: Orientation Group, USAF.
5. *Explorations in Creative Thinking in Mental Hygiene: I. Alone or in Groups?* Minneapolis, MN: Bureau of Educational Research, University of Minnesota. (*Research Memorandum* BER-58-4.)
6. (With K. N. DeYoung, S. N. Ghei, and H. W. Michie) *Explorations of Creative Thinking in Mental Hygiene: II. Some Characteristics of the More Creative Individuals*. Minneapolis, MN: Bureau of Educational Research, University of Minnesota. (*Research Memorandum* BER-58-6.)
7. *Self-Evaluation of Achievement of Course Objectives: Expected Versus Unexpected*. Minneapolis, MN: Bureau of Educational Research, University of Minnesota. (*Research Memorandum* BER-58-7.)
8. (With H. W. Michie) *Explorations in Creative Thinking in the Early School Years: I. Scoring Manual for "How Good is Your Imagination?"* (Form C). Minneapolis, MN: Bureau of Educational Research, University of Minnesota. (*Research Memorandum* BER-59-1).
9. (With F. B. Baker, K. N. DeYoung, S. N. Ghei, and J. Kincannon) *Explorations in Creative Thinking in Mental Hygiene: I. Alone or in Groups*. Minneapolis, MN: Bureau of Educational Research, College of Education, University of Minnesota.
10. *Educational Psychology 159ss—Personality Development and Mental Hygiene*. Minneapolis, MN: College of Education, University of Minnesota.
11. *How Good is Your Imagination: Preliminary Manual for Appraisal of Creative Thinking in Early School Years*. Minneapolis, MN: Bureau of Educational Research, College of Education, University of Minnesota.

Papers Presented at Seminars/Conferences

1. "Public Relations for the Sanitarian." Address prepared for presentation to Fieldman's Conference, Minnesota Sanitarians' Association, St. Paul, MN, September.
2. Designs for Challenging Ingenuity and Resourcefulness. Paper prepared for presenta-

tion to R.O.T.C. Seminar on College Teaching, University of Minnesota, Minneapolis, MN, September.

1959

Parts of Books, Contributions to Cooperative Volumes

(* Indicates a previously published journal article.)

1. *"Functions of Expressed Disagreement in Small Group Processes." In A. H. Rubenstein and C. J. Haberstroh (Eds.), *Readings in Organization*. Cambridge, MA: School of Industrial Management, Massachusetts Institute of Technology, Pp. 250-258.
2. "Mutual Support and Sacrifices in the Survival of Groups Under Stress: Implications for Social Psychiatry." In J. H. Masserman and J. L. Moreno (Eds.), *Progress in Psychotherapy: Social Psychiatry*. New York, NY: Grune & Stratton, Pp. 131-139.
3. "Explorations in Creative Thinking in the Early School Years: A Progress Report." In C. W. Taylor (Ed.), *The Third University of Utah Research Conference on the Identification of Creative Scientific Talent*. Salt Lake City, UT: University of Utah Press, Pp. 58-71.

Articles in Professional and Research Journals

1. An Experimental Evaluation of "No-Pressure" Influence. *Journal of Applied Psychology*, ***43****(2)*, 109-113.
2. (With G. W. Gustafson) How Minnesota Math Teachers Are Meeting the Challenge. *The Minnesota Journal of Science*, ***2****(3)*, 14-18.
3. Influence of Experienced Members of Small Groups on the Behavior of the Inexperienced. *Journal of Social Psychology*, ***49***, 249-257.
4. Small High Schools and the Improvement of Mathematics and Science Programs. *Educational Administration and Supervision*, ***45****(3)*, 127–134.
5. Current Research on the Nature of Creative Talent. *Journal of Counseling Psychology*, ***6****(4)*, 309-316.
6. Care and Feeding of the Gifted Child. *Alumni News (University of Minnesota)*, ***59****(2)*, 6-8.
7. (With G. Gustafson) How Minnesota Mathematics Teachers are Meeting the Challenge. *The Minnesota Journal of Science*, ***11****(3)*, 14-18.
8. Research Notes From Here and There. *Journal of Counseling Psychology*, ***6****(4)*, 309-316.
9. An Experimental Evaluation of "No-Pressure" Influence [Editor's Comment]. *Social Science Reporter*, ***7****(11)*, 3.

Reports, Manuals, Handbooks, Tests, Instructional Materials

1. *Explorations in Creative Thinking in the Early School Years: II. An Experiment in Training and Motivation*. Minneapolis, MN: Bureau of Educational Research, University of Minnesota. (*Research Memorandum* BER-59-2.)
2. (With J. E. Bowers) *Explorations in Creative Thinking in Early School Years: III. Sex Roles and Appropriateness of Stimuli*. Minneapolis, MN: Bureau of Educational Research, University of Minnesota. (*Research Memorandum* BER-59-3.)
3. (With F. B. Baker and J. E. Bowers) *Explorations in Creative Thinking in the Early*

School Years: IV. Manipulation of Objects and Inventiveness. Minneapolis, MN: Bureau of Educational Research, University of Minnesota. (*Research Memorandum* BER-59-4.)

4. *Explorations in Creative Thinking in the Early School Years: V. An Experimental Study of Peer Sanctions Against Highly Creative Children.* Minneapolis, MN: Bureau of Educational Research, University of Minnesota. (*Research Memorandum* BER-59-5.)
5. *Explorations in Creative Thinking in the Early School Years: VI. Highly Intelligent and Highly Creative Children in a Laboratory School.* Minneapolis, MN: Bureau of Educational Research, University of Minnesota.
6. *Explorations in Creative Thinking in the Early School Years: VII. Talkativeness and Creative Thinking.* Minneapolis, MN: Bureau of Educational Research, University of Minnesota.
7. *Explorations in Creative Thinking in the Early School Years: VIII. IQ and Creativity in School Achievement.* Minneapolis, MN: Bureau of Educational Research, University of Minnesota.
8. *Explorations in Creative Thinking in the Early School Years: IX. Personality Studies of Highly Creative Children.* Minneapolis, MN: Bureau of Educational Research, University of Minnesota.
9. *Explorations in Creative Thinking in the Early School Years: X. Hypotheses about Creativity in Classes for the Gifted.* Minneapolis, MN: Bureau of Educational Research, University of Minnesota.
10. (With H. J. Radig) *The Ask-and-Guess Test: Rationale and Scoring Manual.* Minneapolis, MN: Bureau of Educational Research, University of Minnesota.
11. (With H. J. Palm, N. Palamutlu, and H. J. Radig) *Scoring Manual for a Measure of Inventivlevel.* Minneapolis, MN: Bureau of Educational Research, University of Minnesota.
12. *Explorations in Creative Thinking in Mental Hygiene: III. Effects of Evaluative Set on the Development of New Ideas.* Minneapolis, MN: Bureau of Educational Research, University of Minnesota.
13. *Sex-Role Identification and Creative Thinking.* Minneapolis, MN: Bureau of Educational Research, University of Minnesota.
14. (With J. E. Buzzelli, N. Palamutlu, W. Peterson, L. Teppen, and V. Svensson) *Rewarding Creative Thinking: A Manual for Elementary Teachers.* Minneapolis, MN: Bureau of Educational Research, University of Minnesota.
15. *School Counselors and the Struggle for Men's Minds.* Wright-Patterson Air Force Base, OH: Orientation Group, USAF.
16. *Surviving Emergencies and Extrememe Conditions: A Summary of Six Years of Research.* Unpublished manuscript after six years of research with the Survival Training Unit of the Air Force Personnel and Training Research Centre (Survival School).
17. *Problems and Results of Research in the Development and Measurement of Attitudes.* Minneapolis, MN: Bureau of Educational Research, College of Education, University of Minnesota.
18. *Deliberate Improvement of Creative Thinking in the Primary Grades: An Experimental Evaluation.* Minneapolis, MN: Bureau of Educational Research, College of Education, University of Minnesota.
19. *Outcomes of the Juvenile Officers' Institute: Instruments and Exploratory Evaluation.*

Minneapolis, MN: Juvenile Officers' Institute, Center for Continuation Study, University of Minnesota.

20. (With R. E. Wilk and H. B. Sagen) (Eds.) *Studies in Minnesota Education.* Minneapolis, MN: Minnesota Society for the Study of Education and Eta Chapter of Phi Delta Kappa.
21. *Creativity—Proceedings of the Second Minnesota Conference on Gifted Children.* Minneapolis, MN: College of Education, University of Minnesota.
22. *Educational Psychology 159 Personality Development and Mental Hygiene.* Minneapolis, MN: College of Education, University of Minnesota.

Papers Presented at Seminars/Conferences

1. "Developing Creative Thinking Through School Experiences." Paper for Minneapolis Teacher's League, Minneapolis, MN, May.
2. "Understanding Creativity in Talented Students." Paper prepared for the Summer Guidance Institute Lecture Series on "Understanding the Talented Student," University of Minnesota, Minneapolis, MN, July.

1960

Books and Monographs

1. (Ed.) *Talent and Education.* Minneapolis, MN: University of Minnesota Press.
2. *Creativity.* Minneapolis, MN: University of Minnesota, Center for Continuing Study, General Extension Division.
3. *A Theory of Leadership and Interpersonal Behavior Under Stress.* New York, NY: Holt Rinehart and Winston.
4. (With R. E. Wilk and J. Harmon) (Eds.) *Studies in Minnesota Education.* Minneapolis, MN: Minnesota Society for the Study of Education, Eta Chapter of Phi Delta Kappa and Epsilon Center of Pi Lambda Theta.

Parts of Books, Contributions to Cooperative Volumes

1. "Recent Research and Its Implications for Teacher Education: Gifted Children." In *Thirteenth Yearbook of the American Association of Colleges of Teacher Education.* Washington, DC: American Association of Colleges for Teacher Education, Pp. 64-72.
2. "Religious Education and Creative Thinking." In *Creativity in Religious Education.* Minneapolis, MN: Center for Continuation Study, University of Minnesota, Pp. 1-13.
3. "How to Prepare Research Reports." In *Fourteenth Annual Research Conference in Agricultural Education.* Minneapolis, MN: Department of Agricultural Education, University of Minnesota, Pp. 17-27.
4. "Development of Creativity in Educational Researchers." In *Administration of Educational Research.* Urbana, IL: Committee on Institutional Cooperation, University of Illinois, Pp. 44-46.
5. "Function of Expressed Disagreement in Small Group Processes." In Rubenstein and C. Haberstroh (Eds.), *Some Theories of Organization.* Homewood, IL: The Dorsey Press, Inc. and Richard O. Irwin, Inc., Pp. 250-257.
6. "Personality Dynamics of Under-Self-Evaluation Among Intellectually Gifted College

Freshmen." In E. P. Torrance (Ed.), *Talent and Education*. Minneapolis, MN: University of Minnesota Press, Pp. 165-172.

Articles in Professional and Research Journals

1. Teacher Attitude and Pupil Perception. *The Journal of Teacher Education*, ***11(1)***, 97-102.
2. Recent Books on Creative Thinking. *Minnesota Journal of Education*, ***41(1)***, 4. September.
3. (With W. W. Cook) The Educated Man is Creative. *Minnesota Journal of Education*, ***41(1)***, 17-19.
4. Creative Thinking Through the Language Arts. *Educational Leadership*, ***18(1)***, 13-18.
5. Explorations in Creative Thinking. *Education*, ***81***, 216-220.
6. *Research Newsletter*, ***2(3)***, 196. Minneapolis, MN: College of Education, University of Minnesota.

Reports, Manuals, Handbooks, Tests, Instructional Materials

1. *Struggle for Men's Minds*. Wright-Patterson AFB, OH: USAF Orientation Group.
2. (With J. E. Bowers, H. J. Radig, N. Palamutlu, and P. R. Krishnaiah) *The Minnesota Studies of Creative Thinking in the Early School Years*. Minneapolis, MN: Bureau of Educational Research, University of Minnesota.
3. *A Collection of Ideas for Developing the Creative Thinking Abilities Through the Language Arts in the Fourth, Fifth and Sixth Grades*. Minneapolis, MN: Bureau of Educational Research, University of Minnesota.
4. *Social Studies Objectives of Minnesota Elementary and Secondary School Teachers*. Minneapolis, MN: Bureau of Educational Research, University of Minnesota.
5. *Educational Achievement of the Highly Intelligent and the Highly Creative: Eight Partial Replications of the Getzels-Jackson Study*. Minneapolis, MN: Bureau of Educational Research, University of Minnesota. (*Research Memorandum* BER-60-15.)
6. *Changing Reactions of Girls in Grades Four Through Six to Tasks Requiring Creative Scientific Thinking*. Minneapolis, MN: Bureau of Educational Research, University of Minnesota. (*Research Memorandum* BER-60-12.)
7. *Social Stress in Homogeneous and Heterogeneous Groups in the Intermediate Grades*. Minneapolis, MN: Bureau of Educational Research, University of Minnesota. (*Research Memorandum* BER-60-13.)
8. *A Preliminary Analysis of the Evaluative Thinking of Effective and Ineffective Teachers of Experimental Mathematics Courses*. Minneapolis, MN: Bureau of Educational Research, University of Minnesota. (*Research Memorandum* BER-60-16.)
9. (With J. A. Harmon) *Effects of Memory, Evaluative, and Creative Sets on Test Performance*. Minneapolis, MN: Bureau of Educational Research, University of Minnesota. (*Research Memorandum* BER-60-17.)
10. (With P. R. Krishnaiah) *Effects of Competition (Without Practice) Versus Practice (Without Competition) on Fluency and Flexibility*. Minneapolis, MN: Bureau of Educational Research. (*Research Memorandum* BER-60-19.)
11. (With K. Yamamoto, D. Schenitzki, N. Palamutlu, & B. Luther) *Assessing the Creative Thinking Abilities of Children*. Minneapolis, MN: Bureau of Educational Research, University of Minnesota.
12. *Your Ideas Are Important: Material from an Experiment to Help Children Learn to Value Their Creativity*. Minneapolis, MN: Bureau of Educational Research,

University of Minnesota.

13. *Explorations in Creative Thinking in the Early School Years: XIII. Social Stress in Homogeneous and Heterogeneous Groups*. Minneapolis, MN: Bureau of Educational Research, University of Minnesota.
14. *Explorations in Creative Thinking in Mental Hygiene: IV. Need Characteristics of More Creative Mental Hygiene Students*. Minneapolis, MN: Bureau of Educational Research, University of Minnesota.
15. *Objectives and Overview of the Minnesota Studies of Creative Thinking in the Early School Years*. Minneapolis, MN: Bureau of Educational Research, University of Minnesota.
16. *Personality Development of the Highly Creative Child*. Minneapolis, MN: Bureau of Educational Research, University of Minnesota.
17. *Explorations is Creative Thinking in the Early School Years: XI. Changing Reactions of Girls in Grades Four Through Six to Tasks Requiring Creative Scientific Thinking*. Minneapolis, MN: Bureau of Educational Research, University of Minnesota.
18. *An Experimental Attempt to Increase Quality of Ideas*. Minneapolis, MN: Bureau of Educational Research, University of Minnesota.
19. *Application to the Commissioner of Education, U.S. Department of Health, Education and Welfare, for Funds to Support Research Under the Provisions of Public Law 531, 83rd Congress*. Minneapolis, MN: College of Education, University of Minnesota.
20. *Role of Evaluation in Creative Thinking: January 1, 1960 through June 29*. Minneapolis, MN: University of Minnesota.

Papers Presented at Seminars/Conferences

1. "Development of Creativity in Educational Researchers." Paper prepared for conference on administration of educational research, sponsored by Committee on Institutional Cooperation, University of Chicago, held at University of Chicago.
2. "How to Prepare Research Reports." Paper presented to the Department of Agricultural Education, University of Minnesota, St. Paul, MN, August.

1961

Books and Monographs

1. (With V. J. Punsalan) *Creativity: A New Dimension of Intelligence*. Washington, DC: Association for Supervision and Curriculum Development, April. (*CAPCI Bibliography No. 9*.)
2. *New Educational Ideas—Proceedings of the Third Minnesota Conference on Gifted Children*. Minneapolis, MN: University of Minnesota, Center for Continuing Study, General Extension Division.
3. (With R. E. Myers) *Invitation to Thinking and Doing*. Minneapolis, MN: Perceptive Publishing Co.
4. (With R. E. Myers) *Teaching Gifted Elementary Pupils How to Do Research*. Minneapolis, MN: Perceptive Publishing Company.

Parts of Books, Contributions to Cooperative Volumes

1. "A Theory of Leadership and Interpersonal Behavior Under Stress." In L. Petrullo and

B. M. Bass (Eds.), *Leadership and Interpersonal Behavior*. New York, NY: Holt, Rinehart and Winston, Pp. 100-117.

2. "Changing Reactions of Preadolescent Girls to Tasks Requiring Creative Scientific Thinking During a Thirteen Month Period." In E.P. Torrance (Ed.), *Creativity: Third Minnesota Conference on Gifted Children*. Minneapolis, MN: College of Education, University of Minnesota, Pp. 157-167.
3. (With J. Harmon) "Effects of Memory, Evaluative, and Creative Sets on Test Performance." In E.P. Torrance (Ed.), *Creativity: Third Minnesota Conference on Gifted Children*. Minneapolis, MN: College of Education, University of Minnesota, Pp. 119-127.
4. "New Ideas We Have Considered." In E.P. Torrance (Ed.), *Creativity: Third Minnesota Conference on Gifted Children*. Minneapolis, MN: College of Education, University of Minnesota, Pp. 183-185.
5. (With V. J. Punsalan) "Teacher-Initiated and Pupil-Initiated Creative Activities in Grades Three Through Six." In E.P. Torrance (Ed.), *Creativity: Third Minnesota Conference on Gifted Children*. Minneapolis, MN: College of Education, University of Minnesota, Pp. 176-182.
6. "The Evaluative Thinking of Effective and Ineffective Teachers of Experimental Mathematics Courses." In E.P. Torrance (Ed.), *Creativity: Third Minnesota Conference on Gifted Children*. Minneapolis, MN: College of Education, University of Minnesota, Pp. 102-111.
7. 'Development of Creativity in Educational Researchers." In *Administration of Educational Research*. Urbana, IL: Committee on Institutional Cooperation, University of Illinois.
8. "Towards a More Creative Type of Education." In G. Myers and H. E. Samson (Eds.), *Education in Transition*. Minneapolis, MN: College of Education, University of Minnesota.
9. "Team Leadership Through Creative Administration." In *Professional Growth for Administration*. New London, CT: Arthur C. Croft Publications.
10. "The Creative Teacher and the School Team." In *Professional Growth for Teachers*. New London, CT: Arthur C. Croft Publications.
11. "Factors Affecting Creative Thinking in Children: An Interim Research Report." In W. C. Morse and G. Wingo (Eds.), *Readings in Educational Psychology*. Glenview, IL: Scott, Foresman and Co., Pp. 188-193.

Articles in Professional and Research Journals

1. Factors Affecting Creative Thinking in Children: An Interim Research Report. *Merrill-Palmer Quarterly of Behavior and Development*, *7(3)*, 171-180.
2. Priming Creative Thinking in the Primary Grades. *Elementary School Journal*, ***62**(1)*, 34-41.
3. Can Grouping Control Social Stress in Creative Activities? *Elementary School Journal*, ***62**(3)*, 139-145.
4. Curriculum Frontiers for the Elementary Gifted Pupil—Flying Monkeys and Silent Lions. *Exceptional Children*, ***28**(3)*, 119-127.
5. Problems of Highly Creative Children. *Gifted Child Quarterly*, ***5**(2)*, 31-34. (Also appeared in *Education Digest, 27*(3), 40–42.)
6. The Creatively Gifted Are Cause for Concern. *Gifted Child Quarterly*, ***5**(3)*, 79-87.
7. Give the "Devil His Dues." *Gifted Child Quarterly*, ***5**(4)*, 115-118.

8. Stress: When Problems Threaten to Overwhelm the Child, What Can the Teacher Do? *NEA Journal*, December, *50(9)*, 8-11.
9. *Research Newsletters*. Volume 1(1-5), Volume 2(1), Volume 3(1). Minneapolis, MN: Bureau of Educational Research, University of Minnesota.
10. Effects of Memory, Evaluative and Creative Reading Sets on Test Performance. *Journal of Educational Psychology*, ***52***, 207-214.
11. (With P. R. Henrickson) Some Implications for Art Education from the Minnesota Studies of Creative Thinking. *Studies in Art Education*, ***2****(2)*, 36-44.
12. (With P. R. Henrickson) School Discipline and the Creative Personality. *Eastern Art Education Research Bulletin*, ***18****(4)*, 36-42.
13. (With R. E. Myers) Can Teachers Encourage Creative Thinking? *Educational Leadership*, ***19****(3)*, 156-159.

Reports, Manuals, Handbooks, Tests, Instructional Materials

1. (With K. Yamamoto) *Scoring Manual for Evaluating Imaginative Stories*. Minneapolis, MN: Bureau of Educational Research, University of Minnesota.
2. *Status of Knowledge Concerning Education and Creative Scientific Talent*. Minneapolis, MN: Bureau of Educational Research, University of Minnesota. (Part of University of Utah National Science Foundation Project on the Status of Knowledge Concerning Creative Scientific Talent.)
3. (With Staff) *Rewarding Creative Thinking*. Minneapolis, MN: Bureau of Educational Research, University of Minnesota.
4. *Understanding the Fourth Grade Slump in Creative Thinking—Period Covered by Report: September 1, 1960 to December 31, 1960*. Minneapolis, MN: University of Minnesota. Progress Report on OE #994.
5. (With Staff) *Research Memoranda and Other Reports of the BER* (10 reports related to creativity research at the Bureau of Educational Research). Minneapolis, MN: Bureau of Educational Research, College of Education, University of Minnesota.
6. (With K. Yamamoto, D. Schenitzki, N. Palamutlu, and B. Luther) *Assessing the Creative Thinking Abilities of Children*. Minneapolis, MN: Bureau of Educational Research, College of Education, University of Minnesota.
7. *Revised Ask-and-Guess Test: Juvenile Officer Role Behavior Test: Item Classification: Juvenile Officer Personality Test*. Minneapolis, MN: Bureau of Educational Research, College of Education, University of Minnesota.
8. *Coding Guide for Analyzing Concepts of Divergency*. Minneapolis, MN: Minnesota Studies of Creative Behavior, College of Education, University of Minnesota.
9. *Counseling and Guiding Creative Talent*. Minneapolis, MN: Bureau of Educational Research, College of Education, University of Minnesota.
10. (With J. Ross) *Improving Social Studies Education in Minnesota*. Minneapolis, MN: College of Education, University of Minnesota.
11. *Educational Psychology—Personality Theory and Mental Hygiene*. Minneapolis, MN: College of Education, University of Minnesota.

Articles in Popular or Trade Type Journals and Magazines—Applications of Research

1. The Creative Teacher and the School Team. *Professional Growth for Teachers*, April, 1-2.
2. Team Leadership Through Creative Administration. *Professional Growth for*

Administrators, April, 1-2.

3. The Creative Teacher and the School Team: Problems and Pleasures for the Principal. *Professional Growth for Principals*, April, 2.

Papers Presented at Seminars/Conferences

1. "Are the Gifted Being Challenged to Think and Learn Creatively?" Paper for California Association for the Gifted, Sacramento, CA, October.
2. "Counseling Highly Gifted Individuals." Paper for Minnesota Counseling and Guidance Institute, Minneapolis, MN, November.
3. "Discussion and Workshop on Problems of Education for Creative Thinking." Paper for Greater Toronto Council for Exceptional Children, Toronto, Canada, October.
4. "Giving Your Child a Chance to Learn and Think Creatively." Presentation for Southwood School PTA, Bloomington, MN, November.
5. "Identifying Creative Talent." Paper for the University of Georgia Creativity Conference, Athens, GA, January.
6. "Mental Health Problems of Highly Creative Individuals." Paper for American Psychological Association, New York, NY, August.
7. "What Research Tells Us About Creative Thinking During the Elementary School Years." Paper for Northeastern Minnesota Education Association, Duluth, MN, October.
8. "Creativity: Identification and Promotion in Teacher Education Programs." Paper presented at the American Personnel and Guidance Association Meeting, Denver, CO, March.
9. "Research Methodology and Strategy in Studying the Measurement and Development of the Creative Abilities." Paper for American Educational Research Association, Chicago, IL, February.

Foreword(s)/Preface(s), Book Reviews and TV Interviews

1. Interview with E. Paul Torrance by Harry Reasoner. *Calendar Show* Recording. Columbia Broadcasting System-TV, November 15.
2. Interview with E. Paul Torrance by Harry Reasoner. *Calendar Show* Recording. Columbia Broadcasting System-TV, December 19.

1962

Books and Monographs

1. *Guiding Creative Talent*. Englewood Cliffs, NJ: Prentice-Hall.
2. (With R. E. Myers) *Teacher's Manual for Invitations to Speaking and Writing Creatively*. Minneapolis, MN: Perceptive Publishing Company.
3. (With R. E. Myers) *Invitations to Speaking and Writing Creatively*. Minneapolis, MN: Perceptive Publishing Company.
4. (With R. E. Myers) *Teaching Gifted Elementary Pupils How to Do Research*. Eugene, OR: Perceptive Publishing Company.
5. *Guiding Creative Talent* (Japanese translation). Tokyo, Japan: Prentice-Hall.
6. *Spanish Edition of Creativity*. Imbrasa, Instituicao Brasileira de Difusao Cultural S. A.
7. (Ed.) *Studies in Minnesota Education*. Minneapolis, MN: Minnesota Society for the Study of Education.

Parts of Books, Contributions to Cooperative Volumes

(* Indicates a previously published journal article.)

1. "Factors Affecting Creative Thinking in Children: An Interim Report." In W. C. Morse and G. M. Wingo (Eds.), *Readings in Educational Psychology*. Chicago, IL Scott, Foresman, Pp. 183-188.
2. *"Rewarding Creative Activity in the Classroom." In W. B. Barbe and T. M. Stephens (Eds.), *Attention to the Gifted a Decade Later*. Columbus, OH: Superintendent of Public Instruction, Pp. 23-29.
3. "Explorations in Creative Thinking in the Early School Years." In C. W. Taylor and F. Barron (Eds.), *Scientific Creativity: Its Recognition and Development*. New York, NY: John Wiley, Pp. 173-183.
4. "Measurement and Development of Creative Thinking Abilities." In G.Z.F. Bereday & J. A. Lauwerys (Eds.), *The Gifted Child—The Yearbook of Education*. New York, NY: Harcourt, Brace and World, Inc., Pp. 125-142.

Articles in Professional and Research Journals

1. Rewarding Creative Thinking. *Education Digest*, ***27****(9)*, 45-48.
2. Fostering Creative Thinking During the High School Years. *The High School Journal*, ***45****(7)*, 281-288.
3. (With R. E. Myers) Teaching Gifted Elementary Pupils Research Concepts and Skills. *Gifted Child Quarterly*, ***6***, 1-6.
4. Review of Gardner Murphy's "Freeing Intelligence Through Teaching." *Teachers College Record*, ***63***, 492.
5. Review of Sargent's "The Gifted: Educational Resources." *Personnel and Guidance Journal*, ***40****(5)*, 489-490.
6. Review of Freehill's "Gifted Children: Their Psychology and Education." *Personnel and Guidance Journal*, ***40****(6)*, 573-574.
7. Who Is the Underachiever? *NEA Journal*, November, ***51****(8)*, 15-17.
8. Cultural Discontinuities and the Development of Originality in Thinking. *Exceptional Children*, ***29****(1)*, 2-13.
9. Testing and Creative Talent. *Educational Leadership*, ***20***, 7-10.
10. The Creative Mind in an Academic Environment. *The Moderator*, ***1****(1)*, 22-25.
11. With the Researchers: Creative Thinking of Children. *The Journal of Teacher Education*, ***13****(4)*, 448-460.
12. Must Creative Development Be Left to Chance? *Gifted Child Quarterly*, Summer, ***6****(2)*, 41-44.
13. Non-Test Ways of Identifying the Creatively Gifted. *Gifted Child Quarterly*, ***6***, 71-75.
14. Ten Ways of Helping Young Children Gifted in Creative Writing and Speech. *Gifted Child Quarterly*, ***6****(2)*, 121-127.
15. Teaching Gifted Elementary Pupils Research Concepts and Skills. *The Gifted Child Quarterly*, ***6****(1)*, 1-5.
16. Educator Urges "Creative" Learning During Vacation. *United Press International Newsfeatures*, ***4****(258), 1*.
17. The Teacher's Invention Process. *California Journal of Instructional Improvement*, ***5****(4)*, 13-14.

Reports, Manuals, Handbooks, Tests, Instructional Materials

1. (With J. Ross) *Improving Social Studies Education in Minnesota*. Minneapolis, MN: Bureau of Educational Research, University of Minnesota.
2. (With K. Yamamoto & D. D. Hultgren) *Some Outcomes of the 1961 Juvenile Officers and Judges Institutes*. Minneapolis, MN: Center for Continuation Study, University of Minnesota.
3. (With K. Yamamoto, H. B. Sagen, & D. D. Hultgren) *Preliminary Evaluation of the 1961 Juvenile Judges and Officers Institute*. Minneapolis, MN: Center for Continuation Study, University of Minnesota.
4. (With B. F. Cunnington) *Teachers' Manual for Programmed Experiences in Creative Thinking*. Minneapolis, MN: Bureau of Educational Research, College of Education, University of Minnesota.
5. (With R. E. Myers) *An Experimental Training Program in the Language Arts*. Minneapolis, MN: Bureau of Educational Research, University of Minnesota.
6. (With A. O. Prakash) *Preliminary Evaluation of the 1962 Juvenile Court Judges Institute*. Minneapolis, MN: Center for Continuation Study, University of Minnesota.
7. (With H. B. Sagen) *Effects of Written Vs. Oral Administration of the Ask-and-Guess Test in the Intermediate Grades*. Minneapolis, MN: Bureau of Educational Research, College of Education, University of Minnesota.
8. *Creative Students: How They Can Be Identified, What Makes Them Different, and What Happens to Them in Schools Today?* Minneapolis, MN: Bureau of Educational Research, College of Education, University of Minnesota.
9. *Being a Creative Individual in a Computer Age*. Minneapolis, MN: Bureau of Educational Research, College of Education, University of Minnesota.
10. *Guidance and Creativity*. Minneapolis, MN: Bureau of Educational Research, College of Education, University of Minnesota.
11. *Scoring Guide for Incomplete Figures Test in Form NVA, Minnesota Tests of Creative Thinking*. Minneapolis, MN: Department of Educational Psychology, University of Minnesota.
12. *Administration and Scoring Manual for Abbreviated Form VII, Minnesota Tests of Creative Thinking*. Minneapolis, MN: Bureau of Educational Research, College of Education, University of Minnesota.
13. *Development and Evaluation of Recorded Programmed Instruction in Creative Thinking in the Fourth Grade: December 15, 1961 to December 31, 1962*. Minneapolis, MN: University of Minnesota. OE Grant No. 7-22-0400-162.0, Progress Report.
14. *Discussion and Workshop on Problems of Education for Creative Thinking*. Material for the University of Georgia Creativity Conference, Athens, GA.

Articles in Popular or Trade Type Journals and Magazines—Applications of Research

1. Is Creativity Really Important? *Hennepin MEA Highlighter*, May 15.
2. Keeping Creative Talent Alive. *London Times Educational Supplement*, July 27, 2462:110.

Papers Presented at Seminars/Conferences

1. "Cultural Discontinuities and the Development of Originality of Thinking." Paper presented at meeting of National Association of Educators of Gifted Children,

Columbus, OH, April.
2. "Controversial Issue in Education: Grouping for Instruction." Paper presented at Annual Institute of DuPage Valley Division of Illinois Education Association, October.
3. "Guiding Creative Talent and Problems of Housing." Paper prepared for presentation to the Sixth National Conference for the Improvement of Instruction in Housing for Land Grant Universities, October.
4. "Ten Things Parents Can Do to Foster Creative Writing and Speaking in Children." Paper presented to the St. Paul Chapter of the American Association of University Women, October.
5. "Freeing the Creative Thinking Abilities Through Teaching." Paper for Classroom Teacher Work Conference, Georgia Center for Continuing Education, The University of Georgia, Athens, GA, January.

1963

Books and Monographs

1. *Education and the Creative Potential.* Minneapolis, MN: University of Minnesota Press.
2. (With R. E. Myers) *Can You Imagine?* Albany, OR: Perceptive Publishing Company.

Parts of Books, Contributions to Cooperative Volumes

(* Reprinted from published journal articles are indicated by an asterisk.)

1. (With K. Arsan) "Experimental Studies of Homogeneous and Heterogeneous Groups for Creative Scientific Tasks." In W. W. Charters, Jr. and N. L. Gage (Eds.), *Readings in the Social Psychology of Education.* Boston, MA: Allyn and Bacon, Pp. 133-140.
2. *"Creative Thinking Through the Language Arts." In L. D. Crow and A. Crow (Eds.), *Readings in Human Learning.* New York, NY: David McKay, Pp. 436-441.
3. *"Priming Creative Thinking in the Primary Grades." In J. H. Seidman (Ed.), *Educating for Mental Health.* New York, NY: Thomas Y. Crowell Co., Pp. 318-325.
4. (With J. A. Harmon) "Effects of Memory, Evaluative and Creative Reading Sets on Test Performance." In J. M. Seidman (Ed.), *Educating for Mental Health.* New York, NY: Thomas Y. Crowell Co., Pp. 326-339.
5. "Stress: When Problems Threaten to Overwhelm the Child, What Can the Teacher Do?" In L. D. Crow and A. Crow (Eds.), *Mental Hygiene for Teachers: A Book of Readings.* New York, NY: Macmillan, Co., Pp. 102-108.
6. "The Gifted Child." In *The Encyclopedia of Mental Health.* New York, NY: Franklin Watts, Pp. 667-678.
7. "Problems of Highly Creative Children." In L. Crow and A. Crow (Eds.), *Educating the Academically Able.* New York, NY: David McKay Company, Inc., Pp. 240-245.

Articles in Professional and Research Journals

1. Conditions for Creative Learning. *Childhood Education,* ***39****(8),* 367-370.
2. Developing Creative Science Talent. *Proceedings of the Minnesota Academy of Sciences,* ***30****(1),* 83-88.
3. Are There Tops in Our Cages? *American Vocational Journal,* March, ***38***, 20-22.
4. Helping Gifted Children Read Creatively. *Gifted Child Quarterly,* ***7****(1),* 3-8.

5. Changing Reactions of Preadolescent Girls to Tasks Requiring Creative Scientific Thinking. *Journal of Genetic Psychology*, ***102***, 217-223.
6. The Creative Personality and the Ideal Pupil. *Teachers College Record*, ***65****(30)*, 220-226.
7. Adventuring in Creativity. *Childhood Education*, ***40****(2)*, 79-87.
8. What Kind of Person Do You Want Your Gifted Child to Become? *Gifted Child Quarterly*, *7*, 87-91.
9. Toward the More Humane Education of Gifted Children. *Gifted Child Quarterly*, *7*, 135-145.

Reports, Manuals, Handbooks, Tests, Instructional Materials

1. (With A. O. Prakash) *Preliminary Evaluation of the 1962 Juvenile Court Judges Institute*. Minneapolis, MN: Center for Continuation Study, University of Minnesota.
2. (With A. O. Prakash) *Summary of Some Immediate Outcomes of the 1962 Court Judges and Juvenile Officers Institutes*. Minneapolis, MN: Center for Continuation Study.
3. *Twelve Hundred Letters: Problems in Communicating Research Results*. Minneapolis, MN: Bureau of Educational Research, University of Minnesota.
4. *Preliminary Manual for the Personal-Social Motivation Inventory*. Minneapolis, MN: Bureau of Educational Research, University of Minnesota.
5. *Administration and Scoring Manual for Abbreviated Form VII, Minnesota Tests of Creative Thinking*. Minneapolis, MN: Bureau of Educational Research, University of Minnesota.
6. *Administration and Scoring Guide for the Squares Test*. Minneapolis, MN: Bureau of Educational Research, University of Minnesota.
7. (With H. R. Wallace) *Scoring Guide for Small Business Form Ask-and-Guess Test*. Minneapolis, MN: Bureau of Educational Research, University of Minnesota.
8. *Teachers' Manuals for Programmed Experiences in Creative Thinking, Volume II*. Minneapolis, MN: Bureau of Educational Research, University of Minnesota.
9. *Creativity and the Teaching of History*. Minneapolis, MN: Bureau of Educational Research, College of Education, University of Minnesota.
10. *Administrator Personalities Which Hamper Creative Growth*. Minneapolis, MN: Bureau of Educational Research, College of Education, University of Minnesota.
11. *The Measurement of Creative Behavior in Children*. Minneapolis, MN: Bureau of Educational Research, College of Education, University of Minnesota.
12. *Scoring Guide for the Picture Construction Test (Triangles)*. Minneapolis, MN: Bureau of Educational Research, College of Education, University of Minnesota.
13. *What Research Says to the Teacher: Creativity*. Washington, DC: National Education Association. AERA-ACT Pamphlet No. 28.
14. *Teachers' Manuals for Programmed Experiences in Creative Thinking*. Minneapolis, MN: Bureau of Educational Research, College of Education, University of Minnesota.

Papers Presented at Seminars/Conferences

1. "Walter W. Cook's Contribution to Thinking About the Development of a Research Climate." Paper presented at meeting of the Minnesota Society for the Study of Education, University of Minnesota, Minneapolis, MN, December.
2. "How Teachers Recognize and Guide Creativity in Children." Paper presented at Washington State Department of Public Instruction, Central Region ASCD

Conference on "Education of the Gifted and Creative Child," January.

3. "The Learning Process in Religious Education." Paper presented to the Education Division of the Sunday School Board of the South Baptist Convention, Nashville, TN, December.

Foreword(s)/Preface(s) and Book Reviews

1. Review of "Creativity and Psychological Health" by F. Barron. *Contempoary Psychology*, ***8***.
2. Essay review: "Creativity and Intelligence: Explorations with Gifted Students" by Getzels and Jackson. *The School Review*, ***71****(1)*, 112-115.
3. Review of "Personality Factors on the College Campus" by R. L. Sutherland, W. H. Holtzman, E. A. Koile and B. K. Smith (Eds.) *Contemporary Psychology*, ***8***, 164-165.
4. Complex Topic, Complex Talk. (Review of *Personality Factors on the College Campus: Review of a Symposium*)˙ *Contemporary Psychology*, ***8***, 164-165.
5. Essay Review of Getzels and Jackson's *Creativity and Intelligence. School Review*, ***71***, 112-115.
6. A Step Toward Survival (Review of *Psychology for Survival: Human Reactions to the Catastrophes of War*). *Contemporary Psychology*, ***8***, 346-347.

1964

Books and Monographs

1. (With R. J. Goldman) *The Meaning and Relevance of Learning Readiness for Curriculum Building in Christian Education*. Nashville, TN: Education Division, Baptist Sunday School Board.

Parts of Books, Contributions to Cooperative Volumes

(* Indicates a previously published journal article.)

1. "Education and Creativity." In C. W. Taylor (Ed.), *Creativity: Progress and Potential.* New York, NY: McGraw-Hill Book Company, Pp. 49-128.
2. "The Creative Child." In J. S. Roucek (Ed.), *The Difficult Child*. New York, NY: Philosophical Library, Pp. 1-15.
3. *"Individual Differences in Relation to Creativity." In M. Rasmussen (Ed.), *Individualizing Education*. Washington, DC: Association for Childhood Education in International, Pp. 15-20.
4. "Guiding Creative Talent and Problems of Housing." In *Proceedings of the Sixth Conference for the Improvement of Instruction in Housing in Land-Colleges and Universities*. Minneapolis, MN: Center for Continuation Study, University of Minnesota, Pp. 41-48.
5. "The Minnesota Studies of Creative Thinking: 1959-62." In C. W. Taylor (Ed.), *Widening Horizons in Creativity*. New York, NY: John Wiley & Sons, Inc., Pp. 125-144.
6. *"Creative Thinking in Children." In J. L. French (Ed.), *Educating the Gifted: A Book of Readings*. New York, NY: Holt, Rinehart and Winston, Inc., Pp. 407-428.
7. "Developing Creative Readers." In R. G. Stauffer (Ed.), *Dimensions of Critical Reading*. Newark, DE: Reading Study Center, University of Delaware, Pp. 59-74.
8. *"Flying Monkeys and Silent Lions." In V. D. Anderson, P. S. Anderson, F. Ballatine, and

V. M. Howes (Eds.), *Readings in the Language Arts*. New York, NY: Macmillan Company, Pp. 455-468.

Articles in Professional and Research Journals

1. Summer: Time for Self-Initiated Learning. *Gifted Child Quarterly*, ***8****(2)*, 59-63.
2. Seven Guides to Creativity. *Journal of Health, Physical Education, Recreation*, April, ***36****(4)*, 26-27, 68.
3. What Kinds of People Do We Want Gifted Children to Become? *High School Journal*, ***48****(2)*, 88-93.
4. Realistic Re-Creation of Models of Creatively Gifted Persons. *Gifted Child Quarterly*, ***8***, 111-114, 122.
5. Multiphasic Study of Creativity. *Contemporary Psychology*, ***9****(7)*, 277-278.
6. Identifying the Creatively Gifted Among Economically and Culturally Disadvantaged Children. *Gifted Child Quarterly*, ***8****(4)*, 171-176.
7. Arts Education and Human Potential. *Western Arts Association Bulletin*, ***48****(4)*, 22-32.
8. Providing for a More Humane Education of Gifted Children. *Teacher Education*, ***26****(3)*, 14-26.
9. (With R. Gupta) Audiotape Experiment in Creative Thinking. *Audiovisual Instruction*, ***9****(10)*, 685.
10. The Gifted Child. Article prepared for the *Encyclopedia of Education*.

Reports, Manuals, Handbooks, Tests, Instructional Materials

1. *Role of Evaluation in Creative Thinking*. (Report on Project 725, Cooperative Research Branch, U. S. Office of Education.) Minneapolis, MN: Bureau of Educational Research, University of Minnesota.
2. (With R. Gupta) *Development and Evaluation of Recorded Programmed Experiences in Creative Thinking in the Fourth Grade*. (Report on Project Conducted Under New Educational Media Branch, U. S. Office of Education.) Minneapolis, MN: Bureau of Educational Research, University of Minnesota.
3. (With J. C. Gowan) *The Reliability of the Minnesota Tests of Creative Thinking*. Minneapolis, MN: Bureau of Educational Research, University of Minnesota.
4. *Creative Problem Solving in Mental Health and Personality Development*. Minneapolis, MN: Perceptive Publishing Co.
5. *Evaluation of the Juvenile Court Judges Institute, the Juvenile Officers Institute and the Principals Workshop on Problems of the Economically and Culturally Deprived Child*. Minneapolis, MN: Center for Continuation Study, Extensions Division.
6. *Children Are Creative—If*... Minneapolis, MN: Bureau of Educational Research, College of Education, University of Minnesota.
7. *Creative Teaching Makes a Difference*. Minneapolis, MN: Bureau of Educational Research, College of Education, University of Minnesota.
8. *Creative Women*. Minneapolis, MN: Bureau of Educational Research, College of Education, University of Minnesota.
9. *Exploring the Limits on the Automation of Guided, Planned Experiences in Creative Thinking*. Minneapolis, MN: Bureau of Educational Research, College of Education, University of Minnesota.
10. *Fostering Creativity at Church*. Minneapolis, MN: Bureau of Educational Research, College of Education, University of Minnesota.

11. *Giving Children a Chance to Learn Creatively* (draft of script for TV presentation for Boone County, IA). Minnepolis, MN: Bureau of Educational Research, College of Education, University of Minnesota.
12. *How Favorable are the Values of Art Educators in the Creative Approach?* Minneapolis, MN: Bureau of Educational Research, College of Education, University of Minnesota.
13. *Implications of Creativity Research Findings for Instructional Media.* Minneapolis, MN: Bureau of Educational Research, College of Education, University of Minnesota.
14. (With R.E. Myers) *Teachers' Guide to Invitations to Thinking and Doing*. New York: Ginn and Company.
15. *Individual Difference in Relation to Creativity.* Minneapolis, MN: Bureau of Educational Research, College of Education, University of Minnesota.
16. *Outdoor Education and Human Potential.* Minneapolis, MN: Bureau of Educational Research, College of Education, University of Minnesota.
17. *Education and Studies of the Creative Thinking Abilities.* Minneapolis, MN: Bureau of Educational Research, College of Education, University of Minnesota.
18. *Encouragement of Creative Learning Makes a Difference.* Minneapolis, MN: Bureau of Educational Research, College of Education, University of Minnesota.
19. *Creative Problem Solving in Mental Health and Personality Development.* Minneapolis, MN: Perspective Publishing Co.
20. *Bringing the Creative Thinking Abilities into Play in Reading.* Minneapolis, MN: Bureau of Educational Research, College of Education, University of Minnesota.
21. *Guidelines for Creative Teaching.* Minneapolis, MN: Bureau of Educational Research, College of Education, University of Minnesota.

Articles in Popular or Trade Type Journals and Magazines—Applications of Research

1. The Role of Camping in Developing Creativeness. *Camping Magazine*, ***36****(5)*, 13-15.
2. Respecting Children's Questions and Ideas. *The Instructor*, September, **74**, 37, 129.
3. Asking Provocative Questions. *The Instructor*, October, **74**, 35, 72, 78.
4. Recognizing and Valuing Original Ideas. *The Instructor*, November, **74**, 27, 96.
5. Developing Ability to Elaborate. *The Instructor*, December, **74**, 21, 57.
6. No Time for Talent: Why the Creative Student is Out of Step in School. *The National Observer*, January 13, ***3****(2)*, 20.
7. The Wonder and Magic of the Preschool Child's Thinking. *Growing*, October-December, ***17****(1)*, 6-11.
8. Had a Creative Thought Lately? *Church Administration*, December, ***6****(11)*, 14-15.
9. Barriers to Creativity. *Church Administration*, December, ***6****(12)*, 18-19.
10. Questions About Creativity. *Baptist Training Union Magazine*, December, ***30****(12)*, 10-13.

Papers Presented at Seminars/Conferences

1. "What Teachers and Counselors Can Do About Identifying Creative Potential." Paper prepared for presentation to South Dakota Statewide Guidance Conference, South Dakota State University, Brookings, SD, October.
2. "Intellectual Potential of Women." Paper prepared for Minnesota Women's Week, Coffman Union, University of Minnesota, Minneapolis, MN, February.
3. "Creative Teaching Makes A Difference." The Florence S. Dunlop Memorial Lecture, Ontario Council for Exceptional Children, Port Credit, Ontario, Canada.

4. "Continuity in the Creative Development of Young Children." Paper presented at The Institute for the Exploration of Early Childhood Education, Wheelock College, Boston, MA, November.

Foreword(s)/Preface(s) and Book Reviews

1. Review of *Creativity and Intelligence: Explorations with Gifted Children* by J. W. Getzels and P. W. Jackson. *American Journal of Psychology*, 153-154.
2. Introduction to the Japanese edition of *Guiding Creative Talent* by E. Paul Torrance. Minneapolis, MN: Bureau of Educational Research, College of Education, University of Minnesota.

1965

Books and Monographs

1. *Rewarding Creative Behavior: Experiments in Classroom Creativity*. Englewood Cliffs, NJ: Prentice-Hall.
2. *Mental Health and Constructive Behavior*. Belmont, CA: Wadsworth Publishing Co.
3. *Instructor's Manual for Constructive Behavior: Stress, Personality, and Mental Health*. Belmont, CA: Wadsworth Publishing Co.
4. *Gifted Children in the Classroom*. New York: Macmillan Company.
5. (With R. D. Strom) *Mental Health and Achievement*. New York, NY: John Wiley.
6. (With B. F. Cunnington) *What Makes Creativity Grow?* (Imagi/Craft in creative development). Lexington, MA: Ginn and Compnay.
7. *Gifted Children in the Classroom* (Spanish edition). Buenos Aires, Argentina: Editional Paidos.
8. *Gifted Children in the Classroom* (Japanese translation). New York, NY: Macmillan Company.
9. *A New Movement in Education: Creative Development*. Boston, MA: Ginn and Company.
10. *Applications of Creativity Research in the Elementary School*. New York: The New World Foundation.
11. (With R. E. Myers) *Teachers' Guide to For Those Who Wonder*. Eugene, OR: Perceptive Publishing Co.
12. *For Those Who Wonder*. Eugene, OR: Perceptive Publishing Co.
13. *The New Science and Mathematics Curricula*. Tokyo, Japan: New Educational Technology.

Parts of Books, Contributions to Cooperative Volumes

(* Indicates a previously published journal article.)

1. *"Problems of Highly Creative Children." In W. A. Barbe (Ed.), *Psychology and Education of the Gifted: Selected Readings*. New York, NY: Appleton-Century-Crofts, Pp. 276-281.
2. *"Are There Tops in Our Cages?" In W. A. Barbe (Ed.), *Psychology and Education of the Gifted*. New York: Appleton-Century-Crofts, Pp. 137-142.
3. *(With R. E. Myers) "Teaching Gifted Elementary Pupils Research Skills and Concepts."

In I. J. Gordon (Ed.), *Human Development: Readings in Research*. Chicago, IL: Scott, Foresman and Co., Pp. 245-249.

4. *"Understanding Creativity in Talented Students." In J. C. Gowan and G. D. Demos (Eds.), *The Guidance of Exceptual Children*. New York: David McKay, Pp. 86-91.
5. "Exploring the Limits on the Automation of Guided, Planned Experiences in Creative Thinking." In J. S. Roucek (Ed.), *Guide to Automated Instruction*. New York: Philosophical Library.
6. *"Curriculum Frontiers for the Elementary Gifted Pupil—Flying Monkeys and Silent Lions." In J. J. Gallagher (Ed.), *Teaching Gifted Students: A Book of Readings*. Boston, MA: Allyn and Bacon, Pp. 210-214.
7. "The Measurement of Creative Behavior in Children." In M. J. Aschner and C. E. Bish (Eds.), *Productive Thinking in Education*. Washington, DC: National Education Association, Pp. 199-216.
8. "Orientation to Further Intellectual Development." In *Orientation Directors Conference*. Minneapolis, MN: University of Minnesota, Pp. 159-179.
9. "Are There Open Tops in the Cages?: Using Educational Resources." In E. P. Torrance and R. D. Strom (Eds.), *Mental Health and Achievement*. New York, NY: John Wiley & Sons, Pp. 70-82.
10. "Different Ways of Learning for Different Kinds of Children." In E. P. Torrance and R. D. Strom (Eds.), *Mental Health and Achievement*. New York: John Wiley & Sons, Pp. 253-262.
11. "Motivating Children with School Problems." In E. P. Torrance and R. D. Strom (Eds.), *Mental Health and Achievement*. New York: John Wiley, Pp. 338-353.
12. "Implications of Creativity Research Findings for Instructional Media." In C. W. Taylor (Ed.), *Instructional Media and Creativity*. New York: John Wiley & Sons, Inc., Pp. 147-178.
13. "Creativity: Looking for the Unexpected." In W. van der Eyken (Ed.), *New Education*. London, England: Bracken House, Pp. 6-9.
14. "Fostering Creative Behavior." In R. D. Strom (Ed.), *The Inner City Classroom*. Columbus, OH: Charles E. Merrill, Pp. 57-74.
15. "Evaluation of Some Immediate Outcomes of the 1965 Principals." In *Workshop on Problems of the Economically and Culturally Deprived Child*. Minneapolis, MN: Center for the Continuation of Study, University of Minnesota.

Articles in Professional and Research Journals

1. Motivating the Creatively Gifted Among Economically and Culturally Disadvantaged Children. *Gifted Child Quarterly*, ***9***, 9-12, 29-30.
2. Basic Four in Psychology. *NEA Journal*, ***54****(1)*, 15-17.
3. Encouragement of Creative Learning Makes a Difference. *Educational Techniques* ***4***, 12-16 (Japanese).
4. Review: Organizing Educational Research: An Exploration. *Journal of Higher Education*, ***36***, 237-238.
5. Classroom Incident: Consultant's Comments. *NEA Journal*, April, ***54****(4)*, 47-48.
6. (With J. C. Gowan) An Intercultural Study of Non-Verbal Ideational Fluency. *Gifted Child Quarterly*, ***9***, 13-15, 29.
7. Guidelines for Creative Teaching. *High School Journal*, ***48****(8)*, 459-464.
8. Bringing Creative Thinking into Play. *Education*, ***85****(9)*, 547-550.

9. (With D. J. Davis) How Favorable Are the Values of Art Educators to the Creative Person? *Studies in Art Education*, ***6****(2)*, 42-53.
10. Education and Studies of Creative Thinking Abilities. *New Education*, ***1****(7)*, 6-9 (England).
11. Scientific Views on Creativity and Its Development. *Daedalus Journal of the American Academy of Arts and Sciences*, ***94***, 663-681.
12. Art Education and Creative Potential. *Western Art Association Bulletin*, ***48***, 22-31.
13. A Strange Road to the Truth. *Contemporary Psychology*, ***11***, 22, 24.
14. Helping the Creatively Gifted Girl Achieve Her Potentiality. *Journal of the National Association of Women Deans and Counselors*, ***29****(1)*, 28-33.
15. We Know Enough to Teach More Creatively Than We Do. *Gifted Child Quarterly*, ***9***, 59-63, 75.
16. (With N. C. Aliotti) Accuracy, Task Effectiveness, and Emergence of a Social-Emotional Resolver of One and Two-Expert Groups. *Journal of Psychology*, ***61***, 161-170.
17. (With D. C. Dauw) Mental Health Problems of Three Groups of Highly Creative High School Seniors and a Comparable Unselected Group. *Gifted Child Quarterly*, ***9****(3)*, 123-127, 130.
18. (With D. C. Dauw) Aspirations and Dreams of Three Groups of Creatively Gifted High School Seniors and a Comparable Unselected Group. *Gifted Child Quarterly*, ***9****(4)*, 177-183.
19. (With E. Hansen) The Question-Asking Behavior of Highly Creative and Less Creative Basic Business Teachers Identified by a Paper-and-Pencil Test. *Psychological Reports*, ***17***, 815-818.
20. Continuity in the Creative Development of Young Children. *Wheelock College Alumnae Quarterly*, Spring, 10-16.
21. Identifying Talent Among the Disadvantaged. *The Education Digest*, ***30****(7)*, 8-11.
22. Accuracy, Task Effectiveness, and Emergence of a Social-Emotional Resolver as a Function of One-and-Two Expert Groups. *The Journal of Psychology*, ***61***, 161-170.
23. Something Old, Something New. *Contemporary Psychology*, ***11****(6)*, 311-312.
24. Seven Guides to Creativity. *Journal of Health, Physical Education, Recreation*, ***36****(4)*, 26-27, 68.
25. The Creative Child from Education and the Creative Potential. *World*, ***5****(2)*, 36-44.

Reports, Manuals, Handbooks, Tests, Instructional Materials

1. (With B. F. Cunnington) *Sounds and Images: Teachers' Guide and Recorded Text* (Elementary Version). Boston, MA: Ginn and Co.
2. (With B. F. Cunnington) *Sounds and Images: Teachers' Guide and Recorded Text* (Adult Version). Boston, MA: Ginn and Co.
3. (With B. F. Cunnington) *Messages for the Millions and Commander of Communciation: Teachers' Guide and Recorded Text*. Boston, MA: Ginn and Co.
4. (With B. F. Cunnington) *All-Around American (The Benjamin Franklin Story)*. Boston, MA: Ginn and Co.
5. (With B. F. Cunnington) *Superman of Steam (The Robert Fulton Story)*. Boston, MA: Ginn and Co.
6. (With B. F. Cunnington) *Wings for the World (The Wright Brothers Story)*. Boston, MA: Ginn and Co.
7. (With B. F. Cunnington) *Wizard on Wheels (The Henry Ford Story)*. Boston, MA: Ginn and Co.

8. (With B. F. Cunnington) *Master of Miracles (The Thomas Edison Story)*. Boston, MA: Ginn and Co.
9. (With B. F. Cunnington) *Survival Scientist (The Vilhjalmar Stefansson Story)*. Boston, MA: Ginn and Co.
10. (With B. F. Cunnington) *Captains of Courage (The Lewis and Clark Story)*. Boston, MA: Ginn and Co.
11. (With B. F. Cunnington) *Sweetheart of the Skies (The Amelia Earhart Story)*. Boston, MA: Ginn and Co.
12. (With B. F. Cunnington) *Polar Pilot (The Richard Byrd Story)*. Boston, MA: Ginn and Co.
13. (With B. F. Cunnington) *Giovanni and the Giant*. Boston, MA: Ginn and Co.
14. (With B. F. Cunnington) *The Dog They Named King*. Boston, MA: Ginn and Co.
15. (With B. F. Cunnington) *The Blue Crystal*. Boston, MA: Ginn and Co.
16. (With B. F. Cunnington) *The Minstrel's Christmas*. Boston, MA: Ginn and Co.
17. (With R. E. Myers) *Invitations to Thinking and Doing* (Workbook of Exercises). Boston, MA: Ginn and Co.
18. (With R. E. Myers) *Teachers' Guide: Invitations to Thinking and Doing*. Boston, MA: Ginn and Co.
19. (With R. E. Myers) *Invitations to Speaking and Writing Creatively* (Workbook of Exercises). Boston, MA: Ginn and Co.
20. (With R. E. Myers) *Invitations to Speaking and Writing Creatively: Teachers' Guide*. Boston, MA: Ginn and Co.
21. (With R. E. Myers) *Can You Imagine?* Boston, MA: Ginn and Co.
22. *A New Movement in Education: Creative Development*. Boston, MA: Ginn and Co.
23. (With A. Kinkaid) *Scoring Guide for Verbal Form B: Minnesota Test of Creative Thinking*. Minneapolis, MN: Department of Educational Psychology, University of Minnesota.
24. (With E. Kennedy) *Guide for Scoring Originality for the Malayan Version of the Non-Verbal Form A: Minnesota Tests of Creative Thinking*. Minneapolis, MN: Department of Educational Psychology, University of Minnesota.
25. (With J. J. Wu) *Scoring Guide for Evaluating the Originality of Responses of Malayan Subjects on Verbal Form A: Minnesota Tests of Creative Thinking*. Minneapolis, MN: Department of Educational Psychology, University of Minnesota.
26. (With M. Pesci) *Scoring Guide for Evaluating the Originality of Responses of Norwegian Subjects on Non-Verbal Tests of Creative Thinking*. Minneapolis, MN: Department of Educational Psychology, University of Minnesota.
27. (With G. R. Eastwood) *Problem-Making Test: Manual*. Minneapolis, MN: Department of Educational Psychology, University of Minnesota.
28. *Implications of Creativity Research Findings for Instructional Media*. Report to New World Foundation, New York, NY.
29. *Some Immediate Outcomes of the 1965 Principal's Workshop on Problems of Educating Culturally Disadvantaged Children*. Minneapolis, MN: Center for Continuing Education, University of Minnesota.
30. *Some Immediate Outcomes of the 1965 Juvenile Court Judges Institute*. Minneapolis, MN: Center for Continuing Education, University of Minnesota.
31. (With N. C. Aliotti) *Changes in Self-Concepts as a Problem Solver in an Experimental Program for Potential School Dropouts*. Minneapolis, MN: Minnesota Studies of Creative Behavior.

32. (With G. Witt) *Experimental Grouping on the Basis of Creative Abilities and Motivations*. Minneapolis, MN: Department of Educational Psychology, University of Minnesota.
33. (With C. A. Tan) *Guide for Scoring "Ding Dong Bell" Version of The Ask-And-Guess Test.* Minneapolis, MN: Minnesota Studies of Creative Behavior, University of Minnesota.
34. (With D. Werblo) *Historical Research Experiences Concerning One's Own Development and Chances in Self-Evaluation of Gifted Children.* Minneapolis, MN: Bureau of Educational Research, College of Education, University of Minnesota.
35. *Implications of Creativity Research Findings for Instructional Media*. Minneapolis, MN: University of Minnesota.
36. (With G. J. Middents) *Cross-Cultural Studies of Children's Perceptions of Divergency: Analysis of Imaginative Stories of Children in Malaya*. Minneapolis, MN: Minneosta Studies of Creative Behavior, Department of Educational Psychology, University of Minnesota.
37. *Guide for Scoring Dot-Squares Test for Originality*. Minneapolis, MN: Minnesota Studies in Creative Behavior, Department of Educational Psychology, University of Minnesota.
38. *Preliminary Guide for Scoring the Dot-Squares Test for Originality*. Minneapolis, MN: Minnesota Studies in Creative Behavior, Department of Educational Psychology, University of Minnesota.
39. (With B. Bleedorn) *Persistence of Effects of Guided, Planned Experiences in Creative Thinking in the Fourth Grade*. Minneapolis, MN: Department of Educational Psychology, College of Education, University of Minnesota.
40. *Problem Solving Attitudes and Self-Concepts of Beginning Junior High School Students*. Minneapolis, MN: University of Minnesota.
41. (With G. Luthra and C. A. Tan) *Evaluation of Some Immediate Outcomes of the 1965 Principals Workshop on Problems of the Economically and Culturally Deprived Child*. Minneapolis, MN: Centre for Continuation Study, Extension Division, University of Minnesota.
42. *Applications of Creativity*. Minneapolis, MN: Bureau of Educational Research, College of Education, University of Minnesota.

Articles in Popular or Trade Type Journals and Magazines—Applications of Research

1. Searching for the Truth with the Methods of Descriptive Research. *The Instructor*, May, **74**, 13.
2. Searching for the Truth with the Methods of Experimental Research. *The Instructor*, June, **74**, 11, 101.
3. Unevaluated Practice and Experimentation. *The Instructor*, January, **74**, 27, 105.
4. Developing Creative Readers. *The Instructor*, February, **74**, 23, 38.
5. Guided, Planned Experiences. *The Instructor*, March, **74**, 19, 156.
6. Searching for the Truth with the Methods of the Historian. *The Instructor*, April, **74**, 27, 110.
7. How to be Creative in Your Church. *Church Administration*, January, *7(1)*, 22-23.
8. Fostering Creativity at Home. *Every Day With Beginners*, ***10****(2)*, 4-9.
9. Fostering Creativity at Church. *The Beginner Leader*, ***9****(2)*, 4-8.
10. Children Are Creative — If —. *Living With Children*, ***9****(2)*, 20-23.

11. Developing Women's Natural Gifts. *Women's Education*, ***4**(1)*, 1, 7.
12. Are You Growing? *Beginner Teacher*, ***35**(3)*, 58-62.
13. The Creative Child. *World*, April, ***5**(2)*, 36-44. (India).
14. Creative Ways of Learning. *Twin Citian*, August, ***8**(1)*, 14-15, 42-43.
15. Searching for the Truth with the Methods of Descriptive Research. *The Instructor*, May, ***74***, 13.
16. Searching for the Truth with the Methods of Experimental Research. *The Instructor*, June, ***74***, 11, 101.
17. Brainwashing or Brainstorming. *It Starts in the Classroom* (the public relations newsletter for classroom teachers), 3.
18. For Your Enrichment, Fostering Creativity at Home. *Every Day with Beginners*, ***10**(2)*, 4-9.

Papers Presented at Seminars/Conferences

1. "Creativity in American Education." Paper presented at the Creative American Symposium, Clarke College, Dubuque, IA, March.
2. "The World of the Different Investigator and Educator." Paper presented for panel on "Creative Mental Health Focuses on the Divergent, Deviate, and Different Student," American Personnel and Guidance Association, Leamington Hotel, Minneapolis, MN, April.
3. "Guidelines to Learning: Primaries and Juniors." Paper presented for Texas State Sunday School Convention, Tyler, TX, April.
4. "Helping Creatively Gifted Girls Achieve Their Potentialities." Paper for National Association of Women Deans and Counselors, Minneapolis, MN, April.
5. "Concerned Teaching Makes a Difference." Paper presented for Texas State Sunday School Convention, First Baptist Church, Tyler, TX, April.
6. "Different Predictors, Criteria, and Routes to Criteria." Paper prepared for the annual meetings of the American College Personnel Association, Leamington Hotel, Minneapolis, MN, April.
7. "How to be Creative in Your Church." Paper for Texas State Sunday School Convention, Tyler, TX, April.
8. "Introducing Innovation: Instructional Media." Paper prepared for American Personnel and Guidance Association, Curtis Hotel, Minneapolis, MN, April.
9. "Creativity in Utilizing Sources and Resources in Learning." Paper presented for 1965 Bicentennial Convention, National League for Nursing, San Francisco, CA, May.
10. "Implications of Creativity Research for Counseling Psychology." Paper prepared for presentaton at annual meetings of the American Psychological Association, Chicago, IL, September.
11. "Orientation to Further Intellectual Development." Paper presented for 18th Annual Orientation Directors Conference, Minneapolis, MN, October.
12. "Creativity in American Education." Paper prepared for Clark College Colloquium, Dubuque, IA.

Foreward(s)/Preface(s) and Book Reviews

1. Creativity in a Cage—Book Review of *Ruhleben: A Prison Camp Society* by J. Davidson Ketchum. *Contemporary Psychology*, ***12**(3)*, 146, 148.

1966

Books and Monographs

1. *Gifted Children in the Classroom* (Japanese translation). Tokyo, Japan: Kokudo-Sha.
2. (With R. E. Myers) *Creativity Booklets*. Boston, MA: Ginn and Company.

Parts of Books, Contributions to Cooperative Volumes

(* Indicates a previously published journal article.)

1. "Techniques and Materials for Developing Creative Readers." In F. E. Williams (Ed.), *First Seminar on Productive Thinking in Education*. St. Paul, MN: Creativity Project, Macalester College, Pp. 41-52.
2. *"Conditions for Creative Learning." In M. Rasmussen (Ed.), *Readings for Childhood Education*. Washington, DC: Association for Childhood Education International, Pp. 151-158.
3. *"Adventuring in Creativity." In M. Rasmussen (Ed.), *Readings from Childhood Education*. Washington, DC: Association for Childhood Education International, Pp. 187-196.
4. "Fostering Creative Behavior." In R. D. Strom (Ed.), *The Inner-City Classroom: Teacher Behavior*. Columbus, OH: Charles E. Merrill Books, Inc., Pp. 57-74.
5. "Implications of Creativity Research Findings for Instructional Media." In C. W. Taylor (Ed.), *Instructional Media and Creativity*. New York, NY: John Wiley, Pp. 147-178.
6. "Motivating the Creatively Gifted Among Economically and Culturally Disadvantaged Children." In J. C. Gowan and G. D. Demos (Eds.), *The Disadvantaged and Potential Dropout*. Springfield, IL: Charles C. Thomas, Pp. 301-309.
7. "How to be a More Creative Person." In *Proceedings of the Eleventh Annual Meeting of the Southern Baptist Religious Education Association*. Detroit, MI, May 23-24, Pp. 1-14.
8. *"Creative Learning." In J. M. Seidman (Ed.), *Readings in Educational Psychology*. New York, NY: Houghton Mifflin.
9. "Identifying Creative Potential in Children." In H. A. Otto (Ed.), *Explorations in Human Potentialities*. Springfield, IL: Charles C. Thomas, Pp. 240-248.
10. *"Developing Creative Readers." In M. L. King, B. D. Ellinger, and W. Wolf (Eds.), *Critical Reading*. Philadelphia, PA: J. B. Lippincott, Pp. 100-114.
11. "History of the Concept 'Guided Learning' and Its Application in Teaching for Creative Development." In R. H. Ojemann and K. Pritchett (Eds.), *Giving Emphasis to Guiding Learning*. Cleveland, OH: Educational Research Council of Greater Cleveland, Pp. 6-47.
12. "Improving Personal Skills." In *Proceedings of the 11th Annual Meeting of Southern Baptist Religious Education Association*. Detroit, Michigan, Pp. 20-31.
13. (With P. Henrickson) "Some Implications for the Art Education from Minnesota Studies of Creative Thinking." In W. L. Brittain (Ed.), *Creativity and Art Education*. Washington, DC: National Art Association, Pp. 18-26.

Articles in Professional and Research Journals

1. Problem-Solving Attitudes and Self-Concepts of Beginning Junior High School Students. *Guidance Journal*, ***4****(3)*, 74-86.
2. Something Old, Something New. *Contemporary Psychology*, ***11***, 311-312.

3. (With D. C. Dauw) Attitude Patterns of Creatively Gifted High School Seniors. *Gifted Child Quarterly*, ***10***, 53-57.
4. (With G. Witt) Experimental Grouping on the Basis of Creative Abilities and Motivations. *Gifted Child Quarterly*, ***10***, 9-14.
5. Stress-Seeking as a Factor in High Achievement. *Gifted Child Quarterly*, ***10***, 169-173.
6. (With R. T. Johnson) Gifted Thirteen-Year-Olds in Two Cultures: Greater London and Greater Twin Cities (USA). *Gifted Child Quarterly*, ***10***, 125-131.
7. (With D. Werblo) Experiences in Historical Research and Changes in Self Evaluations of Gifted Children. *Exceptional Chidren*, ***33****(3)*, 137-142.
8. Does Evaluative Feedback Facilitate Creative Thinking? *ADA Division 2 Newsletter*, July-August, 1-2.
9. Comments on Classroom Incident What Would You Have Done? *NEA Journal*, ***55****(3)*, 37-38.
10. Explorations in Human Potentialities edited by Herbert Otto. *The Social Studies*, ***59****(3)*, 125-126.
11. Attitude Patterns of Creatively Gifted High School Students. *The Gifted Child Quarterly*, ***10***, 53-57.

Reports, Manuals, Handbooks, Tests, Instructional Materials

1. *Torrance Tests of Creative Thinking: Norms-Technical Manual* (Research Edition). Princeton, NJ: Personnel Press. (Translated and published in French)
2. *Some Immediate Outcomes of the 1965 Juvenile Police Officers' Institute*. Minneapolis, MN: Center for Continuing Education, University of Minnesota.
3. (With R. E. Myers) *For Those Who Wonder* (Pupil Ideabook and Teacher Guide). Boston, MA: Ginn and Co.
4. (With R. E. Myers) *Plots, Puzzles, and Adventures in Self-Expression* (Pupil Ideabook and Teacher Guide). Boston, MA: Ginn and Co.
5. *Torrance Tests of Creative Thinking: Administration and Scoring Guide for Verbal Form A*. Princeton, NJ: Personnel Press.
6. *Torrance Tests of Creative Thinking Administration and Scoring Guide for Figural Form A*. Princeton, NJ: Personnel Press.
7. *Torrance Tests of Creative Thinking: Administration and Scoring Guide for Verbal Form B*. Princeton, NJ: Personnel Press.
8. *Torrance Tests of Creative Thinking Administration and Scoring Guide for Figural Form B*. Princeton, NJ: Personnel Press.
9. *Preliminary Manual for the "What Kind of Person Are You?" Test*. Minneapolis, MN: Minnesota Studies of Creative Behavior.
10. *Scoring Guide for the Tom Piper Version of the Ask-and-Guess Test*. Minneapolis, MN: Minnesota Studies of Creative Behavior.
11. *Scoring Guide for the Ding Dong Bell Version of the Ask-and-Guess Test*. Minneapolis, MN: Minnesota Studies of Creative Behavior.
12. *Self-Perceptions of Southern Baptist Religious Educators with Implications for Their Creative Functioning*. Minneapolis, MN: Minnesota Studies of Creative Behavior.
13. (With E. Parent) *Characteristics of Mathematics Teachers That Affect Students' Learning*. (Final Report on Cooperative Research Project 1020). Washington, DC: United States Office of Education.
14. (With C. A. Tan) *Scoring Guide for "How Good is Your Imagination?"* (Form A).

Minneapolis, MN: Minnesota Studies of Creative Behavior, Department of Educational Psychology, College of Education, University of Minnesota.

15. (With S. Eubank) *Examiner's Manual and Booklets for the Torrance Tests of Creative Thinking: Mother Goose Problems for Young Children*. Athens, GA: Georgia Studies of Creative Behavior.
16. (With N. C. Aliotti) *Guide for Scoring "Little Boy Blue" Version of the Ask-and-Guess Test*. Athens, GA: Department of Educational Psychology, Georgia Studies of Creative Behavior.
17. *Ideas for Creative Ways of Teaching*. Berkley, CA: University of California.
18. *Thinking Creatively with Words*—Booklets A and B. Princeton, NJ: Personnel Press, Inc.
19. *Thinking Creatively with Pictures*—Figural Forms A and B. Princeton, NJ: Personnel Press, Inc.
20. *Torrance Tests of Creative Thinking Directions Manual and Scoring Guides, Figural Form A*. Princeton, NJ: Personnel Press, Inc.
21. *Torrance Tests of Creative Thinking* (Egyptian translation). Princeton, NJ: Personnel Press, Inc.
22. *Torrance Tests of Creative Thinking* (Spanish translation). Princeton, NJ: Personnel Press, Inc.
23. *Torrance Tests of Creative Thinking— Verbal Forms A and B* (Turkish Translation). Princeton, NJ: Personnel Press, Inc.
24. *Torrance Tests of Creative Thinking* (Marathi translation). Princeton, NJ: Personnel Press, Inc.

Articles in Popular or Trade Type Journals and Magazines—Applications of Research

1. Sounds Without Words. *Music for Primaries*, ***1****(1)*, 4-5.
2. Identifying Talent. *Accent on Talent*, ***1****(2)*, 3, 7.
3. Does Evaluative Feedback Facilitate Creative Thinking? *Teaching of Psychology Newsletter*, 1.

Papers Presented at Seminars/Conferences

1. "What Do We Want: Creative Development or Coerced Behavior?" DeKalb County (Georgia) Education Association, October.
2. "Comparative Studies of Stress-Seeking in the Imaginative Stories of Preadolescents in Twelve Different Cultures." Invitational Conference on Stress-Seeking in Man, Sponsored by Bureau of Social Science Research and Supported by Office of Scientific Research of the United States Air Force, Washington, DC, November 11.
3. "Contribution of Creativity Research to Education." Indianapolis Public Schools, Indianapolis, IN, December 6.

Foreword(s)/Preface(s) and Book Reviews, and TV Interviews

1. Foreword. In J. A. Smith, *Setting Conditions for Creative Teaching*. Boston, MA: Allyn and Bacon, Pp. v-viii.
2. Book Review: "Teaching the Disadvantaged by J. O. Loretan and S. Umans." *The Social Studies*, ***58****(6)*, 286.
3. Book Review: "Instructional Media and Creativity by C. Taylor and F. E. Williams." *The Journal of Teacher Education*, ***18****(1)*, 121-122.

4. Interview with E. Paul Torrance by Harry Reasoner. "Calendar Show" on *Today*. Columbia Broadcasting System, February 25.

THE GEORGIA YEARS

1967

Books and Monographs

1. (With J. C. Gowan and G. D. Demos) *Creativity: Its Educational Implications*. New York, NY: John Wiley & Sons. (Translated and published in Spanish)

Parts of Books, Contributions to Cooperative Volumes

(* Indicates a previously published journal article.)

1. *(With E. Hansen) "The Question-Asking Behavior of Highly Creative and Less Creative Basic Business Teachers." In D. H. Clark (Ed.), *The Psychology of Education*. New York, NY: Free Press, Pp. 83-86.
2. *"The Creative Personality and the Ideal Pupil." In L. Nelson and B. Psaltis (Eds.), *Fostering Creativity*. New York, NY: Academic Readings.
3. *"Nurture of Creative Talents." In R. L. Mooney and T. A. Razik (Eds.), *Explorations in Creativity*. New York, NY: Harper and Row, Pp. 185-195.
4. *"Their Stories Tell Their Feelings: Problems of Highly Creative Children." In H. W. Bernard and W. C. Huckins (Eds.), *Readings in Educational Psychology*. Cleveland, OH: World Publishing Co., Pp. 95-98.
5. *"Scientific Views of Creativity and Factors Affecting Its Growth." In J. Kagan (Ed.), *Creativity and Learning*. Boston, MA: Houghton Mifflin, Pp. 73-91.
6. *"Problem-Solving Attitudes and Self-Concepts of Beginning Junior High School Students." In H. W. Bernard and W.C. Huckins (Eds.), *Readings in Educational Psychology*. Cleveland, OH: World Publishing Co., Pp. 78-88.
7. *"Cultural Discontinuities and the Development of Originality." In J. I. Roberts (Ed.), *School Children in the Urban Slum*. New York, NY: Free Press, Pp. 99-114.
8. "How Gifted High School Students Can Continue Growing Intellectually." In J. C. Gowan and E. P. Torrance (Eds.), *Educating the Ablest*. Itasca, IL: F. E. Peacock Publishers, Inc., Pp. 103-110.
9. "Ten Ways of Helping Young Children Gifted in Creative Writing and Speech." In I. M. Teidt and S. W. Teidt (Eds.), *Readings on Contemporary English in the Elementary School*. Englewood Cliffs, NJ: Prentice Hall, Inc., Pp. 159-169.

Articles in Professional and Research Journals

1. The Minnesota Studies of Creative Behavior: National and International Extensions. *Journal of Creative Behavior*, ***1***, 137-154.
2. (With E. Ryan) Training in Elaboration. *Journal of Reading*, ***11***, 27-32.
3. Helping Gifted Children Through Mental Health Information and Concepts. *The Educational Digest*, ***33****(2)*, 34-37.
4. Continuing Intellectual Development After High School. *Gifted Child Quarterly*,

11, 133-139.

5. Nurture of Creative Talents. *Theory into Practice*, ***5****(4)*, 168-173.
6. Independent Study as an Instrumental Tool. *Theory into Practice*, ***5****(5)*, 217-221. (Reprinted in *Education Digest*, ***33***, 27-30.)
7. (With J. Goldsmith) The Plea of the Gifted — for Teachers to Teach. *Gifted Child Quarterly*, ***11****(4)*, 205-208.
8. Creativity in a Cage. *Contemporary Psychology*, ***12***, 146-147.
9. Uniqueness and Creativeness: The School's Role. *Educational Leadership*, ***24****(6)*, 493-496.
10. Consultant's Comments on Classroom Incidents: What Would You have Done? *NEA Journal*, January, ***56****(1)*, 58-59.
11. Mental Health and Creative Functioning. *Gifted Child Quarterly*, ***11***, 71-78.
12. The Minnesota Studies of Creative Behavior: National and International Extensions. *The Journal of Creative Behavior*, ***1****(2)*, 137-154.

Reports, Manuals, Handbooks, Tests, Instructional Materials

1. *Understanding the Fourth Grade Slump in Creative Thinking*. (Report of Cooperative Research Project 994). Washington, DC: United States Office of Education.
2. (With L. R. Fortson and L. E. Orcutt) *The Creative-Aesthetic Approach to School Readiness and Measured Creative Growth*. Athens, GA: Research and Development Center in Educational Stimulation, University of Georgia.
3. (With R. J. Goldman) *Creative Development in a Segregated Negro School in the South*. Athens, GA: Georgia Studies of Creative Behavior, University of Georgia.
4. *Originality Scoring Guide for Western Samoan Version, Form VA and NVA, Torrance Tests of Creative Thinking*. Athens, GA: Georgia Studies of Creative Behavior, University of Georgia.
5. *Originality Scoring Guide for German Version, Form VA, Torrance Tests of Creative Thinking*. Athens, GA: Georgia Studies of Creative Behavior, University of Georgia.
6. *Originality Scoring Manual for German Version, Form NVA, Torrance Tests of Creative Thinking*. Athens, GA: Georgia Studies of Creative Behavior, University of Georgia.
7. *Originality Scoring Manual for India Version, Form VA, Torrance Tests of Creative Thinking*. Athens, GA: Georgia Studies of Creative Behavior, University of Georgia.
8. *Originality Scoring Manual for India Version, Form NVA, Torrance Tests of Creative Thinking*. Athens, GA: Georgia Studies of Creative Behavior, University of Georgia.
9. *Minnesota Studies of Creative Behavior: 1958-1966*. Athens, GA: Georgia Studies of Creative Behavior, University of Georgia.
10. *Examples of Learning Experiences in Reading and Literature to Facilitate Creative Behavior*. Athens, GA: Georgia Studies of Creative Behavior, University of Georgia.
11. *Influence of an Experimental Pre-Primary Program Upon Ability to Read a Picture Upon Entry to First Grade*. Athens, GA: Research and Development Center in Educational Stimulation, University of Georgia.
12. (With C. A. Tan and T. Allman) *Verbal Originality and Teacher Behavior: A Predictive Validity Study*. Athens, GA: Georgia Studies of Creative Behavior, University of Georgia.
13. (With J. P. Torrance) (adapted from an Inventory by Oliver E. Graebner) *Ideas About God*. Athens, GA: Georgia Studies of Creative Behavior, University of Georgia.
14. (With J. P. Torrance) *Interview Form—Ideas About and Definition of Concept of God*. Athens, GA: Georgia Studies of Creative Behavior, University of Georgia.

15. (With J. Khatena and L. E. Orcutt) *Originality Scoring Guide for Australian Version, Form VA, Torrance Tests of Creative Thinking*. Athens, GA: Georgia Studies of Creative Behavior, College of Education, University of Georgia.
16. *Reprints and Drafts of Paper Relevant to International Workshop Paper of Influence of Different Types of Test Items on Student Learning*. Athens, GA: College of Education, Department of Educational Psychology, University of Georgia.

Articles in Popular or Trade Type Journals and Magazines—Applications of Research

1. Learning Difficulties of Gifted Children. *Gifted Children Newsletter*, October, ***10****(1)*, 13-22.
2. Creativity: Turning the Kids On. *Offspring*, November, ***9****(1)*, 4-13.
3. Things That Block Creativity. *The Baptist Student*, ***46****(8)*, 11-13.
4. Listening for Pictures. *Music for Primaries*, ***2****(1)*, 7-8.
5. (With J. P. Torrance) Telling Stories and Painting Pictures with Sounds. *Music for Primaries*, ***2****(2)*, 10-12.
6. Let's Tell Sound Stories. *Music for Primaries*, ***2****(3)*, 10-12.
7. Sound of Leaves. *Music for Primaries*, ***2****(4)*, 15-17.
8. Recognizing and Acknowledging Creative Talent. *Children's Music Leader*, ***2****(4)*, 27-28.

Papers Presented at Seminars/Conferences

1. "Influence of the Elementary School Principal on the Creative Development of Children." Georgia Association of Elementary School Principals, Georgia Educational Association, Atlanta, GA, March.
2. "Learning Difficulties of Gifted Children and Youth." Georgia Council on Exceptional Children, Georgia Education Association, Atlanta, GA, March.
3. "Influence on a Student's Learning of the Type of Test Administered." International Workshop on Eeducational Testing, Pdagogisches Zentrum, May 16-24.
4. "New Type Test Items for Assessing Creative Potentialities." International Workshop on Educational Testing, Pädagogisches Zentrum, May 16-24.
5. "Recognizing and Acknowledging the Creative Potentialities of Disadvantaged Children." Georgia Association for Supervision and Curriculum Development, Georgia Center for Continuing Education, January.
6. "The Assessment of the Creative Person." Telelecture for NDEA Institute, Creativity in Industrial Arts, Kent State University, Kent, OH, June 28.
7. "Working with Creative Children." Seventeenth Annual Principals' Work Conference, Georgia Center for Continuing Education, Athens, GA, July 18.
8. "The Nature of Creative Thinking." Conference on Teaching Creativity, Appalachian State University, Boone, NC, October 27.
9. "Developing Skills in Creative Thinking." Conference on Teaching Creativity, Appalachian State University, Boone, NC, October 28.
10. "Creative Development Through Reading Activities in the Elementary School." Workshop for Washington County Elementary School Teachers, Sandersville, GA, August.
11. "Needs in Education for Sub-Doctoral Personnel in Psychology." Paper prepared for panel on "Providing Psychological Services with Sub-Doctoral Personnel" at the annual meeting of the Georgia Psychology Association, Stone Mountain Inn, Stone Mountain, GA.

Foreword(s)/Preface(s) and Book Reviews

1. Book Review: "Instructional Media and Creativity" by C. Taylor and F. Williams. *The Journal of Teacher Education*, ***28(1)***, 121-122.
2. Book Review: "Taylor, Calvin W. and Frank Williams (Eds.), Instructional Media and Creativity." *Journal of Teacher Education*, ***18***, 121-122.

1968

Books and Monographs

1. (With R E. Myers) *Stretch Exercises for Developing Concepts and Imagination*. Minneapolis, MN: Perceptive Publishing Co.
2. *Creative Learning*. Berlin: Verlag Julius Beltz.

Parts of Books, Contributions to Cooperative Volumes

(* Indicates a previously published journal article.)

1. "Comparative Studies of Stress-Seeking in the Imaginative Stories of Preadolescents in Twelve Different Subcultures." In S. Z. Klausner (Ed.), *Why Man Takes Chances: Studies in Stress-Seeking*. New York, NY: Doubleday & Co., Pp. 195-233.
2. *"Ten Ways of Helping Young Children Gifted in Creative Writing and Speech." In I. M. Tiedt and S. W. Tiedt (Eds.), *Readings in Contemporary English in the Elementary School*. Englewood Cliffs, NJ: Prentice-Hall, Pp. 159-169.
3. *"Conditions for Creative Growth." In L. D. Haskew and J. C. McLendon (Eds.), *This is Teaching* (3rd Ed.). Glenview, IL: Scott, Foresman, Pp. 329-333.
4. "Creative Abilities of Elementary School Children." In W. B. Michael (Ed.), *Teaching for Creative Endeavor*. Bloomington, IN: University of Indiana Press, Pp. 3-24.
5. *"Emerging Concepts of Giftedness." In J. S. Renzulli and W. G. Vassar (Eds.), *The Gifted Child in Connecticut: Practical Suggestions for Program Development*. Hartford, CT: Connecticut Department of Education, Pp. 4-10.
6. "Flying Monkeys, Silent Lions and School Psychologists." In M. Jessen (Ed.), *Sensitivity, Creativity, Innovation*. California Association of School Psychologists and Psychometrists, Pp. 2-12.
7. "Neue Item-Arten zur Erfassung Kreativer Denkhähigkeiten." In K. Ingenkamp and T. Marsolek (Eds.), *Möglichkeiten und grenzen der testwendung in der schule*. Berlin: Verlag Julius Beltz, Pp. 325-343.
8. "Einfluss and Wirkung der Verschiedenen Testarten auf den Nachfolgenden Lernprozess." In K. Ingenkamp and T. Marsolek (Eds.), *Möglichkeiten und grenzen der testanwendung in der schule*. Berlin: Verlag Julius Beltz, Pp. 839-852.
9. "Must Pre-Primary Educational Stimulation be Incompatible with Creative Development?" In F. E. Williams (Ed.), *Creativity at Home and in School*. St. Paul, MN: Macalester College, Pp. 54-73.
10. "Group Dynamics and Creative Functioning." In C. W. Taylor (Ed.), *Climate for Creativity* (Report of the Seventh National Research Conference on Creativity). Salt Lake City, UT: Department of Psychology, University of Utah, Pp. 279-338.
11. "Motivating and Guiding Creative Reading." In T. Clymer and N. M. Wyatt (Eds.), *Teachers Edition: May I Come In?* Boston, MA: Ginn and Company, Pp. 15-21.

12. (With J. A. Harmon) "Effects of Memory, Evaluative and Creative Reading Sets on Test Performance." In R. G. Huh (Ed.), *Studies in Educational Psychology*. Boston, MA: Blaisdell Publishing Company, Pp. 460-468.

Articles in Professional and Research Journals

1. Testing the Educational and Psychological Development of Students from Other Cultures and Subcultures. *Review of Educational Research*, ***38***, 71-76.
2. (With L. R. Fortson) Creativity Among Young Children and the Creative-Aesthetic Approach. *Education*, ***89****(1)*, 27-30.
3. Human Intelligence: The Culture-Related View. *Science Teacher*, ***35****(6)*, 21-23.
4. A Longitudinal Examination of the Fourth-Grade Slump in Creativity. *Gifted Child Quarterly*, ***12***, 195-199.
5. Creativity and its Educational Implications for the Gifted. *Gifted Child Quarterly*, ***12****(2)*, 67-78.
6. Examples of Rationales of Test Tasks for Assessing Creative Abilities. *Journal of Creative Behavior*, ***2***, 165-178.
7. Deans, Counselors, and Creative Students. *Journal of National Association of Women Deans and Counselors*, ***31****(4)*, 145-153.
8. Creativity Research and Its Implications for the Gifted. *Gifted Child Quarterly*, ***12***, 67-78.
9. Finding Hidden Talents Among Disadvantaged Children. *Gifted Child Quarterly*, ***12***, 131-137.
10. (With L. R. Fortson and C. Diener) Creative-Aesthetic Ways of Developing Intellectual Skills Among Five-Year-Olds. *Journal of Research and Development in Education*, ***1****(3)*, 58-69.
11. How Gifted High School Students Can Continue Growing Intellectually. *Gifted Child Quarterly*, ***12***, 3-9.

Reports, Manuals, Handbooks, Tests, Instructional Materials

1. *Minnesota Studies of Creative Behavior: 1958-1966*. Greensboro, NC: Creativity Research Institute, The Richardson Foundation.
2. (With N. C. Aliotti) *Influence of a One-Year Experience in a Pre-Primary Program of Educational Stimulation on Creative Thinking Ability Upon Entry to First Grade*. Athens, GA: Research and Development Center in Educational Stimulation, University of Georgia.
3. *Attitudes Concerning Creative Thinking and Reactions to Creative Problem Solving Procedures: Responses to the University of Georgia Regional TTT Task Force Conference*. Athens, GA: College of Education, University of Georgia.
4. (With N. C. Aliotti) *The Picture Interpretation Test: Selected Correlates*. Athens, GA: Research and Development Center in Educational Stimulation, University of Georgia.
5. (With M. E. Freeman) *Group Size and Question Asking Performance of Pre-Primary Children*. Athens, GA: Research and Development in Educational Stimulation, University of Georgia.
6. *Influence of Two Types of Structure on Small Group Behavior Among Five-Year-Old Children*. Athens, GA: Department of Educational Psychology, College of Education, University of Georgia.
7. (With M. H. Ray) *Influence on a One-Year Experience in a Pre-Primary Program of Educational Stimulation on Cooperative Behavior*. Athens, GA: Research and

Development Center for Educational Stimulation, University of Georgia.
8. *Moral and Religious Growth and Understanding in Children.* Athens, GA: Department of Educational Psychology, College of Education, University of Georgia.
9. (With V. K. Phillips) *Influence of a "Cognitive-Structured" Curriculum on the Development of Casual Thinking.* Athens, GA: Department of Educational Psychology, College of Education, University of Georgia.
10. (With H. Sorkey and J. G. Coone) *Evaluation of the Experienced Teacher Fellowship Program: The University of Georgia, September 1967-August 1968.* Athens, GA: College of Education, University of Georgia.
11. *Revised Scoring Guide for Starkweather's Test of Originality.* Athens, GA: Georgia Studies of Creative Behavior, College of Education, University of Georgia.
12. *Torrance Tests of Creative Thinking—Directions Manual and Scoring Guide, Figural Test Booklet B.* Princeton, NJ: Personnel Press, Inc.
13. *Original Art Work for Creative Positives of Disadvantaged.* Unpublished.
14. (With J. P. Torrance) *I Can Imagine.* Unpublished materials developed by the Torrances to encourage use of imagination to help solve problems.
15. *Parents and the Creative Development of Pre-Primary Children.* Unpublished article for unpublished manuscript for *I Can Imagine*, Department of Educational Psychology, University of Georgia, Athens, GA.

Articles in Popular or Trade Type Journals and Magazines—Applications of Research

1. Singing and Reading with Imagination. *Children's Music Leader*, ***3****(2)*, 32-33.
2. What is Honored in a Culture Will Be Cultivated There. *Gifted Children Newsletter*, ***10***, 16-21.
3. Academic Achievement as a Factor in Emotional Adjustment in Secondary School. *High School Journal*, ***51****(7)*, 281-287.
4. Respect Children's Questions and Ideas. *Children's Music Leader*, ***3****(1)*, 29.
5. Creative Functioning and Mental Health. *Accent on Talent*, ***2****(3)*, 4-5.
6. (With R. E. Myers) Teachers' Strategy Sheet—Techniques for Promoting a Variety of Mental Abilities While Teaching Subject Matter. *Accent on Talent*, ***2****(3)*, 7.
7. Human Intelligence: The Culture-Related View. *Science Teacher*, ***35****(6)*, 21-23.
8. Winter Music. *Music for Primaries*, ***3****(1)*, 6-7.
9. Like the Thing Happening. *Music for Primaries*, ***3****(2)*, 6-8.
10. Saying it with Movement. *Music for Primaries*, ***3****(3)*, 14-15.
11. You Can Make a Story. *Music for Primaries*, ***3****(4)*, 12-13.
12. Improving Behavior with Creative Use of Music. *Children's Musice Leader*, ***3****(3)*, 28.
13. Conditions for Creative Learning. *Resource*, ***8****(4)*, 4-6.
14. Creativity and Its Relationship to Achievement and Motivation. *TAG Gifted Children Newsletter*, November, ***11***, 21-33.

Papers Presented at Seminars/Conferences

1. "Creative Teaching." Address to Professional Growth Winter Conference, Putnam County Public Schools, Eatonton, GA, January 12.
2. "What High School Students Can Do to Develop Their Creative Talents." Athens Chapter, Georgia Governor's Honors Program, Athens High School, January 15.
3. "Fostering Creativity in Young Children and its Implications for Teacher Training."

Twenty-First Teacher Education Conference, University of Georgia Center for Continuing Education, January 18.

4. "Creative Ways of Learning in Early Childhood Education." Twenty-First Teacher Education Conference, University of Georgia Center for Continuing Education, January 18.
5. "What Parents of Pre-School Children Can Do to Encourage Creative Development." Parents and Teachers Association, College Avenue Experimental Kindergarten, Athens, GA, February 6.
6. "Psychological Foundations in Undergraduate and Five-Year Teacher Education Programs." Paper prepared for Professional Education Committee of the Georgia State Department of Education, March 25.
7. "Proposed Roles for Elementary School Principals in Developing Creatively Gifted Children." Principals Association, San Diego Public Schools, San Diego, CA, March 18.
8. "Flying Monkeys, Silent Lions, and School Psychologists." Paper presented to California Association of School Psychologists and Psychometrists, Anaheim, CA, March 20.
9. "Understanding the Child Who Learns in a Different Way." Address to parents of gifted elementary pupils, San Diego Public Schools, San Diego, CA, March 18.
10. "New Goals for Early Childhood Education and Their Attainment." Paper presented at Early Childhood Education Conference, Fort Valley State College, Fort Valley, GA, April 19.
11. "Innovations in Creative Dramatics with Pre-Primary and Disadvantaged Children." Paper presented to NDEA Workshop in Creative Dramatics, University of Minnesota, Minneapolis, MN, June 28.
12. "Creativity: Implications for the Education of Gifted Children." Keynote address to National Association for Gifted Children, Chicago, IL, May 1.
13. "Identification of Creative Talent." Educators Seminar, State Department of Education, Hato Rey, Puerto Rico, May 6.
14. "Development of Creative Potentialities Through Education." Educators Seminar, State Department of Education, San Juan, Puerto Rico, May 7.
15. "Developing the Skills of Teaching Creatively." Educators Seminar, State Department of Education, San Juan, Puerto Rico, May 8.
16. "Human Potentialities for Creativity." Harvard University Institute for Administrators of Pupil Personnel Services, Cambridge, MA, July 15.
17. "Creativity and Its Relationship to Achievement and Motivation." Conference on Pupil Achievement and Motivation, University of Georgia Center for Continuing Education, April 27.
18. "Scholarship and Christian Theology: Today and Tomorrow." College Faculty Conference, Southern Baptist Convention, Toccoa, GA, August 3.
19. "Identification and Development of Creativity in Children." Thirteenth Professional Institute for School Psychologists, Division 16, American Psychological Association, August 26-29.
20. "Providing Experiences for Creative Writing." Northeast Georgia Instructional Center Inservice Education Workshop, Cleveland, GA, September 23.
21. "Creative Strategies in Teaching Disadvantaged Children." Branch Meeting, International Reading Association, Augusta, GA, October 7.

Foreword(s)/Preface(s) and Book Reviews

1. Book Review: *Explorations in Human Potentialities*, edited by Herbert A. Otto. *The Social Studies*, ***59***, 125-126.
2. Book Review: *Psychology in Community Settings: Clinical, Education, Vocational, Social Aspects* by S. B. Sarason, M. Levine, I. I. Goldenberg, D. L. Cherlin and E. M. Bennett. *The Social Studies*, ***59****(1)*, 41.
3. Book Review: *A Theory of Psychological Reactance* by Jack W. Brehm. *American Journal of Psychology*, *81*, 133-134.

1969

Books and Monographs

1. *Dimensions of Early Learning: Creativity*. Belmont, CA: Fearon Publishers.
2. (With W. F. White) *Issues and Advances in Educational Psychology*. Itasca, IL: Peacock Publishers.
3. *Teaching Skills for Creative Ways of Learning*. Chicago, IL: Science Research Associates.
4. *Spanish Edition of Guiding Creative Talent*. Buenos Aires, Argentina: Edition'al Troguel Sa.
5. *Ideas About God*. Nashville, TN: Sunday School Board of the Southern Baptist Convention.

Parts of Books, Contributions to Cooperative Volumes

(* Indicates a previously published journal article.)

1. *"Explorations in Creative Thinking." In S. H. Frey and E. S. Haugen (Eds.), *Readings in Classroom Learning*. New York, NY: American Book Company, Pp. 206-212.
2. "Motivating and Guiding Creative Reading." In T. Clymer and V. W. Jones (Eds.), *Teachers Edition: Seven is Magic*. Boston, MA: Ginn and Company, Pp. 15-21.
3. *"Adventuring in Creativity." In R. H. Jones and B. F. Walker (Eds.), *Educational Perspectives of the Elementary School*. Dubuque, IA: William C. Brown, Pp. 201-210.
4. *"Fostering Creativity During the High School Years." In D. Rogers (Ed.), *Issues in Adolescent Psychology*. New York, NY: Appleton-Century-Crofts, Pp. 231-238.
5. *"Explorations in Creative Thinking." In R. C. Sprinthall and N. A. Sprinthall (Eds.), *Educational Psychology: Selected Readings*. New York, NY: Van Nostrand-Reinhold, Pp. 250-254.
6. "Influence on a Student's Learning of the Type of Test Being Administered." In K. Ingenkamp (Ed.), *Developments in Educational Testing, Vol. 2*. London: University of London Press, Pp. 315-325.
7. "New Type of Items for Measuring the Creative Thinking Abilities." In K. Ingenkamp (Ed.), *Developments in Educational Testing, Vol. 1*. London: University of London Press, Pp. 293-309.
8. *"Their Stories Tell Their Feelings: Problems of Highly Creative Children." In H. F. Clarizio (Ed.), *Mental Health and the Educative Process: Selected Readings*. Chicago, IL: Rand McNally, Pp. 215-220.
9. "How Creativity Development Can Awaken Unrecognized Potential." In L. Hertz (Ed.), *Developing Unawakened and Unrecognized Potential*. St Paul, MN: State Department of Education, Pp. 8-20.

10. *(With R. E. Myers) "Teaching Gifted Elementary Pupils Research Skills and Concepts." In W. L. Herman, Jr. (Ed.), *Current Research in Elementary School Social Studies*. New York, NY: Macmillan Company, Pp. 350-356.
11. "Lernprozesse bei Problem Lösendem und Schöpferischen Verhalten." In *Band 4: Lernen und Eriziehung*. Berlin, West Germany: Colloquim Verlag.
12. *"Issues in the Identification and Encouragement of Gifted Disadvantaged Children." In F. Standage (Ed.), *Creativity and the Disadvantaged Student*. Morehead, KY: Operation Talent Search, Morehead State University.

Articles in Professional and Research Journals

1. (With N. C. Aliotti) Sex Differences in Levels of Performance and Test-Retest Reliability of the Torrance Tests of Creative Thinking. *Journal of Creative Behavior*, ***3(1)***, 52-57.
2. (With J. Khatena) Originality and Imagery in Identifying Creative Talent in Music. *Gifted Child Quarterly*, ***13(1)***, 3-8.
3. What is Honored: Comparative Studies of Creative Achievement and Motivation. *Journal of Creative Behavior*, ***3(3)***, 149-154.
4. (With L. Harris) The Incomplete Story-Situation as a Technique for Studying Children's Thinking. *College of Education Record* (University of North Dakota), ***55(1)***, 4-10.
5. Peer Influence on Preschool Children's Willingness to Try Difficult Tasks. *Journal of Psychology*, ***72***, 189-194.
6. Curiosity of Gifted Children and Performance on Timed and Untimed Tests of Creativity. *Gifted Child Quarterly*, ***13***, 155-158.
7. Prediction of Adult Creative Achievement Among High School Seniors. *Gifted Child Quarterly*, ***13***, 223-229.
8. It's Time You Learned to Eat Peas With a Fork! *Theory into Practice*, ***8(5)***, 332-333.
9. Comparative Studies of Creativity in Children. *Educational Leadership*, ***27***, 146-148.
10. Creative Positives of Disadvantaged Children and Youth. *Gifted Child Quarterly*, ***13***, 71-81.
11. Beyond Learning Theory. *Contemporary Psychology*, ***14***, 530-531.
12. (With R. N. Walker) Identification and Development of Creativity in Children. *The School Psychologist*, ***23(1)***, 33-43.

Reports, Manuals, Handbooks, Tests, Instructional Materials

1. *A Three-Year Study of Continuity of Creative Growth Under a Cognitive-Structured Approach to Educational Stimulation*. Athens, GA: Research and Development Center in Educational Stimulation, University of Georgia.
2. *A Three-Year Study of the Effects of the Creative-Aesthetic Approach to the Creative Development of Pre-Primary Children*. Athens, GA: Research and Development Center in Educational Stimulation, University of Georgia.
3. *Administration and Scoring Guide for Mother Goose Problems Test*. Athens, GA: Georgia Studies of Creative Behavior.
4. *Examples of Learning Experiences for Ghetto Children in Reading to Facilitate Creative Behavior*. Athens, GA: Georgia Studies of Creative Behavior, University of Georgia.
5. *Hierarchy of Creative Thinking Skills Relevant to Reading*. Athens, GA: Georgia Studies of Creative Behavior, University of Georgia.
6. (With H. Sorkey and G. Strag) *Evaluation of The University of Georgia 1968-1969 Experienced Teacher Fellowship Program in School Psychology*. Athens, GA:

Department of Educational Psychology, College of Education, University of Georgia.

7. *A Three-Year Study of the Influence of a Creative-Aesthetic Approach to School Readiness and Beginning Reading and Arithmetic on Creative Development.* Athens, GA: Research and Development Center in Educational Stimulation, University of Georgia.
8. (With J. P. Torrance and V. K. Phillips) *Dictionary of Responses for Figural Form A, Torrance Tests of Creative Thinking.* Athens, GA: Georgia Studies of Creative Behavior, College of Education, University of Georgia.

Articles in Popular or Trade Type Journals and Magazines—Applications of Research

1. (With J. P. Torrance) Softest, Shortest, Slowest, Smallest... *Music for Primaries, 4(1)*, 22-23.
2. (With J. P. Torrance) Good Feelings, Bad Feelings. *Music for Primaries, 4(2)*, 14-15.
3. Games with Sounds. *Music for Primaries, 4(3)*, 14-15.
4. Sounds of Discovery. *Music for Primaries, 4(4)*, 10-11.
5. Issues in the Identification and Encouragement of Disadvantaged Gifted Children. *TAG Gifted Children Newsletter*, March, ***11**(2)*, 48-55.
6. Use Songs for Creative Growth. *Children's Music Leader, 4(1)*, 29.
7. Will Creatively Gifted High School Seniors Behave Creatively Seven Years Later? *TAG Gifted Children Newsletter, **12**(1)*, 24-31.
8. Issues in the Identification and Encouragement of Gifted Disdvantaged Children. *Gifted Children Newsletter, **11**(2)*, 48-55.
9. Creative Functioning and Mental Health. *Accent on Talent*, ***1 and 2***, 52-53.

Papers Presented at Seminars/Conferences

1. "Issues in Identifying and Developing Creative Children Among Disadvantaged Groups." Operation Talent Search Workshop, Morehead State University, Morehead, KY, January 17.
2. "Learning Processes Involved in Creative Activities in the Classroom." College of Education Faculty, Morehead State University, Morehead, KY, January 17.
3. "Classroom Teachers Working with Creative Children." Classroom Teachers Delegate Assembly, Center for Continuing Education, University of Georgia, Athens, GA, February 1.
4. "Motivating and Guiding Creative Reading." Conference on New Materials in Reading, Statler-Hilton Hotel, Boston, MA, February 3.
5. "Ideas for Preparing Reading Materials to Facilitate Creative Behavior Among Ghetto Children." Urban Reading Program Conference, Statler-Hilton Hotel, Boston, MA, March 28.
6. "Creative Stimulation at the Pre-Primary and Primary Levels." Pre-Primary and Follow Through Teachers Inservice Workshop, Atlanta Public Schools, Atlanta, GA, April 2.
7. "Creativity and the Learning Process." Institute for the Dissemination of a Unique Experimental Inservice Training Program Developed by the Chicago Creativity Project, Chicago Public Schools, Sherman House, Chicago, IL, April 15.
8. "How Creativity Development Can Awaken Unrecognized Potential." Conference on Developing Unawakened and Unrecognized Potential, Division of Instruction,

Minnesota State Department of Education, University of Minnesota, Minneapolis, MN, April 26.
9. "Human Potentialities for Creativity." Harvard University Institute for Administrators of Pupil Personnel Services, July 15.
10. "Group Dynamics and Creativity in Curriculum Improvement." Address to Bartow County Educators, Cartersville, GA, October 23.
11. "Human Relations Training for Primary and Pre-Primary Children." Address to workers in Project Follow Through, Miami, FL, October 27.
12. "Group Dynamics and Creativity in the Solution of Problems of School Desegregation." Address to School Principals, Miami Public Schools, Miami, FL, October 28.
13. "Encouraging Creative Growth to Direct Change." Address to Silver Anniversary Conference of Florida Supervisors of Instruction, October 27-28, Miami Beach, FL.
14. "Creativity Research and Higher Education." Paper presented at the annual meetings of the American Association for the Advancement of Science, December 29, Boston, MA.
15. "Creative Reading." Paper presented to the nineteenth annual meeting of the National Reading Conference, Atlanta, GA, December 4.

Foreword(s)/Preface(s) and Book Reviews

1. Book Review: Freeman, J., Butcher, H.J., and Christie, T. *Creativity: A Selective Review of Research*. London: Society for Research in Higher Education. *International Review of Education*, ***15***, 363-364.
2. Book Review: Cropley, A. J. *Creativity*. *International Review of Education*, ***15****(4)*, 499-500.
3. Preface. In A. Beaudot (Ed.), *La Creativité a L'école*. Paris: Presses Universitaires de France, Pp. 5-6.

1970

Books and Monographs

1. *Encouraging Creativity in the Classroom*. Dubuque, IA: William C. Brown.
2. (With R. E. Myers) *Creative Learning and Teaching*. New York, NY: Harper and Row. (Translated and published in Spanish)
3. *The Creative Teacher at Work*. Lexington, MA: Ginn and Company.
4. *Encouraging Creativity in the Classroom* (Japanese translation). Dubuque, IA: William C. Brown (Japanese translation rights through Charles E. Tuttle Co., Inc.).
5. (With R. E. Myers) *What if a Duck is not a Duck?* Lexington, MA: Ginn and Company.

Parts of Books, Contributions to Cooperative Volumes

(* Indicates a previously published journal article.)

1. "What It Means to Become Human." In M. M. Scobey and G. Graham (Eds.), *To Nurture Humanness*. Washington, DC: Association for Supervision and Curriculum Development, Pp. 3-10.
2. *"Cause for Concern." In P. E. Vernon (Ed.), *Creativity*. Middlesex, England: Penguin Books, Pp. 355-370.
3. "Moral and Religious Growth." In C. Ingle (Ed.), *Children and Conversion*. Nashville,

TN: Broadman Press, Pp. 98-111.

4. *"Adventuring in Creativity." In J. F. Ohles (Ed.), *Principles and Practices of Teaching: Selected Readings*. New York, NY: Random House, Pp. 148-159.
5. "Achieving Socialization without Sacrificing Creativity." In C. Taylor (Ed.), *Educational Challenges of Creativity*. Salt Lake, UT: Institute for Behavior Research in Creativity (Ninth International Research Conference on Creativity held in Buffalo-Niagara Falls, NY).
6. "Emerging Concepts of Giftedness." In W. Vasser and J. Renzulli (Eds.), *The Gifted Child in Connecticut*. Storrs, CT: Connecticut State Department of Education, Pp. 7-17.
7. "Unique Needs of the Creative Child and Adult." In *The Gifted and Talented: Their Education and Development* (78th yearbook of the National Society for the Study of Education). Chicago, IL: The National Society for the Study of Education, Pp. 352-371.

Articles in Professional and Research Journals

1. Influence of Dyadic Interaction on Creative Functioning. *Psychological Reports*, ***26***, 391-394.
2. Group Size and Question Performance of Preprimary Children. *Journal of Psychology*, ***74***, 71-75.
3. (With J. C. Gowan, J. J. Wu, and N. C. Aliotti) Creative Functioning of Monolingual and Bilingual Children in Singapore. *Journal of Educational Psychology*, ***61****(1)*, 72-75.
4. Individual Differences in Creativity Among Secondary School Students. *High School Journal*, ***53****(8)*, 129-139.
5. Creativity Research and Higher Education. *Educational Trends* (India), ***5****(2)*, 1-10.
6. (With J. Khatena) "What Kind of Person Are You?": A Brief Screening Device for Identifying Creatively Gifted Adolescents and Adults. *Gifted Child Quarterly*, ***14***, 71-75.
7. Stimulation, Enjoyment, and Originality in Dyadic Creativity. *APA Experimental Publication System, No. 246-34*.
8. Dyadic Interaction as a Facilitator of Gifted Performance. *Gifted Child Quarterly*, ***14****(3)*, 139-143.
9. Freedom to Manipulate Objects and Question-Asking Performance of Six-Year-Olds. *Young Children*, ***26****(2)*, 93-97.
10. Achieving Socialization without Sacrificing Creativity. *Journal of Creative Behavior*, ***4***, 183-189.
11. (With C. A. Tan and T. Allman) Verbal Originality and Teacher Behavior. *Journal of Teacher Education*, ***21****(3)*, 336-341.
12. Small Group Behavior of 5-Year-Old Children Under Three Kinds of Educational Stimulation. *Journal of Experimental Education*, ***38****(4)*, 79-82.
13. Gifted Children Can Read Statistics. *Gifted Child Quarterly*, ***14****(1)*, 3-7, 40-41.
14. Broadening Concepts of Giftedness in the 70's. *Gifted Child Quarterly*, ***14***, 199-208.
15. (With M. Grossman) A Creativity Workshop for Disadvantaged Children. *Art Education*, ***23****(5)*, 32-33.

Reports, Manuals, Handbooks, Tests, Instructional Materials

1. (With V. K. Phillips) *Results from the Fourth Year of a Study of Continuity of Creative Growth Under a Cognitively-Structured Approach to Educational Stimulation*. Athens, GA: Research and Development Center in Educational Stimulation.

2. (With V. K. Phillips) *Preliminary Administration and Scoring Guide: What Could It Be?* Athens, GA: Georgia Studies of Creative Behavior.
3. (With J. Khatena) *Technical-Norms Manual for "What Kind of Person Are You?"* Athens, GA: Georgia Studies of Creative Behavior.
4. (With W. R. Nash) *A Preliminary Evaluation of the Effects of Reading 360 on Creative Development and Functioning at the First Grade Level.* Athens, GA: Georgia Studies of Creative Behavior, Department of Educational Psychology, College of Education, University of Georgia.
5. *Report to the President—White House Conference on Children* (E. P. Torrance was Chairman of Forum). Washington, DC: U.S. Government Printing Office.
6. *Self-Study of the Department of Educational Psychology, Measurement and Research, College of Education, The University of Georgia.* Athens, GA: Department of Educational Psychology, College of Education, University of Georgia.

Articles in Popular or Trade Type Journals and Magazines—Applications of Research

1. The Magic of Singing Pictures. *Music for Primaries, **5**(1)*, 9-11.
2. Sound and Movement, Poems, and Songs. *Music for Primaries, **5**(2)*, 14-15.
3. (With J. P. Torrance) A Trip into the World of Sound. *Music for Primaries, **5**(3)*, 10-11.
4. Thinking Up Round Music Makers. *Music Makers, **1**(1)*, 10-11.
5. (With J. P. Torrance) Keep Creativity Alive. *Resource, **11**(4)*, 18-19.
6. The Teacher as a Teacher. *Collegiate Teacher, **1**(1)*, 104-105.

Papers Presented at Seminars/Conferences

1. "Creative Positives of Disadvantaged Children and Youth." Address to the students and faculty of Alabama Agricultural and Mechanical College, Normal, AL, December 9.
2. "Widening the Child's World Through Creative Reading." Paper presented to Association for Childhood Education International, Atlanta, GA, April 3.
3. "Guiding Creative Reading." Address to Mississippi Reading Supervisors, Mississippi State Department of Education, Jackson, MS, April 4.
4. "Emergence of Identity: Selected Aspects—A Background Paper." Paper for 1970 White House Conference on Children.

1971

Books and Monographs

1.(With J. C. Gowan) *Educating the Ablest.* Itasca, IL: Peacock Publishers.

Parts of Books, Contributions to Cooperative Volumes

(* Indicates a previously published journal article.)

1. *"Nurture of Creative Talents." In G. A. Davis and J. A. Scott (Eds.), *Training Creative Thinking.* New York, NY: Holt, Rinehart and Winston, Pp. 208-219.
2. *"Examples of Rationales of Test Tasks for Assessing Creative Abilities." In G. Q. Davis and J. A. Scott (Eds.), *Training Creative Thinking.* New York, NY: Holt, Rinehart and Winston, Pp. 276-289.

3. "Epilogue: Creativity in American Education, 1865-1965." In R. D. Strom (Ed.), *Teachers and the Learning Process*. Englewood Cliffs, NJ: Prentice-Hall, Pp. 370-381.
4. "Psychology of Gifted Children and Youth." In W. M. Cruickshank (Ed.), *Psychology of Exceptional Children and Youth*. Englewood Cliffs, NJ: Prentice-Hall, Pp. 528-564.
5. "Creativity in the Education Process." In G. S. Lesser (Ed.), *Psychology and Educational Practice*. Glenview, IL: Scott, Foresman and Company, Pp. 217-241.
6. "The Creative Person." In L. C. Deighton (Ed.), *Encyclopedia of Education, Vol. 2*. New York, NY: Macmillan Company, Pp. 552-557.
7. *"Uniqueness and Creativeness: The School's Role." In R. R. Leeper and N. Atkins (Eds.), *Curricular Concern in a Revolutionary Era*. Washington, DC: Association for Supervision and Curriculum Development, Pp. 48-51.
8. *(With D. C. Dauw) "Attitude Patterns of Creatively Gifted High School Seniors." In R. E. Muus (Ed.), *Adolescent Behavior and Society*. New York, NY: Random House, Pp. 113-138.
9. "Long-Range Prediction Studies and International Applications of the Torrance Tests of Creative Thinking." In *Proceedings of the XVII International Association of Applied Psychologists,* 1889-1895.

Articles in Professional and Research Journals

1. Stimulation, Enjoyment, and Originality in Dyadic Creativity. *Journal of Educational Psychology*, ***62****(1)*, 45-49.
2. (With J. Khatena) Attitude Patterns and the Production of Original Verbal Images: A Study of Construct Validity. *Gifted Child Quarterly*, ***15***, 117-122.
3. Are the Torrance Tests of Creative Thinking Biased Against or in Favor of Disadvantaged Groups? *Gifted Child Quarterly*, ***15***, 75-81.
4. Some Validity Studies of Two Brief Screening Devices for Studying the Creative Personality. *Journal of Creative Behavior*, ***5****(2)*, 94-103.
5. Developmental Changes in Sources of Consensual Validation in Pre-Adolescence. *Gifted Child Quarterly*, ***15***, 3-10.
6. "Structure" Can Improve the Group Behavior of Five-Year-Old Children. *Journal of Elementary Education*, ***72****(2)*, 102-106.
7. (With C. Walker and T. S. Walker) A Cross-Cultural Study of the Perception of Situational Causality. *Journal of Cross-Cultural Psychology*, **2**, 401-404.
8. Identity: The Gifted Child's Major Problem. *Gifted Child Quarterly*, ***15***, 147-155.
9. Is Bias Against Job Changing Bias Against Giftedness? *Gifted Child Quarterly*, ***15****(2)*, 244-248.
10. ****Creativity and Infinity. *Journal of Research and Development in Education, 4(3)*, 35-41.**
11. Revue Psychologie. *Les Editions du Centre de Psychologie Applique*, ***21****(4)*, 271-276.
12. Freedom-Control Orientation and Need for Structure in Group Creativity. *Sciences de l'Art* (Paris University), ***8****(1)*, 61-64.
13. (With V. K. Phillips) Divergent Thinking, Remote Association, and Concept Attainment Strategies. *The Journal of Psychology*, *77*, 223-228.

Reports, Manuals, Handbooks, Tests, Instructional Materials

1. *Preliminary Manual for Opinion Questionnaire: Culturally and Economically Disadvantaged Children and Youth*. Athens, GA: Georgia Studies of Creative Behavior.

2. *Technical Manual—Short Form (Creative Motivation Scale) of the Personal-Social Motivation Inventory*. Athens, GA: Georgia Studies of Creative Behavior.
3. *Creative Ways of Teaching*. New York, NY: McGraw-Hill Book Company. (*Sound Seminar* 78232. Cassette 81649).
4. *The Creative Positives of Disadvantaged Children and Youth*. New York, NY: McGraw-Hill Book Company. (*Sound Seminar* 78233. Cassette 81650).
5. *Working with Creatively Gifted Children*. New York, NY: McGraw-Hill Book Company. (*Sound Seminar* 78235. Cassette 81652).
6. *Highlight Summary of the 12-Year Follow-Up of the University of Minnesota High School Studies of Creative Behavior*. Athens, GA: Georgia Studies of Creative Behavior, College of Education, University of Georgia.
7. *Recommendations Concerning the Georgia Governor's Honors Program; Report to Governor Jimmy Carter*. Athens, GA: Department of Educational Psychology, College of Education, University of Georgia.
8. *U.S. and Japan Comparison on SOLAT Scale*. Tokyo, Japan: The Mainichi Press.
9. *Bibliography for the Torrance Tests of Creative Thinking*. Athens, GA: Georgia Studies of Creative Behavior, College of Education, University of Georgia.
10. (With R. Peters, E. Phillips, and J. Loney) *Evaluation of the 1971 Dudley Park Creativity Workshop*. Athens, GA: Department of Educational Psychology and Athens Human Relations Council, University of Georgia.

Articles in Popular or Trade Type Journals and Magazines—Applications of Research

1. Inquiry and Creative Thinking in Teaching the Faith. *Lutheran Education*, ***106****(7)*, 330-334.
2. The Forgotten Children. *Early Years*, ***1****(1)*, 66-67, 75-77, 91, 94.
3. The Courage to Be Creative. *Retail Credit Company Inspection News*, July-August, ***56****(4)*, 8-11.
4. (With J. P. Torrance) Sounds and Thinking. *Music Makers*, ***1****(2)*, 14-15.
5. A Poem About a Sound. *Music Makers*, ***1****(3)*, 20-21.
6. Words, Sounds, Pictures. *Music Makers*, ***1****(4)*, 22-23.

Papers Presented at Seminars/Conferences

1. "Long-Range Prediction Studies and International Applications of the Torrance Tests of Creative Thinking." Paper presented at the XVIIth International Congress of Applied Psychology, Liege, Belgium, July 25-30.
2. "Creativity Within Your Grasp." Paper presented at meeting of Maine Elementary-Kindergarten-Nursery Educators, Portland, ME, October 7.
3. "Will Reading Become Obsolete?" Paper presented at meeting of Maine Reading Association, Portland, ME, October 8.
4. "The New Superstar: The Creative Teacher." Paper presented at University of Michigan School of Education Golden Jubilee, Ann Arbor, MI, October 23.
5. "The Encouragement of Creativity in the Urban Schools." Seminar at School of Education, Georgia State University, November 3.
6. "The Process of Involvement in the Creative Learning of Children." Graduate Seminar, College of Education, University of New Mexico, Albuquerque, NM, December 5.

7. (With L. K. Hall) "Assesing the Further Reaches of the Creative Potential." Lecture and visual aids presented at Maharashi University, IA.

1972

Books and Monographs

1. *Guiding Creative Talent* (Japanese translation). Tokyo, Japan: Meiji-Tosho.

Parts of Books, Contributions to Cooperative Volumes

(* Indicates a previously published journal article.)

1. *"Different Ways of Learning for Different Kinds of Children." In D. E. Hamacheck (Ed.), *Human Dynamics in Psychology and Education* (2nd Ed.). Boston, MA: Allyn and Bacon.
2. "Group Dynamics and Creative Functioning." In C. W. Taylor (Ed.), *Climate for Creativity*. New York, NY: Pergamon Press, Pp. 75-96.
3. *"What is Honored in a Country Will be Cultivated There." In J. O Whittaker (Ed.), *Recent Discoveries in Pyschology*. Philadelphia, PA: W. B. Prentice-Hall, Pp. 128-149.
4. "Problems in Maintaining Creativity." In F. B. McMahon (Ed.), *Psychology: Perspectives on the Hybrid Science*. Englewood Cliffs, NJ: Prentice-Hall, Pp. 128-149.
5. "Potentially Creative Youth." In R. H. Frederickson and J. W. M. Rothney (Eds.), *Recognizing and Assisting Multi-Potential Youth*. Columbus, OH: Charles E. Merrill, Pp. 2-19.
6. "Characteristics of Creatively Gifted Children and Youth." In E. P. Trapp and P. Himmelstein (Eds.), *Readings on the Exceptional Child* (2nd Ed.). New York, NY: Appleton-Century-Crofts, Pp. 273-291.
7 (With J. C. Gowan) "Educating the Ablest: A Book of Readings on the Education of Gifted Children." In M. E. Chisholm (Ed.), *Education Book List, 1971-1972*. Washington, DC: Pi Lambda Theta, P. 27.

Articles in Professional and Research Journals

1. (With C. B. Bruch) Reaching the Creatively Gifted. *National Elementary Principal*, ***51****(5)*, 69-75.
2. Creative Kids. *Today's Education*, ***61****(1)*, 25-28.
3. Tendency to Produce Unusual Visual Perspective as a Predictor of Creative Achievement. *Perceptual and Motor Skills*, ***34***, 911-915.
4. Creative Young Women in Today's World. *Exceptional Children*, ***38****(8)*, 597-603.
5. Influence of Alternate Approaches to Pre-Primary Educational Stimulation and Question-Asking Skills. *Journal of Educational Research*, ***65****(5)*, 204-206.
6. (With R. W. Peters) Dyadic Interaction of Preschool Children and Performance on a Constructive Task. *Psychological Reports*, ***30***, 747-750.
7. Predictive Validity of "Bonus" Scoring for Combinations on Repeated Figures Tests of Creative Thinking. *Journal of Psychology*, ***81***, 167-171.
8. Training Teachers and Leaders to Recognize and Acknowledge Creative Behavior Among Disadvantaged Children. *Gifted Child Quarterly*, ***16****(1)*, 3-10.
9. (With J. P. Torrance) Combining Creative Problem-Solving with Creative Expressive

Activities in the Education of Disadvantaged Young People. *Journal of Creative Behavior*, ***6****(1)*, 1-10.

10. What Kinds of Groups Make a Psychology of Groups? *Contemporary Psychology*, ***17****(5)*.
11. Freedom—Control Orientation and Need for Structure in Group Creativity. *Sciences de L'Art*, ***8***, 61-64.
12. Predictive Validity of the Torrance Tests of Creative Thinking. *Journal of Creative Behavior*, ***6****(4)*, 236-252.
13. The Creative Child. *PTA Magazine*, ***67****(4)*, 24-27.
14. (With H. Langgulung) The Development of Causal Thinking of Children in Mexico and the United States. *Journal of Cross-Cultural Psychology*, ***3***, 315-320.
15. (With V. K. Phillips) Development of Ego Control Through Creative Activities. *Gifted Child Quarterly*, ***16****(4)*, 271-274.
16. ****Career Patterns and Peak Creative Achievements of Creative High School Students 12 Years Later. *Gifted Child Quarterly*, *16*, 75-88.**
17. An Alternative to Compensatory Education. *Educational Horizons*, ***50****(4)*, 176-182.
18. ****Can We Teach Children to Think Creatively? *Journal of Creative Behavior*, *6(2)*, 114-143.**
19. Un Resume Historique du Developpement des Tests de Pensee Creative de Torrance. *Revue de Psychologie Applique* (Paris, France), ***22****(4)*, 203-218.
20. Review of "What Groups Constitute the Psychology of Small Group Behavior?" by M. E. Shaw. *Contemporary Psychology*, ***17****(5)*, 282-283.
21. (With R. W. Peters) Dyadic Interaction of Preschool Children and Performance on a Construction Task. *Psychological Reports*, ***30***, 747-750.

Reports, Manuals, Handbooks, Tests, Instructional Materials

1. *Montrez Votre Imagination avec des Mots. Forms A and B.* Paris, France: Les Editions du Centre de Psychologie Appliquée.
2. *Montrez Votre Imagination avec des Dessins. Forms A and B.* Paris, France: Les Editions du Centre de Psychologie Appliquée.
3. *Manual: Tests de Pensée Créative.* Paris, France: Les Editions du Centre de Psychologie Appliquée.
4. *Module on Creative Teaching* (secondary form). Athens, GA: Department of Educational Psychology, College of Education, University of Georgia.
5. (With V. K. Phillips, W. Rungsinan, and N. Dehlavi) *Evaluation of Some Affect Objectives in Undergraduate Courses in Educational Psychology.* Athens, GA: Department of Educational Psychology, University of Georgia.
6. *Proposed Work as Scholar-in-Residence, United States Commission on Civil Rights.* Athens, GA: Department of Educational Psychology, University of Georgia.
7. *A Petition to the Graduate School of the University of Georgia Requesting Approval to Offer the Doctor of Philosophy Degree in Educational Psychology.* Submitted by the Department of Educational Psychology, Measurement and Research, University of Georgia, Athens, GA.
8. *Predicting the Adult Creative Behavior of High School Students (1959-1971).* Athens, GA: Georgia Studies of Creative Behavior, College of Education, University of Georgia.
9. *Opinion on Creative Learning and Teaching.* Athens, GA: Department of Educational Psychology, University of Georgia.

10. (With V. K. Phillips) *Opinion on Creative Learning and Teaching*. Athens, GA: Department of Educational Psychology, Georgia Studies of Creative Behavior.
11. *Each One is "Special."* Unpublished manuscript prepared at request of editors of Early Years.
12. *Creative Teaching: Indian Teacher Training Project in Secondary Social Science Education*. Athens, GA: University of Georgia.
13. *Narrative Account of Career*. Athens, GA: Department of Educational Psychology, University of Georgia.
14. *Predictive Creative Behavior, 1959-1971* (unpublished manuscript). Athens, GA: Georgia Studies of Creative Behavior.
15. *Torrance Tests of Creative Thinking Directions Manual and Scoring Guide, Figural Test Booklet A, 1972 Revision*. Lexington, MA: Personnel Press, Ginn and Company.
16. *Slovenian Translation Torrance Tests of Creative Thinking, Figural Form A*.
17. *Slovenian Translation Torrance Tests of Creative Thinking, Verbal Form A*.
18. *German Translation of Creative Writing Test*. Minneapolis, MN: Bureau of Educational Research, University of Minnesota.
19. (With K. DeYoung) *Experimental Form: Life Experience Inventory*. Minneapolis, MN: Bureau of Educational Research, University of Minnesota, July 1958 (reprinted by Athens, GA: Georgia Studies of Creative Behavior, College of Education, University of Georgia).

Papers Presented at Seminars/Conferences

1. "Becoming a Productive Creative Scholar." Annual Scholar's Banquet, Georgia Military College, Milledgeville, GA, March 22.
2. "The Creative Problem Solving Process in Education." County Supervisors and Department Heads, Volusia County Schools, Daytona Beach, FL, March 13.
3. "Building Teaching Methods and Curricula on the Creative Positives of Disadvantaged Children." Special Teachers, Volusia County Schools, Daytona Beach, FL, March 13
4. "Creatively Gifted Children in Today's Schools." Elementary Teachers, Volusia County Schools, Daytona Beach, FL, March 14.
5. "Can We Teach Children to Think?" Invited paper at annual meeting of American Educational Research Association, Chicago, IL, April 5.
6. "Career Patterns and Peak Creative Achievements of Creatively Gifted High School Students Twelve Years Later." Invited address, Psi Chi, Southeastern Psychological Association, Atlanta, GA, April 7.
7. "Studies of the Predictive Validity of the Torrance Tests of Creative Thinking." Paper presented at the annual meeting of the Georgia Psychological Association, Macon, GA, May 6.

Foreword(s)/Preface(s) and Book Reviews

1. Book Review: *Creativity and the Teacher*, by John Foster and Creativity and Education by Hugh Lytton. *Educational Studies*, *3*, 239-241.

1973

Books and Monographs

1. (With J. P. Torrance) *Is Creativity Teachable?* Bloomington, IN: Phi Delta Kappa Foundation.

2. (With R. D. Strom) *Education for Affective Achievement.* Chicago, IL: Rand McNally.
3. *The Creative Teacher at Work.* Lexington, MA: Ginn and Company.

Parts of Books, Contributions to Cooperative Volumes

(* Indicates a previously published journal article.)

1. *"Some Consequences of Power Differences in Decision-Making in Permanent and Temporary Groups." In R. Ofshe (Ed.), *Interpersonal Behavior in Small Groups.* Englewood Cliffs, NJ: Prentice-Hall, Pp. 176-183.
2. *"Creative Kids." In R. A. Magoon (Ed.), *Education and Psychology: Past, Present, and Future.* Columbus, OH: Charles E. Merrill, Pp. 96-100.
3. *"Ten Ways of Helping Young Children Gifted in Creative Writing and Speech." In R. R. Ruddell, E. J. Ahern, E. K. Hartson, and J. E. Taylor (Eds.), *Resources in Reading-Language Instruction.* Englewood Cliffs, NJ: Prentice-Hall, Pp. 250-258.
4. "Overview of Research in the Creativity Domain." In E. P. Torrance (Ed.), *Critical Appraisal of Research in the Creativity Domain.* Fort Worth, TX: Institute of Behavioral Research, Texas Christian University.
5. *"La Validite Predictive des Tests de Pensee Creative." In A. Beaudot (Ed.), *La Creativite Recherches Americaines.* Paris, France: Dunod.
6. *(With D. C. Dauw) "Reves et Aspirations de Trois Groupes d'Adolescents Creatifs et d'un Groupe Temoin Comparable." In A. Beaudot (Ed.), *La Creativite Recherches Americaines.* Paris, France: Dunod.
7. "Factors Affecting Creative Thinking Among Children: An Interim Research Report." In M. Bloomberg (Ed.), *Creativity: Theory and Research.* New Haven, CT: College and University Press, Pp. 141-151.
8. "Achieving Socialization Without Sacrificing Creativity." In B. J. Franklin and F. J. Kohout (Eds.), *Social Psychology and Everyday Life.* New York, NY: David McKay, Pp. 416-422.
9. "Can We Teach Children to Think Creatively?" *Creativity in Teaching.* Ajmer, India: National Council of Educational Research and Training, Pp. 118-134.
10. "Different Ways of Learning for Different Kinds of Children." In R. D. Strom and E. P. Torrance (Eds.), *Education for Affective Achievement.* Chicago, IL: Rand McNalley and Co., Pp. 251-261.
11. "I was a Block and Nobody Builded Me!" In R. D. Strom and E. P. Torrance (Eds.), *Education For Affective Achievement.* Chicago, IL: Rand McNally and Co., Pp. 301-311.
12. (With J. C. Gowan, V. K. Phillips, D. J. Davis, N. C. Aliotti, and D. Treffinger) "Creativity: An Overview." In E. P. Torrance (Ed.), *Needed Research on Creativity: A Special Report of the USOE Sponsored Grand Study: Critical Appraisal of Research in Personality, Emotions, Motivation Domain.* Fort Worth, TX: Texas Christian University, Institute of Behavioral Research.

Articles in Professional and Research Journals

1. Assessment of Disadvantaged Minority Group Children. *School Psychology Digest, 2(4),* 3-10.
2. Emergence of Identity Through Expressive Activities. *Elementary English,* ***50***, 849-852, 870.
3. Conversation Pieces: Tourist-Tripping in a Child's Secret World. *Early Years,* ***4****(1),* 46, 47, 82.

4. Non-Test Indicators of Creative Talent Among Disadvantaged Children. *Gifted Child Quarterly*, ***17***, 3-9.
5. What Gifted Disadvantaged Children Can Teach Their Teachers. *Gifted Child Quarterly*, ***17***, 243-249.
6. (With C. B. Bruch and J. A. Morse) Improving Predictions of the Adult Creative Achievement of Gifted Girls by Using Autobiographical Information. *Gifted Child Quarterly*, ***17****(2)*, 91-95.
7. (With G. Halpin and G. Halpin) Effects of Blindness on Creative Thinking Abilities of Children. *Developmental Psychology*, ***9****(2)*, 268-274.
8. (With G. Halpin and G. Halpin) High School Experiences Related to the Creative Personality. *High School Journal*, ***57****(3)*, 101-111.
9. (With G. Halpin and G. Halpin) Comparison of Creative Thinking Abilities of Blind and Deaf Children. *Perceptual and Motor Skills*, ***37***, 154.
10. (With G. Halpin and G. Halpin) Effects of Sex, Race and Age on Creative Thinking Abilities of Blind Children. *Perceptual and Motor Skills*, ***37***, 389-390.
11. Creativity Within Your Grasp. *Educating Children*, ***18****(2)*, 9-12.
12. Suspended Evaluation on Imagination. *Contemporary Psychology*, ***18***, 676-677.
13. Creativity in Communication with Young Children. *Research in Education*, July, ED 073 835.
14. (With H. Langgulung) A Cross-Cultural Study of Children's Conceptualizations of Situational Causality in India, Western Samoa, Mexico, and the United States. *Journal of Social Psychology*, ***89***, 175-183.
15. (With R. W. Peters) Effects of Triadic Interaction on Performance of Five-Year-Old Disadvantaged Children. *Psychological Reports*, ***32***, 755-758.
16. Commitment to Creativity in Education. *McGill Journal of Education*, ***8****(1)*, 3-12.
17. A Glossary for Tourists Tripping in a Child's Secret World. *Early Years*, ***4****(1)*, 46-47, 82.
18. A Brief History of the Development of the Torrance Tests of Creative Thinking Abilities. *Revue de Psychologie Applique*.
19. Sociodrama as a Creative Problem-Solving Approach to Studying the Future. *The Journal of Creative Behavior*, ***9****(3)*, 182-195.
20. Career Patterns and Peak Creative Achievements of Creative High School Students Twelve Years Later. *The Educational Trends*, ***8****(1-4)*, 114-128 (edited and published by T. N. Raina, St. Anselm's Press, Ajmer, India).
21. Cross-Cultural Studies of Creative Development in Seven Selected Societies. *The Educational Trends*, ***8****(1-4)*, 28-28 (edited and published by T. N. Raina, St. Anselm's Press, Ajmer, India).

Reports, Manuals, Handbooks, Tests, Instructional Materials

1. (With J. Khatena) *Norms-Technical Manual: Thinking Creativity with Sounds and Words.* (Research Edition) Lexington, MA: Personnel Press/Ginn and Company.
2. (With J. Khatena and B. F. Cunnington) *Thinking Creatively with Sounds and Words: Directions Manual and Scoring Guide (Adult Form).* Lexington, MA: Personnel Press/Ginn and Company.
3. (With J. Khatena and B. F. Cunnington) *Thinking Creatively with Sounds and Words: Directions Manual and Scoring Guide (Children's Form).* Lexington, MA: Personnel Press/Ginn and Company.
4. (With V. K. Phillips and A. Hudgins) *Bibliography: Torrance Tests of Creative Thinking.*

Athens, GA: Georgia Studies of Creative Behavior.

5. (With V. K. Phillips) *Preliminary Norms-Technical Manual for Opinions on Creative Learning and Teaching*. Athens, GA: Georgia Studies of Creative Behavior.
6. *Magic Net* (16 mm film). Monmouth, OR: Teaching Research Oregon System of Higher Education.
7. *Life Experiences Inventory* (teacher edition). Athens, GA: Georgia Studies of Creative Behavior, University of Georgia.
8. (With J. R. Bing) *Module on Creative Teaching* (elementary form). Athens, GA: Department of Educational Psychology, University of Georgia.
9. (With W. R. Allen) *Images of the Future: Effects of Race, Sex, and Alienation*. Athens, GA: Department of Educational Psychology, University of Georgia.
10. *Twenty Questions About the Future*. Unpublished questionnaire.
11. *Directions Manual and Scoring Guide, Forms IIA and IIB*. Lexington, MA: Personnel Press, Ginn and Company.
12. *Italian Translation of Torrance Tests of Creative Thinking*. Mario Vitali, Italy: Via Giovanni da Compione.
13. *Israeli translation of Torrance Tests of Creative Thinking*. Bensenville, IL: Scholastic Testing Service.

Articles in Popular or Trade Type Journals and Magazines—Applications of Research

1. Elizabeth Drews' Strategy for Reaching Top Education Priorities. *Phi Delta Kappan*, ***50***, 208-209.
2. What is Creative Thinking? *Forum* (J. C. Penney), Fall-Winter, 4-5.

Papers Presented at Seminars/Conferences

1. "Position Paper: Emergent Concepts Concerning Culturally Different Gifted Children." Washington, DC: The Foundation for Exceptional Children, August 1.
2. "Teaching as a Creative Occupation." Paper presented to Gateway Council of English and Reading Teachers, Sonoma State University, Santa Rosa, CA, April 6.
3. "Creative Exploration of Literature Through Movement, Sculpture, Music, Writing, and Drama." Paper presented to Gateway Council of English and Reading Teachers, Sonoma State University, Santa Rosa, CA, April 7.
4. "Creative Behaviors of Disadvantaged Children and Youth." Paper presented to The Association for the Gifted, Council on Exceptional Children International, Dallas, TX, April 27.
5. "Education, the Individual and the Future." Seminars produced in co-operation with the Florida Citizens Committee for the Promotion of the Humanities, Saint Leo College, and the Univesity of South Florida, May 17.
6. "Images of Creatively Gifted Children." Hillsborough County Society for the Gifted, University of South Florida, Tampa, FL, May 17.
7. "Is Creativity Research in Education Dead?" Paper presented to Invitational Conference on Creativity: A Quarter Century Later, Center for Creative Leadership, Greensboro, NC, May 24-26.
8. "Developing Creative Potentials in a Multi-Ethnic Setting." Paper presented to Ninth Annual Reading Conference, Loyola University, New Orleans, LA, November 3.
9. "Let's Celebrate!" Creativity workshop, University of Georgia, Alumni Foundation,

Atlanta, GA, June 8.

10. "Educational Alternatives for Culturally Different Gifted Students." Paper presented to TAG-GAGE Southeastern Regional Conference on the Gifted, Atlanta, GA, December 1.
11. "The Role of Creativity in Mental Health in the Rural South." Speech given at Mental Health in the Rural South Symposium, Erskine College, Due West, SC.

Foreword(s)/Preface(s) and Book Reviews

1. Foreword. In B. Rowen, *The Children We See*. New York: Holt, Rinehart and Winston, Pp. v-vi.
2. *Creativity and the Teacher* by John Foster and *Creativity in Education* by Hugh Lytton. *Educational Studies*, ***3***, 239-241.
3. Book Review: "Man in Isolation and Confinement by J. E. Rassmussen (Ed.)." *Contemporary Psychology*, ***19****(10)*, 711-712.
4. Book Review: "Learning Together by E. M. Drews." *Phi Delta Kappan*, ***60****(3)*, 208-209.

1974

Books and Monographs

1. *Predicting Creative Behavior*. Buffalo, NY: D.O.K. Publishers.
2. (With J. P. Torrance) *Pode-se ensiwar creatividade?* Sao Paulo, Brazil: Editora Pedagogica e Universitaria Ltda.

Parts of Books, Contributions to Cooperative Volumes

(* Indicates a previously published journal article.)

1. *"Broadening Concepts of Giftedness in the '70s." In S. A. Kirk and S. E. Lord (Eds.), *Exceptional Children: Educational Resources and Perspectives*. Boston, MA: Houghton Mifflin, Pp. 186-196.
2. *"Creativity and Infinity." In G. A. Davis and T. F. Warren (Eds.), *Psychology of Education*. Lexington, MA: D. C. Heath, Pp. 431-439.
3. *"Conditions for Creative Learning." In E. Ostrovsky (Ed.), *Self-Discovery and Self-Awareness*. New York, NY: John Wiley, Pp. 76-78.
4. "Learning Styles and Creativity." In R. C. Sprinthall and N. A. Sprinthall (Eds.), *Educational Psychology: A Developmental Approach*. Reading, MA: Addison-Wesley, Pp. 367-379.
5. Ten Ways of Helping Young Children Gifted in Creative Writing and Speech. In R. B. Ruddel, E. J. Aheern, E. K. Hartson, and J. Taylor (Eds.), *Resources and Reading-Language Instruction*. Englewood Cliffs, NJ: Prentice-Hall, Pp. 250-261.

Articles in Professional and Research Journals

1. Status of Creativity Research: Early 1974. *Educational Trends* (India), ***8****(1-4)*, 3-7.
2. Cross-Cultural Studies of Creative Development in Seven Selected Societies. *Educational Trends* (India), ***8***, 28-38.
3. Career Patterns and Peak Creative Achievements of Creative High School Students Twelve Years Later. *Educational Trends* (India), ***8***, 114-128.

4. (With W. R. Nash) Creative Reading and Questioning Abilities of Young Children. *Journal of Creative Behavior*, ***8(1)***, 15-19.
5. Interscholastic Brainstorming and Creative Problem Solving Competition for the Creatively Gifted. *Gifted Child Quarterly*, ***18***, 3-7.
6. Differences Are Not Deficits. *Teachers College Record*, ***75(4)***, 471-488.
7. (With G. Halpin and G. Halpin) Relationships Between Creative Thinking Abilities and a Measure of the Creative Personality. *Educational and Psychological Measurement*, ***34***, 75-82.
8. Ways Gifted Children Can Study the Future. *Gifted Child Quarterly*, ***18***, 65-71.
9. Creative Young Women in Today's World. *Educational Horizons*, ***52(3)***, 117-122.
10. Readiness of Teachers of Gifted to Learn from Culturally Different Gifted Children. *Gifted Child Quarterly*, ***18***, 137-142.
11. Retooling Education for Creative Talent: How Goes It? *Gifted Child Quarterly*, ***18***, 233-239.
12. Creative Kids. *Growing Minds* (New Delhi, India), ***4(1-2)***, 23-27.
13. La Interaccion Dual en las Funciones de Pensamiento Creativo y de Solucion de Problemas. *La Educacion Hoy*, ***2(11)***, 413-416.
14. Creativity in Communication with Young Children. *Educational Trends* (India), ***9***, 1-11.
15. The Risk of Being a Great Teacher. *Educational Journal*, ***2***, 5-11.
16. Assessment of Disadvantaged Minority Group Children. *Educational Horizons*, ***52(4)***, 197-201.
17. How Isolated and Confined is Isolation and Confinement Research? *Contemporary Psychology*, *19*, 711-712.

Reports, Manuals, Handbooks, Tests, Instructional Materials

1. *Norms-Technical Manual: Torrance Tests of Creative Thinking*. (Revised Edition) Lexington, MA: Personnel Press/Ginn and Company.
2. *Directions and Scoring Manual for Figural Form B of Torrance Tests of Creative Thinking*. Lexington, MA: Personnel Press/Ginn and Company.
3. *Directions and Scoring Manual for Verbal Form A of Torrance Tests of Creative Thinking*. (Revised Edition) Lexington, MA: Personnel Press/Ginn and Company.
4. *Directions and Scoring Manual for Verbal Form B of Torrance Tests of Creative Thinking*. (Revised Edition) Lexington, MA: Personnel Press/Ginn and Company.
5. (With A. Hudgins and B. Frost) *1974 Supplement: Bibliography on the Torrance Tests of Creative Thinking*. Athens, GA: Georgia Studies of Creative Behavior.
6. *Preliminary Manual for "What Do You Believe About Disadvantaged Children?"* Athens, GA: Georgia Studies of Creative Behavior.
7. (With A. Hudgins) *Administration and Scoring Guide for the Squares Test* (1974 Revision). Athens, GA: Georgia Studies of Creative Behavior.
8. *Thinking Creatively in Movement and Action* (Research Edition). Athens, GA: Georgia Studies of Creative Behavior.
9. *Thinking Creatively about the Future* (Research Edition, Forms A and B). Athens, GA: Georgia Studies of Creative Behavior.
10. *Thinking Creatively about Learning and Teaching* (Research Edition, Forms A and B). Athens, GA: Georgia Studies of Creative Behavior.
11. *Notes on Sociodrama as a Creative Problem Solving Procedure for Studying the Future*. Athens, GA: Georgia Studies of Creative Behavior, University of Georgia.

12. *Resource Materials on an Orientation to Psychological Foundations of Education.* Athens, GA: Department of Educational Psychology, University of Georgia.
13. *Resource Materials on Testing Predictions: Instructional Plans Based on Learning Hypotheses.* Athens, GA: Department of Educational Psychology, University of Georgia.
14. *Georgia Studies of Creative Behavior: A Brief Summary of Activities and Results (1966-1974).* Athens, GA: Georgia Studies of Creative Behavior, University of Georgia.
15. *Preliminary Notes on Sociodrama as a Creative Problem Solving Approach to Studying the Future.* Athens, GA: Georgia Studies of Creative Behavior, University of Georgia.
16. *Future-Oriented Problem Solving.* Athens, GA: Georgia Studies of Creative Behavior, University of Georgia.
17. *What The University of Georgia Undergraduate Majors in Education Believe About Disadvantaged Children.* Athens, GA: Department of Educational Psychology, University of Georgia.
18. *Resource Materials for Teaching Skills of Observation.* Athens, GA: Department of Educational Psychology, University of Georgia.
19. (With W. R. Allen) *Images of the Future: Effects of Race, Sex, and Alienation.* Athens, GA: Department of Educational Psychology, University of Georgia.
20. *Torrance Tests of Creative Thinking* (Japanese translation).
21. *Punjabi translation of the Torrance Tests of Creative Thinking, Figural Form A.* Published with permission by Ripudaman Singh (originally published by Princeton, NJ: Personnel Press in 1966).
22. *Resource Materials on Using Information to Generate Hypotheses.* Athens, GA: Department of Educational Psychology, University of Georgia.
23. (With W. R. Nash) *Country Sounds Big City Sounds* (teacher's guide and recorded text accompanies reel-to-reel tapes). Lexington, MA: Ginn and Company.
24. (With W. R. Nash) *Zoo Sounds* (teacher's guide and recorded text accompanies reel-to-reel tapes). Lexington, MA: Ginn and Company.

Articles in Popular or Trade Type Journals and Magazines—Applications of Research

1. Recognize and Acknowledge Creative Talent. *Children's Music Leader*, *4*(2), 6-7.

Papers Presented at Seminars/Conferences

1. "Creativity and the Need to Communicate." Paper presented to Virginia Education Association Language Arts Conference, Charlottesville, VA, March 2.
2. "Sociodrama as a Vehicle for Creative Problem Solving." Address to 21st Annual Creative Problem Solving Institute, State University College, Buffalo, NY, June.
3. "What Happens When Children Read Creatively?" Address to Annual Peabody Reading Conference, George Peabody Teachers College, Nashville, TN, June 28.
4. "Developing the Skills of Creative Thinking." Address to Metropolitan Atlanta Private Schools, Lovett School, Atlanta, GA, August 30.
5. "How Shall We Look at Children?" Keynote address to Southwestern Association of Episcopal Schools, Galveston, TX, November 15.
6. "Marvels of the Mind: Creativity." Keynote address to Texas Association for the Education of Gifted Children, Austin, TX, November 17.
7. "Excellence Evaluation: Excellence of Daffodils is not Weight." Lecture presented at

University of Connecticut, Storrs, CT.

8. (With P. Ashton) "Integrating Educational Psychology into a Competency Based Program of Teacher Education." Paper presented at the Annual Meeting of the American Educational Research Association, Chicago, IL, April.
9. (With P. Ashton) "Personality and Creativity: A Multi-Factor Approach." Paper presented at the Annual Meeting of the American Educational Research Association, Chicago, IL, April.

Foreword(s)/Preface(s) and Book Reviews

1. *The Child's World of Make-Believe* by Jerome L. Singer. *American Educational Research Journal*, ***11***, 429-431.
2. *Perception and Understanding in Young Children* by Peter Bryant. *Opening Education*, ***1***, 42-44.
3. Interaction with a Textbook: Review of *Self-Discovery and Social Awareness* by E. Ostrovsky. *Contemporary Psychology*, ***20****(6)*, 486-487.

1975

Books and Monographs

1. (With W. F. White) *Issues and Advances in Educational Psychology*. (Second Edition) Itasca, IL: F. E. Peacock Publishers.
2. (With W. F. White) *Teacher's Guide for Issues and Advances in Educational Psychology*. Itasca, IL: F. E. Peacock Publishers.
3. Spanish Edition of *Creative Learning and Teaching*. Spain: Santillana S. A. De Ediciones.
4. Spanish Edition of *Creativity: Its Educational Implications*. Salamanca-Madrid, Spain: Ediciones Anaya.
5. Japanese Edition: *Encouraging Creativity in the Classroom*. Tokyo, Japan (Full bibliographic information unavailable).

Parts of Books, Contributions to Cooperative Volumes

(* Indicates a previously published journal article.)

1. "Mastery of Stress and Attainment of Human Dignity." In R. N. Cassel and R. L. Heichberger (Eds.), *Leadership Development: Theory and Practice*. North Quincy, MA: Christopher Publishing House, Pp. 180-211.
2. *"Predictive Validity of the Torrance Tests of Creative Thinking." In J. K. Dissinger and C. R. Arnold (Eds.), *Studies in the Psychological Foundations of Excpetionality*. Monterey, CA: Brooks/Cole, Pp. 20-25.
3. "Four Promising Practices for Teaching Gifted Disadvantaged Children." In J. F. Miley, I. S. Sato, et al., *Promising Practices: Teaching the Disadvantaged Gifted*. Ventura, CA: National/State Leadership Training Institute on the Gifted and Talented.
4. "Proposed Higher Education Alternatives: New Opportunity Centers." In *Alternate Admissions Criteria for Minority Students, Part II*. Atlanta, GA: Institute for Higher Educational Opportunity, Southern Regional Education Board.
5. *(With C. Walker and T. S. Walker) "A Cross-Cultural Study of the Perception of

Situational Causality." In H. C. Lindgren (Ed.), *Children's Behavior.* Palo Alto, CA: Mayfield Publishing Co.

6. *"Peer Influences on Preschool Children's Willingness to Try Diffcult Tasks." In H. C. Lindgren (Ed.), *Children's Behavior.* Palo Alto, CA: Mayfield Publishing Co.
7. *"Emerging Concepts of Giftedness." In W. B. Barbe and J. S. Renzulli (Eds.), *Psychology and Education of the Gifted.* New York, NY: John Wiley.
8. *"Problems of Highly Creative Children." In W. B. Barbe and J. S. Renzulli (Eds.), *Psychology and Education of the Gifted.* New York, NY: John Wiley.
9. *"Creative Teaching Makes a Difference." In W. B. Barbe and J. S Renzulli (Eds.), *Psychology and Education of the Gifted.* New York, NY: John Wiley.
10. *(With J. Khatena) "What Kind of Person Are You?": A Brief Screening Device for Identifying Creatively Gifted Adolescents and Adults." In W. B. Barbe and J. S. Renzulli (Eds.), *Psychology and Education of the Gifted.* New York, NY: John Wiley.
11. "Creativity Research in Education: Still Alive." In I. A. Taylor and J. W. Getzels (Eds.), *Perspectives in Creativity.* Chicago, IL: Aldine Publishing Company.
12. "Creativity and Infinity." In D. R. Clasen (Compiled), *Teaching for Thinking: Creativity in the Classroom Book of Readings.* Madison, WI: University of Wisconsin-Extension, Madison Education Extension Programs, Pp. 25-33.
13. "Integrating Abilities and Feeling in Learning." In P. Trapp and P. Himelstein (Eds.), *Readings on the Exceptional Child.* Itasca, IL: F. E. Peacock Publishers Inc., Pp. 331-337.
14. "Creative Kids." In M. Palardy (Ed.), *Teaching Today.* New York, NY: MacMillan Publishing Co., Pp. 388-392.

Articles in Professional and Research Journals

1. Assessing Children, Teachers and Parents Against the Ideal Child Criterion. *Gifted Child Quarterly, **19***, 130-139.
2. Some Guiding Principles in Evaluating Excellence. *Creativity Newsletter* (Aligarh Muslim University, India), ***3**(2)*, 1-10.
3. Sociodrama as a Creative Problem-Solving Approach to Studying the Future. *Journal of Creative Behavior, **9**(3)*, 183-188.
4. Are Creatively Gifted Children Different? *NCAGT Quarterly Journal, **1**(1)*, 5-10.
5. (With R. J. Goldman and J. P. Torrance) The Meaning and Relevance of Learning Readiness for Curriculum Construction in Christian Education: A Study Paper (with R. J. Goldman and J. P. Torrance). *Character Potential, **7**(3)*, 118-142.
6. Helping Gifted Children Through Mental Health Information and Concepts. *NCAGT Quarterly Journal, **3**(3)*, 16-22.
7. Creativity and Its Educational Implications for the Gifted. *NCAGT Quarterly Journal, **1**(4)*, 5-18.
8. (With R. J. Goldman and J. P. Torrance) The Meaning and Relevance of Learning Readiness for Curriculum Construction in Christian Education: A Study Paper. *Character Potential: A Record of Research, **7**(3)*, 118-142.
9. Working with Disadvantaged Gifted. *National/State Leadership Training Institute on the Fifted and Talented Bulletin, **2**(2)*, 4-5.

Reports, Manuals, Handbooks, Tests, Instructional Materials

1. *Four Promising Practices for Teaching Gifted Disadvantaged Students.* Athens, GA:

Georgia Studies of Creative Behavior.

2. *Preliminary Manual: Ideal Child Checklist*. Athens, GA: Georgia Studies of Creative Behavior, Department of Educational Psychology.
3. *Research Edition: Administration, Scoring for Norms Manual, Thinking Creatively in Action and Movement*. Athens, GA: Georgia Studies of Creative Behavior, Department of Educational Psychology, University of Georgia.
4. *Proposed Higher Education Alternatives: New Opportunity Centers in Alternate Admissions Criteria Minority Students, Part II*. Atlanta, GA: Institute for Higher Educational Opportunity, Southern Regional Educational Opportunity.
5. *Give the Gifted Children of the World a Chance to Solve Future Problems*. Athens, GA: Department of Educational Psychology, University of Georgia.
6. (With R. Peters, E. Phillips, and J. Loney) *Evaluation of the 1971 Dudley Park Creativity Workshop*. Athens, GA: Department of Educational Psychology, University of Georgia.
7. *In Defense of the Admission of Students in Educational Psychology to Doctoral Programs from Non-Degree and Unclassified Postgraduate Status*. Athens, GA: Department of Educational Psychology, University of Georgia.
8. *Notes on the World Coference on Gifted Children* (and related materials). Conference held in London, England, September 8-12, 1975.
9. *Preliminary Edition: Streamlined Scoring and Interpretation Guide and Norms Manual for Figural Form B, Torrance Tests of Creative Thinking*. Athens, GA: Georgia Studies of Creative Behavior, University of Georgia.
10. *Torrance Tests of Creative Thinking* (Japanese translation). Tokyo, Japan: Tokyo Shinni.

Articles in Popular or Trade Type Journals and Magazines—Applications of Research

1. Making Music Communicate. *Music Leader*, ***5**(2)*, 6-7.
2. Creative? Me? *Youth Leadership*, ***5**(2)*, 35-38.

Papers Presented at Seminars/Conferences

1. "Creativity: Today and Tomorrow." Address to annual meeting of the Southeastern Conference of Elementary School Principals, Birmingham, AL, February 20.
2. "What Are the Creative Reading Skills?" Address to Continuing Education Conference, Middle Tennessee State University, March 6.
3. "Use of Sociodrama in Teaching Creative Problem Solving Skills." Address to Continuing Education Conference, Middle Tennessee State University, March 6.
4. "Understanding and Developing Creative Reading Skills." Regional Reading Association and Cabell County Reading Council, Huntington, WV, March 19.
5. "Strategies for Teaching Gifted and Talented Students." Address to Project Gifted and Talented, Huntington, WV, March 20.
6. "In Special Education, More of the Same is Not Enough." Address to Fourth Annual Special Education Conference, Marshall University, Huntington, WV, March 20.
7. "Facilitating Creative Behavior in Schools." Address to National Association of School Psychologists, Atlanta, GA, April 1.
8. "Promising Practices for Teaching Disadvantaged Gifted Students." Address to National Training Laboratory on the Gifted and Talented, Atlanta, GA, April 4-6.
9. "Helping the Gifted to Explore the Future." Address to Georgia State University,

Atlanta, GA, April 3.
10. "Using the Creative Processes in Nursing Education." Address to School of Nursing, Grady Hospital, Atlanta, GA, April 4.
11. "Programming for the Disadvantaged Gifted Student." Address to Chattanooga Public Schools, Chattanooga, TN, April 7.
12. "Mainstreaming Gifted Students in the Middle School." Address to J. B. Brown Middle School, Chattanooga, TN, April 8.
13. "Programming for Gifted and Talented Students: More and Better of the Same is Not Enough." Address to University of Tennessee at Chattanooga, TN, April 8.
14. "Assessing the Strengths of Disadvantaged Students." Address to Evaluators in Vocational Education, State Department of Education, Macon, GA, July 30.
15. "Techniques and Strategies for Career Motivation." Address to Georgia Vocational Association, Atlanta, GA, August 7.
16. "Gifted Students Study the Future." Address to World Conference on Gifted Children, London, England, September 12.
17. "Adapting the Torrance Tests of Creative Thinking to Identify Gifted Handicapped Students." Address at Education Center for the Arts, New Haven, CT, December 10-11.
18. "New Developments in Creativity Research." Address at Southern Connecticut College, New Haven, CT, December 10.
19. "Issues on the Psychology of Giftedness." Address to Georgia Psychological Association, Atlanta, GA, December 9.
20. "To Solve Problems, Get Away from 'More and Better of the Same.'" Revision of the address presented before the Southeastern Conference of Elementary School Principals.

Foreword(s)/Preface(s) and Book Reviews

1. Interaction with a Textbook (Review of *Self-Discovery and Social Awareness* by Everett Ostrovsky). *Contemporary Psychology*, ***20***, 486-487.
2. Review of *Perception and Understanding in Young Children: An Experimental Approach* by Peter Bryant. *Opening Education*, ***1***, 42-44.

1976

Books and Monographs

1. (With R. E. Myers). La Ensenanza Creativa. *Creative Learning and Teaching*. New York, NY: Dodd, Mead.
2. *Guiding Creative Talent*. Reprint II. Huntington, NJ: Robert E. Krieger Publishing Company.
3. (With J. C. Gowan and G. D. Demos) *Implicaciones Educativas de la Creatividad*. Salamanca, Spain: Ediciones Anaya.

Parts of Books, Contributions to Cooperative Volumes

1. (With C. Bruch and T. Goolsby) "Gifted Children Study the Future." In J. Gibson and P. Chennels (Eds.), *Gifted Children Looking To Their Future*. London: Latimer New

Dimensions Ltd., Pp. 182-204.
2. "Problems of Highly Creative Children." In W. Barbe and J. Renzulli (Eds.), *Psychology and Education of the Gifted*. New York, NY: Irvington Publishers Inc., and Halsted Press, Pp. 214-219.
3. (With J. Khatena) "What Kind of Person Are You? A Brief Screening Device for Identifying Creatively Gifted Adolescents and Adults." In W. Barbe and J. Renzulli (Eds.), *Psychology and Education of the Gifted*. New York, NY: Irvington Publishers, Inc., and Halsted Press, Pp. 274-279.
4. "Creative Teaching Makes a Difference." In W. Barbe and J. Renzulli (Eds.), *Psychology and Education of the Gifted*. New York, NY: Irvington Publishers, Inc., and Halsted Press, Pp. 460-473.
5. "Can We Teach Children To Think Creatively?" In A. Biondi and S. Parnes (Eds.), *Assessing Creative Growth: Book II*. Great Neck, NY: Creative Synergetics Associates, Ltd., Pp. 131-167.
6. "Examples and Rationales of Test Tasks for Assessing Creative Abilities." In A. Biondi and S. Parnes (Eds.), *Assessing Creative Growth*. Great Neck, NY: Creative Synergetics Associates, Ltd., Pp. 53-68.
7. "Education, the Individual, and the Future." In S. Kaplan and D. Sisk (Eds.), *The Problems of the Individual in an Increasingly Urban Environment*. Tampa, FL: Florida Citizens Committee for the Promotion of the Humanities.
8. "Education and Creativity." In A. Rothenberg and C. R. Hausman (Eds.), *The Creativity Question*. Durham, NC: Duke University Press.
9. "Creativity and Mental Health." In S. Arieti and Chrzanowski (Eds.), *New Dimensions in Psychiatry*, Vol. 2. New York, NY: Basic Books.
10. "Ways to Enhance Creative Thinking." In D. E. Hamachek (Ed.), *Human Dynamics in Psychology and Education: Selected Readings* (Third Edition). Boston, MA: Allyn and Bacon.
11. "Evaluation of Two Career Education Approaches in the Psychological Foundations of Education." In A. F. Perrodin and R. Bruce (Eds.), *Helping Prospective Teachers Attain Career Education Teacher Competencies*. Athens, GA: College of Education, University of Georgia.

Articles in Professional and Research Journals

1. What Gifted Disadvantaged Children Can Teach Their Teachers. *North Carolina Association for Gifted and Talented Quarterly Journal*, ***2****(1)*, 19-26.
2. Os Bem-Dotados E O Futuro. *INEP of Brazil*, 325-339.
3. The School Principal and Creative Change. *North Carolina Association for the Gifted and Talented Quarterly Journal*, ***2****(3)*, 1-14.
4. ****Students of the Future: Their Abilities, Achievements, and Images of the Future. *Creative Child and Adult Quarterly*, *1*, 76-90.**
5. Give the Gifted Children of the World a Chance to Solve Future Problems. *Talents and Gifts*, ***18****(3)*, 22-24.
6. (With C. Bruch and J. P. Torrance) Interscholastic Futuristic Creative Problem Solving. *Journal of Creative Behavior*, ***10****(2)*, 117-125.
7. Future Careers for Gifted and Talented Students. *Gifted Child Quarterly*, ***20***, 142-156.
8. The School Principal and Creative Change: More of the Same is Not Enough. *Creative Child and Adult Quarterly*, ***1***, 76-90.

9. (With C. B. Bruch and T. M. Goolsby) Os ben-dotad os e o futuro. *Revista Brasileira de Estudos Pedagogicos*, ***61****(139)*, 319-346.
10. Creativity Testing in Education. *Creative Child and Adult Quarterly*, ***1****(3)*, 136-148.
11. The Creative Child in the Family: Each One is "Special." *Creative Child and Adult Quarterly*, ***1***, 195-198.

Reports, Manuals, Handbooks, Tests, Instructional Materials

1. *Creativity Testing in Education*. Athens, GA: Department of Educational Psychology, University of Georgia.
2. (With F. Kaufmann and J. P. Torrance) *Preliminary Feedback on Pre-Program Assessment of Needs*. For the 1976 Governor's Honors Program, North Georgia College. Athens, GA: Department of Educational Psychology, University of Georgia.
3. (With F. Kaufmann and J. P. Torrance) *You Are There! Year 2001 Images of Future Careers*. Athens, GA: Department of Educational Psychology, University of Georgia.
4. *Future Problem Solving and Career Education*. A publication of the Pre-Service Teacher Training in Career Education Project. Athens, GA: College of Education, University of Georgia.
5. (With A. Rungsinan) *Administration, Scoring, Norms Manual: Thinking Creatively in Action and Movement*. Athens, GA: Georgia Studies of Creative Behavior, Department of Educational Psychology, University of Georgia.
6. *Sociodrama in Career Education*. A publication of the Pre-Service Teacher Training Career Education Project. Athens, GA: College of Education, University of Georgia.
7. *Discovering and Using the Strengths of the Disadvantaged and Culturally Different in Career Education*. A publication of the Pre-Service Teacher Training in Career Education Project. Athens, GA: College of Education, University of Georgia.
8. (With J. Khatena) *Khatena-Torrance Creative Perception Inventory*. Chicago, IL: Stoelting Company.
9. (With T. O'Keefe, V. Hutchins, M. Wilson, F. Kaufmann, and O. E. Ball) Final Report: Pre-Service Training Project in Career Education for EPY 304 - Learning and Motivation. In *Helping Prospective Teachers Attain Career Education Teacher Competencies*. A publication of the Pre-Service Teacher Training in Career Education Project. Athens, GA: College of Education, University of Georgia, 17-199.
10. *A Preliminary Checklist of Creative Positives of Disadvantaged Students in Vocational Education*. Athens, GA: Georgia Studies of Creative Behavior, Department of Educational Psychology, University of Georgia.
11. (With F. Kaufmann, S. Gibbs, and J. P. Torrance) *Preliminary Report: Evaluation of the 1976 Institute of Career Development of the Governor's Honors Program*. Athens, GA: Department of Educational Psychology, University of Georgia, December. (For Georgia State Department of Education)
12. (With T. Riegel and C. Reynolds) *Preliminary Manual: Your Style of Learning and Thinking*. Athens, GA: Department of Educational Psychology, College of Education, University of Georgia.
13. (With F. Kaufmann, S. Gibbs, and J. P. Torrance) *Summary: Preliminary Evaluation of the 1976 Institute of Career Development of Governor's Honors Program*. Athens, GA: Department of Educational Psychology, College of Education, University of Georgia for Georgia State Department of Education, Division of Curriculum Development, and Atlanta, GA: Pupil Personnel Services, Office of Instructional Services.

14. (With T. O'Keefe, V. Hutchins, M. Wilson, F. Kaufmann, and O. E. Ball) *Evaluation of an Experimental Course in Educational Psychology with Applications in Career Education*. Athens, GA: Pre-Service Teacher Training in Career Education Project of Education, University of Georgia.
15. Spanish Translation of *Torrance Tests of Creative Thinking*. Lexington, MA: Personnel Press.
16. (With T. Riegel and C. R. Reynolds) *Preliminary Manual: Your Style of Learning and Thinking*. Athens, GA: Department of Educational Psychology, University of Georgia.
17. *Proposed Higher Educational Alternatives: New Opportunity Centers*. Athens, GA: Department of Educational Psychology, University of Georgia.
18. (With NEA Staff) *El creatividad: Una manera de aprender*. (Spanish translation of film-strip text with pictures.) National Education Association of the United States.
19. *Suggestions for Positive Verbal Reinforcers for Activities 1-4 of the Torrance Tests of Creative Thinking Verbal Form*. Unpublished paper.
20. *Sociodrama in Career Education*. Athens, GA: Pre-Service Teacher Training in Career Education Project, College of Education, University of Georgia.
21. *Discovering and Using the Strengths of the Disadvantaged and Culturally Different in Career Education*. Athens, GA: Pre-Service Teacher Training in Career Education Project, College of Education, University of Georgia.
22. *A Preliminary Checklist of Creative Positives of Disadvantaged Students in Vocational Education*. Athens, GA: Georgia Studies of Creative Behavior, Department of Educational Psychology.
23. *Handbook for Training Future Problem Solving Teams and Conducting Future Problem Solving Bowls*. Athens, GA: Georgia Studies of Creative Behavior, Department of Educational Psychology, University of Georgia. (Being used by leaders in World Council on Gifted Children in 20 different countries)
24. *Creatividate: Medidas, Testes e Avaliacacoes*. Sao Paulo, Brazil: IBRASA—Instituicao Brasileora de Difusao Cultural.
25. Japanese Edition: *Torrance Tests of Creative Thinking*. M. J. Kobayashi, Sophia University, Tokyo, Japan.
26. Marathi Edition: *Torrance Tests of Creative Thinking*. V. K. Kothurkar, University of Poona, Poona, India.
27. Iranian Edition: *Torrance Tests of Creative Thinking*. Jamal Haghigi-Mobarek, Iran.
28. *Discovering and Using the Strengths of the Disadvantaged and Culturally Different in Career Education*. Athens, GA: College of Education, University of Georgia.
29. (With J. P. Torrance) *The 1976-1977 Future Problem Solving Program*. Athens, GA: Department of Educational Psychology, University of Georgia.
30. (With S. Gibbs and O. E. Ball) *Cumulative Bibliography on the Torrance Tests of Creative Thinking*. Athens, GA: Georgia Studies of Creative Behavior, Department of Educational Psychology, University of Georgia.
31. (With J. Khatena) *Manual for Khatena-Torrance Creative Perception Inventory—CAT. #24534*. Chicago, IL: Stoelting Company.

Articles in Popular or Trade Type Journals and Magazines—Applications of Research

1. Where Am I Going? *Gifted Education Newsletter*, ***2****(2)*, 2-3.

2. Believing in Santa Claus Encourages Children to Think. *The Atlanta Journal/The Atlanta Constitution*, December 25, 1-8.

Papers Presented at Seminars/Conferences

1. "Career Education of Gifted and Talented Students: Their Images of the Future." Address to Commissioner's National Conference on Career Education, Houston, TX, November 9.
2. "Beyond Computers: Future Careers for Gifted Students." Address to Eastern Regional Conference on Gifted Children, Philadelphia, PA, March 26.
3. "Today's Students' Images of the Future." Paper prepared for Eighth Western Symposium on Learning: Creative Thinking. Bellingham, WA: Western Washington State College, October 8.
4. "Future Careers of Gifted and Talented Students." Address at Gifted and Talented Child Conference, Texas A and M University, College Station, TX, November 5.
5. "Sociodrama in a Creative Drama Program." Address to New Orleans Public Schools, New Orleans, LA, January 19.
6. "Implementation of a Model for Teaching Creative Thinking Skills." Address to Title I Teachers, New Orleans Public Schools, New Orleans, LA, January 20.
7. "Learning About the Future Through Language Arts." Address to National Conference on Language Arts in the Elementary School, National Council of English Teachers, Atlanta, GA, March 6.
8. "Using Creativity to Identify Gifted and Talented Children." Address to North Carolina Association for the Gifted, March 20.
9. "The Eternal Struggle Between Creativity and Conformity." Address to Athens Chapter, American Association of University Women, October 11.
10. "Uses of Creativity Testing in Education." Paper presented to Jones Fellows, College of Education, Texas Tech University, Lubbock, TX, November 4.
11. "College Students of the Future: Their Abilities, Achievements, and Images of the Future." Presentation to the Faculty and Students, Texas Tech University, Lubbock, TX, November 4.
12. "Creative Problem Solving Approaches as Teaching Methodologies." Seminar presentation to School of Environmental Design Faculty Educational Seminar, Calloway Building, University Botanical Gardens, Athens, GA, November 12.
13. "Creative Education and Futurism: Progress in Retooling." Address to First International Seminar on Creativity, Universidad Politecnica, Valencia, Spain, November 22-27. (Jointly sponsored by UNESCO and the Spanish Universities)
14. "Assessment of Creativity and Dance Education." Address to Regional Conference, National Dance Association, University of Georgia, Athens, GA, December 4.
15. (With L. M. Bolen) "The Influence on Creative Thinking of Locus of Control, Cooperation, and Sex." Paper presented to American Psychological Association, Washington, DC.

Foreword(s)/Preface(s) and Book Reviews

1. Foreword to F. E. Williams, *Teachers Without Fear*. Buffalo, NY: D.O.K. Publishers, Pp. 10-11.
2. Review. Arieti, Silvano. Book review of *Creativity: The Magic Synthesis*. New York, NY: Basic Book Publications.

3. Foreword. In R. B. Noller, S. J. Parnes and A. M. Biondi. *Creative Actionbook*. New York, NY: Charles Scribner's and Sons.
4. Synthesizing About the Magic Synthesis. *Contemporary Psychology*.
5. Is Stimulation Enough? A Review of *The Psychology of Creativity*, a 16mm Color Film. *Contemporary Psychology*, ***18***(12), 676–677.

1977

Books and Monographs

1. *Discovery and Nurturance of Giftedness in the Culturally Different*. Reston, VA: Council for Exceptional Children.
2. *Creativity in the Classroom: What Research Says to the Teacher*. Washington, DC: National Education Association.

Parts of Books, Contributions to Cooperative Volumes

1. "Creativity and Mental Health." In S. Arieti and G. Chrzanowski (Eds.), *New Dimensions in Psychiatry: A World View, Vol. 2*. New York, NY: John Wiley, Pp. 196-211.
2. "Today's Students' Images of the Future." In S. L. Carmean and B. L. Grover (Eds.), *Creative Thinking*. Eighth Western Symposium on Learning. Bellingham, WA: Western Washington University, Pp. 5-21.
3. "Ways to Enhance Creative Thinking." In D. E. Hamacheck (Ed.), *Human Dynamics in Psychology and Education: Selected Readings*. Boston, MA: Allyn and Bacon, Pp. 98-103.
4. "Creatively Gifted and Disadvantaged Gifted Students." In J. C. Stanley, W. C. George, and H. Scalano (Eds.), *The Gifted and the Creative: A Fifty Year Perspective*. Baltimore, MD: John Hopkins University Press, Pp. 173-196.
5. "Creativity and the Older Adult." In J. E. Montgomery, A. Vesely, and Bradley C. Courtenay (Eds.), *Environments, Creativity and Aging*. Athens, GA: Proceedings of the Fourth Annual Georgia Conference on Aging, University of Georgia Center for Continuing Education. (Also appeared in *The Creative Child and Adult Quarterly, 11*(3), 136–144.)
6. "After Twenty-five Years—What Do We Know About Creativity?" In B. Mehdi (Ed.), *Creativity in Teaching and Learning*. Report of workshop conducted at the Regional College of Education, Mysore, printed by G. H. Rama Rao at Mysore Printing and Publishing House, Mysore, India, Pp. 113-117.

Articles in Professional and Research Journals

1. Synthesizing about the "Magic Synthesis." *Contemporary Psychology*, ***22(4)***, 257-258.
2. Uses of Ceativity Testing in Education. *Gifted Child Quarterly*, ***1(3)***, 136-148.
3. (With C. R. Reynolds and T. Reigel) A Bibliography for Interdisciplinary Research on Lateral Cerebral Specialization and Interhemispheric Integration and Processing of Information. *The Gifted Child Quarterly*, ***21(4)***, 574-585.
4. (With F. Kaufmann) Teacher Education for Career Education of the Gifted and Talented. *Gifted Child Quarterly*, ***21(2)***, 176-185.
5. (With V. R. Phillips) Originality on the Rorschach Inkblot Test and the Creative Personality (abstract). *The Journal of Creative Behavior*, ***11(2)***, 144.

6. (With P. Ashton) Educational Psychology: The Crux of an Interdisciplinary Field-Based Approach to Teacher Education. *Teachers College Record*, ***78****(4)*, 437-445.
7. (With C. Grim) Race and Sex Bias in Interpreting Creativity Test Results of Children. *Journal of Creative Behavior*, ***11***, 212.
8. (With S. Holloway) The Sounds and Images Test as a Predictor of Musical Talent. *Journal of Creative Behavior*, ***11***, 148.
9. (With J. Morris) Ability to Use Freedom Allowed by Rules by Advantaged and Disadvantaged Children. *Journal of Creative Behavior*, ***11***, 215.
10. (With V. K. Phillips) Levels of Originality at Earlier and Later Stages of Creativity Test Tasks. *Journal of Creative Behavior*, ***11***, 147.
11. (With W. Rungsinan) Scoring Originality in Creativity Tests for Culturally Different Samples. *Journal of Creative Behavior*, ***121***, 217.
12. Evaluation Criteria Listed by E. Paul Torrance. *National/State Leadership Training Institute on the Gifted and Talented Bulletin*, ***4****(7)*, 1, 7.

Reports, Manuals, Handbooks, Tests, Instructional Materials

1. *Streamlined Scoring and Interpretation Guide and Norms Manual for Figural Form B, Torrance Tests of Creative Thinking*. Athens, GA: Georgia Studies of Creative Behavior, University of Georgia.
2. (With F. Kaufmann, S. Gibbs, O. E. Ball, and J. P. Torrance) *Evaluation of Career Awareness Component, Georgia Governor's Honors Program: A Follow-up Study of Participants and Their High School Teachers*. Athens, GA: Department of Educational Psychology, University of Georgia for Georgia State Department of Education, Division of Curriculum, and Atlanta, GA: Development and Pupil Personnel Services.
3. (With S. Williams and J. P. Torrance) *Handbook for Training Future Problem Solving Teams*. Athens, GA: Department of Educational Psychology, University of Georgia.
4. (With C. R. Reynolds, T. Reigel, and O. E. Ball) *Your Style of Learning and Thinking, Forms A and B: Preliminary Norms, Abbreviated Technical Notes, Scoring Keys, and Selected References*. Athens, GA: Department of Educational Psychology, University of Georgia.
5. (With C. R. Reynolds) *Results of Pre-Program Futures Attitude Survey and Thinking Creatively About the Future Career Awareness Component*. Report prepared for State Department of Education. Atlanta, GA.
6. *Uses of Creativity Testing in Education*. Athens, GA: Georgia Studies of Creative Behavior, Department of Educational Psychology, University of Georgia.
7. (With C. R. Reynolds, O. E. Ball, and J. P. Torrance) *Preliminary Feedback on Pre-Program Assessment of Needs: 1977 Governor's Honors Program, Career Awareness Component*. Paper prepared for State Department of Education of Georgia. Athens, GA: Department of Educational Psychology, University of Georgia.
8. (With O. E. Ball) *A Workbook for Streamlined Scoring of Figural Form A of the Torrance Tests of Creative Thinking*. Athens, GA: Georgia Studies of Creative Behavior, University of Georgia.
9. (With S. Gibbs) *Third Revision: Administration, Scoring and Norms Manual: Thinking Creatively in Action and Movement*. Athens, GA: Department of Educational Psychology, University of Georgia.
10. (With C. R. Reynolds, B. Jones, S. Gibbs, R. Y. Horng, and J. P. Torrance) *Evaluation*

of the 1977 Career Awareness Component of the Georgia Governor's Honors Program. Prepared for Division of Curriculum Development and Pupil Personnel Services, Office of Instructional Services, Atlanta, GA.

11. (With C. R. Reynolds, T. Riegel, and O. E. Ball) *Your Style of Learning and Thinking, Form B, Egyptian Translation*. Athens, GA: Department of Educational Psychology, University of Georgia.
12. (With F. Kaufmann, S. Gibbs, O. E. Ball, and J. P. Torrance) *Evaluation of Career Awareness Component of the Georgia Governor's Honors Program: A Follow-up Study of Participants and Their High School Teachers*. Athens, GA: Department of Educational Psychology, University of Georgia, for Georgia State Department of Education, Division of Curriculum Development and Pupil Personnel Services.
13. (With S. Gibbs and O. E. Ball) *Cumulative Bibliography on the Torrance Tests of Creative Thinking*. Athens, GA: Georgia Studies of Creative Behavior, University of Georgia.
14. *Images of the Future: Scenarios and Soliloquies of Future Careers*. Athens, GA: Department of Educational Psychology, University of Georgia.
15. *American Indian Adaptation of the Torrance Tests of Creative Thinking*. Duluth, MN: Indian Education Department, Duluth Indian School District #709.

Articles in Popular or Trade Type Journals and Magazines—Applications of Research

1. Making Music Communicate. *The Church Musician, **29**(2)*, 42-44.
2. (With Mainliner Staff) Creativity. *Mainliner*, 41.
3. (With National/State Leadership Training Institute on the Gifted and Talented Staff) Georgia Career Development Programs Evaluated. *National/State Leadership Training Institute on the Gifted and Talented Bulletin, **4**(4)*, 3.
4. Enriching Images of the Future for Gifted Students. *Gifted Education Newsletter, **3**(4)*, 3-9.

Papers Presented at Seminars/Conferences

1. "Gifted Children of the Future: Predictions and Proposed Solutions." Address to Second World Conference on Gifted Children, San Francisco, CA, August 2.
2. "Scenario of Gifted/Talented Education: 2002." Paper presented before annual meeting of the National Association for Gifted Children, Sheraton Island Harbor Hotel, San Diego, CA, October 20.
3. "Opinionnaire on Creative Learning and Teaching." In Bager Mehdi (Ed.), *Creativity in Teaching and Learning*. Report of workshop conducted at the Regional College of Education, Mysore, printed by G. H. Rama Rao at Mysore Printing and Publishing House, Mysore, India. Pp. 113-117.
4. "Dance Dynamics and Creativity Assessment." Paper prepared for the National Dance Association, Athens, GA.
5. "Preparing Teachers for Future Educational Settings." Paper presented before the Association of Teacher Educators, February 4, Hotel Hilton, Atlanta, GA.
6. "Encouraging Developments in Education." Address to Georgia Alumni Chapter, Pi Lambda Theta, Athens, GA, January 29.
7. "Science Teaching and Students' Images of the Future: Some Suggested Implications." Address before General Session, National Association for Research in Science

Teaching, Cincinnati, OH, March 22.

8. "Images of the Future and Their Implications for Education." Address to West Chester State College Conference on Gifted and Talented Children, West Chester, PA, April 5.
9. "Emerging Trends in the Education of Gifted and Talented Children." Address to West Chester State College Conference on Gifted and Talented Children, West Chester, PA, April 5.
10. "Images of the Future: Guides to Action!" Honors Day address, Georgia College at Milledgeville, GA, May 4.
11. "Assessing the Elusive Elements of Gifted Programs: Can It Be Done?" Address to Evaluation Institute, National Leadership Training Institutes for the Gifted and Talented, Los Angeles, CA, May 23.
12. "Use of Creative Problem Solving in Administering Evaluation Programs." Address to Evaluation Institute, National Leadership Training Institutes for the Gifted and Talented, Los Angeles, CA, May 24.
13. "Defining the Horizons of Gifted Education." Address to Evaluation Institute, National Leadership Training Institutes for the Gifted and Talented, Los Angeles, CA, May 25.
14. "Programs for Creatively Gifted Students." Address to Curriculum Institute, National Leadership Training Institutes for the Gifted and the Talented, Teachers College Columbia University, New York, NY, June 20.
15. "New Concepts in Identifying Creatively Gifted Students." Address to Curriculum Institute, National Leadership Training Institutes for the Gifted and the Talented, Teachers College Columbia University, New York, NY, June 20.
16. "Using Sociodrama in Solving Problems of Programming for Gifted Students." Address to Curriculum Institute, National Leadership Training Institutes, Teachers College Columbia University, New York, NY, June 20.
17. "New Scoring Concepts for Evaluating the Figural Form of the Torrance Tests of Creative Thinking." Address to Creative Problem Solving Institute, Buffalo, NY, June 21.
18. (With J. P. Torrance and S. L. Williams) "The Future Problem Solving Program." Address to Creative Problem Solving Institute, Buffalo, NY, June 22.
19. "Your Style of Learning and Thinking and Its Relationship to Creative Problem Solving." Address to Creative Problem Solving Institute, Buffalo, NY, June 23.
20. "Sociodrama as a Creative Problem Solving Process." Address to Creative Problem Solving Institute, Buffalo, NY, June 23.
21. "Development of Images of the Future." Invited address, American Psychological Association, San Francisco, CA, August 30.

Foreword(s)/Preface(s) and Book Reviews

1. Foreword. In F. E. Williams, *Teachers Without Fear*. Buffalo, NY: D.O.K. Publishers.

1978

Books and Monographs

1. (With S. Sato, A. Ando, and M. Kobayashi) *Research in Creativity in Japan in Honor of E. P. Torrance*. Tokyo, Japan: Tokyo Shini Publishers.
2. *Sociodrama and the Creative Process*. Book 14 of a 14-part series, produced by the Life Science Division of Geigy Pharmaceuticals.

Parts of Books, Contributions to Cooperative Volumes

1. "Peer Influences on Preschool Childrens' Willingness to Try Difficult Tasks." In B. S. McClinton and B. G. Meier (Eds.), *Beginnings: Pyschology of Early Childhood*. St. Louis, MO: The C. V. Mosby Company, Pp. 33-35.
2. "Ways of Discovering Gifted Black Children." In A. Y. Baldwin, G. H. Gear, and L. J. Lucito (Eds.), *Educational Planning for the Gifted: Overcoming Cultural, Geographic, and Socioeconomic Barriers*. Reston, VA: Council for Exceptional Children, Pp. 29-33.
3. "The Georgia Studies of Creative Behavior." In S. Sato and A. Onda (Eds.), *Creative Ability: Development and Evaluation*. Tokyo: Tokyo Shinri Company (Japanese Language).

Articles in Professional and Research Journals

1. A View from Myopia. *The Gifted Child Quarterly*, ***22(2)***, 157-159.
2. Five Models for Constructing Creativity Instructional Materials. *Creative Child and Adult Quarterly*, ***3***, 8-14.
3. (With O. E. Ball) Culture and Tendencies to Draw Objects in Internal Visual Perspective. *Perceptual and Motor Skills*, ***47***, 1071-1075.
4. (With L. Bolen) The Influence on Creative Thinking of Locus of Control, Cooperation, and Sex. *Journal of Clinical Psychology*, ***34(4)***, 903-907.
5. (With R. D. Clements and C. Dallas) Black Students and the Visual Arts. *The Negro Educational Review*, ***29(3-4)***, 255-263.
6. (With S. A. Kandil) Further Verification of High Creative Potential Among Emotional Disturbed and Behavior Disordered Children. *Journal of Creative Behavior*, ***12(4)***, 280.
7. (With C. R. Reynolds) Perceived Changes in Styles of Learning and Thinking (Hemisphericity) Through Direct and Indirect Learning. *The Journal of Creative Behavior*, ***12(4)***, 247-252.
8. Giftedness in Solving Future Problems. *Journal of Creative Behavior*, ***12(2)***, 75-86.
9. (With C. R. Reynolds) Images of the Future of Gifted Adolescents: Effects of Alienation and Specialized Cerebral Functioning. *Gifted Child Quarterly*, ***22***, 40-54.
10. (With J. Carter) Teacher Effect in Using Creative Thinking Exercises with Sixth Graders. *The Journal of Creative Behavior*, ***12(3)***, 217.
11. (With S. Mourad) Some Creativity and Style of Learning and Thinking Correlates of Guglielino's Self-Directed Learning Readiness Scale. *Psychological Reports*, ***43***, 1167-1171.
12. Gifted Children of the Future: Predictions and Proposed Solutions. *Creative Network*, ***4(3)***, 1-17.
13. Five Models for Constructing Creativity Instructional Materials. *Creative Child Quarterly*, ***3***, 8-14.
14. (With S. Mourad) Self-Directed Learning Readiness Skills of Gifted Students and Their Relationships to Thinking Creatively About the Future. *The Gifted Child Quarterly*, ***22(2)***, 180-186.
15. Giftedness in Solving Future Problems. *The Journal of Creative Behavior*, ***12(2)***, 75-86.
16. (With A. W. White) The Effects of Psychomotor Warm-up Upon Creative Thinking in Second Grade. *The Creative Child and Adult Quarterly*, ***3(4)***, 212-215.
17. Dare We Hope Again? *Gifted Child Quarterly*, ***22***, 292-312.

18. Healing Qualities of Creative Behavior. *Creative Child and Adult Quarterly*, ***3***, 146-158.
19. (With J. P. Torrance) Future Problem Solving: National Interscholastic Competition and Curriculum Project. *Journal of Creative Behavior*, ***12***, 87-89.
20. (With J. P. Torrance) Developing Creativity Instructional Materials According to the Osborn-Parnes Creative Problem Solving Model. *Creative Child and Adult Quarterly*, ***3***, 80-90.
21. (With S. C. Heindel) Performance and Hedonic Differences Under Dyadic and Individual Conditions. *Journal of Creative Behavior*, ***12***, 223.

Reports, Manuals, Handbooks, Tests, Instructional Materials

1. *Annual Reports: Department of Educational Psychology, Measurement and Research, 1966-1978.* Athens, GA: College of Education, University of Georgia.
2. (With C. R. Reynolds, O. E. Ball, and T. Riegel) *Your Style of Learning and Thinking, Revised Norms-Technical Manual.* Athens, GA: Department of Educational Psychology, University of Georgia.
3. *Effects of a Career Development Institute on the Images of the Future of Gifted Adolescents.* Athens, GA: Department of Educational Psychology, University of Georgia.
4. *Developing Future Career Images.* Athens, GA: Department of Educational Psychology, University of Georgia.
5. *Annual Report of the Department of Educational Psychology, Measurement and Research, 1977-1978.* Athens, GA: College of Education, Department of Educational Psychology, University of Georgia.
6. (With A. Vesely) *Art for Older Americans: A Partial Evaluation.* Prepared for Northeast Georgia Area Planning and Development Commission, 305 Research Drive, Athens, GA.
7. (With O. E. Ball) *A Workbook for Streamlined Scoring of Figural Form B, Torrance Tests of Creative Thinking.* Athens, GA: Georgia Studies of Creative Behavior, Department of Educational Psychology, University of Georgia.
8. *Searching for Images of Futures: Award Winning Scenarios.* Athens, GA: Program in Gifted/Talented Education, Department of Education, University of Georgia.
9. (With O. E. Ball) *Everything You Always Wanted to Know About Scoring the Figural A, Torrance Tests of Creative Thinking.* Athens, GA: Studies of Creative Behavior, Department of Educational Psychology, University of Georgia.
10. (With S. Mourad) *Some Preliminary Norms for Selected Groups of Gifted Children and Adults as Guglielmino's Self-Directed Learning Readiness Scale.* Athens, GA: Department of Educational Psychology, College of Education, University of Georgia.
11. (With J. P. Torrance, S. J. Williams, and R. Y. Horng) *Handbook for Training Future Problem Solving Teams.* Athens, GA: Department of Educational Psychology, University of Georgia.
12. Afrikaan Version of *Torrance Tests of Creative Thinking, Verbal and Figural Forms A and B.* Princeton, NJ: Personnel Press, Inc.
13. Hungarian Translation of the *Torrance Tests of Creative Thinking.* Princeton, NJ: Personnel Press, Inc.
14. Mexican Translation of the *Torrance Tests of Creative Thinking, Figural Form A and Verbal Form A.* Lexington, MA: Reproduced with permission of the Author by

Personnel Press, Inc.

15. *Award-Winning Scenarios, Future Problem Solving Program*. Athens, GA: Sponsored by Program in Gifted/Talented Education, Department of Educational Psychology, University of Georgia.
16. *Self-Directed Learning Readiness Scale*. Japanese Translation by S. Sato.
17. *Annual Report of Professional Activities*. Athens, GA: Department of Educational Psychology, University of Georgia.
18. (With J. P. Torrance and R. Y. Horng) *Scoring Guide: Future Problem Solving Program*. Athens, GA: Georgia Studies of Creative Behavior, Department of Educational Psychology, University of Georgia.
19. (With O. E. Ball) *Third Revision: Streamlined Scoring and Interpretation Guide and Norms Manual for Figural Form A, Torrance Tests of Creative Thinking*. Athens, GA: Georgia Studies of Creative Behavior, University of Georgia.

Articles in Popular or Trade Type Journals and Magazines—Applications of Research

1. Helping Your G/C/T Child Learn About the Future. *G/C/T*, ***1****(1)*, 25, 28-29.
2. Unique Needs of the Creative Child and Adult. The National Society for the Study of Education, Chicago, IL, 353-371.
3. Future Problem Solving Program 1978-79. *GSG Bulletin* (Georgia Supporters of the Gifted), No. 1, 13.

Papers Presented at Seminars/Conferences

1. "Dare We Hope Again." Paper presented for National Forum on Minority/Disadvantaged Gifted and Talented, U.S. Office of Education, Office of Gifted and Talented, Washington, DC.
2. "Torrance Tests of Creative Thinking." Paper presented for seminar with graduate students in education, University of Tokyo, Japan.
3. "Scenario of Gifted and Talented Education: 2003." Paper presented at annual Maryland ESEA Title IV public meeting on gifted and talented, Baltimore, MD: John Hopkins University, May 20.
4. "The Torrance Tests of Creative Thinking in Research." Paper presented to Japanese researchers in education and psychology, Tokyo, Japan, December 16.
5. "Healing Power of Creative Behavior." Abbreviated form of a paper presented at the National Association for Music Therapy, Atlanta, GA.
6. "Education for Fostering Creativity." Paper presented for Open Meeting, Japan Society for the Promotion of Science, Tokyo, Japan.
7. "Future of Differentiated Programs for the Education of Gifted and Talented Students." Presentation to Statewide Conference on Gifted Education, Maryland State Department of Education, Baltimore, MD, May 20.
8. "Who is Gifted?" Presentation to Programs for the Gifted and the Talented, Montclair School Board, Montclair, NJ, May 25.
9. (With F. Reisman) "Comparison of Children's Performance on the Torrance Tests of Creative Thinking and Selected Piagetian Tasks." Paper presented to CEC First World Conference on Future Special Education, Stirling, Scotland, June 29.
10. "The Scenario and Soliloquy Methods in Language Education." Address to Seventh Annual Conference on Teaching the English Language Arts, Georgia Center for

Continuing Education, July 28.

11. "Future Issues in Gifted/Talented Education." Presentation to Advanced Leadership Institute on the Gifted and the Talented, Honolulu, HI, August 7.
12. "Identification and Application of Creative Problem Solving Techniques to Individual Study Plans." Presentation to Advanced Leadership Training Institute on the Gifted and the Talented, Honolulu, HI, August 7.
13. "What Happens When Gifted Students Study the Future." Presentation to Association for the Gifted Midwest Regional Conference, Eastern Michigan University, Ypsilanti, MI, October 13.
14. "Healing Qualities of Creative Behavior and the Music Therapist." Presentation to National Association of Music Therapists, Marriott Motor Hotel, Atlanta, GA, November 13.
15. "Education for Creativity." Open lecture for education professors, researchers, and teachers, Tokyo, Japan, December 14.
16. "A Model for Studying Creative Behavior." Presentation to Department of Educational Psychology, University of Tokyo, Japan, December 15.
17. "Measurement in Creativity Research." Presentation to Tokyo Education and Psychology Research Association, Tokyo, Japan, December 16.
18. "Training for Creative Achievement." Presentation to Center for Creative Development, Institute for Business Management, Tokyo, Japan, December 18.
19. "New Developments in Creativity Research." Open seminar for educators, psychologists, and journalists, Osaka, Japan, December 25.

Foreword(s)/Preface(s) and Book Reviews

1. Foreword. In *Advantaged/Disadvantaged Gifted.* (Presentation for the Third National Conference on Disadvantaged.) National/State Leadership Training Institute of the Gifted and Talented, Ventura County, CA. Pp. xi-xii.
2. Foreword. In J. Khatena, *The Creatively Gifted Child: Suggestions for Parents and Teachers.* New York, NY: The Vantage Press.

1979

Books and Monographs

1. *The Search for Satori and Creativity.* The Creative Education Foundation, Inc., in association with Creative Synergetic Associates, Ltd. Buffalo, NY: Bearly Limited (also translated into Japanese).
2. (With S. Sato) *U.S. and Japan Comparison of Your Styles of Learning and Thinking.* Japan Education Press.
3. *The Search for Satori and Creativity.* (Japanese translation) Buffalo, NY: Creative Education Foundation, Inc., in association with Great Neck, NY: Synergetic Associates, Ltd.
4. *Children Soar: Seeking for Creativity* (Japanese). Tokyo: Japanese Britannica.
5. *Kodomo wa Haneru—Sozousei no Kyouiku o Motomete.* (Translated by Saburo Sato). All articles by E. P. Torrance on young children. Tokyo: Nippon Britannica.
6. *Creativity of Young Children* (Japanese Language). Osaka, Japan: Reed Publishing Company and Encyclopedia Britannica.

Parts of Books, Contributions to Cooperative Volumes

1. "Unique Needs of the Creative Child and Adult." In A. H. Passow (Ed.), *The Gifted and Talented.* Chicago, IL: University of Chicago Press.
2. "Some Creative Dimensions to the Issue of Identification." In J. J. Gallagher, J. C. Gowan, A. H. Passow, and E. P. Torrance (Eds.), *Issues in Gifted Education.* Ventura County Superintendent of Schools Office, Ventura, CA, (N/SLTI/GT), Pp. 1-26.
3. "Future Problem Solving." In *"Futures" in Gifted Education.* The Fourth Annual Conference, Western Exchange for Gifted and Talented, Idaho State Department of Education.
4. (With C. R. Reynolds) "Images of the Future of Gifted Adolescents: Effects of Alienation and Specialized Cerebral Functioning." In J. C. Gowan, J. Khatena, and E. P. Torrance (Eds.), *Educating the Ablest.* Itasca, IL: F. E. Peacock Publishers, Inc., Pp. 431-445.
5. (With C. Bruch and J. A. Morse) "Improving Predictions of the Adult Creative Achievements of Gifted Girls by Using Autobiographical Information." In J. C. Gowan, J. Khatena, and E. P. Torrance (Eds.), *Educating the Ablest.* Itasca, IL: F. E. Peacock Publishers, Inc., Pp. 366-383.
6. "Creative Positives of Disdvantaged Children and Youth." In J. C. Gowan, J. Khatena and E. P. Torrance (Eds.), *Educating the Ablest.* Itasca, IL: F. E. Peacock Publishers, Inc., Pp. 341-365.
7. "Creativity and its Educational Implications for the Gifted." In J. C. Gowan, J. Khatena and E. P. Torrance (Eds.), *Educating the Ablest.* Itasca, IL: F. E. Peacock Publishers, Inc., Pp. 298-311.
8. (With R. E. Myers) "Teaching Gifted Elementary Pupils Research Concepts and Skills." In J. C. Gowan, J. Khatena and E. P. Torrance (Eds.), *Educating the Ablest.* Itasca, IL: F. E. Peacock Publishers, Inc., Pp. 131-138.
9. "Gifted Children of the Future: Predictions and Proposed Solutions." In J. J. Gallagher (Ed.), *Gifted Children: Reaching Their Potential.* Jerusalem, Israel: Kollek and Sons, Ltd., Pp. 55-84.
10. "A Three-Stage Model for Teaching for Creative Thinking." In A. E. Lawson (Ed.), *The Psychology of Teaching for Thinking and Creativity.* Columbus, OH: ERIC Clearinghouse for Science, Mathematics and Environmental Education (7th AETS Yearbook), Pp. 226-253.
11. "Future Problem Solving." In *Future in Gifted Education.* The Fourth Annual Conference, Western Exchange for Gifted and Talented, Idaho State Department of Education.

Articles in Professional and Research Journals

1. (With S. Mourad) Role of Hemisphericity in Performance on Selected Measures of Creativity. *The Gifted Child Quarterly,* ***23****(1),* 44-54.
2. (With S. Mourad) Construct Validity of the Self-Directed Learning Readiness Scale. *Journal for the Education of the Gifted,* ***3***, 93-104.
3. Developing Creativity Instructional Materials According to the Sociodrama Model. *Creative Child and Adult Quarterly,* ***4***, 9-19.
4. (With C. Bruch and D. G. Langham) Genesa as an Aid to Incubation/Imagery and Brain/Mind Function. *Gifted Child Quarterly,* ***23****(4),* 19.
5. (With N. Dehlavi) Iranian Mothers' Perception of the Ideal Child. *GATE (Gifted and Talented Education),* ***1***, 107-111.

6. Education for the Gifted in 2004. *The Education Digest*, ***44****(8)*, 51-53.
7. Images of the Future. *Language Arts*, ***56****(3)*, 228-229.
8. ****An Instructional Model for Enhancing Incubation. *Journal of Creative Behavior*, *13(1)*, 23-39.**
9. Intensive Approach Alters Learning Styles in Gifted. *Brain and Mind*, ***4****(20)*, 2.
10. (With J. P. Torrance). Future Problem Solving: National Interscholastic Competition and Curriculum Project. *Journal of Creative Behavior*, ***12****(2)*, 87-89.
11. The Creative Challenge of Graduate Students in Education in Japan. *Osaka City University, Education Journal*, *5*, May, 1-3.
12. Creative Education in the Future. *Shyougaku Kan Press*, ***34***, 90-102.
13. Education for the Gifted in 2004. *The Education Digest*, ***44****(8)*, 51-53.
14. (With S. Sato) Figural Creative Thinking Abilities of United States and Japanese Majors in Education. *Creative Child and Adult Quarterly*, ***4***, 216-221.
15. Commentary: Images of the Future. *Language Arts*, ***56****(3)*, 228-229.
16. Resistance to Premature Gestalt Closure as a Possible Indicator of Incubation Ability (abstract). *The Journal of Creative Behavior*, ***13****(1)*, 59.
17. Preface. Photographs of children in "Creative Kindergarten." *Journal of Research and Development in Education*, ***12****(3)*, University of Georgia.
18. Lessons from "Giftedness and Creativity From a Nation of 110 Million Overachievers." *The Yomini*, Osaka, Japan, October.
19. (With C. R. Reynolds and B. Kaltsounis) A Children's Form of Your Style of Learning and Thinking: Preliminary Norms and Technical Data. *The Gifted Child Quarterly*, ***23****(4)*, 757-766.
20. Looking to the Future: Scenario of G/C/T Education: 2004. *G/C/T*, ***2****(6)*, 2, 4, 56-57.
21. Styles of Learning and Thinking—Comparative Studies Between Japanese and American Students. *Naigai Kyoiku* (Jiji Press), No. 3090, 10-15 (Japanese language).
22. The Need for Self-Directed Learning in Education. *Bunken Journal*, June, No. 169, 12-28 (Japanese language).
23. Psychology of Educating for the Future. *Research Journal, Institute of Education, Osaka Teachers College*, ***14***, 5-13 (Japanese language).
24. (With C. R. Reynolds) Perceived Changes in Styles of Learning and Thinking (Hemisphericity) Through Direct and Indirect Training. *Journal of Creative Behavior*, ***12***, 247-252.
25. Differences in Japanese and United States Styles of Thinking. *Creative Child and Adult Quarterly*, ***4***, 145-151.
26. Evaluating the Elusive Aspects of Career Education. *Journal of Research and Development in Education*, ***12****(3)*, 93-102.

Reports, Manuals, Handbooks, Tests, Instructional Materials

1. (With N. Sandwith, S. Gibbs, O. E. Ball, B. Frost, and D. Frost) *Cumulative Bibliography on the Torrance Tests of Creative Thinking*. Athens, GA: Georgia Studies of Creative Behavior, Department of Educational Psychology, University of Georgia.
2. *Scoring Guide: Future Problem Solving Program*. Lincoln, NE: Future Problem Solving Program, Box 94987, Centennial Mall South.
3. *U.S. and Japan Comparison on SOLAT Scale*. Osaka (August), Tokyo (September). Mainichi Press.
4. (With J. P. Torrance, S. J. Williams, R. Y. Horng, and A. Crabbe) *Handbook for Training*

Future Problem Solving Teams. Lincoln, NE: Future Problem Solving, Box 94987, 301 Centennial Mall South.

5. *Some Highlights from the Georgia Studies of Creative Behavior: 1970-1979*. Athens, GA: Department of Educational Psychology, University of Georgia.
6. Report to Japan Society for the Promotion of Science.
7. *Annual Report of Professional Activities*. Athens, GA: Department of Educational Psychology, University of Georgia.
8. (With J. P. Torrance) *Mastering and Using Creative Problem Solving*. Athens, GA: Department of Educational Psychology, University of Georgia.

Articles in Popular or Trade Type Journals and Magazines—Applications of Research

1. Looking Into the Future: Scenario of G/C/T Education, 2004. *G/C/T*, ***2****(4)*, 56-57.
2. (With O. E. Ball) Which Gifted Students Apply What They Learn in Special Programs? *G/C/T/Quarterly*, ***7***, 7-9, 62.
3. Future Issues in Gifted/Talented Education. *National/State/Leadership Training Institute on the Gifted and Talented*, ***6****(4)*, 3.
4. Would You Like to Become a Writer? *Wambat (A Journal of Young People's Writing and Art)*, ***1****(1)*, 6.
5. I Remember G.M.C... *Through These Gates: Georgia Military College, 1879-1979 (Centennial Issue)*, ***1****(2)*, 14-15.
6. Education for "Creativity": An Interview with E. P. Torrance. (Japanese interviewer S. Inui) *Private College News (Shigaku News)*.
7. D. Lynch (Ed.), The Search for Satori and Creativity by E Paul Torrance is reviewed. *The Creativity Newsletter*, ***4***.
8. S. Sato, Profile of E. Paul Torrance. *Jiji Press*, October, 10-15.
9. S. Sato, Interview with E. Paul Torrance. *Shigaku News Company*, ***214***, 3-27.

Papers Presented at Seminars/Conferences

1. "The Necessity of Self-Directed Learning in Education." Address presented at Osaka Teachers College, Educational Research Center, February. *Burken Journal No. 169*, June, Burken Publishing Co.
2. Lecture by Paul Torrance and panel discussion. *Research Journal, Institute of Education, Osaka Teachers College, 14*, 2-38.
3. "Conditions for Creative Development." Paper presented at Annual Meeting of New York State Music Educations, New York State University College at Potsdam.
4. "Education Osaka (Kyoiku Osaka)." Looking for a new approach to deal with (educational) problems. The summary of the lecture by E. Paul Torrance. Osaka, Japan: Osaka City Board of Education.
5. "Role of Measurement and a Model for Studying Creative Behavior." Presentation to graduate students and faculty, Osaka City University, Japan, January 9.
6. "Nature of Creative Thinking and Its Assessment." Presentation to Educational Foundations, Osaka City University, Japan, January 10.
7. "Education for Creative Development." Presentation to Educational Psychology Department, Kansai University, Osaka, Japan, January 11.
8. "Measurement and Conceptualization of Creative Behavior." Presentation to School of Education, Kensei-Gakuin University, January 12.

9. "Parents and Teachers in Educating for Creativity." Lecture Series, Nishinomiya School Board, Nishinomiya, Japan, January 13.
10. "Encouraging the Creativity of Preschool Children." Presentation at Otani-Kyushu Junior College, Kurume, Japan, January 16.
11. "Role of Measurement in the Study of Creative Behavior." Presentation to School of Education, Hiroshima University, Hiroshima, Japan, January 22.
12. "Creative Behavior of Elementary School Children." Presentation to Nara Women's University, Nara, Japan, January 23.
13. "Roles of Teachers and Administrators in the Development of Creative Thinking Skills." Presentation at Nara Prefecture In-Service Education Center, Nara, Japan, January 24.
14. "Education for Creative Development." Presentation to School of Education, Shimane University, Matsue, Japan, January 27.
15. "Parents and Teachers in the Creative Development of Children." Presentation to parents and teachers open meeting, Matsue, Japan, January 27.
16. "Role of Measurement in Developing a Science of Creative Behavior." Presentation at Osaka (National) Graduate University, Faculty of Human Sciences, Osaka, Japan, January 29.
17. "Psychotherapeutic Effects of Creative Behavior." Presentation to Japan Association of Counselors, Noguchi Memorial Hall, Tokyo, Japan, January 30.
18. "Encouraging the Creativity of Kindergarten Children." Presentation to Yokohama Kindergarten Teachers Association, Yokohama, Japan, January 31.
19. "The Role of Administrators in Educating for Creativity in the Kindergarten." Presentation to Kindergarten Directors' Association, Hakone, Japan, February 1.
20. "New Developments in Creativity Research." Presentation at Osaka City University, Osaka, Japan, February 6.
21. "Understanding and Encouraging the Creativity of Kindergarten Children." Presentation to Annual In-Service Education Program, New Osaka City Kindergarten Association, February 7.
22. "Creativity and the Development of Readiness for Self-Directed Learning." Osaka National College of Education, February 9.
23. "Parents and Teachers in the Creative Development of Kindergarten Children." Presentation to kindergarten parents and teachers, Uzi, Japan, February 13.
24. "Curriculum Reforms of the 1960s and '70s and Predictions for the 1980s." Presentation to School of Education, Nagoya University, Nagoya, Japan, February 14.
25. "Education for Creative Development of Young Children." Presentation to Eastern Japan Kindergarten Association, Kyoto, Japan, February 15.
26. "Parents and Teachers in the Creative Development of Kindergarten Children." Presentation to parents and teachers, Kitano Temma Kindergarten, Kyoto, Japan, February 16.
27. "Keeping Alive the Creativity of Children Through the Primary School." Presentation to parents and teachers, Tarui Primary School, near Wakayama, Japan, February 17.
28. "Encouraging the Creativity of Preschool Children." Presentation to Institute for Preschool Education and National Taiwan Normal University, Taipei, Taiwan, February 24.
29. "Keeping Alive the Creativity of Preschool Children." Presentation at Institute for Preschool Years, Pintung Teachers College, Pintung, Taiwan, February 25.
30. "Keeping Alive the Creativity of High School Students." Presentation at Kaosiung

Teachers College, Kaosiung, Taiwan, February 26.

31. "Education for Creativity." Kwang-Hua School, Tainan, Taiwan, February 26.
32. "Current Developments in the Education of Gifted and Talented Students." Presentation at Taiwan Provincial College of Education at Changhua, Taiwan, February 27.
33. "The Challenge of Creatively Gifted Children." Presentation to Piedmont Consortium on Gifted and Talented Students, Greenwood, SC, March 23.
34. "Role of Creative Thinking in the Reading Process." Presentation to International Reading Association, Atlanta, GA, April 25.
35. "Sociodrama and Future Problem Solving." Presentation at National Future Problem Solving Bowl, University of Nebraska at Lincoln, NE, April 19-21.
36. "The Scenario and Sociodramatic Techniques in Studying the Future." Presentation at National Future Problem Solving Bowl, University of Nebraska at Lincoln, NE, April 19-21.
37. "Goals of the Future Problem Solving Program." Presentation at National Future Problem Solving Bowl, University of Nebraska at Lincoln, NE, April 19-21.
38. "Creativity and Hemisphericity." Presentation at College of Education, University of Nebraska at Omaha, NE, April 19.
39. "Educational Needs of the Gifted and the Talented." Presentation at College of Education, University of Nebraska at Omaha and the Omaha Public Schools, April 18.
40. "Serving the Unmet Needs of Gifted Children." Presentation to Clarke County Association for Gifted Children, May 21.
41. "The Future Problem Solving Program." Presentation at Conference on Futures in Gifted Education, Western Exchange for Gifted, Idaho State Department of Education, Coeur d'Alene, ID, May 10 (Telelecture).
42. "Creativity and Well Being in Japan." Presentation at Creative Problem Solving Institute, New York State University College at Buffalo, NY, June 15-22.
43. "Evaluating the Future Problem Solving Program." Presentation at Institute on Gifted and Talented, University of Connecticut, Storrs, CT, August 10-11.
44. "Some Lessons on Creativity and Giftedness from a Nation of 115 Million Overachievers." Presentation at Institute on Gifted and Talented, University of Connecticut, Storrs, CT, August 10-11.
45. "Measuring Creative Thinking." Presentation at Conference on the Education of Gifted Children, Kelowna-Rutland Club of Rotary International, Kelowna, B.C., Canada, September 29.
46. "The Future of Education for the Gifted." Presentation at Conference on the Education of Gifted Children, Kelowna-Rutland Club of Rotary International, Kelowna, B.C., Canada, September 29.
47. "Educating for Fostering Creativity." Presentation at Conference on Applied Thinking Skills, Rochester Public Schools, Rochester, NY, October 11.
48. "More Than the Ten Rational Thinking Processes." Presentation at Conference on Applied Thinking Skills, Rochester Public Schools, Rochester, NY, October 11.
49. "The Nature of Creativity: Its Process." Presentation to New York State Association of Music Educators, State University College at Potsdam, NY, October 12.
50. "Teaching as a Creative Occupation." Presentation to New York State Association of Music Educators, State University College at Potsdam, NY, October 13.
51. "Measurement of Creative Potential." Presentation to New York State Association of

Music Educators, State University College at Potsdam, NY, October 13.

52. "Helping Gifted Students Enlarge, Enrich, and Make More Accurate Their Images of the Future." Alabama Association for Gifted and Talented, Mobile, AL, November 3.
53. "Learning About Giftedness and Creativity in a Nation of 115 Million Overachievers." Alabama Association for Gifted and Talented, Mobile, AL, November 3.
54. (With L. K. Hall) "Assessing the Further Reaches of Creative Potential." Presentation at Conference on Creative Intelligence, Marahishi International University, Firfield, IA, December 7.

Foreword(s)/Preface(s) and Book Reviews

1. Book Review: *Education and Ecstasy* by G. B. Leonard. *The Collegiate Teacher*, ***1****(1)*, 104-105.

1980

Parts of Books, Contributions to Cooperative Volumes

1. "Georgia Studies of Creative Behavior: A Brief Summary of Results." In M. K. Raina (Ed.), *Creativity Research: International Perspective*. New Delhi, India: Publication Department, National Council of Educational Research and Training.
2. "After Twenty-five Years, What Do We Know About Creativity?" In M. K. Raina (Ed.), *Personal Perspective*. New Delhi, India: Publication Department, National Council of Educational Research and Training.
3. "A Three-Stage Model for Teaching for Creative Thinking." In A. E. Lawson (Ed.), *The Psychology of Teaching for Thinking and Creativity*. Columbus, OH: ERIC Clearinghouse for Science, Mathematics and Environmental Education (7th AETS Yearbook), Pp. 226-253.
4. "Psychology of Gifted Children and Youth." In W. M. Cruickshank (Ed.), *Psychology of Exceptional Children and Youth*. Englewood Cliffs, NJ: Prentice-Hall, Pp. 469-496.
5. "Extending the Identification of Giftedness: Other Talents, Minority and Handicapped Groups." In *Educating the Preschool/Primary Gifted and Talented*. S/N-LTI-G/T, Ventura County School System, CA, Pp. 43-58.

Articles in Professional and Research Journals

1. (With D. Treffinger and O. E. Ball) Guidelines for Training Creativity Test Administrators and Scorers. *Journal of Creative Behavior*, ***14****(1)*, 47-55.
2. D. Lynch, Education's Paul Torrance Says It Is Time to Encourage Supra-Rational Creativity. *FOCUS Creativity*, ***2****(3)*, 4.
3. J. Paul. Educating the Gifted. (An interview with E. Paul Torrance) *American Educator*, ***4****(2)*, 6-9.
4. (With F. K. Reisman) Alternative Procedures for Assessing Intellectual Strengths of Young Children. *Psychological Reports*, ***46***, 227-230.
5. Japanese Attitudes on Giftedness and Creativity. *The Education Digest*, ***45****(9)*, 29-32.
6. ****Creativity and Futurism in Education: Retooling. *Education, 100(4)*, 298-311.**
7. (With L. K. Hall) Assessing the Further Reaches of Creative Potential. *The Journal of Creative Behavior*, ***14****(1)*, 1-19.

8. Lessons About Giftedness and Creativity From a Nation of 115 Million Overachievers. *Gifted Child Quarterly*, ***24(1)***, 10-16.
9. Japanese Attitudes on Giftedness and Creativity. *The Education Digest*, ***45(9)***, 29-32.
10. (With R. V. Horng) Creativity and Style of Learning and Thinking Characteristics of Adaptators and Innovators. *Creative Child and Adult Quarterly*, ***5(2)***, 80-85.
11. (With W. R. Allen) Racial and Sex Differences in Images of the Future. *Perceptual and Motor Skills*, ***50***, 285-286.
12. Educating the Gifted in the 1980's: Removing the Limits on Learning. *Journal for the Education of the Gifted*, ***4***, 43-49.
13. Growing Up Creatively Gifted: A 22-Year Longitudinal Study. *The Creative Child and Adult Quarterly*, ***5(3)***, 148-159.
14. (With S. A. Kandil) Effects of Verbal Reinforcement and Race on the Performance of Emotionally Handicapped Children. *Exceptional Children*, ***46(4)***, 296-297.
15. Ten Questions About Creativity (translated into Japanese by S. Sato). *Reed*, ***168***, 36-40.
16. More Than the Ten Rational Processes. *Creative Child and Adult Quarterly*, ***5***, 9-19.
17. (With O. E. Ball) Effectiveness of New Materials Developed for Training the Streamlined Scoring of the Torrance Tests of Creative Thinking, Figural A and B Forms. *The Journal of Creative Behavior*, ***14(3)***, 199-203.

Reports, Manuals, Handbooks, Tests, Instructional Materials

1. *Addresses and Present Occupations of Teachers and Students Participating in the University of Minnesota and Sidney Pratt Elementary School Longitudinal (1958-1980) Study of Creative Behavior.* Athens, GA: Georgia Studies of Creative Behavior, University of Georgia.
2. (With O. E. Ball) *A Workbook for Streamlined Scoring of Figural Form A of the Torrance Tests of Creative Thinking.* Athens, GA: Georgia Studies of Creative Behavior, Department of Educational Psychology, University of Georgia.
3. *Annual Report of Professional Activities of Alumni Foundation, Distinguished Professor E. Paul Torrance, April 1979-April 1980.* Athens, GA: Department of Educational Psychology, University of Georgia.
4. *Torrance Tests of Creative Thinking (TTCT) and Thinking Creatively With Sounds and Words (TCSW).* Bensenville, IL: Scholastic Testing Service, Pp. 19-20.
5. *Preliminary Norms-Technical Manual for Your Style of Learning and Thinking - Form C.* Athens, GA: Department of Educational Psychology, University of Georgia.
6. *Assessing Creative Potential.* Bensenville, IL: Scholastic Testing Service.
7. (With O. E. Ball) *Fourth Revision: Streamlined Scoring and Interpretation Guide and Norms Manual for Figural Form A, Torrance Tests of Creative Thinking.* Athens, GA: Georgia Studies of Creative Behavior, University of Georgia.
8. (With J. P. Torrance) *Participating Students Evaluate the 1979-1980 Georgia Future Problem Solving Program.* Athens, GA: Georgia Studies of Creative Behavior, University of Georgia.
9. (With J. P. Torrance) *Want a Future Problem Solving Bowl? Decisions That Have to Be Made.* Athens, GA: Georgia Studies of Creative Behavior, University of Georgia.
10. Italian Translation of the *Torrance Tests of Creative Thinking*. Bensenville, IL: Scholastic Testing Service.
11. (With T. H. Wu and T. Ando) *Preliminary Norms-Technical Manual: Demonstrator Form A, Torrance Tests of Creative Thinking.* Athens, GA: Georgia Studies of

Creative Behavior, University of Georgia.

12. *Administration, Scoring, and Norms Manual: Thinking Creatively in Action and Movement, Fifth Revision.* Athens, GA: Georgia Studies of Creative Behavior, Department of Educational Psychology, University of Georgia.

13. (With O. E. Ball) *Streamlined Scoring and Interpretation Guide and Norms Manual for Figural Form A, Torrance Tests of Creative Thinking, Fourth Revision.* Athens, GA: Georgia Studies of Creative Behavior, University of Georgia.

14. (With C. R. Reynolds) *Preliminary Norms-Technical Manual for Your Style of Learning and Thinking—Form C.* Athens, GA: Department of Educational Psychology, University of Georgia.

15. (With J. P. Torrance and A. B. Crabbe) *Handbook for Training Future Problem Solving Teams: 1980-81 Edition.* Lincoln, NE: Future Problem Solving Program.

16. (With B. Blume, J. Maryanoplis, F. Murphey, and J. Rogers) *Teaching Scenario Writing.* Lincoln, NE: Future Problem Solving Program.

17. (With J. P. Torrance) *Participating Teachers Evaluate the Georgia Future Problem Solving Program, 1978-1980.* Athens, GA: Georgia Studies of Creative Behavior, Department of Educational Psychology, University of Georgia.

Articles in Popular or Trade Type Journals and Magazines—Applications of Research

1. J. P. Torrance Admires Sonia Johnson. *University of Minnesota Alumni Association Letter,* November.
2. What Might We Learn From the Japanese About Giftedness and Creativity? *G/C/T,* May/June, 2-9.
3. (With *U.S. News and World Report* Staff) For Many, Being Gifted Brings Life-Long Struggle. *U.S. News and World Report,* December.

Papers Presented at Seminars/Conferences

1. "Growing Up Creatively Gifted: A 22-Year Longitudinal Study." Address prepared for presentation to the faculty and students of the University of Wisconsin at River Falls, WI, October 29.
2. "Highlights of the Georgia Studies of Creative Behavior, 1970-80." Presentation to International Conference on Creativity Research, La Jolla, CA, January 4-6.
3. (With J. P. Torrance) "New Concepts in Creativity Evaluation." Presentation at Winterfest, Creative Problem Solving Institute, University of California at San Diego, CA, January 3-7.
4. "Measuring the Creative Behavior of Preschool Children." Presentation at Conference on Creativity and the Gifted/Talented, National/State Leadership Training Institute on the Gifted/Talented, Houston, TX, March 20.
5. "Creative Intelligence and An Agenda for the '80s." Viktor Lowenfeld Memorial Lecture, National Association of Art Educators, Atlanta, GA, April 2. (Also in *Art Education, 33*(7), 8–15.)
6. "Challenges in Solving Future Problems." Presentation at National Future Problem Solving Bowl, University of Nebraska at Lincoln, NE, April 30.
7. "The Use of Scenarios in Sociodrama." Presentation at National Future Problem Solving Bowl, University of Nebraska at Lincoln, NE, May 1.
8. "Education of the Gifted in the '80s." Address at Symposium for the Education of the

Gifted, University of Nebraska, June 16.

9. "The Georgia Future Problem Solving Program." Address at Symposium for new Georgia teachers of the gifted, Georgia Department of Education, Atlanta Biltmore Hotel, Atlanta, GA, August 15.
10. "Developing Creative Reading Skills." Address at Appalachian State University Reading Conference, Boone, NC, September 11.
11. "Meeting the Needs of Creatively Gifted Students." Address to Department of Special Education, Appalachian State University, Boone, NC, September 11.
12. "Conducting Longitudinal Studies of Creative Behavior." Address at Agnes Scott College, Marietta, GA, September 18.
13. "The Challenge of Educating Gifted Students in the '80s." Address at Agnes Scott College, Marietta, GA, September 18.
14. "Highlights of the Georgia Studies of Creative Behavior: 1970-1980." Address at State University of New York at Albany, NY, September 26.
15. "Identifying Creatively Gifted Students." Address to New York State Association for the Advocacy of the Gifted, Albany, NY, September 26.
16. "No Limits to Learning: The Challenge of the '80s in Educating the Gifted." Address to New York State Association for the Advocacy of the Gifted, Albany, NY, September 27.
17. "Growing Up Creatively Gifted: A 22-Year View." University of Wisconsin at River Falls, October 29.
18. "Predicting the Creative Achievements of Elementary School Children and What Their Teachers Did to Make a Difference." Address to National Association for Gifted Children, Minneapolis, MN, October 30.

Foreword(s)/Preface(s) and Book Reviews

1. (With J. P. Torrance) Foreword. In B. Eberle and B. Stanish, *CPS for Kids: A Resource Book for Teaching Creative Problem Solving to Children*. Buffalo, NY: D.O.K. Publishers.
2. Foreword. In B. O. Richmond and R. H. Kicklighter, *Children's Adaptive Behavior Scale*. Atlanta, GA: Humanics, Inc.

1981

Books and Monographs

1. *Creativity: Its Educational Implications* (Second Edition). (Edited with J. C. Gowan and J. Khatena) Dubuque, IA/Toronto, Ontario: Kendall/Hunt.
2. (Japanese Edition) *Highest Levels of Thinking and Creativity*. Tokyo, Japan: Tokyo Shinri.
3. (With J. P. Torrance) *Is Creativity Teachable?* North Sydney, Australia: Department of Education, New South Wales Government.

Parts of Books, Contributions to Cooperative Volumes

1. (With B. Kaltsounis and C. R. Reynolds) "A Children's Form of Your Style of Learning and Thinking: Preliminary Norms and Technical Data." In J. C. Gowan, J. Khatena,

and E. P. Torrance (Eds.), *Creativity: Its Educational Implications*. Dubuque, IA: Kendall/Hunt, Pp. 178-187.

2. "Emerging Concepts of Giftedness." In W. Barbe and J. Renzulli (Eds.), *Psychology and Education of the Gifted (Third Edition)*. New York: Irvington Publishers, Pp. 47-54.
3. "Creative Teaching Makes a Difference." In W. Barbe and J. Renzulli (Eds.), *Psychology and Education of the Gifted (Third Edition)*. New York: Irvington Publishers, Pp. 433-447.
4. "Giftedness in Solving Future Problems." In W. Barbe and J. Renzulli, *Psychology and Education of the Gifted (Third Edition)*. New York, NY: Irvington Publishers, Pp. 294-303.
5. "Use of Sociodrama in Teaching Emotionally Troubled Children." In M. M. Wood (Ed.), *Developmental Therapy Sourcebook: Vol 2—Fantasy and Make Believe*. Baltimore, MD: University Park Press, Pp. 137-157.
6. "Sociodrama as a Creative Problem-Solving Approach to Studying the Future." In J. C. Gowan, J. Khatena, and E. P. Torrance (Eds.), *Creativity: Its Educational Implications (Second Edition)*. Dubuque, IA: Kendall/Hunt, Pp. 294-304.
7. "Role of Hemisphericity in Performance on Selected Measures of Creativity." In J. C. Gowan, J. Khatena, and E. P. Torrance (Eds.), *Creativity: Its Educational Implications (Second Edition)*. Dubuque, IA: Kendall/Hunt, Pp. 264-271.
8. "Understanding Creativity in Talented Students." In J. C. Gowan, J. Khatena, and E. P. Torrance (Eds.), *Creativity: Its Educational Implications*. Dubuque, IA: Kendall/Hunt, Pp. 207-211.
9. "Toward the More Humane Education of Gifted Children." In J. C. Gowan, J. Khatena, and E. P. Torrance (Eds.), *Creativity: Its Educational Implications*. Dubuque, IA: Kendall/Hunt, Pp. 6-18.
10. "Non-Test Ways of Identifying the Creatively Gifted." In J. C. Gowan, J. Khatena, and E. P. Torrance (Eds.), *Creativity: Its Educational Implications*. Dubuque, IA: Kendall/Hunt, Pp. 165-170.
11. "Ten Ways of Helping Young Children Gifted in Creative Writing and Speech." In J. C. Gowan, J. Khatena, and E. P. Torrance (Eds.), *Creativity: Its Educational Implications*. Dubuque, IA: Kendall/Hunt, Pp. 144-151.
12. "Creative Teaching Makes a Difference." In J. C. Gowan, J. Khatena, and E. P. Torrance (Eds.), *Creativity: Its Educational Implications*. Dubuque, IA: Kendall/Hunt, Pp. 99-108.
13. "Some Guiding Principles in Evaluating Excellence." In J. C. Gowan, J. Khatena, and E. P. Torrance (Eds.), *Creativity: Its Educational Implications*. Dubuque, IA: Kendall/Hunt, Pp. 47-54.
14. "Testing the Creativity of Preschool Children." In *The Faces and Forms of Creativity*. Los Angeles, CA: National/State Leadership Training Institute on the Gifted and the Talented, Pp. 65-80.
15. (With L. K. Ball) "Assessing the Further Reaches of Creative Potential." In *The Faces and Forms of Creativity*. Los Angeles, CA: National/State Leadership Training Institute on the Gifted and the Talented, Pp. 81-98.
16. "Encouraging Creativity in Young Children." In D. K. Osborn (Ed.), *Parent's Viewpoint*. Chicago, IL: World Book Childcraft International, p. 2.

Articles in Professional and Research Journals

1. (With J. W. Townsend and J. J. Wu) Role of Creative Ability Style in the Production of

Humor Among Adults. *The Journal of Creative Behavior*, ***15(4)***, 280-281.
2. (With F. K. Reisman and B. Floyd) Performance on Torrance's Thinking Creatively in Action and Movement as a Predictor of Cognitive Development of Young Children. *The Creative Child and Adult Quarterly*, ***6(4)***, 205-209.
3. (With J. P. Torrance) Educating Gifted, Talented and Creative Students for the Future. *American Middle School Education*, ***4(1)***, 39-46.
4. Implications of Whole-Brained Theories of Learning and Thinking for Computer-Based Instruction. *Journal of Computer-Based Instruction*, ***4***, 99-105.
5. ****(With T. Wu) A Comparative Longitudinal Study of the Adult Creative Achievements of Elementary School Children Identified as Highly Intelligent and as Highly Creative. Reprinted by permission from the *Creative Child and Adult Quarterly*, *6(2)*, 71-76.**
6. (With R. A. Black) Developing Creativity Instructional Materials According to the de Bono Thinking Skill Model. *Creative Child and Adult Quarterly*, ***6***, 8-12.
7. "Sounds and Images" Imagery as a Potential Indicator of Style of Learning and Thinking. *Journal of Creative Behavior*, ***15***, 279.
8. Empirical Validation of Criterion-Referenced Indicators of Creative Ability Through a Longitudinal Study. *Creative Child and Adult Quarterly*, ***6***, 136-140.
9. ****Predicting the Creativity of Elementary School Children (1958-1980)—and the "Teachers Who Made the Difference." *Gifted Child Quarterly*, *25(2)*, Spring, 55-62.**

Reports, Manuals, Handbooks, Tests, Instructional Materials

1. *Torrance Tests of Creative Thinking Scoring Guides, Verbal Form B and Figural Form A*. (Chinese Translation by J. J. Wu). Taipei, Taiwan, ROC.
2. *Administration, Scoring and Norms Manual—Thinking Creatively in Action and Movement*. Bensenville, IL: Scholastic Testing Service.
3. (With Scholastic Testing Service Staff) *Torrance Tests of Creative Thinking, Thinking Creatively with Sounds and Words, Thinking Creatively in Action and Movement*. Bensenville, IL: Scholastic Testing Service.
4. Testing the Creativity of Preschool Children. In "The Faces and Forms of Creativity." (Proceedings of the First National Conference on Creativity and Gifted/Talented) *N/S-LTI-G/T*, 65-80.
5. *Torrance Tests of Creative Thinking, Thinking Creatively in Action and Movement—Tests and Administration, Scoring and Norms Technical Manual*. Bensenville, IL: Scholastic Testing Service.
6. (With M. Dogan and R. Y. Horng) *Cumulative Bibliography on the Torrance Tests of Creative Thinking*. Athens, GA: Georgia Studies for Creative Behavior, Department of Educational Psychology, University of Georgia.
7. Misconceptions About Creativity in Gifted Education: Removing the Limits on Learning. *N/S-LTI-G/T Bulletin*, Los Angeles, CA, *8(3)*, 2, 6-7.
8. *Annual Report of Professional Activities of Alumni Foundation, Distinguished Professor E. Paul Torrance, April 1980-1981*. Athens, GA: Department of Educational Psychology, University of Georgia.
9. (W. Ching-chi, K. Chyuan-feng, W. Ching-ren, and D. Shing-shyang) *Torrance Tests of Creative Thinking Manuals, Verbal B and Figural Form A Manual* (Chinese Translation). Taipei, Taiwan, R.O.C.: Yeuan-liou.

Articles in Popular or Trade Type Journals and Magazines—Applications of Research

1. Misperceptions About Creativity in Gifted Education: Removing the Limits to Learning. *Bulletin, N/S-LTI-G/T,* ***8****(3)*, 2, 6-7.

Papers Presented at Seminars/Conferences

1. "Growing Up Creatively Gifted With Learning Disabilities." Paper prepared for the 1981 International Conference of the Association for Children and Adults with Learning Disabilities, Atlanta, GA, February 20.
2. "Implications of Dual-hemisphere, Cognitive, and Learning Theories for Planning Computer-Based Instruction." Presentation for Conference of Association for the Development of Computer-Based Instruction, "Computer-Based Instruction: Frontiers for Thought." Atlanta, GA, March.
3. "Some Misperceptions About Creativity in the Education of the Gifted." Address to National Curriculum Conference, National/State Leadership Training Institute for the Gifted and the Talented, Baltimore, MD, January 24.
4. "Psychometric Correlates of Your Style of Learning and Thinking." Address at Whole Brained Being Conference, Key West, FL (Florida International University), February 26.
5. "Implications of Whole Brained Theories of Learning and Thinking for Computer-Based Instruction." Address to Association for the Development of Computer-Based Instructional Systems, Atlanta, GA, March 4.
6. "Ten Implications of Creativity Research for the Education of Gifted Children." Address at Second National Conference on Creativity in Gifted Education, Memphis, TN, March 21.
7. "Challenging Images of the Future." Address at National Future Problem Solving Bowl, University of Nebraska, Lincoln, NE, May 14.
8. "New Developments in Creativity in Gifted Education." Address at Texas Conference on Gifted/Talented Education, Trinity University, San Antonio, TX, June 2.
9. "Teaching Gifted Students to Solve Future Problems." Address at Texas Conference on Gifted/Talented Education, San Antonio, TX, June 3.
10. "Strategies for Enhancing the Creative Growth of the Gifted/Talented." Address at Widener College, Chester, PA, November 1.

Foreword(s)/Preface(s) and Book Reviews

1. Foreword. In Joseph Renzulli, Sally Reis and Linda Smith (Eds.), *The Revolving Door Model.* Mansfield Center, CT: Creative Learning Press, Inc., P. i.

1982

Parts of Books, Contributions to Cooperative Volumes

1. "Growing Up Creatively Gifted with Learning Disabilities." In W. M. Cruickshank and J. W. Lerner (Eds.), *Coming of Age*. Syracuse, NY: Syracuse University Press, Pp. 24-35.
2. "Hochbegabungskonzepte." In K. K. Urban (Ed.), *Hochbegabte Kinder.* Heidelberg, West Germany: G. Schindele Verlag, Pp. 31-40.

3. "Hochbegabte Kinder Identifizieren." In K. K. Urban (Ed.), *Hochbegabte Kinder.* Heidelberg, West Germany: G. Schindele Verlag, Pp. 56-63.
4. "Misperceptions About Creativity in Gifted Education: Removing the Limits on Learning." In *Curricula for the Gifted.* Ventura, CA: National/State Leadership Training Institute for the Gifted and the Talented, Pp. 59-74.
5. "Some Implications of Creativity Research for Gifted Education." In *Creativity Research and Educational Planning.* Ventura, CA: National/State Leadership Training Institute for the Gifted and the Talented, Pp. 21-30.
6. "Identifying and Capitalizing on the Strengths of Culturally Different Children." In C. R. Reynolds and T. B. Gutkin (Eds.), *The Handbook of School Psychology.* New York, NY: John Wiley, Pp. 481-500.
7. "Sociodrama: Teaching Creative Problem Solving as a Therapeutic Technique." In C. R. Reynolds and T. B. Gutkin (Eds.), *The Handbook of School Psychology.* New York, NY: John Wiley, Pp. 591-598.

Articles in Professional and Research Journals

1. (With E. Cowger) Further Examination of the Quality of Changes in Creative Functioning Resulting From Meditation (Zazen) Training. *Creative Child and Adult Quarterly,* ***7***, 211-213.
2. Hemisphericity and Creative Functioning. *Journal of Research and Development in Education,* ***15****(3)*, 29-37.
3. Education for "Quality Circles" in Japanese Schools. *Journal of Research and Development in Education,* ***15****(2)*, 11-15.
4. Future Problem Solving and Quality Circles in Schools. *New Jersey Education Association Review,* ***56****(1)*, 20-23.
5. Sounds and Images Productions of Elementary School Pupils as Predictors of the Creative Achievements of Young Adults. *The Creative Child and Adult Quarterly,* ***7****(1)*, 9-14.
6. (With R. D. Clements, P. L. Dwinnell, and J. T. Kidd) Evaluation of Some of the Effects of a Teen Drama Program on Creativity. *Journal of Creative Behavior,* ***16***, 206-210.
7. Ten Lessons on the Development of Giftedness and Talent from Japan. *Gifted International,* ***1****(1)*, 61-72.

Reports, Manuals, Handbooks, Tests, Instructional Materials

1. (With L. K. Hall and V. Connell) *Cumulative Bibliography on the Torrance Tests of Creative Thinking: 1982 Supplement.* Athens, GA: Georgia Studies of Creative Behavior, Department of Educational Psychology, University of Georgia.
2. (E. P. Torrance et al.) *International Bibliography on Stimulating Creativity.* (Prepared for World Conference on Gifted and Talented Children) Athens, GA: Torrance Studies of Creative Behavior.
3. (J. P. Torrance, C. Anderson, A. Crabbe, et al.) *Scoring Guide: Future Problem Solving Program (Draft for Discussion).* Future Problem Solving Program, Coe College, Cedar Rapids, IA.
4. (With J. Presbury and M. W. Henderson) *Children of the World—Hopeful, But Worried.* Athens, GA: Georgia Studies of Creative Behavior, University of Georgia.
5. *A Retrospective Look at the Minnesota and Georgia Studies of Creative Behavior.* Athens, GA: Georgia Studies of Creative Behavior, Department of Educational Psychology,

University of Georgia.

6. Misperceptions About Creativity in Gifted Education: Removing the Limits on Learning. In "Curriculum for the Gifted" (Selected Proceedings of the First National Conference on Curriculum for the Gifted/Talented) *N/S-LTI-G/T*, Ventura County School System, Ventura County, CA, Pp. 59-70.
7. Some Implications of Creativity Research for Gifted Education. In "Creativity Research and Education Planning." (Proceedings from the Second National Conference on Creativity of Gifted and Talented) Ventura County Superintendent of Schools Office, Ventura County, CA.
8. (With J. P. Torrance, C. Anderson, and A. Crabbe) *Scoring Guide: Future Problem Solving Program*. Future Problem Solving Program, Coe College, Cedar Rapids, IA.
9. *International Scenario Writing Project: List of U.S.A. Award Winners*. Athens, GA: Georgia Studies of Creative Behavior, Department of Educational Psychology, University of Georgia.
10. *International Bibliography on Stimulating Creativity*. Prepared for World Conference on Gifted and Talented Children. Athens, GA: Georgia Studies of Creative Behavior, Department of Educational Psychology, University of Georgia.

Articles in Popular or Trade Type Journals and Magazines—Applications of Research

1. Future Problem Solving and Quality Circles in Schools. *New Jersey Education Association, **56**(1)*, 20-23.
2. Ask the Experts (Use of Fantasy). *Gifted Children Newsletter, **5**(4)*, 17-18.
3. Ask the Experts (Futurism vs. Special Interests). *Gifted Children Newsletter, **3**(10)*, 17-18
4. (With Leadership Training Staff) Meeting of the Minds in Georgia. *N/S-LTI-G/T Bulletin, **6***, 2.

Papers Presented at Seminars/Conferences

1. "The Mandate: A New Image of Teaching." Address at Summit Education Conference, South Carolina State College, Orangeburg, SC, November 19.
2. "The Importance of Falling in Love With 'Something.'" Athens, GA: Elmer Schacht Lecture, Athens Academy.
3. "America's Energy is Mindpower." Address to Louisiana Association for Gifted and Talented Students, Louisiana State University, Baton Rouge, LA, March 6.
4. "Recent Developments and Future Problems of the Future Problem Solving Program." Address at Creative Problem Solving Institute, La Jolla, CA, January 9.
5. "Reflections on 'The Search for Satori and Creativity.'" Address at Creative Problem Solving Institute, La Jolla, CA, January 10.
6. "Your Search for Your Creativity." Address at Presbyterian College, Laurinburg, NC, January 26. (telelecture)
7. "Creativity in Communications." Address to University of Georgia Communications Club, Athens, GA, January 26.
8. "Studying Creativity." Address to Department of Educational Psychology, Texas A & M University, College Station, TX, February 4.
9. "Quality Circles: A Proposal for Improving the Quality of Life in American Schools." Address to Louisiana Association for Gifted and Talented Students, Louisiana State University, Baton Rouge, LA, March 6. (Also given at Third National Conference on

Creativity in Gifted Education, Minneapolis, MN, March 20.)

10. "Creativity in Gifted Education." Address at New Orleans University, New Orleans, LA, March 8.
11. "Misconceptions About Creativity in Education." Address at New Orleans University, New Orleans, LA, March 8.
12. "Problems in Writing Books for Publication." Address to University of Georgia College of Education Faculty and Graduate Students, Athens, GA, March 9.
13. "Teaching for Creative Development." Address at Victoria (TX) In-Service Education Program for Teachers of Gifted/Talented Students, Victoria, TX, March 12.
14. "Fall In Love With Your Dream." Address at Fourth Annual Elmer C. Schacht Lecture, Athens Academy, Athens, GA, March 16.
15. "A Retrospective Look at the Minnesota and Georgia Studies of Creative Behavior." Address at Third National Conference on Creativity in Gifted Education, Minneapolis, MN, March 19.
16. "Using Creative Problem Solving Models in Designing Instructional Materials for Gifted Students." Address at Third National Conference on Gifted Education, Minneapolis, MN, March 20.
17. "How Parents Might Nurture the Creativity of Young Children." Address at United States Air Force Management School, Wright-Patterson Air Force Base, OH, May 6. (telelecture)
18. "Solving the Problems of the Space Age and Living in Space." Address at National Future Problem Solving Bowl, Coe College, Cedar Rapids, IA, June 2.
19. "Helping Gifted Children 'Fall in Love' with Something and Pursue it with Excellence." Address at Summer Institute, National/State Leadership Training Institute on the Gifted and the Talented, Georgia Center, University of Georgia, Athens, GA, July 2.
20. "What Happens When Children Study the Future." Address at Kephart Memorial Seminar, Aspen, CO, July 5.
21. "A Retrospective View of the Minnesota and Georgia Studies of Creative Behavior." Address at Northern Colorado University, Greeley, CO, July 7.
22. "Training Teams in the Future Problem Solving Program." Address at Georgia College, Milledgeville, GA, July 14.
23. "Implications of Creativity Research for the Education of Gifted and Talented Children." Address at Pacific Lutheran University, Tacoma, OR, October 7.
24. "Improving the Technology for Teaching Gifted and Talented Students Creatively." Address at Regional Conference, Seattle-Tacoma Area, Pacific Lutheran University, Tacoma, OR, October 8.
25. "Assessing and Nurturing the Creative Potential of Disadvantaged Children." Address to Georgia Association for School Psychologists, Lake Jackson, GA, October 15.
26. "The Role of Mentors in Creative Achievement: A Longitudinal Study." Address to National Association for Gifted Children, New Orleans, LA, October 21.
27. "Meeting the Needs of Creatively Gifted Children." Address at Regional Conference of The Association for the Gifted, Tulsa, OK, December 2.

Foreword(s)/Preface(s) and Book Reviews

1. Foreword. In D. J. Shallcross and D. A. Sisk, *The Growing Person*. Englewood Cliffs, NJ: Prentice-Hall.
2. Preface. In M. M. Frasier and J. A. Carland, *Dictionary of Gifted, Talented and Creative*

Educational Terms. New York: Trillium Press, Pp. iv-v.
3. Book Review: *Educational Psychology of the Gifted* by Joe Khatena. *Journal of Mental Imagery*, ***6***, 251-252.

1983

Parts of Books, Contributions to Cooperative Volumes

1. "Creative Motivation Scale." In B. Weinstein (Ed.), *20 Ways to Be More Creative in Your Job*. New York, NY: Simon and Schuster, Inc., Pp. 16-19.
2. "Your Style of Learning and Thinking—Form C." In R. L. Lewis (Ed.), *Inductive Preaching: Activities Guidebook*. Wilmore, KY: Inductive Preaching Today, Asbury Theological Seminary, Pp. 27-31.
3. (K. Morita, Japanese Translation) "Future Images and Characteristics of Gifted Children Around the World." In *The Year 2010: International Scenario Writing Contest*. Tokyo, Japan: International Society for Intelligence.

Articles in Professional and Research Journals

1. Reply from Paul Torrance. *CREATA, Gifted Child Education*, ***1****(2)*, 8-9.
2. (With M. M. Frasier) Style of Learning and Thinking and Biographical Inventory Measures. *Creative Child and Adult Quarterly*, ***8***, 206-210.
3. The Role of Mentors in Creative Achievement. *Creative Child and Adult Quarterly*, ***8****(1)*, 8-16.
4. Status of Creative Women: Past, Present, Future. *Creative Child and Adult Quarterly*, ***8***, 135-144.

Reports, Manuals, Handbooks, Tests, Instructional Materials

1. *Future Career Images: Award-Winning Scenarios in the Georgia Division of the International Scenario Writing Contest, 1982-1983*. Athens, GA: Georgia Future Problem Solving Program, Georgia Studies of Creative Behavior, Department of Educational Psychology, University of Georgia.
2. *Annual Report of Professional Activities of Alumni Foundation, Distinguished Professor E. Paul Torrance, April 1982-April 1983*. Athens, GA: Department of Educational Psychology, University of Georgia.
3. *One Hundred Reasons for Having Georgia Future Problem Solving Week: One Hundred Ideas for Observing Georgia Future Problem Solving Week*. (Ideas developed by participants in the Ninth Georgia Future Problem Solving Bowl held at the University of Georgia, Athens, GA).
4. (With Georgia Future Problem Solving Program students) *Future Images, 1983 Award-Winning Scenarios in the Georgia Statewide Scenarios Writing Contest*. Athens, GA: Georgia Future Problem Solving Program, Georgia Studies of Creative Behavior.
5. *Teaching Scenario Writing* (Revised Edition). Cedar Rapids, IA: Future Problem Solving Program, Coe College.
6. *100 Reasons for Having Georgia Future Problem Solving Week and 100 Suggested Activities for Georgia Future Problem Solving Week*. Athens, GA: Georgia Future Problem Solving Program.

7. (With O. E. Ball) *Streamlined Scoring and Interpretation Guide and Norms-Technical Manual for Figural Forms A and B, Torrance Tests of Creative Thinking.* Bensenville, IL: Scholastic Testing Service.
8. (With O. E. Ball) *Workbook for the Streamlined Scoring of Figural Form A, Torrance Tests of Creative Thinking.* Bensenville, IL: Scholastic Testing Service.
9. (With O. E. Ball) *Workbook for the Streamlined Scoring of Figural Form B, Torrance Tests of Creative Thinking.* Bensenville, IL: Scholastic Testing Service.
10. *America's Energy is Mindpower.* Baton Rouge, LA: Louisiana Association for the Gifted and Talented.

Articles in Popular or Trade Type Journals and Magazines—Applications of Research

1. Solutions for Unsolvable Problems. *The Student, 42(11),* 15-16.
2. ****The Importance of Falling in Love With Something. *Creativity Network Newsletter, 4(2),* 2.**
3. Leisure Time Society of 2001. In *On the Eve of 2001: Images of the Future.* Scotia, New York: Albany-Schoharie-Schenactady Boces, Scotia-Glenville School District, 31-32.
4. "Quality Circles" for Quality Programs. *Gifted Children Newsletter, 4(1),* 1-3, 8.
5. Future Problem Solving Bowls and Scenarios by South African Students. *Creata Gifted Child Education,* September, Cape Town, South Africa, Vol. 1, No. 2, 8-9.
6. Needed: A New Concept of Giftedness. *Creativity Network Newsletter,* 3-4.

Papers Presented at Seminars/Conferences

1. "Future Images and Characteristics of Gifted Children Around the World." Paper prepared for Fifth World Conference on Gifted Children, Manila, Philippines, August 5.
2. "The Role of Creativity in the Education of the Gifted: A Position Paper." In *Proceedings of the Seminar on Certification for the Field of Gifted.* Presented for the Georgia Certification Conference on the Education of the Gifted, Holiday Inn, Gainsville, GA, October 14, Pp. 31-51.
3. "Pre-Dawn of Talents Unlimited." Paper presented for Third Conference on Talents Unlimited, Mobile County Board of Education, Mobile, AL, October 20.
4. "Developing Programs for Creatively Gifted and Culturally Different Gifted Children." Address to Palm Springs Public Schools, Palm Springs, CA, January 11.
5. "Creativity and a Changing View of Teaching." Address at Oglethorpe University, Atlanta, GA, February 8.
6. "New Developments in the Study of Creativity." Address to Department of Educational Psychology, Texas A & M University, February 17. (telelecture)
7. "International Contributions to the Study of Creativity." Address at Fourth National Conference on Creativity in Gifted Education, Dallas, TX, March 18.
8. "The Sounds and Images Test as a Predictor of Creative Achievement: A Longitudinal Study." Address at Fourth National Conference on Creativity in Gifted Education, Dallas, TX, March 19.
9. "The Status of Creative Women: Past, Present and Future." Address to President's Commission on the Status of Women, Mississippi State University, Starkville,

MS, March 22.

10. "Role of Creativity in My Life." Address to President's Commission on the Status of Women, Mississippi State University, Starkville, MS, March 23.
11. "Barry F. Box: His Outreach." Dedication of the Box Building, Department of Educational Psychology, Mississippi State University, Starkville, MS, March 23.
12. "History and Culture: Their Contributions to the Study of Creativity." Address at College of Education, Mississippi State University, Starkville, MS, March 24.
13. "Emerging Developments in the Education of Gifted Children." Paper presented at annual meeting of the Georgia Supporters of the Gifted, History Village, Athens, GA, April 8.
14. "Creativity and Coping with Change." Paper presented at University of Georgia Campus Ministers, Episcopal University Center, May 12.
15. "Helping Children Who Fall in Love with Something." Paper presented at Georgia Society for the Study of Early Childhood Education, Georgia Center of Continuing Education, Athens, GA, May 14.
16. "Issues Regarding Creativity in Curriculum and Instruction." Paper presented at University of Georgia Seminar on Curriculum and Supervision, Athens, GA, May 18.
17. "New Directions in the Future Problem Solving Program." Paper presented at National Future Problem Solving Bowl, Coe College, Cedar Rapids, IA, May 30.
18. "Images of the Future of Gifted Children: Implications for Educating Them." Paper presented at National Leadership Training Institute for the Gifted and the Talented, Georgia Center for Continuing Education, Athens, GA, July 1.
19. "How Shall We Respond to the Dreams of the Future of Gifted Children?" Paper presented at Confratute `83, University of Connecticut, Storrs, CT, July 21.
20. Curriculum Implications of the Images of the Future of Gifted Children." Leadership Training Institute on the Gifted and the Talented, Queen Kapiolan Hotel, Honolulu, HI, July 29.
21. "An Overview of 25 Years of Creativity Research." Paper presented at Philippine Normal University, Manila, Philippines, August 4.
22. "Assessing Creative Potential." Telelecture at Widener College, PA, October 23.
23. "Educating for Creative Achievement and Living." Meet the Scholars Series, College of Education Alumni Seminar, University of Georgia, Athens, GA, October 28.
24. "New Research Findings Regarding the Education of the Gifted and Talented." Paper presented to Georgia Educational Research Association, Ramada Inn, Athens, GA, November 19.

Foreword(s)/Preface(s) and Book Reviews

1. Foreword. In Audrey W. Lederman and Dan Craig Lederman, *Mission: Serendipity!* Buffalo, NY: D.O.K. Publishers.
2. Foreword. In Jim Goodacre, Jay Heale, Forbes Smith and Ellen Smith (Eds.), *Wakening Word '82: Creative Writing of Primary School Children.* Three Anchor Bay, South Africa: Ellerton Primary School.
3. Foreword. In R. B. Noller and B. R. Frey, *Mentoring: An Annotated Bibliography.* Buffalo, NY: Bearly Limited.

1984

Books and Monographs

1. *Mentor Relationships: How They Aid Creative Achievement, Endure, Change and Die.* Buffalo, NY: Bearly Limited.
2. (With A. Crabbe and J. P. Torrance) *Ten Years of Future Problems (1974-1984).* Cedar Rapids, IA: Future Problem Solving Program, Coe College.
3. (With R. E. Myers) *Wondering: Invitations to Think About the Future for Primary Grades.* Mansfield Center, CT: Creative Learning Press, Inc.
4. (With J. P. Torrance and A. Crabbe) *Fifty Plus Fuzzies.* Cedar Rapids, IA: Future Problem Solving Program.

Parts of Books, Contributions to Cooperative Volumes

1. "My Recollections of Georgia Military College." In R. G. Hendrickson (Ed.), *Through These Gates Passed the Great Class of 1934.* Milledgeville, GA: Georgia Military College.
2. "Quality Circles: A Proposal for Improving the Quality of the Education of the Gifted by Improving the Quality of Life in Schools." In *New Directions of Creativity Research.* Ventura, CA: Ventura County Superintendent of Schools Office, Pp. 29-34.
3. "A Retrospective View of the Minnesota and Georgia Studies of Creative Behavior." In *New Directions in Creativity Research.* Ventura, CA: Ventura County Superintendent of Schools Office, Pp. 65-74.

Articles in Professional and Research Journals

1. (With J. Presbury) The Criteria of Success in 242 Studies of Creativity. *The Creative Child Quarterly, **9**(4)*, 238-243.
2. The Increasing Loss of Creative Women from Education. *Creativity Network, **5**(3)*, 3.
3. (With H. Okabayashi) Role of Style of Learning and Thinking and Self-Directed Learning Readiness in the Achievement of Gifted Students. *Journal of Learning Disabilities, **17**(2)*, 104-107.
4. Some Products of Twenty-Five Years of Creativity Research. *Educational Perspectives, **22**(3)*, 3-8.
5. The Role of Creativity in the Identification of the Gifted and Talented. *Gifted Child Quarterly, **28**(4)*, 153-156.

Reports, Manuals, Handbooks, Tests, Instructional Materials

1. *Reliability and Validity Data and Revised Bibliography for Human Information Processing Survey.* Bensenville, IL: Scholastic Testing Service, Inc.
2. (With L. Hall and V. Connell) *Supplements to Cumulative Bibliography on the Torrance Tests of Creative Thinking.* Athens, GA: Torrance Studies of Creative, Gifted, and Future Behaviors, Aderhold Hall, College of Education, University of Georgia.
3. (With O. E. Ball) *Streamlined Scoring Workbook, Figural A, Torrance Tests of Creative Thinking.* Bensenville, IL: Scholastic Testing Service, Inc.
4. (With Georgia Future Problem Solving students) *Future Images, 1984 Award-Winning Scenarios in the Georgia Statewide Scenario Writing Contest.* Athens, GA: Georgia Future Problem Solving Program, Georgia Studies of Creative Behavior.

5. (With W. Taggart) *Human Information Processing Survey (HIPS)*. Bensenville, IL: Scholastic Testing Service, Inc.
6. (With W. Taggart) *Human Information Processing Survey (HIPS) (Management Training Edition)*. Bensenville, IL: Scholastic Testing Service, Inc.
7. (With O. E. Ball) *Torrance Tests of Creative Thinking Streamlined (Revised) Manual, Figural A and B*. Bensenville, IL: Scholastic Testing Service, Inc.
8. (E. P. Torrance et al.) *International Network of Gifted Children and Their Teachers Network Newsletter*. Athens, GA: Georgia Studies of Creative Behavior, Department of Educational Psychology, University of Georgia, **1**(1).
9. *Educating for Creative Behavior: 25 Provocative Research Results*. Athens, GA: Torrance Studies of Creative, Gifted and Future Behavior, University of Georgia.
10. *Faculty Activities Report, 1983-1984*. Athens, GA: College of Education, Department of Educational Psychology, University of Georgia.
11. (With C. B. Bruch) *Selected Papers of E. Paul Torrance: Genesa Analyses-Essence and Three Primary Components*. Athens, GA: Torrance Studies of Gifted, Creative and Future Behavior, Department of Educational Psychology, University of Georgia.
12. (With A. Nalls) *International Network of Gifted Children and Their Teachers Network Newsletter*. Athens, GA: Torrance Studies for Gifted, Creative and Future Behaviors, University of Georgia, **2**(1).

Articles in Popular or Trade Type Journals and Magazines—Applications of Research

1. (With J. Presbury and M. W. Henderson) Those Worried, Hopeful, Gifted Children of the World. *G/C/T*, ***32***, 9-18.
2. J. H. Presbury and M. Henderson, If You Haven't Met Them Yet, It's Time to Visit E. Paul Torrance and Pansy Nigh Torrance. *G/C/T*, ***32***, 2-8.
3. SAT Scores Go Down—Creativity Scores Go Up. *Creativity Network*, ***5****(2)*, 2, 5.

Papers Presented at Seminars/Conferences

1. "The Search for a Nation's Treasure." In *Retirement Celebration for Dr. E. Paul Torrance, March 23, 1985*. Keynote address at the National Association for Gifted Children, St. Louis, MO. Athens, GA: College of Education, University of Georgia.
2. "Designing and Using Psychometric Data to Guide the Teaching of Creative Behavior." Paper presented to the Inquiry Group on Applied Psychometrics and Clinical Assessment, Texas A & M University, College Station, TX, February 6.
3. "Helping Creatively Gifted Children." Paper presented at Palm Springs Unified School District, Palm Springs, CA, January 12.
4. "Twenty-five Provocative Findings from 25 Years of Creativity Research." Paper presented at University of Houston at Clear Lake, Clear Lake, TX, February 7.
5. "Creativity: Search for Satori." Paper presented at Oklahoma City University, Oklahoma City, OK, February 24.
6. "The Concept of Creative Intelligence and the Future Definition of Giftedness." Paper presented at Fifth National Conference on Creativity in Gifted Education, Holiday Inn (Mart), Chicago, IL, March 17.
7. "How Parents Might Help Gifted Children Maintain Their Creativity." Paper presented at Gwinnett County Board of Education, Gwinnett County, Georgia, March 22.

8. "Beyond 1984 as Predicted by the Children of the World." Paper presented at Seventh Southern Regional Conference of the World Future Society, Urban Life Center, Georgia State University, Atlanta, GA, March 31.
9. "Conditions for Invention and Innovation." Telelecture at Widener College, PA, January 28.

Foreword(s)/Preface(s) and Book Reviews

1. Foreword. In M. K. Raina, *Education of the Left and the Right: Implications of Hemispheric Specialization*. New Delhi, India: Allied Publishers Private Limited.
2. Foreword. In Bernice Bleedorn with Sara McKelvey, *Humor: Lessons in Laughter for Learning and Living*. Buffalo, NY: D.O.K. Publishers.
3. Prologue. In F. Bellon, O. M. Dadamia, and J. Martinez, *La Creatividad en la Educacion*. Madrid, Spain: Editorial Escuela Espanola.

RETIREMENT YEARS

1985

Parts of Books, Contributions to Cooperative Volumes

1. "Future Images and Characteristics of Gifted and Talented Children Around the World." In A. H. Roldan (Ed.), *Gifted Children, Youth, and Adults: Their Social Perspectives and Culture*. Manila, Philippines: Reading Dynamics, Inc.
2. "Teaching Creative and Gifted Learners." In M. R. Wittrock (Ed.), *Handbook of Teaching*. New York, NY: Macmillan, Pp. 1-34.
3. "Educating for Creative Behavior." In *25 Provocative Research Results*. Athens, GA: Department of Educational Psychology, College of Education, University of Georgia, Pp. 45-53.

Articles in Professional and Research Journals

1. Creative Retirement Provides a Fair Chance to Grow. *Creative Child and Adult Quarterly*, ***10****(4)*, 214-222.
2. Who is Gifted? *Illinois Council for the Gifted Journal*, ***4***, 2-3.
3. Left, Right, and Integrated Brain Dominance. *Journal of Children and Youth*, ***5****(3)*, 33.
4. Creative Power in Networking. *Creativity Network*, ***6****(6)*, 1.

Reports, Manuals, Handbooks, Tests, Instructional Materials

1. *Message to the 1985 World Council for Gifted and Talented Children, Hamburg, Germany*. Athens, GA: Department of Educational Psychology, University of Georgia.
2. (With J. P. Torrance) *Over the Years: Research Insights of E. Paul Torrance*. In Retirement Celebration for E. Paul Torrance, March 23, 1985. Athens, GA: College of Education, University of Georgia, Pp. 25-42.
3. *Faculty Activities Report (1983-1984)*. Athens, GA: Department of Educational Psychology, College of Education, University of Georgia.

Articles in Popular or Trade Type Journals and Magazines—Applications of Research

1. A Change in Concepts of Intelligence. *Human Intelligence International Newsletter*, ***6****(2)*, 9.

Papers Presented at Seminars/Conferences

1. "A Fair Chance to Grow." March, 23. First annual E. Paul Torrance Lecture, Georgia Center for Continuing Education, University of Georgia, Athens, GA.
2. "Creativity Talent Search." Paper presented to the Sixth National Conference of Creativity and the Gifted/Talented, Atlanta, GA.

1986

Books and Monographs

1. (With R. E. Myers) *Imagining: Invitations to Think About the Future for Intermediate Grades*. Mansfield Center, CT: Creative Learning Press.

Articles in Professional and Research Journals

1. A Service for the Creatively Gifted. *Creativity Network Newsletter*, *7*, 4-5.
2. Glimpses of the "Promised Land." *Roeper Review*, ***8****(4)*, 246-251.
3. (With B. G. Clinton) S.E.A.M.: A Training Program for Developing Problem Identification Skills. *Journal of Creative Behavior*, ***20****(2)*, 77-80.
4. ****(With H. T. Safter) Are Children Becoming More Creative? *Journal of Creative Behavior*, *20(1)*, 1-13.**
5. (With A. M. Solimon) Styles of Learning and Thinking of College Students in the Japanese, United States and Kuwait Cultures. *Creative Child and Adult Quarterly*, ***11****(4)*, 196-204.
6. Intense Emotional Experience—Impetus to Creation. *Creative Child and Adult Quarterly*, ***11****(3)*, 130-137.
7. (With Z. L. Rockenstein) Styles of Thinking and Creativity. *Gifted International*, ***4****(1)*, 37-49.

Foreword(s)/Preface(s) and Book Reviews

1. Review. Shaughnessy, M. F. Book review of *Mentor Relationships: How They Aid Creative Achievement, Endure, Change and Die*. *Creative Child and Adult Quarterly*, ***11****(3)*, 184-185.

1987

Books and Monographs

1. (With D. Weiner, J. Presbury, and M. W. Henderson) *Save Tomorrow for the Children*. Buffalo, NY: Bearly Limited.

Parts of Books, Contributions to Cooperative Volumes

1. "Teaching for Creativity." In S. G. Isaksen (Ed.), *Frontiers of Creativity Research: Beyond the Basics*. Buffalo, NY: Bearly Limited, Pp. 189-215.

Articles in Professional and Research Journals

1. A Climate for Inventing. *Creative Child and Adult Quarterly*, ***12****(3)*, 230-236.
2. (With J. A. Wright) Sociometric Audience Technique as a Device for Maximizing Creativity in Problem Solving in Large Groups. *Creative Child and Adult Quarterly*, ***17****(3)*, 147-151.
3. Some Evidence Regarding Development of Cerebral Lateralization. *Perceptual and Motor Skills*, ***64***, 262.
4. Future Career Image as a Predictor of Creative Achievement in a 22-year Longitudinal Study. *Psychological Reports*, ***60***, 2.

Reports, Manuals, Handbooks, Tests, Instructional Materials

1. *Survey of the Uses of the Torrance Tests of Creative Thinking*. Bensenville, IL: Scholastic Testing Service.
2. (With D. Treffinger and O. E. Ball) *Guidelines for Administration and Scoring: Comments on Using the Torrance Tests of Creative Thinking*. Bensenville, IL: Scholastic Testing Service.
3. *1987 Supplement, Torrance Tests of Creative Thinking Cumulative Bibliography*. Athens, GA: Georgia Studies of Creative Behavior.
4. *Using the Torrance Tests of Creative Thinking to Guide the Teaching of Creative Behavior*. Bensenville, IL: Scholastic Testing Service.
5. *Guidelines for Administration and Scoring/Comments on Using the Torrance Tests of Creative Thinking*. Bensenville, IL: Scholastic Testing Service.

Articles in Popular or Trade Type Journals and Magazines—Applications of Research

1. Creativity and the Arts. *TEMPO* (Texas Association for the Gifted and Talented), *7(3)*, 8-9.
2. *Creative Minds Unlimited* (A newsletter of TAG, Phillippines), ***1****(1)*.
3. Teaching for Getting Beyond Aha! (Part I). *N/S-LTI-G/T Bulletin*, ***14****(1)*, 2-5.
4. Teaching for Getting Beyond Aha! (Part II). *N/S-LTI-G/T Bulletin*, ***14****(3)*, 1-4.

Papers Presented at Seminars/Conferences

1. (With R. Y. Horng) "Imagery Abilities, Sex, and Intelligence as Predictors of Creative Thinking Abilities." Draft of a paper presented at 3rd International Imagery Conference, Japan, July 2-5.

1988

Parts of Books, Contributions to Cooperative Volumes

1. "The Nature of Creativity as Manifest in its Testing." In R. G. Sternberg (Ed.), *The Nature of Creativity: Contemporary Perspectives*. New York: Cambridge

University Press, Pp. 43-75.

2. (With Z. L. Rockenstein) "Styles of Thinking and Creativity." In R. R. Schmeck (Ed.), *Learning Strategies and Learning Styles*. New York, NY: Plenum Publishing, Pp. 275-290.
3. (With J. P. Torrance) "Creativity and Teaching Concepts of God." In D. Ratcliff (Ed.), *Handbook of Preschool Religious Education*. Birmingham, AL: Religious Education Press, Pp. 224-247.
4. "Teaching for 'Getting Beyond Aha!'" In I. Sato (Ed.), *Priorities in Curriculum Planning for the Gifted/Talented*. Ventura, CA: Ventura County Superintendent of Schools Office, Pp. 23-28.

Articles in Professional and Research Journals

1. (With M. C. Murdock) Using the Torrance Sociodramatic Models as a Vehicle for Negotiation. *Creative Child and Adult Quarterly*, ***13****(2)*, 108-114.
2. Comments on Education for Quality Circles in Japanese Schools (in Chinese). *Educational Administration*, ***5****(1)*, 64-66.

Reports, Manuals, Handbooks, Tests, Instructional Materials

1. *Style of Learning and Thinking: Administrator's Manual—Elementary and Youth Forms*. Bensenville, IL: Scholastic Testing Service.
2. *Directions Manual for Figural Test A of Torrance Tests of Creative Thinking* (in Chinese). Bensenville, IL: Scholastic Testing Service.
3. *Norms and Technical Manual of Torrance Tests of Creative Thinking* (in Italian). Bensenville, IL: Scholastic Testing Service.
4. *Directions Manual for Verbal Test A of Torrance Tests of Creative Thinking* (in Chinese). Bensenville, IL: Scholastic Testing Service.

Articles in Popular or Trade Type Journals and Magazines—Applications of Research

1. (With J. Presbury, A. J. Benson, and J. Fitch) Children and Creativity. *NASP Communique*, ***17****(3)*, 24-25.

Foreword(s)/Preface(s) and book Reviews

1. Foreword. In J. Hayes and M. M. Sebastian, *Critical Thinking Problem Solving: Grade 5-6*. Minneapolis, MN: Judy/Instructo.

1989

Parts of Books, Contributions to Cooperative Volumes

1. "A Reaction to 'Gifted Black Students: Curriculum and Teaching Strategies.'" In C. J. Maker and S. W. Schiever (Eds.), *Critical Issues in Gifted Education: Defensible Programs for Cultural and Ethnic Minorities, Vol. II*. Austin, TX: Pro-ed, Pp. 270-274.
2. "Thinking Creatively." In J. G. Beamont (Ed.), *Brain Power: Unlock the Power of Your Mind*. New York, NY: Harper and Row, Pp. 212-217.

Articles in Professional and Research Journals

1. On the Shoulders of Giants: What Humans Can Become. *Educational Forum*, ***53****(2)*, 117-124.
2. (With K. Goff) A Quiet Revolution. *Journal of Creative Behavior*, ***23****(2)*, 136-144.
3. (With H. T. Safter) The Long Range Predictive Validity of the Just Suppose Test. *Journal of Creative Behavior*, ***23****(4)*, 219-223.
4. Creating a Brighter Future. *Thresholds in Education*, ***24****(2)*, 2-3.
5. (With C. B. Clements and K. Goff) Mind-Body Learning Among the Elderly: Arts, Fitness and Incubation. *Educational Forum*, ***54****(1)*, 124-133.

Reports, Manuals, Handbooks, Tests, Instructional Materials

1. *Manual and Guide for Evaluating Form A of Torrance Tests of Creative Thinking* (in Italian). Bensenville, IL: Scholastic Testing Service.
2. *Torrance Tests of Creative Thinking* (Verbal A and Figural A Tests with Score Sheets; in Italian). Bensenville, IL: Scholastic Testing Service.

Articles in Popular or Trade Type Journals and Magazines—Applications of Research

1. (With K. Goff and F. Kaufmann) Thinking About the Future. *Gifted Child Today*, November/December Issue, 48-50.
2. (With J. Juntune) The Beginning Years. *Focus*, (1), 3-5.
3. (With K. Goff) Fostering Academic Creativity in Gifted Students. *ERIC Flyer Files*.
4. Are We Teaching Our Children to Think About the Future? *G/C/T*, ***12****(6)*, 48-50.
5. Pansy Nigh Torrance, 1913-1988. *N/S-LTI-G/T Quarterly Bulletin*, ***16****(1)*, 3-4.

Foreword(s)/Preface(s) and Book Reviews

1. Foreword. In G. W. Millar, *Developing Student Questioning Skills*. Bensenville, IL: Scholastic Testing Services.
2. Foreword. In J. Hayes and M. M. Sebastian, *Mr. Thinker's Pet Store*. Minneapolis, MN: Judy/Instructo (Grade 1).
3. Foreword. In J. Hayes and M. M. Sebastian, *Super Solvers Circus*. Minneapolis, MN: Judy/Instructo (Grade 2).
4. Foreword. In J. Hayes and M. M. Sebastian, *Thinkersville Zoo*. Minneapolis, MN: Judy/Instructo (Grade 3).
5. Foreword. In J. Hayes and M. M. Sebastian, *Welcome Quick Wits*. Minneapolis, MN: Judy/Instructo (Grade 4).
6. Foreword. In J. Hayes and M. M. Sebastian, *Exploring Thinking*. Minneapolis, MN: Judy/Instructo (Grades 5 and 6).
7. Foreword. In R. C. Morris and B. A. Smith (Eds.), *Gifted Education: Creating a Brighter Future* (pp. 2-3). *Thresholds in Education*, ***15****(2)*, 18.
8. Foreword. *Thresholds in Education*, ***15****(2)*, 2-3.

1990

Books and Monographs

1. (With K. Goff) *Fostering Academic Creativity in Gifted Students.* Reston, VA: ERIC Clearinghouse on Handicapped and Gifted Children.
2. (With H. T. Safter) *The Incubation Model of Teaching.* Buffalo, NY: Bearly Limited.

Parts of Books, Contributions to Cooperative Volumes

1. "The Creative Scholars Mentors Program." In C. W. Taylor (Ed.), *Expanding Awareness of Creative Potential Worldwide.* Salt Lake City, UT: Brain Talent-Powers Press, Pp. 56-58.
2. (With P. A. Haensly) "Assessment of Creativity in Children and Adolescents." In C. R. Reynolds and R. W. Kamphaus (Eds.), *Handbook of Psychological and Educational Assessment of Children: Intelligence and Achievement.* New York, NY: Guilford Press, Pp. 697-719.
3. "Be A Great Teacher!" In A. C. Ornstein (Ed.), *Strategies for Effective Thinking.* New York, NY: Harper & Row, P. 565.
4. (With K. Goff) "Working with Adult Learners." In C. Clements (Ed.), *The Arts/Fitness Quality of Life Program for Elderly Persons With and Without Developmental Disabilities.* Athens, GA: University of Georgia, Pp. 8-9.
5. (With K. Goff) "Brainstorming and Asking Provocative Questions." In C. Clements (Ed.), *The Arts/Fitness Quality of Life Program for Elderly Persons With and Without Developmental Disabilities.* Athens, GA: The University of Georgia, Pp. 15-20.
6. "Professional Viewpoint—Be A Great Teacher." In A. C. Ornstein (Ed.), *Strategies for Effective Teaching.* New York, NY: Harper & Row, P. 565.
7. (With J. Presbury, J. H. Benson, and A. J. Fitch) "Children and Creativity." In A. Thomas (Ed.), *Handouts.* National Association of School Psychologists.

Articles in Professional and Research Journals

1. (With K. Goff and H. Okabayashi) Japanese Creative Problem Solving Methods. *Creative Child and Adult Quarterly,* ***15****(4),* 173-182.
2. (With J. Juntune) An Interview: The Importance of Creativity in Society. *Focus,* ***191***, 3-6, 8.

Reports, Manuals, Handbooks, Tests, Instructional Materials

1. (With O. E. Ball) *Torrance Tests of Creative Thinking: Norms-Technical Manual, Figural (Streamlined) Forms A and B.* Bensenville, IL: Scholastic Testing Service.
2. *Manual for Scoring and Interpreting Results: Torrance Tests of Creative Thinking, Verbal Forms A and B.* Bensenville, IL: Scholastic Testing Service.
3. *Torrance Tests of Creative Thinking: To the Test User.* Bensenville, IL: Scholastic Testing Service.
4. *Torrance Tests of Creative Thinking, Figural Form A and Verbal Form A, and Administration Manual for Torrance Tests of Creative Thinking, Form A*(translated into Portuguese).
5. (With K. Goff) *Cumulative Bibliography on the Torrance Tests of Creative Thinking.* Athens, GA: Georgia Studies of Creative Behavior.

Articles in Popular or Trade Type Journals and Magazines—Applications of Research

1. Questions and Answers with Dr. Torrance. *Newsletter for the Torrance Creative Scholars Programs*, ***3****(1)*, 2.
2. (With K. Goff) Fostering Academic Creativity in Gifted Students. *ERIC Flyer File*.

Foreword(s)/Preface(s) and Book Reviews

1. Review. "High-Tech, Aesthetics, Art, and Art Education." Review of F. H. Farley and R. W. Neperud (Eds.), *The Foundations of Aesthetics, Art, and Art Education*. *Contemporary Psychology*, ***35****(10)*, 995-996.
2. Foreword. In J. W. Eby and J. F. Smutny, *A Thoughtufl Overview of Gifted Education*. New York, NY: Longman.

1991

Parts of Books, Contributions to Cooperative Volumes

1. (With E. J. Caropreso) "Assessment of Preschool Giftedness: Intelligence and Creativity." In B. A. Bracken (Ed.), *The Psychoeducational Assessment of Preschool Children*. Boston, MA: Allyn and Bacon, Pp. 430–449.

Articles in Professional and Research Journals

1. Creatively Gifted, Disadvantaged Children: Their Desperate Need for Mentors. *Illinois Council for the Gifted Journal*, ***10***, 4-5.
2. Beyonders and Their Characteristics. *Creative Child and Adult Quarterly*, ***16****(2)*, 69–79.
3. (With K. Goff) Maintaining Creativity in the Later Years. *Creative Child and Adult Quarterly*, ***16****(1)*, 5-16.
4. (With J. Presbury, A. J. Benson, and J. Fitch) What Can Children's Creative Writing Tell Us About Their Cognitive Development? *Journal of Creative Behavior*, ***25***, 244-249.
5. (With K. Goff) The Georgia Studies of Creative Behavior: Venturing into Studies of Creativity in Elders. *Generations*, 53-54.
6. (With K. Goff) Healing Qualities of Imagery and Creativity. *Journal of Creative Behavior*, ***25***, 296-303.

Reports, Manuals, Handbooks, Tests, Instructional Materials

1. *Torrance Tests of Creative Thinking Pensando Criativamente*.
2. (With K. Goff) *Mentor's Guide and Protégé's Handbook*. Bensenville, IL: Scholastic Testing Service.

1992

Parts of Books, Contributions to Cooperative Volumes

1. (With K. Goff) "Maintaining Creativity in Later Years." In *Bridging Networks in Georgia: Alternatives for Aging Persons with Developmental Disabilities*. (Selected Conference Proceedings, May 8-10, 1991) University Affiliated Program for Persons with

Developmental Disabilities, University of Georgia, Pp. 80-102.

2. (With K. Goff) "A Quiet Revolution." In S. J. Parnes (Ed.), *A Source Book for Creative Problem-Solving*. Buffalo, NY: Creative Education Foundation, Pp. 78-84.
3. (With K. Goff and H. Okabayashi) "The Japanese Innovate—KJ and NM: Japanese Creative Problem Solving Methods." In S. J. Parnes (Ed.), *A Source Book for Creative Problem-Solving*. Buffalo, NY: Creative Education Foundation, Pp. 274-281.
4. "Play the Futurist: Sociodrama as a Creative Problem-Solving Approach to Studying the Future." In S. J. Parnes (Ed.), *A Source Book for Creative Problem-Solving*. Buffalo, NY: Creative Education Foundation, Pp. 393-401.
5. (With E. J. Caropreso) "Assessment of Preschool Giftedness: Intelligence and Creativity." In B. A. Bracken (Ed.), *The Psycho-Educational Assessment of Preschool Children*. Needham Heights, MA: Allyn and Bacon, Pp. 430-449.

Articles in Professional and Research Journals

1. (With K. Goff) Enhancing Creativity in Older Adults. *Journal of Creative Behavior*, ***26***, 40-49.
2. A National Climate for Creativity and Invention. *Gifted Child Today*, ***15****(1)*, 10-14.
3. Creatively Gifted, Learning Disabled Individuals. *Educational Forum*, ***56****(4)*, 399-404.
4. Invited Reaction: "Hidden" Information in Corporate Creativity in Japan. *Human Resource Development Quarterly*, ***3****(3)*, 235-238.

Reports, Manuals, Handbooks, Tests, Instructional Materials

1. (With L. H. Rose) *Cumulative Bibliograhy of Thinking Creatively in Action and Movement (TCAM)*. Athens, GA: Georgia Studies of Creative Behavior.
2. (With Hsin-tai Lin and L. H. Rose) *Cumulative Bibliography: Khatena-Torrance Creative Perception Inventory*. Athens, GA: Georgia Studies of Creative Behavior.
3. (With L. H. Rose) *Cumulative Bibliography: Thinking Creatively with Sounds and Words (TCSW)*. Athens, GA: Georgia Studies of Creative Behavior.
4. (With O. E. Ball and H. T. Safter) *Torrance Tests of Creative Thinking Streamlined Scoring Guide, Figural A and B*. Bensenville, IL: Scholastic Testing Service, Inc.
5. (With J. Lee) *Additions to the Cumulative Bibliography on the Torrance Tests of Creative Thinking (Fall 1990–Summer 1992)*. Athens, GA: Georgia Studies of Creative Behavior.
6. (With L. H. Rose and J. Lee) *International Impact: 1985-1991*. Athens, GA: Georgia Studies of Creative Behavior.
7. *Torrance Tests of Creative Thinking Streamlined Scoring Guide Figural Forms A and B*. Bensenville, IL: Scholastic Testing Service.
8. *Torrance Tests of Creative Thinking, Figural A* (translated into Finnish).

Articles in Popular or Trade Type Journals and Magazines—Applications of Research

1. How Glorious It Would Be! *Advent Devotions 1992*. Athens, GA: First Baptist Church.

Foreword(s)/Preface(s) and Book Reviews

1. Foreword. In C. S. Micklus, *OMermania! Encouraging Humor and Creativity Using Odyssey of the Mind Problems*. Glassboro, NJ: Creative Competitions.

1993

Books and Monographs

1. (With H. T. Safter) *Making the Creative Leap Beyond...* Buffalo, NY: Bearly Limited (in press).

Foreword(s)/Preface(s) and Book Reviews

1. Understanding Creativity: Where to Start? *Psychological Inquiry—An International Journal of Peer Commentary and Review.* *4*(3), 232–234.

1994

Books and Monographs

1. *Creativity—Just Wanting to Know.* Pretoria, South Africa: Benedic Books.
2. (with R.E. Myers) *Creativity—What Next? Futeristic Scenerios for Creative Problem Solving.* Tucson, AZ: Zephyr Press.

1995

Books and Monographs

1. (in press) *Why Fly? A Philosophy of Creativity.* Norwood, NJ: Ablex.
2. (With M.C. Murdock, & D. Fletcher) *Creative Problem Solving Through Role-Playing.* Pretoria, South Africa: Benedic Books (in press).

Appendix B

QUESTIONNAIRE

In 1992, a questionnaire was sent out to many of Dr. Torrance's friends, students, and colleagues, accompanied by the following letter:

> Dear Participant:
>
> As you know, Dr. E. Paul Torrance has made a singular impact on education and psychology through his seminal research in the area of creativity. He began his academic career as Director of the Bureau of Educational Research at the University of Minnesota from 1958 to 1966. At that time, he returned to his native Georgia as Chairman of the Educational Psychology Department at the University of Georgia and continued his research and teaching until his retire ment in 1985. Currently, he is still actively engaged in applying his research to enhancing the quality of life for senior citizens. He also has a number of books in various stages of development.
>
> Dr. Torrance has published more than 1,500 articles and 35 books. Perhaps his greatness can best be measured by the disciples he has taught through the years who are influencing millions of people all over the world. There is a need to write a comprehensive account of his life and works—a biography. Presently, it does not exist. Dr. Torrance has agreed to work with me on this important project.

The questionnaire consisted of the following questions:

Personal Impressions:

1. What is it in Dr. Torrance's persona that impressed you most?
2. Relate a personal anecdote that occurred between you and Dr. Torrance that is vivid and memorable.

Significant Contributions:

1. In what ways has Dr. Torrance's research/work affected your thinking/professional career?
2. What is the most significant thing you have learned from Dr. Torrance?

Appendix C

DESCRIPTION OF CREATIVE FACTORS AND CREATIVE STRENGTHS

RATIONAL FACTORS

These factors have largely resulted from the work of J. P. Guilford and represent a rational view of the creative process. These factors include fluency, flexibility, originality, and elaboration.

Creative Factor A

- Produce and consider many alternatives. (Or: Think of lots and different kinds of ideas.)

Description

This factor actually involves two creative elements: *fluency* and *flexibility*. Fluency is simply the production of a number of ideas. Flexibility has to do with an individual's ability to shift mental categories or to produce and consider ideas and alternatives that are categorically different from one another.

Creative Factor B

- Be Original. (Or: Be inventive!)

Description

Originality is the ability to produce ideas that are different and unique. It requires looking beyond the obvious and mundane to the novel and inventive.

Rarity and unusualness of response characterize this factor.

Creative Factor C

• Elaborate. (Or: Add some extras.)

Description

The addition of detail to an idea, plan, or drawing is *elaboration*. It involves the embellishment of whatever is being produced. It is the "flesh" that rounds out the "skeleton" of an idea.

SUPRARATIONAL FACTORS

Creative Strengths

Since 1979, Paul Torrance and his associates have developed a set of factors that fall outside the realm of pure reason. These factors move creativity toward the further reaches of creative potential and are termed creative strengths. Torrance's tests utilize these factors in the scoring scheme.

Creative Strength #1

• Highlight the Essence. (Or: Get to the heart of the matter.)

Description

This ability requires a whole range of subskills from simplification and clarification to condensation and summarization. It involves a process of distinguishing between relevant and irrelevant material. The ultimate goal of highlighting the essence is to identify the dominant problem or idea.

Creative Strength #2

• Keep Open. (Or: Don't take the easiest way out.)

Description

In order to prevent premature closure, an individual must resist the natural impulse to accept the first idea or solution that comes to mind. Deferment of judgment until a problem is fully understood and a number of solutions have been explored is crucial to avoiding premature closure.

Creative Strength #3

- Be Awarene of Emotions. (Or: Know and express your feelings.)

Description

Feelings affect thinking and creative production. Emotional commitment is required and emotional factors play a role in the achievement of a genuine breakthrough or "aha." Many ideas and solutions related to a problem originate in emotions. Although the most meaningful creative insight will arise in conjunction with knowledge and persistence, without the ability to tap the emotions, it may not occur at all.

Creative Strength #4

- Put Your Ideas in Context. (Or: Get the big picture.)

Description

Ideas do not function in isolation from other ideas. This creative strength is the ability to see the relationship between and recognize the large-scale implications of ideas and events.

Creative Strength #5

- Combine and Synthesize. (Or: Get it together.)

Description

This strength is an ability to bind an array of ideas and factors together to develop a new idea. The new idea is more than sum of the parts that make it up. The parts may be very diverse, and the process of connecting and joining them in a novel and pleasing combination is the essence of this creative strength.

Creative Strength #6

- Visualize It Richly and Colorfully. (Or: See things in all their splendor.)

Description

Creative production demands an ability to visualize concepts, ideas, processes, and plans. The visualizations need not be original but are of necessity vivid, distinct, intense, and colorful. The image produced often appeals to and stimulates more than one of the sense modalities.

Creative Strength #7

• Fantasize. (Or: Use your imagination.)

Description

Fantasizing is the ability to go beyond what is real into the realm of imagination. The ability to extend one's thoughts beyond concrete reality and, just for a while, to believe the impossible possible is the essence of fantasy. It is an ability that can wither quickly under the pressure to conform and face up to reality.

Creative Strength #8

• Enrich Imagery. (Or: Feel it, smell, it, touch it, taste it, hear it.)

Description

Imagery is enriched when more than one sense modality is incorporated in the experience. Idea flow appears to be increased when an individual is kinesthetically and auditorally active.

Creative Strength #9

• Have an Unusual Visual Perspective. (Or: Seeing things from a different angle.)

Description

An *unusual visual perspective* is achieved when an individual perceives an object, person, or event in a different and new light. A creative individual may look at everyday objects and see something novel and exciting. This ability is one of the single most effective predictors of adult creative achievement.

Creative Strength #10

• Have an Internal Visual Perspective. (Or: Don't judge a book by its cover!)

Description

An *internal visual perspective* is attained by examining inner elements of an object, problem, or idea. An interest in what makes a machine "tick" or determining the core components of an idea is an internal visual perspective. This ability involves looking beyond exteriors to hidden possibilities.

Creative Strength #11

- Breakthrough—Extend the Boundaries. (Or: Break habit thinking.)

Description

Breaking away from an image or idea to go beyond its boundaries is what is meant by *breakthrough*. It requires looking past the problems or images themselves to the systems that they function in and around. It involves removing barriers imposed by habit and tradition and reformulating the problem or solution.

Creative Strength #12

- Have a Sense of Humor. (Or: Laugh a little.)

Description

Humor involves an ability to see incongruities, to combine ideas or images in an unusual way, or to surprise. The most important component of this strength is not necessarily the ability to produce humor but to see and pick up on the humor in situations, events, and images. The ability to see humor, or to be humorous, requires a certain detachment that is similar to the critical perspective necessary to look at problems and situations in a creative way.

Creative Strength #13

- Decentrism—Glimpse Infinity. (Or: Get out your crystal ball.)

Description

Decentrism simply means a concern for things outside of the self. It involves a concern for the future and a willingness to adapt to changes that the future holds and to be a part in shaping the future. An acceptance of the uncertainty of the future and remaining open to it is an important component of this creative strength.

Appendix D

SIGNIFICANT EVENTS, HONORS AND DISTINCTIONS IN THE LIFE OF E. PAUL TORRANCE

"I don't deserve all those awards, but I have arthritis, deteriorated discs, ataxia, an enlarged prostate, a hernia, and I don't deserve them either."

—Christmas Letter from E. Paul Torrance, December 1985

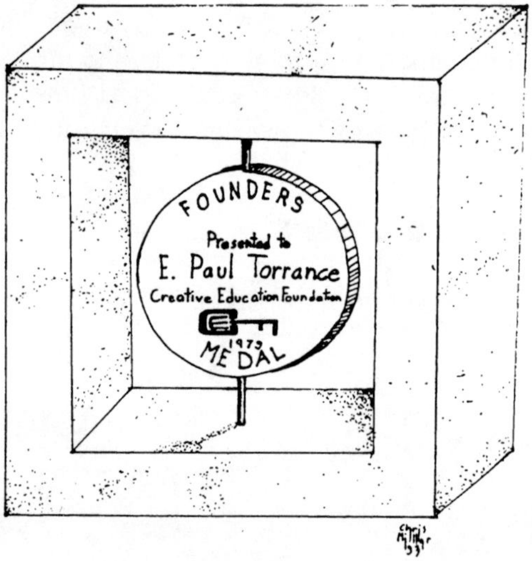

1915

- Born on October 8 in Baldwin County near Milledgeville, Georgia, to Ellis Watson and Jimmie Pearl Ennis Torrance—the first of two children. Woodrow Wilson was President, and the population of the United States was 74.5 million.

1916

- Walked in June, at age 9 months.

1923

- Began attending Union Point School at age 7. Walked 3 miles each way.

1928

- Won $10 award for essay on "Baldwin County Products" and a medal for citizenship and scholarship from the Sons of the American Revolution.

1929

- Graduated from the elementary grades at Union Point School as the top student (First Honor Graduate).

1930

- Won first place in a Latin contest and a medal for an essay from the Sons of the American Revolution.

1931

- Graduated from the junior high school division of Union Point School as the top student (First Honor Graduate).
- Won Third Place in 100-yard dash in District Meet.

1933

- Voted Most Intellectual Cadet in high school at Georgia Military College.

1934

- Won a medal for oratory and graduated from Georgia Military College High School as the top student (First Honor Graduate).

1936

- Graduated from Georgia College as the top student (First Honor Graduate), earning an Associate in Arts (A.A.) degree.
- Held first teaching position at Midway Vocational High School (Grades 8 and 9) in Hardwick, Georgia.
- Received first teaching certificate (Non-Professional Junior College Teacher's Certificate) from the State of Georgia Department of Education.

1937

- Began teaching Latin, French, Algebra, Geometry, and History at Georgia Military College, and remained there until 1941.
- Received Provisional High School Teacher's Certificate from State of Georgia Department of Education.

1938

- Received Professional High School Teacher's Certificate from State of Georgia Department of Education.

1940

- Graduated from Mercer University, Bachelor of Arts (A.B.), summa cum laude.
- First journal article published in *Scholastic Editor.*

1942

- Appointed representative for all the Armed Services at Georgia Military College.

1944

- Graduated with a Master of Arts (M.A.) degree with a major in educational psychology from the University of Minnesota. The thesis topic was "Predicting and Measuring Success in Plane Geometry."
- Named principal of the high school at Georgia Military College.

1945

- Accepted a job at the University of Minnesota Student Counseling Bureau, working with disabled veterans. Drafted into the U.S. Army and assigned to the Psychiatry and Sociology Division as a psychiatric social worker.

1946

- Developed a vocational guidance program for men who were dishonorably discharged from the Army. This involved a good deal of individual testing.
- Released from the U.S. Army in July to accept a position as a counselor of disabled veterans at Kansas State College in Manhattan, Kansas.

1947

- Appointed Dean of Men at Kansas State College, with additional counseling duties.

1948

- Entered the University of Michigan on a Horace J. Rackham Fellowship and began work on a doctorate.
- Elected to Phi Delta Kappa.

1949

- Accepted position as Director of the Counseling Bureau and Professor of Psychology at Kansas State College in Manhattan, Kansas. Taught courses in counseling and mental health.
- Elected member of Division of Counseling and Guidance of the American Psychological Association.

1951

- Received a Doctor of Philosophy (Ph.D.) degree in educational psychology from the University of Michigan at Ann Arbor. The dissertation was entitled "Self-Concepts and Their Significance in the Learning and Adjustment of College Freshmen."

- Accepted position with U.S. Air Force as Director of Survival Research Field Unit at Camp Carson in Colorado Springs, Colorado. Learned the importance of experiential factors in learning.

1952

- Moved with the Air Force Survival School to Reno, Nevada, and studied men's reactions to survival exercises in the Sierra Nevada Mountains.

1953

- Headed team to study fighter interceptor pilot combat effectiveness. This involved conducting interviews and administering psychological tests to jet aces, near aces, and pilots who made no hits in Korea. Published two articles on the psychological aspects of survival.

1954

- Completed fighter interceptor study, and on May 31, the study appeared in *Time Magazine*—"The Portrait of an Ace." Published articles on aspects of survival that were widely quoted in group dynamics and sociology texts.

1956

- Published a number of articles on stress reaction to hot and cold conditions, pressure on POWs, and psychological interrogation.

1958

- Appointed Director of the Bureau of Educational Research at the University of Minnesota in Minneapolis.
- Held first of three Minnesota conferences on the gifted. Conducted a statewide study on the qualifications of mathematics and science teachers and how they were responding to the ascent of Sputnik. Initiated a longitudinal study of creative talent in the University of Minnesota Laboratory Elementary School and the Sidney Pratt Elementary School.

1959

- Married Pansy Nigh on November 25.
- Launched a longitudinal study of creative talent in the University of Minnesota High School.

1960

- Launched a cross-cultural study of creative development in India, Australia, Norway, Germany, and Western Samoa, and in the United States in both black and white populations.
- Participated in the Space Age Conference on Education with Margaret Mead.

1961

- Received national recognition when *Look Magazine* published an article about Torrance—"The Creative Child" by Chandler Brossard and John Vachone. The article brought 1,200 letters and phone calls, and the ire of some leaders in gifted education and educational psychology.
- Named by Department of Health, Education, and Welfare to the Nursing Research Study Section.

1962

- Published first book on creativity—*Guiding Creative Talent* (Prentice-Hall). The book was chosen by the American Personnel and Guidance Association as the most outstanding study in quality and significance to members during the year 1963. Also, selected by Educators' Book Club as Book of the Month for July.
- Elected as Fellow, Division 15, Educational Psychology, in American Psychological Association.
- Awarded membership in the American Society of Group Psychotherapy and Psychodrama.
- Listed in *Who's Who in America*, *Contemporary Authors*, *American Men of Science*, *Who's Who in American Education*, *Leaders in Education*, *Outstanding Educators*, and *Dictionary of International Biography*.
- Named Distinguished Visiting Educator, University of Delaware.

1963

- Won American Personnel and Guidance Association Award for Outstanding Research (*Guiding Creative Talent*).
- *Education and the Creative Potential* selected by *Book List* (published by National Education Association) as outstanding book.
- Cited by Department of Health, Education, and Welfare for service to the Nursing Research Study Section.

1964

- Elected Active Member of the New York Academy of Sciences.

1965

- Published teacher resource materials to enhance children's creativity.
- Received job offer from The University of Georgia; acceptance postponed to the Fall of 1966.
- Named to editorial board of the *Journal of Creative Behavior.*
- Participated in Institutional Conference on "Stress Seeking in Man," Bureau of Social Research, Office of Scientific Research of the U.S. Air Force.
- *Rewarding Creative Behavior: Experiments in Classroom Creativity* selected as Book of the Month Club for April.

1966

- Returned to native Georgia as chair and professor of Educational Psychology Department, College of Education, The University of Georgia.
- Published *Torrance Tests of Creative Thinking* (Personnel Press).
- Elected to the Board of Governors of the Association for the Gifted.

1967

- Agreed to work with Ginn and Company as a Creativity Consultant for their reading series (Reading 360 and eventually 720) and social studies series.
- Elected as member to the Committee of Psychology in Schools by the Council of Representatives of the American Psychological Association.
- Cited by the National Association for Gifted Children for pioneer work in identifying and developing creative abilities in children.

- Received grant for first Experienced Teachers Program to train 20 experienced teachers to be school psychologists.
- Listed in *Dictionary of International Biography* and cited for distinguished service to Educational Psychology.

1968

- Received second grant from the United States Office of Education for Experienced Teachers Fellowship in School Psychology.
- Received grant from the United States Office of Education for research in Gifted Education.

1969

- Received recognition from Ginn and Company's consultants, authors, editors, artists, and graphics people through their endorsement of a creativity strand for their reading publication.
- Elected Fellow status, Division 10, Psychology of the Arts, American Psychology Association.
- Appointed Colleague of the Creative Education Foundation.

1970

- Appointed by the President of the United States to be Forum Chairman of Early Childhood Group of the White House Conference on Children.
- Established and organized first creativity workshop for disadvantaged children.
- Appointed Adjunct Professor of the Union Graduate School (Union for Experimenting Colleges and Universities).

1971

- Made recommendations to Governor Jimmy Carter about the Governor's Honor Program.
- *Guiding Creative Behavior* was translated into Spanish.

1972

- *Creative Learning and Teaching* listed in *Education Book List* (Pi Lambda

Theta and National Education Association).

- Received Outstanding Alumnus Award at Georgia Military College in Education.
- Cited by Psi Chi, National Honor Society in Psychology, for outstanding contributions to the advancement of the science of psychology and for encouraging, stimulating, and maintaining scholarship in all academic fields.
- Listed in *Outstanding Educators in America*.
- Named to Board of Advisors for Humanizing Education.
- Certified as a Charter Member of the Georgia Association for Gifted Children.

1973

- Reappointed to the University of Georgia Graduate Faculty.
- Named Alumni Foundation Distinguished Professor by President of the University of Georgia for outstanding achievement in teaching, research, and service.
- Received citation from Creative Leadership Center, Smith Richardson Foundation, for outstanding contribution to creativity research during the past 25 years.
- Received award for distinguished contributions to the advancement and understanding of gifted children and youth from the Association for the Gifted, Council for Exceptional Children International.
- Received joint citation, with Pansy, from the National Association for Gifted Children, in recognition of their programs for disadvantaged gifted boys and girls.

1974

- Listed in *Who's Who in the World*.
- Received award from the Athens Alumni Chapter, Kappa Delta Pi fraternity, for outstanding contributions, attainments, service, and leadership in educational psychology and community leadership.
- Founded the Future Problem Solving Program.
- Named by the University of Wisconsin at Oshkosh as EDUCARE Distinguished Visiting Professor.
- Received award for Excellence as a Teacher Educator, Kappa Delta Pi.
- Elected to the Board of Directors of the American Society for Group Psychotherapy and Psychodrama.
- Received Distinguished Achievement Award for excellence in educational journalism from Educational Press Association of America, All-America Awards Program.
- Honored by Kappa Alpha Psi for leadership and achievement in career.

- Named to Editorial Advisory Board, University of Georgia Press.
- Elected to Board of Trustees of the Creative Education Foundation.

1975

- Received Compatriot in Education Award from Kappa Delta Pi for contributions to the field of education.
- Accepted as a member into the National Association for School Psychologists.
- Received certificate of recognition from Office of Career Education, United States Office of Education, for significant contributions to the Commissioner's National Conference on Career Education.
- Received certificate of recognition from Office of Education for the Gifted and Talented for significant contributions to the education of gifted and talented youth.

1976

- Listed in *International Who's Who*.
- Listed in *Personalities of the South* (Bicentennial Edition) in recognition of past achievements and outstanding service to community and state.
- Received Bicentennial Award, Beta Chapter, Kappa Delta Pi, for contributions as a Teacher Educator.

1977

- Received Distinguished Service award from Georgia Military College.
- Presented invited address to Division 15 (Educational Psychology) of the American Psychological Association.
- Appointed as a Member of the National Association of School Psychologists.

1978

- Received award from Sertoma Club for outstanding service to mankind—Advanced Institute in Gifted Education, Honolulu, Hawaii.
- Received Distinguished Scholar Award from the National Association for Gifted Children.
- Cited by Phi Delta Kappa as one of 10 top contributors of significant research in the United States and Canada.
- Cited by Institution of Scientific Information as one of 100 most cited

social scientists.

- Appointed Visiting Scholar for the Japanese Society for the Promotion of Science to visit Japanese universities and encourage international cooperation in scientific research.
- Honored by S. Sato and A. Onda, who dedicated their book, *Creative Potential: Its Development and Evaluation*, to E. Paul Torrance.
- Honored by Department of Educational Psychology (Measurement and Research), College of Education, University of Georgia, for 12 years of dedicated service as department chairman.

1979

- Spent two months in Japan as a guest of the Japanese Society for the Promotion of Research.
- Spent two weeks in Taiwan.
- Published *Search for Satori and Creativity* (Creative Education Foundation).
- Awarded the Phoenix Medal by the University of Hiroshima.
- Awarded key to Osaka by the Mayor and received citation for contributions to infant education.
- Received *festschrift* book from Japanese creativity researchers during visit to Japan.
- Elected Associate Fellow in National Academy of Physical Education.
- Awarded Founders Medal of the Creative Education Foundation and received citation for contribution to creative education.
- Received Honor's Day recognition for superior teaching, University of Georgia.
- Received citation of merit from National/State Leadership Training Institute on the Gifted and Talented.
- Received award from National Association for Gifted Children for direction of outstanding dissertation research (Jonathan Edwards).
- Listed in *International Authors* and *Writers Who's Who.*
- Listed in *Men of Achievement.*
- Received Odyssey of the Mind Creativity Award for the development and promotion of human creativity.
- Received citation from Atlanta Capital of the Age of Enlightenment for contributions towards creating an ideal society.
- Received award from National Association of Gifted Children for outstanding research of the year.

1980

- Completed data collection for 22-year follow-up study on creative behavior of elementary students (first studied in 1958).

- Nursed Pansy, who had a massive stroke on returning from Future Problem Solving Workshop in Savannah, Georgia.
- Cited by the National Association for Gifted Children for establishing the National Future Problem Solving Program and Bowl.
- New listing in *Who's Who in America* and *Who's Who in the World.*
- Received Viktor Lowenfeld Medal and Citation for contribution to research in art education.
- Participated as honored guest with 16 of the teachers in the 22-year longitudinal study at the opening of the National Association for Gifted Children Conference in Minneapolis.

1981

- *Search for Satori and Creativity* was translated into Japanese by Tokyo Shinri Publishing Company.
- Received award, with Pansy, from the Georgia Supporters of the Gifted for local, national, and international contributions to gifted education.
- Received Distinguished Scholar Award given by the National Association for Gifted Children.
- Acknowledged for outstanding professional contributions in the *Advisor.*

1982

- The Torrance Center for Creative Studies, Educational Psychology Department, University of Georgia, was conceptualized.
- Conducted International Scenario Writing Contest involving 16 countries.
- Received award, with Pansy, from Center for Creative Studies, College of St. Thomas, University of Minnesota, for original contributions to the understanding of creative behavior.
- Invited to become an Advisor on the United States Congressional Advisory Board.
- Received Arthur Lipper Award of the World Olympics of the Mind for outstanding original contributions to the development of human creativity.
- Received award, with Pansy, from the National Future Problem Solving Program for the creation of the program and continued support.
- Elected Honorary Member of the Georgia Association of School Psychologists and cited for contributing to the establishment and development of school psychology in Georgia.
- Received award from the Institute for the Arts and Humanities for original contributions to the education of gifted children.
- Recognized by College of Education, University of Georgia, for superior teaching.

1983

- Established the International Network of Gifted Children and Their Teachers.
- Honored by the World Conference for the Gifted and Talented.
- Elected to *Who's Who in the World.*
- Elected to *Who's Who in Frontier Science and Technology.*

1984

- Nursed Pansy, who began having strokes on February 20.
- Had a stroke himself on November 10.
- Torrance Archives were established at Hargrett Library, University of Georgia.
- The Torrance Center for Creative, Gifted, and Future Studies was established in the College of Education, University of Georgia.
- Received award at the University of Houston at Clear Lake with citation for contributions to understanding and educating creative children.
- Received award from the World Council on Gifted and Talented Children for contribution to the understanding and education of gifted and talented children.
- Received plaque of appreciation from the University of Stellenbosch for participating and making possible the International Conference on Education for the Gifted.

1985

- Honored at retirement banquet, March 23, University of Georgia.
- Board of Regents approved Emeritus title.
- Inducted into Hall of Fame by National Association for Creative Children and Adults.
- Honored by dedication of July/August/September Leadership Training Institute of National/State Leadership Training Institute on Gifted and Talented.
- Honored by Thelma Epley, who dedicated her book, *Futuristics: A Handbook for Teachers of the Gifted and Talented*, to E. Paul Torrance.
- Received Bicentennial Medal from University of Georgia for serving the university with high distinction.
- Honored by a proclamation from the Governor of the State of Georgia for his lifelong commitment to education.
- Received award from Ohio Association for Gifted Children.

1988

- Pansy Nigh Torrance died on November 13.
- The National Association for Gifted Children's Creativity Award was named "The E. Paul Torrance Award."
- The Creativity Symposium of the American Psychological Association was dedicated to E. Paul Torrance and J. P. Guilford.
- Listed in *Who's Who in the World.*
- Received Emeritus Membership in Phi Delta Kappa.

1989

- Named "Notable Alumnus" by Georgia Military College.
- Received commendation for creative altruism from Institute of Noetic Sciences.
- Received Honorary Life Membership from Georgia Supporters for the Gifted.
- Honored by John A. Glover, Roy R. Ronning, and Cecil R. Reynold, who dedicated their book, *Handbook of Creativity*, to E. Paul Torrance.
- Honored by the National/State Leadership Training Institute on the Gifted and Talented for dedicated service on the Advisory Committee.

1990

- Listed in *Who Who's in America.*
- Nominated for 8th Annual Inspiration Awards, City of Athens Mayor's Office, Clarke County Board of Commissioners, and Athens Community Council on Aging.

1991

- Nominated for Donald J. Quigly Excellence in Education Award.
- Awarded Lifetime Membership and Beyond by Creative Education Foundation.

1992

- Honored by Gary Davis, who dedicated the Third Edition of *Creativity Is Forever* to E. Paul Torrance.

1993

- Honored by the Baldwin County Retired Teachers' Association for his contributions and dedication to the education of children in his state and nation.
- Honored by National Association for the Gifted Children for his significant contributions to the field of Gifted Education and to the development of their organization.

1994

- Honored by American Creativity Association for lifetime achievement in education and creativity research (first recipient of ACA's National Achievement Award).
- Award for outstanding contribution to research, theory, and practice in creative thinking by Sixth International Conference on Thinking at the Massachusetts Institute of Technology.

NAME INDEX

A

Aderhold, Dr. A.C., 109
Aftreth, Dr. Orville, 62
Al-Baili, Mohammed Abdulla, 167
Aldrin, Edwin "Buzz," 108
Aliedin, Mohamed, 158
Allman, T., 65, *106*
Alvino, Dr. James, 137, 138
Anderson, Gordon, 23
Anderson, John P., 95
Anderson, Karl, 48
Anderson, Shirley, 191
Ando, Terutsugu, 159, 229
Andrews, Alice, 209
Andrews, Lewis, 209
Antenon, Wayne, 112
Appleton, Jon, 118, 188, 189
Arnold, Rose, 208
Arsan, Dr. Kevsar, 66
Arsan, Dietmar, 66
Atlas, Charles, 217

B

Badaway, Mohammed, 190, 208, 222
Baldwin, Adam, 109
Ball, O.E., 49, *106,* 208
Barnes, Agnes, 15
Barron, Frank, 50, 54, 68
Bashaw, Dr. Louis, 208
Bateson, Willard, 27
Baycura, Peter, 101
Bellinger, Gladys, 209
Bellón, Francisco Menchén, 156, 229, 240
Benson, Art, 100
Bergeson, B.E., 102
Binet, Alfred, 237
Bivins, P.N., 22
Black, Alan, 208
Blake, Dr. Katherine, 166
Blatz, William, 76
Bledsoe, Dr. Joe, 142
Bleedorn, Berenice "Bee," 95, 96, 97, 134, 137, 148, 154, 155, 164, *176,* 202, 208, 229, 230
Boring, E.G., 88
Bolton, Eurie Bell, 20
Bond, Guy, 93
Borrow, Henry, 56
Bowers, John, 56
Bowers, Raymond, 37
Bracken, Bruce, 158, *176,* 224
Braunes, Harry, 154
Briggs, J., 243
Broadley, Margaret, 45, 46, *104*
Broome, Faith, 75
Brossard, Chandler, 73, 74, *104*
Brown, Major Hilton, 22
Bruce, Robert, 3
Bruch, Kay, 125, 134, 166, 171
Bryhgelson, Dr. Bryng, 57
Bryan, Craig, 206
Bryan, Doris, 206
Buccino, Alfonse, 184, *238*
Burton, Bessie, 12, 86
Burton, Richard, 108
Bush, George, 192
Buswell, Harriet, 208
Butler-Por, Nava, xv, 164, 232

Butts, Dr. David, 206

C

Cambell, Dr. Angus, 28
Camden, Tom, 174, 184
Carroll, John, 131, 199, 200, 208
Carter, Jimmy, 108, 139, 140
Chase, Naomi, 94
Chergosky, Don, 207
Christian, Robert, 22
Church, Dr. Jack, 116
Clark, Bob, 116
Clarke, Dean John, 21
Clements, Dr. Bob, 120, 133, *177,* 200, 205, *238*
Clymer, Ted, 65, 93, 113
Collins, D., *239*
Conn, Eleanor, 209
Connell, Vicki, 173, 203, 209
Cook, A.N., *17*
Cook, Dr. Walter, 22, 23, 43, 44, 45, 47, 56, 93, 94, *104*
Coone, J., *179*
Copernicus, Nicolas, 45, 63, 88
Cordell, Lew, 209
Cordell, Lorena, 209
Crabbe, Dr. Anne, 137, 209
Cramond, *177,* 208
Cunnington, Bert, 69, 83, 84, *105,* 126, 168, *179*
Curry, Bill, 208
Curry, Jim, 208
Curtin, Dr. James, 62, 94, 99

D

Darley, John, 22
Darwin, Charles, 45
Das, J.P., 127, *177*
Daumal, Rene, 197, *238*
Dauw, Dean, 47, *104*
Davis, Deborah, 165
Davis, Gary A., xv
Davis, O.L., 99
Davison, Fred, 109, 138, 165
Dawson, Richard, 68
Decker, Major Bert, 100
De Gaulle, Charles, 108
Delisle, James, 122, *177,* 236, *238*
DeSchepper, Jimmy, 73
Dewey, John, 45
DeYoung, Kenneth, 47, 105
Dorough, Otis, 15
Dorsey, Grace, 101
Dugan, Willis, 94
Dwinell, Pat, 208, 226, 227
Dyer, T., *177*

E

Eckert, Ruth, 95
Eby, J.W., 229, *238*
Edison, Thomas, 46, 63
Edwards, Jon, 208
Edwards, Marcia, 93, 102
Eggen, P.D., 236, *238*
Eisenhower, Dwight, 42
Eisenhower, Milton, 26
Ennis, Jimmie Pearl, 2
Eggleston, Claude, 28
El-Dreny, Dr. Hesseen Abedel-Azia, 226, *238*
Ennis, Charlie "Chunk" Owens, 4
Ennis, Winnifred, 4

F

Falk, Carolyn, xiv
Faubus, Gov. Orval, 42
Ferguson, Major, 21
Festinger, Leon, 37
Flack, Jerry, 208, 227, 228
Flanders, Ned, 93
Fletcher, David, 129, 148, *179*
Forlano, George, 25
Fortson, Dr. Laura, 113
Foster, Florence, 86
Fox, Lynn, 126, *177*
Frasier, Dr. Mary, 165, 171, 174, *177,* 181, 183, 195, 196, 209, *239*
Freccia, Liba, 102
Freeman, Orville, 42, 43
French, Dr. Robert, 35, 37
Friedel, Marie, 209
Frost, Robert, 41
Fujita, George, 208

G
Gardner, John, 89
Garret, H., *238*
Garnick, Martin, 74
Gates, Dr. Arthur, 93
Gatch, Dr. Vera, 26
George, W.C., *178*
Gesell, 68, *104*
Getzels, G.W., 80
Ghandi, Indira, 108
Ghei, Som Nath, 47, 52
Gibbs, Suzanne, 226
Glauser, V., *177*
Glotzbach, Charles, 26, 28, 43, 56, 59, 60, 93
Glotzbach, Helen, 60
Goetz, Judith, 128
Goff, K., *177, 179*, 189, 201, 205, 208
Gold, Marvin, 176, *177*
Goldman, Juliette, 159
Goldman, Ronald, 72, *106*
Gordon, Ira, 28
Gowan, Dr. John, 85
Gray, P., *239*
Green, Gwendolyn, 68
Gregory, John, 21
Gretzky, Wayne, 34, *243*
Guetzgow, Dr. Harold, 28
Guglielmino, Lucy, 132
Guilford, Dr. J.P., 45, 50, 53, 69, 96, *105*, 234
Gupta, Ram, 83, 88, 96, 102, *106*

H
Haganah, Theta, 93
Halbauer, Charles, 56
Halbauer, Ruthetta, 56
Hall, Eleanor, xiv
Hall, Lyman, 109
Harris, Dale, 95
Harmon, Judson, 69
Harnell, Thomas, 37
Harris, Joe Chandler, 2
Harris, Joe Frank, 137, 184
Hastie, Reid, 94, 99
Hawkins, Charles, 56
Henderson, B., 177
Henderson, M., *105*, 133, 136, 163, 176, 235
Henrickson, Paul, 53, 54, 55, 208
Hermelin, Dr., 158
Hill, Julius, 27
Himsl, Ralph, 50, *105*, 170
Hitchcock, Alfred 108
Holland, John, 68, 120, *177*
Holmes, Thomas J., 101
Hooker, Clifford, 94
Hoomes, Eleanor, 176
Hooper, Peggy, 118, 208
Houseman, Howard, 37
Howieson, Noel, 131, 132
Huntley, S., 196, *239*
Hudspeth, R., 162, *177*
Humphrey, Hubert, 43, 90, 91, 92
Hutchinson, Lee Ann, 139

I
Inni, S., 145
Isaacs, Ann F., 185, 209
Iverson, Barbara, 100
Iverson, Noel, 69
Ivey, Marilyn, 208

J
Jackson, Jennine, 221
Jackson, Michael, 204
Jackson, R., 151, *177*, 220
Jansen, Claire John, 74
Jarvis, Greg, 152
Jenkins, David, 25
Jenkins, Col. Joseph H., 15, 22
Jensen, Dr. Arthur, 62
Johnson, Aileen, 166, 167
Johnson, Lyle, 98, 208, 234
Johnson, Lyndon, 108
Johnson, Marvin, 168
Johnson, Richard, 66, 69
Johnson, Vincent, 68
Jones, Quincy, 151
Juntune, Joyce, 154, 209

K
Kalushev, Georgi, 150
Karoussos, John, 87

Kauchak, D., 236, *238*
Kaufmann, Felice, 139, 189, 208
Kaufmann, Dr. John D., 120
Keller, Robert, 94, 102, 103
Kelly, Dr. Harold, 28, *209*
Kennedy, John, 4
Ketchum, Hank, 35
Khatena, Joe, 85, 125, 127, 154, 155, *179,* 208, 228
Kincaid, Adrienne, 151, 208
Kingston, Albert, 170, 171
Kitagawa, Masae, 147
Kitagawa, Sadayuki, 147
Knight, Otis, 21
Kolesinski, Mary, 126, *179*
Krieger, Myrrl, H., 102

L

LaForge, G.R., 40
Lathrop, Robert, 57
Lee, Chris, 150, 141, *177*
Lemay, General Curtis, 29, 32
Lemmon, Dr. Bill, 26
Lewis, Dr. Gail, 166, 167, 171, 181, 208
Lienard, Dr. Margaret, 75
Lin, Hsin-tai, *179*
Lindgren, H.C., *239*
Littleford, Anda, 60, 71,
Littleford, Laura, 60, 70, 71, 80, 231
Littleford, Rev. Warren 60
Livingston, Robert, M.D., 158
Lowry, R.W., 67
Luther, Balderjav, 66
Luthra, Gargi, 69

M

Macagnoni, Virginia, 208
MacEachern, Don, 98
MacKinnon, Donald W., 99
Maker, June, 157, *177,* 225, 234
Marechal, Dr. Hans, 32
Marland, Sydney, 78, *105*
Martin, Charlie, 176
Mason, R., *40*
May, Mrs. Alma, 101
May, Rollo, 87
McAuliffe, 191, 198, 218
McCarthy, Bernice, 126, *179*
McClusky, Howard, 28
McCracken, Jamie, 201
McCullar, C.B., 226
McDonald, F.J., *239*
McKelvey, Sarah, 154, *176*
McKenzie, Commander Colonel, 33
McNair, Ron, 192
McNeil, J., *177*
Mead, Margaret, 51
Meigs, Josiah, 110
Michie, Harold, 52
Middents, Gerald, 153, 154, 178, 208
Millar, Chris, 53
Millar, G.W., 73, 76, *105,* 166, 167, 169, *178,* 208
Millar, Vivian, 227
Miller, Harold, 75
Mitchell, Dr. Bruce, 158
Mitchell, Phillip, 27, 29
Mitchell, Dr. Dorothy, 26, 28
Moehlman, Dr.Arthur, 28
Montessori, 45
Moonana, Mrs. Reginald E., 74
Moran, "Uncle Billy," 11
Moran, Dr. O.F., 2
Moreno, Dr. Jacob, 26, 36, 148
Moreno, Zerka, 148
Morrill, J.L., 43
Murdoch, Mary, 129, 148, 179, 180, 189, 190
Murray, Dr. Elwood, 27
Myers, Garry C., 101
Myers, Rod, 69, 79, 80, 82, 83, 98, *105,* 168, *177,* 208, 232, *239*

N

Nakagawa, Kyoko, 167
Nash, Dr. Bill, 133, 192, 208, 214, 222
Neethling, Kobus, xiv, 156, 208, 232, 234, 237
Nelson, Christopher, 125, 201, 208
Newcomb, Theodore, 28
Nicholson, G., *239*
Nicklaus, Jack, 108
Nicola, Grigoire, 208
Nightingale, Earl, 35, *40*

Nixon, Richard, 205
Noller, Ruth, 184, 209
Nozu, Matsue, 219
Nozu, Yoshio, 147, 234, 219

O

O'Brien, Dr. William, 218
O'Connor, Johnson, 45, 46, *105*
O'Connor, Neil, 158
Onda, Akira, 146, 147, *177*
Omond, Jock L.. 158
Onizuka, Ellison, 192
Orcutt, Larry, 126
Orcutt, Lee, 126
Osbourne, Alex F., 100, 134, 236

P

Palmer, Jack, 218
Palmer, Ross, 209
Parker, Dr. Jeannete, 166, 167, 176, 208
Parnes, Bea, 209
Parnes, Sydney, 134, 169, 209, 230
Passi, B.K., 167
Passow, Harry, xiii, 153, 161, 227, 229, 233, 234
Paterson, Donald, 22
Pattishall, Evan, 27
Pekar, Diana, 7
Pekar, John, 2
Pelletier, Dr. Peter, 142
Peterson, Richard, 69
Petrullio, Luigi, 29
Platz, Mary Lee, 133, 208
Poole, Patrick H., 74
Poppleston, John, 37
Popper, Sam, 94
Por, Nava Butler, 164, 234
Postnick, Diane, 132
Presbury, J., xv, *105,* 133, 163, 176, 198, 199, 208, 218, 225, 234, 235
Price, J.M., *105*
Punsulan, Victoria, 66

R

Radigi, Herman, 60
Raina, M.K., xiv, 153, 154, 167, *177,* 208, 226, 234
Ray, Claude, 14
Reagan, Ronald, 191, 197, 227
Reilly, J.M., 171
Reilly, R., *243*
Reid, Alastair, 53, *105*
Reissman, Dr. Frederico, 142
Rentz, "Slap," 14, 19
Renzulli, Joe, 115, 122, 160, 165, 174, *177,* 231, 237, *239*
Resnick, Judy, 192
Reynolds, Cecil, 214, 231
Reynolds, Maynard, 57, 80, 85, 88, 89, 93, 96, 97
Richards, Julie, 129
Richardson, Dr. Edwin, 38
Richmond, Bert, 108, 111, 112, 160, 209
Riegel, Ted, 126, 208
Riley, Jack, 208
Rockenstein, Zoa, 189
Rogers, Carl, 87
Rogers, Jerry, 138
Roldan, Aurora, xiv, 225
Rorscharch, Herman, 237
Rose, Laura, 126, *179,* 208
Rose, Dr. Susan, 87
Rosser. R., *239*
Ruben, H.L., 125, *178, 239*
Rufi, John, 23
Runco, Dr. Mark, 236
Rust, J.O., *178*
Ryan, Nolan, 34, 53

S

Safter, Tammy, 160, 164, *179,* 189, 208, 210
Sanders, Carl E., 108
Satterfield, Neil, 208
Sato, Irving, 116, 165, 169, 179, 209
Sato, Sabura, 86, 144, 146, 148, *177, 179,* 189, 208
Schacter, Stan, 36
Schaller, Suzanne, 226
Scherer, R., *239*
Schiever, S., 157, *177*
Schilchter, Carol, 209, 236, 237
Schwartz, Dr. Bernie, 120, *178*
Scohee, Dick, 175, 192, 193, 194, 196, 198

Shallcross, Doris, 157, 209
Shaughnessy, Michael, 153, *178*
Shelton, Arthur Henley, 100
Sherman, General W.T., 2
Shy, Robin, 171, 173
Sisk, Dorothy, 209
Sless, Bernard, 25
Sloop, Dr. Betty, 136, 229
Smalley, Dr., 21
Smith, Dora, 94
Smith, Ellen, 86, 87, 157
Smith, Jamie, 126, 179
Smith, Krystle, 138
Smith, Lillian, 13, *17*
Smith, Michael, 192, *239*
Smutny, Joan Franklin, xiii, 229, *238*
Solano, C.H., *178*
Soliman, Abdalla, 158, 167, 208
Solorzano, L., *239*
Sorkey, *179*
Spratlin, Leatha, 209, 227, 228
Stamp, Alma, 3
Stamp, Guy, 3, 5
Stamp, Johnny, 3
Stanley, Dr. Julian, 155, *178*
Stein, Morris, 226
Stern, Sam, 202
Stevens, Howard, 208
Stevens, Norma, 208
Stewart, Dr. Emily, 159, 226
Stiles, Ezra, 109
Strom, Harry, 116, 169
Strom, Robert, 209, 214
Strom, Shirley, 215
Strother, Holland, 12
Strother, Mrs. Holland, 12
Strupp, Hans, 37
Summerhill, Ray, 27
Super, Donald, 36
Swicord, Barbara, 176, 208
Swint, Tom, 9

T

Taggart, Barbara, 127, *179*
Taggart, Bill, 127, *179*
Tan, C.A., 65, *106*
Tara, S. Nayana, 208
Taylor, Anne, 208
Taylor, Calvin, 46, 47, 50, 57, 58, 68, 80, 100, *105,* 154
Taylor, Elizabeth, 108
Taylor, J., *243*
Templeton, David, 208
Thagard, Dr. Norm, 197, 198
Thomley, Betty, 60
Thomas, Garth, 25
Thorne, Dr. Ren, 16, 22
Thurstone, 46
Toeman, Zerka, 26
Torrance, Ellen, 9, 11, 16, 61, 208, 211
Torrance, Ellis William, 211, 212, 213
Torrance, James Robert, 3
Torrance, Jessie Pansy Nigh, 21, 57, 58, 59, 60, 61, 62, 71, 72, 85, 90, 92, 98, 104, *106,* 107, 108, 118, 134, 136, 138, 139, 144, 147, 148, 154, 160, 168, 175, 176, 180, 184, 185, 186, 187, 188, 189, 190, 200, 201, 202, 205, 206, 207, 208, 209, 210, 211, 218, 219, 222, 224, 225, 230, 231, 241
Treffinger, Don, xiii, 120, 160, 169, *179,* 203, 209
Trotter, Dr. Virginia, 166, 184
Trow, Dr. Clark, 28
Turner, Faith, 208
Turner, Harry, 208

U

Ulrich, Darlene, 68
Uusikyla, Kari Tapid, 167

V

Vachon, John, 73
Vinson, Carl, 16
Volsky, Ted, 56

W

Wachowiak, 120, 177
Walden, Major Herbert, 22
Walker, Herschel, 222
Wardell, Dorolese, 68, 94
Warmath, Murray, 226
Waterstreet, Mary, 200

Weaver, Wendell W., 170
Weschler, David, 237
Weschler, Solange, 223, 226
Werblo, Dorothy Funk, 208
Werner, D., *177,* 208
Westrim, Walter, 197
Whitfield, George, 109
White, William, 209
Willman, Conchita Tan, 208
Williams, Emmet, 82
Williams, Frank, 154
Williams, Dean Joseph, 102, 107, 141
Williamson, Dean, 23
Williamson, E.G., 22, 93
Williams, Wilbur, 27
Wilk, Roger, 56, 57, 93, 102, 103
Wilson, Dr. Robert, 126, 209
Wilson, Woodrow, 4
Wolf, Dr. Alexander, 25, 26
Wolfe, Thomas, 189
Woolf, Jeanne, 26
Woolf, Dr. Maurice, 25, 26, 28
Wren, Gilbert, 22, 44, 56, 94

Y

Yamamoto, Kaoru, 52, 55, 60, 66, 68, 208
Yeatts-Thomas, Pearline, xiii, 141, 181
Young, Captain Keith, 29, 36

Z

Zander, Dr. Albert, 28, 36, 43
Ziller, Robert, 35, *40*